A History of the American Constitution

Daniel A. Farber
Henry J. Fletcher Professor of Law
University of Minnesota

Suzanna Sherry
Professor of Law
University of Minnesota

West Publishing Company
Saint Paul   New York   Los Angeles   San Francisco

Copyediting: Julie Bach
Composition: Northwestern Printcrafters

COPYRIGHT ©1990   By WEST PUBLISHING COMPANY
50 W. Kellogg Boulevard
P.O. Box 64526
St. Paul, MN 55164-1003

97 96 95 94 93 92 91 90   8 7 6 5 4 3 2 1 0

Library of Congress Cataloging-in-Publication Data

Farber, Daniel A., 1950-
   A history of the American constitution / Dan Farber, Suzanna Sherry.
      p.   cm.
   Includes bibliographical references.
   ISBN 0-314-56768-2
   1. United States—Constitutional history.   I. Sherry, Suzanna.   II. Title.
KF4541.F29   1990
342.73-029—dc20   89-37878
(347.30229)   CIP

To the memory of
my grandparents,
Ben and Esther Farber.

DAF

———

To Paul.

SS

Table of Contents

Table of Cases

The principal cases are in *italic* type. Cases sited or discussed are in roman type.

Preface

This book was conceived in the fall of 1986. On the eve of the bicentennial, President Reagan's nomination of Associate Justice William H. Rehnquist to replace retiring Chief Justice Warren Burger (as well as the nomination of Antonin Scalia to replace Rehnquist as an associate justice) reignited the long-smoldering debate over "originalism": to what extent the Supreme Court is bound to follow the intent of the original framers in interpreting the Constitution.

Steeped in the celebratory atmosphere of the Constitution's two-hundredth birthday and conscious of the accelerating argument over originalism, one of us decided to offer in the spring of 1987 a historical seminar entitled "The Summer of 1787." We were shocked to discover, however, that despite the bicentennial issuance of everything from birthday buttons to liberty beach towels, the only paperback edition of Madison's *Notes of Debates in the Federal Convention* was out of print and not expected to be republished. Deeming the hardcover version—plus additional sources to provide historical context—beyond the ordinary student budget, we did a quick and dirty cut-and-paste on Madison's *Notes*, organizing the debates by topic and deleting those we found overly repetitive or of minimal significance. That effort was the first draft of this book.

Three years and countless drafts later, with the addition of the Reconstruction Amendments and a considerable amount of our own text to explicate the primary sources, our original excerpts from Madison's *Notes* have become a usable resource for constitutional history. Between us, we have taught the materials three times, and have been pleased with the student response each time.

Versions of three chapters have previously appeared in print. A version of chapter 1 was published as Sherry, *The Intellectual Origins of the Constitution: A Lawyers' Guide to Contemporary Historical Scholarship*, 5 Constitutional Comm. 323 (1988). A version of chapter 9 was published as Farber & Muench, *The*

Ideological Origins of the Fourteenth Amendment, 1 Constitutional Comm. 235 (1984). A version of chapter 14 was published as Farber, *The Originalism Debate: A Guide for the Perplexed*, 49 Ohio St. L.J. 1085 (1989).

We are grateful to a number of people for the help they provided us in writing this book. Dean Robert A. Stein of the University of Minnesota Law School supported our project from the beginning and helped us find a publisher, as well as providing necessary summer grants and leave time. He also encouraged the scholarly and collegial atmosphere at Minnesota in which we both thrive. Portions of Part 2 of the book are derived from an earlier research project one of us did with John Muench. Marti Blake, Harriett Carlson, and Jean Castle spent many hours typing manuscripts, laboriously cutting and pasting (and recutting and repasting ad infinitum) Madison's *Notes*, and deciphering illegible copies of the *Congressional Globe*. Joan Humes (Minnesota J.D. 1990) provided invaluable research assistance locating sources, checking and rechecking our citations, and generally keeping the manuscript readable and consistent. Mark Wilson (Minnesota J.D. 1988) was helpful in researching and writing background memoranda for some of the chapters. Finally, we would like to thank our students at Minnesota and Stanford, whose participation in the seminars refined our understanding and kept us enthusiastic when the project seemed interminable.

A Note On Sources

Remember that most of the events described in this book happened more than a century ago, and many of them more than two centuries ago. Although written records of the debates and proceedings exist, some of them may be less than scrupulously accurate.[1] Keep that fact in mind when reading them.

THE FEDERAL CONVENTION: 1787

The only records of the debates in the Federal Convention in 1787 are the notes taken by individual delegates and published later. The official *Journal of the Convention*, kept by an elected secretary, was published in 1819. Unfortunately, it contains only a record of the delegates' votes, and no notes on the debates themselves.

James Madison took the most extensive notes, which were published in 1840 after his death. While most modern historians believe that his notes are a relatively faithful account of the debates as far as they go, they are clearly incomplete: the delegates debated for about five hours a day, but Madison's notes for any one day take only a few minutes to read aloud.[2]

Other delegates took notes, including Robert Yates, John Lansing, and Alexander Hamilton of New York, Rufus King of Massachusetts, William Paterson of New Jersey, James McHenry of Maryland, and William Pierce of Georgia. Some fragments of these notes have survived, but their accuracy is questionable. Unless otherwise indicated, all excerpts from Convention debates in chapters 2 through 8 are from Madison's notes.

Madison's notes have been republished in many editions. We have used the Tansill edition of the notes. That edition has been published separately a number of times, but was originally published as part of *Documents Illustrative of the Formation of the Union of American States*, 69th Congress, 1st Session, House Document No. 398, Government Printing Office, 1927. Tansill in turn relied on G. Hunt and J. Scott, *The Debates in the Federal Convention of 1787*, Oxford University Press, 1920. In preparing his edition of the notes, Tansill checked the Hunt and Scott edition against Madison's original transcript and added footnotes documenting every difference. In the interest of readability, we have omitted those footnotes. The Tansill volume is also the source of our excerpts from the notes of the other delegates, except for Lansing's notes. Lansing's notes are not reprinted in Tansill, but may be found in James H. Hutson, ed., *Supplement to Max Farrand's The Records of the Federal Convention of 1787*, Yale University Press, 1987.

THE RATIFICATION DEBATES: 1787–1788

Four main sources of information about the debate over ratification of the Constitution are extant. There are records of the debates in the state ratifying conventions; newspaper and circular essays by various opponents (and a few supporters) of the proposed Constitution; the *Federalist Papers* written in support of the Constitution by James Madison, Alexander Hamilton, and John Jay; and private correspondence among the principal actors in the ratification process. The essays and letters (including the *Federalist Papers*) are expressions of opinion and have survived as written. The accuracy of the records of debates in the state ratifying conventions is doubtful, as the reporters were often partisans themselves or hired by partisan participants. Thomas Lloyd, for example, who recorded the debates in Pennsylvania and Maryland, was paid by Federalists to delete all Anti-Federalist speeches from his report of the Pennsylvania Convention.

Virtually all of the ratification documents excerpted in chapters 7 and 8 are available from multiple sources. For the convenience of the reader, we have established a hierarchy of sources. Each document is identified by its location in the highest source in which it appears.

All of the debates in the state ratifying conventions are labeled by state and date, and identified by their location in Jonathan Elliot, *Debates in the State Conventions on the Adoption of the Federal Constitution*, J. B. Lippincott, 1891. Each excerpt is labeled by volume number and page number(s) in Elliot. For a few states, the Wisconsin Historical Society has supplemented Elliot by returning to his original sources and also to the private journals of participants in the debates. As that work progresses, it will provide a useful additional source of the debates in the state conventions. We have not used any excerpts from that work, however, as the Pennsylvania volume—the only one already available for a major state convention—does not add much to the Elliot excerpts we have included. Although the Wisconsin Historical Society work has been done under different editors, it is cited here as John P. Kaminski and Gaspare J. Saladino, eds., *The Documentary History of the Ratification of the Constitution*, Wisconsin Historical Society, 1976–present.

For *Federalist Papers* and private letters, no individual source is given. *Federalist Papers* are identified by number and by author. Letters are identified by sender, recipient, and date. So many editions of both the *Federalist Papers* and the letters of the various framers exist that this identifying information is sufficient to allow the reader to locate the document in virtually any edition.

Each excerpt from published Anti-Federalist essays is identified by author, essay number if relevant, and date of first publication. Although most of these essays are available from many sources, the most complete source is Herbert J. Storing, ed., The *Complete Anti-Federalist*, University of Chicago Press, 1981. For the convenience of the reader, we have further identified Anti-Federalist documents with Storing's own three-digit numbering system, to locate the document within his seven-volume set. His system includes the volume number, a number corresponding to each author within the volume, and a number corresponding to each portion of the author's work. The numbering system is copyright (c) 1981 by the University of Chicago, and is used with permission.

Miscellaneous other works that do not appear in Storing are similarly identified by author, essay number, and date of first publication. For the convenience of the reader, they are also identified by their location (volume and page) in Philip B. Kurland and Ralph Lerner, eds., *The Founders' Constitution*, University of Chicago Press, 1987.

THE BILL OF RIGHTS: 1789–1791

The documentary evidence on the Bill of Rights is even sketchier than the evidence on the drafting and ratification of the 1787 Constitution. Debates in the House of Representatives in the early years of the federal republic are recorded in Gales and Seaton, eds., *The Debates and Proceedings in the Congress of the United States*, 1834, also called *Annals of Congress*. The accuracy of the *Annals* is open to some question, as they were prepared by Thomas Lloyd, whose lack of integrity has been noted above and whose ability to record the proceedings had declined by 1789 due to excessive drinking.[3]

Locating particular debates in the 1789 House is further complicated by the fact that *two* printings of the first two volumes of the *Annals of Congress* exist. They are identical except for pagination, running page titles, and back titles. The printing with the running page title "History of Congress" conforms to the remaining volumes of the series while the printing with the running page title "Gales & Seaton's History of Debates in Congress" does not. To aid the reader in locating excerpts in either printing, we have included the date of the debate in all excerpts and footnote citations in chapter 8. The page numbers in footnote citations are from the "History of Congress" series. House resolutions and committee reports are taken from Volume V of *A Documentary History of the Constitution of the United States of America*, U.S. Bureau of Rolls and Library; Department of State, 1905.

The Senate sat in closed session until 1794, so there are no records of their debates over the Bill of Rights. Excerpts and discussions of Senate motions and votes in chapter 8 are taken from the *Senate Journal*, reprinted in *History of Congress; Exhibiting a Classification of the Proceedings of the Senate, and the House of Representatives, from March 4, 1789, to March 3, 1793*, Lea & Blanchard, 1843.

RECONSTRUCTION AMENDMENTS: 1865–1873

By 1865, the *Annals of Congress* had been replaced by the *Congressional Globe*, a much more faithful account of congressional debates. Both House and Senate debates are recorded in the *Globe*. The full debates over the Reconstruction Amendments are not collected in any one source and are available only by paging through the *Globe*. All excerpts in chapters 10 through 12 are taken from the *Globe*, and are identified by date. Footnote citations include the number of the Congress and session number as well.

FOOTNOTES

1. For an account of some of the questions about the accuracy of the historical record, see James H. Hutson, *The Creation of the Constitution: The Integrity of the Documentary Record*, 65 Tex. L. Rev. 1 (1986).

2. Hutson has calculated that a typical one-hour discussion uses approximately 6,000-8,000 words. Madison's notes average less than 600 words per hour of debate, suggesting that he recorded less than ten percent of the daily debates. *Id*. at 34.

3. *See id*. at 36.

Editorial Note

Throughout the book we have indicated deletions within any document by ellipses. Editorial decisions to begin or end the excerpt in the middle of the document are not marked. Decisions to begin or end a particular individual's speech or judicial opinion in the middle are also not marked. Footnotes and citations are sometimes deleted without notice.

Introduction

No one book can truly live up to the title, *A History of the American Constitution*. Constitutional history is far too broad to be fully discussed in a single volume or even in a dozen. The history of the Constitution is both a part of and a reflection of the larger history of the United States—social, economic, political, and so on. The history of the Constitution, like any historical project, can also be written from the bottom up rather than the top down, as a story of the people and individual conflicts involved in significant changes in the Constitution or its interpretation. Constitutional history, moreover, often refers specifically to the historical development of Supreme Court case law and its place in American society.

This book focuses on a single aspect of constitutional history: the drafting and ratification of the written Constitution. Created in several stages and still evolving, the United States Constitution is the product of three centuries of American political and intellectual history. The people who wrote and ratified each part of the Constitution drew on philosophical influences of their day to argue about the language, the purpose, the meaning, and the necessity of the provisions they were adopting. Those debates are the primary sources that form the core of this book. They are supplemented with textual explanations and background to place the debates in historical context.

This aspect of constitutional history is significant for many reasons. It is a vital part of American history, and especially of American legal history. Examining the views and beliefs of the framers of the Constitution sheds light on the historical circumstances that prompted constitutional provisions, and may serve to illuminate the original meaning of the language of those provisions. Integrating the history of the writing of the Constitution with the history of its interpretation—the standard fare of any constitutional law course—lends an added dimension to constitutional doctrine.

We have divided the book into three parts, to correspond with the three main phases of development of the Constitution. Part 1 (chapters 1 through 8)

xxi

covers the period from 1787 to 1791, when both the body of the Constitution and the Bill of Rights were adopted. The first chapter is an introductory discussion of the ideological influences of the late eighteenth century that puts the framers' debates in historical perspective. Chapter 2 provides an overview of the issues facing the delegates to the Federal Convention in Philadelphia in 1787, including the thorny question of their own authority to do more than amend the Articles of Confederation. The heart of the delegates' debates—taken from Madison's notes of the Convention—is found in chapters 3 through 6. Those chapters are arranged topically: chapter 3 covers the judiciary, chapter 4 the executive, and chapter 5 the legislature. Chapter 6 deals separately with the question of slavery. Chapter 7 is an account of the long ratification process of the 1787 Constitution, and includes excerpts from Federalist and Anti-Federalist writings and speeches. Finally, the last chapter in part 1 presents a history of the Bill of Rights, the first ten amendments to the Constitution.

Part 2 (chapters 9 through 12) covers the "Reconstruction Revolution," the period from 1865 to 1873 when the Thirteenth, Fourteenth, and Fifteenth amendments were adopted. Chapter 9 is an introduction to the intellectual and historical forces that influenced the Reconstruction politicians. Chapter 10 focuses on the Thirteenth Amendment, which outlawed slavery. Chapter 11 deals with the Fourteenth Amendment and its statutory precursor, the 1866 Civil Rights Act. The Fifteenth Amendment is covered in chapter 12.

The last part of the book (chapters 13 and 14) focuses on the uses of the historical evidence presented in the first two parts. Chapter 13 discusses the twentieth-century Supreme Court's use of constitutional history in interpreting the written document. Chapter 14 surveys the voluminous contemporary literature on the "originalism" debate: whether the original intent of the framers of the Constitution should be dispositive in determining the current meaning of the constitutional language. Thus part 3 extends the history of the Constitution into the late twentieth century and frames the question of the relevance of the earlier history to contemporary constitutional issues.

PART ONE

1787-1791

INTRODUCTION TO PART ONE

The Constitution of the United States is a short document—it runs only sixteen pages in the Appendix—but it was created over the course of two centuries. Thus, different parts of the Constitution reflect different historical eras. We have chosen in this book to consider the history of the Constitution in three distinct parts. Part 1 covers the original Constitution of 1787 as well as the first ten amendments (the Bill of Rights) adopted all at once in 1791. Part 2 covers the Thirteenth, Fourteenth, and Fifteenth amendments, the so-called "Reconstruction Amendments" adopted shortly after the Civil War. Part 3 brings the history of the Constitution up to date by discussing modern judicial and scholarly use of historical evidence in interpreting the written text.

In this first part, we present excerpts from debates on the drafting and ratification of the 1787 Constitution and the 1791 Bill of Rights. Only eleven years old in 1787, the new American nation was already experiencing difficulties with its first national constitution, the Articles of Confederation. So in May of 1787, twelve of the thirteen states sent delegates to the Federal Convention to draft a new constitution. Chapters 2 through 6 deal with the debates in that Convention. The document produced by the Convention was not put into effect until it was ratified by individual conventions in the states; chapter 7 focuses on the debates over ratification. Because many people were still unsatisfied with the new Constitution, Congress proposed twelve amendments in 1789 as one of its first orders of business; ten of the twelve amendments were sucessfully ratified in 1791. Chapter 8 covers those amendments, known collectively as the Bill of Rights.

Before we turn to the events of 1787, however, we must explore the historical and philosophical background of eighteenth-century American beliefs and politics. Chapter 1 is a brief history of the intellectual origins or the Constitution and the ideological forces present in 1787 America.

1

The Intellectual Origins of the Constitution

INTRODUCTION

The history of the American Constitution begins in 1215. When King John acceded to the demands of his nobles and signed the Magna Carta, he did more than acknowledge many of the rights that would eventually become a part of the American Constitution. The events at Runnymede signaled the start of a new era in theories of government. The progress from John's reluctant acceptance of limits on his previously absolute authority to the written American Constitution is a series of increasingly sophisticated steps in the establishment of government under law.

The Magna Carta remained Britain's only written form of constitution for almost five hundred years. During those centuries, a tradition of constitutionalism nevertheless flourished. Those opposed to the exercise of royal or parliamentary authority often based their arguments on Britain's unwritten "ancient constitution," or common law, custom, and tradition. They sought to establish that the king's own powers were derived from, and thus subordinate to, this law. Though these arguments were usually unsuccessful, the notion of constitutional limitations on governmental authority became part of English rhetoric and political philosophy. By the beginning of the seventeenth century, appeal to the "ancient constitution," which had allegedly existed since "time immemorial," was a standard political argument.

The momentous events of the seventeenth century catapulted English constitutionalism into the modern era, but in forms ultimately unacceptable to the American colonists. The Interregnum, the Glorious Revolution of 1688 (ending the reign of the Stuarts), and the 1689 Bill of Rights and its companion acts, settled both the limits on royal prerogative and the absolute supremacy of Parliament. Limited government came to mean the Crown limited by Parliament and the rights of the people safeguarded by the vaunted "mixed constitution." A balance among the monarchic (Crown), aristocratic (Lords), and democratic (Commons) elements was thought to ensure the preservation of liberty, and no further checks on parliamentary supremacy were thought necessary. The British constitution was both a description of existing institutions—including laws, customs, and traditions as well as the balance of power—and a declaration of fundamental principles. Neither of these aspects of the constitution served much to limit Parliament.

Throughout this period, numerous political philosophers tried to spell out the principles on which the system was (or in their view should have been) based. The Enlightenment's rationalist rejection of the divine right of kings, Cromwell's assumption of power, and the Glorious Revolution with its ouster of the Stuarts opened new avenues for discussion about sovereignty and power. Competing visions of the basis for or origin of sovereignty (was sovereignty based on raw power or consent of the governed?) and its ultimate location (did it reside in Parliament or in the constitution?) led Hobbes and Locke, Blackstone and Bolingbroke, and Harrington and Montesquieu to devise and refine intricate and conflicting theories of government based on rational Enlightenment principles, rather than on the pre-Enlightenment religious tradition.

The American colonies, settled in the early seventeenth century and coming of political age in the eighteenth, thus inherited diverse and sophisticated theories of government. Throughout the eighteenth century, however, American development and interpretation of these political theories began to diverge from their British sources. Although Americans relied heavily on British thinkers, they were selective in their philosophical inspirations and radical in their applications.

Three circumstances most shaped the prism through which the colonists viewed British political philosophy: political exclusion, geographic situation, and a resulting perceived cultural uniqueness. Together, these factors allowed—and sometimes demanded—that Americans develop their own political culture.

The colonies' political and geographic isolation led them, sometimes in spite of their own intentions, to establish cohesive communities that were often more egalitarian than the relatively hierarchical English structures. It led them, especially after the mid-1760s, to favor theories that stressed natural law rather than civil or socially-created law in order to dispute the validity of their political dependency. It led them to embrace English Opposition theories that rejected the conventional view of legislative supremacy. It evoked a new emphasis on a constitution as a limiting principle which gradually superseded the traditional view of a constitution as a description. It enabled them to adopt Enlightenment rationalism with enthusiasm by allowing them to ignore or reject aspects inconsistent with their circumstances.

Separated from England by a vast ocean, confident that the continent would provide unlimited land, and oppressed by English rule but unencumbered by the practical political realities of large-scale self-government, the colonists came to view themselves and their institutions as uniquely virtuous and rational—and in particular peril from the corrupting force of England. Echoing the sentiments of many of his compatriots, John Adams wrote in 1765:

> The liberties of mankind and the glory of human nature is in their keeping. America was designed by Providence for the theatre on which man was to make his true

figure, on which science, virtue, liberty, happiness and glory were to exist in peace.[1]

By the 1760s, this divergence of colonial political theory from its British antecedents began pointing ineluctably toward separation from Great Britain. By the Revolution, the American social and political structure so differed—in both ideal and real forms—from that of Great Britain that Americans could view themselves as restoring rather than destroying, maintaining rather than altering, political liberty and the social order through revolution. This chapter tells the story of these interwoven strands of political philosophy and their American interpretations. It is this story that forms the background against which the American Constitution was written and ratified.

Contemporary historians disagree about the amount of influence various philosophical sources had on Americans between 1760 and 1787. Until the late 1960s, most historians thought that the philosophical inspiration for the American Revolution came almost solely from the work of John Locke. The Constitution was similarly seen primarily as a product of Lockean liberalism. Depending on the historian's own political views, the Constitution was described sometimes as a selfish attempt to protect private property and sometimes as a brilliant beginning of the capitalist individualism that made America great, but always as traceable almost directly to John Locke.

Beginning in 1967 with the publication of Bernard Bailyn's *The Ideological Origins of the American Revolution*, historians began identifying additional philosophical sources for both the Revolution and the Constitution. For the past two decades, many historians have argued that classical republicanism, especially in the form passed down through English Opposition theories of the seventeenth and early eighteenth century, had a greater intellectual influence than Locke on the American Revolution. While this emphasis on "republicanism" (both "republicanism" and "liberalism" are defined later in this chapter) is currently the predominant school of thought, some historians still stress Locke's influence to a greater or lesser degree. Moreover, there is great debate about the timing of the transformation from classical republicanism to Lockean liberalism; some historians believe it was complete by 1787 and others contend that America is still somewhat republican.

In our narrative we have chosen to follow a version of the most popular historiographical approach: that classical republicanism was the most significant influence until after the Revolution, but that by 1787 Lockean liberalism provided a strong counterinfluence that overshadowed but did not eradicate republican sentiment. We have also tried, however, to give full descriptions of other influences to allow readers to draw their own conclusions as they trace the different schools of thought present in the Constitutional Convention.

"A CONSPIRACY AGAINST THE RIGHTS OF HUMANITY"

Sources

Thomas Jefferson was perhaps the most well-read American of the eighteenth century. His library contained almost 5,000 volumes in 1815, when he sold the entire collection to the Library of Congress. It is a tribute to him, and an illustration of the many influences on the American Constitution, that his library contained the work of every writer mentioned in this chapter. While his collection was unique, it contained works that were well-known sources of inspiration for many Americans. Speaking an eighteenth-century language of corruption and conspiracy, of virtue and vigilance, Americans drew on a multitude of philosophical sources to construct their own science of politics. They learned perhaps the most from the "Country" or Opposition party of England. Members of that party, which existed in various forms from the early seventeenth century through the tumultous period of the American Revolution, looked primarily to James Harrington (the author of a 1656 utopian tract titled *The Commonwealth of Oceana*) for their ideas. Elements of Harrington's philosophy can be traced backward through Niccolo Machiavelli to the ancient republics, and forward through John Trenchard and Thomas Gordon (the authors of *Cato's Letters*, published between 1720 and 1724), Viscount Bolingbroke (Henry Saint-John), and James Burgh. Throughout most of the seventeenth century, the Opposition party consisted primarily of Whigs opposed to royal encroachments on parliamentary authority. After the Glorious Revolution of 1688 removed the Stuarts, put the Whig party in power, and established the supremacy of Parliament, the "Country" party included those few Whigs who felt that not enough had been done, and some Tories who opposed the new "Court" party that had come to power.

Variously called Old Whigs, Real Whigs, and Commonwealthmen, the Opposition party had few adherents in Great Britain after the Glorious Revolution of 1688. Whig ideas were tremendously influential in America, however; in pamphlets that served as primary vehicles of popular political expression during both the pre-Revolutionary period and the ratification struggle after the Constitutional Convention, many writers took either Whiggish pseudonyms or, in imitation of the English Whigs, classical ones.

A related source of American political ideas was the Continental Enlightenment philosophers. Only Montesquieu and Rousseau are well-known today, but colonial Americans also read and relied on such forgotten Enlightenment figures as Grotius, Pufendorf, Vattel, and Burlamaqui. Montesquieu, the most frequently cited of any philosopher during the ratification period, in turn drew drew on the English Bolingbroke as well as on his own Continental contemporaries.

One of the more influential philosophers is also one of the hardest to categorize. John Locke, whose *Two Treatises of Government* was first published in 1690, has been allied both with and against some of the Old Whigs. He has been hailed as the spirit of 1776 but not of 1787, as the spirit of 1787 but not of 1776, and as the spirit of both, and of neither. His work has been praised as bringing the Enlightenment to America, castigated as leading Americans into a narrow and short-sighted vision of politics, and relegated to the status of a minor influence on the Revolutionary or constitutional periods. Whether or not Americans drew their inspiration directly from his writings, Locke's ideas wound through American thought of both periods. As we shall see, different elements of his theories were prominent at different times.

Finally, Americans looked to the magnificent English common lawyers: Edward Coke, Henry de Bracton, and William Blackstone. From the early seventeenth century to the eve of the Revolution, Americans could turn to these English lawyers, judges, and commentators for a principled historical explication of English common law. Many prominent figures of the Revolution and more than half the delegates to the Constitutional Convention were lawyers or legally trained—and to Americans in the latter half of the eighteenth century, to be legally trained meant to be steeped in English common law. The most important lesson Americans learned from the common lawyers, however, was methodological rather than substantive. They admired Blackstone's *Commentaries*, for example, not so much for its content as for its scientific method of drawing general principles from a vast body of judicial decisions.

These different strands of thought contained myriad variations and nuances, and were often inconsistent with one another. Americans added their own inventions. From this seamless web grew more theories, with different patriots espousing different views at different times. The history of the American Constitution is a history of ideas. The rest of this chapter surveys the ideas that inspired Americans between 1774, when the Revolution began to seem inevitable, and 1787, when fifty-five men sat down in Philadelphia to write a constitution.

Corruption

For most eighteenth-century Americans, politics could be reduced to its essential character: a constant struggle between power and liberty. They looked at history—at the history of the ancient republics, Europe, and, increasingly, England—and saw a pattern of governmental tyranny stifling the liberty of the people. The source of this tyranny was corruption. Until the 1760s, Americans considered themselves fortunate to be under English rule, for the English "mixed constitution" was a safeguard against corruption. More and more influenced by the "Country" party, however, Americans began to see corruption even in England. In 1774, a writer in the Philadelphia *Pennsylvania Packet* described the English constitution as "the mighty ruin of a once noble fabrick."[2] Such was the result of corruption.

Primarily derived from Opposition theory, the term corruption did not have the rather limited meaning of moral subversion we assign it today. It meant virtually any distortion of the proper balance of power orchestrated by forces within the government. Any part of government could become corrupt. Parliament was corrupt when it became dependent on the king, whether that dependency arose from individual indebtedness or institutional subordination. Evidence of the Crown's corruption lay in its increasing use of patronage, ministerial persuasiveness, and electoral influence—rather than the constitutionally mandated (but clumsy) "prerogative"—to achieve its goals, notwithstanding parliamentary objections. A writer in the Boston *New England Chronicle* described royal corruption:

> It is upon this principle that the King of Great-Britain is absolute; for though he doth not act without the parliament, by places, pensions, honours and promises, he obtains the sanction of the parliament for doing as he pleases. The ancient form is preserved, but the spirit of the constitution is evaporated.[3]

The language of the colonists, like the writings of the Opposition party, was peppered with code words for the symptoms of corruption: placemen, standing armies, bishops, aristocrats, luxury, monopolies, stock-jobbers. Although each term originally had a specific meaning, they came to be used as epithets, hurled at enemies for their emotive effect.

Although English and American Whigs thought that power tended inevitably toward corruption, the corrosive effect of corruption was not viewed as random or unchanneled. Taught by the Enlightenment to reject the workings of Providence as sufficient explanation, eighteenth-century writers blamed the ways of men. Americans, like their "Country" teachers, saw in the English government a deliberate conspiracy against liberty. Thomas Jefferson wrote of "a deliberate, systematical plan of reducing us to slavery."[4] William Henry Drayton described "a conspiracy against the rights of humanity."[5] As every modern criminal lawyer knows, the existence of a conspiracy allows every false move to be branded as a high crime. Thus the American colonists were suspicious or "jealous" of every parliamentary or royal act, however minor, that might be construed as a step in the conspiracy.

Good Whigs on both sides of the Atlantic knew that certain forms of government provided some protection against corruption. Any device that made the legislature more accountable to its constituents offered hope. Members of the Opposition party called for shorter parliamentary sessions, which would have afforded a more frequent opportunity for electors to throw out corrupt legislators. They also demanded the right to instruct their representatives, in order to control their votes on particular issues.

Another method of discouraging legislative corruption lay in the nature of the legislature itself. The English Parliament had, over the centuries, become less directly representative. Rather than a group of individual members speaking for their local constituents, Parliament had become a national legislature. Edmund Burke described it favorably:

> Parliament is a *deliberative* assembly of *one* nation with *one* interest, that of the whole, where, not local purposes, not local prejudices ought to guide, but the general good, resulting from the general reason of the whole.[6]

Burke's theory was especially grating to the colonists because it served as a justification for their exclusion from Parliament. Following Burke's lead, England could argue that Americans did not need direct representation in Parliament because they had "virtual representation": members of Parliament were looking out for colonial interests though they were not actually elected by the colonies.

Most Americans, following the "Country" party rejection of Burke's deliberative assembly, held instead that representatives in Parliament were "creatures" only of the constituents who elected them, and were strictly accountable to those electors. The colonies thus rejected the British theory of "virtual representation." They also, in creating their own colonial assemblies, tried to avoid a Burkean legislature. As a result, colonial assemblies were condemned by their British contemporaries as

> plain illiterate husbandmen, whose views seldom extended farther than to the regulation of highways, the destruction of wolves, wildcats and foxes, and the advancement of the other little interests of the particular counties which they were chosen to represent.[7]

Despite the American rejection of virtual representation, however, colonial assemblies were still badly malapportioned.

"Country" ideology also recommended another device to guard against distortion of the balance of government: strict separation of powers. Both Bolingbroke and Montesquieu spoke of the independence of the different branches of government, and often suggested that keeping the functions of each branch separate would prevent mingling of power and the resulting loss of liberty. The "mixed constitution," by contrast, established a system more of checks and balances. Each branch represented a different segment of society (the Crown, the aristocracy, and the masses) rather than exercising a different function. Restraint and harmony, for the dominant English party (the "Court" party), came from relations among the personnel and constituencies of the different branches of government. Americans preferred Montesquieu's vision of separate functions. Americans believed that the English constitution was an insufficient safeguard against corruption. Again, however, the theory was an imperfect representation. In both Montesquieu's description of an ideal constitution and early American practice, the authority and powers of each branch were not rigidly separate.

Corruption not only destroyed the liberties of a people, it sapped their strength. A people subverted by corruption were unable to repel foreign invasions or to protest further subversion of the constitution by the government. Once enslaved by a corrupt regime, a republic ceased to exist. Ancient Greek and Roman republics and contemporary Polish and Danish republics had perished in this way. By the early 1770s, Americans were certain that the English republic was in imminent danger of the same fate. They rebelled to save themselves from the English conspiracy against liberty.

Liberty

If corruption was the predator, liberty was the victim. Liberty meant many things, and in speaking of it Americans often used ideas not only of Opposition thinkers but of Locke and Montesquieu. Sometimes they fused these into a single, value-laden concept with interchangeable meaning and great rhetorical effect. When Patrick Henry galvanized Virginians by demanding liberty or death, his listeners could interpret his words as encompassing a number of interrelated ideas.

The simplest meaning of liberty was individual liberty: the capacity to exercise natural rights. That definition, however, concealed basic ambiguities. With their focus on the looming destruction of natural rights, neither English nor American Whigs spent much time describing the rights themselves. The second of *Cato's Letters*—the Opposition tract read by nearly every literate American of the period—said that liberty was "the Power which every man has over his own Actions, and his Right to enjoy the Fruit of his Labour, Art, and Industry."[8] Various writers identified the right to conscience (primarily religious liberty) as an inalienable right. All the rights protected by English common law and the "ancient constitution"—including jury trials and other procedural protections, and some freedom of speech—were held to be inalienable rights. In part, eighteenth-century natural lawyers did not need to specify particular rights because they believed them to be self-evident, or, in historian Bernard Bailyn's description, "inherent in people as such . . . [and] distilled from reason and justice."[9]

Perhaps the most thorough discussion of natural rights available to the founding generation was Locke's account of natural law. According to Locke, in the state of nature (prior to political society and government) all men began as equals.[10] They were equally free from the authority of another and equally vulnerable to the "invasion" of another. This vulnerability and the consequent disruption of natural liberty is what led men to leave the state of nature and enter into a compact to form civil or political society. By entering the social compact, men cede to their governors some rights. There are, however, certain natural and inalienable rights that cannot be ceded.

From this account of the origins of political society, Locke derived his theory of government. Government is a compact with limited purposes and limited effects. For classical republicans—typified best in this instance by Aristotle—government and society are not distinct, but merge into a single concept: a "regime," with pervasive involvement in the lives of citizens. For Locke, in contrast, the only legitimate purpose of government is the purpose for which it is formed: to protect citizens' enjoyment of their natural and inalienable rights. These include life, liberty—in a narrower sense than the general capacity to exercise all natural rights—and property.

But what did Locke mean by life, liberty, and property? Certainly Americans took him to include freedom of conscience and freedom from arbitrary laws. Locke also noted that even after entering the civil compact, each man still has "*Liberty* to dispose, and order . . . his Person, Actions, Possessions and his whole Property, within the Allowance of those Laws under which he is."[11] Thus liberty in society is somewhat narrower than it is in the state of nature. Regardless, the right to self-preservation can never be legitimately stifled, although it is possible to read Locke as allowing government to limit the means by which this right can be exercised.

Locke's theory of property rights is especially complex. Although each man has a natural right to the fruits of his own labor, there are limits to the amount any individual may accumulate. Property is originally given to man (by God) in common. It is only by his own labor that a man acquires individual property rights. Labor thus becomes the basis for all property rights, and Locke saw two limits on acquisition: no individual can acquire more property than he can improve by his labor or more than he can use. Thus, nothing should be allowed to spoil, or "perish . . . uselessly."[12] Moreover, Locke's premises that man must live in society and that self-preservation necessarily implies the preservation of society led him to attach the proviso that a man can only acquire property by his labor if "there is enough, and as good left in common for others."[13]

The Lockean theory of limited acquisition was consistent with other influences on American ideology. Many eighteenth-century thinkers considered property a political or civil right, rather than an inalienable natural right. An early English radical declared in 1647:

> The Law of God doth not give me property, nor the Law of Nature, but property is of human constitution. I have a property and this I shall enjoy. Constitution founds property.[14]

Government regulation of property rights—sometimes to the point of confiscation—was thus permissible, and extensive. In the New England colonies, for example, public post roads were established by narrowing existing privately owned throughways, and then giving back to the owners the strips obtained by the narrowing. As historian Forrest McDonald has described it, the colonial government "compensated landowners for taking part of their land by letting them keep the remainder of their land."[15]

Locke's ideas on property rights were agreeable to the American colonists because they reflected an even greater influence on American definitions of liberty: classical republicanism. According to the prevailing "Country" ideology of classical republicanism, the purpose of property ownership was to benefit the whole community rather than the individual owner. Owning land instilled virtues necessary for active citizenship: an attachment to the community, self-sufficiency, stability, and wisdom. Thus Jefferson advocated abolishing primogeniture (whereby only the oldest son could inherit real property) in order to broaden the base of citizenship. Land ownership, when accompanied by labor and improvement, also benefited the community by increasing productivity and plenty. Since land ownership primarily benefited the community, individual owners were expected to obey the community's regulations.

Thus both Locke and the "Country" party writers found some government regulation of property appropriate. The apparent congruence of their views, however, is misleading; their differences are more significant than their similarities. Where Locke emphasized individual rights as the basis for natural law, classical republican or "Country" ideology subordinated individual liberty to the needs of the community (although the needs of the community sometimes called for the exercise of individual liberty). The Continental Enlightenment philosophers also wrote copiously on natural law and natural rights, but again from a more community-oriented perspective. With their primarily classical outlook, most Americans—at least through the late 1770s—selectively embraced the less individualist aspects of Locke. This emphasis may have changed somewhat by 1787, as we shall see. But during the colonial and early independent era, the classical outlook also led Americans away from specific definitions of natural rights. Individual liberty was rarely defined more specifically than (in the words of one Revolutionary American) "a power of acting agreeable to the laws which are made and enacted by the consent of the PEOPLE, and in no ways inconsistent with the natural rights of a single person, or the good of the society."[16]

Thus colonial Americans rarely defined natural rights because defining anything in terms of *individual* rights was something of a rarity. Another reason natural rights were not well-defined in the 1760s and 1770s is that individual liberty was, for many, not as important as civil or political liberty. Political liberty was essentially the right of the people to participate in self-government. Even a cursory glance at the Declaration of Independence, for example, reveals that the rights demanded and the injuries protested are primarily public, not private. The grievances include the king's various interferences with legislative attempts to pass laws "wholesome and necessary for the public good" and his obstruction of justice.

The theory, then, was that the greater the diffusion of political liberty, the more ideal the society. Americans viewed their society as more naturally adapted to liberty. America was in fact somewhat more egalitarian than most European nations, and property (a republican prerequisite for political citizenship) was more broadly distributed. The existence of slavery was essentially ignored. The colonists felt—any evidence to the contrary notwithstanding—both uniquely free and in unique danger from the English threat to political liberty.

Political liberty in a republic was, moreover, inextricably intertwined with the purposes of republican government. At this point, some terminology must be clarified. The term "republican" has two meanings. Eighteenth-century Americans used "republic" or "republican form of government" to describe merely the *form* of government: a republic was the antithesis of a monarchy. Twentieth-century historians, however, use "republican" (especially when modified by the adjectives "classical" or "Jeffersonian") to describe a school of thought prevalent at the time. The discussion of property rights shows that classical republican or "Country" ideology differed significantly from the liberalism of Locke. Note that "liberalism" also has a specialized meaning: it does not refer to the underlying ideology of the modern welfare state (one of its modern meanings) but rather to the individualistic philosophy derived from Locke that was dominant in the United States in the late nineteenth century.

The problem is that eighteenth-century Americans had no single word to describe either their own "Country" or republican outlook, or its liberal opposite, and so we must use the modern terms. In the first sentence in the preceding paragraph, for example, "republic" is used in its eighteenth-century sense, and "republican" in its twentieth-century sense. For the convenience of the reader, we will use "republic" only to describe the form of government, and "republican" only to label the school of thought. Remember, though, that the eighteenth-century thinkers whose works you will be reading use both terms interchangeably. "Liberal" and "liberalism"—which were generally not used in the eighteenth century—are used here as the antithesis of republicanism, and not in their more common modern political sense.

A republic (the type of government), then, can be either liberal or republican (depending on whether it is mostly Lockean or mostly "Country"). Americans, for example, were influenced by both Locke and the classical republicans in demanding changes in the form of government. Rejecting a monarchy or a mixed government, they were determined to create a republic, or government based on the people. The type of republic they envisioned, however, depended on the extent to which they adopted Lockean or "Country" goals.

Unlike Locke, who viewed protection of individual liberty as the sole purpose of government, the classical republicans thought that all government "ought to be calculated for the general good . . . of the community."[17] The public good, not private liberty, was the most important goal of republican government. Political liberty consisted not only of the capacity to participate in government, but also of living under a government that put the good of the community ahead of the good of any individual.

It is here that Locke's emphasis on individual liberty and the "Country" or classical republican emphasis on community are most in conflict. At least through 1776, however, there was little recognition of this conflict. American revolutionaries believed that only corrupt governors, or "idiots or self-murderers" among the people, would put selfish interests ahead of the interests of the nation.[18]

Despite this somewhat naive belief that conflicting individual interests would not seriously hamper pursuit of the communal good, the underlying conflict still existed. For Locke, the good of the whole was defined by the good of individuals—the more freedom individuals had to pursue their own interests, the better off was the nation. For republicans, the good of the whole was greater than the aggregated good of individuals. Classical republicans conceived of society in organic terms, rather than in mechanistic terms. The whole was therefore more than the sum of its parts; the community had its own existence and its own needs. Political liberty involved more than the greatest possible amount of individual liberty. Good republican government might transform individuals; good liberal (Lockean) government merely protected them. Historian John Diggins has described the difference:

> Between Machiavelli and Locke lies the dilemma of American politics. Classical political philosophy aims to discipline man's desires and raise him far above his vulgar wants; liberalism promises to realize desires and satisfy wants. The first is more noble, the second more attainable.[19]

Much of the first half of this book consists of the public debate over this dilemma and solutions to it.

It was in fact political liberty in all of its manifestations that was most threatened by the corruption of the English constitution and the excesses of Parliament. And the way in which Americans sought to protect their liberty from the corrupting force across the Atlantic was the creation and maintenance of public virtue.

Virtue

In 1776, Americans believed that a republic had only one defense against conspiracy against liberty: the "virtue" of its people. As we have seen, political liberty required both public participation in government and a government dedicated to the public good. The maintenance of political liberty demanded that individuals subordinate their private interests to the welfare of the community. This willingness to sacrifice private interests to the public good was called virtue. John Adams described in 1776 the need for what he termed "public virtue":

> [P]ublic virtue is the only foundation of republics. There must be a positive passion for the public good, the public interest, honor, power, and glory, established in the minds of the people, or there can be no republican government, nor any real liberty; and this public passion must be superior to all private passions. Men must be ready, they must pride themselves, and be happy to sacrifice their private pleasures, passions, and interests, nay, their private friendships and dearest connections, when they stand in competition with the rights of society.[20]

Adams believed a republic to be the most fragile form of government, requiring constant vigilance against both corruption and lack of virtue.

How did a society cultivate virtue? Americans thought themselves naturally virtuous as a result of their circumstances, so they did not explore this question as fully as they might have. Their "Country" predecessors were too busy lamenting governmental corruption to spend much time on public virtue. We can, however, draw out some common themes.

Broad distribution of land ownership was believed to be essential for creating and maintaining a virtuous population, because tilling the land made men virtuous. Jefferson was perhaps the most eloquent expositor of this premise:

> Cultivators of the earth are the most valuable citizens. They are the most vigorous, the most independent, the most virtuous, and they are tied to their country and wedded to its liberty and interests, by the most lasting bonds.[21]

Those who owned land were best able to see how their private interests were bound up with the good of the community. Despite the fact that many landowners were also slave owners, Jefferson (himself the owner of many slaves) thought that those with property learned lessons of virtue more easily than those deprived of property, because the latter lacked a concrete connection to the community. The unpropertied class included both those too poor to own land and those engaged in trade or commerce rather than farming. Both groups, thought Jefferson, were inclined to be less virtuous than the yeoman farmer.

Another means of inculcating virtue was education. A people could be taught to value liberty and to understand how serving the public good served liberty:

> Where learning prevails in a community, liberality of sentiment, and zeal for the publick good, are the grand characteristicks of the people. . . .
>   If we would maintain our dear bought rights inviolate, let us diffuse the spirit of literature: Then will self interest, the governing principle of a savage heart, expand and be transferred into patriotism: Then will each member of the community consider himself as belonging to one common family, whose happiness he will ever be zealous to promote.[22]

Public virtue also depended on a fundamental premise of equality. Eighteenth-century Americans meant many things by the term "equality." With Locke, they believed men were born equal because, in the most basic sense, none had any superior claim to rule over others. Despite its apparent breadth, this eighteenth-century egalitarianism was extremely limited. It did not lead many Americans to conclude that slavery was wrong. Nor did most American republicans extend equality to those who did not participate in the political process, including women, Indians, children, and—in some places at some times—those who lacked property qualifications for voting. More important, Americans defined equality in a moral sense: they believed men to be equally bound by moral duties and equally endowed with moral sensibility. It was this moral equality that allowed the American republicans to place their faith in the virtue of (some of) the people. Jefferson, for example, stated repeatedly that man was innately moral and innately capable of public virtue:

> Man was destined for society. His morality, therefore, was to be formed to this object. He was endowed with a sense of right and wrong, merely relative to this. This sense is as much a part of his nature, as the sense of hearing, seeing, feeling. . . . It may be strengthened by exercise, as may any particular limb of the body.[23]

Thus Jefferson, like most of his contemporaries, believed that inborn moral sensibility might be brought out by the right circumstances and the right education. There were not many, however, who had the ability—to say nothing of the wealth and the leisure—to pursue the development of virtue to the extent necessary to sustain a republic. The eighteenth-century republicans on both sides of the Atlantic expected that a "natural aristocracy" would spring up to govern the country. Composed of those with extraordinary talent, the natural aristocracy would exemplify both virtue and restraint. They would put the good of the community before their own selfish interests and protect liberty from the selfishness of individuals and the corruption of governors. At the same time, since they would derive their pre-eminent role from natural talents rather than artificial distinctions, they would be in an ideal position to guide and govern the masses.

For Revolutionary Americans, as for their "Country" cousins and classical republican ancestors, the best foundation for a flourishing republic was to increase the supply of virtue: to make better people. In 1776, this looked like an easy task, because Americans perceived themselves to be uniquely virtuous and therefore uniquely suited to a republic.

> [In America] the moral basis of a healthy, liberty-preserving polity seemed already to exist in the unsophisticated lives of the independent, uncorrupted, landowning yeoman farmers who comprised so large a part of the colonial population.[24]

The main threat to this utopia came from outside, from the corrupting force in England. Once the connection to England was severed, Americans expected their natural virtue would allow them to regain the basis for their republic. As the next section shows, they were quickly disillusioned.

"THE EXCESSES OF DEMOCRACY"

When jealousy of their liberty and their virtue led Americans to take the extreme step of declaring to a "candid world" their grievances and their independence, they entered into the process of creating new governments with great enthusiasm but little experience. In addition to their Opposition politics, the colonial experience with British rule left the newly independent American people with two firm determinations. They would never again be subject to a monarch, and they would be careful to enact written constitutions to mark the limits of governmental authority.

Between 1776 and 1778, eleven states drafted new constitutions, and one of these states, South Carolina, drafted two. By 1787, two more states had revised their first efforts. In 1777, the Continental Congress drafted and submitted to the states the first national constitution, the Articles of Confederation, which took effect in 1781. The provisions of these early constitutions are discussed in greater detail in subsequent chapters. In this section, we will instead focus on the changes in intellectual trends occasioned by the colonies' first experience with self-government.

The Revolution inspired a public passion that confounded the expectations of those who led it. Between 1776 and 1787 there took place what historian Gordon Wood has called "the democratization of the American mind." The egalitarian and anti-aristocratic rhetoric of the Revolutionary writers, directed initially at English institutions, was taken as the standard of government by an ever expanding segment of the public. The reading public, and hence the politically active public, broadened to include more than the elite ranks of educated gentlemen who had composed it in the 1760s and early 1770s. Self-government, which originally meant rule by an elite body of the people, gradually came to mean rule by a much broader segment of society.

In essence, the terms "republic" (rule by the people instead of a monarch) and "democracy" (rule by the masses instead of the elite), which to the Revolutionary generation had been similar but severable, became synonomous in the public mind. Many of the leaders of the Revolution were shocked by this merging of two terms that to them had opposite connotations:

> For if "republic" conjured up for many the positive features of the Commonwealth era and marked the triumph of virtue and reason, "democracy"—a word that denoted the lowest order of society as well as the form of government in which the commons ruled—was generally associated with the threat of civil disorder and the early assumption of power by a dictator.[25]

By the 1780s, politics was no longer the exclusive domain of educated gentlemen. Moreover, the expected natural aristocracy failed to arise, depriving classical republicans of their governing class.

The new republic, no longer threatened by corruption, faced a hitherto neglected danger: licentiousness. *Licentiousness,* or anarchy, occurred when the people abused their power. If the people—on whom the republic rested—were selfish individuals who put their own interests ahead of those of the community, they could wreak havoc on a system that depended on public virtue. Public liberty—especially in the sense of a government dedicated to the public good—required both a vigilance against governmental corruption and a willingness to sacrifice individual interests. A republic might perish as easily from unrestrained selfishness as from corruption.

Both English and American Whigs had always warned of the dangers of the excesses of democracy, but these did not seem a realistic threat until after the Revolution. By the mid-1780s, however, many American thinkers were more worried about licentiousness than about corruption. Benjamin Rush, an eminent Pennsylvania doctor, commented in 1787:

> In our opposition to monarchy, we forgot that the temple of tyranny has two doors. We bolted one of them by proper restraints; but we left the other open, by neglecting to guard against the effects of our own ignorance and licentiousness.[26]

Evidence of licentiousness took many forms. It could be seen in the economic bickering among states that sapped the war effort and helped cause a peacetime recession in 1785–1786. It was manifest in the development of "factions": groups in the legislature with different, selfish interests. The most common example of licentiousness was the legislature of Rhode Island, also known as Rogue Island. There they carried trends in other states toward debtor relief, paper money, and other popular measures so far as to propose redistribution of property every thirteen years.

For those who despaired of the people's virtue, the last straw was Shays' Rebellion. The economic depression that swept the country in 1785–1786 hit rural residents hard. High interest rates and a low money supply increased bankruptcies and made it difficult for farmers to pay their public and private debts. They blamed urbanites, and especially the lawyers and the court system, for taking advantage of rural poverty: "Like Drones they fatten on the Lab'rers toil/Defraud the Widow and the Orphans spoil."[27] Farmers pressed—unsuccessfully—for various forms of debtor relief, including collection delays, court reforms, an increased money supply (often by state issuance of paper currency), and low taxes.

The crisis came to a head in rural western Massachusetts late in the summer of 1786. There a group of disgruntled farmers, led by Daniel Shays, took up arms to demand court reform and debtor relief. They drew up a list of grievances and began drilling, but were quickly crushed by the militia. Word of the rebellion spread, however, and the rebels' cause was further harmed by exaggerated accounts of their intentions. Henry Knox, serving as the superintendent of war, wrote to George Washington that the Shaysites had intended to march on Boston, loot the Bank of Massachusetts, and then march southward redistributing property. Washington did not keep this news to himself, and the rumor spread quickly. The whole rebellion—truth and fiction—was viewed by the educated elite as an example of the excesses of democracy caused by the decline in virtue. One of Washington's aides condemned the "licentious spirit prevailing among many of the people; a levelling principle; a desire of change."[28] Abigail Adams wrote to Jefferson that "these commotions" (meaning specifically Shays' Rebellion) were caused by "Luxury and extravagance."[29] As the definition of "the people" broadened to include those with less inclination toward virtue—generally those with less wealth and education—the paradigm of classical republicanism began to collapse. No longer confident that the innate (if dormant) virtue of the people would triumph, many in the period between 1776 and 1787 turned away from the "Country" world-view with its theories of corruption and virtue. If the republican experiment was to be saved, a new theory of government would have to be devised, for virtue was in short supply. The problem was no longer simply governmental corruption, which could be defeated. The problem was that people were inevitably prey to selfishness and self-interest; Americans had irretrievably lost their virtue.

Some, of course, remained committed republicans. Although often no more democratic than their disillusioned counterparts, they retained their faith in the virtue of the people despite their disagreement with many popular measures. Rather than abandoning republicanism, they attempted to create a more virtuous public. America could be put on the right track, could regain her virtue, if only the proper steps were taken. They continued to advocate Whig measures and espouse "Country" ideology. Others, however, abandoned hope, and turned to alternative theories of government to support the republic. This difference of opinion would persist throughout the Constitutional Convention and the ratification debates, and would influence American politics well into the nineteenth century.

Those who lost faith in the American people did not have to look far for inspiration. Locke's liberal individualism provided a ready-made theory that fit the times perfectly. Montesquieu's theory of separation of powers contained a new counterpoint of checks and balances. And a little known English writer named Bernard Mandeville provided a springboard for a theory of government based not on virtue but on vice. Together, these thinkers allowed disillusioned republicans (now liberals) to construct a new "science of politics," basing government not on man as he ought to be but on man as he often is: ignoble, self-interested, and ignorant.

As we have seen, Locke's theory of limited acquisition of property was compatible with a republican perspective. His theory of a limited-purpose government, however, provided an alternative to the republican vision of an encompassing regime. It could also serve to transform the classical republican community of citizens into a modern liberal collection of individuals.

For classical republicans, the community and the government were joined in a common endeavor of promoting individual and civic virtue. Law and morality were necessarily intertwined. No part of individual life could be marked off as separate from the community, and no part of communal life was beyond the reach of the government acting on behalf of the community. This was the classical vision of government: an integrated "regime" rather than a functionally separate "government." Additionally, republicans put the community at the center and considered individuals as parts of a larger whole. Individuals were expected to subordinate their private interests to the good of the community.

Americans saw in Locke's work a way to turn this scheme on its head. His derivation of government (political society) from the state of nature allowed the conclusion that individuals were prior to, and superior to, the societies they formed. Individuals came first; their needs and rights were the basis for—and the limits of—political society. Instead of individuals subordinating their private interests to the needs of the community, the very purpose of the community was to give individuals freedom to pursue their private interests. Government was thus limited to the purpose for which it was formed: protecting individuals from their neighbors' viciousness in order to permit them to engage in private pursuits.

Limiting the role of government to facilitating individual desires also meant that law and morality could now be separated. The sphere of law included only protection of individual liberty. It no longer encompassed fostering the private or public virtue necessary to public liberty. Lockean liberalism thus transformed both the role and the purposes of government.

Transformations, however, do not happen overnight. Many who turned to Locke still held dear republican principles. For them, Bernard Mandeville and those who followed him provided a theoretical scheme to justify condoning individual selfishness without compromising the public good. In 1714 Mandeville published *The Fable of the Bees*, expanded from a shorter version published in 1705. Its subtitle was guaranteed to capture the imagination of the disillusioned republicans: *Private Vices, Public Benefits*.

Mandeville's satirical attack on the "Country" preoccupation with virtue purported to show how the selfish and unvirtuous motivations of individual bees still resulted in a productive beehive.

> Millions endeavouring to supply
> Each other's lust and vanity . . .
> Thus every part was full of vice,
> Yet the whole mass a paradise.[30]

The Fable of the Bees scandalized Mandeville's contemporaries, but it had a significant influence. Both Adam Smith and David Hume denied any reliance on Mandeville, yet their economic and political theories clearly owe a debt to his linking of private vices and public benefits. Smith explained how individual selfishness might operate, as if by the workings of "an invisible hand," to promote the public economy.

Hume relied on a similar theory to advocate constructing a government based on vice:

> [I]n contriving any system of government, and fixing the several checks and controuls of the constitution, every man ought to be supposed a *knave*, and to have no other end, in all his actions, than private interest. By this interest we must govern

him, and, by means of it, make him, notwithstanding his insatiable avarice and ambition, co-operate to public good.[31]

Hume's advice would be taken to heart by many at the Constitutional Convention.

Neither Hume nor Mandeville explained, however, how constitution writers might turn individual vices into public benefits. It was all very well to
speculate that a selfish citizen could be induced to "co-operate to public
good," but in the absence of civic virtue, how could this be accomplished?

Ever innovative and adaptive, the liberals turned back to Montesquieu for
the new purpose of complementing the theories of Locke and Hume. Montesquieu himself would have been horrified. He was an admirer of Bolingbroke and a thoroughgoing republican who feared only corruption and
trusted only virtue. But in his explication of separation of powers lay the
seeds of a more complex theory. For those who read carefully Montesquieu's
description of the ideal form of government—and not merely his general
statements about the necessity of separating the branches of government—a
new doctrine of checks and balances began to emerge. The functions of the
different branches might be deliberately mingled in such a way as to counter,
rather than foster, individual ambition and lust for power. Montesquieu's
ideal government in fact gave the three branches of government overlapping
power: the legislature had impeachment power, and the executive was given
authority to veto laws. Checks and balances could be redefined as a way of
mingling power to provide each branch with a safeguard against the ambitions and encroachments of the other branches.

With these rudiments of a structure of government that might combat licentiousness, those who despaired of "Country" ideology could turn to its
opposite: the "Court" party, which had held power in England since the Glorious Revolution. Members of this party, like many Americans after their own
Revolution, were beginning to explore the possibility of substituting self-
interestedness for virtue. Unsurprisingly, "Court" ideology embodied notions highly offensive to "Country" Whigs:

> Its characteristics were a strong and stable executive representing a guaranteed
> Protestant monarchy in parliament, and a steady diminution of political competi-
> tiveness; its means included compromised elections, a Septennial (replacing a Tri-
> ennial) Act extending the duration of parliaments, and a system of political man-
> agement in which patronage played a visible if not an oversignificant part.[32]

Before the 1780s, almost no patriotic American would endorse such a program. By 1787, "Court" ideology, backed up by the liberalism of Locke and
Hume, was at least as well-represented in the Constitutional Convention as
the "Country" party—and probably more so. Whiggish republicans, Lockean
liberals, and a few stray monarchists brought their different visions of government and society to Philadelphia in the summer of 1787. How their competing views were played out in the Constitutional Convention in Philadelphia, and then in the state conventions, is the story of the next six chapters of
this book.

FOOTNOTES

1. *1 Diary and Autobiography of John Adams* 282 (L. Butterfield, L. Faber and W. Garrett eds. 1961).

2. Philadelphia *Pennsylvania Packet*, August 8, 1774, quoted in Gordon Wood, *The Creation of the American Republic, 1776–1787* 32 (1969) [hereinafter *Creation*].

3. Boston *New England Chronicle*, September 5, 1776, quoted in *id*. at 33–34.

4. Thomas Jefferson, *A Summary View of the Rights of British America* (1774), in 1 *Papers of Thomas Jefferson* 125 (Julian P. Boyd ed. 1955).

5. Charge to the Grand Jury, Charleston, April 23, 1776, quoted in Wood, *Creation*, at 39.

6. Edmund Burke, *Speech to the electors of Bristol*, quoted in Bernard Bailyn, *The Ideological Origins of the American Revolution* 163 (1967) [hereinafter *Origins*] (emphasis in original).

7. Quoted in Bailyn, *Origins*, at 165.

8. 2 John Trenchard and Thomas Gordon, *Cato's Letters* 245 (1723).

9. Bailyn, *Origins*, at 77.

10. It is illustrative of the chasm between our world and that of the framers that Locke—as well as his American followers—thought that only men had political rights. In this book we are therefore deliberately using male nouns and pronouns, which in most cases are meant to convey the *exclusion* of women in the eighteenth century (in contrast to the modern tendency to insist that generic male pronouns *include* women).

11. John Locke, *Two Treatises of Government*, 2d Treatise § 87 (1690) (emphasis in original).

12. *Id*. at § 46.

13. *Id*. at § 27.

14. Speech by Henry Ireton (1647), quoted in J.G.A. Pocock, *The Machiavellian Moment: Florentine Political Thought and the Atlantic Republican Tradition* 375 (1975) [hereinafter *Machiavellian Moment*].

15. Forrest McDonald, *Novus Ordo Seclorum: The Intellectual Origins of the Constitution* 23 (1986) [hereinafter *Novus Ordo*].

16. John Allen, *The Watchman's Alarm to Lord N---h* (1774), quoted in Bailyn, *Origins*, at 77 (emphasis in original).

17. 1 Kate M.Rowland, *The Life of George Mason* 431 (1892).

18. John Sullivan to Meshech Weare, December 11, 1775, quoted in Wood, *Creation*, at 56.

19. John Diggins, *The Lost Soul of American Politics: Virtue, Self-Interest and the Foundations of Liberalism* 16 (1984).

20. John Adams to Mercy Warren, April 16, 1776.

21. Thomas Jefferson to John Jay, August 23, 1785.

22. "The Worcester Speculator," in the *Worcester Magazine*, October 1787, reprinted in 1 *American Political Writing During the Founding Era, 1760–1805* at 699, 701 (Charles S. Hyneman and Donald S. Lutz eds. 1983).

23. Thomas Jefferson to Peter Carr, August 10, 1787.

24. Bailyn, *Origins*, at 51–52.

25. Bailyn, *Origins*, at 282.

26. Benjamin Rush, *An Address* (1787), quoted in McDonald, *Novus Ordo*, at 3.

27. "Aristedes," in the *Boston Gazette*, April 17, 1786, quoted in Jackson Turner Main, *The Antifederalists: Critics of the Constitution 1781–1788* 57 (1961) [hereinafter *Antifederalists*].

28. David Humphreys to George Washington, November 9, 1786, quoted in Main, *Antifederalists*, at 62.

29. Abigail Adams to Thomas Jefferson, January 29, 1787, in 11 *Papers of Thomas Jefferson* 86 (Julian P. Boyd ed. 1955).

30. Bernard Mandeville, *The Fable of the Bees* 30, 33 (Douglas Garman ed. 1934).

31. David Hume, *Essays, Moral, Political and Literary* 117-18 (T.H. Green and T.H. Grose eds. 1889).

32. Pocock, *Machiavellian Moment*, at 478.

CHAPTER TWO

Creating a National Government

CALLING THE CONVENTION

The Constitutional Convention of 1787 was not really a fair test of the competing ideologies described in the preceding chapter; the deck was stacked. Those who were most appalled by lack of virtue among the people—and therefore most likely to turn away from republicanism and toward liberalism—were of course likely to be in the forefront of the movement for constitutional change. As these former Whigs turned more and more toward "Court" ideology, some of them also began to focus on the need for a strong national government. Moreover, those dissatisfied (for other reasons) with the loose confederation in place during the 1780s also looked toward a strong central government. Thus, although the relationships between "Court" and nationalism and between "Country" and anti-nationalism were complex and not always predictable, liberalism and nationalism came to be allied more and more. Both movements developed largely as a reaction to events in the decade prior to 1787. The preceding chapter described the turn toward liberalism; this one will survey the turn toward nationalism.

In 1777, the Second Continental Congress finally proposed to the states the Articles on Confederation, which had been two years in the drafting. The limited nature of the Articles as a governing document was evident even in the preamble:

> To All to whom these Presents shall come, we the undersigned Delegates of the States affixed to our Names send greeting. . . . [T]he Delegates of the United States of America in Congress assembled did on the fifteenth day of November [1777] . . . agree to certain articles of Confederation and perpetual Union between the States of Newhampshire, Massachusetts-bay, Rhodeisland and Providence Plantations, Connecticut, New York, New Jersey, Pennsylvania, Delaware, Maryland, Virginia, North-Carolina, South-Carolina and Georgia[.]

In the thirteen articles that followed, this first United States constitution declared the sovereignty and mutual friendship of the several states, and set up a rudimentary national government. The Articles established a unicameral Congress with each state having one vote; delegates were paid by their states and were subject to recall. Congress was given, and the states prohibited from exercising, most foreign relations powers, including the power to wage war. Miscellaneous provisions, such as those requiring each state to give full faith and credit to the judicial proceedings of another, and making Congress a court of last resort for territorial disputes among states, were designed to reduce friction among the states. As discussed more fully in the last section of this chapter, amending the Articles required the consent of all thirteen state legislatures.

Under the Articles of Confederation, Congress had almost no power over domestic affairs. It had no authority to regulate commerce or to tax. Even the powers it did have were virtually unenforceable: the only enforcement provision was included in Article XIII, which declared that "Every state shall abide by the determinations of the united states in congress assembled, on all questions which by this confederation are submitted to them." This left enforcement to the states, many of whom acted as if compliance with Article XIII was wholly optional.

The central problem of the national government under the Articles of Confederation was its lack of coercive power. Unable to tax the states or the people, Congress could only raise money by requisitioning funds from states that often refused its requests. During the war, state reluctance to contribute money exacerbated General Washington's problems: the terrible winter at Valley Forge was due as much to an inability to purchase supplies as it was to the inclement weather.

The war left the Confederation in debt. Soldiers were retired or discharged while still owed pay. George Washington in 1782 lamented the injustice of the unpaid debts:

> When I see such a Number of Men goaded by a thousand stings of reflexion on the past, and of anticipation on the future, about to be turned into the World, soured by penury and what they call the ingratitude of the Public, involved in debts, without one farthing of Money to carry them home, after having spent the flower of their days and many of them their patrimonies in establishing the freedom and Independence of their Country, and suffered every thing that human Nature is capable of enduring on this side of death . . . I cannot avoid apprehending that a train of Evils will follow, of a very serious and distressing Nature.[1]

Congress was also unable to repay foreign loans taken to support the war effort. Despite Robert Morris's brilliant tenure as superintendent of finance, repeated efforts to impose a federal tax, and continual cycles of congressional printing and devaluing of currency, the situation did not improve. In 1786, a delegate to the Continental Congress wrote home that "the Treasury now is literally without a penny."[2]

Debt was not the Confederation's only problem. Trade suffered under both foreign and domestic restrictions. England and Spain imposed trade restrictions that narrowed the markets for American exports. Moreover, foreign nations posed a constant threat to the fragile American confederation. Although European nations negotiated officially only with representatives of the national government, there were tensions among the states regarding foreign relations. Congress had no power to regulate foreign or interstate commerce, so commercial treaties between foreign countries and the Confederation were of little value. Additionally, individual states dealt harshly with foreign residents (especially British subjects) despite congressional overtures of friendship. Foreign nations thus tended to mistrust American treaties. This mistrust, together with an uproar over John Jay's negotiations with Spain regarding the Mississippi (discussed in detail in chapter 5), weakened the foreign relations authority of the Continental Congress. There was also fear that foreign importuning—especially in the form of foreign gold—might seduce inhabitants in the Western territories into alliances that would prove fatal to an American union.

Domestic

Domestic relations were little better. Many states engaged in commercial discrimination against their neighbors. Each state and its industries essentially attempted to profit at the expense of less fortunate states and industries. The Northern port states (especially New York and Pennsylvania) imposed import duties on foreign goods, a financial benefit to New York that was borne by consumers in states where the goods eventually ended up. Southern states tried to gain an advantage in exporting their goods. Lacking a shipping industry of their own to transport their crops to foreign markets, they encouraged British shipping by taxing exports lightly or not at all. Although all the states explicitly exempted the goods produced in other states from the import duties imposed on foreign goods, some states still imposed higher tariffs on goods imported from sister states than on domestic goods. States with ports and navigable rivers charged ships from other states higher navigation fees than were charged to local ships. Congress was impotent to intervene, and the bickering continued. The combination of a high national debt, increasing trade deficits, and economic infighting among the states caused a nationwide recession in 1785–1786.

All these economic woes, due primarily to the weakness of the national government, created a growing impetus for change. A few early efforts at cooperation were made. In 1785, Pennsylvania eliminated many of its most discriminatory tariffs. In March of the same year, representatives from Maryland and Virginia met in Alexandria and drafted the Mount Vernon Compact. Under the compact, ships of each state could enter the bays and rivers of the other without paying tolls or port duties. The two states also assumed joint responsibility for navigation on the Potomac. Both legislatures quickly ratified the compact, and the Maryland legislature invited Pennsylvania and Delaware to participate in further joint endeavors.

In January of 1786, the Virginia legislature took a further step forward. Acting on a bill proposed by John Tyler (but possibly written by James Madison), the legislature called for a national convention. Delegates from Virginia were to meet with delegates from other states to "consider how far a uniform system in their commercial regulations may be necessary for their common interest and permanent harmony." Virginia's invitation was sent to executives of the other states, and Annapolis, Maryland, was chosen as the site of the meeting. Madison explained in a later letter to Jefferson that he had favored Annapolis because of its central location, its rural character, and its distance from New York, where Congress sat. According to Madison, "[i]t was thought prudent to avoid the neighborhood of Congress, and the large commercial towns, in order to disarm the adversaries to the object of insinuations of influence from either of these quarters."[3]

On September 11, 1786, five states—not including Maryland itself, which declined to participate on the ground that "[i]nnovations in government . . . are dangerous"[4]— convened the Annapolis Convention. They met for only three days and concluded that substantive action was "inadvisable" in light of "so partial and defective a representation." Instead, "[d]eeply impressed . . . with the magnitude and importance" of reaching an interstate agreement on trade, they called for another convention.

> Under this impression, Your Commissioners, with the most respectful deference, beg leave to suggest their unanimous conviction, that it may essentially tend to advance the interests of the union, if the States, by whom they have been respectively delegated, would themselves concur, and use their endeavours to procure the concurrence of the other States, in the appointment of Commissioners, to meet at Philadelphia on the second Monday in May next, to take into consideration the situation of the United States, to devise such further provisions as shall appear to them necessary to render the constitution of the Federal Government adequate to the exigencies of the Union; and to report such an Act for that purpose to the United States in Congress assembled, as when agreed to, by them, and afterwards confirmed by the Legislatures of every State, will effectually provide for the same.[5]

On February 21, 1787, using almost identical language, the Continental Congress called for a convention of delegates to meet in Philadelphia on the second Monday in May.

WRITING THE RULES

On Monday, May 14, 1787—the second Monday in May—the Virginia instigators of this momentous meeting arrived at the Pennsylvania State House at Sixth and Chestnut streets in Philadelphia. Here the Declaration of Independence had been signed almost eleven years before, and the building would soon be renamed Independence Hall to commemorate the event. It had been built in the 1730s. Typical of that era, the construction had been financed largely by private money that had not been fully repaid until 1761. On May 14, however, the State House was almost empty. Besides the Virginians, only the Pennsylvania delegates showed up. Most of the latter had simply walked from their homes.

Contrary to popular belief, the weather in Philadelphia was mild that summer. The average temperature in May was 62 degrees. Robert Morris reported that May 14 was "cloudy and dull with driz'ling Rain at times," and a Philadelphia meteorologist recorded the mean temperature that day as 57 degrees. Even in August, the hottest month, the average temperature in Philadelphia was only 74.5 degrees, which was about half a degree cooler than normal.[6]

The Convention began on May 25, 1787, more than a week later than scheduled, by electing George Washington president and establishing rules of procedure. In order to "provide against . . . licentious publications," the convention resolved:

> That no copy be taken of any entry on the journal during the sitting of the House without leave of the House.
> That members only be permitted to inspect the journal.

> That nothing spoken in the House be printed, or otherwise published or communicated without leave.

The rules provided for strict secrecy and were apparently followed rigorously. The Convention Journal, which recorded only motions and votes, was not published until 1819. Besides the official journal kept by the secretary, other delegates took notes of the debates. Some notes by Madison, Yates, Lansing, King, Paterson, Hamilton, Pierce, and McHenry have survived. Madison's notes are by far the most extensive, and almost certainly the most accurate. Despite frequent requests that he publish his notes, Madison refused to do so, and they were not published until 1840, after his death. Yates's notes, the first to be published (in 1821), were liberally edited before publication by Edmond C. Genet, an unscrupulous New Yorker who ran against Madison for the Republican presidential nomination in 1808. Recent scholarship has shown that Genet's partisan editorial hand virtually destroyed the accuracy of Yates's original notes. A comparison between Genet's version and the sole two surviving pages of Yates's original shows that Genet "omitted half of the material on the sheets and altered every sentence that he published."[7] The other delegates took notes sporadically, and only fragments have survived.

Despite all these note-takers, the proceedings in Independence Hall were kept absolutely confidential. Delegates faithfully observed the strictures of secrecy, even when writing to colleagues. Rufus King of Massachusetts wrote to Nathan Dane, then representing Massachusetts in Congress:

> I think that I informed you that by an early order of the Convention the members are restrained from communicating any thing done in convention during the time of their session. . . . I am therefore prevented from writing to you with that freedom which otherwise I should do, as well for your information of the proceedings of the convention, as to obtain your sentiments on points of consequence which must here receive their discussion.[8]

Outsiders had so little idea what was occurring within doors that at one point Philadelphians speculated that the delegates were negotiating with the second son of George III as a possible monarch for the United States. As the materials in chapter 4 will show, that speculation was wildly inaccurate. The delegates faithfully kept their discussions and their differences to themselves until well after the Convention. Even the Congress had no idea of the substance of the proceedings. Robert Burton, a North Carolina delegate to Congress visiting Philadelphia at the time, wrote to a friend: "the Convention sitting here are so very private that there is no telling what business they are on."[9]

At the Convention, even an occasional carelessness drew a stern response. President Washington reportedly chastised the entire Convention as if they were schoolchildren when an anonymous scrap of notes was found on the floor of the hall:

> Gentlemen. I am sorry to find that some one member of this body has been so neglectful of the secrets of the convention as to drop in the State House a copy of their proceedings, which by accident was picked up and delivered to me this morning. I must entreat the gentlemen to be more careful, [lest] our transactions get into the newspapers and disturb the public repose by premature speculations. I know not whose paper it is, but there it is. Let him who owns it take it.

The paper remained where Washington had placed it, and the miscreant never confessed.

Maintaining absolute secrecy among fifty-five men with political ambitions and widely divergent views was possible only because of the nature of the gathering. All of the delegates were gentlemen, to whom politics was serious but private business. Most were veterans of the political pamphlet literature of the Revolution, who "conceived of their readership as restricted and aristocratic, as being made up of men essentially like themselves."[10] During the Revolutionary era, limited readership was a natural consequence of low literacy rates and few newspapers. Thus, only gentlemen were active in politics. By 1787, however, the potential readership of political writing, and hence the politically active segment of the community, had grown significantly. If the "ignorant vulgar," as John Randolph called the masses in 1774, were to be excluded from any aspect of politics in 1787, a conscious effort at secrecy was required. The delegates to the Federal Convention knew, moreover, that any candid discussion of the ills of the American polity would inevitably touch on sensitive issues, including, for example, the dangers of too much democracy. Such discussions were possible only in secrecy.

If the rule of strict secrecy was an agreeable one to eighteenth-century gentlemen, so were the flexible procedural rules. These included rules regarding reconsideration of issues, the Convention's decision to proceed as a Committee of the Whole and thus to relax rules of parliamentary procedure, and the practice of assigning difficult questions to smaller committees even less constrained by procedural rules. Such rules allowed delegates to reason with one another and to change their minds without losing face, and made writing the constitution a truly cooperative effort. To these men of letters, the writing of a constitution, like any other eighteenth-century writing, was not an opportunity for individual aggrandizement: "The true gentleman of letters . . . writes for a small group of social peers, circulates drafts among those peers for correction, avoids publication until agreement is reached, and leaves his work unsigned."[11]

Madison also noted a rule that had been debated even before the Convention began. Twelve states sent delegations consisting of from two (New Hampshire) to eight (Pennsylvania) representatives. With different populations and different sized delegations, how was each state's vote to be counted? They decided that each state would cast a single vote. Madison explained the reasons in his notes:

> Previous to the arrival of a majority of the States, the rule by which they ought to vote in the Convention had been made a subject of conversation among the members present. It was pressed by [Gouverneur] Morris and favored by Robert Morris and others from Pennsylvania, that the large States should unite in firmly refusing to the small states an equal vote, as unreasonable, and as enabling the small States to negative every good system of Government, which must in the nature of things, be founded on a violation of that equality. The members from Virginia, conceiving that such an attempt might beget fatal altercations between the large & small States, and that it would be easier to prevail on the latter, in the course of the deliberations, to give up their equality for the sake of an effective Government, than on taking the field of discussion to disarm themselves of the right & thereby throw themselves on the mercy of the large States, discountenanced & stifled the project.

Each state's vote was determined by a simple majority decision among the state's attending delegates. Occasionally a state's delegation was evenly divided, leaving that state with no official vote at all. Having thus reached a consensus on some rules and a compromise on others, on May 29 the Convention turned to the task that would occupy it for the next four months.

HOW MUCH TO ALTER?

Edmund Randolph "opened the main business" of the Convention on May 29 by presenting and defending fifteen resolutions that formed the core of what came to be called the "Virginia Plan." The Virginia delegates had arrived at Independence Hall on May 14, the date set for the opening of the Convention, only to find that few other delegates were present. Lacking a quorum for the Convention, the Virginia contingent spent the next week setting down on paper their hopes for the new government. Although Madison was almost surely the chief architect, his fellow Virginian, Edmund Randolph, presented the result of the week's labors in his own name.

Tuesday, May 29

Mr. Randolph: He expressed his regret, that it should fall to him, rather than those, who were of longer standing in life and political experience, to open the great subject of their mission. But, as the convention had originated from Virginia, and his colleagues supposed that some proposition was expected from them, they had imposed this task on him.

He then commented on the difficulty of the crisis, and the necessity of preventing the fulfilment of the prophecies of the American downfal.

He observed that in revising the foederal system we ought to inquire 1. into the properties, which such a government ought to possess, 2. the defects of the confederation, 3. the danger of our situation & 4. the remedy.

1. The Character of such a government ought to secure 1. against foreign invasion: 2. against dissentions between members of the Union, or seditions in particular states: 3. to procure to the several States, various blessings, of which an isolated situation was incapable: 4. to be able to defend itself against incroachment: & 5. to be paramount to the state constitutions.

2. In speaking of the defects of the confederation he professed a high respect for its authors, and considered them, as having done all that patriots could do, in the then infancy of the science, of constitu-

tions & of confederacies,—when the inefficiency of requisitions was unknown—no commercial discord had arisen among any states—no rebellion had appeared as in Massts.—foreign debts had not become urgent—the havoc of paper money had not been foreseen—treaties had not been violated—and perhaps nothing better could be obtained from the jealousy of the states with regard to their sovreignty.

He then proceeded to enumerate the defects: 1. that the confederation produced no security against foreign invasion; congress not being permitted to prevent a war nor to support it by their own authority—Of this he cited many examples; most of which tended to shew, that they could not cause infractions of treaties or of the law of nations, to be punished: that particular states might by their conduct provoke war without controul; and that neither militia nor draughts being fit for defence on such occasions, inlistments only could be successful, and these could not be executed without money.

2. that the foederal government could not check the quarrels between states, nor a rebellion in any, not having constitutional power nor means to interpose according to the exigency:

3. that there were many advantages, which the U. S. might acquire, which were not attainable under the confederation—such as a productive impost—counteraction of the commercial regulations of other

nations—pushing of commerce ad libitum—&c &c.

4. that the foederal government could not defend itself against the incroachments from the states.

5. that it was not even paramount to the state constitutions, ratified, as it was in may of the states.

3. He next reviewed the danger of our situation, appealed to the sense of the best friends of the U. S. —the prospect of anarchy from the laxity of govern-

ment every where; and to other considerations.

4. He then proceeded to the remedy; the basis of which he said must be the republican principle

He proposed as conformable to his ideas the following resolutions, which he explained one by one.

[The Convention then voted to refer the Randolph resolutions to a Committee of the Whole.]

In Madison's original notes, the resolutions themselves follow Randolph's eloquent defense of them. Since Madison copied out each resolution at the time it was discussed by the Convention, the complete resolutions are omitted here but may be found in the Appendix. The resolutions are in Madison's handwriting, with no corrections or additions. The speech defending them, by contrast, is full of interlineations and is in Randolph's handwriting. Madison acknowledged that "This abstract of the Speech was furnished to J.M. by Mr. Randolph," but made no similar comment regarding the resolutions, suggesting that he in fact wrote them.

The excerpts in this book are taken directly from published copies of Madison's handwritten notes. You will notice that he was in some ways a sloppy note-taker: there are numerous misspellings and inconsistencies, and occasional words omitted or repeated. In order to give the reader the full flavor of the historical record, we have not corrected these inaccuracies.

Randolph's resolutions were strongly nationalist. Both branches of the federal legislature were apportioned according to population. Their powers were broad and largely undefined, and included both a negative on state laws and the authority to legislate "in all cases to which the separate States are incompetent, or in which the harmony of the United States may be interrupted by the exercise of individual Legislation." Both a national judiciary and a national executive were to be established, the latter to be appointed by the national legislature. Resolution 8 provided that the executive and members of the judiciary should combine to form a Council of Revision with veto power over both state and national legislatures. Ratification of the new Constitution was to be by popularly elected conventions in the states rather than by the state legislatures.

Randolph's eloquent defense of his Virginia plan did not persuade the representatives of the smaller states, and they immediately began attacking the underlying nationalism of the plan. Their primary objection was to the creation of an independent *national* government to replace the *confederated* alliance of the thirteen states. In fact, the delegates argued vehemently over Gouverneur Morris's suggestion that the delegates agree preliminarily "that a *national* Government ought to be established consisting of a *supreme* Legislative, Executive & Judiciary." The younger Pinckney wondered whether Randolph and Morris "meant to abolish the State Governments altogether." With several of the smaller states still not in attendance, the nationalists prevailed by a majority of six to one— New York was divided, and only Connecticut voted against Morris's proposal.

After losing on the basic question of whether the new government would be national or federal, the anti-nationalists spent the next three weeks fighting a rear-guard action. With little or no opposition, the Randolph resolutions were passed with few changes. The Committee of the Whole reported the slightly amended Virginia plan, reprinted in the Appendix, on June 13. The delegates reconvened in Convention in order to consider the report more formally, and immediately adjourned for the day. Had the Convention begun to consider the Virginia plan the next day the momentum was such that it might well have been adopted within another few weeks.

Instead, on June 14, the anti-nationalists belatedly realized that decisive action was necessary if the confederation was not to become a consolidation. William Paterson of New Jersey took the lead:

> [He] observed to the Convention that it was the wish of several deputations, particularly that of N. Jersey, that further time might be allowed them to contemplate the plan reported from the Committee of the Whole, and to digest one purely federal, and contradistinguished from the reported plan.

Paterson presented the New Jersey plan on June 15, and the Convention again immediately adjourned. Madison reported that the plan was a direct consequence of the nationalist assault:

> [T]his plan had been concerted among the deputations or members thereof, from Connecticut, N.Y., N.J., Del. and perhaps Mr. Martin from Maryland who made with them a common cause on different principles. Connecticut & N.Y. were against a departure from the principle of the Confederation, wishing rather to add a few new powers to Congress than to substitute a National Government. The States of N.J. and Delaware were opposed to a National Government because its patrons considered a proportional representation of the States as the basis of it. The eagourness displayed by the members opposed to a National Government from these different motives began now to produce serious anxiety for the result of the Convention. Mr. Dickenson said to Mr. Madison—You see the consequence of pushing things too far. Some of the members from the small States wish for two branches in the General Legislature, and are friends to a good National Government; but we would sooner submit to a foreign power than submit to be deprived of an equality of suffrage, in both branches of the legislature, and thereby be thrown under the domination of the large States.

The New Jersey plan, which is reprinted in the Appendix, incorporated some aspects of the Virginia plan, but limited federal power to a much greater degree. No new federal legislature was established; the powers of the Continental Congress—in which states were equally represented—were somewhat enlarged instead. The New Jersey plan required a supermajority for the exercise of even those powers. The executive was to be a creature of the legislature, appointed by and removable at the will of Congress. The judiciary would consist only of a Supreme Court, with very limited jurisdiction.

The great contrast between the Virginia and New Jersey plans is immediately apparent to any reader, and was so to the delegates. They resumed consideration as a Committee of the Whole on June 16 with a comparison of the two plans. Their debates that day illustrate how far apart the delegates were on even the most basic issues.

Saturday, June 16

Mr. Lansing called for the reading of the 1st. resolution of each plan, which he considered as involving principles directly in contrast; that of Mr. Patterson says he sustains the sovereignty of the respective States, that of Mr. Randolph distroys it: the latter requires a negative on all the laws of the particular States; the former, only certain general powers for the general good. The plan of Mr. R. in short absorbs all power except what may be exercised in the little local matters of the States which are not objects worthy of the supreme cognizance. He grounded his preference of Mr. P.'s plan, chiefly on two objections agst. that of Mr. R.

1. want of power in the Convention to discuss & propose it.

2 the improbability of its being adopted. 1. He was decidedly of opinion that the power of the Convention was restrained to amendments of a federal nature, and having for their basis the Confederacy in being. The Act of Congress The tenor of the Acts of the States, the Commissions produced by the several deputations all proved this. And this limitation of the power to an amendment of the Confederacy, marked the opinion of the States, that it was unnecessary & improper to go farther. He was sure that this was the case with his State. N. York would never have concurred in sending deputies to the convention, if she had supposed the deliberations were to turn on a consolidation of the States, and a National Government.

2. was it probable that the States would adopt & ratify a scheme, which they had never authorized us to propose? and which so far exceeded what they regarded as sufficient? We see by their several Acts particularly in relation to the plan of revenue proposed by Cong. in 1783, not authorized by the Articles of Confederation, what were the ideas they then entertained. Can so great a change be supposed to have already taken place. To rely on any change which is hereafter to take place in the sentiments of the people would be trusting to too great an uncertainty. We know only what their present sentiments are. And it is in vain to propose what will not accord with these. The States will never feel a sufficient confidence in a general Government to give it a negative on their laws. The Scheme is itself totally novel. There is no parallel to it to be found. The authority of Congress is familiar to the people, and an augmentation of the powers of Congress will be readily approved by them.

Mr. Patterson, said as he had on a former occasion given his sentiments on the plan proposed by Mr. R. he would now avoiding repetition as much as possible give his reasons in favor of that proposed by himself. He preferred it because it accorded 1. with the powers of the Convention, 2 with the sentiments of the people. If the confederacy was radically wrong, let us return to our States, and obtain larger powers, not assume them of ourselves. I came here not to speak my own sentiments, but the sentiments of those who sent me. Our object is not such a Governmt. as may be best in itself, but such a one as our Constituents have authorized us to prepare, and as they will approve. If we argue the matter on the supposition that no Confederacy at present exists, it can not be denied that all the States stand on the footing of equal sovereignty. All therefore must concur before any can be bound. If a proportional representation be right, why do we not vote so here? If we argue on the fact that a federal compact actually exists, and consult the articles of it we still find an equal Sovereignty to be the basis of it. He reads the 5th. art: of Confederation giving each State a vote—& the 13th. declaring that no alteration shall be made without unanimous consent. This is the nature of all treaties. What is unanimously done, must be unanimously undone. It was observed [by Mr. Wilson] that the larger States gave up the point, not because it was right, but because the circumstances of the moment urged the concession. Be it so. Are they for that reason at liberty to take it back. Can the donor resume his gift without the consent of the donee. This doctrine may be convenient, but it is a doctrine that will sacrifice the lesser States. The large States acceded readily to the confederacy. It was the small ones that came in reluctantly and slowly. N. Jersey & Maryland were the two last, the former objecting to the want of power in Congress over trade: both of them to the want of power to appropriate the vacant territory to the benefit of the whole.—If the sovereignty of the States is to be maintained, the Representatives must be drawn immediately from the States, not from the people: and we have no power to vary the idea of equal sovereignty. The only expedient that will cure the difficulty, is that of throwing the States into Hotchpot. To say that this is impracticable, will not make it so. Let it be tried, and we shall see whether the Citizens of Massts. Pena. & Va. accede to it. It will be objected that Coercion will be impracticable.

But will it be more so in one plan than the other? Its efficacy will depend on the quantum of power collected, not on its being drawn from the States, or from the individuals; and according to his plan it may be exerted on individuals as well as according that of Mr. R. A distinct executive & Judiciary also were equally provided by his plan. It is urged that two branches in the Legislature are necessary. Why? for the purpose of a check. But the reason of the precaution is not applicable to this case. Within a particular State, where party heats prevail, such a check may be necessary. In such a body as Congress it is less necessary, and besides, the delegations of the different States are checks on each other. Do the people at large complain of Congs.? No, what they wish is that Congs. may have more power. If the power now proposed be not eno', the people hereafter will make additions to it. With proper powers Congs. will act with more energy & wisdom than the proposed Natl. Legislature; being fewer in number, and more secreted & refined by the mode of election. The plan of Mr. R. will also be enormously expensive. Allowing Georgia & Del. two representatives each in the popular branch the aggregate number of that branch will be 180. Add to it half as many for the other branch and you have 270. members coming once at least a year from the most distant as well as the most central parts of the republic. In the present deranged state of our finances can so expensive a system be seriously thought of? By enlarging the powers of Congs. the greatest part of this expence will be saved, and all purposes will be answered. At least a trial ought to be made.

Mr. Wilson entered into a contrast of the principal points of the two plans so far he said as there had been time to examine the one last proposed. These points were 1. in the Virga. plan there are 2 & in some degree 3 branches in the Legislature: in the plan from N. J. there is to be a *single* legislature only—2. Representation of the people at large is the basis of the one:—the State Legislatures, the pillars of the other—3. proportional representation prevails in one:—equality of suffrage in the other—4. A single Executive Magistrate is at the head of the one:—a plurality is held out in the other.—5. in the one the majority of the people of the U. S. must prevail:—in the other a minority may prevail. 6. the Natl. Legislature is to make laws in all cases to which the separate States are incompetent &-:—in place of this Congs. are to have additional power in a few cases only—7. A negative on the laws of the States:—in place of this coertion to be substituted—8. The Executive to be removeable on impeachment & conviction;—in one plan: in the other to be removeable at the instance of majority of the Executives

of the States—9. Revision of the laws provided for in one:—no such check in the other—10. inferior national tribunals in one:—none such in the other. 11. In ye. one jurisdiction of Natl. tribunals to extend &c—; an appellate jurisdiction only allowed in the other. 12. Here the jurisdiction is to extend to all cases affecting the Nationl. peace & harmony: there, a few cases only are marked out. 13. finally ye. ratification is in this to be by the people themselves:—in that by the legislative authorities according to the 13 art: of Confederation.

With regard to the *power of the Convention*, he conceived himself authorized to *conclude nothing*, but to be at liberty to *propose any thing*. In this particular he felt himself perfectly indifferent to the two plans.

With *regard to the sentiments of the people*, he conceived it difficult to know precisely what they are. Those of the particular circle in which one moved, were commonly mistaken for the general voice. He could not persuade himself that the State Govts. & Sovereignties were so much the idols of the people, nor a Natl. Govt. so obnoxious to them, as some supposed. Why sd. a Natl. Govt. be unpopular? Has it less dignity? will each Citizen enjoy under it less liberty or protection? Will a Citizen of *Delaware* be degraded by becoming a Citizen of the *United States*? Where do the people look at present for relief from the evils of which they complain? Is it from an internal reform of their Govts.? no, Sir. It is from the Natl. Councils that relief is expected. For these reasons he did not fear, that the people would not follow us into a national Govt. and it will be a further recommendation of Mr. R.'s plan that it is to be submitted to *them*, and not to the *Legislatures*, for ratification.

proceeding now to the 1st point on which he had contrasted the two plans, he observed that anxious as he was for some augmentation of the federal powers, it would be with extreme reluctance indeed that he could ever consent to give powers to Congs. he had two reasons either of wch. was sufficient. 1. Congs. as a Legislative body does not stand on the people. 2. it is a *single* body. 1. He would not repeat the remarks he had formerly made on the principles of Representation. he would only say that an inequality in it, has ever been a poison contaminating every branch of Govt. In G. Britain where this poison has had a full operation, the security of private rights is owing entirely to the purity of Her tribunals of Justice, the Judges of which are neither appointed nor paid, by a venal Parliament. The political liberty of that Nation, owing to the inequality of representation is at the mercy of its rulers. He means not to insinuate that there is any parallel between the situation of that Country & ours at present. But it is a lesson we ought not to disregard, that the smallest bodies in G. B. are notoriously the most corrupt. Every other source of influence must also be stronger in small than large bodies of men. When Lord Chesterfield had told us that one of the Dutch provinces had been seduced into the views of France, he need not have added, that it was not Holland, but one of the *smallest* of them. There are facts among ourselves which are known to all. Passing over others, he will only remark that the *Impost,* so anxiously wished for by the public was defeated not by any of the *larger* States in the Union. 2. *Congress is a single Legislature.* Despotism comes on Mankind in different Shapes, sometimes in an Executive, sometimes in a Military, one. Is there no danger of a Legislative despotism? Theory & practice both proclaim it. If the Legislative authority be not restrained, there can be neither liberty nor stability; and it can only be restrained by dividing it within itself, into distinct and independent branches. In a single House there is no check, but the inadequate one, of the virtue & good sense of those who compose it.

On another great point, the contrast was equally favorable to the plan reported by the Committee of the whole. It vested the Executive powers in a single Magistrate. The plan of N. Jersey, vested them in a plurality. In order to controul the Legislative authority, you must divide it. In order to controul the Executive you must unite it. One man will be more responsible than three. Three will contend among themselves till one becomes the master of his colleagues. In the triumvirates of Rome first Caesar, then Augustus, are witnesses of this truth. The Kings of Sparta, & the Consuls of Rome prove also the factious consequences of dividing the Executive Magistracy. Having already taken up so much time he wd. not he sd. proceed to any of the other points. Those on which he had dwelt, are sufficient of themselves: and on a decision of them, the fate of the others will depend.

Mr. Pinkney, the whole comes to this, as he conceived. Give N. Jersey an equal vote, and she will dismiss her scruples, and concur in the Natil. system. He thought the Convention authorized to go any length in recommending, which they found necessary to remedy the evils which produced this Convention.

The next day, June 18, was an unproductive but entertaining one. The delegates first voted to postpone consideration of the Paterson plan in order to consider a substitute motion by Dickinson explicitly limiting the work of the Convention to revising the Articles of Confederation.

At this point in the debates, Alexander Hamilton stood up to give his most substantial speech of the Convention. Speaking for several hours, with appropriate historical illustrations, he advocated an extremely powerful centralized government, complete with life-tenured senate and executive. He proposed to make the states mere administrative units, with even their governors appointed by the national government. He even suggested that states were an unnecessary luxury:

> If they were extinguished, he was persuaded that great economy might be obtained by substituting a general Gov't. He did not mean however to shock the public opinion by proposing to such a measure. On the other hand he saw no *other* necessity for declining it.

His disdain for state sovereignty extended to popular sovereignty as well. According to Yates's notes—and partially corroborated by Madison—he referred to popular governments as "pork still, with a little change of sauce." Hamilton's suggestions made even the strongest nationalists look moderate, and perhaps that was his intention. In any event, the convention essentially ignored his remarks, reacting to his oratory "rather as if they had taken a day off to attend the opera."[12]

The next day the Committee of the Whole voted six to four to reject Dickinson's limiting motion, and then turned back to the Paterson plan for a final day. Madison's impassioned defense of the Virginia plan provides one of the best illustrations of his overall theory of government at this time.

Tuesday, June 19

Mr. Madison: Proceeding to the consideration of Mr. Patterson's plan, he stated the object of a proper plan to be twofold. 1. to preserve the Union. 2. to provide a Governmt. that will remedy the evils felt by the States both in their united and individual capacities. Examine Mr. P.s plan, & say whether it promises satisfaction in these respects.

1. Will it prevent those violations of the law of nations & of Treaties which if not prevented must involve us in the calamities of foreign wars? The tendency of the States to these violations has been manifested in sundry instances. The files of Congs. contain complaints already, from almost every nation with which treaties have been formed. Hitherto indulgence has been shewn to us. This can not be the permanent disposition of foreign nations. A rupture with other powers is among the greatest of national calamities. It ought therefore to be effectually provided that no part of a nation shall have it in its power to bring them on the whole. The existing Confederacy does not sufficiently provide against this evil. The proposed amendment to it does not supply the omission. It leaves the will of the States as uncontrouled as ever.

2. Will it prevent encroachments on the federal authority? A tendency to such encroachments has been sufficiently exemplified, among ourselves, as well in every other confederated republic antient and Modern. By the federal articles, transactions with the Indians appertain to Congs. Yet in several instances, the States have entered into treaties & wars with them. In like manner no two or more States can form among themselves any treaties &c. without the consent of Congs. Yet Virga. & Maryd. in one instance—Pena. & N. Jersey in another, have entered into compacts, without previous application or subsequent apology. No State again can of right raise troops in time of peace without the like consent. Of all cases of the league, this seems to require the most scrupulous observance. Has not Massts., notwithstanding, the most powerful member of the Union, already raised a body of troops? Is she not now augmenting them, without having even deigned to apprise Congs. of Her intention? In fine—Have we not seen the public land dealt out to

Cont. to bribe her acquiescence in the decree constitionally awarded agst. her claim on the territory of Pena.? for no other possible motive can account for the policy of Congs. in that measure?—If we recur to the examples of other confederacies, we shall find in all of them the same tendency of the parts to encroach on the authority of the whole.

. . .

3. Will it prevent trespasses of the States on each other? Of these enough has been already seen. He instanced Acts of Virga. & Maryland which give a preference to their own Citizens in cases where the Citizens of other States are entitled to equality of privileges by the Articles of Confederation. He considered the emissions of paper money & other kindred measures as also aggressions. The States relatively to one an other being each of them either Debtor or Creditor; The creditor States must suffer unjustly from every emission by the debtor States. We have seen retaliating acts on this subject which threatened danger not to the harmony only, but the tranquility of the Union. The plan of Mr. Paterson, not giving even a negative on the acts of the States, left them as much at liberty as ever to execute their unrighteous projects agst. each other.

4. Will it secure the internal tranquility of the States themselves? The insurrections in Massts. admonished all the States of the danger to which they were exposed. Yet the plan of Mr. P. contained no provisions for supplying the defect of the Confederation on this point. According to the Republican theory indeed, Right & power being both vested in the majority, are held to be synonimous. According to fact & experience, a minority may in an appeal to force be an overmatch for the majority. 1. If the minority happen to include all such as possess the skill & habits of military life, with such as possess the great pecuniary resources, one third may conquer the remaining two thirds. 2. one third of those who participate in the choice of rulers may be rendered a majority by the accession of those whose poverty disqualifies them from a suffrage, & who for obvious reasons may be more ready to join the standard of sedition than that of the established Government.

3. where slavery exists, the Republican Theory becomes still more fallacious.

5. Will it secure a good internal legislation & administration to the particular States? In developing the evils which vitiate the political system of the U. S. it is proper to take into view those which prevail within the States individually as well as those which affect them collectively: Since the former indirectly affect the whole; and there is great reason to believe that the pressure of them had a full share in the motives which produced the present Convention. Under this head he enumerated and animadverted on 1. the multiplicity of the laws passed by the several States. 2. the mutability of their laws. 3. the injustice of them. 4. the impotence of them: observing that Mr. Patterson's plan contained no remedy for this dreadful class of evils, and could not therefore be received as an adequate provision for the exigences of the Community.

. . .

The great difficulty lies in the affair of Representation; and if this could be adjusted, all others would be surmountable. It was admitted by both the gentlemen from N. Jersey [Mr. Brearly and Mr. Patterson] that it would not be *just to allow Virga.* which was 16 times as large as Delaware an equal vote only. Their language was that it would not be *safe for Delaware* to allow Virga. 16 times as many votes. The expedient proposed by them was that all the States should be thrown into one mass and a new partition be made into 13 equal parts. Would such a scheme be practicable? The dissimilarities existing in the rules of property, as well as in the manners, habits and prejudices of the different States, amounted to a prohibition of the attempt.

. . .

The prospect of many new States to the Westward was another consideration of importance. If they should come into the Union at all, they would come when they contained but few inhabitants. If they shd. be entitled to vote according to their proportions of inhabitants, all would be right & safe. Let them have an equal vote, and a more objectionable minority than ever might give law to the whole.

On a question for postponing generally the 1st. proposition of Mr. Patterson's plan, it was agreed to: N. Y. & N J. only being no—

On the question moved by Mr. King whether the Committee should rise & Mr. Randolphs propositions be re-reported without alteration, which was in fact a question whether Mr. R's should be adhered to as preferable to those of Mr. Patterson: Massts. ay. Cont. ay. N. Y. no. N. J. no. Pa. ay. Del. no. Md. divd. Va. ay. N. C. ay. S. C. ay. Geo. ay.

Despite this decisive nationalist victory, the anti-nationalists had destroyed the nationalists' momentum. What had taken three weeks to pass in principle would now take three months to hammer out in detail.

Topics For Discussion

1. What do you think would have happened if the proceedings of the Federal Convention had been open to the public? Given the climate of the times (discussed in chapter 1), what sort of constitution (if any) might have resulted? Would that constitution have been better or worse—or about the same—as the one the Convention produced? In what ways?

2. Read carefully Madison's fourth numbered argument on June 19 regarding republican theory. What is he saying about slavery? What are his views of limited suffrage? Who governs in his "republican" society?

3. Note Madison's comment regarding the voting rules in the Convention itself. He purports to have made a wise political decision. Did it work? What would you have done in his position?

4. Eighteenth-century American fiction, poetry, and drama has sometimes been criticized as "selfless": literarily weak because insufficiently personal and lacking an individual viewpoint. Viewing the Constitution as literature, can you see how the weaknesses of early American fiction become the strengths of a frame of government?

5. Imagine any group of modern politicians writing a Constitution. What would the process and the result look like?

6. Make a list of the anti-nationalist objections to the Virginia plan, especially as noted by Paterson on June 16. What compromises might alleviate anti-nationalist concerns? How do those compromises change Randolph's original structure?

THE CONVENTION'S AUTHORITY TO ACT

Although the rejection of the New Jersey plan and the consequent commitment to a relatively nationalist government tentatively resolved one overarching dispute among the delegates, another remained to trouble them throughout the debates. This involved the crucial issue of the Convention's own authority vis-à-vis both the existing states and the citizenry. Did they have the power to do any more than merely suggest amendments to the existing Articles of Confederation? Article XIII of that document provided:

> And the Articles of this confederation shall be inviolably observed by every state, and the union shall be perpetual; nor shall any alteration of any kind hereafter be made in any of them; unless such alteration be agreed to in a congress of the united states, and be afterwards confirmed by the legislatures of every state.

Congress had called the Convention "for the sole and express purpose of revising the Articles of Confederation" and for reporting suggested amendments to Congress and the state legislatures. Almost all of the state resolutions authorizing delegates mirrored this or similar language. Delaware even restricted its delegates by explicitly prohibiting them from considering any amendment to the portion of Article V that stated: "In determining Questions in the United States in Congress Assembled each State shall have one Vote."

That many delegates were contemplating more than merely revising or amending the Articles is clear throughout the Convention. The proposals for a federal executive and judiciary, for vastly increased congressional power, and above all, for two houses of Congress in at least one of which states would be represented in proportion to their population, were so different from the Articles of Confederation that they could scarcely be called "amendments."

The clearest indication that the new constitution was not merely an amendment to the old was in the proposed method of ratification. Randolph's original proposal for ratification, unchanged for much of the summer (and little changed in substance after that) read:

> Resolved that the amendments which shall be offered to the confederation by the Convention, ought at a proper time or times, after the approbation of Congress be submitted to an assembly or assemblies of representatives, recommended by the several legislatures, and be expressly chosen by the People to consider and decide thereon.

The Articles of Confederation required the consent of all state legislatures to amendments; Randolph's plan, which required neither unanimity nor state legislative approbation, was a marked departure. The question arose again and again: did the Convention have the authority to disregard the will of Congress, the Articles of Confederation, and their own instructions, and to propose to the people an entirely new constitution?

The question of their own authority was particularly troublesome to the delegates because of the lack of precedent. Since prior constitutions had been written and ratified largely by state legislatures, the very idea of a "constitutional convention" was novel. In order to justify exceeding their instructions and producing a new constitution, the delegates had to explain not only their own status, but the very nature of the document they were writing. The debates over the Convention's authority—which focused primarily on the proposed method of ratification of the new constitution—illustrate the much deeper philosophical project that formed one of the Convention's major achievements: to define the relationship between a democratic nation and its constitution. That central issue colors all the debates over the particulars of the new constitution. Thus, though the delegates' vision of their creation evolved slowly throughout the summer, we cover the whole course of their debates over ratification methods in this preliminary chapter in order to lay a philosophical framework for the debates over details.

In the view of the Enlightenment-educated delegates to the Federal Convention, the Convention's authority depended in part on the nature of the complex relationships among the thirteen states, their citizens, and the Confederation. Where did final authority, or sovereignty, lie?

Sovereignty was an evolving concept to the men at the Convention. As the discussion in chapter 1 suggests, they were on the brink of a new consciousness. Having abandoned the classical notion of an integrated regime, they were still unsure of the sources of authority for the more limited government they were constituting. Sovereignty certainly no longer derived from a divine right of kings. Did it flow from the individual states, who had, with the final ratification of the Articles of Confederation in 1781, entered a compact with one another?

The idea that sovereignty might lie in the people was still relatively novel in 1787. Popular participation in the creation of constitutions—one indicator of popular sovereignty—was rare. Ten of the twelve state constitutions adopted between 1776 and 1778 were enacted by ordinary legislative means, and the other two were drafted by specially elected conventions and implemented without popular ratification. Of the five of these early constitutions that made provision for amendments, three provided for amendment by the legislature. Only two state constitutions adopted prior to 1787—Massachusetts' in 1780 and New Hampshire's in 1784—were ratified by the people.

Thus the delegates to the Federal Convention began their debates with no clear idea that taking their proposed constitution to the people might obviate the difficulties arising from gaps in the Convention's authority. Instead, they focused at first on the role of the states. That question implicated a much broader philosophical inquiry regarding the "state of nature" and the relationships among the thirteen independent states.

If the Articles of Confederation created a binding compact among previously independent states, then the delegates, as agents of their respective states, had no authority to go beyond it. If the colonies separated from Great Britain as *united* states, on the other hand, then there was more room to argue whether the state legislatures could limit the authority of representatives of the whole nation. This question had a philosophical aspect as well as a practical, political one. What the delegates argued about was the theoretical status of the newly independent colonies at the moment of separation. Were they, as Luther Martin suggested, "in a state of Nature toward each other"? Much depended on the answer.

The framers, like most eighteenth-century American thinkers, took seriously Locke's notion of the state of nature as the original, pre-political condition of mankind. In the absence of organized political society, all men were free and equal, and possessed certain inalienable rights. According to Locke's theories, government was formed by the consent of the governed, primarily to provide protection of these inalienable rights. To be legitimate, any government established out of this state of nature must respect both equality and natural rights. Further rights, however, were civil in origin and could be rescinded.

The question whether the colonies reverted to the pre-political state of nature on their independence from Great Britain posed several related problems. If the people of each state were held to have severed all political ties and to have reverted to a state of nature, then all civilly granted rights, especially property rights, were at risk. Two theories common in the period avoided this danger. First, each colony might be considered a continuously existing political society, severing only its ties to another nation. Second, each state, in writing its own constitution between 1776 and 1778, might be considered an immediately reconstituted political society, implicitly or explicitly re-establishing the laws and rights of the old colony. Many state constitutions in fact incorporated by reference English statutory and common law. By 1787, then, it was clear that independence did not necessarily imply a state of nature within each state.

Less clear was whether severing ties with Great Britain also severed the ties between states, and thus whether the states themselves, as sovereign nations, were in a state of nature toward one another. The implications of this debate were much broader than simply defining the authority of the Convention. Some states owned vast tracts of western land, granted by the crown and often largely uninhabited by white settlers. Reversion to a collective state of nature might erase this previous ownership in much the same way it negated individual ownership. In 1777, for example, Maryland claimed that Virginia's western lands belonged to Americans at large and not to Virginia. From 1775 through 1784, settlers in these and other Crown-granted territories argued that separation from Great Britain dissolved their ties to various states. They made unsuccessful bids to found new and independent states, calling themselves "Vermont," "Kentucky," "Westsylvania," and "Franklin." Although none of these attempts were successful at the time, the state of nature debate raged on.

In 1787 there was still a great gap between those who thought the states had seceded independently and those who thought they had seceded united. That dispute affected the Convention's entire discussion of both its authority and the method of ratification. During the debates, however, a subtle transformation took place. The delegates began by discussing the Convention's legitimacy in terms of the rights of states vis-à-vis one another. They often focused on practical considerations for want of a theoretical justification of Randolph's proposal. Then at some point during the summer, their focus shifted to the legitimating effect of popular ratification and a theory of popular sovereignty. In the excerpts below, try to trace the idea of popular sovereignty as it turns from a practical argument to a philosophical principle.

Tuesday, June 5

Propos. 15 for *"recommending Conventions under appointment of the people to ratify the new Constitution"* &c. being taken up.

Mr. Sharman thought such a popular ratification unnecessary: the articles of Confederation providing for changes and alterations with the assent of Congs. and ratification of State Legislatures.

Mr. Madison thought this provision essential. The articles of Confedn. themselves were defective in this respect, resting in many of the States on the Legislative sanction only. Hence in conflicts between acts of the States, and of Congs. especially where the former are of posterior date, and the decision is to be made by State tribunals, an uncertainty must necessarily prevail, or rather perhaps a certain decision in favor of the State authority. He suggested also that as far as the articles of Union were to be considered as a Treaty only of a particular sort, among the Governments of Independent States, the doctrine might be set up that a breach of any one article, by any of the parties, absolved the other parties from the whole obligation. For these reasons as well as others he thought it indispensable that the new Constitution should be ratified in the most unexceptionable form, and by the supreme authority of the people themselves.

Mr. Gerry observed that in the Eastern States the Confedn. had been sanctioned by the people themselves. He seemed afraid of referring the new system to them. The people in that quarter have at this time the wildest ideas of Government in the world.

They were for abolishing the Senate in Massts. and giving all the other powers of Govt. to the other branch of the Legislature.

Mr. King supposed that the last article of ye. Confedn. rendered the legislature competent to the ratification. The people of the Southern States where the federal articles had been ratified by the Legislatures only, had since *impliedly* given their sanction to it. He thought notwithstanding that there might be policy in varying the mode. A Convention being a single house, the adoption may more easily be carried thro' it, than thro' the Legislatures where there are several branches. The Legislatures also being to lose power, will be most likely to raise objections. The people having already parted with the necessary powers it is immaterial to them, by which Government they are possessed, provided they be well employed.

Mr. Wilson took this occasion to lead the Committee by a train of observations to the idea of not suffering a disposition in the plurality of States to confederate anew on better principles, to be defeated by the inconsiderate or selfish opposition of a few States. He hoped the provision for ratifying would be put on such a footing as to admit of such a partial union, with a door open for the acession of the rest.

Mr. Pinkney hoped that in case the experiment should not unanimously take place nine States might be authorized to unite under the same Governt.

The propos. 15. was postponed nem. cont.

On June 12, Proposition 15 was adopted with no further debate. When Paterson introduced his New Jersey plan three days later, however, the debate over ratification began again. Paterson's plan did not specify a method of ratification, but he clearly intended that it be submitted to the state legislatures as provided in the Articles of Confederation. The difference between the Randolph and Paterson plans rested partly on their proposed methods of ratification.

Much of the discussion on June 16, reprinted in the preceding section of this chapter, consisted of a debate over the authority of the Convention. As you will recall from those excerpts, Lansing and Paterson objected to the Randolph plan because of the "want of power in the Convention to discuss & propose it." Wilson noted that the Convention's authority to *propose*, unlike its power to *conclude*, was unlimited. It was Edmund Randolph himself who gave the most stirring—and the most radical—defense of his plan:

> Mr. Randolph, was not scrupulous on the point of power. When the salvation of the Republic was at stake, it would be treason to our trust, not to propose what we found necessary. . . . There are certainly seasons of a peculiar nature where the ordinary cautions must be dispensed with; and this is certainly one of them. He would not as far as depended on him leave any thing that seemed necessary, undone. The present moment is favorable, and is probably the last that will offer.

Although Madison here discreetly reported that Randolph "was not scrupulous on the point of power," Yates's notes give a fuller description of Randolph's eloquent speech:

> There are great seasons when persons with limited powers are justified in exceeding them, and a person would be contemptible not to risk it. . . . I am certain that a national government must be established, and this is the only moment when it can be done—And let me conclude by observing, that the best exercise of power is to exert it for the public good.

Yates's notes also give an interesting rendition of Paterson's defense of his own plan:

> But if the subsisting confederation is so radically defective as not to admit of amendment, let us say so and report its insufficiency, and wait for enlarged powers. We must, in the present case, pursue our powers, if we expect the approbation of the people. I am not here to pursue my own sentiments of government, but of those who have sent me; and I believe that a little practical virtue is to be preferred to the finest theoretical principles, which cannot be carried into effect.

Despite Randolph's impassioned plea, the debate over ratification continued.

Tuesday, June 19

Mr . Madison: It had been alledged [by Mr. Patterson], that the Confederation having been formed by unanimous consent, could be dissolved by unanimous Consent only. Does this doctrine result from the nature of compacts? does it arise from any particular stipulation in the articles of Confederation? If we consider the federal union as analogous to the fundamental compact by which individuals compose one Society, and which must in its theoretic origin at least, have been the unanimous act of the component members, it can not be said that no dissolution of the compact can be effected without unanimous consent. A breach of the fundamental principles of the compact by a part of the Society would certainly absolve the other part from their obligations to it. If the breach of *any* article by *any* of the parties, does not set the others at liberty, it is because, the contrary is *implied* in the compact itself, and particularly by that law of it, which gives an indifinite authority to the majority to bind the whole in all cases. This latter circumstance shews that we are not to consider the federal Union as analogous to the social compact of individuals: for it if were so, a Majority would have a right to bind the rest, and even to form a new Constitution for the whole, which the Gents. from N. Jersey would be among the last to admit. If we consider the federal Union as analogous not to the social compacts among individual men: but to the conventions among individual States. What is the doctrine resulting from these conventions? Clearly, according to the Expositors of the law of Nations, that a breach of any one article, by any one party, leaves all the other parties at liberty, to consider the whole convention as dissolved, unless they choose rather to compel the delinquent party to repair the breach.

. . .

He observed that the violations of the federal articles had been numerous & notorious. Among the most notorious was an act of N. Jersey herself; by

which she *expressly refused* to comply with a constitutional requisition of Congs. and yielded no farther to the expostulations of their deputies, than barely to rescind her vote of refusal without passing any positive act of compliance. He did not wish to draw any rigid inferences from these observations. He thought it proper however that the true nature of the existing confederacy should be investigated, and he was not anxious to strengthen the foundations on which it now stands.

Later that day the Convention rejected the New Jersey plan. The delegates immediately became enbroiled in bitter disputes over the substantive provisions of the Randolph resolutions, and did not return to the question of ratification until July 23.

Monday, July 23

Resol: 19. "referring the new Constitution to Assemblies to be chosen by the people for the express purpose of ratifying it" was next taken into consideration.

Mr. Elseworth moved that it be referred to the Legislatures of the States for ratification. Mr. Patterson 2ded. the motion.

Col. Mason considered a reference of the plan to the authority of the people as one of the most important and essential of the Resolutions. The Legislatures have no power to ratify it. They are the mere creatures of the State Constitutions, and can not be greater than their creators. And he knew of no power in any of the Constitutions, he knew there was no power in some of them, that could be competent to this object. Whither then must we resort? To the people with whom all power remains that has not been given up in the Constitutions derived from them. It was of great moment he observed that this doctrine should be cherished as the basis of free Government. Another strong reason was that admitting the Legislatures to have a competent authority, it would be wrong to refer the plan to them, because succeeding Legislatures having equal authority could undo the acts of their predecessors; and the National Govt. would stand in each State on the weak and tottering foundation of an Act of Assembly. There was a remaining consideration of some weight. In some of the States the Govts. were not derived from the clear & undisputed authority

of the people. This was the case in Virginia. Some of the best & wisest citizens considered the Constitution as established by an assumed authority. A National Constitution derived from such a source would be exposed to the severest criticisms.

Mr. Randolph. One idea has pervaded all our proceedings, to wit, that opposition as well from the States as from individuals, will be made to the System to be proposed. Will it not then be highly imprudent, to furnish any unnecessary pretext by the mode of ratifying it. Added to other objections agst. a ratification by Legislative authority only, it may be remarked that there have been instances in which the authority of the Common law has been set up in particular States agst. that of the Confederation which has had no higher sanction than Legislative ratification.—Whose opposition will be most likely to be excited agst. the System? That of the local demagogues who will be degraded by it from the importance they now hold. These will spare no efforts to impede that progress in the popular mind which will be necessary to the adoption of the plan, and which every member will find to have taken place in his own, if he will compare his present opinions with those brought with him into the Convention. It is of great importance therefore that the consideration of this subject should be transferred from the Legislatures where this class of men, have their full influence to a field in which their efforts can be less mischeivous. It is moreover worthy of consideration that some of the States are averse to any change in their Constitution, and will not take the requisite steps, unless expressly called upon to refer the question to the people.

Mr. Gerry. The arguments of Col. Mason & Mr. Randolph prove too much. they prove an unconstitutionality in the present federal system even in some of the State Govts. Inferences drawn from such a source must be inadmissible. Both the State Govts. & the federal Govt. have been too long acquiesced in, to be now shaken. He considered the Confederation to be paramount to any State Constitution. The last article of it authorizing alterations must consequently be so as well as the others, and every thing done in pursuance of the article must have the same high authority with the article. — Great confusion he was confident would result from a recurrence to the people. They would never agree on any thing. He could not see any ground to suppose that the people will do what their rulers will not. The rulers will either conform to, or influence the sense of the people.

. . .

Mr. Elseworth. If there be any Legislatures who should find themselves incompetent to the ratification, he should be content to let them advise with their constitutents and pursue such a mode as wd. be competent. He thought more was to be expected from the Legislatures than from the people. The prevailing wish of the people in the Eastern States is to get rid of the public debt; and the idea of strengthening the Natl. Govt. carried with it that of strengthening the public debt. It was said by Col. Mason 1. that the Legislatures have no authority in this case. 2. that their successors having equal authority could rescind their acts. As to the 2d. point he could not admit it to be well founded. An Act to which the States by their Legislatures, make themselves parties, becomes a compact from which no one of the parties can recede of itself. As to the 1st. point, he observed that a new sett of ideas seemed to have crept in since the articles of Confederation were established. Conventions of the people, or with power derived expressly from the people, were not then thought of. The Legislatures were considered as competent. Their ratification has been acquiesced in without complaint. To whom have Congs. applied on subsequent occasions for further powers? To the Legislatures; not to the people. The fact is that we exist at present, and we need not enquire how, as a federal Society, united by a charter one article of which is that alterations therein may be made by the Legislative authority of the States. It has been said that if the confederation is to be ob-

served, the States must *unanimously* concur in the proposed innovations. He would answer that if such were the urgency & necessity of our situation as to warrant a new compact among a part of the States, founded on the consent of the people; the same pleas would be equally valid in favor of a partial compact, founded on the consent of the Legislatures.

Mr. Williamson thought the Resoln.:[19   ] so expressed as that it might be submitted either to the Legislatures or to Conventions recommended by the Legislatures. He observed that some Legislatures were evidently unauthorized to ratify the system. He thought too that Conventions were to be preferred as more likely to be composed of the ablest men in the States.

Mr. Govr. Morris considered the inference of Mr. Elseworth from the plea of necessity as applied to the establishment of a new System on ye. consent of the people of a part of the States, in favor of a like establishnt. on the consent of a part of the Legislatures as a non sequitur. If the Confederation is to be pursued no alteration can be made without the unanimous consent of the Legislatures: Legisiative alterations not conformable to the federal compact, would clearly not be valid. The Judges would consider them as null & void. Whereas in case of an appeal to the people of the U.S., the supreme authority, the federal compact may be altered by a *majority of them;* in like manner as the Constitution of a particular State may be altered by a majority of the people of the State. The amendmt moved by Mr. Elseworth erroneously supposes that we are proceeding on the basis of the Confederation. This Convention is unknown to the Confederation.

Mr. King thought with Mr. Elseworth that the Legislatures had a competent authority, the acquiescence of the people of America in the Confederation, being equivalent to a formal ratification by the people. He thought with Mr. E—also that the plea of necessity was as valid in the one case as in the other. At the same time he preferred a reference to the authority of the people expressly delegated to Conventions, as the most certain means of obviating all disputes & doubts concerning the legitimacy of the new Constitution; as well as the most likely means of drawing forth the best men in the States to decide on it. He remarked that among other objections made in the State of N. York to granting powers to Congs. one had been that such powers as would operate within the State, could not be reconciled to the Constitution; and therefore were not grantible by the Legislative authority. He considered it as of some consequence also to get rid of the scruples which some members of the State Legisla-

tures might derive from their oaths to support &
maintain the existing Constitutions.

Mr. Madison thought it clear that the Legislatures
were incompetent to the proposed changes. These
changes would make essential inroads on the State
Constitutions, and it would be a novel & dangerous
doctrine that a legislature could change the constitution under which it held its existence. There
might indeed be some Constitutions within the
Union, which had given a power to the Legislature
to concur in alterations of the federal Compact. But
there were certainly some which had not; and in the
case of these, a ratification must of necessity be obtained from the people. He considered the difference between a system founded on the Legislatures
only, and one founded on the people, to be the true
difference between a *league* or *treaty*, and a *Constitution*. The former in point of *moral* obligation might be
as inviolable as the latter. In point of *political operation*, there were two important distinctions in favor
of the latter. 1. A law violating a treaty ratified by a

pre-existing law, might be repected by the Judges as
a law, though an unwise or perfidious one. A law
violating a constitution established by the people
themselves, would be considered by the Judges as
null & void. 2. The doctrine laid down by the law of
Nations in the case of treaties is that a breach of any
one article by any of the parties, frees the other parties from their engagements. In the case of a union
of people under one Constitution, the nature of the
pact has always been understood to exclude such an
interpretation. Comparing the two modes in point
of expediency he thought all the considerations
which recommended this Convention in preference
to Congress for proposing the reform were in favor
of State Conventions in preference to the Legislatures for examining and adopting it.

On question on Mr. Elseworth's motion to refer
the plan to the Legislatures of the States

N. H. no. Mas. no. Ct. ay. no. Pa. no. Del. ay.
Md. ay. Va. no. N. C. no. S. C. no. Geo. no.

The Convention then agreed to popular ratification, and left the details of
the entire document to the appropriately named Committee on Detail. That
committee was elected by ballot on July 24, and consisted of John Rutledge of
South Carolina, Edmund Randolph of Virginia, Nathaniel Gorham of Massachusetts, Oliver Ellsworth of Connecticut and James Wilson of Pennsylvania.
Between July 26 and August 6, while the Convention took its longest recess of
the summer, these five men took the general principles agreed to in Convention and produced a comprehensive first draft of the Constitution. Their draft
contained twenty-three separate articles, but at approximately 3,700 words
was only three-quarters as long as the final version.

Not much is known about the work of the Committee on Detail. The evidence suggests that Randolph wrote its first effort. Wilson probably produced a second draft after careful discussion among the members. After approval by the rest of the committee, the draft was sent to prominent
Philadelphia printers John Dunlap and David Claypoole. Despite the fact that
these men also owned a Philadelphia newspaper, the *Pennsylvania Packet*,
they printed only enough copies for the delegates as requested. They also
kept quiet about their task; this fact has led historian Clinton Rossiter to comment that Dunlap and Claypoole "must have been the most trusted men of
their profession in the history of the Republic."[13]

The Committee on Detail's draft provided that the Constitution would be
"laid before the United States in Congress assembled, for their approbation,"
and then ratified by state conventions. The number of state ratifications required was left blank, and the Convention spent most of August 30 (when
they finally reached those sections of the draft) debating how many state ratifications would be required to make the document effective. Seven, eight,
nine, ten, and thirteen were suggested. Madison even proposed filling the
blank with "any seven or more States entitled to thirty three members at least

in the House of Representatives" because this "would require the concurrence of a majority both of the States and [the] people." After Mason suggested that nine was preferable because it had been required "in all great cases under the Confederation" and was thus "familiar to the people," the Convention agreed to require nine ratifications.

When the Convention turned to the necessity of the approbation of Congress, however, the simmering dissatisfaction of several delegates could no longer be contained. The Convention quickly voted eight to three to delete the requirement of congressional approbation. Morris and Pinckney then pushed the issue too far by proposing to add that "the several Legislatures ought to provide for the calling of Conventions in their respective States as speedily as circumstances will permit." Martin responded by accusing them of a disingenuous motive: "He believed [the people] would not ratify it unless hurried into it by surpize."

After the Convention rejected the Morris–Pinckney motion, Gerry moved for a postponement, perhaps to curb the rancor or perhaps out of dissatisfaction with the progress of the debate. Mason seconded the motion and "declar[ed] that he would sooner chop off his right hand than put it to the Constitution as it now stands." Not to be outdone, Morris also supported the postponement, explaining that "he had long wished for another Convention, that will have the firmness to provide for a vigorous government, which we are afraid to do." The motion for a postponement failed, however, and the Convention ultimately approved the ratification provisions as amended.

That resolution lasted only a little over a week, however. At the next opportunity, Gerry brought the question up for reconsideration.

Monday, September 10

Mr. Gerry moved to reconsider art: XXI and XXII. from the latter of which "for the approbation of Congs." had been struck out. He objected to proceeding to change the Government without the approbation of Congress, as being improper and giving just umbrage to that body. He repeated his objections also to an annulment of the confederation with so little scruple or formality.

Mr. Hamilton concurred with Mr. Gerry as to the indecorum of not requiring the approbation of Congress. He considered this as a necessary ingredient in the transaction. He thought it wrong also to allow nine States as provided by art XXI. to institute a new Government on the ruins of the existing one. He wd. propose as a better modification of the two articles (XXI & XXII) that the plan should be sent to Congress in order that the same if approved by them, may be communicated to the State Legislatures, to the end that they may refer it to State Conventions; each Legislature declaring that if the Con-

vention of the State should think the plan ought to take effect among nine ratifying States, the same shd. take effect accordingly.

Mr. Gorham. Some States will say that nine States shall be sufficient to establish the plan, others will require unanimity for the purpose. And the different and conditional ratifications will defeat the plan altogether.

Mr. Hamilton. No Convention convinced of the necessity of the plan will refuse to give it effect on the adoption by nine States. He thought this mode less exceptionable than the one proposed in the article, and would attain the same end.

Mr. Fitzimmons remarked that the words "for their approbation" had been struck out in order to save Congress from the necessity of an Act inconsistent with the Articles of Confederation under which they held their authority.

Mr. Randolph declared, if no change should be made in the this part of the plan, he should be obliged to dissent from the whole of it. He had from the beginning he said been convinced that radical changes in the system of the Union were necessary. Under this conviction he had brought forward a set of republican propositions as the basis and outline of a reform. These Republican propositions had however, much to his regret, been widely, and in his opinion, irreconcileably departed from. In this state of things it was his idea and he accordingly meant to propose, that the State Conventions shd. be at liberty to offer amendments to the plan; and that these should be submitted to a second General Convention, with full power to settle the Constitution finally. He did not expect to succeed in this proposition, but the discharge of his duty in making the attempt, would give quiet to his own mind.

Mr. Wilson was against a reconsideration for any of the purposes which had been mentioned.

Mr. King thought it would be more respectful to Congress to submit the plan generally to them; than in such a form as expressly and necessarily to require their approbation or disapprobation. The assent of nine States be considered as sufficient; and that it was more proper to make this a part of the Constitution itself, than to provide for it by a supplemental or distinct recommendation.

Mr. Gerry urged the indecency and pernicious tendency of dissolving in so slight a manner, the solemn obligations of the articles of confederation. If nine out of thirteen can dissolve the compact, Six out of nine will be just as able to dissolve the new one hereafter.

Mr. Sherman was in favor of Mr. King's idea of submitting the plan generally to Congress. He thought nine States ought to be made sufficient: but that it would be best to make it a separate act and in some such form as that intimated by Col: Hamilton, than to make it a particular article of the Constitution.

On the question for reconsidering the two article, XXI & XXII—

N. H. divd. Mas. no. Ct. ay. N. J. ay. Pa. no. Del. ay. Md. ay. Va. ay. N. C. ay. S. C. no. Geo. ay.

No new arguments were offered during reconsideration, and the two articles remained unchanged.

Although the Convention thus resolved the question of its own authority, both that issue and the debate over the state of nature were to recur. During the subsequent ratification debates, Antifederalists seized on the Convention's lack of power as a convenient criticism of the Constitution (discussed in chapter 7). The eventual ratification of the Constitution, however, made moot the question of the Convention's authority.

In 1789, Congress definitively settled the state of nature debate. One of the earliest disputes in the House of Representatives concerned a petition to deny a seat to William Smith of South Carolina on the ground that he had not been a citizen of the United States for the required seven years. Smith had been born in South Carolina while it was still a colony, and had been sent to school in England as a child in 1770. Despite his efforts to return during the Revolution, a series of mishaps (including being orphaned and being shipwrecked) delayed his return until November 1783. He had been back in South Carolina for less than six years at the time he was elected to the House.

The petition contesting his election argued that Smith had, like all colonists, been born a citizen of Great Britain. He could only acquire American citizenship by participation in the Revolution, by oath of fidelity, by tacit consent, or by adoption, none of which he had done prior to 1783. The petition concluded: "[M]any . . . dangerous consequences, would, as your petitioner apprehends, follow from the establishment of a precedent, by which it was acknowledged, that a native of this country might be a citizen of the United States before he lived under their Government."[14]

James Madison took this assertion that the Revolution created a discontinuity of citizenship as a reiteration of the position that the colonies had reverted to a total state of nature on separation from Great Britain. He had rejected that position in 1787, and he disputed it now. Beginning with the proposition that Smith was a citizen of South Carolina from his birth, Madison argued that Smith had remained a citizen from that day forward. Any contrary conclusion, according to Madison, was based on the erroneous assumption that the Revolution had broken all bonds of allegiance, and not just the bonds between American citizens and the king of Great Britain. He characterized his opponents as subscribing to an erroneous assumption:

> [My] reasoning [about which bonds of allegiance were broken] will hold good, unless it is supposed that the separation which took place between these States and Great Britain, not only dissolved the union between those countries, but dissolved the union among the citizens themselves: that the original compact, which made them altogether one society, being dissolved, they could not fall into pieces, each part making an independent society; but must individually revert into a state of nature[.] [15]

He described his own views as quite different: "I conceive the colonies remained as a political society, detached from their former connexion with another society, without dissolving into a state of nature."[16] James Jackson of Georgia disputed Madison's premises, arguing that "the whole allegiance or compact [was] dissolved" on independence, throwing the individual states back into a state of nature.[17]

The House voted thirty-six to one to seat Smith, and effectively silenced further debate about whether the United States had ever been in a state of nature. The issue did not arise again until the crisis of slavery and the doctrine of nullification made the definition of states' rights crucial, and raised again the question of the nature of the compact. Before we return to that philosophical thicket, however, we must consider in detail the writing of the 1787 Constitution itself.

Topics For Discussion

1. Compare the Articles of Confederation and the Constitution. What differences between the documents are signified by the differences in form and substance of their preambles? Note that Randolph forgives the authors of the Articles their mistakes on the theory that they were written "in the then infancy of the science, of constitutions, & of confederacies." Is he correct in implying that by 1787 things had changed? Would the preamble of the Constitution have been controversial or uncontroversial at the beginning of the Convention? In other words, was the preamble a reflection of changes in the political climate between 1777 and 1787, or was it fought out in the Convention itself?

2. In what ways did the Convention deal with its apparent lack of authority? How did the responses of the delegates develop over the summer? Look especially at the debates on July 23. What *is* this Constitution they are writing, according to Ellsworth or Gerry? According to Mason, Gouverneur Morris, or King? Recall the description of the British constitution in chapter 1. Note also that when the supremacy clause was first introduced by Luther Martin on July 17, the Constitution itself was not made supreme. It was only on August 23 that that change was made, without debate. Does this tell you anything further about what the delegates thought they were writing?

3. Recall Randolph's lack of scruples "on the point of power" and his eloquent speech on June 16. What would have happened had that speech been made public at the end of the Convention? What would happen if a congressional committee, an administrative agency, or some body such as the National Security Council made such an argument today, in defense of some action it had taken? Are there differences?

4. Notice Randolph's reversal: he opens the Convention by proposing popular ratification and closes it by unsuccessfully moving for legislative ratification. What happened?

5. Consider the various discussions on the nature of the compact and the binding character of the Constitution. Did the Southern states act unconstitutionally when they seceded from the Union at the start of the Civil War? What would the men at the Federal Convention have thought of that action? If they could have predicted it, might they have altered their proposed constitution? How?

6. Compare Madison's speech on June 19 regarding the nature of the confederation with his speech in the House of Representatives. Had his thinking changed?

7. There have recently been calls for a new convention pursuant to Article V to amend the Constitution. These modern demands are usually limited to proposing a particular amendment, such as one requiring a balanced budget or prohibiting school busing. If Congress were to call for a convention to propose particular, specified amendments to the Constitution, what do you think would happen? Would the convention be limited to those amendments? Could it, like its predecessor, exceed its instructions? Why or why not? Should such a convention proceed in the same shroud of secrecy that surrounded the first convention? Could it maintain the secrecy? Why or why not?

FOOTNOTES

1. Washington to Secretary of War Lincoln, October 2, 1782, quoted in Edmund C. Burnett, *The Continental Congress* 552 (1941).

2. Rufus King to Elbridge Gerry, June 18, 1786, quoted in Forrest McDonald, *Novus Ordo Seclorum: The Intellectual Origins of the Constitution* 171 (1985).

3. Quoted in Shirley Baltz, *A Closer Look at the Annapolis Convention* 5 (1986) [hereinafter *Annapolis Convention*].

4. *Maryland Senate Votes and Proceedings of the November Session, 1785,* quoted in Baltz, *Annapolis Convention,* at 8.

5. *Proceedings of the Commissioners to Remedy Defects of the Federal Government, Annapolis, Maryland, 1786,* in *Documents Illustrative of the Formation of the Union of the American States* 39, 42–43 (Charles Tansill ed. 1927).

6. *Supplement to Max Farrand's The Records of the Federal Convention of 1787.* 325–327 (James. H. Hutson, ed. 1987) [hereinafter *Farrand Supplement*].

7. James H. Hutson, *The Creation of the Constitution: The Integrity of the Documentary Record,* 65 Tex. L. Rev. 1, 12 (1986).

8. Rufus King to Nathan Dane, June 16, 1787, in *Farrand Supplement,* at 79–80.

9. Robert Burton to John Gray Blount, May 30, 1787, in *Farrand Supplement,* at 35.

10. Gordon S. Wood, *The Democratization of Mind in the American Revolution*, in *The Moral Foundations of the American Republic* at 109, 115 (Robert H. Horwitz, 3d ed. 1986).

11. Robert A. Ferguson, *"We Do Ordain and Establish": The Constitution as Literary Text*, 29 Wm. & Mary L. J. 3, 18 (1987); *see also* Michael M. Warner, *Textuality and Legitimacy in the Printed Constitution*, 97 Proc. Am. Antiquarian Soc. 59, 74 (1987). ("Anonymity, in the republican culture of print, does not designate cowardice, but public virtue.")

12. John P. Roche, *The Founding Fathers: A Reform Caucus in Action*, 55 Am. Polit. Sci. Rev. 799, 807 (1961).

13. Clinton Rossiter, *1787: The Grand Convention* 202 (1987).

14. 1 *Annals of Cong.* 404 (May 22, 1789).

15. *Id.* at 405.

16. *Id.*

17. *Id.* at 407.

CHAPTER THREE

The Federal Judiciary

INTRODUCTION

As the previous chapter has shown, Americans in 1787 were not yet experienced at writing a constitution or establishing new institutions of government. They were extremely experienced, however, in one aspect of government, which the states had been perfecting since the colonies were settled: the judicial system. Great Britain and the newly independent states all had longstanding and complex judicial systems. Each state had a somewhat different structure, but all had basic underlying similarities. These judicial structures were familiar to the delegates to the Federal Convention: thirty-four of the fifty-five delegates were lawyers or law trained. Thus the Convention delegates were able to draw on a vast pool of knowledge and experience without encountering significant disputes among themselves.

Article III on the judiciary was therefore the least controversial and most easily drafted of all the major provisions in the Constitution. Most of the disputes that occurred were arguments over the breadth of the federal government, as the next section of this chapter will show. The Convention was also concerned with technical details, such as the mode of appointing judges, which in the state systems differed widely. Only one proposal involving the federal judiciary engendered much controversy: Madison's suggested Council of Revision, treated separately in the last section of this chapter.

Consensus on the shape of the judiciary stemmed only partly from the delegates' familiarity with similar legal systems. The lack of controversy was also due to the delegates' view of the minor role they expected the judiciary to play. The history of the judiciary to 1787 was truly a history of the "least dangerous branch" (Hamilton's description of the federal judiciary in the *Federalist Papers*). This was largely because the judiciary was, in England as well as in the colonies and independent states, the least independent of the three branches of government. Especially in America, when judges did act inde-

51

pendently they were usually viewed as defending the people's rights against excesses of the other branches. This view of the judiciary, discussed in greater detail in the last section of this chapter, led the delegates to believe they had little to fear from judicial independence.

American courts during the colonial period were localized, with strong ties to the local communities. Less complex than the English system, they were still elaborate structures of numerous inferior and appellate courts with specialized jurisdiction. Jurisdictional divisions, including allocation of subject matter among higher and lower courts, constituted the primary differences among judicial systems of the thirteen colonies.

All the colonial courts were overseen, however, by final appeals to the Judicial Committee of the Privy Council—that is, the king acting with his council. Even though the Privy Council jurisdiction was seldom exercised, this royal prerogative overshadowed colonial courts. Within each colony, the court of final appeal was usually either the governor acting alone or with his council, or the assembly. Lower courts were inferior to the other branches of government both at home and in England. Moreover, the branches of government were not well separated: "The basic lower court was a *governing court*," performing various administrative and nonjudicial tasks.[1]

The British government also generally forbade the colonies from establishing life-tenured judges, which served as a further check on judicial independence. In several colonies efforts were made to establish life-tenured judges, but these efforts were usually rebuffed by the Crown. The most notorious example of an unsuccessful attempt to evade this rule occurred in New York. Peter Zenger's original defense counsel in his trial for seditious libel was not Andrew Hamilton, who took the case to trial, but James Alexander and William Smith. They began their defense by objecting to the court's jurisdiction. They argued that the judges were not properly commissioned because they were not granted life tenure, as required under the Act of Settlement (which had been held inapplicable to the colonies). They were disbarred for their pains, and were not reinstated until nearly two years later, long after Zenger himself had been acquitted. Chief Justice DeLancey made it clear that colonial efforts to free judges from their dependence on the royal governors were not appreciated:

> [Y]ou thought to have gained a great deal of applause and popularity by opposing this Court . . . but you have brought it to that point that either we must go from the bench or you from the bar: Therefore we exclude you and Mr. Alexander from the bar.[2]

The dispute over judicial tenure was so significant that it was listed in the Declaration of Independence as one of the "Facts submitted to a candid World."

The limitations on judicial independence rankled the colonists, and after 1776 the newly independent states attempted to remedy the problem. Most of the state constitutions provided for tenure during good behavior, and some protected judicial salaries from legislative caprice. Article XXX of the Maryland Bill of Rights of 1776 is typical:

> That the independency and uprightness of Judges are essential to the impartial administration of justice, and a great security to the rights and liberties of the people; wherefore the Chancellor and Judges ought to hold commissions during good be-

havior; . . . That salaries, liberal, but not profuse, ought to be secured to the Chancellor and the Judges, during the continuance of their commissions, in such manner, and at such times, as the Legislature shall hereafter direct, upon consideration of the circumstances of this State.

Most of the states, however, retained some mechanism for removing judges at the will of either the executive or the legislature (or both). In Maryland, for example, the same article provided that judges could be removed on the concurrence of the governor and two-thirds of each house of the legislature. In Rhode Island, judges who had invalidated a legislative enactment (a subject more fully discussed in the last section of this chapter) were called before the legislature to explain their action. When they refused to do so, they were removed from office.

Moreover, while judges gained some independence from the other branches, the judicial system as a whole remained vulnerable to legislative or executive interference. Although the state constitutions often explicitly recognized the doctrine of separation of powers and directed that each branch be independent, the principle was honored more in the breach than in the observance. Legislatures frequently reversed judicial decisions: they "freely vacated judicial proceedings, suspended judicial actions, annulled or modified judgments, cancelled executions, reopened controversies, authorized appeals, granted exemptions from the standing law, expounded the law for pending cases, and even determined the merits of disputes."[3] Thomas Jefferson commented that the legislature "in many instances, decided rights which should have been left to judiciary controversy. . . ."[4] As Forrest McDonald reports, "few Americans except lawyers trusted a truly independent judiciary."[5]

The rudimentary federal judicial system established by the Articles of Confederation also had limited and largely ineffectual authority. Seeking to fill the void left by the elimination of the appellate jurisdiction of the Privy Council, the Articles established congressional jurisdiction in three crucial areas: piracy, admiralty, and disputes between states. The Congress quickly delegated its jurisdiction over piracy to the state courts. Admiralty jurisdiction was first exercised by the Congress itself, taking appellate jurisdiction over admiralty cases originally heard in the state courts. In 1780, Congress established a national court of appeals for admiralty, called the "Court of Appeals in cases of capture." Since this court had only appellate jurisdiction, however, enforcement of its decrees was left to the states, which sometimes simply refused to comply with the federal decision. The system thus worked rather poorly.

Federal jurisdiction over disputes between states was exercised by Congress itself, under the absurdly cumbersome procedure described in Article IX of the Articles of Confederation. The complaining state was first to appear before Congress, which would assign a day for a hearing.

[The states involved] shall then be directed to appoint by joint consent, commissioners or judges to constitute a court for hearing and determining the matter in question: but if they cannot agree, congress shall name three persons out of each of the united states, and from the list of such persons each party shall alternately strike out one, the petitioners beginning, until the number shall be reduced to thirteen; and from that number no less than seven, nor more than nine names as congress shall direct, shall in the presence of congress be drawn out by lot, and the

persons whose names shall be so drawn or any five of them, shall be commissioners or judges, to hear and finally determine the controversy. . . .

The procedure has been described as "knocking out the brains of the committee" because in reducing the number of judges from thirty-nine to thirteen,
each side sought to eliminate its opponent's ablest supporters.[6] It actually was
used three times, once averting a war between Pennsylvania and Connecticut
over western lands.

As you read the materials in the next section, try to trace the consequences
of this early American judicial experience. To what extent did the experience
with England make life tenure and salary protections uncontroversial? How
well did the delegates sort out and perfect judicial independence and separation of powers? How did the experience under the Articles of Confederation
affect the debates over federal jurisdiction? How great a role did the delegates
expect the judiciary to take in governing the nation? How independent did
they expect judges to be?

CREATION AND SCOPE OF THE FEDERAL JUDICIARY

The Virginia Plan proposed by Edmund Randolph at the beginning of the
Convention called for a national judiciary similar in many respects to the
structure eventually described in Article III of the finished Constitution. Appointed by the national legislature but largely independent, judges of a supreme court and inferior courts were to have fairly broad jurisdiction over
matters of national importance:

> Resd. that a National Judiciary be established to consist of one or more supreme
> tribunals, and of inferior tribunals to be chosen by the National Legislature, to hold
> their offices during good behaviour; and to receive punctually at stated times fixed
> compensation for their services, in which no increase or diminution shall be made
> so as to affect the persons actually in office at the time of such increase or diminu-
> tion. that the jurisdiction of the inferior tribunals shall be to hear & determine in the
> first instance, and of the supreme tribunal to hear and determine in the dernier re-
> sort, all piracies & felonies on the high seas, captures from an enemy; cases in
> which foreigners or citizens of other States applying to such jurisdictions may be
> interested, or which respect the collection of the National revenue; impeachments
> of any National officers, and questions which may involve the national peace and
> harmony.

The discussion began harmoniously enough on Monday, June 4. With no
debate, the Convention added "one or more" before "inferior tribunals." The
next day, however, the delegates began arguing about the mode of appointment and the creation of inferior tribunals.

Tuesday, June 5

The words, "one or more" were struck out before
"inferior tribunals" as an amendment to the last
clause of Resoln. 9th. The Clause—"that the Na-

tional Judiciary be chosen by the National Legislature," being under consideration.

Mr. Wilson opposed the appointmt. of Judges by

the National Legisl: Experience shewed the impropriety of such appointmts. by numerous bodies. Intrigue, partiality, and concealment were the necessary consequences. A principal reason for unity in the Executive was that officers might be appointed by a single, responsible person.

Mr. Rutlidge was by no means disposed to grant so great a power to any single person. The people will think we are leaning too much towards Monarchy. He was against establishing any national tribunal except a single supreme one. The State tribunals are most proper to decide in all cases in the first instance.

Doct. Franklin observed that two modes of chusing the Judges had been mentioned, to wit, by the Legislature and by the Executive. He wished such other modes to be suggested as might occur to other gentlemen; it being a point of great moment. He would mention one which he had understood was practiced in Scotland. He then in a brief and entertaining manner related a Scotch mode, in which the nomination proceeded from the Lawyers, who always selected the ablest of the profession in order to get rid of him, and share his practice among themselves. It was here he said the interest of the electors to make the best choice, which should always be made the case if possible.

Mr. Madison disliked the election of the Judges by the Legislature or any numerous body. Besides, the danger of intrigue and partiality, many of the members were not judges of the requisite qualifications. The Legislative talents which were very different from those of a Judge, commonly recommended men to the favor of Legislative Assemblies. It was known too that the accidental circumstances of presence and absence, of being a member or not a member, had a very undue influence on the appointment. On the other hand he was not satisified with referring the appointment to the Executive. He rather inclined to give it to the Senatorial branch, as numerous eno' to be confided in—as not so numerous as to be governed by the motives of the other branch; and as being sufficiently stable and independent to follow their deliberate judgments. He hinted this only and moved that the *appointment by the Legislature* might be struck out, & a blank left to be hereafter filled on maturer reflection. Mr. Wilson seconds it. On the question for striking out. Massts. ay. Cont. no. N. Y. ay. N. J. ay. Pena. ay. Del. ay. Md. ay. Va. ay. N. C. ay. S. C. no. Geo. ay.

.   .   .

Mr. Rutlidge havg. obtained a rule for reconsideration of the clause for establishing *inferior* tribunals under the national authority, now moved that that part of the clause in propos. 9. should be expunged: arguing that the State Tribunals might and ought to be left in all cases to decide in the first instance the right of appeal to the supreme national tribunal being sufficient to secure the national rights & uniformity of Judgmts.: that it was making an unnecessary encroachment on the jurisdiction of the States and creating unnecessary obstacles to their adoption of the new system.—**Mr. Sherman** 2ded. the motion.

Mr. Madison observed that unless inferior tribunals were dispersed throughout the Republic with *final* jurisdiction in *many* cases, appeals would be multiplied to a most oppressive degree; that besides, an appeal would not in many cases be a remedy. What was to be done after improper Verdicts in State tribunals obtained under the biassed directions of a dependent Judge, or the local prejudices of an undirected jury? To remand the cause for a new trial would answer no purpose. To order a new trial at the Supreme bar would oblige the parties to bring up their witnesses, tho' ever so distant from the seat of the Court. An effective Judiciary establishment commensurate to the legislative authority, was essential. A Government without a proper Executive & Judiciary would be the mere trunk of a body, without arms or legs to act or move.

Mr. Wilson opposed the motion on like grounds. he said the admiralty jurisdiction ought to be given wholly to the national Government, as it related to cases not within the jurisdiction of particular states, & to a scene in which controversies with foreigners would be most likely to happen.

Mr. Sherman was in favor of the motion. He dwelt chiefly on the supposed expensiveness of having a new set of Courts, when the existing State Courts would answer the same purpose.

Mr. Dickinson contended strongly that if there was to be a National legislature, there ought to be a national Judiciary, and that the former ought to have authority to institute the latter.

On the question for Mr. Rutlidge's motion to strike out "inferior tribunals"

Massts. divided. Cont. ay. N. Y. divd. N. J. ay. Pa. no. Del. no. Md. no. Va. no. N. C. ay. S. C. ay. Geo. ay.

Mr. Wilson & Mr. Madison then moved, in pursuance of the idea expressed above by Mr. Dickinson, to add to Resol: 9. the words following "that the National Legislature be empowered to institute inferior tribunals." They observed that there was a distinction between establishing such tribunals absolutely, and giving a discretion to the Legislature to establish or not establish them. They repeated the necessity of some such provision.

Mr. Butler. The people will not bear such innovations. The States will revolt at such encroachments. Supposing such an establishment to be useful, we must not venture on it. We must follow the example of Solon who gave the Athenians not the best Govt. he could devise; but the best they wd. receive.

Mr. King remarked as to the comparative expence that the establishment of inferior tribunals wd. cost infinitely less than the appeals that would be prevented by them.

On this question as moved by Mr. W. & Mr. M.

Mass. ay. Ct. no. N. Y. divd. N. J. ay. Pa. ay. Del. ay. Md. ay. Va. ay. N. C. ay. S. C. no. Geo. ay.

Wednesday, June 13

Resol: 9 being resumed

The latter parts of the clause relating to the jurisdiction of the Natil. tribunals, was struck out nem. con in order to leave full room for their organization.

Mr. Randolph & **Mr. Madison**, then moved the following resolution respecting a National Judiciary, viz "that the jurisdiction of the National Judiciary shall extend to cases, which respect the collection of the national revenue, impeachments of any national officers, and questions which involve the national peace and harmony" which was agreed to.

Mr. Pinkney & **Mr. Sherman** moved to insert after the words "one supreme tribunal" the words "the Judges of which to be appointed by the national Legislature."

Mr. Madison, objected to an appt. by the whole Legislature. Many of them were incompetent Judges of the requisite qualifications. They were too much influenced by their partialities. The candidate who was present, who had displayed a talent for business in the legislative field, who had perhaps assisted ignorant members in business of their own, or of their Constituents, or used other winning means, would without any of the essential qualifications for an expositor of the laws prevail over a competitor not having these recommendations, but possessed of every necessary accomplishment. He proposed that the appointment should be made by the Senate, which as a less numerous & more select body, would be more competent judges, and which was sufficiently numerous to justify such a confidence in them.

Mr. Sharman & **Mr. Pinkney** withdrew their motion, and the appt. by the Senate was agd. to nem. con.

The Committee of the Whole then submitted to the Convention the following resolutions regarding the judiciary:

11 Resolved. that a national Judiciary be established to consist of One Supreme Tribunal. The Judges of which to be appointed by the second Branch of the National Legislature. to hold their offices during good behaviour to receive, punctually, at stated times, a fixed compensation for their services: in which no encrease or diminution shall be made so as to affect the persons actually in office at the time of such encrease or diminution

12 Resolved.That the national Legislature be empowered to appoint inferior Tribunals.

13 Resolved. that the jurisdiction of the national Judiciary shall extend to cases which respect the collection of the national revenue: impeachments of any national officers: and questions which involve the national peace and harmony.

That still did not satisfy some delegates, however, and the debate over both issues continued.

Wednesday, July 18

Resol. 11 "that a Natl. Judiciary be establd. to consist of one supreme tribunal." agd. to nem. con.

"The Judges of which to be appointd. by the 2d branch of the Natl. Legislature."

Mr. Ghorum, wd. prefer an appointment by the 2d branch to an appointmt. by the whole Legislature; but he thought even that branch too numerous, and too little personally responsible, to ensure a good choice. He suggested that the Judges be appointed by the Execuve. with the advice & consent of the 2d branch, in the mode prescribed by the constitution of Masts. This mode had been long practised in that country, & was found to answer perfectly well.

Mr. Wilson, still wd. prefer an appointmt. by the Executive; but if that could not be attained, wd. prefer in the next place, the mode suggested by Mr. Ghorum. He thought it his duty however to move in the first instance "that the Judges be appointed by the Executive." Mr. Govr. Morris 2ded the motion.

Mr. L. Martin was strenuous for an appt. by the 2d branch. Being taken from all the States it wd. be best informed of characters & most capable of making a fit choice.

Mr. Sherman concurred in the observations of Mr. Martin, adding that the Judges ought to be diffused, which would be more likely to be attended to by the 2d branch, than by the Executive.

Mr. Mason. The mode of appointing the Judges may depend in some degree on the mode of trying impeachments of the Executive. If the Judges were to form a tribunal for that purpose, they surely ought not to be appointed by the Executive. There were insuperable objections besides agst. referring the appointment to the Executive. He mentioned as one, that as the Seat of Govt. must be in some one State, and the Executive would remain in office for a considerable time, for 4, 5, or 6 years at least, he would insensibly form local & personal attachments within the particular State that would deprive equal merit elsewhere, of an equal chance of promotion.

Mr. Ghorum. As the Executive will be responsible in point of character at least, for a judicious and faithful discharge of his trust, he will be careful to look through all the States for proper characters. The Senators will be as likely to form their attachments at the seat of Govt. where they reside, as the Executive. If they can not get the man of the particular State to which they may respectively belong,

they will be indifferent to the rest. Public bodies feel no personal responsibility, and give full play to intrigue & cabal. Rh. Island is a full illustration of the insensibility to character, produced by a participation of numbers, in dishonorable measures, and of the length to which a public body may carry wickedness & cabal.

Mr. Govr. Morris supposed it would be improper for an impeachmt. of the Executive to be tried before the Judges. The latter would in such case be drawn into intrigues with the Legislature and an impartial trial would be frustrated. As they wd. be much about the Seat of Govt. they might even be previously consulted & arrangements might be made for a prosecution of the Executive. He thought therefore that no argument could be drawn from the probability of such a plan of impeachments agst. the motion before the House.

Mr. Madison, suggested that the Judges might be appointed by the Executive with the concurrence of ⅓ at least, of the 2d branch. This would unite the advantage of responsibility in the Executive with the security afforded in the 2d branch agst. any incautious or corrupt nomination by the Executive.

Mr. Sherman, was clearly for an election by the Senate. It would be composed of men nearly equal to the Executive, and would of course have on the whole more wisdom. They would bring into their deliberations a more diffusive knowledge of characters. It would be less easy for candidates to intrigue with them, than with the Executive Magistrate. For these reasons he thought there would be a better security for a proper choice in the Senate than in the Executive.

Mr. Randolph. It is true that when the appt. of the Judges was vested in the 2d branch an equality of votes had not been given to it. Yet he had rather leave the appointmt. there than give it to the Executive. He thought the advantage of personal responsibility might be gained in the Senate by requiring the respective votes of the members to be entered on the Journal. He thought too that the hope of receiving appts. would be more diffusive if they depended on the Senate, the members of which wd. be diffusively known, than if they depended on a single man who could not be personally known to a very great extent; and consequently that opposition to the System, would be so far weakened.

Mr. Bedford thought there were solid reasons

agst. leaving the appointment to the Executive. He must trust more to information than the Senate. It would put it in his power to gain over the larger States, by gratifying them with a preference of their Citizens. The responsibility of the Executive so much talked of was chimerical. He could not be punished for mistakes.

Mr. Ghorum remarked that the Senate could have no better information than the Executive. They must like him, trust to information from the members belonging to the particular State where the Candidates resided. The Executive would certainly be more answerable for a good appointment, as the whole blame of a bad one would fall on him alone. He did not mean that he would be answerable under any other penalty than that of public censure, which with honorable minds was a sufficient one.

On the question for referring the appointment of the Judges to the Executive, instead of the 2d branch
Mas. ay. Cont. no. Pa. ay. Del. no. Md. no. Va. no. N. C. no. S. C. no.—Geo. absent.

Mr. Ghorum moved "that the Judges be nominated and appointed by the Executive by & with the advice & consent of the 2d branch & every such nomination shall be made at least   days prior to such appointment." This mode he said had been ratified by the experience of 140 years in Massachussts. If the appt. should be left to either branch of the Legislature, it will be a mere piece of jobbing.

Mr. Govr. Morris 2ded & supported the motion.

Mr. Sherman thought it less objectionable than an absolute appointment by the Executive; but disliked it as too much fettering the Senate.

Question on Mr. Ghorum's motion
Mas. ay. Cont. no. Pa. ay. Del. no. Md. ay. Va. ay. N. C. no. S. C. no. Geo. absent.

Mr. Madison moved that the Judges should be nominated by the Executive, & such nomination should become an appointment if not disagreed to within   days by ⅔ of the 2d branch **Mr. Govr. Morris** 2ded the motion. By common consent the consideration of it was postponed till tomorrow.

"To hold their offices during good behavior" & "to receive fixed salaries" agreed to nem: con:

"In which [salaries of Judges] no increase or diminution shall be made so as to affect the persons at the time in office."

Mr. Govr. Morris moved to strike out "or increase." He thought the Legislature ought to be at liberty to increase salaries as circumstances might require, and that this would not create any improper dependence in the Judges.

Docr. Franklin was in favor of the motion. Money may not only become plentier, but the business of

the department may increase as the Country becomes more populous.

Mr. Madison. The dependence will be less if the *increase alone* should be permitted, but it will be improper even so far to permit a dependence Whenever an increase is wished by the Judges, or may be in agitation in the legislature, an undue complaisance in the former may be felt towards the latter. If at such a crisis there should be in Court suits, to which leading members of the Legislature may be parties, the Judges will be in a situation which ought not to suffered, if it can be prevented. The variations in the value of money, may be guarded agst. by taking for a standard wheat or some other thing of permanent value. The increase of business will be provided for by an increase of the number who are to do it. An increase of salaries may be easily so contrived as not to affect persons in office.

Mr. Govr. Morris. The value of money may not only alter but the State of Society may alter. In this event the same quantity of wheat, the same value would not be the same compensation. The Amount of salaries must always be regulated by the manners & the style of living in a Country. The increase of business can not, be provided for in the supreme tribunal in the way that has been mentioned. All the business of a certain description whether more or less must be done in that single tribunal. Additional labor alone in the Judges can provide for additional business. Additional compensation therefore ought not to be prohibited.

On the question for striking out "or increase"
Mas. ay. Cont. ay. Pa. ay. Del. ay. Md. ay. Va. no. N. C. no. S. C. ay. Geo. absent.

The whole clause as amended was then agreed to nem: con:

12. Resol: "that Natl. Legislature be empowered to apoint inferior tribunals"

Mr. Butler could see no necessity for such tribunals. The State Tribunals might do the business.

Mr. L. Martin concurred. They will create jealousies & oppositions in the State tribunals, with the jurisdiction of which they will interfere.

Mr. Ghorum. There are in the States already federal Courts with jurisdiction for trial of piracies &c. committed on the Seas. No complaints have been made by the States or the Courts of the States. Inferior tribunals are essential to render the authority of the Natl. Legislature effectual

Mr. Randolph observed that the Courts of the States can not be trusted with the administration of the National laws. The objects of jurisdiction are such as will often place the General & local policy at variance.

Mr. Govr. Morris urged also the necessity of such a provision

Mr. Sherman was willing to give the power to the Legislature but wished them to make use of the State Tribunals whenever it could be done, with safety to the general interest.

Col. Mason thought many circumstances might arise not now to be foreseen, which might render such a power absolutely necessary.

On question for agreeing to 12. Resol: empowering the National Legislature to appoint "inferior tribunals." Agd. to nem. con.

13. Resol: "Impeachments of national officers" were struck out" on motion for the purpose. "The jurisdiction of Natl. Judiciary." Several criticisms having been made on the definition; it was proposed by Mr. Madison so to alter as to read thus— "that the jurisdiction shall extend to all cases arising under the Natl. laws: And to such other questions as may involve the Natl. peace & harmony," which was agreed to nem. con.

Saturday, July 21

The motion made by Mr. Madison July 18. & then postponed, "that the Judges shd. be nominated by the Executive & such nominations become appointments unless disagreed to by ⅔ of the 2d. branch of the Legislature," was now resumed.

Mr. Madison stated as his reasons for the motion. 1. that it secured the responsibility of the Executive who would in general be more capable & likely to select fit characters than the Legislature, or even the 2d. b. of it, who might hide their selfish motives under the number concerned in the appointment.—2. that in case of any flagrant partiality or error, in the nomination it might be fairly presumed that ⅔ of the 2d. branch would join in putting a negative on it. 3. that as the 2d. b. was very differently constituted when the appointment of the Judges was formerly referred to it, and was not to be composed of equal votes from all the States, the principle of compromise which had prevailed in other instances required in this that their shd. be a concurrence of two authorities, in one of which the people, in the other the States, should be represented. The Executive Magistrate wd. be considered as a national officer, acting for and equally sympathising with every part of the U. States. If the 2d. branch alone should have this power, the Judges might be apointed by a minority of the people, tho' by a majority, of the States, which could not be justified on any principle as their proceedings were to relate to the people, rather than to the States: and as it would moreover throw the appointments entirely into the hands of ye Northern States, a perpetual ground of jealousy & discontent would be furnished to the Southern States.

Mr. Pinkney was for placing the appointmt. in the 2d. b. exclusively. The Executive will possess neither the requisite knowledge of characters, nor confidence of the people for so high a trust.

Mr. Randolph wd. have preferred the mode of apointmt. proposed formerly by Mr. Ghorum, as adopted in the Constitution of Massts. but thought the motion depending so great an improvement of the clause as it stands, that he anxiously wished it success. He laid great stress on the responsibility of the Executive as a security for fit apointments. Appointments by the Legislatures have generally resulted from cabal, from personal regard, or some other consideration than a title derived from the proper qualifications. The same inconveniencies will proportionally prevail, if the appointments be be referred to either branch of the Legislature or to any other authority administered by a number of individuals.

Mr. Elseworth would prefer a negative in the Executive on a nomination by the 2d. branch, the negative to be overruled by a concurrence of ⅔ of the 2d. b. to the mode proposed by the motion; but preferred an absolute appointment by the 2d. branch to either. The Executive will be regarded by the people with a jealous eye. Every power for augmenting unnecessarily his influence will be disliked. As he will be stationary it was not to be supposed he could have a better knowledge of characters. He will be more open to caresses & intrigues than the Senate. The right to supersede his nomination will be ideal only. A nomination under such circumstances will be equivalent to an appointment.

Mr. Govr. Morris supported the motion. 1. The States in their corporate capacity will frequently have an interest staked on the determination of the Judges. As in the Senate the States are to vote the Judges ought not to be appointed by the Senate.

Next to the impropriety of being Judge in one's own cause, is the appointment of the Judge. 2. It had been said the Executive would be uninformed of characters. The reverse was ye. truth. The Senate will be so. They must take the character of candidates from the flattering pictures drawn by their friends. The Executive in the necessary intercourse with every part of the U. S. required by the nature of his administration, will or may have the best possible information. 3. It had been said that a jealousy would be entertained of the Executive. If the Executive can be safely trusted with the command of the army, there cannot surely be any reasonable ground of Jealousy in the present case. He added that if the objections agst. an appointment of the Executive by the Legislature, had the weight that had been allowed there must be some weight in the objection to an appointment of the Judges by the Legislature or by any part of it.

Mr. Gerry. The appointment of the Judges like every other part of the Constitution shd. be so modelled as to give satisfaction both to the people and to the States. The mode under consideration will give satisfaction to neither. He could not conceive that the Executive could be as well informed of characters throughout the Union, as the Senate. It appeared to him also a strong objection that ⅔ of the Senate were required to reject a nomination of the Executive. The Senate would be constituted in the same manner as Congress. And the appointments of Congress have been generally good.

Mr. Madison, observed that he was not anxious that ⅔ should be necessary to disagree to a nomination. He had given this form to his motion chiefly to vary it the more clearly from one which had just been rejected. He was content to obviate the objection last made, and accordingly so varied the motion as to let a majority reject.

Col. Mason found it his duty to differ from his colleagues in their opinions & reasonings on this subject. Notwithstanding the form of the proposition by which the appointment seemed to be divided between the Executive & Senate, the appointment was substantially vested in the former alone. The false complaisance which usually prevails in such cases will prevent a disagreement to the first nominations. He considered the appointment by the Executive as a dangerous prerogative. It might even give him an influence over the Judiciary department itself. He did not think the difference of interest between the Northern and Southern States could be properly brought into this argument. It would operate & require some precautions in the case of regulating navigation, commerce & imposts; but he could not see that it had any connection with the Judiciary department.

On the question, the motion now being that the executive should nominate, & such nominations should become appointments unless disagreed to by the Senate"

Mas. ay. Ct. no. Pa. ay. Del. no. Md. no. Va. ay. N. C. no. S. C. no. Geo. no.

On question for agreeing to the clause as it standards by which the Judges are to be appointed by 2d. branch

Mas. no. Ct. ay. Pa. no. Del. ay. Md. ay. Va. no. N. C. ay. S. C. ay. Geo. ay.

No further changes were made in the Randolph resolutions regarding the judicial branch, and the Committee on Detail then proceeded to flesh out the resolutions adopted by the whole Convention. That committee's draft, delivered on August 6, describes aspects of the judiciary in Article IX, section 1, and the whole of Article XI. The draft of the Committee on Detail is reprinted in the Appendix; you should review Articles IX and XI at this point.

While the Convention continued to debate the Committee on Detail's draft, various delegates submitted written suggestions to be referred back to that committee. On August 20, Charles Pinckney submitted a long list of suggested revisions. He proposed, among other things, that:

Each branch of the Legislature, as well as the supreme Executive shall have authority to require the opinions of the supreme Judicial Court upon important questions of law, and upon solemn occasions. . . .

The Jurisdiction of the supreme Court shall be extended to all controversies between the U.S. and an individual State, or the U.S. and the Citizens of an individual State.

On August 22, the committee reported back, incorporating Pinckney's suggested expansion of Supreme Court jurisdiction in the draft before the Convention. The committee did not adopt his suggestion that the other branches be authorized to request opinions of the Supreme Court.

The Convention began discussing Article IX of the Committee on Detail draft on August 23. Unable to reach a compromise on the treaty ratification provisions, they referred the whole article to a committee. The roles of the legislature and executive in both treaty ratification and judicial appointment remained unclear until late in the Convention. Both issues were inextricably linked to the mode of electing the president, on which the delegates could not agree.

Temporarily stymied on judicial appointment, the Convention turned to other provisions regarding the judiciary.

Monday, August 27

Art: XI. being taken up.

Doct. Johnson suggested that the judicial power ought to extend to equity as well as law — and moved to insert the words "both in law and equity" after the words "U.S." in the 1st line, of sect. I.

Mr. Read objected to vesting these powers in the same Court.

On the question

N. H. ay. Mas. absent. Ct. ay. N. J. abst. P. ay. Del. no. Md. no. Virga. ay. N. C. abst. S. C. ay. Geo. ay.

On the question to agree to Sect. 1. art. XI, as amended.

N H. ay. Mas. abst. Ct. ay. Pa. ay. N. J. abst. Del. no. Md. no. Va. ay. N. C. abst. S. C. ay. Geo. ay.

Mr. Dickinson moved as an amendment to sect. 2. art XI. after the words "good behavior" the words "provided that they may be removed by the Executive on the application by the Senate and House of Representatives."

Mr. Gerry 2ded. the motion

Mr. Govr. Morris thought it a contradiction in terms to say that the Judges should hold their offices during good behavior, and yet be removeable without a trial. Besides it was fundamentally wrong to subject Judges to so arbitrary an authority.

Mr. Sherman saw no contradiction or impropriety if this were made part of the constitutional regulation of the Judiciary establishment. He observed that a like provision was contained in the British Statutes.

Mr. Rutlidge. If the Supreme Court is to judge between the U. S. and particular States, this alone is an insuperable objection to the motion.

Mr. Wilson considered such a provision in the British Government as less dangerous than here, the House of Lords & House of Commons being less likely to concur on the same occasions. Chief Justice Holt, he remarked, had *successively* offended by his independent conduct, both houses of Parliament. Had this happened at the same time, he would have been ousted. The judges would be in a bad situation if made to depend on every gust of faction which might prevail in the two branches of Govt.

Mr. Randolph opposed the motion as weakening too much the independence of the Judges.

Mr. Dickinson was not apprehensive that the Legislature composed of different branches constructed on such difference principles, would improperly unite for the purpose of displacing a Judge.

On the question for agreeing to Mr. Dickinson's Motion

N. H. no. Mas. abst. Ct. ay. N. J. abst. Pa. no. Del. no. Md. no. Va. no. N. C. abst. S. C. no. Geo. no.

On the question on Sect. 2. art: XI as reported. Del & Maryd. only no.

Mr. Madison and **Mr. McHenry** moved to reinstate the words "increased or" before the word "diminished" in the 2d. sect. art XI.

Mr. Govr. Morris opposed it for reasons urged by him on a former occasion —

Col: Mason contended strenuously for the motion. There was no weight he said in the argument drawn from changes in the value of the metals, because this might be provided for by an increase of salaries so made as not to affect persons in office, and this was the only argument on which much stress seemed to have been laid.

Genl. Pinkney. The importance of the Judiciary will require men of the first talents: large salaries will therefore be necessary, larger than the U.S. can allow in the first instance. He was not satisfied with the expedient mentioned by Col: Mason. He did not think it would have a good effect or a good appearance, for new Judges to come in with higher salaries than the old ones.

Mr. Govr. Morris said the expedient might be evaded & therefore amounted to nothing. Judges might resign, and then be reappointed to increased salaries.

On the question

N. H. no. Ct. no. Pa. no. Del. no. Md. divd. Va. ay. S. C. no. Geo. abst. also Masts. N. J. & N. C.

.   .   .

Mr. Madison & **Mr. Govr. Morris** moved to insert after the word "controversies" the words "to which the U. S. shall be a party." which was agreed to nem: con:

Docr. Johnson moved to insert the words "this Constitution and the" before the word "laws"

Mr. Madison doubted whether it was not going too far to extend the jurisdiction of the Court generally to cases arising under the Constitution & whether it ought not to be limited to cases of a Judiciary Nature. The right of expounding the Constitution in cases not of this nature ought not to be given to that Department.

The motion of Docr. Johnson was agreed to nem: con: it being generally supposed that the jurisdiction given was constructively limited to cases of a Judiciary nature.

On motion of **Mr. Rutlidge** the words "passed by the Legislature" were struck out, and after the words "U.S." were inserted nem. con: the words "and treaties made or which shall be made under their authority" conformably to a preceding amendment in another place.

The clause "in cases of impeachment," was postponed.

Mr. Govr. Morris wished to know what was meant by the words "In all the cases before mentioned it [jurisdiction] shall be appellate with such exceptions &c," whether it extended to matters of fact as well as law—and to cases of Common law as well as Civil law.

Mr. Wilson. The Committee he believed meant facts as well as law & Common as well as Civil law. The jurisdiction of the federal Court of Appeals had he said been so construed.

Mr. Dickinson moved to add after the word "appellate" the words both as to law & fact which was agreed to nem: con:

Mr. Madison & **Mr. Govr. Morris** moved to strike out the beginning of the 3d sect. "The jurisdiction of the supreme Court" & to insert the words "the Judicial power" which was agreed to nem: con:

The following motion was disagreed to, to wit to insert "In all the other cases before mentioned the Judicial power shall be exercised in such manner as the Legislature shall direct"

Del. Virga. ay. N. H. Con. P. M. S.C. G no

On a question for striking out the last sentence of sect. 3. "the Legislature may assign &c."

N. H. ay. Ct. ay. Pa. ay. Del. ay. Md. ay. Va. ay. S. C. ay. Geo. ay.

Mr. Sherman moved to insert after the words "between Citizens of different States" the words, "between Citizens of the same State claiming lands under grants of different States"—according to the provision in the 9th. Art: of the Confederation—which was agreed to nem: con:

Tuesday, August 28

Art XI Sec. 3 It was moved to strike out the words "it shall be appellate" & to insert the words "the supreme Court shall have appellate jurisdiction,"—in order to prevent uncertainty whether "it" referred to the *supreme Court*, or to the *Judicial power*.

On the question

N. H. ay. Mas. ay. Ct. ay. N. J. abst. Pa. ay. Del. ay. Md. no. Va. ay. N C ay. S. C. ay. Geo. ay.

Sect. 4. was so amended nem: con: as to read "The trial of all crimes (except in cases of impeachment) shall be by jury, and such trial shall be held in the State where the said crimes shall have been committed; but when not committed within any State, then the trial shall be at such place or places as the Legislature may direct." The object of this amendment was to provide for trial by jury of offences committed out of any State.

Mr. Pinkney, urging the propriety of securing the benefit of the Habeas corpus in the most ample manner, moved "that it should not be suspended but on the most urgent occasions, & then only for a limited time, not exceeding twelve months"

Mr. Rutlidge was for declaring the Habeas Corpus inviolable. He did not conceive that a suspension could ever be necessary at the same time through all the States.

Mr. Govr. Morris moved that "The privilege of

the writ of Habeas Corpus shall not be suspended; unless where in cases of Rebellion or invasion the public safety may require it."

Mr. Wilson doubted whether in any case a suspension could be necessary, as the discretion now exists with Judges, in most important cases to keep in Gaol or admit to Bail.

The first part of Mr. Govr. Morris' motion, to the word "unless" was agreed to nem: con:—on the remaining part;

N. H. ay. Mas. ay. Ct. ay. Pa. ay. Del. ay. Md. ay. Va. ay. N. C. no. S. C. no. Geo. no.

The delegates may also have considered an issue which does not appear in Madison's notes. George Mason's papers (in the Library of Congress) contain a "Draft Resolution" attributed by an unknown hand to John Blair of Virginia. The resolution's language closely resembles the language of Article XI, which the Convention was considering on August 27 and 28. It also contains an intriguing additional paragraph:

> In all other Cases not otherwise provided for the *Superior* State Courts shall have original Jurisdiction, and an Appeal may be made to the Supreme Court in all Cases where the Subject in Controversy—or the Decree of Judgment of the State Court shall be of the value of one thousand Dollars and in Cases of less value the Appeal shall be to the High Court of Appeals, Court of Errors or other Supreme Court of the State where the suit shall be tryed[.][7]

It is not clear when the "Draft Resolution" was written, or whether it was ever discussed by the Convention. The similarity between the resolution and the Committee on Detail's Article XI, however, is suggestive.

On September 4, the Committee of Eleven[8] made its report on the presidency. In addition to a crucial compromise on the mode of election discussed in chapter 4, the committee report proposed that the power to appoint judges be given to the president acting by and with the advice and consent of the Senate. The compromise on the appointment power was adopted unanimously after a short debate on September 7.

Friday, September 7

"He shall nominate &c Appoint Ambassadors &c."

Mr. Wilson objected to the mode of appointing, as blending a branch of the Legislature with the Executive. Good laws are of no effect without a good Executive; and there can be no good Executive without a responsible appointment of officers to execute. Responsibility is in a manner destroyed by such an agency of the Senate. He would prefer the council proposed by Col: Mason, provided its advice should not be made obligatory on the President.

Mr. Pinkney was against joining the Senate in these appointments, except in the instance of Ambassadors whom he thought ought not to be appointed by the President.

Mr. Govr. Morris said that as the President was to nominate, there would be responsibility, and as the Senate was to concur, there would be security. As Congress now make appointments there is no responsibility.

Mr. Gerry. The idea of responsibility in the nomination to offices is chimerical. The President can not know all characters, and can therefore always plead ignorance.

Mr. King. As the idea of a Council proposed by Col. Malson has been supported by Mr. Wilson, he would remark that most of the inconveniencies charged on the Senate are incident to a council of Advice. He differed from those who thought the Senate would sit constantly. He did not suppose it was meant that all the minute officers were to be appointed by the Senate, or any other original source, but by the higher officers of the departments to

which they belong. He was of opinion also that the people would be alarmed at an unnecessary creation of new Corps which must increase the expence as well as influence of the Government.

On the question on these words in the clause viz—"He shall nominate & by & with the advice and consent of the Senate, shall appoint ambassadors, and other public ministers (and Consuls) Judges of the Supreme Court." Agreed to nem: con: the insertion of "and consuls" having first taken place.

Topics for Discussion

1. Consider the delegates' discussion of the mode of appointment, especially the debates between those who favored appointment by the Senate and those who favored appointment by the executive. Article II, section 2 reflects their resolution of the question: the president "shall nominate, and by and with the Advice and Consent of the Senate, shall appoint" judges. What does "Advice and Consent" mean in this context? How great a role did the delegates envision for the Senate in the confirmation process? Should it be limited to ensuring that the nominee is qualified and that the nomination is not the result of "intrigue" or "partiality"?

2. Since 1789, the Senate has in fact rejected approximately one Supreme Court nominee out of five, for a variety of reasons. What reasons are legitimate? In particular, what things should senators consider if they are to fulfill the role envisioned by the framers? May the Senate reject a nominee on ideological grounds? Should it? Does it matter whether the nominee is the first or the fifth appointment by a particular president? Does it matter whether the nominee will swing the balance of the Court in one direction or another? Does it matter how extreme the nominee's views are? How should a senator decide what ideological views are too extreme? May senators oppose a nominee on the basis of that nominee's likely votes on particular issues? Does the margin by which the nominating president won the most recent election matter? Do the results of any intervening senatorial election matter?

3. In her confirmation hearings before the Senate Judiciary Committee in 1981, Justice Sandra Day O'Connor answered numerous questions about her personal views on such matters as federalism, abortion, and judicial activism. When Senator East asked her to endorse or reject a statement made by the dissent in *Roe v. Wade*, however, she refused:

> For me to join in that criticism [of the majority opinion] would be perhaps perceived as an improper exercise of my function right now, as a nominee to the Court, for the simple reason that I suspect we have not seen the last of that doctrine, or holding, or case, and that indeed we are very likely to have the matter come back before the Court in one form or another.[9]

She similarly refused to comment on other particular issues she thought would come before the court. Was her refusal in keeping with the expectations of the framers? To what extent does a nominee's refusal to comment on cases that might come before the Court foster separation of powers and judicial independence?

4.   Consider the progress of the discussions of appointment of judges. To what extent does the final compromise reflect the large states' unwillingness to give power to a congressional body in which states are equally represented? To what extent might it have been a necessary part of the committee of Eleven's overall proposal on the executive? Do your answers to these questions affect your views of the role the Senate should play in judicial appointments?

5. The delegates discussed the state judiciaries in two contexts: deciding whether there should be lower federal courts, and deciding whether to give the Supreme Court appellate jurisdiction over law and fact. Did the delegates trust the state judiciaries? Why or why not? Do the same problems exist today? Modern judges and constitutional scholars frequently disagree over the extent to which every plaintiff asserting a federally protected right should be guaranteed a federal forum. What light do these debates shed on that question? Does it help to know that general federal question jurisdiction was not conferred by statute until 1875?

6.   Consider Pinckney's rejected proposal that the other branches of government be authorized to request judicial opinions "upon important questions of law, and upon solemn occasions." Note also Madison's concern that the Court's jurisdiction ought to be limited "to cases of a Judiciary Nature." In 1793, President Washington formally requested the justices' opinion on the legal limits of American neutrality in the war between England and France. The justices refused, and explained their reasons in a letter to the president:

> [T]he three departments of government . . . being in certain respects checks upon each other, and our being judges of a court in the last resort, are considerations which afford strong arguments against the propriety of our extra-judicially deciding the questions alluded to, especially as the power given by the Constitution to the President, of calling on the heads of departments for opinions, seems to have been *purposely* as well as expressly united to the *executive* department.

This refusal eventually ripened into a doctrine stating that the federal courts will not issue advisory opinions, but will decide only actual cases and controversies. Is that doctrine consistent with the language and history of Article III? If so, why did President Washington, who was a member of the Constitutional Convention, request an advisory opinion? Note that two other Convention delegates, James Wilson and John Blair, were associate justices at the time. To what extent might this have affected their decision? Why do you think the justices failed to cite any of the relevant debates in support of their conclusion?

7.   The reach of the exceptions clause of Article III is still an open question. In allocating appellate jurisdiction to the Supreme Court "with such Exceptions, and under such Regulations as the Congress shall make," how much power does the Constitution grant Congress to limit Supreme Court jurisdiction? Trace the exceptions clause from its inception in the Committee on Detail through the brief discussions on August 27 and 28. Was it meant to give Congress power to eliminate Supreme Court jurisdiction over controversial subject matters such as abortion, school prayer, or school busing? Bills have frequently been proposed to do so. Would the framers have approved such bills?

How much does your answer rely on the discussions of the exceptions clause, and how much on the general discussions of separation of powers? Can the outlines of the separation of powers argument be gleaned from the document itself, without recourse to the debates?

8. Notice that North Carolina, South Carolina, and Georgia voted in favor of Rutledge's motion striking inferior courts. South Carolina then voted against even Madison's compromise allowing Congress to establish inferior courts. These three states were large and growing states, with vast western lands and an interest in a strong national government, and thus were aligned with the Madisonian camp. Why did they vote against him on this issue? What objection might they have had to lower federal courts? Consider the judicial role in the civil rights movement of the 1950s and 1960s. Were their fears justified?

THE COUNCIL OF REVISION

The delegates' vision of the federal judiciary is evident as much in what they did not do as in what they did. The Council of Revision—one of Madison's greatest failures—is a striking example of this. Apprehensive that the executive alone would not be firm enough to oppose the legislature, Madison wished to join the president and members of the Supreme Court in a Council of Revision that would have veto power over legislative enactments. This council was first proposed in Randolph's May 29 resolutions:

> 8. Res[olved] that the Executive and a convenient number of the National Judiciary, ought to compose a Council of revision with authority to examine every act of the National Legislature before it shall operate, & every act of a particular Legislature before a Negative thereon shall be final; and that the dissent of the said Council shall amount to a rejection, unless the Act of the National Legislature be again passed, or that of a particular Legislature be again negatived by _____ of the members of each branch.

The council was thus to review both positive federal enactments and the federal legislature's veto of state laws (the latter is discussed in chapter 5). Madison or one of his fellow nationalists proposed this Council of Revision four separate times, and each time it was soundly defeated. The excerpts below illustrate Madison's difficulty in compromising on important issues. This difficulty is further explored in the context of apportionment in the Senate, discussed in chapter 5.

The debates over the Council of Revision provide much more than an insight into Madison's inability to compromise, however. These discussions, together with a brief colloquy on the ex post facto clause, are the best evidence of the delegates' views on the practice of judicial review. Judicial review is the process by which courts examine legislative or executive acts for consistency with the Constitution, invalidating those acts that conflict with the Constitution. It is the cornerstone of modern constitutional law, and has become the most important aspect of federal court jurisdiction. The framers' views of its existence and scope have been a matter of judicial and scholarly debate for most of this century. To what extent did the framers anticipate that courts would review the constitutionality of statutes? If they expected courts to engage in the practice of judicial review, how did they think courts would go about interpreting the vague and open-ended clauses of the Constitution?

The debates on the Council of Revision provide some answers, but they must be considered in the context of eighteenth-century judicial theory and practice.

American judicial review began with the theories of Sir Edward Coke, an English judge and legal commentator of the late sixteenth and early seventeenth century. While most of his contemporaries believed in the absolute supremacy of Parliament, Coke held that acts of Parliament inconsistent with fundamental law were void. His most celebrated declaration of this principle came in 1610, in *Dr. Bonham's Case*: "when an act of Parliament is against common right and reason, or repugnant, or impossible to be performed, the common law will controul it, and adjudge such Acts to be void[.]"[10] Parliamentary enactments were thus subject to a higher law.

Coke's rather rambling description of what makes a statute void, and of the content of this higher law, was echoed in contemporaneous discussions of fundamental law. Viscount Bolingbroke, for example, described the English constitution as

> that Assemblage of Laws, Institutions and Customs, derived from certain fix'd Principles of Reason, directed to certain fix'd Objects of publick Good, that compose the general System, according to which the Community hath agreed to be govern'd.[11]

All of these descriptions of fundamental law, which might be paraphrased as custom mediated by reason, necessarily depend on *unwritten* law: England had (and still has) no written constitution. For Coke and the other English Opposition thinkers, positive legislative enactments were subordinate to unwritten, fundamental law.

Coke's theory, along with similar arguments of Bolingbroke and other "Country" party thinkers, were not well-accepted in England. English constitutional law was more influenced by Sir William Blackstone, who reasoned:

> [I]f the parliament will positively enact a thing to be done which is unreasonable, I know of no power in the ordinary forms of the constitution, that is vested with authority to control it. . . .

Although there were some nuances and inconsistencies, by and large Parliament was supreme. As one 1701 case commented, "an act of parliament can do no wrong, though it may do several things that look pretty odd."[13] By the second half of the eighteenth century, Blackstone's view had eclipsed that of Coke.

The American colonists, however, were greatly taken with the Opposition views of Coke and Bolingbroke. The notion that fundamental law might be superior to legislative enactments was attractive to the colonists, especially since it provided a principled basis on which to challenge such abhorred statutes as the Stamp Act. The American infatuation with Coke had global consequences, as Parliament's continuing defiance of fundamental law came to be viewed more and more as unlawful. When James Otis argued to the Massachusetts court in 1761 that it ought not issue writs of assistance (which gave Crown officials broad authority to search homes), he grounded his argument on the fundamental right of citizens to be secure in their houses. He repeated the by then common argument that "[a]n act against the Constitution is void: an act against natural equity is void: and if an act of Parliament should be made [authorizing writs of assistance], it would be void."[14] John Adams later characterized this speech as the genesis of the Revolution: "Then and there the child Independence was born."[15] The doctrine of higher-law limits on Parliament was one precursor to the "inalienable rights" and "self-evident truths" of the Declaration of Independence.

The English Opposition definitions of natural law were also popular in the colonies. Alexander Hamilton wrote in 1774:

> The sacred rights of mankind are not to be rummaged for, among old parchments, or musty records. They are written, as with a sun beam, in the whole *volume* of human nature, . . . and can never be erased or obscured[.][16]

Moreover, American thinkers as early as the 1760s began embellishing Coke's theory of the supremacy of fundamental law with an idea that was only obliquely suggested by Coke himself: that the *judiciary* might be charged with enforcing the society's fundamental law against legislative or executive usurpations. The royal hegemony over colonial courts prevented any practical application of this theory prior to 1776. When independence was declared, however, the new states had in place all the necessary elements to support a theory of judicial review.

In the 1780s, the state courts turned theory into practice. Between 1780 and 1787 the courts of seven states reviewed state statutes for constitutionality. Five statutes were invalidated, one was upheld, and one was given a questionable interpretation in order to avoid any conflict with higher law. The opinions and arguments echoed those of Coke and Bolingbroke. Judges and lawyers cited nearly indiscriminately: written state constitutions or charters, the "fundamental laws of England," the "law of nations," Blackstone's *Commentaries*, the Magna Carta, the Declaration of Independence, "general principles binding on all governments," "common right and reason," "inalienable rights," "natural justice," and the "relations of universal society."[17]

This was the background against which the delegates to the Federal Convention began discussing the proper role of the judiciary in the constitutional scheme. As you read the debates, consider the various delegates' statements in the context of this historical framework. To what extent did the delegates anticipate judicial review? How did they expect the federal courts to exercise their powers? What makes a law unconstitutional or invalid?

Monday, June 4

First Clause of Proposition 8th. relating *to a Council of Revision* taken into consideration.

Mr. Gerry doubts whether the Judiciary ought to form a part of it, as they will have a sufficient check agst. encroachments on their own department by their exposition of the laws, which involved a power of deciding on their Constitutionality. In some States the Judges had actually set aside laws as being agst. the Constitution. This was done too with general approbation. It was quite foreign from the nature of ye. office to make them judges of the policy of public measures. He moves to postpone the clause in order to propose "that the National Executive shall have a right to negative any Legislative act which shall not be afterwards passed by _____ parts of each branch of the national Legislature."

Mr. King second the motion, observing that the

Judges ought to be able to expound the law as it should come before them, free from the bias of having participated in its formation.

Mr. Wilson thinks neither the original proposition nor the amendment go far enough. If the Legislative Exetv. & Judiciary ought to be distinct & independent. The Executive ought to have an absolute negative. Without such a self-defense the Legislature can at any moment sink it into non-existence. He was for varying the proposition in such a manner as to give the Executive & Judiciary jointly an absolute negative.

On the question to postpone in order to take Mr. Gerry's proposition into consideration it was agreed to, Massa. ay. Cont. no. N. Y. ay. Pa. ay. Del. no. Maryd. no. Virga. no. N. C. ay. S. C. ay. Ga. ay.

The notes of William Pierce of Georgia give a slightly fuller account of King's opposition to the Council of Revision:

> Mr. King was of opinion that the Judicial ought not to join in the negative of a Law, because the Judges will have the expounding of those Laws when they come before them; and they will no doubt stop the operation of such as shall appear repugnant to the constitution.

The Convention then debated and approved an executive veto, with no judicial participation. Two days later, Wilson raised again the possibility of including judges in the veto power.

Wednesday, June 6

Mr. Wilson moved to reconsider the vote excluding the Judiciary from a share in the revision of the laws, and to add after "National Executive" the words "with a convenient number of the national Judiciary"; remarking the expediency of reinforcing the Executive with the influence of that Department.

Mr. Madison 2ded. the motion. He observed that the great difficulty in rendering the Executive competent to its own defence arose from the nature of Republican Govt. which could not give to an individual citizen that settled pre-eminence in the eyes of the rest, that weight of property, that personal interest agst. betraying the national interest, which appertain to an hereditary magistrate. In a Republic personal merit alone could be the ground of political exaltation, but it would rarely happen that this merit would be so pre-eminent as to produce universal acquiescence. The Executive Magistrate would be envied & assailed by disappointed competitors: His firmness therefore wd. need support. He would not possess those great emoluments from his station, nor that permanent stake in the public interest which wd. place him out of the reach of foreign corruption: He would stand in need therefore of being controuled as well as supported. An asso-

ciation of the Judges in his revisionary function wd. both double the advantage and diminish the danger. It wd. also enable the Judiciary Department the better to defend itself agst. Legislative encroachments. Two objections had been made 1st. that the Judges ought not to be subject to the bias which a participation in the making of laws might give in the exposition of them. 2dly. that the Judiciary Departmt. ought to be separate & distinct from the other great Departments. The 1st. objection had some weight; but it was much diminished by reflecting that a small proportion of the laws coming in question before a Judge wd. be such wherein he had been consulted; that a small part of this proportion wd. be so ambiguous as to leave room for his prepossessions; and that but a few cases wd. probably arise in the life of a Judge under such ambiguous passages. How much good on the other hand wd. proceed from the perspicuity, the conciseness, and the systematic character wch. the Code of laws wd. receive from the Judiciary talents. As to the 2d. objection, it either had no weight, or it applied with equal weight to the Executive & to the Judiciary revision of the laws. The maxim on which the objection was founded required a separation of the Executive as well as of the Judiciary from the Legislature

& from each other. There wd. in truth however be no improper mixture of these distinct powers in the present case. In England, whence the maxim itself had been drawn, the Executive had an absolute negative on the laws; and the supreme tribunal of Justice [the House of Lords] formed one of the other branches of the Legislature. In short whether the object of the revisionary power was to restrain the Legislature from encroaching on the other co-ordinate Departments, or on the rights of the people at large; or from passing laws unwise in their principle, or incorrect in their form, the utility of annexing the wisdom and weight of the Judiciary to the Executive seemed incontestable.

Mr. Gerry thought the Executive, whilst standing alone wd. be more impartial than when he cd be covered by the sanction & seduced by the sophistry of the Judges.

Mr. King. If the Unity of the Executive was preferred for the sake of responsibility, the policy of it is as applicable to the revisionary as to the Executive power.

Mr. Pinkney had been at first in favor of joining the heads of the principal departmts the Secretary of War, of foreign affairs &—in the council of revision. He had however relinquished the idea from a consideration that these could be called in by the Executive Magistrate whenever he pleased to consult them. He was opposed to an introduction of the Judges into the business.

Col. Mason was for giving all possible weight to the revisionary institution. The Executive power ought to be well secured agst. Legislative usurpations on it. The purse & the sword ought never to get into the same hands whether Legislative or Executive.

Mr. Dickenson. Secrecy, vigor & despatch are not the principal properties reqd. in the Executive. Important as these are, that of responsibility is more so, which can only be preserved; by leaving it singly to dicharge its functions. He thought too a junction of the Judiciary to it, involved an improper mixture of powers.

Mr. Wilson remarked, that the responsibility required belonged to his Executive duties. The revisionary duty was an extraneous one, calculated for collateral purposes.

Mr. Williamson, was for substituting a clause requiring ⅔ for every effective act of the Legislature, in place of the revisionary provision.

On the question for joining the Judges to the Executive in the revisionary business, Mass. no. Cont. ay. N. Y. ay. N. J. no. Pa. no. Del. no. Md. no. Va. ay. N. C. no. S. C. No. Geo. no.

Here again Madison's notes are interestingly supplemented by those of another delegate. Alexander Hamilton described Pinckney's principal opposition to the council:

> Principle—Danger that the Executive by too frequent communication with the judicial may corrupt it—They may learn to enter into his passions—

As Madison's notes show, the council was defeated again. Wilson raised it for the third time on July 21; Madison raised it one final time on August 15.

Saturday, July 21

Mr. Wilson moved as an amendment to Resoln. 10. that the supreme Natl. Judiciary should be associated with the Executive in the Revisionary power." This proposition had been before made and failed: but he was so confirmed by reflection in the opinion of its utility, that he thought it incumbent on him to make another effort: The Judiciary ought to have an opportunity of remonstrating agst. projected encroachments on the people as well as on themselves. It had been said that the Judges, as expositors of the Laws would have an opportunity of defending their constitutional rights. There was weight in this observation; but this power of the Judges did not go far enough. Laws may be unjust, may be unwise, may be dangerous, may be destructive; and yet may not be so unconstitutional as to justify the Judges in refusing to give them effect. Let them have a share in the Revisionary power, and they will have an opportunity of taking notice of these characters of a law, and of counteracting, by the weight of their opinions the improper views of the Legislature.—

Mr. Madison 2ded the motion

Mr. Ghorum did not see the advantage of employing the Judges in this way. As Judges they are not to be presumed to possess any peculiar knowledge of the mere policy of public measures. Nor can it be necessary as a security for their consitutional rights. The Judges in England have no such additional provision for their defence, yet their jurisdiction is not invaded. He thought it would be best to let the Executive alone be responsilbe, and at most to authorize him to call on Judges for their opinions.

Mr. Elseworth approved heartily of the motion. The aid of the Judges will give more wisdom & firmness to the Executive. They will possess a systematic and accurate knowledge of the Laws, which the Executive can not be expected always to possess. The law of Nations also will frequently come into question. Of this the Judges alone will have competent information.

Mr. Madison considered the object of the motion as of great importance to the meditated Constitution. It would be useful to the Judiciary departmt. by giving it an additional opportunity of defending itself agst. Legislative encroachments; It would be useful to the Executive, by inspiring additional confidence & firmness in exerting the revisionary power: It would be useful to the Legislature by the valuable assistance it would give in preserving a consistency, conciseness, perspicuity & technical propriety in the laws, qualities peculiarly necessary; & yet shamefully wanting in our republican Codes. It would moreover be useful to the Community at large as an additional check agst. a pursuit of those unwise & unjust measures which constituted so great a portion of our calamities. If any solid objection could be urged agst. the motion, it must be on the supposition that it tended to give too much strength either to the Executive or the Judiciary. He did not think there was the least ground for this apprehension. It was much more to be apprehended that notwithstanding this co-operation of the two departments, the Legislature would still be an overmatch for them. Experience in all the States had evinced a powerful tendency in the Legislature to absorb all power into its vortex: This was the real source of danger to the American Constitutions; & suggested the necessity of giving every defensive authority to the other departments that was consistent with republican principles.

Mr. Mason said he had always been a friend to this provision. It would give a confidence to the Ex-

ecutive, which he would not otherwise have, and without which the Revisionary power would be of little avail.

Mr. Gerry did not expect to see this point which had undergone full discussion, again revived. The object he conceived of the Revisionary power was merely to secure the Executive department agst. legislative encroachment. The Executive therefore who will best know and be ready to defend his rights ought alone to have the defence of them. The motion was liable to strong objections. It was combining & mixing together the Legislative & the other departments. It was establishing an improper coalition between the Executive & Judiciary departments. It was making Statesmen of the Judges; and setting them up as the guardians of the Rights of the people. He relied for his part on the Representatives of the people as the guardians of their Rights & interests. It was making the Expositors of the Laws, the Legislators which ought never to be done. A better expedient for correcting the laws, would be to appoint as had been done in Pena. a person or persons of proper skill, to draw bills for the Legislature.

Mr. Strong thought with Mr. Gerry that the power of making ought to be kept distinct from that of expounding, the laws. No maxim was better established. The Judges in exercising the function of expositors might be influenced by the part they had taken, in framing the laws.

Mr. Govr. Morris. Some check being necessary on the Legislature, the question is in what hands it should be lodged. On one side it was contended that the Executive alone ought to exercise it. He did not think that an Executive appointed for 6 years, and impeachable whilst in office wd. be a very effectual check. On the other side it was urged that he ought to be reinforced by the Judiciary department. Agst. this it was objected that Expositors of laws ought to have no hand in making them, and arguments in favor of this had been drawn from England. What weight was due to them might be easily determined by an attention to facts. The truth was that the Judges in England had a great share in ye. Legislation. They are consulted in difficult & doubtful cases. They may be & some of them are members of the Legislature. They are or may be members of the privy Council, and can there advise the Executive as they will do with us if the motion succeeds. The influence the English Judges may have in the latter capacity in strengthening the Executive check can not be ascertained, as the King by his influence in a manner dictates the laws. There is one difference in the two Cases however which disconcerts all reasoning from the British to our proposed Constitution. The British Executive has so

great an interest in his prerogatives and such powerful means of defending them that he will never
yield any part of them. The interest of our Executive
is so inconsiderable & so transitory, and his means
of defending it so feeble, that there is the justest
ground to fear his want of firmness in resisting incroachments. He was extremely apprehensive that
the auxiliary firmness & weight of the Judiciary
would not supply the deficiency. He concurred in
thinking the public liberty in greater danger
from Legislative usurpations than from any other
source. It had been said that the Legislature ought
to be relied on as the proper Guardians of liberty.
The answer was short and conclusive. Either bad
laws will be pushed or not. On the latter supposition no check will be wanted. On the former a
strong check will be necessary: And this is the
proper supposition. Emissions of paper money, lar-
gesses to the people—a remission of debts and similar measures, will at some times be popular, and
will be pushed for that reason At other times such
measures will coincide with the interests of the Legislature themselves, & that will be a reason not less
cogent for pushing them. It may be thought that the
people will not be deluded and misled in the latter
case. But experience teaches another lesson. The
press is indeed a great means of diminishing the
evil, yet it is found to be unable to prevent it altogether.

Mr. L. Martin. Considered the association of the
Judges with the Executive as a dangerous innovation; as well as one which could not produce the
particular advantage expected from it. A knowledge
of Mankind, and of Legislative affairs cannot be presumed to belong in a higher deger degree to the
Judges than to the Legislature. And as to the Constitutionality of laws, that point will come before the
Judges in their proper official character. In this character they have a negative on the laws. Join them
with the Executive in the Revision and they will
have a double negative. It is necessary that the Supreme Judiciary should have the confidence of the
people. This will soon be lost, if they are employed
in the task of remonstrating agst. popular measures
of the Legislature. Besides in what mode & proportion are they to vote in the Council of Revision?

Mr. Madison could not discover in the proposed
association of the Judges with the Executive in the
Revisionary check on the Legislature any violation
of the maxim which requires the great departments
of power to be kept separate & distinct. On the contrary he thought it an auxiliary precaution in favor
of the maxim. If a Constitutional discrimination of
the departments on paper were a sufficient security
to each agst. encroachments of the others, all fur-

ther provisions would indeed be superfluous. But
experience had taught us a distrust of that security;
and that it is necessary to introduce such a balance
of powers and interests, as will guarantee the provisions on paper. Instead therefore of contenting
ourselves with laying down the Theory in the Constitution that each department ought to be separate
& distinct, it was proposed to add a defensive
power to each which should maintain the Theory in
practice. In so doing we did not blend the departments together. We erected effectual barriers for
keeping them separate. The most regular example
of this theory was in the British Constitution. Yet it
was not only the practice there to admit the judges
to a seat in the legislature, and in the Executive
Councils, and to submit to their previous examination all laws of a certain description, but it was a
part of their Constitution that the Executive might
negative any law whatever; a part of *their* Constitution which had been universally regarded as calculated for the preservation of the whole. The objection agst. a union of the Judiciary & Executive
branches in the revision of the laws, had either no
foundation or was not carried far enough. If such a
Union was an improper mixture of powers, or such
a Judiciary check on the laws, was inconsistent with
the Theory of a free Constitution, it was equally so
to admit the Executive to any participation in the
making of laws; and the revisionary plan ought to
be discarded altogether.

Col. Mason Observed that the defence of the Executive was not the sole object of the Revisionary
power. He expected even greater advantages from
it. Notwithstanding the precautions taken in the
Constitution of the Legislature, it would still so
much resemble that of the individual States, that it
must be expected frequently to pass unjust and pernicious laws. This restraining power was therefore
essentially necessary. It would have the effect not
only of hindering the final passage of such laws; but
would discourage demagogues from attempting to
get them passed. It had been said [by Mr. L. Martin]
that if the judges were joined in this check on the
laws, they would have a double negative, since in
their expository capacity of Judges they would have
one negative. He would reply that in this capacity
they could impede in one case only, the operation of
laws. They could declare an unconstitutional law
void. But with regard to every law however unjust
oppressive or pernicious, which did not come
plainly under this description, they would be under
the necessity as Judges to give it a free course. He
wished the further use to be made of the Judges, of
giving aid in preventing every improper law. Their
aid will be the more valuable as they are in the habit

and practice of considering laws in their true principles, and in all their consequences.

Mr. Wilson. The separation of the departments does not require that they should have separate objects but that they should act separately tho' on the same objects. It is necessary that the two branches of the Legislature should be separate and distinct, yet they are both to act precisely on the same object.

Mr. Gerry had rather give the Executive an absolute negative for its own defence than thus to blend together the Judiciary & Executive departments. It will bind them together in an offensive and defensive alliance agst the Legislature, and render the latter unwilling to enter into a contest with them.

Mr. Govr. Morris was surprised that any defensive provision for securing the effectual separation of the departments should be considered as an improper mixture of them. Suppose that the three powers, were to be vested in three persons, by compact among themselves; that one was to have the power of making, another of executing, and a third of judging the laws. Would it not be very natural for the two latter after having settled the partition on paper, to observe, and would not candor oblige the former to admit, that as a security agst. legislative acts of the former which might easily be so framed as to undermine the powers of the two others, the two others ought to be armed with a veto for their own defence, or at least to have an opportunity of stating their objections agst. acts of encroachment? And would any one pretend that such a right tended to blend & confound powers that ought to be separately exercised? As well might it be said that If three neighbours had three distinct farms, a right in each to defend his farm agst. his neighbours, tended to blend the farms together.

Mr. Ghorum. All agree that a check on the Legislature is necessary. But there are two objections agst. admitting the Judges to share in it which no

observations on the other side seem to obviate. The 1st. is that the Judges ought to carry into the exposition of the laws no prepossessions with regard to them.

2d. that as the Judges will outnumber the Executive, the revisionary check would be thrown entirely out of the Executive hands, and instead of enabling him to defend himself, would enable the Judges to sacrifice him.

Mr. Wilson. The proposition is certainly not liable to all the objections which have been urged agst. it. According [to Mr. Gerry] it will unite the Executive & Judiciary in an offensive & defensive alliance agst. the Legislature. According to Mr. Ghorum it will lead to a subversion of the Executive by the Judiciary influence. To the first gentleman the answer was obvious; that the joint weight of the two departments was necessary to balance the single weight of the Legislature. To the 1st. objection stated by the other Gentleman it might be answered that supposing the prepossion to mix itself with the exposition, the evil would be overbalanced by the advantages promised by the expedient. To the 2d. objection, that such a rule of voting might be provided in the detail as would guard agst. it.

Mr. Rutlidge thought the Judges of all men the most unfit to be concerned in the revisionary Council. The Judges ought never to give their opinion on a law till it comes before them. He thought it equally unnecessary. The Executive could advise with the officers of State, as of war, finance &c. and avail himself of their information & opinions.

On Question on Mr. Wilson's motion for joining the Judiciary in the Revision of laws it passed in the negative—

Mas. no. Cont. ay. N. J. not present. Pa. divd. Del. no. md. ay. Va. ay. N. C. no. S. C. no. Geo. divd.

Wednesday, August 15

Mr. Pinkney opposed the interference of the Judges in the Legislative business: it will involve them in parties, and give a previous tincture to their opinions.

Mr. Mercer heartily approved the motion. It is an axiom that the Judiciary ought to be independent of that department. The true policy of the axiom is that legislative usurpation and oppression may be obviated. He disapproved

of the Doctrine that the Judges as expositors of the Constitution should have authority to declare a law void. He thought laws ought to be well and cautiously made, and then to be uncontroulable.

Mr. Gerry. This motion comes to the same thing with what has been already negatived.

Question on the Motion of Mr. Madison.

N. H. no. Mass. no. Ct. no. N. J. no. Pa. no. Del.

ay. Maryd. ay. Virga. ay. N. C. no. S. C. no. Geo. no.

. . .

Mr. **Dickenson** was strongly impressed with the remark of Mr. Mercer as to the power of the Judges to set aside the law. He thought no such power ought to exist. He was at the same time at a loss what expedient to substitute. The Justiciary of Arragon he observed became by degrees, the lawgiver.

Mr. **Govr. Morris**, suggested the expedient of an absolute negative in the Executive. He could not agree that the Judiciary which was part of the Executive, should be bound to say that a direct violation of the Constitution was law. A controul over the legislature might have its inconveniences. But view the danger on the other side. The most virtuous Citizens will often as members of a legislative body concur in measures which afterwards in their private capacity they will be ashamed of. Encroachments of the popular branch of the Government ought to be guarded agst.

. . .

Mr. **Sherman**. Can one man be trusted better than all the others if they all agree? This was neither wise nor safe. He disapproved of Judges meddling in politics and parties. We have gone far enough in forming the negative as it now stands.

The debates over the Council of Revision are good evidence that many of the delegates expected courts to engage in judicial review of at least federal legislation. They also provide some evidence of the anticipated manner of constitutional interpretation. More direct discussion of how judges would be expected to view legislation occurred during a debate over the ex post facto clause of article I, section 9.

Wednesday, August 22

Mr. **Gerry** & Mr. **McHenry** moved to insert after the 2d. sect. Art: 7, the Clause following, to it, "the Legislature shall pass no bill of attainder nor any ex post facto law."

Mr. **Gerry** urged the necessity of this prohibition, which he said was greater in the National than the State Legislature, because the number of members in the former being fewer were on that account the more to be feared.

Mr. **Govr. Morris** thought the precaution as to ex post facto laws unnecessary; but essential as to bills of attainder

Mr. **Elseworth** contended that there was no lawyer, no civilian who would not say that ex post facto laws were void of themselves. It can not then be necessary to prohibit them.

Mr. **Wilson** was against inserting any thing in the Constituion as to ex post facto laws. It will bring reflexions on the Constitution—and proclaim that we are ignorant of the first principles of Legislation, or are constituting a Government which will be so.

The question being divided, The first part of the motion relating to bills of attainder was agreed to nem. contradicente.

On the second part relating to ex post facto laws—

Mr. **Carrol** remarked that experience overruled all other calculations. It had proved that in whatever light they might be viewed by civilians or others, the State Legislatures had passed them, and they had taken effect.

Mr. **Wilson**. If these prohibitions in the State Constitutions have no effect, it will be useless to insert them in this Constitution. Besides, both sides will agree to the principle, & will differ as to its application.

Mr. **Williamson**. Such a prohibitory clause is in the Constitution of N. Carolina, and tho it has been violated, it has done good there & may do good here, because the judges can take hold if it.

Docr. Johnson thought the clause unnecessary, and implying an improper suspicion of the National Legislature.

Mr. Rutlidge was in favor of the clause.

On the question for inserting the prohibition of ex post facto laws.

N. H. ay. Mas. ay. Cont. no. N. J. no. Pa. no. Del. ay. Md. ay. Virga ay N. C. divd S. C. ay. Geo. ay.

James McHenry of Maryland summarized the opposition to the clause slightly differently:

> Moved that the legislature should pass no ex post facto laws or bills of attainder.
>
> Gouverneur Morris Wilson Dr. Johnson etc thought the first an unnecessary guard as the principles of justice law et[c] were a perpetual bar to such. To say that the legislature shall not pass an ex post facto law is the same as to declare they shall not do a thing contrary to common sense—that they shall not cause that to be crime which is no crime.
>
> Carried in the affirmative.

The records of the Convention provide one other insight into the framers' expectations regarding future judicial interpretation of the Constitution. In the Committee on Detail, Edmund Randolph apparently produced a working paper to guide the committee's drafting process. He began by describing the basic principles that ought to govern the committee.

> In the draught of a fundamental constitution, two things deserve attention:
>
> **1.** To insert essential principles only, lest the operations of government should be clogged by rendering those provisions permanent and unalterable, which ought to be accomodated to times and events. and
>
> **2.** To use simple and precise language, and general propositions, according to the example of the (several) constitutions of the several states. (For the construction of a constitution of necessarrily differs from that of law)[18]

The rest of the working paper sets out a rough outline of the substantive provisions of the Constitution.

Topics for Discussion

1. Some scholars have suggested that the Convention's rejection of a Council of Revision is evidence that the delegates did not intend judges to have any role in determining the constitutionality of statutes. They suggest that *Marbury v. Madison*, 5 U.S. (1 Cranch) 137, 2 L. Ed. 60 (1803), in which Chief Justice John Marshall explicitly established and defended the practice of judicial review, is a usurpation of authority. After reading these debates, do you think that is a valid interpretation of the Convention's action? Why or why not?

2. Since judicial review has in fact been an unbroken practice of the federal courts for almost two hundred years, the question whether the framers anticipated it is of largely historical interest. There is, however, continuing modern controversy over the manner in which the power of judicial review should be exercised. As chapter 14 discusses in detail, there is great dispute about whether judges should interpret the Constitution solely by looking at the intent of the framers, or whether they should engage in a more flexible method of interpretation and adapt the Constitution to contemporary circumstances.

What light do these debates shed on that question? How did the framers expect the Constitution to be interpreted? Does Randolph's guide to the drafting process help? Is it consistent with the views expressed in the Convention?

3. In constructing the framers' understanding of constitutional interpretation, you might focus on particular statements by various delegates. Look carefully at Madison's defense of his council on June 6. Assuming that the majority viewed judicial review as an adequate substitute for the rejected council, what role can you ascribe to the judges in passing on the validity of statutes? What qualities should they bring to their task? How are those qualities manifested in judicial opinions invalidating statutes?

4. The delegates discussed the nature of unconstitutional laws at several points. Look at Wilson's initial speech on July 21, at Mason's lengthy defense of the council the same day, and at the discussion of ex post facto laws on August 22. Recall the English Opposition theory and the early state instances of judicial review. What makes a statute unconstitutional? Did the delegates view the written constitution as the sole source of higher law? To what extent should judges invalidate unwise laws? laws inconsistent with "natural rights"? Can you use these debates to construct an argument supporting or opposing substantive due process?

5. Consider Gouverneur Morris's arguments on August 15 in favor of some check on the legislature. To what extent does judicial review now fulfill the role Morris envisioned for the executive veto? To what extent does the executive veto do so? Did other delegates share Morris's views?

FOOTNOTES

1. Lawrence M. Friedman, *A History of American Law* 45 (1973) (emphasis in original).

2. Quoted in Joseph H. Smith, *An Independent Judiciary: The Colonial Background*, 124 U. Pa. L. Rev. 1104, 1116 (1976).

3. Edward S. Corwin, *The Progress of Constitutional Theory Between the Declaration of Independence and the Meeting of the Philadelphia Convention*, in *The Confederation and the Constitution: The Critical Issues* 14 (Gordon S. Wood ed. 1973).

4. Thomas Jefferson, *Notes on the State of Virginia, Query XIII* in *The Life and Selected Writings of Thomas Jefferson* 238 (Adrienne Koch and William Peden eds. 1944).

5. Forrest McDonald, *Novus Ordo Seclorum: The Intellectual Origins of the Constitution* 85 (1985).

6. John P. Frank, *Historical Bases of the Federal Judicial System*, 23 Ind. L. J. 236, 243 n. 33 (1948).

7. From *Supplement to Max Farrand's The Records of the Federal Convention of 1787* 245 (James H. Hudson ed. 1987).

8. This committee, selected "by ballot" on August 31 to consider various controversial issues that had been postponed, consisted of Nicholas Gilman (New Hampshire), Rufus King (Massachusetts), Roger Sherman (Connecticut), David Brearley (New Jersey), Gouverneur Morris (Pennsylvania), John Dickinson (Delaware), Daniel Carroll (Maryland), James Madison (Virginia), Hugh Williamson (North Carolina), Pierce Butler (South Carolina), and Abraham Baldwin (Georgia).

9. *The Supreme Court of the United States: Hearings and Reports on Successful and Unsuccessful Nominations of Supreme Court Justices by the Senate Judiciary Committee, 1983 Supplement* at 219 (Roy M. Merskey and J. Myron Jacobstein eds. 1983).

10. 77 Eng. Rep. 646, 652 (K.B. 1610).

11. Bolingbroke, *A Dissertation Upon Parties* (1735), quoted in Julius Goebel, Jr., *History of the Supreme Court of the United States: Antecedents and Beginnings to 1801* 89 (1971).

12. 1 W. Blackstone, *Commentaries* *91.

13. *City of London v. Wood*, 12 Mod. Rep. 669, 687–88 (1701).

14. 2 *The Works of John Adams* 522 (Charles Adams ed. 1851).

15. John Adams to William Tudor, March 29, 1817.

16. 1 *Papers of Alexander Hamilton* 122 (Harold C. Syrett ed. 1961) (emphasis in original).

17. The cases, in chronological order and identified by date and state (but not by particular court) are: *Holmes v. Walton* (N.J. 1780), unreported but described in Scott, *Holmes v. Walton, The New Jersey Precedent*, 4 Am. Hist. Rev. 456 (1899); *Commonwealth v. Caton*, 4 Call 5 (Va. 1782); *Rutgers v. Waddington* (N.Y. 1784), unreported but described in J. Goebel, *The Law Practice of Alexander Hamilton: Documents and Commentary* 393–419 (1964); *The Symsbury Case*, 1 Kirby 444 (Conn. 1785); the "Ten-Pound Cases" (N.H. 1786), unreported but described in 2 W. Crosskey, *Politics and the Constitution in the History of the United States* 969–71 (1953); *Trevett v. Weeden* (R.I. 1786), unreported but described in James Varnum, *The Case, Trevett Against Weeden* (Providence 1787); *Bayard v. Singleton*, 1 N.C. 5, 1 Martin 42 (N. Car. 1787).

18. This document, along with other papers of the Committee on Detail, is found in 2 Max Farrand, *The Records of the Federal Convention of 1787* 137 (1911). (Portions in parentheses were crossed out in the original).

CHAPTER FOUR

The Federal Executive

INTRODUCTION

Between 1760 and 1787, the country experienced several dramatically different types of executive government. Much of the revolutionary fervor that helped end the colonial period arose from American dissatisfaction with the excesses of a strong executive. The new state constitutions of 1776–1778, like the Articles of Confederation, evidenced a determined effort to limit executive power. During the Confederation era, however, there was a gradual metamorphosis in the state governments toward a stronger, more effective executive, a change that paralleled the general recognition of the ineffectiveness of government under the Articles.

In the colonial period, the royal governors constituted an executive that was in some ways even stronger than the king himself. Because various acts derived from the Glorious Revolution of 1688 did not apply to the colonies, the governors exercised some powers denied to the king in England. Governors were permitted to regulate legislative elections, and to appoint legislators to positions in the cabinet and the judiciary. They held powerful controls over the assemblies, including the right to reject the speaker of the house, the right to determine the time and place of the legislative sessions, the right to dissolve the legislature, and an absolute veto over colonial laws. Although the king possessed some (but not all) of these controls over Parliament, no monarch had dared to exercise much direct control since 1688. Other executive powers not exercised by the governor—such as administering the colonial treasury and the colonial armed forces—were held by other agents of the Crown.

The executive branch also held control over the judicial branch. Most colonial judges were appointed by the Crown, and served at the pleasure of the governor. The governor and his council constituted the highest colonial court of appeal in civil cases.

Unlike the elected assemblies, the royal governors were appointed by the Crown. The governor's commission bound him to uphold English law and to disallow any law inconsistent with it. He also received "instructions" from the Crown, which detailed what he should do regarding certain specific issues. The only popular check on the executive was the fact that the legislature determined his salary.

When the colonies threw off the yoke of royal authority in 1776, a counter-reaction set in. After the Revolution, new state constitutions drastically limited the executive power. Both their experience with royal governors and the "Country" politics that prevailed in the new republic (discussed in chapter 1) led Americans to place most of the powers of government in the hands of the legislature rather than the executive. As James Wilson commented:

> The executive and the judicial as well as the legislative authority was now the child of the people; but, to the two former, the people behaved like stepmothers. The legislature was still discriminated by excessive partiality; and into its lap, every good and precious gift was profusely thrown.[1]

State executives were deliberately kept weak. Most state executives were chosen by the legislature; only New York originally provided for a popularly elected executive. Short terms of office kept the executive under control of the legislature: most states placed the maximum term of office at one year, and two states forbade re-election. Many states further weakened the executive by dividing authority between a governor and a council.

The new state constitutions stripped executives of virtually all the powers exercised by the royal governors. Executives were given few specific powers, and often even these were subject to legislative interference or oversight. The Virginia constitution of 1776, for example, gave the executive the pardon power, some control over the militia "under the laws of the country," and a few minor appointments. The Virginia constitution made clear that the executive's powers were extremely limited:

> [H]e shall, with the advice of a Council of State, exercise the executive powers of government, according to the laws of this Commonwealth; and shall not, under any pretence, exercise any power or prerogative, by virtue of any law, statute or custom of England.

Most state executives thus were mere creatures of the legislature. There was one glaring exception to this rule: New York. Unlike many of his counterparts in other states, the governor of New York ruled without a general council. He worked with a senatorial council on appointment matters, and with the judiciary in the Council of Revision that vetoed legislative enactments, but otherwise he exercised executive powers alone. The constitution gave him a three-year term, the longest of any state executive. He was elected by the people rather than by the legislature, and was re-eligible without any limitations. George Clinton was thus able to hold the governorship of New York from 1777 through 1795 and to serve as a vigorous leader. He was so strong, in fact, that he hand-picked two of the delegates to the Federal Convention, John Lansing and Robert Yates.

Some citizens of other states gradually became dissatisfied with their weak executives and began imitating New York's system. One primary concern was the efficient and effective maintenance of the war effort. Governors who held office for only a year could not develop adequate experience, staffs, or procedures to handle the complexities of running a state at war with Great Britain. As strong and popular governors in many states were forced to retire by constitutional mandate, people began to realize the disadvantages of too weak an executive.

Two later state constitutions (written after the independence-inspired flurry of constitutions in 1776–1778) increased the power of the executive branch. The 1780 Massachusetts constitution, unlike that state's unratified 1778 draft constitution, gave the governor a veto over legislative enactments, more control over the militia, and the power to appoint most judges. The 1776 New Hampshire constitution had not established an executive at all; the 1784 revision filled that gap with a "President" who lacked veto power but otherwise held all the powers of the Massachusetts governor.

By 1787, then, executive powers ranged from states with early constitutions and weak executives through the moderate constitutions of New Hampshire and Massachusetts to Governor Clinton's strong reign in New York. The "Country" and colonial hatred of a strong executive still lingered, however, among some delegates to the Federal Convention, and even those who favored a strong executive rejected the model of the British monarch. As they structured a federal executive, the delegates were divided more by pure reason than by political interest or ideology:

> [The executive branch] was not a matter that divided the delegates into opposing interests. Issues of presidential power, unlike those of representation, commercial regulation, or slavery, were not questions about which the delegates could know whether their constituents would benefit from particular outcomes. . . . One's view on any particular question depended on one's other assumptions about how the executive would function—assumptions that could be elaborated only in part at the convention and would evolve in full only with the gradual development of the office of president.[2]

The delegates approached the task of creating a federal executive with few concrete ideas and much uncertainty.

INVENTING THE EXECUTIVE

The delegates' uncertainty was evident from the very first. Randolph's plan had only a single resolution concerning the executive branch, and provided such an elastic description that the executive could take almost any form:

> 7. Resolved that a National Executive be instituted; to be chosen by the National Legislature for the term of _____ years, to receive punctually at stated times, a fixed compensation for the services rendered, in which no increase or diminution shall be made so as to affect the Magistracy, existing at the time of increase or diminution, and to be ineligible a second time; and that besides a general authority to execute the National laws, it ought to enjoy the Executive rights vested in Congress by the Confederation.

Resolution 7 left open the length of the executive's term and even the number of individuals who would comprise the executive, referring to the chief executive as "it" rather than "he." Only three points were firmly established: that the executive would be paid, that he or it would be appointed by the national legislature, and that the executive would be ineligible for a second term.

Agreement on the first was trivial and on the last two short-lived, as the delegates began discussing Randolph's proposed executive.

Friday, June 1

Mr. Pinkney was for a vigorous Executive but was afraid the Executive powers of the existing Congress might extend to peace & war &c., which would render the Executive a monarchy, of the worst kind, to wit an elective one.

Mr. Wilson moved that the Executive consist of a single person. **Mr. C Pinkney** seconded the motion, so as to read "that a National Ex. to consist of a single person, be instituted.

A considerable pause ensuing and the Chairman asking if he should put the question, **Docr. Franklin** observed that it was a point of great importance and wished that the gentlemen would deliver their sentiments on it before the question was put.

Mr. Rutlidge animadverted on the shyness of gentlemen on this and other subjects. He said it looked as if they supposed themselves precluded by having frankly disclosed their opinions from afterwards changing them, which he did not take to be at all the case. He said he was for vesting the Executive power in a single person, tho' he was not for giving him the power of war and peace. A single man would feel the greatest responsibility and administer the public affairs best.

Mr. Sherman said he considered the Executive magistracy as nothing more than an institution for carrying the will of the Legislature into effect, that the person or persons ought to be appointed by and accountable to the Legislature only, which was the depository of the supreme will of the Society. As they were the best judges of the business which ought to be done by the Executive department, and consequently of the number necessary from time to time for doing it, he wished the number might not be fixed but that the legislature should be at liberty to appoint one or more as experience might dictate.

Mr. Wilson preferred a single magistrate, as giving most energy dispatch and responsibility to the office. He did not consider the Prerogatives of the British Monarch as a proper guide in defining the Executive Powers. Some of these prerogatives were of Legislative nature. Among others that of war & peace &c. The only powers he conceived strictly Executive were those of executing the laws, and appointing officers, not appertaining to and appointed by the Legislature.

Mr. Gerry favored the policy of annexing a Council to the Executive in order to give weight & inspire confidence.

Mr. Randolph strenuously opposed a unity in the Executive magistracy. He regarded it as the foetus of monarchy. We had he said no motive to be governed by the British Governmt. as our prototype. He did not mean however to throw censure on that Excellent fabric. If we were in a situation to copy it he did not know that he should be opposed to it; but the fixt genius of the people of America required a different form of Government. He could not see why the great requisites for the Executive department, vigor, despatch & responsibility could not be found in three men, as well as in one man. The Executive ought to be independent. It ought therefore in order to support its independence to consist of more than one.

Mr. Wilson said that unity in the Executive instead of being the fetus of monarchy would be the best safeguard against tyranny. He repeated that he was not governed by the British Model which was inapplicable to the situation of this Country; the extent of which was so great, and the manners so republican, that nothing but a great confederated Republic would do for it.

Mr. Wilson's motion for a single magistrate was postponed by common consent, the Committee seeming unprepared for any decision on it; and the first part of the clause agreed to, viz—"that a National Executive be instituted."

Mr. Madison thought it would be proper, before a choice shd. be made between a unity and a plurality in the Executive, to fix the extent of the Executive authority; that as certain powers were in their nature Executive, and must be given to that departmt. whether administered by one or more persons, a definition of their extent would assist the judgment in determining how far they might be safely entrusted to a single officer. He accordingly moved that so much of the clause before the Committee as related to the powers of the Executive shd. be struck out & that after the words "that a national Executive ought to be instituted" there be inserted the words following viz. "with power to carry into effect the national laws, to appoint to offices in cases not otherwise provided for, and to execute such other powers "not Legislative nor Judiciary in their nature," as may from time to time be delegated by the national Legislature." The words "not legislative nor judiciary in their nature" were added to the proposed amendment in consequence of a suggestion by Genl. Pinkney that improper powers might otherwise be delegated.

Mr. Wilson seconded this motion—

Mr. Pinkney moved to amend the amendment by striking out the last member of it; viz: "and to execute such other powers not Legislative nor Judiciary in their nature as may from time to time be delegated." He said they were unnecessary, the object of them being included in the "power to carry into effect the national laws."

Mr. Randolph seconded the motion.

Mr. Madison did not know that the words were absolutely necessary, or even the preceding words— "to appoint to offices &c. the whole being perhaps included in the first member of the proposition. He did not however see any inconveniency in retaining them, and cases might happen in which they might serve to prevent doubts and misconstructions.

In consequence of the motion of Mr. Pinkney, the question on Mr. Madison's motion was divided; and the words objected to by Mr. Pinkney struck out; by the votes of Connecticut, N. Y. N. J. Pena. Del. N. C. & Geo. agst. Mass. Virga. & S. Carolina the preceding part of the motion being first agreed to; Connecticut divided, all the other States in the affirmative.

The next clause in Resolution 7, relating to the mode of appointing, & the duration of, the Executive being under consideration,

Mr. Wilson said he was almost unwilling to declare the mode which he wished to take place, being apprehensive that it might appear chimerical. He would say however at least that in theory he was for an election by the people. Experience, particularly in N. York & Massts., shewed that an election of the first magistrate by the people at large, was both a convenient & successful mode. The objects of choice in such cases must be persons whose merits have general notoriety.

Mr. Sherman was for the appointment by the Legislature, and for making him absolutely dependent on that body, as it was the will of that which was to be executed. An independence of the Executive on the supreme Legislature, was in his opinion the very essence of tyranny if there was any such thing.

The delegates then spent some time discussing the president's term of office, and whether he should be eligible for re-election. The debate was between those in favor of a short term (three years) with continued eligibility and those in favor of a longer term (seven years) with a limit of one term. The first vote was five to four in favor of the longer term.

The next day, Saturday, June 2, Wilson fired the opening salvo of what was to become a summer-long battle over the method of selecting the president. He suggested a complicated method of mediated popular election by which the voters of each "district" would select electors who would then choose the president. He also reiterated his arguments in favor of election by the people rather than by federal or state legislatures. His suggestion was soundly rejected, with only his own state and Maryland voting for it. By the same overwhelming vote, the Convention then approved election of the president by the national legislature.

At this point, Benjamin Franklin interrupted to make a long speech. He had, "being very sensible of the effect of age on his memory," written out his speech, and Wilson read it aloud for him. The gist of it was that the executive should not be paid, lest the Constitution "sow the seeds of contention, faction & tumult, by making our posts of honor, places of profit." According to Madison, "no debate ensued" on Franklin's motion, which was postponed: "It was treated with great respect, but rather for the author of it, than from any apparent conviction of its expediency or practicability." The delegates then resumed their debate.

Saturday, June 2

Mr. Dickenson moved "that the Executive be made removeable by the National Legislature on the request of a majority of the Legislatures of individual States." It was necessary he said to place the power of removing somewhere. He did not like the plan of impeaching the Great officers of State. He did not know how provision could be made for removal of them in a better mode than that which he had proposed. He had no idea of abolishing the State Governments as some gentlemen seemed inclined to do. The happiness of this Country in his opinion required considerable powers to be left in the hands of the States.

Mr. Bedford seconded the motion.

Mr. Sherman contended that the National Legislature should have power to remove the Executive at pleasure.

Mr. Mason. Some mode of displacing an unfit magistrate is rendered indispensable by the fallibility of those who choose, as well as by the corruptibility of the man chosen. He opposed decidedly the making the Executive the mere creature of the Legislature as a violation of the fundamental principle of good Government.

Mr. Madison & Mr. Wilson observed that it would leave an equality of agency in the small with the great States; that it would enable a minority of the people to prevent ye. removal of an officer who had rendered himself justly criminal in the eyes of a majority; that it would open a door for intrigues agst. him in States where his administration tho' just might be unpopular, and might tempt him to pay court to particular States whose leading partizans he might fear, or wish to engage as his partizans. They both thought it bad policy to introduce such a mixture of the State authorities, where their agency could be otherwise supplied.

Mr. Dickenson considered the business as so important that no man ought to be silent or reserved. He went into a discourse of some length, the sum of which was, that the Legislative, Executive, & Judiciary departments ought to be made as independent as possible; but that such an Executive as some seemed to have in contemplation was not consistent with a republic: that a firm Executive could only exist in a limited monarchy. In the British Govt. itself the weight of the Executive arises from the attachments which the Crown draws to itself, & not merely from the force of its prerogatives. In place of these attachments we must look out for something else. One source of stability is the double branch of the Legislature. The division of the Country into distinct States formed the other principal source of stability. This division ought therefore to be maintained, and considerable powers to be left with the States. This was the ground of his consolation for the future fate of his Country. Without this, and in case of a consolidation of the States into one great Republic, we might read its fate in the history of smaller ones. A limited Monarchy he considered as *one* of the best Governments in the world. It was not *certain* that the same blessings were derivable from any other form. It was certain that equal blessings had never yet been derived from any of the republican form. A limited Monarchy however was out of the question. The spirit of the times—the state of our affairs, forbade the experiment, if it were desireable. Was it possible moreover in the nature of things to introduce it even if these obstacles were less insuperable. A House of Nobles was essential to such a Govt. could these be created by a breath, or by a stroke of the pen? No. They were the growth of ages, and could only arise under a complication of circumstances none of which existed in this Country. But though a form the most perfect *perhaps* in itself be unattainable, we must not despair. If antient republics have been found to flourish for a moment only & then vanish for ever, it only proves that they were badly constituted; and that we ought to seek for every remedy for their diseases. One of these remedies he conceived to be the accidental lucky division of this Country into distinct States; a division which some seemed desirous to abolish altogether. As to the point of representation in the national Legislature as it might affect States of different sizes, he said it must probably end in mutual concession. He hoped that each State would retain an equal voice at least in one branch of the National Legislature, and supposed the sums paid w..hin each State would form a better ratio for the other branch than either the number of inhabitants or the quantum of property.

A motion being made to strike out "on request by a majority of the Legislatures of the individual States" and rejected, Connecticut, S. Carol: & Geo. being ay, the rest no: the question was taken—

On Mr. Dickenson's motion for making Executive removeable by Natl.; Legislature at request of majority of State Legislatures was also rejected—all the

States being in the negative Except Delaware which gave an affirmative vote.

The question for making ye. Executive ineligible after seven years, was next taken, and agreed to:

Massts; ay. Cont; no. N. Y. ay. Pa. divd. Del. ay. Maryd. ay. Va. ay. N. C. ay. S. C. ay. Geo. no.

Mr. Williamson 2ded. by **Mr. Davie** moved to add to the last Clause, the words—"and to be removeable on impeachment & conviction of malpractice or neglect of duty"—which was agreed to.

Mr. Rutlidge & Mr. C. Pinkney moved that the blank for the no. of persons in the Executive be filled with the words "one person." He supposed the reasons to be so obvious & conclusive in favor of one that no member would oppose the motion.

Mr. Randolph opposed it with great earnestness, declaring that he should not do justice to the Country which sent him if he were silently to suffer the establishmt. of a Unity in the Executive department. He felt an opposition to it which he believed he should continue to feel as long as he lived. He urged 1. that the permanent temper of the people was adverse to the very semblance of Monarchy. 2. that a unity was unnecessary a plurality being equally competent to all the objects of the department. 3. that the necessary confidence would never be re-

posed in a single Magistrate. 4. that the appointments would generally be in favor of some inhabitant near the center of the Community, and consequently the remote parts would not be on an equal footing. He was in favor of three members of the Executive to be drawn from different portions of the Country.

Mr. Butler contended strongly for a single magistrate as most likely to answer the purpose of the remote parts. If one man should be appointed he would be responsible to the whole, and would be impartial to its interests. If three or more should be taken from as many districts, there would be a constant struggle for local advantages. In Military matters this would be particularly mischievous. He said his opinion on this point had been formed under the opportunity he had had of seeing the manner in which a plurality of military heads distracted Holland when threatened with invasion by the imperial troops. One man was for directing the force to the defence of this part, another to that part of the Country, just as he happened to be swayed by prejudice or interest.

The motion was then postpd. the Committee rose & the House Adjd.

Debate over the number of the executive continued the next day, and the delegates eventually voted six to three in favor of a single executive. George Mason was absent during the vote, and when he returned later in the day he gave an impassioned speech against unity in the executive. The speech, his own draft of which is reprinted below, summarizes the arguments on both sides of the debate.

George Mason Draft Speech[3]

The chief Advantages which have been urged in favour of Unity in the Executive, are the Secrecy, the Dispatch, the Vigour and Energy, which the Government will derive from it; especially in time of war.—That these are great Advantages, I shall most readily allow—They have been strongly insisted on by all monarchical Writers—they have been acknowledged by the ablest and most candid Defenders of Republican Government; and it can not be denyed that a Monarchy possesses them in a much greater Degree than a Republic.—Yet perhaps a little Reflection may incline us to doubt whether these

Advantages are not greater in Theory than in Practice—or lead us to enquire whether there is not some pervading Principle in Republican Governments which sets at Naught, and tramples upon this boasted Superiority—as hath been experienced, to their cost, by most Monarchys, which have been imprudent enough to invade or attack their republican Neighbors. This invincible Principle is to be found in the Love the Affection the Attachment of the Citizens to their Laws, to their Freedom, and to their Country—Every Husbandman will be quickly converted into a Soldier, when he knows and feels that he is to fight not in Defence of the Rights of a particular Family, or a Prince; but for his own. This is the true Construction of the pro Aris & focis which has, in all Ages, performed such Wonders— It was this which, in ancient times, enabled the little Cluster of Grecian Republics to resist, and almost constantly to defeat the Persian Monarch—It was this which supported the States of Holland against a Body of veteran Troops thro' a thirty Years War with Spain, then the greatest Monarchy in Europe, and finally rendered them victorious.—It is this which preserves the Freedom and Independence of the Swiss Cantons in the midst of the most powerful Nations—And who that reflects seriously upon the Situation of America, in the Beginning of the late War—without Arms—without Soldiers—without Trade, Money or Credit—in a Manner destitute of all Resources, but must ascribe our Success to this pervading, all-powerful Principle?

Disputes over the executive branch did not play a major role in the contest between the Virginia plan and the New Jersey plan. After rejecting the New Jersey plan, the delegates turned their attention to more controversial matters. They focused almost exclusively on the legislature for the next month; as we will see in the next chapter, it was all they could do to keep the Convention from dissolving as a result of disputes over the legislative branch.

When the delegates finally turned back to the executive branch on July 17, they had before them Randolph's resolutions as amended by the Committee of the Whole.

> 9. Resolved that a national Executive be instituted to consist of a single person. to be chosen by the National Legislature. for the term of seven years. with power to carry into execution the national Laws, to appoint to Offices in cases not otherwise provided for[,] to be ineligible a second time, and to be removable on impeachment and conviction of mal practice or neglect of duty. to receive a fixed stipend, by which he may be compensated for the devotion of his time to public service to be paid out of the national Treasury.

The delegates had, however, altered their views on the appropriate character of the executive branch. As the next chapter will show, some of the debates over the legislature included concerns about too much democracy. By July 17, even those delegates initially opposed to a strong executive began to realize that a strong executive might afford a check on the more democratic legislature.

After an initial skirmish, the delegates agreed on a basic principle: the executive should be independent enough to provide a check on the legislature, but not so strong that he would become a tyrant. At this point they entered a vicious cycle that would continue until September 4. It centered on the mode of election, but implicated virtually all aspects of the character of the executive branch. The problem was that if the executive was appointed by the legislature, he could only be independent if he was ineligible a second time and thus did not need to keep the favor of the legislature. If he was ineligible for a second term, however, he would tend toward tyranny by making the most of his short time in office. Election by the people provided a solution to some of these problems, but created others. As you read the excerpts below, try to trace the delegates' evolving solutions as they went through the step-by-step process of solving each problem only to confront one they thought they had previously resolved. As you go through what might seem to *you* like endless repetitions, imagine *their* mounting frustration.

Tuesday, July 17

"To be chosen by the National Legisl:"

Mr. Governr. Morris was pointedly agst. his being so chosen. He will be the mere creature of the Legisl: if appointed & impeachable by that body. He ought to be elected by the people at large, by the freeholders of the Country. That difficulties attend this mode, he admits. But they have been found superable in N. Y. & in Cont. and would he believed be found so, in the case of an Executive for the U. States. If the people should elect, they will never fail to prefer some man of distinguished character, or services; some man, if he might so speak, of continental reputation. —If the Legislature elect, it will be the work of intrigue, of cabal, and of faction; it will be like the election of a pope by a conclave of cardinals; real merit will rarely be the title to the appointment. He moved to strike out "National Legislature" & insert "citizens of U.S."

Mr. Sherman thought that the sense of the Nation would be better expressed by the Legislature, than by the people at large. The latter will never be sufficiently informed of characters, and besides will never give a majority of votes to any one man. They will generally vote for some man in their own States, and the largest State will have the best chance for the appointment. If the choice be made by the Legislre. A majority of voices may be made necessary to constitute an election.

Mr. Wilson. two arguments have been urged agst. an election of the Executive Magistrate by the people. 1 the example of Poland where an Election of the supreme Magistrate is attended with the most dangerous commotions. The cases he observed were totally dissimilar. The Polish nobles have resources & dependents which enable them to appear in force, and to threaten the Republic as well as each other. In the next place the electors all assemble in one place: which would not be the case with us. The 2d. argt. is that a *majority* of the people would never concur. It might be answered that the concurrence of a majority of people is not a necessary principle of election, nor required as such in any of the States. But allowing the objection all its force, it may be obviated by the expedient used in Masts. where the Legislature by majority of voices, decide in case a majority of people do not concur in favor of one of the candidates. This would restrain the choice to a good nomination at least, and prevent in a great degree intrigue & cabal. A particular objection with him agst. an absolute election by the Legislre. was

that the Exec: in that case would be too dependent to stand the mediator between the intrigues & sinister views of the Representatives and the general liberties & interests of the people.

Mr. Pinkney did not expect this question would again have been brought forward; An Election by the people being liable to the most obvious & striking objections. They will be led by a few active & designing men. The most populous States by combining in favor of the same individual will be able to carry their points. The Natl. Legislature being most immediately interested in the laws made by themselves, will be most attentive to the choice of a fit man to carry them properly into execution.

.   .   .

Col. Mason. It is curious to remark the different language held at different times. At one moment we are told that the Legislature is entitled to thorough confidence, and to indifinite power. At another, that it will be governed by intrigue & corruption, and cannot be trusted at all. But not to dwell on this inconsistency he would observe that a Government which is to last ought at least to be practicable. Would this be the case if the proposed election should be left to the people at large. He conceived it would be as unnatural to refer the choice of a proper character for chief Magistrate to the people, as it would, to refer a trial of colours to a blind man. The extent of the country renders it impossible that the people can have the requisite capacity to judge of the respective pretensions of the Candidates.

.   .   .

Docr. McClurg moved* to strike out 7 years, and insert "during good behavior." By striking out the words declaring him not re-eligible, he was put into a situation that would keep him dependent for ever on the Legislature; and he conceived the independence of the Executive to be equally essential with that of the Judiciary department.

Mr. Govr. Morris 2ded. the motion. He expressed great pleasure in hearing it. This was the way to get a good Government. His fear that so valuable an ingredient would not be attained had led him to take the part he had done. He was indif-

---

*The probable object of this motion was merely to enforce the argument against the re-eligibility of the Executive Magistrate, by holding out a tenure during good behaviour as the alternative for keeping him independent of the Legislature. [Footnote by Madison.]

ferent how the Executive should be chosen, provided he held his place by this tenure.

Mr. Broome highly approved the motion. It obviated all his difficulties

Mr. Sherman considered such a tenure as by no means safe or admissible. As the Executive Magistrate is now re-eligible, he will be on good behavior as far as will be necessary. If he behaves well he will be continued; if otherwise, displaced, on a succeeding election.

Mr. Madison† If it be essential to the preservation of liberty that the Legisl: Execut: & Judiciary powers be separate, it is essential to a maintenance of the separation, that they should be independent of each other. The Executive could not be independent of the Legislure, if dependent on the pleasure of that branch for a reappointment. Why was it determined that the Judges should not hold their places by such a tenure? Because they might be tempted to cultivate the Legislature, by an undue complaisance, and thus render the Legislature the virtual expositor, as well the maker of the laws. In like manner a dependence of the Executive on the Legislature, would render it the Executor as well as the maker of laws: & then according to the observation of Montesquieu, tyrannical laws may be made that they may be executed in a tyrannical manner. There was an analogy between the Executive & Judiciary departments in several respects. The latter executed the laws in certain cases as the former did in others. The former expounded & applied them for certain purposes, as the latter did for others. The difference between them seemed to consist chiefly in two circumstances—1. the collective interest & security were much more in the power belonging to the Executive than to the Judiciary department. 2 in the administration of the former much greater latitude is left to opinion and discretion than in the administration of the latter. But if the 2d. consideration proves that it will be more difficult to establish a rule sufficiently precise for trying the Execut: than the Judges, & forms an objection to the same tenure of office, both considerations prove that it might be more dangerous to suffer a union between the Executive & Legisl: powers, than between the Judiciary & Legislative powers. He conceived it to be absolutely necessary to a well constituted Republic that the two first shd. be kept distinct & independent of each other. Whether the plan proposed by the motion was a proper one was another question,

as it depended on the practicability of instituting a tribunal for impeachmts. as certain & as adequate in the one case as in the other. On the other hand, respect for the mover entitled his propostion to a fair hearing & discussion, until a less objectionable expedient should be applied for guarding agst. a dangerous union of the Legislative & Executive departments.

Col. Mason. This motion was made some time ago, & negatived by a very large majority. He trusted that it wd. be again negatived. It wd. be impossible to define the misbehaviour in such a manner as to subject it to a proper trial; and perhaps still more impossible to compel so high an offender holding his office by such a tenure to submit to a trial. He considered an Executive during good behavior as a softer name only for an Executive for life. And that the next would be an easy step to hereditary Monarchy. If the motion should finally succeed, he might himself live to see such a Revolution. If he did not it was probable his children or grand children would. He trusted there were few men in that House who wished for it. No state he was sure had so far revolted from Republican principles as to have the least bias in its favor.

Mr. Madison, was not apprehensive of being thought to favor any step towards monarchy. The real object with him was to prevent its introduction. Experience had proved a tendency in our governments to throw all power into the Legislative vortex. The Executives of the States are in general little more than Cyphers; the legislatures omnipotent. If no effectual check be devised for restraining the instability & encroachments of the latter, a revolution of some kind or other would be inevitable. The preservation of Republican Govt. therefore required some expedient for the purpose, but required evidently at the same time that in devising it, the genuine principles of that form should be kept in view.

Mr. Govr. Morris was as little a friend to monarchy as any gentleman. He concurred in the opinion that the way to keep out monarchical Govt. was to establish such a Repub. Govt. as wd. make the people happy and prevent a desire of change.

Docr. McClurg was not so much afraid of the shadow of monarchy as to be unwilling to approach it; nor so wedded to Republican Govt. as not to be sensible of the tyrannies that had been & may be exercised under that form. It was an essential object with him to make the Executive independent of the Legislature; and the only mode left for effecting it, after the vote destroying his ineligiblity a second time, was to appoint him during good behavior.

On the question for inserting "during good be-

†The view here taken of the subject was meant to aid in parrying the animadversions likely to fall on the motion of Dr. McClurg, for whom J. M. had a particular regard. The Doctr. though possessing talents of the highest order, was modest & unaccustomed to exert them in public debate. [Footnote by Madison.]

havior" in place of 7 years [with a re-eligiblity] it passed in the negative.

Mas. no. Ct. no. N. J. ay. Pa. ay. Del. ay. Md. no. Va. ay. N. C. no. S. C. no. Geo. no.*

---

*This vote is not be considered as any certain index of opinion, as a number in the affirmative probably had it chiefly in view to alarm those attached to a dependence of the Executive on the Legislature, & thereby facilitate some final arrangement of a contrary tendency. The avowed friends of an Executive, "during good behaviour" were not more than three or four, nor is it certain they would finally have adhered to such a tenure. An independence of the three great departments of each other, as far as possible, and the responsibility of all to the will of the community seemed to be generally admitted as the true basis of a well constructed government. [Footnote by Madison.]

On the motion "to strike out seven years" it passed in the negative.

Mas. ay. Ct. no. N. J. no. Pa. ay. Del. ay. Md. no. Va. no. N. C. ay. S. C. no. Geo. no.*

It was now unanimously agreed that the vote which had struck out the words "to be ineligible a second time" should be reconsidered to-morrow. [On July 18, they agreed to postpone reconsideration until July 19.]

Adjd.

---

*There was no debate on this motion, the apparent object of many in the affirmative was to secure the re-eligibility by shortening the term, and of many in the negative to embarrass the plan of referring the appointment & dependence of the Executive to the Legislature. [Footnote by Madison.]

Thursday, July 19

On reconsideration of the vote rendering the Executive re-eligible a 2d. time, **Mr. Martin** moved to reinstate the words, "to be ineligible a 2d. time."

Mr. Governeur Morris. It is necessary to take into one view all that relates to the establishment of the Executive; on the due formation of which must depend the efficacy & utility of the Union among the present and future States. It has been a maxim in Political Science that Republican Government is not adapted to a large extent of Country, because the energy of the Executive Magistracy can not reach the extreme parts of it. Our Country is an extensive one. We must either then renounce the blessings of the Union, or provide an Executive with sufficient vigor to pervade every part of it. This subject was of so much importance that he hoped to be indulged in an extensive view of it. One great object of the Executive is to controul the Legislature. The Legislature will continually seek to aggrandize & perpetuate themselves; and will sieze those critical moments produced by war, invasion or convulsion for that purpose. It is necessary then that the Executive Magistrate should be the guardian of the people, even of the lower classes, agst. Legislative tyranny, against the Great & the wealthy who in the course of things will necessarily compose the Legislative body. Wealth tends to corrupt the mind & to nourish its love of power, and to stimulate it to oppression. History proves this to be the spirit of the opulent. The check provided in the 2d. branch was not meant as a check on Legislative usurpations of power, but on the abuse of lawful powers, on the propensity in the 1st. branch to legislate too much

to run into projects of paper money & similar expedients. It is no check on Legislative tyranny. On the contrary it may favor it, and if the 1st. branch can be seduced may find the means of success. The Executive therefore ought to be so constituted as to be the great protector of the Mass of the people.—It is the duty of the Executive to appoint the officers & to command the forces of the Republic: to appoint 1. ministerial officers for the administration of public affairs. 2. officers for the dispensation of Justice. Who will be the best Judges whether these appointments be well made? The people at large, who will know, will see, will feel the effects of them. Again who can judge so well of the discharge of military duties for the protection & security of the people, as the people themselves who are to be protected & secured?—He finds too that the Executive is not to be re-eligible. What effect will this have? 1. it will destroy the great incitement to merit public esteem by taking away the hope of being rewarded with a reappointment. It may give a dangerous turn to one of the strongest passions in the human breast. The love of fame is the great spring to noble & illustrious actions. Shut the Civil road to Glory & he may be compelled to seek it by the sword. 2. It will tempt him to make the most of the short space of time allotted him, to accumulate wealth and provide for his friends. 3. It will produce violations of the very constitution it is meant to secure. In moments of pressing danger the tried abilities and established character of a favorite Magistrate will prevail over respect for the forms of the Constitution. The Executive is also to be impeachable. This is a dangerous part of the plan. It will hold him in such dependence that he will be no check on the Legislature, will not be a firm guardian of the people and of the public interest. He will be the tool of a faction, of some leading demagogue in the Legislature. These then are the faults of the Executive establishment as now proposed. Can no better establishmt. be devised? If he is to be the Guardian of the people let him be appointed by the people? If he is to be a check on the Legislature let him not be impeachable. Let him be of short duration, that he may with propriety be re-eligible.

. . .

Mr. Randolph urged the motion of Mr. L. Martin for restoring the words making the Executive ineligible a 2d. time. If he ought to be independent, he should not be left under a temptation to court a re-appointment. If he should be re-appointable by the Legislature, he will be no check on it. His revisionary power will be of no avail. He had always thought & contended as he still did that the danger apprehended by the little States was chimerical; but those who thought otherwise ought to be peculiarly anxious for the motion. If the Executive be appointed, as has been determined, by the Legislature, he will probably be appointed either by joint ballot of both houses, or be nominated by the 1st. and appointed by the 2d. branch. In either case the large States will preponderate. If he is to court the same influence for his re-appointment, will he not make his revisionary power, and all the other functions of his administration subservient to the views of the large States. Besides, is there not great reason

to apprehend that in case he should be re-eligible, a false complaisance in the Legislature might lead them to continue an unfit man in office in preference to a fit one. . . .

. . .

Mr. Wilson. It seems to be unanimous sense that the Executive should not be appointed by the Legislature, unless he be rendered in-eligible a 2d. time: he perceived with pleasure that the idea was gaining ground, of an election mediately or immediately by the people.

Mr. Madison. If it be a fundamental principle of free Govt. that the Legislative, Executive & Judiciary powers should be *separately* exercised, it is equally so that they be *independently* exercised. There is the same & perhaps greater reason why the Executive shd. be independent of the Legislature, than why the Judiciary should: A coalition of the two former powers would be more immediately & certainly dangerous to public liberty. It is essential then that the appointment of the Executive should either be drawn from some source, or held by some tenure, that will give him a free agency with regard to the Legislature. This could not be if he was to be appointable from time to time by the Legislature.

. . .

Mr. Gerry. If the Executive is to be elected by the Legislature he certainly ought not to be re-eligible. This would make him absolutely dependent. He was agst. a popular election. The people are uninformed, and would be misled by a few designing men.

At this point, the delegates voted that the executive should be appointed by electors, who would themselves be selected by the state legislatures. The ratio of electors was postponed, and the question of term and re-eligibility was debated again. At the end of the day, the delegates had determined that the president would serve for six years, and would be eligible for re-election. The next day they established a ratio of electors whereby the smallest states would have one each, the middle states two each, and the largest states three each. The Convention then turned to the question of how to remove the president from office.

Friday, July 20

"to be removeable on impeachment and conviction for mal practice or neglect of duty." see Resol: 9

Mr. Pinkney & **Mr. Govr. Morris** moved to strike out this part of the Resolution. Mr. P. observd. he ought not to be impeachable whilst in office

Mr. Davie. If he be not impeachable whilst in office, he will spare no efforts or means whatever to get himself re-elected. He considered this as an essential security for the good behaviour of the Executive.

Mr. Wilson concurred in the necessity of making the Executive impeachable whilst in office.

Mr. Govr. Morris. He can do no criminal act without Coadjutors who may be punished. In case he should be re-elected, that will be sufficient proof of his innocence. Besides who is to impeach? Is the impeachment to suspend his functions. If it is not the mischief will go on. If it is the impeachment will be nearly equivalent to a displacement, and will render the Executive dependent on those who are to impeach

Col. Mason. No point is of more importance than that the right of impeachment should be continued. Shall any man be above Justice? Above all shall that man be above it, who can commit the most extensive injustice? When great crimes were committed he was for punishing the principal as well as the Coadjutors. There had been much debate & difficulty as to the mode of chusing the Executive. He approved of that which had been adopted at first, namely of referring the appointment to the Natl. Legislature. One objection agst. Electors was the danger of their being corrupted by the Candidates; & this furnished a peculiar reason in favor of impeachments whilst in office. Shall the man who has practised corruption & by that means procured his appointment in the first instance, be suffered to escape punishment, by repeating his guilt?

Docr. Franklin was for retaining the clause as favorable to the Executive. History furnishes one example only of a first Magistrate being formally brought to public Justice. Every body cried out agst. this as unconstitutional. What was the practice before this in cases where the chief Magistrate rendered himself obnoxious? Why recourse was had to assassination in wch. he was not only deprived of his life but of the opportunity of vindicating his character. It wd. be the best way therefore to provide in the Constitution for the regular punishment of the Executive where his misconduct should deserve it, and for his honorable acquittal when he should be unjustly accused.

Mr. Govr. Morris admits corruption & some few other offences to be such as ought to be impeachable; but thought the cases ought to be enumerated & defined:

Mr. Madison thought it indispensable that some provision should be made for defending the Community agst. the incapacity, negligence or perfidy of the chief Magistrate. The limitation of the period of his service, was not a sufficient security. He might lose his capacity after his appointment. He might pervert his administration into a scheme of peculation or oppression. He might betray his trust to foreign powers. The case of the Executive Magistracy was very distinguishable, from that of the Legislature or of any other public body, holding offices of limited duration. It could not be presumed that all or even a majority of the members of an Assembly would either lose their capacity for discharging, or be bribed to betray, their trust. Besides the restraints of their personal integrity & honor, the difficulty of acting in concert for purposes of corruption was a security to the public. And if one or a few members only should be seduced, the soundness of the remaining members, would maintain the integrity and fidelity of the body. In the case of the Executive Magistracy which was to be administered by a single man, loss of capacity or corruption was more within the compass of probable events, and either of them might be fatal to the Republic.

Mr. Pinkney did not see the necessity of impeachments. He was sure they ought not to issue from the Legislature who would in that case hold them as a rod over the Executive and by that means effectually destroy his independence. His revisionary power in particular would be rendered altogether insignificant.

Mr. Gerry urged the necessity of impeachments. A good magistrate will not fear them. A bad one ought to be kept in fear of them. He hoped the maxim would never be adopted here that the chief magistrate could do no wrong.

Mr. King expressed his apprehensions that an extreme caution in favor of liberty might enervate the Government we were forming. He wished the House to recur to the primitive axiom that the three great departments of Govts. should be separate & independent: that the Executive & Judiciary should be so as well as the Legislative: that the Executive should be so equally with the Judiciary. Would this be the case, if the Executive should be impeachable? It had been said that the Judiciary would be impeachable. But it should have been remembered at the same time that the Judiciary hold their places not for a limited time, but during good behaviour. It is necessary therefore that a forum should be established for trying misbehaviour. Was the Executive to hold his place during good behaviour? The Executive was to hold his place for a limited term like the members of the Legislature: Like them particularly the Senate whose members would continue in appointmt. the same term of 6 years he would periodically be tried for his behaviour by his electors, who would continue or discontinue him in trust according to the manner in which he had discharged it. Like them therefore, he ought to be subject to no intermediate trial, by impeachment. He ought not to be impeachable unless he held his office during good behaviour, a tenure which would be most agreeable to him; provided an independent and effectual forum could be devised. But under no circumstances ought he to be impeachable by the Legislature. This would be destructive of his independence and of the principles of the Constitution. He relied on the vigor of the Executive as a great security for the public liberties.

Mr. Randolph. The propriety of impeachments was a favorite principle with him. Guilt wherever found ought to be punished. The Executive will have great opportunitys of abusing his power; particularly in time of war when the military force, and in some respects the public money will be in his hands. Should no regular punishment be provided, it will be irregularly inflicted by tumults & insurrections. He is aware of the necessity of proceeding with a cautious hand, and of excluding as much as possible the influence of the Legislature from the business. He suggested for consideration an idea which had fallen [from Col Hamilton] of composing a forum out of the Judges belonging to the States: and even of requiring some preliminary inquest whether just grounds of impeachment existed.

Doctr. Franklin mentioned the case of the Prince of Orange during the late war. An agreement was made between France & Holland; by which their two fleets were to unite at a certain time & place. The Dutch fleet did not appear. Every body began to wonder at it. At length it was suspected that the Statholder was at the bottom of the matter. This suspicion prevailed more & more. Yet as he could not be impeached and no regular examination took place, he remained in his office, and strengthening his own party, as the party opposed to him became

formidable, he gave birth to the most violent animosities & contentions. Had he been impeachable, a regular & peaceable enquiry would have taken place and he would if guilty have been duly punished, if innocent restored to the confidence of the public.

Mr. King remarked that the case of the Statholder was not applicable. He held his place for life, and was not periodically elected. In the former case impeachments are proper to secure good behaviour. In the latter they are unnecessary; the periodical responsibility to the electors being an equivalent security.

Mr. Wilson observed that if the idea were to be pursued, the Senators who are to hold their places during the same term with the Executive, ought to be subject to impeachment & removal.

Mr. Pinkney apprehended that some gentlemen reasoned on a supposition that the Executive was to have powers which would not be committed to him: He presumed that his powers would be so circumscribed as to render impeachments unnecessary.

Mr. Govr. Morris's opinion had been changed by the arguments used in the discussion. He was now sensible of the necessity of impeachments, if the Executive was to continue for any time in office. Our Executive was not like a Magistrate having a life interest, much less like one having an hereditary interest in his office. He may be bribed by a greater interest to betray his trust; and no one would say that we ought to expose ourselves to the danger of seeing the first Magistrate in forign pay, without being able to guard agst. it by displacing him. One would think the King of England well secured agst. bribery. He has as it were a fee simple in the whole Kingdom. Yet Charles II was bribed by Louis XIV. The Executive ought therefore to be impeachable for treachery; Corrupting his electors, and incapacity were other causes of impeachment. For the latter he should be punished not as a man, but as an officer, and punished only by degradation from his office. This Magistrate is not the King but the prime-Minister. The people are the King. When we make him amenable to Justice however we should take care to provide some mode that will not make him dependent on the Legislature.

It was moved & 2ded. to postpone the question of impeachments which was negatived. Mas. & S. Carolina only being ay.

On ye. Question, Shall the Executive be removeable on impeachments &c.?

Mas. no. Ct. ay. N. J. ay. Pa. ay. Del ay. Md. ay. Va. ay. N. C. ay. S. C. no. Geo. ay.

The delegates then spent a day discussing the veto power, focusing primarily on Wilson's renewed motion for a Council of Revision. One more day was devoted to the last of Randolph's original resolutions, the method of ratification of the new constitution. At the end of the day, just before the delegates voted to send the amended resolutions to the Committee on Detail, Houston and Spaight reopened the whole issue of the executive by moving to reconsider the method of appointment.

They began their reconsideration the next morning. Virtually all the delegates repeated their earlier arguments, and the Convention voted seven states to four (New Hampshire's delegates having arrived the day before) to reinstate appointment by the national legislature.

At that point, Martin and Gerry moved to reinstate the ineligibility provision, and the whole debate began again. The discussions over the next few days were nearly identical to those of the preceding few days. As Gouverneur Morris observed in desperation on July 24, after almost a week of discussing very little except the executive:

> It is most difficult of all rightly to balance the Executive. Make him too weak: The Legislature will usurp his powers. Make him too strong: He will usurp on the Legislature.

After another fruitless day, Morris again pinpointed the problem:

> The evils to be guarded against in this case are 1. the undue influence of the Legislature. 2. instability of Councils. 3. misconduct in office. To guard against the first, we run into the second evil. We adopt a rotation which produces instability of Councils. To avoid Scylla we fall into Charibdis.

After going around in circles several more times, they gave up and temporarily agreed to appointment by the legislature, ineligibility for a second term, and impeachment for "mal-practice or neglect of duty." The Committee on Detail, which made its report on August 6, changed little.[4] That committee rewrote the grounds for impeachment, changing "mal-practice or neglect of duty" to "treason, bribery or corruption"; added the president of the Senate as backup chief executive should the president die, resign, become unable to discharge his duties, or be impeached; and assigned to the president almost all of the specific powers ultimately listed in Article II, except the powers (shared with the Senate) to appoint judges and ambassadors, and to enter into treaties.

When the convention addressed the committee's work on the executive, in late August, the battle began again. The committee had filled in many of the powers of the executive branch, adding another item to the delegates' disputes: without knowing how he was to be elected, many delegates could not decide whether certain powers were appropriately assigned to the president. On August 23, for example, the delegates argued over whether the Senate or the president should have the power to conclude treaties. The committee's draft gave the power to the Senate alone, but Madison and others suggested that the president ought to be given the power. Both then and later, some delegates objected to presidential treaty power because they were unhappy about how the president was selected. Issues of presidential power will be discussed in the next section. The Convention was also still deadlocked on the familiar questions of how the president ought to be elected, whether he ought to be eligible for a second term, and whether and how he ought to be impeachable.

After another fruitless week of the same arguments, the Convention decided, on August 31, to refer the executive branch to a committee, along with miscellaneous minor disputes. The committee, elected by ballot, consisted of one member from each state: Nicholas Gilman (New Hampshire), Rufus King (Massachusetts), Roger Sherman (Connecticut), David Brearley (New Jersey), Gouverneur Morris (Pennsylvania), John Dickinson (Delaware), Daniel Carroll (Maryland), James Madison (Virginia), Hugh Williamson (North Carolina), Pierce Butler (South Carolina), and Abraham Baldwin (Georgia).

Little is known about the workings of this committee, but its solution to the problem of electing the executive was presented on September 4. With some amendments, that solution ultimately satisfied the concerns of all the delegates.

Tuesday, September 4

Mr. Brearly from the Committee of eleven made a further partial Report as follows

. . .

(4) . . .

'He shall hold his office during the term of four years, and together with the vice-President, chosen for the same term, be elected in the following manner, viz. Each State shall appoint in such manner as its Legislature may direct, a number of electors equal to the whole number of Senators and members of the House of Representatives to which the State may be entitled in the Legislature. The Electors shall meet in their respective States, and vote by ballot for two persons, of whom one at least shall not be an inhabitant of the same State with themselves; and they shall make a list of all the persons voted for, and of the number of votes for each, which list they shall sign and certify and transmit sealed to the Seat of the Genl. Government, directed to the President of the Senate—The President of the Senate shall in that House open all the certificates; and the votes shall be then & there counted. The Person having the greatest number of votes shall be the President, if such number be a majority of that of the electors; and if there be more than one who have such majority, and have an equal number of votes, then the Senate shall immediately choose by ballot one of them for President: but if no person have a majority, then from the five highest on the list, the Senate shall choose by ballot the President. And in every case after the choice of the President,

the person having the greatest number of votes shall be vice-president: but if there should remain two or more who have equal votes, the Senate shall choose from them the vice-President. The Legislature may determine the time of choosing and assembling the Electors, and the manner of certifying and transmitting their votes.'

. . .

Mr. Gorham disapproved of making the next highest after the President, the vice-President, without referring the decision to the Senate in case the next highest should have less than a majority of votes. as the regulation stands a very obscure man with very few votes may arrive at that appointment

Mr. Sherman said the object of this clause of the report of the Committee was to get rid of the ineligibility, which was attached to the mode of election by the Legislature, & to render the Executive independent of the Legislature. As the choice of the President was to be made out of the five highest, obscure characters were sufficiently guarded against in that case; and he had no objection to requiring the vice-President to be chosen in like manner, where the choice was not decided by a majority in the first instance

Mr. Madison was apprehensive that by requiring both the President & vice President to be chosen out of the five highest candidates, the attention of the electors would be turned too much to making candidates instead of giving their votes in order to a definitive choice. Should this turn be given to the business, the election would, in fact be consigned to the Senate altogether. It would have the effect at the same time, he observed, of giving the nomination of the candidates to the largest States.

Mr. Govr. Morris concurred in, & enforced the remarks of Mr. Madison.

Mr. Randolph & **Mr. Pinkney** wished for a particular explanation & discussion of the reasons for changing the mode of electing the Executive.

Mr. Govr. Morris said he would give the reasons of the Committee and his own. The 1st. was the danger of intrigue & faction if the appointmt. should be made by the Legislature. 2. the inconveniency of an ineligibility required by that mode in order to lessen its evils. 3. The difficulty of establishing a Court of Impeachments, other than the Senate which would not be so proper for the trial nor the other branch for the impeachment of the President, if appointed by the Legislature, 4. No body had appeared to be satisfied with an appointment by the Legislature. 5. Many were anxious even for an immediate choice by the people. 6. the indispensible necessity of making the Executive independent of the Legislature. — As the Electors would vote at the same time throughout the U. S. and at so great a distance from each other, the great evil of cabal was avoided. It would be impossible also to corrupt them. A conclusive reason for making the Senate instead of the Supreme Court the Judge of impeachments, was that the latter was to try the President after the trial of the impeachment.

Col: Mason confessed that the plan of the Committee had removed some capital objections, particularly the danger of cabal and corruption. It was liable however to this strong objection, that nineteen times in twenty the President would be chosen by the Senate, an improper body for the purpose

Mr. Butler thought the mode not free from objections, but much more so than an election by the Legislature, where as in elective monarchies, cabal faction & violence would be sure to prevail.

Mr. Pinkney stated as objections to the mode 1. that it threw the whole appointment in fact into the hands of the Senate. 2. The Electors will be strangers to the several candidates and of course unable to decide on their comparative merits. 3. It makes the Executive reeligible which will endanger the public liberty. 4. It makes the same body of men which will in fact elect the President his Judges in case of an impeachment.

Mr. Williamson had great doubts whether the advantage of reeligibility would balance the objection to such a dependence of the President on the Senate for his reappointment. He thought at least

the Senate ought to be restrained to the *two* highest on the list

Mr. Govr. Morris said the principal advantage aimed at was that of taking away the opportunity for cabal. The President may be made if thought necessary ineligible on this as well as on any other mode of election. Other inconveniences may be no less redressed on this plan than any other.

Mr. Baldwin thought the plan not so objectionable when well considered, as at first view. The increasing intercourse among the people of the States, would render important characters less & less unknown; and the Senate would consequently be less & less likely to have the eventual appointment thrown into their hands.

Mr. Wilson. This subject has greatly divided the House, and will also divide people out of doors. It is in truth the most difficult of all on which we have had to decide. He had never made up an opinion on it entirely to his own satisfaction. He thought the plan on the whole a valuable improvement on the former. It gets rid of one great evil, that of cabal & corruption; & Continental Characters will multiply as we more & more coalesce, so as to enable the electors in every part of the Union to know & judge of them. It clears the way also for a discussion of the question of reeligiblity on its own merits, which the former mode of election seems to forbid. He thought it might be better however to refer the eventual appointment to the Legislature than to the Senate, and to confine it to a smaller number than five of the Candidates. The eventual election by the Legislature wd. not open cabal anew, as it would be restrained to certain designated objects of choice, and as these must have had the previous sanction of a number of the States: and if the election be made as it ought as soon as the votes of the electors are opened & it is known that no one has a majority of the whole, there can be little danger of corruption. Another reason for preferring the Legislature to the Senate in this business, was that the House of Reps. will be so often changed as to be free from the influence & faction to which the permanence of the Senate may subject that branch.

Mr. Randolph preferred the former mode of constituting the Executive, but if the change was to be made, he wished to know why the eventual election was referred to the *Senate* and not to the *Legislature?* He saw no necessity for this and many objections to it. He was apprehensive also that the advantage of the eventual appointment would fall into the hands of the States near the Seat of Government.

Mr. Govr. Morris said the *Senate* was preferred because fewer could then, say to the President, you owe your appointment to us. He thought the President would not depend so much on the Senate for his re-appointment as on his general good conduct.

The further consideration of the Report was post- poned that each member might take a copy of the remainder of it.

viz. Electral Collge

Wednesday, September 5

The Report made yesterday as to the appointment of the Executive being taken up. **Mr. Pinkney** renewed his opposition to the mode, arguing 1. that the electors will not have sufficient knowledge of the fittest men, & will be swayed by an attachment to the eminent men of their respective States. Hence 2dly. the dispersion of the votes would leave the appointment with the Senate, and as the President's reappointment will thus depend on the Senate he will be the mere creature of that body. 3. He will combine with the Senate agst. the House of Representatives. 4. This change in the mode of election was meant to get rid of the ineligibility of the President a second time, whereby he will become fixed for life under the auspices of the Senate

Mr. Gerry did not object to this plan of constituting the Executive in itself, but should be governed in his final vote by the powers that may be given to the President.

Mr. Rutlidge was much opposed to the plan reported by the Committee. It would throw the whole power into the Senate. He was also against a re-eligibility. He moved to postpone the Report under consideration & take up the original plan of appointment by the Legislature, to wit. "He shall be elected by joint ballot by the Legislature to which election a majority of the votes of the members present shall be required: He shall hold his office during the term of seven years; but shall not be elected a second time."

On this motion to postpone

N. H. divd. Mas. no. Ct. no. N. J. no. Pa. no. Del. no. Md. no. Va. no. N. C. ay. S. C. ay. Geo. no.

Col. Mason admitted that there were objections to an appointment by the Legislature as originally planned. He had not yet made up his mind, but would state his objections to the mode proposed by the Committee. 1. It puts the appointment in fact into the hands of the Senate, as it will rarely happen that a majority of the whole votes will fall on any one candidate: and as the Existing President will always be one of the 5 highest, his re-appointment will of course depend on the Senate. 2. Considering the powers of the President & those of the Senate, if a coalition should be established between these two branches, they will be able to subvert the Constitution—The great objection with him would be removed by depriving the Senate of the eventual election. He accordingly moved to strike out the words "if such number be a majority of that of the electors."

Mr. Williamson 2ded. the motion. He could not agree to the clause without some such modification. He preferred making the highest tho' not having a majority of the votes, President, to a reference of the matter to the Senate. Referring the appointment to the Senate lays a certain foundation for corruption & aristocracy.

Mr. Govr. Morris thought the point of less consequence than it was supposed on both sides. It is probable that a majority of votes will fall on the same man. As each elector is to give two votes, more than ¼ will give a majority. Besides as one vote is to be given to a man out of the State, and as this vote will not be thrown away, ½ the votes will fall on characters eminent & generally known. Again if the President shall have given satisfaction, the votes will turn on him of course, and a majority of them will reappoint him, without resort to the Senate: If he should be disliked, all disliking him, would take care to unite their votes so as to ensure his being supplanted.

Col. Mason those who think there is no danger of there not being a majority for the same person in the first instance, ought to give up the point to those who think otherwise.

Mr. Sherman reminded the opponents of the new mode proposed that if the small states had the advantage in the Senate's deciding among the five highest candidates, the large States would have in fact the nomination of these candidates

On the motion of Col: Mason

N. H. no. Mas. no. Ct. no. N. J. no. Pa. no. Del. no. Md. ay. Va. no. N. C. ay. S. C. no. Geo. no.

Mr. Wilson moved to strike out "Senate" and insert the word "Legislature"

Mr. Madison considered it as a primary object to render an eventual resort to any part of the Legislature improbable. He was apprehensive that the proposed alteration would turn the attention of the large States too much to the appointment of candidates, instead of aiming at an effectual appointment of the officer, as the large States would predominate in the Legislature which would have the final choice out of the Candidates. Whereas if the Senate in which the small States predominate should have this final choice, the concerted effort of the large States would be to make the appointment in the first instance conclusive.

Mr. Randolph. We have in some revolutions of this plan made a bold stroke for Monarchy. We are now doing the same for an aristocracy. He dwelt on the tendency of such an influence in the Senate over the election of the President in addition to its other powers, to convert that body into a real & dangerous Aristocracy.

Mr. Dickinson was in favor of giving the eventual election to the Legislature, instead of the Senate. It was too much influence to be superadded to that body.

On the question moved by Mr. Wilson

N. H. divd. Mas. no. Ct. no. N. J. no. Pa. ay. Del. no. Md. no. Va. ay. N. C. no. S. C. ay. Geo. no.

Thursday, September 6

Mr. Gerry proposed, as the President was to be elected by the Senate out of the five highest candidates, that if he should not at the end of his term be re-elected by a majority of the Electors, and no other candidate should have a majority, the eventual election should be made by the Legislature. This he said would relieve the President from his particular dependence on the Senate for his continuance in office.

Mr. King liked the idea, as calculated to satisfy particular members & promote unanimity, & as likely to operate but seldom.

Mr. Read opposed it, remarking that if individual members were to be indulged, alterations would be necessary to satisfy most of them.

Mr. Williamson espoused it as a reasonable precaution against the undue influence of the Senate.

Mr. Sherman liked the arrangement as it stood, though he should not be averse to some amendments. He thought he said that if the Legislature were to have the eventual appointment instead of the Senate, it ought to vote in the case by States, in favor of the small States, as the large States would have so great an advantage in nominating the candidates.

Mr. Govr. Morris thought favorably of Mr. Gerry's proposition. It would free the President from being tempted in naming to Offices, to Conform to the will of the Senate, & thereby virtually give the appointments to office, to the Senate.

Mr. Wilson said that he had weighed carefully the report of the Committee for remodelling the constitution of the Executive; and on combining it with other parts of the plan, he was obliged to consider the whole as having a dangerous tendency to aristocracy; as throwing a dangerous power into the hands of the Senate. They will have in fact, the appointment of the President, and through his dependence on them, the virtual appointment to offices; among others the offices of the Judiciary Department. They are to make Treaties; and they are to try all impeachments. In allowing them thus to make the Executive & Judiciary appointments, to be the Court of impeachments, and to make Treaties which are to be laws of the land, the Legislative, Executive & Judiciary powers are all blended in one branch of the Government. The power of making Treaties involves the case of subsidies, and here as an additional evil, foreign influence is to be dreaded. According to the plan as it now stands, the President will not be the man of the people as he ought to be, but the Minion of the Senate. He cannot even appoint a tide-waiter without the Senate. He had always thought the Senate too numerous a body for making appointments to office. The Senate, will moreover in all probability be in constant Session. They will have high salaries. And with all those powers, and the President in their interest, they will depress the other branch of the Legislature, and aggrandize themselves in proportion. Add to all this, that the Senate sitting in conclave, can by holding up to their respective States various and improbable candidates, contrive so to scatter their votes, as to bring the appointment of the President ultimately before themselves. Upon the whole, he thought the new mode of appointing the President, with some amendments, a valuable improvement; but he could never agree to purchase it at the price of the ensuing parts of the Report, nor befriend a system of which they make a part.

Mr. Govr. Morris expressed his wonder at the observations of Mr. Wilson so far as they preferred the plan in the printed Report to the new modification of it before the House, and entered into a comparative view of the two, with an eye to the nature of Mr. Wilsons objections to the last. By the first the Senate he observed had a voice in appointing the President out of all the Citizens of the U.S: by this they were limited to five candidates previously nominated to them, with a probability of being barred altogether by the successful ballot of the Electors. Here surely was no increase of power. They are now to appoint Judges nominated to them by the President. Before they had the appointment without any agency whatever of the President. Here again was surely no additional power. If they are to make Treaties as the plan now stands, the power was the same in the printed plan. If they are to try impeachments, the Judges must have been triable by them before. Wherein then lay the dangerous tendency of the innovations to establish an aristocracy in the Senate? As to the appointment of officers, the weight of sentiment in the House, was opposed to the exercise of it by the President alone; though it was not the case with himself. If the Senate would act as was suspected, in misleading the States into a fallacious disposition of their votes for a President, they would, if the appointment were withdrawn wholly from them, make such representations in their several States where they have influence, as would favor the object of their partiality.

Mr. Williamson. replying to Mr. Morris: observed that the aristocratic complexion proceeds from the change in the mode of appointing the President which makes him dependent on the Senate.

Mr. Clymer said that the aristocratic part to which he could never accede was that in the printed plan, which gave the Senate the power of appointing to offices.

Mr. Hamilton said that he had been restrained from entering into the discussions by his dislike of the Scheme of Govt. in General; but as he meant to support the plan to be recommended, as better than nothing, he wished in this place to offer a few remarks. He liked the new modification, on the whole, better than that in the printed Report. In this the President was a Monster elected for seven years, and ineligible afterwards; having great powers, in appointments to office, & continually tempted by this constitutional disqualification to abuse them in order to subvert the Government. Although he should be made re-eligible, still if appointment by the Legislature, he would be tempted to make use of corrupt influence to be continued in office. It seemed peculiarly desireable therefore that some other mode of election should be devised. Considering the different views of different States, & the different districts Northern Middle & Southern, he concurred with those who thought that the votes would not be concentered, and that the appointment would consequently in the present mode devolve on the Senate. The nomination to offices will give great weight to the President. Here then is a mutual connection & influence, that will perpetuate the President, and aggrandize both him & the Senate. What is to be the remedy? He saw none better than to let the highest number of ballots, whether a majority or not, appoint the President. What was the objection to this? Merely that too small a number might appoint. But as the plan stands, the Senate may take the candidate having the smallest number of votes, and make him President.

.   .   .

Mr. Williamson suggested as better than an eventual choice by the Senate, that this choice should be made by the Legislature, voting *by States* and not *per capita.*

Mr. Sherman suggested the House of Reps. as preferable to the Legislature, and moved, accordingly,

To strike out the words "The Senate shall immediately choose &c." and insert "The House of Representatives shall immediately choose by ballot one of them for President, the members from each State having one vote."

Col: Mason liked the latter mode best as lessening the aristocratic influence of the Senate.

On the Motion of Mr. Sherman

N. H. ay. Mas. ay. Ct. ay. N. J. ay. Pa. ay. Del. no. Md. ay. Va. ay. N. C. ay. S. C. ay. Geo. ay.

Unwieldy as it is, the compromise of the Committee of Eleven—the electoral college—still operates today. The electoral college has had a checkered history, however, and has been under attack almost since its inception. In 1796 Federalist John Adams was elected president, and his political enemy (and a Republican) Thomas Jefferson, vice president. In the 1800 presidential race, Thomas Jefferson and his running mate, Aaron Burr, each received 73 electoral votes; the Republican electors had each cast one vote for Jefferson and one for Burr (soundly defeating the Federalist candidate, Adams). It was the only time the electoral college was evenly divided. It took 36 ballots in the House of Representatives to resolve the deadlock and elect Jefferson as president and Burr as vice president. Originally friends, the two became mortal enemies. Each man maintained to his death that the electors had intended *him* to be president and the other vice president.

To avoid a repetition of the Jefferson–Burr uncertainty over which candidate should head the ticket, the Twelfth Amendment was ratified in 1804. That amendment provides that the electors vote separately for president and vice president. Although it is still possible to have a president and vice president of opposing parties, it is now clear which candidate is elected to which position.

The Twelfth Amendment did not resolve all problems with the electoral college, however. Three times since 1800 a candidate losing the popular vote has nevertheless been elected president. In 1824, a four-way race gave Andrew Jackson a plurality of both the popular and the electoral college vote, but no candidate won a majority. John Quincy Adams had run second, William Crawford of Georgia third, and Kentuckian Henry Clay fourth. With no candidate receiving a majority in the electoral college, the election went to the House. After Crawford suffered a debilitating stroke and Clay threw his few states to Adams, the House elected Adams. When the new president appointed Clay to the post of secretary of state, the country cried foul, and Jackson overwhelmingly defeated Adams in an 1828 rematch.

No further elections went to the House, but two other minority presidents were elected by the electoral college. In 1876, Democrat Samuel Tilden beat Republican Rutherford Hayes in the popular vote. Because of disputes over who had won in three Southern states and in Oregon, it was uncertain which man had the majority in the electoral college. A congressional commission determined that all four states should go to Hayes, giving him a 185 to 184 majority in the electoral college. Two factors influenced this outcome. First, Republicans outnumbered Democrats on the congressional commission. Second, the Republicans promised Southern politicians that if the latter acquiesced in Hayes's election, the new Republican administration would stop enforcing the Fifteenth Amendment (giving blacks the right to vote). In 1887, Congress enacted legislation directing that future election disputes were to be resolved by the states(s) involved. That legislation prevented further congressional fixing of elections, but it did nothing to prevent the election of a minority president by the electoral college. The very next year, Republican Benjamin Harrison lost the popular vote to incumbent Grover Cleveland, but won the electoral college. Although that was the last time the college elected a minority president, there have been several close cases in this century.

Topics for Discussion

1. According to the delegates, what attributes contribute to a strong executive? To a weak one? Which delegates favored which type of executive? What are the dangers of too strong an executive? Too weak an executive?

2. Based on their comments about the proposed ratification procedure (in chapter 2) and the federal judiciary (in chapter 3), have you been able to categorize some delegates as more or less nationalist? How do those categories hold up during the debates over the executive branch? Are there "anti-nationalists" who seem aligned with Madison? "Nationalists" who oppose him? What does this tell you about the issues raised by the creation of a national executive?

3. What problems created the delegates' circle of debate? Why did questions on the mode of election and re-eligibility seem to create a "chicken-and-egg" problem?

4. What did the delegates think was wrong with direct popular election? The Constitution did not (and still does not) require that members of the electoral college be popularly elected. A variety of methods have been used, including complicated districting schemes. Until 1824, electors were chosen by the state legislature in most states. Most states switched to popular election in 1824, and since 1892 all the states have conducted popular elections. Have the problems that led the framers to reject direct popular elections materialized? What changes have taken place in American politics and culture to prevent some of the anticipated difficulties?

5. How does the electoral college assuage each of the concerns outlined by the various delegates? Does it serve any other purpose except compromise? What role should the vice president have within the executive branch, given the framers' reasons for creating the office?

6. How did the delegates think the electoral college would function? Has it done so? What has happened? Should the electoral college system be retained? Why or why not? What functions might it serve today?

7. Despite the Convention's decision not to limit presidential re-eligibility, no president served more than two terms until Franklin D. Roosevelt. George Washington began a tradition by declining to run for a third term because he was eager to return to private life. His immediate successors followed his example, and by the twentieth century the tradition was so solid that the few presidents who considered a third term were rebuffed by popular reaction. In 1940, however, after serving two full terms, Roosevelt was at the peak of his popularity. The Supreme Court had only recently capitulated and begun upholding his New Deal, and the country was recovering from the Great Depression and on the brink of war. He was re-elected by an overwhelming majority, and then re-elected for a fourth time in 1944 (he died in 1945 and did not complete his fourth term). On January 3, 1947, the opening day of the first Republican-controlled Congress since Roosevelt (a Democrat) had taken office, Republicans introduced what became the Twenty-second Amendment, limiting the president to two terms. Ratification was completed in 1951. Recently, there have been calls to repeal the Twenty-second Amendment. Should it have been adopted? Should it be repealed?

THE POWERS OF THE PRESIDENT

For most of the Convention, the powers of the executive branch were left virtually open. The original Randolph resolutions gave the executive "a general authority to execute the National laws" and "the Executive rights vested in Congress by the Confederation." The amended Randolph resolutions added little: they gave the executive "power to carry into execution the national Laws, [and] to appoint Offices in cases not otherwise provided for." Both of these powers were agreed to without debate or dissent on July 17.

The delegates did not focus again on the powers of the president until after they had resolved the question of his selection. The September 4 report of the Committee of Eleven included provisions regarding the powers of the president and vice president:

> (6) 'Sect. 3. The vice-president shall be ex officio President of the Senate, except when they sit to try the impeachment of the President, in which case the Chief Justice shall preside, and excepting also when he shall exercise the powers and duties of President, in which case & in case of his absence, the Senate shall chuse a President pro tempore—The vice President when acting as President of the Senate shall not have a vote unless the House be equally divided.'
>
> (7) 'Sect. 4. The President by and with the advice and Consent of the Senate, shall have power to make Treaties; and he shall nominate and by and with the advice and consent of the Senate shall appoint ambassadors, and other public Ministers, Judges of the Supreme Court, and all other Officers of the U.S., whose appointments are not otherwise herein provided for. But no Treaty shall be made without the consent of two thirds of the members present.'
>
> (8) After the words—"into the service of the U.S." in sect. 2. art: 10. add 'and may require the opinion in writing of the principal officer in each of the Executive Departments, upon any subject relating to the duties of their respective offices.'

The delegates turned to these provisions on September 7. Executive power was a less controversial topic than executive selection, in part because the language could be vague and the details left open.

Friday, September 7

Section 3. (see Sepr. 4). "The vice President shall be ex-officio President of the Senate"

Mr. Gerry opposed this regulation. We might as well put the President himself at the head of the Legislature. The close intimacy that must subsist between the President & vice-president makes it absolutely improper. He was agst. having any vice President.

Mr. Govr. Morris. The vice president then will be the first heir apparent that ever loved his father. If there should be no vice president, the President of the Senate would be temporary successor, which would amount to the same thing.

Mr. Sherman saw no danger in the case. If the vice-President were not to be President of the Senate, he would be without employment, and some member by being made President must be deprived of his vote, unless when an equal division of votes might happen in the Senate, which would be but seldom.

Mr. Randolph concurred in the opposition to the clause.

Mr. Williamson, observed that such an officer as vice-President was not wanted. He was introduced only for the sake of a valuable mode of election which required two to be chosen at the same time.

Col: Mason, thought the office of vice-President an encroachment on the rights of the Senate; and that it mixed too much the Legislative & Executive, which as well as the Judiciary departments, ought to be kept as separate as possible. He took occasion to express his dislike of any reference whatever of the power to make appointments to either branch of the Legislature. On the other hand he was averse to vest so dangerous a power in the President alone. As a method for avoiding both, he suggested that a privy Council of six members to the president should be established; to be chosen for six years by the Senate, two out of the Eastern two out of the middle, and two out of the Southern quarters of the

Union, & to go out in rotation two every second year; the concurrence of the Senate to be required only in the appointment of Ambassadors, and in making treaties, which are more of a legislative nature. This would prevent the constant sitting of the Senate which he thought dangerous, as well as keep the departments separate & distinct. It would also save the expence of constant sessions of the Senate. He had he said always considered the Senate as too unwieldy & expensive for appointing officers, especially the smallest, such as tide waiters &c. He had not reduced his idea to writing, but it could be easily done if it should be found acceptable.

On the question shall the vice President be ex officio President of the Senate?

N. H. ay. Mas. ay. Ct. ay. N. J. no. Pa. ay. Del. ay. Mas. no. Va. ay. N. C. abst. S. C. ay. Geo. ay.

The other parts of the same Section (3) were then agreed to.

The Section 4. — to wit, "The President by & with the advice and consent of the Senate shall have power to make Treaties &c"

Mr. Wilson moved to add, after the word "Senate" the words, "and House of Representatives." As treaties he said are to have the operation of laws, they ought to have the sanction of laws also. The circumstance of secrecy in the business of treaties formed the only objection; but this he thought, so far as it was inconsistent with obtaining the Legislative sanction, was outweighed by the necessity of the latter.

Mr. Sherman thought the only question that could be made was whether the power could be safely trusted to the Senate. He thought it could; and that the necessity of secresy in the case of treaties forbade a reference of them to the whole Legislature.

Mr. Fitzimmons 2ded. the motion of Mr. Wilson, & on the question

N. H. no. Mas. no. Ct. no. N. J. no. Pa. ay. Del. no. Md. no. Va. no. N. C. no. S. C. no. Geo. no.

The first sentence as to making treaties was then Agreed to: nem: con:

.   .   .

Section 4. "The President by and with the advice and consent of the Senate shall have power to make Treaties" — "*But no treaty shall be made without the consent of two thirds of the members present*" — this last being before the House.

Mr. Wilson thought it objectionable to require the concurrence of ⅔ which puts it in the power of a minority to controul the will of a majority.

Mr. King concurred in the objection; remarking that as the Executive was here joined in the business, there was a check which did not exist in Congress where The concurrence of ⅔ was required.

Mr. Madison moved to insert after the word "treaty" the words "except treaties of peace" allowing these to be made with less difficulty than other treaties — It was agreed to nem: con:

Mr. Madison then moved to authorise a concurrence of two thirds of the Senate to make treaties of peace, without the concurrence of the President." — The President he said would necessarily derive so much power and importance from a state of war that he might be tempted, if authorised, to impede a treaty of peace. **Mr. Butler** 2ded. the motion

Mr. Gorham thought the precaution unnecessary as the means of carrying on the war would not be in the hands of the President, but of the Legislature.

Mr. Govr. Morris thought the power of the President in this case harmless; and that no peace ought to be made without the concurrence of the President, who was the general Guardian of the National interests.

Mr. Butler was strenuous for the motion, as a necessary security against ambitious & corrupt Presidents. He mentioned the late perfidious policy of the Statholder in Holland; and the artifices of the Duke of Marlbro' to prolong the war of which he had the management.

Mr. Gerry was of opinion that in treaties of peace a greater rather than less proportion of votes was necessary, than in other treaties. In Treaties of peace the dearest interests will be at stake, as the fisheries, territory &c. In treaties of peace also there is more danger to the extremities of the Continent, of being sacrificed, than on any other occasions.

Mr. Williamson thought that Treaties of peace should be guarded at least by requiring the same concurrence as in other Treaties.

On the motion of Mr. Madison & Mr. Butler

N. H. no. Mas. no. Ct. no. N. J. no. Pa. no. Del. no. Md. ay. Va. no. N. C. no. S. C. ay. Geo. ay.

On the part of the clause concerning treaties amended by the exception as to Treaties of peace,

N. H. ay. Mas. ay. Ct. ay. N. J. no. Pa. no. Del. ay. Md. ay. Va. ay. N. C. ay. S. C. ay. Geo. no.

Saturday, September 8

The last Report of Committee of Eleven (see Sepr. 4) was resumed.

Mr. King moved to strike out the "exception of Treaties of peace" from the general clause requiring two thirds of the Senate for making Treaties

Mr. Wilson wished the requisition of two thirds to be struck out altogether If the majority cannot be trusted, it was a proof, as observed by Mr. Ghorum, that we were not fit for one Society.

A reconsideration of the whole clause was agreed to.

Mr. Govr. Morris was agst. striking out the "exception of Treaties of peace" If two thirds of the Senate should be required for peace, the Legislature will be unwilling, to make war for that reason, on account of the Fisheries or the Mississippi, the two great objects of the Union. Besides, if a majority of the Senate be for peace, and are not allowed to make it, they will be apt to effect their purpose in the more disagreeable mode, of negativing the supplies for the war.

Mr. Williamson remarked that Treaties are to be made in the branch of the Govt. where there may be a majority of the States without a majority of the people. Eight men may be a majority of a quorum, & should not have the power to decide the conditions of peace. There would be no danger, that the exposed States, as S. Carolina or Georgia, would urge an improper war for the Western Territory.

Mr. Wilson If two thirds are necessary to make peace, the minority may perpetuate war, against the sense of the majority.

Mr. Gerry enlarged on the danger of putting the essential rights of the Union in the hands of so small a number as a majority of the Senate, representing, perhaps, not one fifth of the people. The Senate will be corrupted by foreign influence.

Mr. Sherman was agst. leaving the rights established by the Treaty of peace, to the Senate, & moved to annex a "proviso that no such rights shd. be ceded without the sanction of the Legislature.

Mr. Govr. Morris seconded the ideas of Mr. Sherman.

Mr. Madison observed that it had been too easy in the present Congress to make Treaties altho' nine States were required for the purpose.

On the question for striking "except Treaties of peace"

N. H. ay. Mas. ay. Ct. ay. N. J. no. Pa. ay. Del. no. Md. no Va. ay. N. C. ay. S. C. ay. Geo. ay.

Mr. Wilson & Mr. Dayton move to strike out the clause requiring two thirds of the Senate for making Treaties—on which,

N. H. no. Mas. no. Ct. divd. N. J. no. Pa. no Del. ay. Md. no. Va. no. N. C. no. S. C. no. Geo. no.

Mr. Rutlidge & Mr. Gerry move that "no Treaty be made without the consent of ⅔ of all the members of the Senate"—according to the example in the present Congs.

Mr. Ghorum. There is a difference in the case, as the President's consent will also be necessary in the New Govt.

On the question

N. H. no. Mass. no. (Mr. Gerry ay) Ct. no. N. J. no. Pa. no. Del. no. Md. no. Va. no. N. C. ay. S. C. ay. Geo. ay.

Mr. Sharman movd. that no Treaty be made without a Majority of the whole number of the Senate. Mr. Gerry seconded him.

Mr. Williamson. This will be less security than ⅔ as now required.

Mr. Sherman. It will be less embarrassing.

On the question, it passed in the negative.

N. H. no. Mas. ay. Ct. ay. N. J. no. Pa. no. Del. ay. Md. no. Va. no. N. C. no. S. C. ay. Geo. ay.

.   .   .

On the question on clause of the Report of the Come. of Eleven relating to Treaties by ⅔ of the Senate. All the States were ay—except Pa. N. J. & Geo. no.

.   .   .

The clause referring to the Senate, the trial of impeachments agst. the President, for Treason & bribery, was taken up.

Col. Mason. Why is the provision restrained to Treason & bribery only? Treason as defined in the Constitution will not reach many great and dangerous offences. Hastings is not guilty of Treason. Attempts to subvert the Constitution may not be Treason as above defined. As bills of attainder which have saved the British Constitution are forbidden, it is the more necessary to extend: the power of impeachments. He movd. to add after "bribery" "or maladministration." Mr. Gerry seconded him.

Mr. Madison So vague a term will be equivalent to a tenure during pleasure of the Senate.

Mr. Govr. Morris, it will not be put in force & can

do no harm. An election of very four years will prevent maladministration.

Col. Mason withdrew "maladministration" &
substitutes "other high crimes & misdemesnors
agst. the State"

On the question thus altered
N. H. ay. Mas. ay. Ct. ay. N. J. no. Pa. no. Del.
no. Md. ay. Va. ay. N. C. ay. S. C. ay. Geo. ay.

Only one executive power gave the delegates much difficulty: the executive
veto. Since the advisability of an executive veto depended more on the delegates' views of legislative competence than on the mode of electing the president, the question of an executive veto arose early in the Convention.

As outlined in chapter 3, Randolph originally proposed to join the executive
and the judiciary in a Council of Revision with veto power over legislation.
On June 4, the convention voted to postpone consideration of the Council of
Revision in order to take up instead Gerry's proposal that "the National Executive shall have a right to negative any Legislative act which shall not be
afterwards passed by _____ parts of each branch of the national Legislature." Wilson and Hamilton immediately moved to delete the last portion of
Gerry's proposal, and leave the executive with an absolute veto that could not
be overridden by the legislature.

Monday, June 4

It was mentioned by **Col: Hamilton** that the King
of G. B. had not exerted his negative since the Revolution.

Mr. Gerry sees no necessity for so great a controul over the legislature as the best men in the
Community would be comprised in the two
branches of it.

Docr. Franklin, said he was sorry to differ from
his colleague for whom he had a very great respect,
on any occasion, but he could not help it on this. He
had had some experience of this check in the Executive on the Legislature, under the proprietary Government of Pena. The negative of the Governor was
constantly made use of to extort money. No good
law whatever could be passed without a private bargain with him. An increase of his salary, or some
donation, was always made a condition; till at last it
became the regular practice, to have orders in his favor on the Treasury, presented along with the bills
to be signed, so that he might actually receive the
former before he should sign the latter. When the
Indians were scalping the western people, and notice of it arrived, the concurrence of the Governor in
the means of self-defence could not be got, till it was
agreed that his Estate should be exempted from taxation: so that the people were to fight for the secu-

rity of his property, whilst he was to bear no share
of the burden. This was a mischievous sort of check.
If the Executive was to have a Council, such a power
would be less objectionable. It was true, the King of
G. B. had not, as was said, exerted his negative
since the Revolution; but that matter was easily explained. The bribes and emoluments now given to
the members of parliament rendered it unnecessary, every thing being done according to the will of
the Ministers. He was afraid, if a negative should be
given as proposed, that more power and money
would be demanded, till at last eno' would be got-
ten to influence & bribe the Legislature into a compleat subjection to the will of the Executive.

Mr. Sherman was agst. enabling any one man to
stop the will of the whole. No one man could be
found so far above all the rest in wisdom. He
thought we ought to avail ourselves of his wisdom
in revising the laws, but not permit him to overule
the decided and cool opinions of the Legislature.

Mr. Madison supposed that if a proper proportion of each branch should be required to overrule
the objections of the Executive, it would answer the
same purpose as an absolute negative. It would
rarely if ever happen that the Executive constituted
as ours is proposed to be would, have firmness eno'

to resist the legislature, unless backed by a certain part of the body itself. The King of G. B. with all his splendid attributes would not be able to withstand ye. unanimous and eager wishes of both houses of Parliament. To give such a prerogative would certainly be obnoxious to the temper of this Country; its present temper at least.

Mr. Wilson believed as others did that this power would seldom be used. The Legislature would know that such a power existed, and would refrain from such laws, as it would be sure to defeat. Its silent operation would therefore preserve harmony and prevent mischief. The case of Pena. formerly was very different from its present case. The Executive was not then as now to be appointed by the people. It will not in this case as in the one cited be supported by the head of a Great Empire, actuated by a different & sometimes opposite interest. The salary too is now proposed to be fixed by the Constitution, or if Dr. F.'s idea should be adopted all salary whatever interdicted. The requiring a large proportion of each House to overrule the Executive check might do in peaceable times; but there might be tempestuous moments in which animosities may run high between the Executive and Legislative

branches, and in which the former ought to be able to defend itself.

Mr. Butler had been in favor of a single Executive Magistrate; but could he have entertained an idea that a compleat negative on the laws was to be given him he certainly should have acted very differently. It had been observed that in all countries the Executive power is in a constant course of increase. This was certainly the case in G. B. Gentlemen seemed to think that we had nothing to apprehend from an abuse of the Executive power. But why might not a Cataline or a Cromwell arise in this Country as well as in others.

Mr. Bedford was opposed to every check on the Legislative, even the Council of Revision first proposed. He thought it would be sufficient to mark out in the Constitution the boundaries to the Legislative Authority, which would give all the requisite security to the rights of the other departments. The Representatives of the people were the best Judges of what was for their interest, and ought to be under no external controul whatever. The two branches would produce a sufficient controul within the Legislature itself.

Franklin then made a long speech opposing the Wilson and Hamilton motion. He studded it with historical illustrations, and noted: "The first man put at the helm will be a good one. No body knows what sort may come afterwards." Every delegate probably agreed with at least part of Franklin's assessment, for it was commonly assumed that George Washington would be the first president.

The delegates then voted to reject an absolute veto. Madison's notes indicate only that the states were unanimous in their rejection, but King's notes show that there were three individual supporters of the absolute veto (and thus of an especially strong executive): himself, Wilson, and Hamilton.

Gerry's limited executive veto was then passed eight to two, and the Convention unanimously agreed on a two-thirds majority of each house as the proportion necessary to override the veto. The resolutions adopted by the Committee of the Whole and presented to the Convention accordingly provided:

10. Resolved that the national executive shall have a right to negative any legislative act: which shall not be afterwards passed unless by two third parts of each branch of the national legislature.

On August 15, after again rejecting a Council of Revision, the Convention voted—with almost no debate—to change two-thirds to three-quarters.

Less than a week before the end of the Convention, the delegates made one last change in the structure of the executive branch. On September 12, after the Committee on Style had already completed its work, they changed the majority necessary to override a presidential veto back to two-thirds. This last-minute change, reversing once again an earlier decision, is illustrative of the Convention's general treatment of the executive branch. It was not so much that they disagreed with one another, but rather than they could not make up their collective mind.

Topics for Discussion

1. Based on the debates in both this section and the preceding one, how do you think the delegates envisioned the role of the president? Has the president generally served this function?

2. As the debates in the preceding section amply illustrate, the founders did not anticipate the existence of political parties. If they had, do you think they would have had the same concerns about the mode of selecting the president? Would they have given him the same powers? What about the executive veto? What purpose was the veto meant to serve? What purpose has it served?

3. Throughout our history, the president and Congress have argued over the boundaries between their powers, especially in the area of foreign relations and war. One of the most recent examples is the Iran-Contra controversy of 1987. During the Constitution's bicentennial summer, Congress held hearings to determine whether the executive branch had acted illegally in selling arms to Iran and channeling the profits to the Nicaraguan rebels, all without congressional knowledge or approval. One prominent executive participant, Marine Lieutenant Colonel Oliver North, argued that the Constitution empowered the president to aid the rebels in this way without consulting Congress. Do the debates shed any light on these sorts of questions? Does it matter whether Congress had explicitly forbidden aid to the rebels? Can Congress limit executive branch activities in foreign affairs?

4. Although the Supreme Court has never definitively settled the boundaries of the president's foreign affairs authority, it has resolved some disputes in the domestic context. In 1952, in *Youngstown Sheet & Tube Co. v. Sawyer*, 343 U.S. 579, 72 S.Ct. 863, 96 L.Ed. 1153 (1952) (The Steel Seizure Case), the Court invalidated President Truman's attempt to seize the nation's steel mills. Acting without the Congress, Truman had seized the steel mills in order to avoid a strike that might disrupt the Korean War effort. In an extremely influential concurring opinion, Justice Jackson noted that there is "a zone of twilight" in which the president and Congress have concurrent authority; within that zone, "any actual test of power is likely to depend on the imperatives of events and contemporary imponderables rather than on abstract theories of law." Is this reasoning consistent with the views of the delegates?

5. The Supreme Court has also resolved the issue of executive privilege. In 1974, a federal district court issued a subpoena to President Nixon, ordering him to turn over certain tapes of White House conversations. The tapes were needed in the ongoing criminal trial of former Nixon aides for conspiracy to obstruct justice, and other federal offenses. The indictment had named the president as an unindicted co-conspirator. Nixon refused to turn over the tapes, claiming that the Constitution granted him either an absolute privilege of immunity from judicial process, or a limited privilege to determine which tapes should be surrendered. The Supreme Court, in *United States v. Nixon*, 418 U.S. 683, 94 S.Ct. 3090, 41 L.Ed.2d 1039 (1974), rejected both claims, and ordered Nixon to surrender the tapes. Was that decision consistent with the intent of the framers? Would a contrary decision have been? The Court also noted, in a controversial footnote, that "the silence of the Constitution . . . is not dispositive," and suggested obliquely that the Constitution gives the president, as well as the legislature, implied powers. Did the delegates think they were granting the president implied powers, or only the specifically enumerated powers?

6. For what offenses should the president be impeachable? Only one president, Andrew Johnson, has been impeached by the House; the Senate then acquitted him by a single vote. The House was considering articles of impeachment against Nixon at the time he resigned. Johnson was impeached for ignoring a statute he believed was unconstitutional. The statute, enacted by a partisan Congress and designed to cripple Johnson's administration because he had failed to carry forward the Reconstruction effort, required the president to obtain the advice and consent of the Senate for removals as well as appointments. The Supreme Court later held a similar act unconstitutional. The articles of impeachment against Nixon focused on the Watergate cover-up and on his refusal to comply with congressional subpoenas. The Supreme Court never ruled on whether the president is privileged against *congressional* subpoenas, a question carefully left open in *U.S. v. Nixon*. Thus both Nixon and Johnson were threatened with impeachment in part because each maintained that his conduct was constitutionally permissible, and the Congress disagreed. If the president and Congress disagree about the constitutionality of a presidential course of conduct, is impeachment an appropriate remedy? What evils was the impeachment provision intended to remedy? If you conclude that Congress should not be able to impeach a president based solely on a reasonable dispute over the constitutionality of the latter's conduct, what alternatives would you suggest?

7. In 1978, in the aftermath of the Watergate scandal, Congress passed the Ethics in Government Act. A central part of the act established procedures for the appointment, by a special court, of a special prosecutor or independent counsel to investigate and prosecute wrongdoing in the executive branch. To guard against a repeat of the "Saturday Night Massacre," Congress included a provision that only the Attorney General could fire an independent counsel, and only for "good cause." In 1988, executive officials under investigation by an independent counsel challenged the scheme as a violation of separation of powers and an infringement on the prerogatives of the executive. In particular, they argued that since investigating and prosecuting criminals was an *executive* function, the act gave the judiciary too much control and the executive branch too little control over an executive branch officer. The Supreme Court, by a vote of seven to one, upheld the statute. *Morrison v. Olson*, 488 U.S., 108 S.Ct. 2597, 101 L.Ed.2d 569, (1988). Do the debates over executive responsibility shed any light on this question?

FOOTNOTES

1. *The Works of James Wilson* 357 (James D. Andrews, ed. 1896).

2. William E. Nelson, *Reason and Compromise in the Establishment of the Federal Constitution, 1787–1801* 3:XLIV Wm. & Mary Q. 458, 468–69 (1987).

3. Taken from *Supplement to Max Farrand's The Records of the Federal Convention of 1787* (James H. Hutson ed. 1987).

4. The Committee on Detail is discussed in more detail in chapter 2.

CHAPTER FIVE

The Federal Legislature

INTRODUCTION

Some of the earliest and most persistent conflicts between the colonists and England involved legislative prerogatives. When Americans protested English acts of oppression, they concomitantly asserted a right to be governed by the colonial legislatures, which were partly popularly elected. Moreover, American and British theories of representation differed, providing another source of friction. As with the executive branch, experiences between 1776 and 1787 contributed to American views of the legislature and caused some modification of earlier theories.

Colonial legislatures, like Parliament, consisted of two branches. The lower house, or assembly, went by different names in the different colonies: House of Burgesses, Delegates, Commons, or Representatives. Elected by the people, members of the lower house were still generally from the wealthiest and most elite families in the colony. They were merchants, lawyers, and large landholders rather than yeoman farmers. They were elected, moreover, not only by their propertied peers, but also by the lower classes. Property qualifications for voting varied, but in most colonies at least two-thirds of white male inhabitants were entitled to vote. Poorer voters often had less influence—a combination of distance from polling places, the lack of secret ballots, and the greater number of representatives allotted to populous commercial centers contrived to increase the likelihood that the wealthy would be elected. But the poor also apparently believed that members of the upper class would be better able to represent the colonists' concerns. Deference to the aristocratic classes was widespread in political life.

Members of the upper house, or Governor's Council, in each colony were similarly aristocratic. Chosen by the Crown or its agents, they were some of the most important men in the colonies. The Randolphs and Lees in Virginia, the Van Rensselaers in New York, and the Bowdoins in Massachusetts—all of whom left their mark on history—were among the families well-represented on the various councils. Councils played a prominent role in governing the colonies. In addition to legislative duties, the councils also performed an executive function in their capacity as advisors to the governors, and a judicial function as the highest courts of appeal in the colonies.

Since the assembly was the only governmental body elected by the colonists, most of the conflict between the colonies and Britain stemmed from disputes over control of that body. Inspired by the English Triennial Act of 1694, some colonies tried to require frequent assembly elections. All such acts were vetoed by the governor or rejected by the Privy Council on review. Many colonies also tried to limit gubernatorial influence over the members of the assembly. These attempts were notably unsuccessful, and governors exerted substantial influence. In Virginia, for example, Governor Spotswood decided in 1713 to create forty new offices to be distributed among members of the assembly. The English Act of Settlement of 1701 barred the king from distributing offices to the House of Commons, but no similar provision limited the royal governors. Many governors followed Governor Spotswood's example, and all colonial attempts to pass laws prohibiting the practice were vetoed.

Americans also disagreed with their British cousins on the very nature of representation. According to the prevailing British theory, exemplified by Edmund Burke, legislatures were deliberative bodies whose allegiance was to the nation rather than to specific constituencies. The underlying premise was that of "virtual representation": since the *interests* of all British citizens were represented in Parliament, the *citizens* themselves did not need to be. Thus, although the colonists, like nine-tenths of the inhabitants of Britain itself, could not vote for members of Parliament, they were all "virtually" represented there. The franchise was an accidental attribute, irrelevant to the great purposes of Parliament.

> [N]one are actually, all are virtually represented in Parliament: for every Member of Parliament sits in the House, not as Representative of his own Constituents, but as one of that august Assembly by which all the Commons of *Great Britain* are represented. Their Rights and their Interests, however his own Borough may be affected by general Dispositions, ought to be the great objects of his Attention, and the only Rules for his Conduct; and to sacrifice these to a partial Advantage in favour of the Place where he was chosen, would be a Departure from his Duty; if it were otherwise, *Old Sarum* would enjoy Privileges essential to Liberty, which are denied to *Birmingham* and to *Manchester*, but as it is, they and the Colonies and all *British* Subjects whatever, have an equal Share in the general Representation of the Commons of *Great Britain*, and are bound by the Consent of the Majority of that House, whether their own particular Representatives consented to or opposed the Measures there taken, or whether they had or had not particular Representatives there.[1]

The colonists rejected both the theory behind, and the practice of, virtual representation. For Americans, representatives were nothing more and nothing less than agents of their constituents. John Adams wrote of representation in 1766:

> It is in reality nothing more than this, the people choose attorneys to vote for them in the great council of the nation, reserving always the fundamentals of the government, reserving also a right to give their attorneys instructions how to vote, and

a right at certain, stated intervals, of choosing a-new, discarding an old attorney, and choosing a wiser and better.[2.]

Thus Burke's vision of a national legislature was inconsistent with American desires for locally controlled representatives. In fact, the colonists repeatedly rejected the notion that even sending colonial representatives to Parliament would be a sufficient safeguard of American interests. The long term of office, during which a colonial representative in London would be virtually isolated from his constituents, would offer little better representation of the colonies than did the actual absence of colonial representatives in Parliament. As part of their program of local control, the colonists also pressed for short terms of office and the right to instruct their representatives.

When the American states gained the opportunity to create legislatures more to their liking, they implemented many of these ideas. In 1776, Adams again expressed the views of many of his compatriots when he described the ideal legislature: "It should be in miniature an exact portrait of the people at large. It should think, feel, reason and act like them."[3] In order to create such a legislature, and to check the power of legislators, the new states uniformly established very short terms of office. Elections for the lower house were held every year in every state except South Carolina, where they were held every other year. Members of the upper house served one-year terms in four states of the nine that had an upper house. In the others, the terms ranged from two years to five years.

Voters in most states also had the right to instruct their representatives and to direct votes on individual issues. Three state constitutions guaranteed such a right. In the others, the right was assumed. Town meetings and county conventions exercised the right, but did so sparingly.

Pennsylvania provided for even more substantial citizen participation in the business of the legislature. Article XV of the 1776 Pennsylvania constitution read:

> To the end that laws before they are enacted may be more maturely considered, and the inconvenience of hasty determinations as much as possible prevented, all bills of public nature shall be printed for the consideration of the people, before they are read in general assembly the last time for debate and amendment; and, except on occasions of sudden necessity, shall not be passed into laws until the next session of assembly; and for the more perfect satisfaction of the public, the reasons and motives for making such laws shall be fully and clearly expressed in the preambles.

Many states further restrained the legislatures by requiring that legislative sessions be open to the public, or that legislative proceedings be published.

After the Revolution, there was also a trend toward relaxation of property qualifications for voting. In general, this took the form of lowering monetary amounts and accepting other forms of property ownership in lieu of land ownership. Perhaps as a result of broader representation—or, as discussed in chapter 1, as a result of broadening political awareness generally—some state legislatures began to take on a truly popular character. They enacted laws that were favored by the masses and unpopular with the wealthy classes: issuance of paper money, debtor protection measures, and various other forms of wealth redistribution. With short terms and popular accountability, the legislatures also tended toward instability; laws were frequently changed. Both the instability and the popular character of the state legislatures troubled some people.

As citizens in the new states agreed on some basic principles of representation, what had been peripheral disagreements became more central. Although most states ultimately adopted a bicameral legislature, there was strong support for unicameral legislatures. Proponents of a single house suggested that the simplest forms of government were best, and a bicameral legislature introduced unnecessary complexity. They were also concerned that an upper house veto might interfere with rule by popular majorities. Four states—Pennsylvania, Connecticut, Rhode Island, and Georgia— had no upper house, although the first two established an executive council with some legislative powers. The national congress established under the Articles of Confederation was also unicameral.

Another growing source of friction was the basis for representation. Before the Revolution, most colonial assemblies were based on equal representation of towns, counties, or parishes. Movements in several states toward representation proportional to population drew sharp criticism. Small towns in rural Massachusetts opposed the proposed Massachusetts constitution of 1780 for this reason:

> Each Town has rights, Liberties and Priviledges peculiar to the same, and as dear to them as those to any other, and which they have as just a right as any others to have guarded and protected. If larger Towns have more to represent them and more Voices in the General Court than the smaller, they will have the Advantage of the smaller; the smaller will not have their Rights equally guarded and protected.

Most states initially kept the town or county system, but incorporated some method of factoring in relative wealth or population in the future. By 1787, almost all states had some form of graduated representation in the lower house.

Representation in the upper house varied considerably from state to state. Some states created special senatorial districts with equal populations. Others allocated senators to existing counties according to such factors as population, wealth, tax revenues, and relative influence. Still others simply gave each county an equal number of senators. The Articles of Confederation, at the insistence of the smaller states, adopted this last provision, and gave each state an equal vote in the unicameral national congress.

By 1787, all Americans—influenced by both reason and experience—held strong views on the proper constitution and character of a legislature. They did not, however, hold identical views; creating a federal legislature was thus one of the most difficult tasks faced by the delegates to the Constitutional Convention.

THE CONVENTION DEADLOCKS

For half the summer, disagreement over the legislative branch was so grave that it threatened to dissolve the Convention. Madison's first concession to the smaller states, noted in chapter 2, was to give each state an equal vote in the Convention itself. In persuading the Pennsylvania delegation not to insist on proportional representation in the Convention, Madison hoped to win the more important point later on: proportional representation in both houses of the national legislature. He was doomed to disappointment, but his persistence and refusal to accept early compromises almost destroyed the Convention.

Debates over the legislature implicated one of the most fundamental disputes in the Convention: whether the new government was to be consolidated or confederated. The small states, and the anti-nationalists (often the same delegates), preferred a confederated government that left the states intact and more or less supreme. The large states and the nationalists (again, an overlapping group) urged more consolidation and more transferring of state powers to the national government. These same issues prompted the New Jersey delegates to provide an alternative to the Randolph plan; the Convention's rejection of the New Jersey plan postponed, but did not eliminate, an eventual showdown.

The key issues arose early. On May 31, the third day of substantive debate, the delegates began discussing how members of the national legislature should be chosen. The dispute over whether the legislators in each house should be popularly elected or chosen by the state legislatures raised two underlying questions.

First, would the new national government represent *states* or *individuals*? This question divided the delegates politically, along both nationalist/anti-nationalist and large-state/small-state lines. Large-state nationalists favored popular elections, both in order to deprive the states of power and to avoid the perceived problem of an overly numerous upper house. To strengthen the national government and simultaneously to avoid the problem of two houses too similar to one another, Randolph's resolutions called for popular election of the first, or lower, house, which would then itself select the members of the second house from candidates nominated by the state legislatures. Both anti-nationalists and delegates from the smaller states opposed this solution.

The second question was a more philosophical debate over the very nature of the legislature: how democratic should it be? On this issue, nationalist sentiments were a less reliable predictor of a delegate's position; many delegates wavered and were hard to categorize. Even the most nationalist delegates were concerned about what Randolph called "the turbulence and follies of democracy." One can trace both questions through the materials that follow, as the delegates discussed modes of election and apportionment in the national legislature.

Thursday, May 31

Resol: 4. first clause "that the members of the first branch of the National Legislature ought to be elected by the people of the several States" being taken up,

Mr. Sherman opposed the election by the people, insisting that it ought to be by the State Legislatures. The people he said, immediately should have as little to do as may be about the Government. They want information and are constantly liable to be misled.

Mr. Gerry. The evils we experience flow from the excess of democracy. The people do not want virtue, but are the dupes of pretended patriots. In Massts. it had been fully confirmed by experience that they are daily misled into the most baneful measures and opinions by the false reports circulated by designing men, and which no one on the spot can refute. One principal evil arises from the want of due provision for those employed in the administration of Governmt. It would seem to be a maxim of democracy to starve the public servants. He mentioned the popular clamour in Massts. for the reduction of salaries and the attack made on that of the Govt. though secured by the spirit of the Constitution itself. He had he said been too republican heretofore: he was still however republican, but had been taught by experience the danger of the levilling spirit.

Mr. Mason, argued strongly for an election of the larger branch by the people. It was to be the grand depository of the democratic principle of the Govts. It was, so to speak, to be our House of Commons— It ought to know & sympathise with every part of the community; and ought therefore to be taken not only from different parts of the whole republic, but also from different districts of the larger members of it, which had in several instances particularly in Virga., different interests and views arising from difference of produce, of habits &c &c. He admitted that we had been too democratic but was afraid we sd. incautiously run into the opposite extreme. We ought to attend to the rights of every class of people. He had often wondered at the indifference of the superior classes of society to this dictate of humanity & policy; considering that however affluent their circumstances, or elevated their situations, might be, the course of a few years, not only might but certainly would, distribute their posterity throughout the lowest classes of Society. Every selfish motive therefore, every family attachment, ought to recommend such a system of policy as would provide no less carefully for the rights and happiness of the lowest than of the highest orders of Citizens.

Mr. Wilson contended strenuously for drawing the most numerous branch of the Legislature immediately from the people. He was for raising the federal pyramid to a considerable altitude, and for that reason wished to give it as broad a basis as possible. No government could long subsist without the confidence of the people. In a republican Government, this confidence was peculiarly essential. He also thought it wrong to increase the weight of the State Legislatures by making them the electors of the national Legislature. All interference between the general and local Governmts. should be obviated as much as possible. On examination it would be found that the opposition of States to federal measures had proceded much more

from the officers of the States, than from the people at large.

Mr. Madison considered the popular election of one branch of the National Legislature as essential to every plan of free Government. He observed that in some of the States one branch of the Legislature was composed of men already removed from the people by an intervening body of electors. That if the first branch of the general legislature should be elected by the State Legislatures, the second branch elected by the first—the Executive by the second together with the first; and other appointments again made for subordinate purposes by the Executive, the people would be lost sight of altogether; and the necessary sympathy between them and their rulers and officers, too little felt. He was an advocate for the policy of refining the popular appointments by successive filtrations, but thought it might be pushed too far. He wished the expedient to be resorted to only in the appointment of the second branch of the Legislature, and in the Executive & judiciary branches of the Government. He thought too that the great fabric to be raised would be more stable and durable, if it should rest on the solid foundation of the people themselves, than if it should stand merely on the pillars of the Legislatures.

Mr. Gerry did not like the election by the people. The maxims taken from the British constitution were often fallacious when applied to our situation which was extremely different. Experience he said had shewn that the State legislatures drawn immediately from the people did not always possess their confidence. He had no objection however to an election by the people if it were so qualified that men of honor & character might not be unwilling to be joined in the appointments. He seemed to think the people might nominate a certain number out of which the State legislatures should be bound to choose.

Mr. Butler thought an election by the people an impracticable mode.

On the question for an election of the first branch of the national Legislature by the people.

Massts. ay. Connect. divd. N. York ay. N. Jersey no. Pena. ay. Delawe. divd. Va. ay. N. C. ay. S. C. no. Georga. ay.

·   ·   ·

The Committee proceeded to Resolution 5. "that the second, [or senatorial] branch of the National Legislature ought to be chosen by the first branch out of persons nominated by the State Legislatures."

Mr. Spaight contended that the 2d. branch ought

to be chosen by the State Legislatures and moved an amendment to that effect.

. . .

Mr. Wilson opposed both a nomination by the State Legislatures, and an election by the first branch of the national Legislature, because the second branch of the latter, ought to be independent of both. He thought both branches of the National Legislature ought to be chosen by the people, but was not prepared with a specific proposition. He suggested the mode of chusing the Senate of N. York to wit of uniting several election districts, for one branch, in chusing members for the other branch, as a good model.

Mr. Madison observed that such a mode would destroy the influence of the smaller States associated with larger ones in the same district; as the latter would chuse from within themselves, altho' better men might be found in the former. The election of Senators in Virga. where large & small counties were often formed into one district for the purpose, had illustrated this consequence Local partiality, would often prefer a resident within the County or State, to a candidate of superior merit residing out of it. Less merit also in a resident would be more known throughout his own State.

Mr. Sherman favored an election of one member by each of the State Legislature.

Mr. Pinkney moved to strike out the "nomination by the State Legislatures." On this question.

Massts. no. Cont. no. N. Y. no. N. J. no. Pena. no. Del. divd. Va. no. N. C. no. S. C. no. Georg. no.

On the whole question for electing by the first branch out of nominations by the State Legislatures, Mass. ay. Cont. no. N. Y. no. N. Jersey. no. Pena. no. Del. no. Virga. ay. N. C. no. S. C. ay. Ga. no.

So the clause was disagreed to & a chasm left in this part of the plan.

Wednesday, June 6

Mr. Pinkney according to previous notice & rule obtained, moved "that the first branch of the national Legislature be elected by the State Legislatures, and not by the people." contending that the people were less fit Judges in such a case, and that the Legislature would be less likely to promote the adoption of the new Government, if they were to be excluded from all share in it.

Mr. Rutlidge 2ded. the motion.

Mr. Gerry. Much depends on the mode of election. In England, the people will probably lose their liberty from the smallness of the proportion having a right of suffrage. Our danger arises from the opposite extreme: hence in Massts. the worst men get into the Legislature. Several members of that Body had lately been convicted of infamous crimes. Men of indigence, ignorance & baseness, spare no pains, however dirty to carry their point agst. men who are superior to the artifices practised. He was not disposed to run into extremes. He was as much principled as ever agst. aristocracy and monarchy. It was necessary on the one hand that the people should appoint one branch of the Govt. in order to inspire them with the necessary confidence. But he wished the election on the other to be so modified as to secure more effectually a just preference of merit. His idea was that the people should nominate certain persons in certain districts, out of whom the State Legislature shd. make the appointment.

Mr. Wilson. He wished for vigor in the Govt., but he wished that vigorous authority to flow immediately from the legitimate source of all authority. The Govt. ought to possess not only 1st. the *force*, but 2dly. the *mind or sense* of the people at large. The Legislature ought to be the most exact transcript of the whole Society. Representation is made necessary only because it is impossible for the people to act collectively. The opposition was to be expected he said from the *Governments*, not from the Citizens of the States. The latter had parted as was observed [by Mr. King] with all the necessary powers; and it was immaterial to them, by whom they were exercised, if well exercised. The State officers were to be the losers of power. The people he supposed would be rather more attached to the national Govt. than to the State Govts. as being more important in itself, and more flattering to their pride. There is no danger of improper elections if made by *large* districts. Bad elections proceed from the smallness of the districts which give an opportunity to bad men to intrigue themselves into office.

Mr. Sherman. If it were in view to abolish the State Govt. the elections ought to be by the people. If the State Govts. are to be continued, it is necessary in order to preserve harmony between the National & State Govts. that the elections to the former shd. be made by the latter. The right of participating in the National Govt. would be sufficiently secured to the people by their election of the State Legislatures. The objects of the Union, he thought were few. 1. defence agst. foreign danger. 2 agst. internal disputes & a resort to force. 3. Treaties with foreign nations. 4 regulating foreign commerce, & drawing revenue from it. These & perhaps a few lesser objects alone rendered a Confederation of the States necessary. All other matters civil & criminal would be much better in the hands of the States. The people are more happy in small than large States. States may indeed be too small as Rhode Island, & thereby be too subject to faction. Some others were perhaps too large, the powers of Govt. not being able to pervade them. He was for giving the General Govt. power to legislate and execute within a defined province.

Col. Mason. Under the existing Confederacy, Congs. represent the *States* not the *people* of the States: their acts operate on the *States,* not the individuals. The case will be changed in the new plan of Govt. The people will be represented; they ought therefore to choose the Representatives. The requisites in actual representation are that the Reps. should sympathize with their constituents; shd. think as they think, & feel as they feel; and that for these purposes shd. even be residents among them. Much he sd. had been alledged agst. democratic elections. He admitted that much might be said; but it was to be considered that no Govt. was free from imperfections & evils; and that improper elections in many instances, were inseparable from Republican Govts. But compare these with the advantage of this Form in favor of the rights of the people, in favor of human nature. He was persuaded there was a better chance for proper elections by the people, if divided into large districts, than by the State Legislatures. Paper money had been issued by the latter when the former were against it. Was it to be supposed that the State Legislatures then wd. not send to the Natl. legislature patrons of such projects, if the choice depended on them.

Mr. Madison considered an election of one branch at least of the Legislature by the people immediately, as a clear principle of free Govt. and that this mode under proper regulations had the additional advantage of securing better representatives, as well as of avoiding too great an agency of the State Governments in the General one.—He differed from the member from Connecticut [Mr. Sharman] in thinking the objects mentioned to be all the principal ones that required a National Govt. Those were certainly important and necessary objects; but he combined with them the necessity of providing more effectually for the security of private rights, and the steady dispensation of Justice. Interferences with these were evils which had more perhaps than any thing else, produced this convention. Was it to be supposed that republican liberty could long exist under the abuses of it practised in some of the States. The gentleman [Mr. Sharman] had admitted that in a very small State, faction & oppression wd. prevail. It was to be inferred then that wherever these prevailed the State was too small. Had they not prevailed in the largest as well as the smallest tho' less than in the smallest; and were we not thence admonished to enlarge the sphere as far as the nature of the Govt. would admit. This was the only defence agst. the inconveniencies of democracy consistent with the democratic form of Govt. All civilized Societies would be divided into different Sects, Factions, & interests, as they happened to consist of rich & poor, debtors & creditors, the landed, the manufacturing, the commercial interests, the inhabitants of this district or that district, the followers of this political leader or that political leader, the disciples of this religious Sect or that religious Sect. In all cases where a majority are united by a common interest or passion, the rights of the minority are in danger. What motives are to restrain them? A prudent regard to the maxim that honesty is the best policy is found by experience to be as little regarded by bodies of men as by individuals. Respect for character is always diminished in proportion to the number among whom the blame or praise is to be divided. Conscience, the only remaining tie, is known to be inadequate in individuals: In large numbers, little is to be expected from it. Besides, Religion itself may become a motive to persecution & oppression.—These observations are verified by the Histories of every Country antient & modern.

. . .

Mr. Read. Too much attachment is betrayed to the State Governts. We must look beyond their continuance. A national Govt. must soon of necessity swallow all of them up. They will soon be reduced to the mere office of electing the National Senate. He was agst. patching up the old federal System: he hoped the idea wd. be dismissed. It would be like putting new cloth on an old garment. The confederation was founded on temporary principles. It cannot last: it cannot be amended. If we do not establish a good Govt. on new principles, we must either go to ruin, or have the work to do over again. The people at large are wrongly suspected of being averse to a Genl. Govt. The aversion lies among interested men who possess their confidence.

Mr. Pierce was for an election by the people as to the 1st. branch & by the States as to the 2d. branch; by which means the Citizens of the States wd. be represented both *individually* & *collectively*.

General Pinkney wished to have a good National Govt. & at the same time to leave a considerable share of power in the States. An election of either branch by the people scattered as they are in many States, particularly in S. Carolina was totally impracticable. He differed from gentlemen who thought that a choice by the people wd. be a better guard agst. bad measures, than by the Legislatures. A majority of the people in S. Carolina were notiriously for paper money as a legal tender; the Legislature had refused to make it a legal tender. The reason was that the latter had some sense of character and were restrained by that consideration. The

State Legislatures also he said would be more jealous, & more ready to thwart the National Govt., if excluded from a participation in it. The Idea of abolishing these Legislatures wd. never go down.

Mr. Wilson, would not have spoken again, but for what had fallen from Mr. Read; namely, that the idea of preserving the State Govts. ought to be abandoned. He saw no incompatibility between the National & State Govts. provided the latter were restrained to certain local purposes; nor any probability of their being devoured by the former. In all confederated Systems antient & modern the reverse had happened; the Generality being destroyed gradually by the usurpations of the parts composing it.

On the question for electing the 1st. branch by the State Legislatures as moved by Mr. Pinkney: it was negatived:

Mass. no. Ct. ay. N. Y. no. N. J. ay. Pa. no. Del. no. Md. no. Va. no. N. C. no. S. C. ay. Geo. no.

Thursday, June 7

The Clause providing for ye. appointment of the 2d. branch of the national Legislature, having lain blank since the last vote on the mode of electing it, to wit, by the 1st. branch, Mr. Dickenson now moved "that the members of the 2d. branch ought to be chosen by the individual Legislatures."

Mr. Sharman seconded the motion; observing that the particular States would thus become interested in supporting the national Governt. and that a due harmony between the two Governments would be maintained. He admitted that the two ought to have separate and distinct jurisdictions, but that they ought to have a mutual interest in supporting each other.

Mr. Pinkney. If the small States should be allowed one Senator only, the number will be too great, there will be 80 at least.

Mr. Dickenson had two reasons for his motion. 1. because the sense of the States would be better collected through their Governments; than immediately from the people at large; 2. because he wished the Senate to consist of the most distinguished characters, distinguished for their rank in life and their weight of property, and bearing as strong a likeness to the British House of Lords as possible; and he thought such characters more likely to be selected by the State Legislatures, than in any other mode.

The greatness of the number nas no objection with him. He hoped there would be 80 and twice 80. of them. If their number should be small, the popular branch could not be balanced by them. The legislature of a numerous people ought to be a numerous body.

.   .   .

Mr. Wilson. If we are to establish a national Government, that Government ought to flow from the people at large. If one branch of it should be chosen by the Legislatures, and the other by the people, the two branches will rest on different foundations, and dissensions will naturally arise between them. He wished the Senate to be elected by the people as well as the other branch, and the people might be divided into proper districts for the purpose & moved to postpone the motion of Mr. Dickenson, in order to take up one of that import.

Mr. Morris 2ded. him.

.   .   .

Mr. Madison, if the motion [of Mr. Dickenson] should be agreed to, we must either depart from the doctrine of proportional representation; or admit into the Senate a very large number of members.

The first is inadmissible, being evidently unjust.   Mass. ay. Ct. ay. N. Y. ay. Pa. ay Del. ay. Md. ay.
The second is inexpedient.   Va. ay N. C. ay. S. C. ay. Geo. ay.

. . .

    On Mr. Dickinson's motion for an appointment of
the Senate by the State Legislatures.

King's notes shed interesting light on Mason's May 31 reference to "[e]very selfish motive [and] every family attachment." According to King, Mason was "in favor of popular choice [in the lower branch], because the first Branch is to represent the People. . . . A portion of Democracy should be preserved; our own children in a short time will be among the general mass." Even Mason, however, favored election of senators by the state legislatures.

On June 21 and 25, the Convention approved what it had done as a Committee of the Whole, quickly agreeing that the Senate was to be elected by the state legislatures and the House by the people. General Pinckney suggested giving to state legislatures the power to determine how members of the House should be selected, but his motion was defeated. The delegates thus quickly compromised by providing that one house would be elected by the people, and the other by the states.

As Madison recognized in a footnote commenting on Dickinson's June 7 motion, however, the method of selection of legislators was intertwined with an even more explosive issue: how the states would be represented in the national legislature. The relationship between the two issues was both practical and theoretical. On a theoretical level, allowing the state legislatures to select federal legislators suggested that states, as well as individuals, should be represented in the national legislature. This was a principle abhorrent to many of the nationalists.

On a practical level, as several delegates noted, election by the state legislatures required either equal representation or a very large Senate. Both King and Pinckney suggested that if the smallest state had one senator, a proportional Senate would have eighty or more members. In fact, the original House of Representatives had sixty-five members based on an imperfect apportionment scheme, so King's and Pinckney's estimates were not far from wrong. As illustrated by the various comments regarding the Senate's aristocratic character, all the delegates expected the Senate to be much smaller than the House. The combination of state legislative selection of senators and proportional representation in the Senate posed a difficult problem.

What made these disputes over representation in the legislature even more acrimonious and difficult to resolve was the defection of the small state nationalists from the Madisonian camp. Despite the willingness of some to create a strong national government, representatives of the smaller states were not willing to turn that government over to the large states—and that is exactly what they thought Madison was trying to do.

States were represented equally in the unicameral Congress of the Articles of Confederation. This irritated the larger states, and most large state delegates arrived at the Convention determined that states would be proportionally represented in both houses of the new Congress. The small state delegates, on the other hand, although they put up only a token fight on the proportional representation in the House, refused to give up on equality in the senate. Thus the real battle between the large and small states was over the composition of the Senate. From early June until mid-July, the delegates were divided according to the size of their respective states, rather than their sentiments on a strong national government.

The large states began by voting as a bloc. Massachusetts, Pennsylvania and Virginia were the pre-eminent large states. Both the Carolinas and Georgia also voted with the large states, because their vast unsettled lands and growing populations led them to believe that they would soon rank among the larger states. The large states were spread throughout the country, so Madison could easily argue that they had little in common and would not unite to the detriment of the smaller states. He suggested instead that the various "factions" that might attempt to gain an advantage in the Congress were based on such things as religious and commercial differences, and not regional or state differences. In other words, he recognized—and tried to convince the other delegates—that a merchant in Philadelphia (in one of the largest states) and one in Baltimore (in one of the smallest) had more in common with each other than either did with rural farmers in his own state.

Notice, however, that there was one vitally important sectional difference originally overlooked by Madison: slave and free states. The significance of slavery will be discussed in the next chapter, but in the materials below, one can occasionally find an anti-nationalist sentiment expressed by a delegate from one of the large southern states, probably prompted by a fear that a powerful national government might interfere with the South's peculiar institution.

The large state bloc, led by Madison and Wilson, outsmarted itself by refusing to compromise. As early as June 7, Charles Pinckney of South Carolina suggested that the Senate be apportioned on a principle of compressed proportionality, giving the largest states three senators and the smallest one. That compromise offer was repeated, mostly by Pinckney, throughout June and early July, but was consistently rebuffed by Madison and Wilson. The materials below illustrate how this refusal to compromise ultimately led to a deadlock on July 2.

Randolph's original resolutions provided for proportional representation in both houses. He left open whether the representation was to be apportioned according to population or wealth, but the delegates could not address that issue until they resolved whether there would be proportional representation at all. A short debate on May 30 merely resulted in a vote to postpone consideration of the question. George Read of Delaware reminded the Convention that "the deputies from Delaware were restrained by their commission from assenting to any change of the rule of suffrage." In the first of many threats issued by various states, he noted that "in case such a change should be fixed on, it might become their duty to retire from the Convention." The delegates agreed to postpone this thorny issue until William Paterson of New Jersey raised it again on June 9 and the debate began in earnest.

Saturday, June 9

Mr. Patterson moves that the Committee resume the clause relating to the rule of suffrage in the Natl. Legislature.

Mr. Brearly seconds him. He was sorry he said that any question on this point was brought into view.

. . .

Virga. with her sixteen votes will be a solid column indeed, a formidable phalanx. While Georgie with her Solitary vote, and the other little States will be obliged to throw themselves constantly into the scale of some large one, in order to have any weight at all. He had come to the convention with a view of being as useful as he could in giving energy and stability to the federal Government. When the proposition for destroying the equality of votes came forward, he was astonished, he was alarmed. Is it fair then it will be asked that Georgia should have an equal vote with Virga. He would not say it was. What remedy then? One only, that a map of the U. S. be spread out, that all the existing boundaries be erased, and that a new partition of the whole be made into 13 equal parts.

Mr. Patterson considered the proposition for a proportional representation as striking at the existence of the lesser States.

. . .

He said there was no more reason that a great individual State contributing much, should have more votes than a small one contributing little, than that a rich individual citizen should have more votes than an indigent one. If the rateable property of A was to

that of B as 40 to 1, ought A for that reason to have 40 times as many votes as B. Such a principle would never be admitted, and if it were admitted would put B entirely at the mercy of A. As A. has more to be protected than B so he ought to contribute more for the common protection: The same may be said of a large State wch. has more to be protected than a small one.

. . .

N. Jersey will never confederate on the plan before the Committee. She would be swallowed up. He had rather submit to a monarch, to a despot, than to such a fate. He would not only oppose the plan here but on his return home do every thing in his power to defeat it there.

Mr. Wilson hoped if the Confederacy should be dissolved, that a *majority*, that a *minority* of the States would unite for their safety. He entered elaborately into the defence of a proportional representation, stating for his first position that as all authority was derived from the people, equal numbers of people ought to have an equal no. of representatives. This principle had been improperly violated in the Confederation, owing to the urgent circumstances of the time. As to the case of A. & B, stated by Mr. Patterson, he observed that in districts as large as the States, the number of people was the best measure of their comparative wealth. Whether therefore wealth or numbers were to form the ratio it would be the same. Mr. P. admitted persons, not property to be the measure of suffrage. Are not the Citizens of Pena. equal to those of N. Jersey? does it require 150 of the former to balance 50 of the latter?

Monday, June 11

The clause concerning the rule of suffrage in the natl. Legislature postponed on Saturday was resumed.

Mr. Sharman proposed that the proportion of suffrage in the 1st. branch should be according to the respective numbers of free inhabitants; and that in the second branch or Senate, each State should have one vote and no more. He said as the States would remain possessed of certain individual

rights, each State ought to be able to protect itself: otherwise a few large States will rule the rest. The House of Lords in England he observed had certain particular rights under the Constitution, and hence they have an equal vote with the House of Commons that they may be able to defend their rights.

. . .

Mr. King & **Mr. Wilson**, in order to bring the

question to a point moved "that the right of suffrage in the first branch of the national Legislature ought not to be according the rule established in the articles of Confederation, but according to some equitable ratio of representation."

. . .

On the question for agreeing to Mr. Kings and Mr. Wilsons motion it passed in the affirmative
Massts. ay. Ct. ay. N. Y. no. N. J. no. Pa. ay.

Del. no. Md. divd. Va. ay. N. C. ay. S. C. ay. Geo. ay.

. . .

Mr. Wilson & **Mr. Hamilton** moved that the right of suffrage in the 2d. branch ought to be according to the same rule as in the 1st. branch. On this question for making the ratio of representation the same in the 2d. as in the 1st. branch it passed in the affirmative:
Massts. ay. Cont. no. N. Y. no. N. J. no. Pa. ay. Del. no. Md. no. Va. ay. N. C. ay. S. C. ay. Geo. ay.

The delegates also agreed that the rule of representation would be according to "the whole number of white and other free citizens and inhabitants" and "three fifths of all other persons . . . except Indians not paying taxes." Their discussion of this basis for proportional representation will be covered in more detail in chapter 6 (on slavery). The resolutions adopted by the Committee of the Whole on June 13 thus read:

> 7. Resolved that the right of suffrage in the first branch of the national Legislature ought not to be according to the rule established in the articles of confederation; but according to some equitable ratio of representation. . . .
> 8. Resolved that the right of suffrage in the second branch of the national Legislature ought to be according to the rule established for the first.

The New Jersey Plan retained the equal representation of the Articles of Confederation. After that plan was rejected on June 19 (see chapter 2), the delegates began a more thorough consideration of the Randolph Plan. They reached Resolution 7 on June 27, and began three weeks of the most bitter debates of the summer.

It began, on June 27, with Luther Martin's diatribe against the nationalists and their plan. The flamboyant Maryland lawyer spoke for over three hours, quoting long passages from Locke and exhausting even his allies. Madison reported that Martin—who as Maryland's attorney general would later argue *McCulloch v. Maryland* before the Supreme Court—spoke "at great length and with great eagerness," and delivered his discourse "with much diffuseness and & considerable vehemence." William Pierce said of Martin that "[t]his gentleman possesses a good deal of information but he has a very bad delivery, and is so extremely prolix, that he never speaks without tiring the patience of all who hear him." Yates reported that "his arguments were too diffuse, and in many instances desultory, [so that it] was not possible to trace him through the whole, or to methodize his ideas into a systematic or argumentative arrangement."

Martin paused only because, according to Madison, "he was too much exhausted he said to finish his remarks." He began again the next day and continued most of the morning. There are persistent rumors, never substantiated or falsified, that he was drunk during both this Convention speech and the *McCulloch* argument.

The Convention essentially ignored Martin, and began serious consideration of the Randolph resolutions on June 28.

Thursday, June 28

Mr. Lansing & Mr. Dayton moved to strike out "not." so that the 7 art: might read that the rights of suffrage in the 1st. branch ought to be according to the rule established by the Confederation."

. . .

Mr. Williamson. thought that if any political truth could be grounded on mathematical demonstration, it was that if the States were equally sovereign now, and parted with equal proportions of sovereignty, that they would remain equally sovereign. He could not comprehend how the smaller States would be injured in the case, and wished some Gentleman would vouchsafe a solution of it. He observed that the small States, if they had a plurality of votes would have an interest in throwing the burdens off their own shoulders on those of the large ones. He begged that the expected addition of new States from the Westward might be kept in view. They would be small States, they would be poor States, they would be unable to pay in proportion to their numbers; their distance from market rendering the produce of their labour less valuable; they would consequently be tempted to combine for the purpose of laying burdens on commerce & consumption which would fall with greatest weight on the old States.

. . .

Mr. Madison. That it is not necessary to secure the small States agst. the large ones he conceived to be equally obvious: Was a combination of the large ones dreaded? this must arise either from some interest common to Va. Masts. & Pa. & distinguishing them from the other States or from the mere circumstance of similarity of size. Did any such common interest exist? In point of situation they could not have been more effectually separated from each other by the most jealous citizen of the most jealous State. In point of manners, Religion, and the other circumstances which sometimes beget affection between different communities, they were not more assimilated than the other States.—In point of the staple productions they were as dissimilar as any three other States in the Union. The Staple of Masts. was *fish*, of Pa. *flower*, of Va. *Tobo.* Was a combination to be apprehended from the mere circumstance of equality of size? Experience suggested no such danger. The journals of Congs. did not present any peculiar association of these States in the votes recorded.

The vote on the Lansing and Dayton motion was then postponed, "at the request of the Deputies of N. York."

At this point, Franklin rose and addressed the Convention. He was concerned, he said, that after five weeks of "close attendance & continual reasonings with each other," the Convention had been unable to come to agreement. Instead of running from ancient to modern history in search of inspiration, as the delegates had been doing, Franklin suggested that they turn to prayer:

> In this situation of this Assembly, groping as it were in the dark to find political truth, and scarce able to distinguish it when presented to us, how has it happened, Sir, that we have not hitherto once thought of humbly applying to the Father of lights to illuminate our understandings? . . .
>
> I therefore beg leave to move—that henceforth prayers imploring the assistance of Heaven, and its blessings on our deliberations, be held in this Assembly every morning before we proceed to business, and that one or more of the Clergy of this City be requested to officiate in that Service[.]

Roger Sherman seconded Franklin's motion, but it was immediately opposed by virtually every other delegate. They made objections that included the offense that might be given to members of different religions, the likelihood that such a move would be perceived by the public as a move of desperation, and the cost of employing a minister. Randolph tried "to give a favorable aspect to [the] measure" by limiting it to a sermon on July 4 and prayers after that. The delegates were reluctant to offend Franklin but unwilling to accept his motion. Madison reported that ultimately, "[a]fter several unsuccessful attempts for silently postponing the matter by adjourning the adjournment was at length carried without any vote on the motion."

By the next day, Franklin's motion was forgotten, and the delegates immediately returned to the substance of the debate.

Friday, June 29

Doctr. Johnson. The controversy must be endless whilst Gentlemen differ in the grounds of their arguments; Those on one side considering the States as districts of people composing one political Society; those on the other considering them as so many political societies. The fact is that the States do exist as political Societies, and a Govt. is to be formed for them in their political capacity, as well as for the individuals composing them. Does it not seem to follow, that if the States as such are to exist they must be armed with some power of self-defence. This is the idea of [Col. Mason] who appears to have looked to the bottom of this matter. Besides the Aristocratic and other interests, which ought to have the means of defending themselves, the States have their interests as such, and are equally entitled to likes means. On the whole he thought that as in some respects the States are to be considered in their political capacity, and in others as districts of individual citizens, the two ideas embraced on different sides, instead of being opposed to each other, ought to be combined; that in *one* branch the *people*, ought to be represented; in the *other* the *States*.

. . .

Mr. Hamilton: [A]s States are a collection of individual men which ought we to respect most, the rights of the people composing them, or of the artificial beings resulting from the composition. Nothing could be more preposterous or absurd than to sacrifice the former to the latter. It has been sd. that if the smaller States renounce their *equality*, they renounce at the same time their *liberty*. The truth is it is a contest for power, not for liberty. Will the men composing the small States be less free than those composing the larger. The State of Delaware having 40,000 souls will *lose power*, if she has $\frac{1}{10}$ only of the votes allowed to Pa. having 400,000: but will the people of Del: *be less free*, if each citizen has an equal vote with each citizen of Pa.

. . .

Mr. Gerry urged that we never were independent States, were not such now, & never could be even on the principles of the Confederation. The States & the advocates for them were intoxicated with the idea of their *sovereignty*. He was a member of Congress at the time the federal articles were formed. The injustice of allowing each State an equal vote was long insisted on. He voted for it, but it was agst. his Judgment, and under the pressure of public danger, and the obstinacy of the lesser States.

The states then voted six to four (with Maryland equally divided) against Lansing's attempt to force equality of representation in what was to become the House of Representatives. They approved the clause as it stood, by the same vote.

Yates's notes contain a more stirring version than Madison's of parts of Hamilton's speech against equality of representation.

The question, after all is, is it our interest in modifying this general government to sacrifice individual rights to the preservation of the rights of an *artificial* being, called States? There can be no truer principles than this—that every individual of the community at large has an equal right to the protection of government.

Late on Friday, June 29, the delegates turned to the most controversial of Randolph's proposals: proportional representation in the Senate. All that day and the next they debated the issue with little progress. Both the large and small states repeated the arguments they had made with regard to proportional representation in the House. By now, however, the small states were desperate. Ellsworth of Connecticut summed up the views of the small state nationalists:

> Let a strong Executive, a Judiciary & Legislative power be created; but Let not too much be attempted; by which all may be lost.

Several of the small states unsuccessfully pressed for a letter to the executive of New Hampshire, whose delegates had not yet arrived. Madison noted that "it was well understood that the object was to add N. Hamshire to the number of States opposed to the doctrine of proportional representation, which it was presumed from her relative size she must be adverse to."

In addition to the arguments made for and against proportional representation in the House, the delegates battled over whether equality in the Senate would allow a minority of the population to control the majority. These and other reasoned arguments were unsuccessful, and the debates gradually degenerated into threats and counterthreats.

Saturday, June 30

Mr. Wilson: If the minority of the people of America refuse to coalesce with the majority on just and proper principles, if a separation must take place, it could never happen on better grounds. The votes of yesterday agst. the just principle of representation, were as 22 to 90 of the people of America.

. . .

[A]n equality [in the second branch] will enable the minority to controul in all cases whatsoever, the sentiments and interests of the majority. Seven States will controul six: Seven States, according to the estimates that had been used, composed $^{24}/_{90}$ of the whole people. It would be in the power then of less than $\frac{1}{3}$ to overrule $\frac{2}{3}$ whenever a question should happen to divide the States in that manner. Can we forget for whom we are forming a Govern-

ment? Is it for *men*, or for the imaginary beings called *States*? Will our honest Constituents be satisfied with metaphysical distinctions? Will they, ought they to be satisfied with being told that the one third compose the greater number of States? The rule of suffrage ought on every principle to be the same in the 2d. as in the 1st. branch.

. . .

Mr. Elseworth. The capital objection of Mr. Wilson "that the minority will rule the majority" is not true. The power is given to the few to save them from being destroyed by the many. If an equality of votes had been given to them in both branches, the objection might have had weight. Is it a novel thing that the few should have a check on the many?

Madison again denied that the large states had any interests in common, noting for the first time that the "great division of interests . . . did not lie between the large & small States: It lay between the Northern & Southern[.]"

He suggested a new compromise: one house to be proportional not counting slaves at all, and the other to be proportional counting slaves as full inhabitants. "By this arrangement," he said, "the Southern Scale would have the advantage in one House, and the Northern in the other." He neglected to note that Virginia would have the greatest number of delegates in *both* houses under this plan. No other delegate supported him.

Gunning Bedford of Delaware suggested that the votes in the Convention showed the large states banding together to the detriment of the small ones. If the large states were given unequal votes, they would ultimately claim unequal power. "Given the opportunity," he argued, "ambition will not fail to abuse it." Yates's report of Bedford's speech is stark:

> [The large states] insist that although the powers of the general government will be increased, yet it will be for the good of the whole; and although the three great States form nearly a majority of the people of America they never will hurt or injure the lesser states. *I do not, gentlemen, trust you.* If you possess the power, the abuse of it could not be checked; and what then would prevent you from exercising it to our destruction?

At the end of the second day of this fruitless debate, the small states threw down an ultimatum. The smallest of the states was Delaware, and her representative, Gunning Bedford, threatened:

> The Large States dare not dissolve the Confederation. If they do the small ones will find some foreign ally of more honor and good faith, who will take them by the hand and do them justice.

With little further debate, the Convention adjourned for the day.

The next day was a Sunday: the delegates had all day to consider Bedford's threat and to negotiate among themselves. And negotiate they must have, because when they returned on Monday morning, the first thing they did was vote on Ellsworth's pending motion for equality of representation in the Senate.

The five small states voted in favor, as was expected. Massachusetts, Pennsylvania, Virginia, and both Carolinas voted against, also as expected. That five to five tie left Georgia, the last to vote, in control. Up to this point, Georgia had voted as part the large state bloc. With a growing population and vast empty lands, the state expected to take a place in the ranks of the largest states within a few years. But on that Monday morning, July 2, Georgia cast a divided vote: William Houstoun voted against equality in the Senate, and Abraham Baldwin voted in favor. The Convention was deadlocked.

Abraham Baldwin, the man who prevented the large states' victory, was a newcomer to Georgia. He had been born and raised in Connecticut, educated at Yale, and he later tutored there. In 1787, he still had strong ties to Connecticut. Perhaps on that intervening Sunday the Connecticut delegates prevailed on him to change his vote in order to force a compromise. Perhaps he was simply unwilling to use ramrod tactics to forge a union that might quickly dissolve. Madison's notes contain no speeches by Baldwin during the few days of concentrated debate on the matter, but Yates reported that Baldwin spoke on June 29:

> It appears to be agreed that the government we should adopt ought to be energetic and formidable, yet I would guard against the danger of becoming too formidable.

The second branch ought not to be elected as the first. Suppose we take the example of the constitution of Massachusetts, as it is commended for its goodness: There the first branch represents the people, and the second its property.

Whatever Baldwin's reasons, his vote that morning shocked all the delegates into taking an unprecedented step. At General Pinckney's suggestion, they sent the question to a committee, hoping that the smaller body would be able to negotiate an acceptable compromise. As Roger Sherman put it:

We are now at a full stop, and nobody he supposed meant that we should break up without doing something. A committee he thought was most likely to hit on some expedient.

Elbridge Gerry was also in favor of commitment: "Something must be done, or we shall disappoint not only America, but the whole world."

Gouverneur Morris thought a committee advisable not only to resolve the deadlock, but to make other changes as well. His speech on July 2 is an important illustration of his and several other delegates' views on the role of the Senate and on the nature of democratic government.

Monday, July 2

Mr. Gov. Morris thought a Com. adviseable as the Convention had been equally divided. He had a stronger reason also. The mode of appointing the 2d. branch tended he was sure to defeat the object of it. What is this object? to check the precipitation, changeableness, and excesses of the first branch. Every man of observation had seen in the democratic branches of the State Legislatures, precipitation—in Congress changeableness, in every department excesses agst. personal liberty private property & personal safety. What qualities are necessary to constitute a check in this case? *Abilities* and *virtue*, are equally necessary in both branches. Something more then is now wanted. 1. the checking branch must have a personal interest in checking the other branch, one interest must be opposed to another interest. Vices as they exist, must be turned agst. each other. 2. It must have great personal property, it must have the aristocratic spirit; it must love to lord it thro' pride, pride is indeed the great principle that actuates both the poor & the rich. It is this principle which in the former resists, in the latter abuses authority. 3. It should be independent.

. . .

The aristocratic body, should be as independent & as firm as the democratic. If the members of it are to revert to a dependence on the democratic choice, the democratic scale will preponderate. All the guards contrived by America have not restrained the Senatorial branches of the Legislatures from a servile complaisance to the democratic. If the 2d. branch is to be dependent we are better without it. To make it independent, it should be for life. It will then do wrong, it will be said. He believed so: He hoped so. The Rich will strive to establish their dominion & enslave the rest. They always did. They always will. The proper security agst. them is to form them into a separate interest. The two forces will then controul each other.

. . .

It should be considered too how the scheme could be carried through the States. He hoped there was strength of mind eno' in this House to look truth in the face. He did not hesitate therefore to say that loaves & fishes must bribe the Demagogues. They must be made to expect higher offices under the general than the State Govts. A Senate for life will be a noble bait. Without such captivating prospects, the popular leaders will oppose & defeat the plan.

Whether motivated by despair or by mere dissatisfaction, most of the delegates favored commitment, and it passed by a nine to two vote. After electing the members of the committee, the convention adjourned for a two-day recess, "[t]hat time might be given to the Committee, and to such as chose to attend to the celebrations on the anniversary of Independence." On July 4, 1787, while the country celebrated, the Committee of Eleven determined whether the nation's eleventh birthday would be its last.

Topics for Discussion

1. What did the various delegates think was wrong with popular senatorial elections? What differences did they anticipate between a popularly elected Senate and a state-chosen Senate? What benefits did they hope to derive from mediated elections?

2. The nationalists opposed elections by state legislatures partly on the fear that such elections would make a proportional senate too large, and thus create pressure for a non-proportional Senate. But if the people in each state vote directly for their (proportionally allocated) senators, as they would for representatives, how does that alleviate the size problem? Did the nationalists expect that popular elections for senators would be by state? How did they envision senatorial elections in order to achieve a small Senate, proportional representation, and popular elections? What does this tell you about their vision of the Senate?

3. The Seventeenth Amendment, ratified in 1913, requires popular elections for the Senate. What changes between 1787 and 1913 prompted that amendment? Have the problems anticipated by the Convention arisen? If not, why not?

4. Consider Madison's speech on June 6. Can you explain his theory of republican government? Do you agree with it? How does it follow from the philosophy of Locke and Hume, discussed in chapter 1? What did he mean by "factions"?

5. Compare Madison's early preference for popular senatorial elections with his June 6 speech and with his views—discussed in chapter 3—on the role of the Senate in selecting judges. What inconsistencies are there? Can you explain them? How did he envision the Senate? Would popular elections have created the Senate he desired?

6. Note that several delegates argued for popular election on the theory that since the national government would operate on individuals rather than on states, the states did not need to be represented. What conclusions can you draw from the fact that the Convention ultimately decided against popular elections? What effect might your conclusions have on the reading of the Tenth Amendment? In *National League of Cities v. Usery*, 426 U.S. 833, 96 S.Ct. 2465, 49 L.Ed.2d 245 (1976), the Supreme Court held that the Tenth Amendment precluded Congress from requiring states to pay their employees the federal minimum wage. In *Garcia v. San Antonio Metropolitan Transit Authority*, 469 U.S. 528, 105 S.Ct. 1005, 83 L.Ed.2d 1016 (1985), the Supreme Court overruled *National League of Cities* and held that Congress could prohibit states from establishing mandatory retirement for state employees before age seventy. Do the debates shed any light on this crucial federalism question? Does the Seventeenth Amendment help?

7. What exactly did the small states fear from a proportionally allocated Senate? Were they worried only about the large states combining? Were their fears well founded? Has the proportional House of Representatives acted as they feared?

8. Wilson and Ellsworth (among others) disagreed on whether equal representation in the Senate would allow a minority to rule the majority. Who has the better argument? The small state delegates insisted that the large states—despite their disparate interests—would combine forces to the detriment of the small ones. Does Wilson's fear depend on a similar observation about the small states? Did the large states have interests in common? Did the small ones? Consider the demographics of the United States today. What sorts of interests, if any, do the less populous states have in common? The more populous states? Are the small states likely to act in concert in the Senate, voting as a bloc to defeat the votes of the more populous states?

9. Assuming that Wilson was right and that equal representation in the senate allows minority rule, are there any provisions of the Constitution that temper the power of the minority? Do they always work? Under what circumstances might Wilson's concerns be valid? In 1986, President Reagan nominated Daniel Manion for a federal judgeship on the Seventh Circuit. After several procedural complexities, the question came to a final vote in the Senate. Vice President Bush broke the forty-nine to forty-nine tie in favor of confirming Manion. Twenty-three states split their votes: one senator in favor, and one against. Of the twenty-six remaining states (Arizona's senators both abstained) half voted wholly for Manion and half wholly against. However, the thirteen states in favor had a total population of approximately thirty-three million, and the thirteen states against had a total population of approximately sixty-three million. Considering both the legislative debates and the debates over judicial selection (discussed in chapter 3), was Manion's confirmation consistent with the spirit of the Constitution?

BREAKING THE DEADLOCK

The decision of the committee of Eleven was a foregone conclusion: the committee was stacked in favor of equal representation in the Senate. It included one delegate from each state—obviously significant when the very issue the committee was to resolve was whether states should be equally represented in the Senate—and its membership consisted of some of the most able and vocal delegates from the small states, but did not include the most uncompromising firebrands from the large states. The small states were represented by Sherman (replacing Ellsworth, who had been selected but fell ill), Yates (*not* Hamilton), Paterson, Bedford, and Martin. The large state representatives included several delegates with nascent anti-nationalist sentiments, some who were relatively unassuming, and none of those who had been most vehemently opposed to equal representation. Massachusetts was represented by the moderate Gerry (who later became an Anti-Federalist), rather than an outspoken nationalist such as King or Gorham. The Pennsylvanians sent Franklin rather than Wilson or Morris. Franklin, in fact, is believed to have proposed the committee's final compromise, which added to Roger Sherman's early suggestion of different modes of representation in the House and Senate the idea that the Senate be forbidden to originate or amend money bills. North Carolina had no superstars, but sent one of their most obscure delegates, William Davie. South Carolina contributed Rutledge rather than one of the forceful Pinckneys. Georgia sent Abraham Baldwin, the man whose change of vote had deadlocked the Convention in the first place. Virginia's contribution was most telling: ignoring the architects of the Virginia plan, Madison and Randolph, Virginia instead sent George Mason, who would later oppose ratification.

All in all, it was a committee designed to conclude that states should be equally represented in the Senate, and it did so. On Thursday, July 5, the committee gave its report, and the delegates began their debates.

Thursday, July 5

Mr. Gerry delivered in from the Committee appointed on Monday last the following Report.

"The Committee to whom was referred the 8th. Resol. of the Report from the Committee of the whole House, and so much of the 7th. as has not been decided on, submit the following Report: That the subsequent propositions be recommended to the Convention on condition that both shall be generally adopted. I. that in the 1st. branch of the Legislature each of the States now in the Union shall be allowed 1 member for every 40,000 inhabitants of the description reported in the 7th. Resolution of the Come. of the whole House: that each State not containing that number shall be allowed 1 member: that all bills for raising or appropriating money, and for fixing the Salaries of the officers of the Governt. of the U. States shall originate in the 1st. branch of of the Legislature, and shall not be altered or amended by the 2d. branch: and that no money shall be drawn from the public Treasury. but in pursuance of appropriations to be orginiated in the 1st branch" II. That in the 2d. branch each State shall have an equal vote."*

---

*This report was founded on a motion in the Committe made by Dr. Franklin. It was barely acquiesced in by the members from the States opposed to an equality of votes in the 2d. branch and was evidently considered by the members on the other side, as a gaining of their point. A motion was made by Mr. Sherman [he acted in place of Mr. Elseworth who was kept away by indisposition.] In the Committee to the following effect "that each State should have an equal vote in the 2d. branch; provided that no decision therein should prevail unless the majority of States concurring should also comprize a majority of the inhabitants of the U. States." This motion was not much deliberated on nor approved in the Committee. A similar proviso had been proposed in the debates on the articles of Confederation in 1777, to the articles giving certain powers to "nine States." See Journals of Congs. for 1777, p. 462. [Footnote by Madison.]

Mr. Ghorum observed that as the report consisted of propositions mutually conditional he wished to hear some explanations touching the grounds on which the conditions were estimated.

Mr. Gerry. The Committee were of different opinions as well as the Deputations from which the Come. were taken, and agreed to the Report merely in order that some ground of accomodation might be proposed. Those opposed to the equality of votes have only assented conditionally; and if the other side do not generally agree will not be under any obligation to support the Report.

Mr. Wilson thought the Committee had exceeded their powers.

Mr. Martin was for taking the question on the whole report.

Mr. Wilson was for a division of the question: otherwise it wd. be a leap in the dark.

Mr. Madison. could not regard the exclusive privilege of originating money bills as any concession on the side of the small States. Experience proved that it had no effect. If seven States in the upper branch wished a bill to be originated, they might surely find some member from some of the same States in the lower branch who would originate it. The restriction as to amendments was of as little consequence. Amendments could be handed privately by the Senate to members in the other house. Bills could be negatived that they might be sent up in the desired shape.

. . .

Mr. Govr. Morris. thought the form as well as the matter of the Report objectionable. It seemed in the first place to render amendments impracticable. In the next place, it seemed to involve a pledge to agree to the 2d. part if the 1st. shd. be agreed to. He conceived the whole aspect of it to be wrong. He came here as a Representative of America; he flattered himself he came here in some degree as a Representative of the whole human race; for the whole human race will be affected by the proceedings of this Convention. He wished gentlemen to extend their views beyond the present moment of time; beyond the narrow limits of place from which they derive their political origin. If he were to believe some things which he had heard, he should suppose that we were assembled to truck and bargain for our particular States.

.   .   .

This Country must be united. If persuasion does not unite it, the sword will. He begged that this consideration might have its due weight. The scenes of horror attending civil commotion can not be described, and the conclusion of them will be worse than the term of their continuance. The stronger party will then make traytors of the weaker; and the Gallows & Halter will finish the work of the sword. How far foreign powers would be ready to take part in the confusions he would not say. Threats that they will be invited have it seems been thrown out.

.   .   .

Mr. Bedford. He found that what he had said as to the small States being taken by the hand, had been misunderstood; and he rose to explain. He did not mean that the small States would court the aid & interposition of foreign powers. He meant that they would not consider the federal compact as dissolved untill it should be so by the Acts of the large States. In this case The consequence of the breach of faith on their part, and the readiness of the small States to fulfill their engagements, would be that foreign Nations having demands on this Country would find it their interest to take the small States by the hand, in order to do themselves justice. This was what he meant. But no man can foresee to what extremities the small States may be driven by oppres-

sion. He observed also in apology that some allowance ought to be made for the habits of his profession in which warmth was natural & sometimes necessary. But is there not an apology in what was said by [Mr. Govr. Morris] that the sword is to unite: by Mr. Ghorum that Delaware must be annxed to Penna. and N. Jersey divided between Pena. and N. York. To hear such language without emotion, would be to renounce the feelings of a man and the duty of a Citizen.

.   .   .

Mr. Gerry. Tho' he had assented to the Report in the Committee, he had very material objections to it. We were however in a peculiar situation. We were neither the same Nation nor different Nations. We ought not therefore to pursue the one or the other of these ideas too closely. If no compromise should take place what will be the consequence. A secession he foresaw would take place; for some gentlemen seem decided on it; two different plans will be proposed; and the result no man could foresee. If we do not come to some agreement among ourselves some foreign sword will probably do the work for us.

Mr. Mason. The Report was meant not as specific propositions to be adopted; but merely as a general ground of accomodation. There must be some accomodation on this point, or we shall make little further progress in the work. Accomodation was the object of the House in the appointment of the Committee; and of the Committee in the Report they had made. And however liable the Report might be to objections, he thought it preferable to an appeal to the world by the different sides, as had been talked of by some Gentlemen. It could not be more inconvenient to any gentleman to remain absent from his private affairs, than it was for him: but he would bury his bones in this City rather than expose his Country to the Consequences of a dissolution of the Convention without any thing being done.

Without taking a vote on the question of money bills, the Convention then turned to the committee's rule of proportionality for the first branch: one representative for every 40,000 inhabitants, counting slaves as three-fifths. Several delegates objected on the ground that (in Gouverneur Morris's words), "property ought to be taken into the estimate as well as the number of inhabitants." Rutledge agreed; echoing Morris, he stated that "[p]roperty was certainly the principle object of Society." Both of them were also concerned that if population was the sole measure of representation, the thirteen original states would soon be outvoted by the large but poor western states to be carved out of the territories. Rutledge noted: "If number should be made the rule of representation, the Atlantic States will be subjected to the Western." The Convention defeated Rutledge's motion to count property nine to one, but the next day they began arguing again over the rule of apportionment. Charles Pinckney of South Carolina raised yet another question about the rule, suggesting that slaves should be counted equally with freemen.

They finally agreed to send the whole question to a committee of five—Gouverneur Morris, Gorham, Randolph, Rutledge, and King—and returned to the origination of money bills, repeating many of the earlier arguments. Wilson pointed out again that the limitation on origination was meaningless: "If both branches were to say yes or no, it was of little consequence which should say yes or no first, which last." Mason defended the limitation on its merits, suggesting that, as the less democratic branch, the Senate should not have power to spend "the people's money." The limitation eventually passed five states to three (with three states divided).

On Saturday, July 7, the delegates turned to the next part of the report: allowing each state one vote in the Senate. Earlier arguments were again repeated, with delegates from the large and small states taking predictable positions. Gerry and Madison got into a minor wrangle over whether the federal legislature's powers or its method of representation should be considered first. The Convention ultimately agreed to postpone the question until after the Committee of Five reported on the method of representation in the House.

With nothing resolved, the Convention again adjourned for its Sunday break. When they returned on Monday morning, the Committee of Five reported on the rule of representation to be followed in the proportional lower house. In that report, each state was allotted a number of representatives roughly corresponding to population, but no fixed rule was established. The report also authorized Congress, "from time to time," to adjust the allocation "upon principles of wealth and number of inhabitants."

All that week the delegates wrangled over the proper measure of representation in the lower house. Minor issues arose—Madison suggested that at sixty-five members the House was too small and moved unsuccessfully to double the number of representatives allotted each state—but the real dispute was over the basis of representation. Was the popular branch of the legislature to represent people or property? The greatest controversy was over how to count those who had attributes of both: slaves. For that reason, the debates between July 9 and July 13 are only summarized here, and are considered in greater detail in chapter 6.

During that week of July 9, the delegates fought over both principle and politics. Some delegates were still worried that any rule of representation that disregarded property would soon result in the predominance of the future western states over the original thirteen. Others countered that it would be unjust to admit new states on anything less than an equal footing, regardless of their poverty.

Still others argued that as a matter of principle, wealthier states should have greater representation, since protection of property was the fundamental object of society. At one time or another, nine different delegates expressed the view that wealth ought to be represented because government was meant to protect property. James Wilson denied such a conclusion: "Again he could not agree that property was the sole or the primary object of Government & Society. The cultivation and improvement of the human mind was the most noble object."

The Convention resubmitted the issue to a second committee, this time composed of a member from each state. After five solid days of discussing virtually nothing but the ratio of proportional representation, the convention finally approved representation on the basis of population, counting slaves as three-fifths. They required Congress, within six years and every ten years subsequently, to take a census and reapportion accordingly. And they removed any reference to wealth from the various descriptions of the House of Representatives. How they reached these decisions is considered in chapter 6.

On Saturday, July 14, the delegates returned to the issue on which they were still at odds: the rule of apportionment in the Senate.

Saturday, July 14

Mr. Wilson traced the progress of the report through its several stages, remarking yt. when on the question concerning an equality of votes, the House was divided, our Constituents had they voted as their representatives did, would have stood as ⅔ agst. the equality, and ⅓ only in favor of it. This fact would ere long be known, and it will appear that this fundamental point has been carried by ⅓ agst. ⅔.

.   .   .

Mr. L. Martin denies that there were ⅔ agst. the equality of votes. The States that please to call themselves large, are the weekest in the Union. Look at Masts. Look at Virga. Are they efficient States? He was for letting a separation take place if they desired it. He had rather there should be two Confederacies, than one founded on any other principle than an equality of votes in the 2d. branch at least.

Mr. Wilson was not surprised that those who say that a minority is more than the majority should say that the minority is stronger than the majority. He supposed that the next assertion will be that they are richer also; though he hardly expected it would be persisted in when the States shall be called on for taxes & troops—

.   .   .

Mr. Pinkney moved that instead of an equality of votes, the States should be represented in the 2d. branch as follows: N. H. by. 2. members. Mas. 4. R. I. 1. Cont. 3. N. Y. 3. N. J. 2. Pa. 4. Del 1. Md. 3. Virga. 5. N. C. 3. S. C. 3. Geo. 2. making in the whole 36.

Mr. Wilson seconds the motion

Mr. Dayton. The smaller States can never give up their equality. For himself he would in no event yield that security for their rights.

Mr. Sherman urged the equality of votes not so much as a security for the small States; as for the State Govts. which could not be preserved unless they were represented & had a negative in the Genl. Government. He had no objection to the members in the 2d. b. voting per capita, as had been suggested by [Mr. Gerry]

Mr. Madison concurred in this motion of Mr. Pinkney as a reasonable compromise.

Mr. Gerry said he should like the motion, but could see no hope of success. An accomodation must take place, and it was apparent from what had been seen that it could not do so on the ground of the motion. He was utterly against a partial confederacy, leaving other States to accede or not accede; as had been intimated.

Mr. King said it was always with regret that he differed from his colleagues, but it was his duty to differ from [Mr. Gerry] on this occasion. He considered the proposed Government as substantially and formally, a General and National Government over the people of America. There never will be a case in which it will act as a federal Government on the States and not on the individual Citizens. And is it not a clear principle that in a free Govt. those who are to be the objects of a Govt. ought to influence the operations of it? What reason can be assigned why the same rule of representation sd. not prevail in the 2d. branch as in the 1st.? He could conceive none.

After further arguments in the same vein, the Convention voted against Pinckney's motion for compressed proportionality in the Senate and adjourned without voting on the committee report. King wrote in his notes: "This Question was taken and to my mortification by the vote of Massachusetts lost."

Another Sunday came, affording another opportunity for negotiation out of doors. On Monday morning, July 16, the delegates began by taking a vote on the committee report. It passed, five states to four. The large states had two defections, which cost them the vote: Massachusetts was divided (Gerry and Strong in favor, King and Gorham against), and North Carolina voted in favor (except Spaight). Two weeks to the day after their deadlock on representation in the Senate, the Convention agreed to a compromise that has lasted ever since.

Later that day, and early the next, the losers made their last feeble attempts to regain the advantage.

Monday, July 16

Mr. Randolph. The vote of this morning [involving an equality of suffrage in 2d. branch] had embarrassed the business extremely.

. . .

[H]e wished the Convention might adjourn, that the large States might consider the steps proper to be taken in the present solemn crisis of the business, and that the small States might also deliberate on the means of conciliation.

. . .

Mr. Rutlidge could see no need of an adjournt. because he could see no chance of a compromise. The little States were fixt. They had repeatedly & solemnly declared themselves to be so. All that the large States then had to do, was to decide whether they would yield or not. For his part he conceived that altho' we could not do what we thought best, in itself, we ought to do something. Had we not better keep the Govt. up a little longer, hoping that another Convention will supply our omissions, than abandon every thing to hazard. Our Constituents will be very little satisfied with us if we take the latter course.

Mr. Randolph & **Mr. King** renewed the motion to adjourn till tomorrow.

On the question. Mas. ay. Cont. no. N. J. ay. Pa. ay. Del. no. Md. ay. Va. ay. N. C. ay, S. C. ay. Geo. divd.

Adjourned

On the morning following before the hour of the convention a number of the members from the larger States, by common agreement met for the purpose of consulting on the proper steps to be taken in consequence of the vote in favor of an equal Representation in the 2d. branch, and the apparent inflexibility of the smaller States on that point. Several members from the latter States also attended. The time was wasted in vague conversation on the subject, without any specific proposition or agreement. It appeared indeed that the opinions of the members who disliked the equality of votes differed so much as to the importance of that point, and as to the policy of risking a failure of any general act of the Convention, by inflexibly opposing it.

. . .

It is probable that the result of this consultation satisfied the smaller States that they had nothing to apprehend from a union of the larger, in any plan whatever agst. the equality of votes in the 2d. branch.

Tuesday, July 17

Mr. Governr. Morris. moved to reconsider the whole Resolution agreed to yesterday concerning the constitution of the 2 branches of the Legislature.

. . .

[T]his motion was not seconded. [It was probably approved by several members, who either de-spaired of success, or were apprehensive that the attempt would inflame the jealousies of the smaller States.]

With the failure of Morris's motion, the Convention closed the book on what was perhaps the most difficult compromise of the summer. One last change completed it. On July 23, the delegates agreed for the first time that senators should vote *per capita* rather than by state. This was suggested by Gouverneur Morris and Rufus King, and made the equality of votes in the Senate somewhat more palatable to the large states.

A few incidental changes were made later. On August 8, after Madison objected that one representative for every forty thousand inhabitants would quickly produce a legislature of unmanageable size, the Convention changed the formula to read "not exceeding 1 for every 40,000." Later the same day they added, without debate or dissent, a clause guaranteeing each state at least one representative.

On September 8, they softened the limitation on money bills and allowed the Senate to amend such bills, although that body was still prohibited from originating them. On September 15, they modified Article V to prohibit future amendments depriving any state of its equal representation in the Senate. And on the last day of the Convention, September 17, after the Constitution had already been printed and was ready to be signed, they made one last change. Gorham moved to change the proportion of representation in the House from not more than one for every forty thousand to not more than one for every thirty thousand. Whether this previously debated change would have succeeded on its own merits, or whether it would have embroiled the delegates in further wrangling, we will never know. For the first and only time during the Convention, President Washington entered the discussion, supporting Gorham's motion. Washington's stature guaranteed immediate and unanimous passage of Gorham's motion.

CONGRESSIONAL POWERS

The delegates had much less difficulty with the powers of the legislature than they did with its make-up. Most of the delegates agreed that the economic chaos of the 1780s was due to congressional impotence; thus there was little debate about many of the powers of Congress. Only two issues evoked much controversy: whether Congress should have the power to veto state laws, and the extent to which additional congressional powers were implied by the enumerated ones.

The Randolph resolutions gave broad but vague powers to the Congress.

6. Resolved that each branch ought to possess the right of originating Acts; that the National Legislature ought to be impowered to enjoy the Legislative Rights vested in Congress by the Confederation & moreover to legislate in all cases to which the separate States are incompetent, or in which the harmony of the United States may be interrupted by the exercise of individual legislation; to negative all laws passed by the several States, contravening in the opinion of the National Legislature the articles of Union; and to call forth the force of the Union against any members of the Union failing to fulfill its duty under the articles thereof.

Both the breadth and vagueness of the resolution troubled some delegates. Most controversial, however, was the power given to Congress to negative state laws.

Thursday, May 31

On the proposition for giving "Legislative power in all cases to which the State Legislatures were individually incompetent."

Mr. Pinkney & **Mr. Rutledge** objected to the vagueness of the term *incompetent*, and said they could not well decide how to vote until they should see an exact enumeration of the powers comprehended by this definition.

Mr. Butler repeated his fears that we were running into an extreme in taking away the powers of the States, and called on Mr. Randolph for the extent of his meaning.

Mr. Randolph disclaimed any intention to give indefinite powers to the national Legislature, declaring that he was entirely opposed to such an inroad on the State jurisdictions, and that he did not think any considerations whatever could ever change his determination. His opinion was fixed on this point.

Mr. Madison said that he had brought with him into the Convention a strong bias in favor of an enumeration and definition of the powers necessary to be exercised by the national Legislature; but had also brought doubts concerning its practicability. His wishes remained unaltered; but his doubts had become stronger. What his opinion might ultimately be he could not yet tell. But he should shrink from nothing which should be found essential to such a form of Govt. as would provide for the safety, liberty and happiness of the community. This being the end of all our deliberations, all the necessary means for attaining it must, however reluctantly, be submitted to.

On the question for giving powers, in cases to which the States are not competent, Massts. ay. Cont. divd. [Sharman no Elseworth ay] N. Y. ay. N. J. ay. Pa. ay. Del. ay. Va. ay. N. C. ay. S. Carolina ay. Georga. ay.

On Friday, June 8, the delegates reconsidered the clause giving the national legislature a veto over state laws. Randolph's proposal was limited to state laws that might violate the federal Constitution, but Pinkney urged that it be strengthened to give the national legislature a veto over *all* state laws. Madison immediately seconded Pinkney's motion, suggesting that a veto was "the mildest expedient that could be devised" for keeping recalcitrant states in line. Several delegates objected to the breadth of Pinkney's proposal and pointed out the practical difficulties of submitting all state laws for congressional approval. Williamson noted specifically that he was "against giving a power that might restrain the States from regulating their internal police." Perhaps that remark convinced the southernmost trio to defect from the large-state bloc. In any case, only Massachusetts, Pennsylvania, and Virginia voted in favor of Pinkney's proposal, and the plan submitted by the Committee of the Whole to the Convention was almost identical to Randolph's original resolutions regarding the powers of legislature.

Before the Convention began further discussion of legislative powers, however, the controversy over apportionment came to a head. The delegates did not turn back to the question of legislative powers until July 16, after voting affirmatively on the great compromise.

Monday, July 16

The 1st member [of the sixth resolution] "That the Nat'l Legislature ought to possess the Legislative Rights vested in Cong. by the Confederation." was agreed to nem. Con.

The next, "And moreover to legislate in all cases to which the separate States are incompetent; or in which the harmony of the U. S. may be interrupted by the exercise of individual legislation," being read for a question

Mr. Butler calls for some explanation of the extent of this power: particularly of the word *incompetent*. The vagueness of the terms rendered it impossible for any precise judgment to be formed.

Mr. Ghorum. The vagueness of the terms constitutes the propriety of them. We are now establishing general principles, to be extended hereafter into details which will be precise & explicit.

Mr. Rutlidge, urged the objection started by Mr. Butler and moved that the clause should be committed to the end that a specification of the powers comprised in the general terms, might be reported.

On the question for a commitment, the States were equally divided.

Mas. no. Cont. ay. N. J. no. Pa. no. Del. no. Md. ay. Va. ay. N. C. no. S. C. ay. Geo. ay. So it was lost.

Tuesday, July 17

Mr. Sherman observed that it would be difficult to draw the line between the powers of the Genl. Legislatures, and those to be left with the States; that he did not like the definition contained in the Resolution, and proposed in place of the words "of individual Legislation" line 4. inclusive, to insert "to make laws binding on the people of the United States in all cases which may concern the common interests of the Union; but not to interfere with the Government of the individual States in any matters of internal police which respect the Govt. of such States only, and wherein the general welfare of the U. States is not concerned."

Mr. Wilson 2ded. the amendment as better expressing the general principle.

Mr. Govr. Morris opposed it. The internal police, as it would be called & understood by the States ought to be infringed in many cases, as in the case of paper money & other tricks by which Citizens of other States may be affected.

Mr. Sherman, in explanation of his idea read an enumeration of powers, including the power of levying taxes on trade, but not the power of *direct taxation*.

Mr. Govr. Morris remarked the omission, and inferred that for the deficiencies of taxes on consumption, it must have been the meaning of Mr. Sherman, that the Genl. Govt. should recur to quotas & requisitions, which are subversive to the idea of Govt.

Mr. Sherman acknowledged that his enumeration did not include direct taxation. Some provision he supposed must be made for supplying the deficiency of other taxation, but he had not formed any.

On Question of Mr. Sherman's motion, it passed in the negative

Mas. no. Cont. ay. N. J. no. Pa. no. Del. no. Md. ay. Va. no. N. C. no. S. C. no. Geo. no.

Mr. Bedford moved that the 2d. member of Resolution 6. be so altered as to read "and moreover to legislate in all cases for the general interests of the Union, and also in those to which the States are separately incompetent," or in which the harmony of the U. States may be interrupted by the exercise of individual Legislation."

Mr. Govr. Morris 2ds. the motion

Mr. Randolph. This is a formidable idea indeed. It involves the power of violating all the laws and constitutions of the States, and of intermeddling with their police. The last member of the sentence is also superfluous, being included in the first.

Mr. Bedford. It is not more extensive or formidable than the clause as it stands: *no state* being *separately* competent to legislate for the *general interest* of the Union.

On question for agreeing to Mr. Bedford's motion, it passed in the affirmative.

Mas. ay. Cont. no. N. J. ay. Pa. ay. Del. ay. Md. ay. Va. no. N. C. ay. S. C. no. Geo. no.

On the sentence as amended, it passed in the affirmative.

Mas. ay. Cont. ay. N. J. ay. Pa. ay. Del. ay. Md. ay. Va. ay, N. C. ay. S. C. no. Geo. no.

The next. "To negative all laws passed by the several States contravening in the opinion of the Nat: Legislature the articles of Union, or any treaties subsisting under the authority of ye. Union"

Mr. Govr. Morris opposed this power as likely to be terrible to the States, and not necessary, if sufficient Legislative authority should be given to the Genl. Government.

Mr. Sherman thought it unnecessary, as the Courts of the States would not consider as valid any law contravening the Authority of the Union, and which the legislature would wish to be negatived.

Mr. L. Martin considered the power as improper & inadmissible. Shall all the laws of the States be sent up to the Genl. Legislature before they shall be permitted to operate?

Mr. Madison Confidence can not be put in the State Tribunals as guardians of the National authority and interests. In all the States these are more or less dependt. on the Legislatures. In Georgia they are appointed annually by the Legislature. In R. Island the Judges who refused to execute an unconstitutional law were displaced, and others substituted, by the Legislature who would be willing instruments of the wicked & arbitrary plans of their masters. A power of negativing the improper laws of the States is at once the most mild & certain means of perserving the harmony of the system.

. . .

Mr. Sherman. Such a power involves a wrong principle, to wit, that a law of a State contrary to the articles of the Union, would if not negatived, be valid & operative.

Mr. Pinkney urged the necessity of the Negative.

On the question for agreeing to the power of negativing laws of States &c" it passed in the negative.

Mas. ay. Ct. no. N. J. no. Pa. no. Del. no. Md. no. Va. ay. N. C. ay. S. C. no Geo. no.

The Convention thus sent to the Committee on Detail a brief and unilluminating description of the powers of Congress. What they got back was a masterpiece.

As the debates excerpted above illustrate, some delegates wanted an enumeration of powers and others were content with general principles. The Committee on Detail chose the former course and produced, in its Article VII, section 1 [reprinted at page 424], an enumeration that contained substantially all of the powers that were ultimately listed in Article I, section 8. The delegates spent only a few days on these powers, and most of the provisions were approved "nem. con."—without opposition. Even the necessary and proper clause, which would cause such rancor later, was accepted with little debate.

They began by debating whether Congress should have the power to tax exports; the Southern states were concerned that Congress might use the power to the South's disadvantage. The question was ultimately left open (to be resolved in connection with the tax on the slave trade, discussed in chapter 6).

The delegates then turned to the other clauses of the Article on congressional power. Two things are of special interest in their debates: the lack of controversy over the particular provisions, and the discussions of implied powers. The considerable legal skills of the various delegates are perhaps most evident in these discussions of technical, largely nonpolitical details.

Thursday, August 16

Clause for regulating commerce with foreign nations &c. agreed to nem. con.

for coining money. agd. to nem. con.

for regulating foreign coin. do. do.

for fixing the standard of weights & measures. do. do.

"To establish post-offices." **Mr. Gerry** moved to add, and post-roads. **Mr. Mercer** 2ded. & on question

N. H. no. Mas. ay. Ct. no. N. J. no. Pena. no. Del. ay. Md. ay. Va. ay N. C. no. S. C. ay. Geo. ay.

Mr. Govr. Morris moved to strike out "and emit bills on the credit of the U. States"—If the United States had credit such bills would be unnecessary: if they had not, unjust & useless.

. . .

Col. Mason had doubts on the subject. Congs. he thought would not have the power unless it were expressed. Though he had a mortal hatred to paper money, yet as he could not foresee all emergences, he was unwilling to tie the hands of the Legislature. He observed that the late war could not have been carried on, had such a prohibition existed.

. . .

On the motion for striking out

N. H. ay. Mas. ay. Ct. ay. N. J. no. Pa. ay. Del. ay. Md. no. Va. ay* N. C. ay. S. C. ay. Geo. ay.

The clause for borrowing money, agreed to nem. con.

---

*This vote in the affirmative by Virga. was occasioned by the acquiescence of Mr. Madison who became satisfied that striking out the words would not disable the Govt. from the use of public notes as far as they would be safe & proper; & would only cut off the pretext for a paper currency, and particularly for making the bills a tender either for public or private debts. [Footnote by Madison.]

Friday, August 17

Art VII. Sect. 1. resumed.

. . .

"To constitute inferior tribunals" agreed to nem. con.

. . .

"To subdue a rebellion in any State, on the application of its legislature."

Mr. Pinkney moved to strike out "on the application of its legislature"

Mr. Govr. Morris 2ds.

Mr. L. Martin opposed it as giving a dangerous & unnecessary power. The consent of the State ought to precede the introduction of any extraneous force whatever.

Mr. Mercer supported the opposition of Mr. Martin.

Mr. Elseworth proposed to add after "legislature" "or Executive."

Mr. Govr. Morris. The Executive may possibly be at the head of the Rebellion. The Genl. Govt. should enforce obedience in all cases where it may be necessary.

Mr. Elseworth. In many cases The Genl. Govt. ought not to be able to interpose, unless called upon. He was willing to vary his motion so as to read, "or without it when the legislature cannot meet."

Mr. Gerry was agst. letting loose the myrmidons of the U. States on a State without its own consent. The States will be the best Judges in such cases.

More blood would have been spilt in Massts. in the late insurrection, if the Genl. authority had intermeddled.

Mr. Langdon was for striking out as moved by Mr. Pinkney. The apprehension of the national force, will have a salutary effect in preventing insurrections.

Mr. Randolph. If the Natl. Legislature is to judge whether the State legislature can or cannot meet, that amendment would make the clause as objectionable as the motion of Mr. Pinkney.

Mr. Govr. Morris. We are acting a very strange part. We first form a strong man to protect us, and at the same time wish to tie his hands behind him, The legislature may surely be trusted with such a power to preserve the public tranquility.

On the motion to add "or without it [application] when the legislature cannot meet"

N. H. ay. Mas. no. Ct. ay. Pa. divd. Del. no. Md. no. Va. ay. N. C. divd. S. C. ay. Geo. ay. So agreed to—

Mr. Madison and **Mr. Dickenson** moved to insert as explanatory, after "State'—"against the Government thereof" There might be a rebellion agst. the U. States—which was Agreed to nem. con.

On the clause as amended

N. H. ay. Mas abst. Ct. ay. Pen. abst. Del. no. Md. no. Va. ay. N. C. no. S. C. no. Georg. ay—so it was lost.

"To make war"

Mr. Pinkney opposed the vesting this power in the Legislature. Its proceedings were too slow. It wd. meet but once a year. The Hs. of Reps. would be too numerous for such deliberations. The Senate would be the best depositary, being more acquainted with foreign affairs, and most capable of proper resolutions. If the States are equally represented in Senate, so as to give no advantage to large States, the power will notwithstanding be safe, as the small have their all at stake in such cases as well as the large States. It would be singular for one authority to make war, and another peace.

Mr. Butler. The objections agst. the Legislature lie in great degree agst. the Senate. He was for vesting the power in the President, who will have all the requisite qualities, and will not make war but when the Nation will support it.

Mr. Madison and **Mr. Gerry** moved to insert "declare," striking out "make" war; leaving to the Executive the power to repel sudden attacks.

Mr. Sharman thought it stood very well. The Executive shd. be able to repel and not to commence war. "Make" better than "declare" the latter narrowing the power too much.

Mr. Gerry never expected to hear in a republic a motion to empower the Executive alone to declare war.

Mr. Elsworth. there is a material difference between the cases of making *war* and making *peace*. It shd. be more easy to get out of war, than into it. War also is a simple and overt declaration. peace attended with intricate & secret negociations.

Mr. Mason was agst. giving the power of war to the Executive, because not safely to be trusted with it; or to the Senate, because not so constructed as to be entitled to it. He was for clogging rather than facilitating war; but for facilitating peace. He preferred "*declare*" to "*make*."

On the motion to insert *declare*—in place of *make*, it was agreed to.

N. H. no. Mas. abst. Cont. no.* Pa. ay. Del. ay. Md. ay. Va. ay. N. C. ay. S. C. ay. Geo. ay.

---

*On the remark by Mr. King that "*make*" war might be understood to "conduct" it which was an Executive function. Mr. Elseworth gave up his objection. and the vote of Cont. was changed to—ay. [Footnote by Madison.]

Saturday, August 18

[T]he House proceeded to the clause "To raise armies."

Mr. Ghorum moved to add "and support" after "raise." Agreed to nem. con. and then the clause agreed to nem. con. as amended

Mr. Gerry took notice that there was no check here agst. standing armies in time of peace. The existing Congs. is so constructed that it cannot of itself maintain an army. This wd. not be the case under the new system. The people were jealous on this head, and great opposition to the plan would spring from such an omission. He suspected that preparations of force were now making agst. it. [he seemed to allude to the activity of the Govr. of N. York at this crisis in disciplining the militia of that State.] He thought an army dangerous in time of peace & could never consent to a power to keep up an indefinite number. He proposed that there shall not be kept up in time of peace more than _____ thousand troops. His idea was that the blank should be filled with two or three thousand.

Instead of "to build and equip fleets"—"to provide & maintain a navy" agreed to nem. con. as a more convenient definition of the power.

"To make rules for the Government and regulation of the land & naval forces," added from the existing Articles of Confederation.

Mr. L. Martin and **Mr. Gerry** now regularly moved "provided that in time of peace the army shall not consist of more than _____ thousand men."

Genl. Pinkney asked whether no troops were ever to be raised untill an attack should be made on us?

At this point, George Washington is rumored to have quipped that the Constitution should also provide that no foreign army of more than three thousand men be permitted to invade the United States. The motion to limit the size of the army was quickly rejected, and the Convention turned to miscellaneous other matters.

Monday, August 20

Mr. Mason moved to enable Congress "to exact sumptuary laws." No Government can be maintained unless the manners be made consonant to it. Such a discretionary power may do good and can do no harm. A proper regulation of excises & of trade may do a great deal but it is best to have an express provision. It was objected to sumptuary laws that they were contrary to nature. This was a vulgar error. The love of distinction it is true is natural; but the object of sumptuary laws is not to extinguish this principle but to give it a proper direction.

Mr. Elseworth. The best remedy is to enforce taxes & debts. As far as the regulation of eating & drinking can be reasonable, it is provided for in the power of taxation.

Mr. Govr. Morris argued that sumptuary laws tended to create a landed Nobility, by fixing in the great-landholders and their posterity their present possessions.

Mr. Gerry. the law of necessity is the best sumptuary law.

On Motion of Mr. Mason "as to Sumptuary laws" N. H. no. Mas. no. Cont. no. N. J. no. Pa. ay. Del. ay. Md. ay. Va. no. N. C. no. S. C. no. Geo. ay.

"And to make all laws necessary and proper for carrying into execution the foregoing powers, and all other powers vested, by this Constitution, in the Government of the U. S. or any department or officer thereof."

Mr. Madison and **Mr. Pinkney** moved to insert between "laws" and "necessary" "and establish all offices," it appearing to them liable to cavil that the latter was not included in the former.

Mr. Govr. Morris, Mr. Wilson, Mr. Rutledge and **Mr. Elseworth** urged that the amendment could not be necessary.

On the motion for inserting "and establish all offices"

N. H. no. Mas. ay. Cont. no. N. J. no. Pa. no. Del. no. Md. ay. Va. no. N. C. no. S. C. no. Geo. no.

The clause as reported was then agreed to nem. con.

On August 23, Charles Pinckney moved to reinsert a provision giving the national legislature the power to veto state laws. His proposal was given short shrift by all except Madison and Wilson. Williamson said that discussing an already defeated provision was "a waste of time." Rutledge commented: "If nothing else, this alone would damn and ought to damn the Constitution." In the face of almost unanimous opposition, Pinckney withdrew his motion.

In early September, the delegates began their final discussions. The question of implied powers, which had been raised obliquely in earlier discussions, began to surface again. James McHenry reported an interesting questions on September 1, on which Madison's notes are unilluminating.

> Is it proper to declare all the navigable waters or rivers and within the U.S. common high ways? Perhaps a power to restrain any State from demanding tribute from citizens of another State in such cases is comprehended in the power to regulate trade between State and State.

McHenry also reported on September 6 an out-of-doors conversation:

> Spoke to Gov Morris Fitzimmons and Mr. Goram to insert a power in the confederation enabling the legislature to erect piers for protection of shipping in winter and to preserve the navigation of harbours. Mr. Gohram against. The other two gentlemen for it. Mr. Gov: thinks it may be done under the words of the 1 clause 1 sect 7 art. amended—"and provide for the common defense and general welfare." If this comprehends such a power, it goes to authorise the legisl. to grant exclusive privileges to trading companies etc.

Madison reported similar debates regarding implied powers on September 14.

Friday, September 14

Docr. Franklin moved to add after the words "post roads" Art. I. Sect. 8. "a power to provide for cutting canals where deemed necessary"

Mr. Wilson 2ded. the motion

Mr. Sherman objected. The expence in such cases will fall on the U. States, and the benefit accrue to the places where the canals may be cut.

Mr. Wilson. Instead of being an expence to the U. S. they may be made a source of revenue.

Mr. Madison suggested an enlargement of the motion into a power "to grant charters of incorporation where the interest of the U. S. might require & the legislative provisions of individual States may be incompetent." His primary object was however to secure an easy communication between the States which the free intercourse now to be opened, seemed to call for. The political obstacles being removed, a removal of the natural ones as far as possible ought to follow. **Mr. Randolph** 2ded. the proposition

Mr. King thought the power unnecessary.

Mr. Wilson. It is necessary to prevent *a State* from obstructing the *general* welfare.

Mr. King. The States will be prejudiced and divided into parties by it. In Philada. & New York, It will be referred to the establishment of a Bank, which has been a subject of contention in those Cit-

ies. In other places it will be referred to mercantile monopolies.

Mr. Wilson mentioned the importance of facilitating by canals, the communication with the Western Settlements. As to Banks he did not think with Mr. King that the power in that point of view would excite the prejudices & parties apprehended. As to mercantile monopolies they are already included in the power to regulate trade.

Col: Mason was for limiting the power to the single case of Canals. He was afraid of monopolies of every sort, which he did not think were by any means already implied by the Constitution as supposed by Mr. Wilson.

The motion being so modified as to admit a distinct question specifying & limited to the case of canals,

N. H. no. Mas. no. Ct. no. N. J. no. Pa. ay. Del. no. Md. no. Va. ay. N. C. no. S. C. no. Geo. ay.

The other part fell of course, as including the power rejected.

Mr. Madison & **Mr. Pinkney** then moved to insert in the list of powers vested in Congress a power—"to establish an University, in which no preferences or distinctions should be allowed on account of Religion."

Mr. Wilson supported the motion

Mr. Govr. Morris. It is not necessary. The exclusive power at the Seat of Government, will reach the object.

On the question

N. H. no. Mas. no. Cont. divd. Dr. Johnson ay. Mr. Sherman no. N. J. no. Pa. ay. Del. no. Md. no. Va. ay. N. C. ay. S. C. ay. Geo. no.

Thus the Convention ultimately left the powers of Congress open-ended.

Miscellaneous other issues regarding the legislature had been resolved earlier. The Convention decided after considerable debate that the legislators should be paid out of the federal treasury rather than by their respective states. All the delegates recognized that dependence on their states for salaries would make the federal legislators subject to greater state control. The dispute was between those who desired such control and those who did not. General Pinckney offered another possibility. He proposed that senators not be paid at all:

> As this . . . branch was meant to represent the wealth of the Country, it ought to be composed of persons of wealth; and if no allowance was to be made the wealthy alone would undertake the service.

He was seconded by Franklin and defeated by the narrow margin of a single state.

The delegates also argued strenuously about whether property qualifications ought to be set for either voters or office-holders. Here the issue was similar to the dispute over representation: to what extent should wealth be represented in the national legislature? Those who argued against property qualifications won their point primarily because the qualifications for voting so differed in the various states that setting a uniform national standard would have been difficult and controversial, as it might have disenfranchised previously qualified citizens in some states.

Other qualifications for members of Congress—age, citizenship, and residency—were little discussed. James Wilson would have preferred not to include a minimum age for representatives and pointed to several men who had "rendered [significant services] in high stations to the public before the age of 25." George Mason defended the age limit: "It had been said that Congress had proved a good school for our young men. It might be so for any thing he knew but if it were, he chose that they should bear the expence of their own education."

Setting the terms of office for senators and representatives gave the Convention some difficulty. Almost all of the delegates agreed that members of the House, as representatives of the people, should have short terms of office, and it was not hard to agree on two-year terms.

There was greater controversy over the Senate. Although most delegates felt that this deliberative body, because of the need for wisdom and stability, should be made up of members with relatively long terms, they could not initially agree on a length. They proposed terms that ranged from three years to life. On June 25 they had already decided that the terms of office of one-third of the senators should expire at a time (the principle of rotation that found its way into the final document). After a short debate, the delegates agreed that seven years was the most appropriate length for a senator's term. At that point, Hugh Williamson of North Carolina, who had once been a professor of mathematics at the College of Philadelphia (which later became the University of Pennsylvania), made an important point: "Mr. Williamson suggest[ed] '6 years' as more convenient for Rotation than 7 years." The other delegates conceded the arithmetical justification, and voted to delete the reference to seven years.

This left them with a choice of either six or nine years. On June 26, Madison gave an impassioned speech in favor of the longer term. In it, he reveals his views of the purposes of the Senate.

Tuesday, June 26

Mr. Madison. In order to judge of the form to be given to this institution, it will be proper to take a view of the ends to be served by it. These were first to protect the people agst. their rulers: secondly to protect the people agst. the transient impressions into which they themselves might be led. A people deliberating in a temperate moment, and with the experience of other nations before them, on the plan of Govt. most likely to secure their happiness, would first be aware, that those chargd. with the public happiness, might betray their trust. An obvious precaution agst. this danger wd. be to divide the trust between different bodies of men, who might watch & check each other.

.   .   .

It wd. next occur to such a people, that they themselves were liable to temporary errors, thro' want of information as to their true interest, and that men chosen for a short term, & employed but a small portion of that in public affairs, might err from the same cause. This reflection wd. naturally suggest that the govt. be so constituted, as that one of its branches might have an oppt. of acquiring a competent knowledge of the public interests.

Madison's position was accepted by only three states (Virginia, Pennsylvania, and Delaware), and the convention settled on six years.

Another issue that troubled the delegates was the extent to which members of Congress should be precluded from holding other national offices during or after their terms. Many delegates were concerned about corruption; they suggested that legislators would use their positions for personal gain. Some delegates wished to preclude legislators from ever holding any other national office. Others argued that this would prevent good men from serving their country. They compromised by prohibiting the legislators from holding other national offices during their terms or holding offices afterward that had been created or financially improved during their terms.

Finally, there were many debates about the exact procedures that should be followed in cases of impeachment. Some delegates mistrusted the Senate, and some the House. Many were worried that neither branch would have enough firmness of purpose to oppose the president. A few were concerned that providing for impeachment would subordinate the president to the legislature. The Convention in fact could not reach agreement on most of the issues arising out of impeachment procedures. The Committee on Detail thus forged on its own the compromise provisions that appear in the Constitution. Although there was some grumbling, the Committee's basic ideas were accepted.

Through a combination of threats, concessions, compromise and cool deliberation, the provisions of Article I were hammered out over the course of four difficult months.

Topics for Discussion

1. Consider the great compromise. Why should states be represented in the federal legislature? Are you persuaded by Wilson's and Hamilton's argument that only natural beings, not artificial entities, should be represented? Why or why not? How does state representation in the Senate—whether by election or appointment—fit into theories of republican government?

2. Why did the great compromise succeed? The small states disliked proportional representation in the House; the large states disliked equal representation in the Senate. The populists disliked mediated elections; the republicans disliked limiting the more deliberative—and the more carefully watched—Senate. The aristocrats disliked taking money decisions away from the wealthy Senate. If everybody disliked something, why did it pass?

3. With the benefit of hindsight, would you support equal representation in the Senate? Assume, as the delegates did, that the Convention would have failed if the small states were not pacified. Can you propose other provisions to counteract the large states' fears about equal representation in the Senate? Consider especially the problem of the Manion confirmation, noted on page 128.

4. Note that a crucial part of the great compromise—the provision limiting Senate action on money bills— passed on July 6 by a vote of five states in favor, three against, and three divided. Population aside, that still meant that a minority of the states present supported the measure. According to Madison, "A Question was then raised whether the question was carried in the affirmative: there being but 5 ays out of 11 States present." The Convention voted nine states to two (Virginia and Massachusetts) that the previous vote did count as an affirmative decision. Were they right to do so? Why do you think that Pennsylvania, which voted against the money bill limit, voted in favor of accepting the affirmative vote? What about the divided states? Recall the discussion in chapter 2 about the mores of eighteenth-century gentlemen. Does that help to explain the nine to two vote?

5. Notice Wilson's reaction on July 5 to the committee report: "[He] thought the Committee had exceeded their powers." Compare that to his position on the powers of the Convention in chapter 2.

6. Based on the material in this chapter, can you describe the purposes each delegate expected or hoped the Senate would serve? How did each delegate's preference for a particular mode of election, particular terms, and particular powers satisfy his goal for the Senate's function? Were nationalists or antinationalists more "democratic"? Why? Recall the discussion in chapter 1 of the differences between American and British legislatures in the 1760s and 1770s. Had anything changed by 1787?

7. Does the current Senate fulfill the role envisioned by any member of the Convention? Consider especially its function as a check on popular tyranny. Does any branch of the federal government serve that function?

8. Read carefully Madison's speech on June 26 in favor of long Senate terms. What functions did he expect the Senate to serve? Are these functions compatible with his views on popular elections? With his desire that both the House and the Senate be popularly elected and proportional? Consider the liberal and republican positions outlined in chapter 1. Where do Madison's views fall, based on this speech? Is your answer consistent with the picture of Madison you have developed in preceding materials?

9. Madison's June 26 speech is also interesting for its methodology. Notice that he argued that "a people deliberating in a temperate moment" would reach the conclusions he favors. Modern philosopher John Rawls uses a similar technique in *A Theory of Justice*, where he suggests that individuals deliberating under a "veil of ignorance" about their own particular desires and circumstances would reach the best principles of justice. Is this a useful technique, for Madison or for Rawls?

10. Notice the dispute about whether the national or state governments were more likely to encroach on the sphere of the other. Which was more likely in 1787? Which is more likely today? What, if anything, has changed?

11. Why did the nationalists favor enabling the national legislature to veto state laws? What were they worried about? Did the final Constitution contain any mechanism that allayed their concerns?

12. How far did the delegates expect congressional power to extend? In 1819, in *McCulloch v. Maryland*, 17 U.S. (4 Wheat.) 316, 4 L.Ed. 579 (1819), Chief Justice John Marshall read the necessary and proper clause very broadly. He interpreted it to mean that Congress could enact any legislation reasonably related to a legitimate purpose. In the twentieth century, application of this principle to the commerce clause has led the court to uphold congressional use of the commerce clause to regulate virtually any subject with any connection to interstate commerce. See especially *Katzenbach v. McClung*, 379 U.S. 294, 85 S.Ct. 377, 13 L.Ed.2d 290 (1964) (Congress may impose an antidiscrimination law on a small local restaurant that served no interstate travellers, but which bought approximately 46% of its food from a local supplier who had procured it from outside the state); *Scarborough v. United States*, 431 U.S. 563, 97 S.Ct. 1963, 52 L.Ed.2d 582 (1977) (Congress may punish a convicted felon for possession of a firearm which had moved in interstate commerce previous to original conviction). Are these expansive interpretations of congressional power consistent with the delegates' expectations?

FOOTNOTES

1. Thomas Whately, *The Regulations lately Made Concerning the Colonies and the Taxes Imposed upon Them, Considered* (1765), in Edmund S. Morgan & Helen M. Morgan, *The Stamp Act Crisis: Prologue to Revolution* 21–22 (1962) (emphasis in original).

2. "The Earl of Clarendon to William Pym," *Boston Gazette*, Jan. 27, 1766, in 3 *Works of John Adams* 481 (Charles Adams ed. 1850–1856).

3. John Adams, *Thoughts on Government* (1776), in 1 *American Political Writing During the Founding Era, 1760–1805*, at 403 (Charles S. Hyneman & Donald S. Lutz eds. 1983).

CHAPTER SIX

Slavery

INTRODUCTION

The American institution of slavery began in 1619, when a Dutch warship sold twenty African slaves to the settlers in Jamestown, Virginia. During the next two centuries, many millions of Africans were brought to the American colonies in chains. By 1760, there were over three hundred thousand slaves in the American colonies; by 1790 there were almost seven hundred thousand. At the time of the Revolution, there were black slaves in every state.

Public attacks on the institution of slavery began as early as the 1750s. In 1751, Benjamin Franklin began a lifelong crusade against slavery. His opposition was most influential in Pennsylvania, where the Quakers also consistently opposed slavery. Samuel Adams worked quietly against slavery in Massachusetts. Over the next two decades, antislavery sentiment grew, especially in those two states. Some patriots began drawing parallels between British violations of natural law and the unnatural institution of slavery.

In 1764, James Otis used slavery and the slave trade as a vehicle for attacking the British rule under which such abominations were permitted. After blaming England for the existence of slavery, he criticized the invidious distinction between blacks and whites.

> Does it follow that 'tis right to enslave a man because he is black? Will short hair curled like wool instead of Christian hair, as 'tis called by those whose hearts are as hard as the nether millstone, help the argument? Can any logical inference in favor of slavery be drawn from a flat nose, a long or short face?[1]

Outside of Pennsylvania and New England, however, Otis's sentiments were the exception rather than the rule in 1764. With the collapse of his tortured theories of the political relationship between the colonies and Great Britain, his influence waned even in the north. For another decade and a half, the growing abolitionist movement was outnumbered throughout the colonies.

Despite American protests against the "slavery" of English rule and the majestic assertion in the Declaration of Independence that "all men are created equal," the colonists rarely connected the ideology of the Revolution with an opposition to slavery. Jefferson's original draft of the Declaration included slavery and the slave trade as grievances against the king, but the clauses were excised by the Continental Congress. Perhaps the fact that Jefferson himself owned over two hundred slaves undercut the justness of his words.

Only after the Revolution did some states—particularly those with few slaves—begin to abolish slavery. The gradual democratization of the new republic, described in chapter 1, illuminated, at least in some states, the inherent inequality of a system by which some inhabitants held others in bondage. The Revolution itself also caused some practical disruption of the institution of slavery. Some slaves were emancipated in order to fight in the army (or because they had already fought bravely), and others simply took advantage of the wartime chaos to escape from bondage. The Northern economy—never as suited to slave labor as the Southern—was changing, and slavery gradually gave way to other labor systems.

The Northern states outlawed slavery in a variety of ways. Only Vermont, not yet a state, made slavery unconstitutional. It declared in Article I of its abortive 1777 Constitution:

> That all men are born equally free and independent, and have certain natural, inherent and unalienable rights, amongst which are the enjoying and defending life and liberty; acquiring, possessing and protecting property, and pursuing and obtaining happiness and safety. Therefore, no male person, born in this country, or brought from over sea, ought to be holden by law, to serve any person, as a servant, slave or apprentice, after he arrives to the age of twenty-one years, nor female, in like manner, after she arrives to the age of eighteen years, unless they are bound by their own consent, after they arrive to such age, or bound by law, for the payment of debts, damages, fines, costs or the like.

Other state constitutions declared the same natural and inalienable right of equality, but did not take the next step of prohibiting slavery.

In Massachusetts, the connection between natural rights and abolition was accomplished by judicial fiat. In a series of cases during the early 1780s, the Massachusetts Supreme Judicial Court ignored the failure of legislative attempts to abolish slavery and interpreted the Massachusetts Constitution's protection of "natural rights" as abolishing slavery. Slavery did not disappear from Massachusetts immediately; by 1787, however, it had virtually no slaves. New Hampshire's experience was similar. After attempts to outlaw slavery by legislation failed, the courts interpreted the New Hampshire Constitution as prohibiting slavery.

Pennsylvania chose a more gradual method of abolition. In 1780, the state legislature enacted a law providing that any slave born after that date would become free on his or her twenty-eighth birthday. Thus the master would be recompensed for the cost of raising the child of a slave by gaining some service. Rhode Island and Connecticut both passed similar statutes in 1784.

In New York and New Jersey, the battle for abolition was not complete by 1787. A bill to abolish slavery gradually had failed in New York in 1785, and would not succeed until 1799. New Jersey waited until 1804 to restrict slavery. In both states, the laws were cautious and conservative, careful to preserve the property rights of slave owners.

Abolition of slavery caused little change in the actual status of Northern blacks. Often indentured for long periods, rarely rising above the poverty line, and always considered less than full citizens, Northern blacks were only technically free. They were politically invisible; the republican image of the citizen as a man of property with a stake in the community could not encompass enslaved or recently freed blacks. In the North as well as the South, racial prejudice was the order of the day. Even most Northern whites assumed that blacks were childlike and uncivilized, with an innate tendency toward idleness and crime. Northern blacks were, moreover, insignificant: in 1776, ninety percent of American blacks lived south of Delaware.

Much has been written about the natural adaptation of slavery to the Southern agricultural economy. Tobacco and rice, the Southern staples, were well suited to cultivation and harvest by large numbers of unskilled slave laborers. The rise of the large plantation engendered growth of the slave population, which in turn ensured that the plantation system would maintain its dominance.

Many Southerners believed that free whites could never be enticed to do the unpleasant and dangerous work performed by slaves. In 1776, Thomas Lynch of South Carolina told the Continental Congress:

> Freemen cannot be got to work in our Colonies; it is not in the ability or inclination of freemen to do the work that the negroes do.[2]

In 1788, Charles Cotesworth Pinckney repeated to the South Carolina ratifying convention an argument he had made earlier. He assured the convention:

> [W]hile there remained one acre of swamp-land uncleared of South Carolina, I would raise my voice against restricting the importation of negroes. I am . . . thoroughly convinced . . . that the nature of our climate, and the flat, swampy situation of our country, obliges us to cultivate our lands with negroes, and that without them South Carolina would soon be a desert waste.[3]

Slavery was, moreover, both an economic system and a method of social control. The fear of slave rebellion led Southern whites to avoid any loosening of control that might move the economy away from a dependence on slave labor. Reliance on slave labor also provided a practical way to avoid the social unrest associated with a large population of working-class whites.

Despite the South's reliance on slavery, there were a few Southern opponents of slavery. Jefferson summed up his opposition to slavery in his 1782 *Notes on Virginia*: "Indeed I tremble for my country when I reflect that God is just." Even Jefferson did not free his own slaves, however.

Southern opponents of slavery were confounded by practical problems. A slave population that in many counties outnumbered the free white population, and a pervasive belief that blacks and whites could never co-exist peacefully in freedom, left serious questions about the aftermath of any move toward emancipation. Jefferson lamented later:

> Nothing is more certainly written in the book of fate, than that these people are to be free; nor is it less certain that the two races, equally free, cannot live in the same government. Nature, habit, opinion have drawn indelible lines of distinction between them.[4]

Other Southerners were appalled by the vision of mass emancipation. A 1785 petition to the Virginia House of Delegates, opposing a movement toward loosening manumission controls, described the anticipated consequences of emancipation as

> [t]he horrors and outrages of all the rapes, murders, robberies, and outrages which a vast multitude of unprincipled, unpropertied, vindictive, and remorseless banditti are capable of perpetrating.[5]

Miscegenation, and the resulting mongrelization of the white race, was another fear.

For all these reasons, Southerners believed that blacks could never be citizens and must instead remain slaves. The only movement in the South toward abolition was Virginia's post-revolutionary decision to permit private manumission, previously restricted. Not many slave-owners took advantage of the provision.

In contrast to slavery, abolition of the slave trade was more widespread even in the South. By 1787, only Georgia and North Carolina still permitted the noxious commerce, and the latter taxed it heavily. The reasons for the lack of controversy were partly economic, partly political, and virtually never moral. States with many slaves feared that the growing ratio of slaves to freemen would undermine the whites' ability to maintain control. Also, in many states, especially Virginia, the high birth rate among the slave population made it more economically advantageous to sell American-born slaves than to import new African blacks.

The varying and uncertain status of slavery inevitably gave it the character of a political pawn. For example, in 1776 the Continental Congress, drafting the Articles of Confederation, struggled with the perennial question of state representation in the national legislature. States were equally represented in the Continental Congress, but the larger states were pressing for change. Virginia proposed a compromise in order to accomplish the goal of proportional representation. Leave each state with a single vote, Virginia suggested, but stipulate that no bill would pass unless supported by enough states to represent a majority of the population. To sweeten the compromise, the Virginians agreed to exclude slaves from the calculation of population, thus reducing their own influence. Patrick Henry had suggested a similar ploy before the first Continental Congress in 1774. From the beginning, then, slaves were considered fair game for political maneuvering. The final Articles of Confederation provided for equal representation of states, and the question of how slaves were to be counted for purposes of representation did not arise again until the Constitutional Convention.

Congress did, however, repeatedly address the question of how slaves were to be counted for purposes of taxation. The original draft of the Articles of Confederation provided that taxes be apportioned among the states on the basis of "the number of Inhabitants of every age, sex and quality, excepting Indians not paying taxes, the number of Inhabitants, of all ages, including negroes and mulattoes in each colony[.]"[6] The Southern delegates immediately objected to including slaves in the calculation, since it would increase the tax burden of slave states. Samuel Chase of Maryland moved to insert "white" before "inhabitants":

> Negroes [are] a species of property, personal estate. If negroes are taken into the computation of numbers to ascertain wealth, they ought to be, in settling the rep-

resentation. The Massachusetts fisheries, and navigation, ought to be taken into consideration. The young and old negroes are a burthen to their owners.[7]

After James Wilson and John Adams disagreed, Thomas Lynch (of South Carolina) and Benjamin Franklin took Southern and Northern positions, respectively, that would be repeated in the Constitutional Convention:

> Lynch. If it is debated, whether their slaves are their property, there is an end of the confederation. Our slaves being our property, why should they be taxed more than the land, sheep, cattle, horses, &c? . . .
> Dr. Franklin. Slaves rather weaken than strengthen the State, and there is therefore some difference between them and sheep; sheep will never make any insurrections.[8]

Notice that in this debate the delegates drew no distinction between slaves and free blacks; the failure to draw such a distinction was commonplace.

Unable to resolve the dispute, Congress simply required that each state's contribution to the national treasury be calculated on the basis of the "value of all land" within the state.

By 1783, it was clear that the land valuation formula of the Articles of Confederation would not work. A congressional committee chaired by Nathaniel Gorham proposed revising the Articles to allocate the tax burden according to population rather than land values. That reopened the question of how to count slaves. The committee proposed "that two blacks be rated as equal to one freeman" (notice the assumed equivalence of blacks and slaves), and on March 28, various delegates countered with suggestions of four to three, four to one, three to one, and three to two. After the last of these was defeated, Madison proposed a ratio of five to three, and the first adoption of the three-fifths compromise was achieved by a vote of seven states to two, with Massachusetts divided. For various reasons having nothing to do with the slave question, however, this proposal to amend the Articles was never ratified by the states. Again, the question of how to count slaves for purposes of taxation would haunt the Convention.

Two further matters complicate any historical understanding of the issue of slavery in 1787. First, the Southern states had a sectional interest not only in slavery, but also in questions having to do with trade. Various sorts of trade restrictions, or "navigation acts," would be likely to enrich Northern merchants at the expense of Southern planters.

Without a shipping industry of their own, the Southern "non-carrying" states were dependent on either Northern or British ships to carry their agricultural products to foreign markets. They feared that the Northern states would place restrictions on British shipping, giving the Northerners a monopoly by which to exploit Southern agriculture. Since the Northern states were also the manufacturing states, the Southerners were also concerned that protective tariffs might promote Northern industry at the expense of Southern ability to purchase cheaper foreign goods.

The "navigation" controversy was crystallized by Secretary for Foreign Affairs John Jay's 1786 negotiations with Spain. After the American Revolution, Spain viewed the new nation as a threat to its own empire. It therefore denied Americans the right to trade with its West Indian colonies, a restriction that most Americans wished removed. At the same time, Spain effectively closed off the Mississippi River to American trade by refusing American ships passage through New Orleans at the mouth of the river. The Mississippi was largely irrelevant to the Northern industries with access to the numerous Atlantic ports, but Southerners regarded free navigation on the Mississippi as essential to their westward expansion.

In 1786, after almost a year of fruitless negotiation, Diego Gardoqui, the Spanish minister to the United States, offered Jay a tempting proposition. Spain would open its empire to American trade if the United States would renounce any rights to navigate the Mississippi for twenty-five years. Jay's instructions specifically forbade him from giving away the Mississippi, so on May 29, 1786, he asked Congress to change his instructions and remove the limitation. On August 29, after a bitter debate, Congress did so. Mississippi navigation was sacrificed for Caribbean trade by a straight sectional vote of seven states to five: Delaware was absent, but every state to the north of her voted in favor and every state to the south voted against. When the subsequent negotiations with Spain produced a treaty essentially giving away the Mississippi, the five Southern states were able to block it only because treaties required the consent of nine states. This incident left the South determined that the next constitution would require a two thirds majority for navigation acts and foreign treaties.

The second complicating factor involved the Northwest Ordinance, passed by Congress in New York on July 13, 1787, while the Convention sat in Philadelphia. That act applied to the western territories north of the Ohio River, which consisted of what is now the states of Ohio, Michigan, Indiana, Illinois, Wisconsin, and the eastern edge of Minnesota. Article VI of the Ordinance provided that:

> There shall be neither Slavery nor involuntary Servitude in the said territory otherwise than in the punishment of crimes, whereof the party shall have been duly convicted; provided always that any person escaping into the same, from whom labor or service is lawfully claimed in any one of the original States, such fugitive may be lawfully reclaimed and conveyed to the person claiming his or her labor or service aforesaid.

Thus at the same time the delegates in Philadelphia were sanctioning the institution of slavery, the Congress in New York was guaranteeing that slavery would not spread to the Northwest Territories.

Several of the framers traveled between New York and Philadelphia. The Journal of the Continental Congress, which unfortunately contains no record of the debates over the Northwest Ordinance, does provide two interesting observations. Four delegates to the Federal Convention were present in Congress on July 13, the day the Ordinance passed. Yates of New York voted against it, but Blount of North Carolina and Few and Pierce of Georgia voted in favor. The Journal also indicates that Article VI was added to the Ordinance only that day (the required "third reading" of the bill), despite the fact that Congress had had the Ordinance before it the preceding day as well (for its "second reading").

In light of the heavy opposition encountered by previous attempts to limit slavery in the territories, the easy passage of the Northwest Ordinance seems peculiar. Southern support of the Ordinance seems even more so, although it may be at least partly explained by a Southern assumption that prohibiting slavery in the northwestern territories implicitly permitted it in the south-western territories. One historian, however, has speculated that there is a relationship between the two compromises on slavery: one in New York and one in Philadelphia, within days of one another. Read the debates carefully for evidence of any connection.

The debates in the Convention focused primarily on four interrelated issues regarding slavery: (1) its continued existence, which the slave states feared might be threatened by some aspects of a strong or Northern-dominated national government; (2) the slave trade, viewed similarly; (3) how slaves were to be counted for purposes of representation and taxation; and (4) the obligations of free states toward runaway slaves escaping from slave states. In addition, the delegates dealt briefly with the fear of slave revolts. One historian has concluded that a total of ten clauses were inserted into the Constitution in consequence of the South's insistence on protection for slavery.[9] Try to trace these various accommodations through the debates.

REPRESENTATION AND TAXATION

The first reference to slavery in the convention came on June 6, when Madison mentioned it in passing. In defending a large republic on the ground that its size would discourage the evils of faction, Madison cited, as an "unjust law" caused by faction, "the mere distinction of colour." He labeled it "a ground of the most oppressive dominion ever exercised by man over man."

The next reference to slavery was considerably more oblique. On June 8 (in a debate excerpted in chapter 5), the Convention discussed whether to give the national legislature a veto over state laws. Hugh Williamson of North Carolina stated that he was "against giving a power that might restrain the States from regulating their internal police." All the delegates present recognized that the "internal police" power referred primarily to the decision whether to permit slavery. The proposed negative was defeated seven states to three, with Delaware divided; Georgia and the Carolinas, which had to that point been voting consistently with Virginia in favor of a strong national government, broke ranks and voted against adding this power to the federal arsenal. This was the first indication that the division between large (or growing) states—including the southernmost trio—and small states might sometimes be replaced by a division along the lines of slavery.

The division between Northern and Southern interests, however, was still not sharp this early in the debates. On June 11, the Convention dealt with the issue surprisingly cursorily.

Monday, June 11

The clause concerning the rule of suffrage in the natl. Legislature postponed on Saturday was resumed.

Mr. Sharman proposed that the proportion of suffrage in the 1st. branch should be according to the respective numbers of free inhabitants; and that in the second branch or Senate, each State should have one vote and no more. He said as the States would remain possessed of certain individual rights, each State ought to be able to protect itself: otherwise a few large States will rule the rest.

Mr. King & **Mr. Wilson**, in order to bring the

question to a point moved "that the right of suffrage in the first branch of the national Legislature ought not to be according the rule established in the articles of Confederation, but according to some equitable ratio of representation." The clause so far as it related to suffrage in the first branch was postponed in order to consider this motion.

. . .

On the question for agreeing to Mr. Kings and Mr. Wilsons motion it passed in the affirmative
Mass. ay. Ct. ay. N. Y. no. N. J. no. Pa. ay. Del. no. Md. divd. Va. ay. N. C. ay. S. C. ay. Geo. ay.
It was then moved by **Mr. Rutlidge** 2ded. by **Mr. Butler** to add to the words "equitable ratio of representation" at the end of the motion just agreed to, the words "according to the quotas of contribution." On motion of **Mr. Wilson** seconded by **Mr. C. Pinckney**, this was postponed; in order to add,

after, after the words "equitable ratio of representation" the words following "in proportion to the whole number of white & other free Citizens & inhabitants of every age sex & condition including those bound to servitude for a term of years and three fifths of all other persons not comprehended in the foregoing description, except Indians not paying taxes, in each State," this being the rule in the Act of Congress agreed to by eleven States, for apportioning quotas of revenue on the States, and requiring a Census only every 5-7, or 10 years.
Mr. Gerry thought property not the rule of representation. Why then shd. the blacks, who were property in the South, be in the rule of representation more than the Cattle & horses of the North.
On the question,—Mass: Con: N. Y. Pen: Maryd. Virga. N. C. S. C. & Geo.: were in the affirmative: N. J. & Del: in the negative.

Perhaps the delegates still hoped to avoid any direct conflict over slavery. On June 2, for example, the Pennsylvania Society for the Abolition of Slavery submitted an address to its president, Benjamin Franklin, and asked him to present it to the Convention. He declined to do so, perhaps because it would have inflamed the Southern delegates.

Pennsylvania Society for the Abolition of Slavery
June 2, 1787

To the revival of [the slave] trade the Society ascribe part of the Obloquy with which foreign Nations have branded our infant States. In vain will be their Pretentions to a love of liberty or a regard for national Character, while they share in the profits of a Commerce that can only be conducted upon Rivers of human tears and Blood.

By all the Attributes, therefore, of the Deity which are offended by this inhuman traffic—by the Union of our whole species in a common Ancestor and by all the Obligations which result from it—by the apprehensions and terror of the righteous Vengeance of God in national Judgements—by the certainty of the great and awful day of retribution—by the efficacy of the Prayers of good Men, which would only insult the Majesty of Heaven, if offered up in behalf of our Country while the Iniquity we deplore continues among us—by the sanctity of the Christian

Name—by the Pleasure of domestic Connections and the pangs which attend [their] Dissolutions—by the Captivity and Sufferings of our *American* bretheren in Algiers which seem to be intended by divine Providence to awaken us to a Sense of the Injustice and Cruelty of dooming our *African* Bretheren to perpetual Slavery and Misery—by a regard to the consistency of principles and Conduct which should mark the Citizens of Republics—by the magnitude and intensity of our desires to promote the happiness of those millions of intelligent beings who will probably cover this immense Continent with rational life—and by every other consideration that religion Reason Policy and Humanity can suggest the Society implore the present Convention to make the Suppression of the African trade in the United States, a part of their important deliberations.[10]

Nevertheless, the question of slavery continued to influence debates over apportionment in the legislature. By the end of June there was increasing recognition that the major division of interests lay between Northern and Southern states, not between large and small states. On June 30, Madison summarized his arguments in favor of proportional representation in the Senate:

Saturday, June 30

Mr. Madison: But he contended that the States were divided into different interests not by their difference of size, but by other circumstances; the most material of which resulted partly from climate, but principally from the effects of their having or not having slaves. These two causes concurred in forming the great division of interests in the U. States. It did not lie between the large & small States: It lay between the Northern & Southern, and if any defensive power were necessary, it ought to be mutually given to these two interests. He was so strongly impressed with this important truth that he had been casting about in his mind for some expedient that would answer the purpose. The one which had occurred was that instead of proportioning the votes of the States in both branches, to their respective numbers of inhabitants computing the slaves in the ratio of 5 to 3, they should be represented in one branch according to the number of free inhabitants only; and in the other according to the whole no. counting the slaves as if free. By this arrangement the Southern Scale would have the advantage in one House, and the Northern in the other. He had been restrained from proposing this expedient by two considerations: one was his unwillingness to urge any diversity of interests on an occasion where it is but too apt to arise of itself—the other was, the inequality of powers that must be vested in the two branches, and which wd. destroy the equilibrium of interests.

On July 2, Charles Pinckney added his South Carolina voice to the growing concern over slavery, a turning point because South Carolina had heretofore considered herself in the "large state" camp:

> [He] thought an equality of votes in the 2d. branch inadmissible. At the same time candor obliged him to admit that the large States would feel a partiality for their own Citizens & give them a preference, in appointments: that they might also find some common points in their commercial interests, and promote treaties favorable to them. There is a real distinction [between] the Northern & Southn. interests. N. Carola. S. Carol: & Geo. in their Rice & Indigo had a peculiar interest which might be sacrificed. How then shall the larger States be prevented from administering the Genl. Govt. as they please, without being themselves unduly subjected to the will of the smaller? By allowing them some but not a full proportion.

At this point, the delegates were temporarily diverted by the escalating controversy over the Senate. The Committee of Eleven, discussed in chapter 5, made its report on the great compromise on July 5. Unable to agree even to that compromise, the delegates sent the issue back to a smaller committee, consisting of Gouverneur Morris, Gorham, Randolph, Rutledge, and King. That committee reported on July 9, and the serious debate over representation in the House began. Two related disputes divided the delegates: whether population or wealth ought to be represented, and how to count slaves in either case.

Monday, July 9

Mr. Govr. Morris delivered a report from the Come. of 5 members to whom was committed the clause in the Report of the Come. consisting of a member from each State, stating the proper ratio of Representatives in the 1st. branch, to be as 1 to every 40,000 inhabitants, as follows viz

"The Committee to whom was referred the 1st. clause of the 1st. proposition reported from the grand Committee, beg leave to report

I. that in the 1st. meeting of the Legislature the 1st. branch thereof consist of 56. members of which Number, N. Hamshire shall have 2. Massts. 7. R.Id. 1. Cont. 4. N. Y. 5. N. J. 3. Pa. 8. Del. 1. Md. 4. Va. 9. N. C. 5. S. C. 5. Geo. 2. —

II. But as the present situation of the States may probably alter as well in point of wealth as in the number of their inhabitants, that the Legislature be authorized from time to time to augment ye. number of Representatives. And in case any of the States shall hereafter be divided, or any two or more States united, or any new States created within the limits of the United States, the Legislature shall possess authority to regulate the number of Representatives in any of the foregoing cases, upon the principles of their wealth and number of inhabitants."

Mr. Sherman wished to know on what principles or calculations the Report was founded. It did not appear to correspond with any rule of numbers, or of any requisition hitherto adopted by Congs.

Mr. Gorham. Some provision of this sort was necessary in the outset. The number of blacks & whites with some regard to supposed wealth was the general guide Fractions could not be observed. The Legislre. is to make alterations from time to time as justice & propriety may require. Two objections prevailed agst. the rate of 1 member for every 40,000 inhts. The 1st. was the Representation would soon be too numerous: the 2d. that the Westn. States who may have a different interest, might if admitted on that principle by degrees, outvote the Atlantic. Both these objections are removed. The number will be small in the first instance and may be continued so; and the Atlantic States having ye. Govt. in their own hands, may take care of their own interest, by dealing out the right of Representation in safe proportions to the Western States. These were the views of the Committee.

Mr. L Martin wished to know whether the Come. were guided in the ratio, by the wealth or number of inhabitants, of the States, or by both;

noting its variations from former apportionments by Congs.

Mr. Govr. Morris & **Mr. Rutlidge** moved to postpone the 1st. paragraph relating to the number of members to be allowed each State in the first instance, and to take up the 2nd. paragraph authorizing the Legislre. to alter the number from time to time according to wealth & inhabitants. The motion was agreed to nem. con.

On Question on the 2nd. paragh. taken without any debate

Masts. ay. Cont. ay. N. Y. no. N. J. no. Pa. ay. Del. ay. Md. ay. Va. ay. N. C. ay. S. C. ay. Geo. ay.

.   .   .

Mr. Williamson, thought it would be necessary to return to the rule of numbers, but that the Western States stood on different footing. If their property shall be rated as high as that of the Atlantic States, then their representation ought to hold a like proportion. Otherwise if their property was not to be equally rated.

Mr. Govr. Morris. The Report is little more than a guess. Wealth was not altogether disregarded by the Come. Where it was apparently in favor of one State, whose nos. were superior to the numbers of another, by a fraction only, a member extraordinary was allowed to the former: and so vice versa. The Committee meant little more than to bring the matter to a point for the consideration of the House.

Mr. Reed asked why Georgia was allowed 2 members, when her number of inhabitants had stood below that of Delaware.

Mr. Govr. Morris. Such is the rapidity of the population of that State, that before the plan takes effect, it will probably be entitled to 2 Representatives

Mr. Randolph. disliked the report of the Come. but had been unwilling to object to it. He was apprehensive that as the number was not to be changed till the Natl. Legislature should please, a pretext would never be wanting to postpone alterations, and keep the power in the hands of those possessed of it. He was in favor of the commitmt. to a member from each State.

Mr. Patterson considered the proposed estimate for the future according to the Combined rule of numbers and wealth, as too vague. For this reason N. Jersey was agst. it. He could regard negroes slaves in no light but as property. They are no free agents, have no personal liberty, no faculty of acquiring property, but on the contrary are themselves property, & like other property entirely at the will of the Master. Has a man in Virga. a number of votes in proportion to the number of his slaves? And if Negroes are not represented in the States to which they belong, why should they be represented in the Genl. Govt. What is the true principle of Representation? It is an expedient by which an assembly of certain individls. chosen by the people is substituted in place of the inconvenient meeting of the people themselves. If such a meeting of the people was actually to take place, would the slaves vote? They would not. Why then shd. they be represented. He was also agst. such an indirect encouragemt. of the slave trade; observing that Congs. in their act relating to the change of the 8 art: of Confed. had been ashamed to use the term "slaves" & had substituted a description.

Mr. Madison, reminded Mr. Patterson that his doctrine of Representation which was in its principle the genuine one, must for ever silence the pretensions of the small States to an equality of votes with the large ones. They ought to vote in the same proportion in which their citizens would do, if the people of all the States were collectively met. He suggested as a proper ground of compromise, that in the first branch the States should be represented according to their number of free inhabitants; and in the 2d. which had for one of its primary objects the guardianship of property, according to the whole number, including slaves.

Mr. Butler urged warmly the justice & necessity of regarding wealth in the apportionment of Representation.

Mr. King had always expected that as the Southern States are the richest, they would not league themselves with the Northn. unless some respect were paid to their superior wealth. If the latter expect those preferential distinctions in Commerce & other advantages which they will derive from the connection they must not expect to receive them without allowing some advantages in return. Eleven out of 13 of the States had agreed to consider Slaves in the apportionment of taxation; and taxation and Representation ought to go together.

Without reaching any conclusions, the Convention recommitted the allocation of representatives to yet another committee.

The committee reported the next day. Its report increased the total number of representatives from fifty-six to sixty-five. Allocation to the seven northernmost states went from thirty-one to thirty-six, and to the five southernmost from twenty-five to twenty-nine. The Southern states were still not satisfied, and Rutledge moved to reduce New Hampshire's representation from three to two.

Tuesday, July 10

Genl. Pinkney. The Report before it was committed was more favorable to the S. States than as it now stands. If they are to form so considerable a minority, and the regulation of trade is to be given to the Genl. Government, they will be nothing more than overseers for the Northern States. He did not expect the S. States to be raised to a majority of representatives, but wished them to have something like an equality. At present by the alterations of the Come. in favor of the N. States they are removed farther from it than they were before. One member had indeed been added to Virga. which he was glad of as he considered her as a Southern State. He was glad also that the members of Georgia were increased.

Mr. Williamson was not for reducing N. Hamshire from 3 to 2. but for reducing some others. The Southn. Interest must be extremely endangered by the present arrangement. The Northn. States are to have a majority in the first instance and the means of perpetuating it.

Mr. Dayton observed that the line between the Northn. & Southern interest had been improperly drawn: that Pa. was the dividing State, there being six on each side of her.

Genl. Pinkney urged the reduction, dwelt on the

superior wealth of the Southern States, and insisted on its having its due weight in the Government.

Mr. Govr. Morris regretted the turn of the debate. The States he found had many Representatives on the floor. Few he fears were to be deemed the Representatives of America. He thought the Southern States have by the report more than their share of representation. Property ought to have its weight, but not all the weight. If the Southn. States are to supply money. The Northn. States are to spill their blood. Besides, the probable Revenue to be ex-

pected from the S. States has been greatly over-rated. He was agst. reducing N. Hamshire.

Mr. Randolph was opposed to a reduction of N. Hamshire, not because she had a full title to three members: but because it was in his contemplation 1. to make it the duty instead of leaving it in the discretion of the Legislature to regulate the representation by a periodical census. 2. to require more than a bare majority of votes in the Legislature in certain cases, & particularly in commercial cases.

The proposal to reduce New Hampshire's entitlement was rejected, as were rapid-fire attempts to increase the representation of first North Carolina, then South Carolina, then Georgia.

The next day, July 11, the Convention turned to Randolph's proposal to require a periodic census and reapportionment. That debate in turn led the delegates back to the previously avoided question of exactly how representatives ought to be allocated. Follow carefully the clause-by-clause progress through the day.

Wednesday, July 11

Mr. Randolph's motion requiring the Legislre. to take a periodical census for the purpose of redressing inequalities in the Representation, was resumed.

Mr. Sherman was agst. shackling the Legislature too much. We ought to choose wise & good men, and then confide in them.

Mr. Mason. The greater the difficulty we find in fixing a proper rule of Representation, the more unwilling ought we to be, to throw the task from ourselves, on the Genl. Legislre. He did not object to the conjectural ratio which was to prevail in the outset; but considered a Revision from time to time according to some permanent & precise standard as essential to ye. fair representation required in the 1st. branch. According to the present population of America, the Northn. part of it had a right to preponderate, and he could not deny it. But he wished it not to preponderate hereafter when the reason no longer continued. From the nature of man we may be sure, that those who have power in their hands will not give it up while they can retain it. On the contrary we know they will always when they can rather increase it. If the S. States therefore should have ¾ of the people of America within their limits,

the Northern will hold fast the majority of Representatives. ¼ will govern the ¾. The S. States will complain: but they may complain from generation to generation without redress. Unless some principle therefore which will do justice to them hereafter shall be inserted in the Constitution, disagreeable as the declaration was to him, he must declare he could neither vote for the system here, nor support it, in his State. Strong objections had been drawn from the danger to the Atlantic interests from new Western States. Ought we to sacrifice what we know to be right in itself, lest it should prove favorable to States which are not yet in existence. If the Western States are to be admitted into the Union, as they arise, they must, he wd. repeat, be treated as equals, and subjected to no degrading discriminations. They will have the same pride & other passions which we have, and will either not unite with or will speedily revolt from the Union, if they are not in all respects placed on an equal footing with their brethren. It has been said they will be poor, and unable to make equal contributions to the general Treasury. He did not know but that in time they would be both more numerous & more wealthy than their Atlantic brethren. The extent & fertility of their soil, made this probable; and though Spain might for a time deprive them of the natural outlet for their productions, yet she will, because she must, finally yield to their demands. He urged that numbers of inhabitants; though not always a precise standard of wealth was sufficiently so for every substantial purpose.

Mr. Williamson was for making it the duty of the Legislature to do what was right & not leaving it at liberty to do or not do it. He moved that Mr. Randolph's proposition be postpond. in order to consider the following "that in order to ascertain the alterations that may happen in the population & wealth of the several States, a census shall be taken of the free white inhabitants and ⅗ths. of those of other descriptions on the 1st. year after this Government shall have been adopted and every year thereafter; and that the Representation be regulated accordingly."

Mr. Randolph agreed that Mr. Williamson's proposition should stand in the place of his. He observed that the ratio fixt for the 1st. meeting was a mere conjecture, that it placed the power in the hands of that part of America, which could not always be entitled to it, that this power would not be voluntarily renounced; and that it was consequently the duty of the Convention to secure its renunciation when justice might so require; by some constitutional provisions. If equality between great & small States be inadmissible, because in that case unequal numbers of Constituents wd. be represented by equal number of votes; was it not equally inadmissible that a larger & more populous district of America should hereafter have less representation, than a smaller & less populous district. If a fair representation of the people be not secured, the injustice of the Govt. will shake it to its foundations. What relates to suffrage is justly stated by the celebrated Montesquieu, as a fundamental article in Republican Govts. If the danger suggested by Mr. Govr. Morris be real, of advantage being taken of the Legislature in pressing moments, it was an additional reason, for tying their hands in such a manner that they could not sacrifice their trust to momentary considerations. Congs. have pledged the public faith to New States, that they shall be admitted on equal terms. They never would nor ought to accede on any other. The census must be taken under the direction of the General Legislature. The States will be too much interested to take an impartial one for themselves.

Mr. Butler & **Genl. Pinkney** insisted that blacks be included in the rule of Representation, *equally* with the Whites: and for that purpose moved that the words "three fifths" be struck out.

Mr. Gerry thought that ⅗ of them was to say the least the full proportion that could be admitted.

Mr. Ghorum. This ratio was fixed by Congs. as a rule of taxation. Then it was urged by the Delegates representing the States having slaves that the blacks were still more inferior to freemen. At present when the ratio of representation is to be established, we are assured that they are equal to freemen. The arguments on ye. former occasion had convinced him that ⅗ was pretty near the just proportion and he should vote according to the same opinion now.

Mr. Butler insisted that the labour of a slave in S. Carola. was as productive & valuable as that of a freeman in Massts., that as wealth was the great means of defence and utility to the Nation they were equally valuable to it with freeman; and that consequently an equal representation ought to be allowed for them in a Government which was instituted principally for the protection of property, and was itself to be supported by property.

Mr. Mason, could not agree to the motion, notwithstand it was favorable to Virga. because he thought it unjust. It was certain that the slaves were valuable, as they raised the value of land, increased the exports & imports, and of course the revenue, would supply the means of feeding & supporting an army, and might in case of emergency become themselves soldiers. As in these important respects they were useful to the community at large, they ought not to be excluded from the estimate of Representation. He could not however regard them as equal to freemen and could not vote for them as such. He added as worthy of remark, that the Southern States have this peculiar species of property, over & above the other species of property common to all the States.

Mr. Williamson reminded Mr. Ghorum that if the Southn. States contended for the inferiority of blacks to whites when taxation was in view, the Eastern States on the same occasion contended for their equality. He did not however, either then or now, concur in either extreme, but approved of the ratio of ⅗.

On Mr. Butlers motion for considering blacks as equal to Whites in the apportionmt. of Representation.

Massts. no. Cont. no. [N. Y. not on floor.] N. J. no. Pa. no. Del. ay. Md. no. Va no. N. C. no. S. C. ay. Geo. ay

Mr. Govr. Morris said he had several objections to the proposition of Mr. Williamson. 1. It fettered the Legislature too much. 2. it would exclude some States altogether who would not have a sufficient number to entitle them to a single Representative. 3. it will not consist with the Resolution passed on Saturday last authorising the Legislature to adjust the Representation from time to time on the principles of population & wealth or with the principles of equity. If slaves were to be considered as inhabitants, not as wealth, then the sd. Resolution would not be pursued: If as wealth, then why is no other wealth but slaves included? These objections may perhaps be removed by amendments. His great objection was that the number of inhabitants was not a proper standard of wealth. The amazing difference between the comparative numbers & wealth of different Countries, rendered all reasoning superfluous on the subject. Numbers might with greater propriety be deemed a measure of stregth, than of wealth, yet the late defence made by G. Britain, agst. her numerous enemies proved in the clearest manner, that it is entirely fallacious even in this respect.

Mr. King thought there was great force in the objections of Mr. Govr. Morris: he would however accede to the proposition for the sake of doing something.

Mr. Rutlidge contended for the admission of wealth in the estimate by which Representation should be regulated. The Western States will not be able to contribute in proportion to their numbers; they shd. not therefore be represented in that proportion. The Atlantic States will not concur in such a plan. He moved that "at the end of   years after the 1st. meeting of the Legislature, and of every   years thereafter, the Legislature shall proportion the Representation according to the principles of wealth & population"

Mr. Sherman thought the number of people alone the best rule for measuring wealth as well as representation; and that if the Legislature were to be governed by wealth, they would be obliged to estimate it by numbers. He was at first for leaving the matter wholly to the discretion of the Legislature; but he had been convinced by the observations of [Mr. Randolph & Mr. Mason,] that the *periods* & the *rule*, of revising the Representation ought to be fixt by the Constitution

Mr. Reid thought the Legislature ought not to be too much shackled. It would make the Constitution like Religious Creeds, embarrassing to those bound to conform to them & more likely to produce dissatisfaction and scism, than harmony and union.

Mr. Mason objected to Mr. Rutlidge motion, as requiring of the Legislature something too indefinite & impracticable, and leaving them a pretext for doing nothing.

Mr. Wilson had himself no objection to leaving the Legislature entirely at liberty. But considered wealth as an impracticable rule.

Mr. Ghorum. If the Convention who are comparatively so little biassed by local views are so much perplexed, How can it be expected that the Legislature hereafter under the full biass of those views, will be able to settle a standard. He was convinced by the arguments of others & his own reflections, that the Convention ought to fix some standard or other.

Mr. Govr. Morris. The argts. of others & his own reflections had led him to a very different conclusion. If we can't agree on a rule that will be just at this time, how can we expect to find one that will be just in all times to come. Surely those who come after us will judge better of things present, than we can of things future. He could not persuade himself that numbers would be a just rule at any time. The remarks of [Mr. Mason] relative to the Western Country had not changed his opinion on that head. Among other objections it must be apparent they would not be able to furnish men equally enlightened, to share in the administration of our common interests. The Busy haunts of men not the remote wilderness, was the proper school of political Talents. If the Western people get the power into their hands they will ruin the Atlantic interests. The Back members are always most averse to the best measures. He mentioned the case of Pena formerly. The lower part of the State had ye. power in the first instance. They kept it in ye. own hands & the Country was ye. better for it. Another objection with him agst. admitting the blacks into the census, was that the people of Pena. would revolt at the idea of being put on a footing with slaves. They would reject any plan that was to have such an effect. Two objections had been raised agst. leaving the adjustment of the Representation from time, to time, to the discretion of the Legislature. The 1. was they would be unwilling to revise it at all. The 2. that by referring to *wealth* they would be bound by a rule which if willing, they would be unable to execute. The 1st. objn. distrusts their fidelity. But if their duty, their honor & their oaths will not bind them, let us not put into their hands our liberty, and all our other great interests: let us have no Govt. at all. 2. If these ties will bind them, we need not distrust the practicability of the rule. It was followed in part by the Come. in the apportionment of Representatives yesterday reported to the House. The best course that could be taken would be to leave the interests of the people to the Representatives of the people.

. . .

On the question on the first clause of Mr. Williamson's motion as to taking a census of the *free* inhabitants; it passed in the affirmative Masts. ay. Cont.

ay. N. J. ay. Pa. ay. Del. no. Md. no. Va. ay. N. C. ay. S. C. no. Geo no.

the next clause as to ⅗ of the negroes considered.

Mr. King. being much opposed to fixing numbers as the rule of representation, was particularly so on account of the blacks. He thought the admission of them along with Whites at all, would excite great discontents among the States having no slaves. He had never said as to any particular point that he would in no event acquiesce in & support it; but he wd. say that if in any case such a declaration was to be made by him, it would be in this. He remarked that in the temporary allotment of Representatives made by the Committee, the Southern States had received more than the number of their white & three fifths of their black inhabitants entitled them to.

Mr. Sherman. S. Carola. had not more beyond her proportion than N. York & N. Hampshire, nor either of them more than was necessary in order to avoid fractions or reducing them below their proportion. Georgia had more; but the rapid growth of that State seemed to justify it. In general the allotment might not be just, but considering all circumstances, he was satisifed with it.

Mr. Ghorum. supported the propriety of establishing numbers as the rule. He said that in Massts. estimates had been taken in the different towns, and that persons had been curious enough to compare these estimates with the respective numbers of people; and it had been found even including Boston, that the most exact proportion prevailed between numbers & property. He was aware that there might be some weight in what had fallen from his colleague, as to the umbrage which might be taken by the people of the Eastern States. But he recollected that when the proposition of Congs. for changing the 8th. art: of Confedn. was before the Legislature of Massts. the only difficulty then was to satisfy them that the negroes ought not to have been counted equally with whites instead of being counted in the ratio of three fifths only.*

Mr. Wilson did not well see on what principle the admission of blacks in the proportion of three fifths could be explained. Are they admitted as Citizens? then why are they not admitted on an equality with White Citizens? are they admitted as property? then why is not other property admitted into the compu-

---

*They were then to have been a rule of taxation only. [Footnote by Madison.]

tation? These were difficulties however which he thought must be overruled by the necessity of compromise. He had some apprehensions also from the tendency of the blending of the blacks with the whites, to give disgust to the people of Pena. as had been intimated by his Colleague [Mr. Govr. Morris]. But he differed from him in thinking numbers of inhabts. so incorrect a measure of wealth. He had seen the Western settlemts. of Pa. and on a comparison of them with the City of Philada. could discover little other difference, than that property was more unequally divided among individuals here than there. Taking the same number in the aggregate in the two situations he believed there would be little difference in their wealth and ability to contribute to the public wants.

Mr. Govr. Morris was compelled to declare himself reduced to the dilemma of doing injustice to the Southern States or to human nature, and he must therefore do it to the former. For he could never agree to give such encouragement to the slave trade as would be given by allowing them a representation for their negroes, and he did not believe those States would ever confederate on terms that would deprive them of that trade.

On Question for agreeing to include ⅗ of the blacks

Massts. no. Cont. ay. N. J. no. Pa. no. Del. no. Mard. no. Va. ay. N. C. ay. S. C. no. Geo. ay

On the question as to taking census "the first year after meeting of the Legislature"

Masts. ay. Cont. no. N. J. ay. Pa. ay. Del. ay. Md. no. Va. ay. N. C. ay. S. ay. Geo. no

On filling the blank for the periodical census, with 15 years," Agreed to nem. con.

Mr. Madison moved to add after "15 years," the words "at least" that the Legislature might anticipate when circumstances were likely to render a particular year inconvenient.

On this motion for adding "at least," it passed in the negative the States being equally divided.

Mas. ay. Cont. no. N. J. no. Pa. no. Del. no. Md. no. Va. ay. N. C. ay. S. C. ay. Geo. ay.

A Change of the phraseology of the other clause so as to read; "and the Legislature shall alter or augment the representation accordingly" was agreed to nem. con.

On the question on the whole resolution of Mr. Williamson as amended.

Mas. no. Cont. no. N. J. no. Del. no. Md. no. Va. no. N. C. no. S. C. no. Geo. no.

Thus at the end of the day, the delegates rejected the entire package they had so painstakingly constructed a clause at a time. Every state objected to some provision, so no state was willing to support the whole.

They returned to the State House the next day, July 12, to do battle again. This time, however, Gouverneur Morris began the day's debates by proposing to add to the Williamson/Randolph motion the proviso that taxation be in proportion to representation. Note that the Articles of Confederation already provided for taxation according to the three-fifths compromise; that Madison's footnote on July 11 described the Articles provision as establishing ''a rule of taxation *only*,'' suggesting that the Williamson proposal would apply to both taxation and representation; and that no delegate had ever suggested separating the bases for taxation and representation. In light of these facts, does Morris's motion add anything? Trace carefully the fate of Morris's motion—supplemented by Randolph—during the July 12 debates.

Thursday, July 12

Mr. Govr. Morris moved to add to the clause empowering the Legislature to vary the Representation according to the principles of wealth & number of inhabts. a ''proviso that taxation shall be in proportion to Representation.''

Mr. Butler contended again that Representation sd. be according to the full number of inhabts. including all the blacks; admitting the justice of Mr. Govr. Morris's motion.

Mr. Mason also admitted the justice of the principle, but was afraid embarrassments might be occasioned to the Legislature by it. It might drive the Legislature to the plan of Requisitions.

Mr. Govr. Morris, admitted that some objections lay agst. his motion, but supposed they would be removed by restraining the rule to *direct* taxation. With regard to indirect taxes on *exports* & imports & on consumption, the rule would be inapplicable. Notwithstanding what had been said to the contrary he was persuaded that the imports & consumption were pretty nearly equal throughout the Union.

General Pinkney liked the idea. He thought it so just that it could not be objected to. But foresaw that if the revision of the census was left to the discretion of the legislature, it would never be carried into execution. The rule must be fixed, and the execution of it enforced by the Constitution. He was alarmed at what was said yesterday, concerning the negroes. He was now again alarmed at what had been thrown out concerning the taxing of exports. S. Carola. has in one year exported to the amount of £600,000 Sterling all which was the fruit of the labor of her blacks. Will she be represented in proportion to this amount? She will not. Neither ought she then to be subject to a tax on it. He hoped a clause would be inserted in the system, restraining the Legislature from a taxing Exports.

Mr. Wilson approved the principle, but could not see how it could be carried into execution; unless restrained to direct taxation.

Mr. Govr. Morris having so varied his Motion by inserting the word ''direct.'' It passd. nem. con. as follows—''provided the always that direct taxation ought to be proportioned to representation.''

Mr. Davie, said it was high time now to speak out. He saw that it was meant by some gentlemen to deprive the Southern States of any share of Representation for their blacks. He was sure that N. Carola. would never confederate on any terms that did not rate them at least as ⅗. If the Eastern States meant therefore to exclude them altogether the business was at an end.

Dr. Johnson, thought that wealth and population were the true, equitable rule of representation; but he conceived that these two principles resolved themselves into one; population being the best measure of wealth. He concluded therefore that ye. number of people ought to be established as the rule, and that all descriptions including blacks *equally* with the whites; ought to fall within the computation. As various opinions had been expressed on the subject, he would move that a Committee might be appointed to take them into consideration and report thereon.

Mr. Govr. Morris. It has been said that it is high time to speak out, as one member, he would candidly do so. He came here to form a compact for the good of America. He was ready to do so with all the States. He hoped & believed that all would enter into such a Compact. If they would not he was ready to join with any States that would. But as the Compact was to be voluntary, it is in vain for the Eastern States to insist on what the Southn. States will never agree to. It is equally vain for the latter to require what the other States can never admit; and he verily believed the people of Pena. will never agree to a representation of Negroes. What can be desired by these States more than has been already proposed; that the Legislature shall from time to time regulate Representation according to population & wealth.

Genl. Pinkney desired that the rule of wealth should be ascertained and not left to the pleasure of the Legislature; and that property in slaves should not be exposed to danger under a Govt. instituted for the protection of property.

The first clause in the Report of the first Grand Committee was postponed.

Mr. Elseworth. In order to carry into effect the principle established, moved to add to the last clause adopted by the House the words following "and that the rule of contribution by direct taxation for the support of the Government of the U. States shall be the number of white inhabitants, and three fifths of every other description in the several States, until some other rule that shall more accurately ascertain the wealth of the several States can be devised and adopted by the Legislature."

Mr. Butler seconded the motion in order that it might be committed.

Mr. Randolph was not satisfied with the motion. The danger will be revived that the ingenuity of the Legislature may evade or pervert the rule so as to perpetuate the power where it shall be lodged in the first instance. He proposed in lieu of Mr. Elseworth's motion, "that in order to ascertain the alterations in Representation that may be required from time to time by changes in the relative circumstances of the States, a census shall be taken within two years from the 1st. meeting of the Genl Legislature of the U.S., and once within the term of every   year afterwards, of all the inhabitants in the manner & according to the ratio recommended by Congress in their resolution of the 18th day of Apl. 1783; [rating the blacks at ⅗ of their number] and, that the Legislature of the U. S. shall arrange the Representation accordingly."—He urged strenuously that express security ought to be provided for including slaves in the ratio of Representation. He

lamented that such a species of property existed. But as it did exist the holders of it would require this security. It was perceived that the design was entertained by some of excluding slaves altogether; the Legislature therefore ought not to be left at liberty.

Mr. Elseworth withdraws his motion & seconds that of Mr. Randolph.

Mr. Wilson observed that less umbrage would perhaps be taken agst. an admission of the slaves into the Rule of representation, if it should be so expressed as to make them indirectly only an ingredient in the rule, by saying that they should enter into the rule of taxation: and as representation was to be according to taxation, the end would be equally attained. He accordingly moved & was 2ded. so to alter the last clause adopted by the House, that together with the amendment proposed the whole should read as follows—provided always that the representation ought to be proportioned according to direct taxation, and in order to ascertain the alterations in the direct taxation which may be required from time to time by the changes in the relative circumstances of the States. Resolved that a census be taken within two years from the first meeting of the Legislature of the U. States, and once within the term of every   years afterwards of all the inhabitants of the U. S. in the manner and according to the ratio recommended by Congress in their Resolution of April 18. 1783; and that the Legislature of the U. S. shall proportion the direct taxation accordingly."

Mr. King. Altho' this amendment varies the aspect somewhat, he had still two powerful objections agst. tying down the Legislature to the rule of numbers. 1. they were at this time an uncertain index of the relative wealth of the States. 2. if they were a just index at this time it can not be supposed always to continue so. He was far from wishing to retain any unjust advantage whatever in one part of the Republic. If justice was not the basis of the connection it could not be of long duration. He must be shortsighted indeed who does not foresee that whenever the Southern States shall be more numerous than the Northern, they can & will hold a language that will awe them into justice. If they threaten to separate now in case injury shall be done them, will their threats be less urgent or effectual, when force shall back their demands. Even in the intervening period, there will   no point of time at which they will not be able to say, do us justice or we will separate. He urged the necessity of placing confidence to a certain degree in every Govt. and did not conceive that the proposed confidence as to a periodical readjustment, of the representation exceeded that degree.

Mr. Pinkney moved to amend Mr. Randolph's motion so as to make "blacks equal to the whites in the ratio of representation." This he urged was nothing more than justice. The blacks are the labourers, the peasants of the Southern States: they are as productive of pecuniary resources as those of the Northern States. They add equally to the wealth, and considering money as the sinew of war, to the strength of the nation. It will also be politic with regard to the Northern States, as taxation is to keep pace with Representation.

Genl. Pinkney moves to insert 6 years instead of two, as the period computing from 1st. meeting of ye. Legis—within which the first census should be taken. On this question for inserting six instead of "two" in the proposition of Mr. Wilson, it passed in the affirmative

Masts. no. Ct. ay. N. J. ay. Pa. ay. Del. divd. Mayd. ay. Va. no. N. C. no. S. C. ay. Geo. no.

On a question for filling the blank for ye. periodical census with 20 years, it it passed in the negative.

Masts. no. Ct. ay. N. J. ay. P. ay. Del. no. Md. no. Va. no. N. C. no. S. C. no. Geo. no.

On a question for 10 years, it passed in the affirmative.

Mas. ay. Cont. no. N. J. no. P. ay. Del. ay. Md. ay. Va. ay. N. C. ay. S. C. ay. Geo. ay.

On Mr. Pinkney's motion for rating blacks as equal to Whites instead of as ⅗—

Mas. no. Cont. no. [Dr. Johnson ay] N. J. no. Pa. no. [3 agst. 2.] Del. no. Md. no. Va. no. N. C. no. S. C. ay. Geo.—ay.

Mr. Randolph's proposition as varied by Mr. Wilson being read for question on the whole.

Mr. Gerry, urged that the principle of it could not be carried into execution as the States were not to be taxed as States. With regard to taxes in imports, he conceived they would be more productive. Where there were no slaves than where there were; the consumption being greater—

Mr. Elseworth. In case of a poll tax there wd. be no difficulty. But there wd. probably be none. The sum allotted to a State may be levied without difficulty according to the plan used by the State in raising its own supplies. On the question on ye. whole proposition; as proportioning representation to direct taxation & both to the white & ⅗ of black inhabitants, & requiring a Census within six years—& within every ten years afterwards.

Mas. divd. Cont. ay. N. J. no. Pa. ay. Del. no. Md. ay. Va. ay. N. C. ay. S. C. divd. Geo. ay.

By a vote of six states to two, with two divided, the Convention thus resolved one of the most difficult issues of the summer.

Although there was some grumbling on July 13, the July 12 vote held. Gouverneur Morris complained that the distinction set up between the Northern and Southern states was "heretical" and "groundless," and advised that if there was in fact a real sectional division, the states ought to "take a friendly leave of each other." Pierce Butler of South Carolina replied that the Southern states were simply seeking security "that their negroes may not be taken from them, which some gentlemen within or without doors, have a very good mind to do." James Wilson, defending the decision to apportion representation on the basis of numbers rather than wealth, stated:

> Again he could not agree that property was the sole or the primary object of Government & society. The cultivation and improvement of the human mind was the most noble object. With respect to this object, as well as to other *personal* rights, numbers were surely the natural & precise measure of Representation.

With little further debate, the delegates voted to remove all reference to wealth from the apportionment provisions, and to rely instead on the three-fifths compromise.

This resolution of the representation question did not end the controversy over slavery. On July 23, shortly before the work of the Convention was submitted to the Committee on Detail, Charles Cotesworth Pinckney (the senior of the two South Carolina Pinckneys) warned the delegates that other issues remained. He "reminded the Convention that if the Committee should fail to insert some security to the Southern States against an emancipation of slaves, and taxes on exports, he should be bound by duty to his State to vote against their Report." His objection to taxes on exports was understood as a way of guarding against an indirect tax on slavery through a federal tax on the products of slave labor.

The Committee on Detail[11] heeded the warning. Their report on August 6 contained a number of provisions that protected the South's peculiar institution. The three-fifths compromise was reflected in various provisions on representation and taxation, some of which were cross-referenced. On August 8, a minor change in one of these cross-references, designed to make the three-fifths formula more explicit, roused the Northern delegates to make one last stand against the compromise.

The committee report had required Congress to allocate representatives to new states "according to the provisions herein after made." At Hugh Williamson's suggestion, the wording was changed to "according to the rule hereafter provided for direct taxation." It was only a technical change, not a substantive one, but it reminded some of the delegates of their continued opposition to the three-fifths rule.

Wednesday, August 8

Mr. King wished to know what influence the vote just passed was meant have on the succeeding part of the Report, concerning the admission of slaves into the rule of Representation. He could not reconcile his mind to the article if it was to prevent objections to the latter part. The admission of slaves was a most grating circumstance to his mind, & he believed would be so to a great part of the people of America. He had not made a strenuous opposition to it heretofore because he had hoped that this concession would have produced a readiness which had not been manifested, to strengthen the Genl. Govt. and to mark a full confidence in it. The Report under consideration had by the tenor of it, put an end to all those hopes. In two great points the hands of the Legislature were absolutely tied. The importation of slaves could not be prohibited—exports could not be taxed. Is this reasonable? What are the great objects of the Genl. System? 1. defence agst. foreign invasion. 2. agst. internal sedition. Shall all the States then be bound to defend each; & shall each be at liberty to introduce a weakness which will render defence more difficult? Shall one part of the U. S. be bound to defend another part, and that other part be at liberty not only to increase its own danger, but to withhold the compensation for the burden? If slaves are to be imported shall not the exports produced by their labor, supply a reve-

nue the better to enable the Genl. Govt. to defend their masters?—There was so much inequality & unreasonableness in all this, that the people of the Northern States could never be reconciled to it. No candid man could undertake to justify it to them. He had hoped that some accomodation wd. have taken place on this subject; that at least a time wd. have been limited for the importation of slaves. He never could agree to let them be imported without limitation & then be represented in the Natl. Legislature. Indeed he could so little persuade himself of the rectitude of such a practice; that he was not sure he could assent to it under any circumstances. At all events, either slaves should not be represented, or exports should be taxable.

Mr. Sherman regarded the slave trade as iniquitous; but the point of representation having been settled after much difficulty & deliberation, he did not think himself bound to make opposition; especially as the present article as amended did not preclude any arrangement whatever on that point in another place of the Report.

Mr. Govr. Morris moved to insert "free" before the word inhabitants. Much he said would depend on this point. He never would concur in upholding domestic slavery. It was a nefarious institution. It was the curse of heaven on the States where it prevailed. Compare the free regions of the Middle

States, where a rich & noble cultivation marks the prosperity & happiness of the people, with the misery & poverty which overspread the barren wastes of Va. Maryd. & the other States having slaves. Travel thro' ye. whole Continent & you behold the prospect continually varying with the appearance & disappearance of slavery. The moment you leave ye. E. Sts. & enter N. York, the effects of the institution become visible, passing thro' the Jerseys & entering Pa. every criterion of superior improvement witnesses the change. Proceed Southwdly & every step you take thro' ye. great region of slaves presents a desert increasing, with ye. increasing proportion of these wretched beings. Upon what principle is it that the slaves shall be computed in the representation? Are they men? Then make them Citizens and let them vote. Are they property? Why then is no other property included? The Houses in this city [Philada.] are worth more than all the wretched slaves which cover the rice swamps of South Carolina. The admission of slaves into the Representation when fairly explained comes to this: that the inhabitant of Georgia and S. C. who goes to the Coast of Africa, and in defiance of the most sacred laws of humanity tears away his fellow creatures from their dearest connections & damns them to the most cruel bondages, shall have more votes in a Govt. instituted for the protection of the rights of mankind, than the Citizen of Pa. or N. Jersey who views with a laudable horror, so nefarious a practice. He would add that Domestic slavery is the most prominent feature in the aristocratic countenance of the proposed Constitution. The vassalage of the poor has ever been the favorite offspring of Aristocracy. And What is the proposed compensation to the Northern States for a sacrifice of every principle of right, of every impulse of humanity. They are to bind themselves to march their militia for the defence of the S. States; for their defence agst. those very slaves of whom they complain. They must supply vessels & seamen in case of foreign Attack. The Legislature will have indefinite power to tax them by excises, and duties on imports: both of which will fall heavier on them than on the Southern inhabitants; for the bohea tea used by a Northern freeman, will pay more tax than the whole consumption of the miserable slave, which consists of nothing more than his physical subsistence and the rag that covers his nakedness. On the other side the Southern States are not be be restrained from importing fresh supplies of wretched Africans, at once to increase the danger of attack, and the difficulty of defence; nay they are to be encouraged to it by an assurance of having their votes in the Natl. Govt. increased in proportion, and are at the same time to have their exports & their slaves exempt from all contributions for the public service. Let is not be said that direct taxation is to be proportioned to representation. It is idle to suppose that the Genl. Govt. can stretch its hand directly into the pockets of the people scattered over so vast a Country. They can only do it through the medium of exports imports & excises. For what then are all these sacrifices to be made? He would sooner submit himself to a tax for paying for all the negroes in the U. States, than saddle posterity with such a Constitution.

Morris's motion failed (it was seconded by Jonathan Dayton of New Jersey, and only that state voted in favor), but his "curse of heaven" speech is perhaps the most stirring oratory of the Convention.

Topics for Discussion

1. What were the major concerns of the Northern states? Did they view slavery as immoral or merely inconvenient? Look closely at the speeches of the Northern delegates, especially those of Gouverneur Morris of Pennsylvania. Pennsylvania was one of the states most strongly opposed to slavery, so Morris's speeches, including the eloquent "curse of heaven" speech on August 8, should provide good evidence of the basis for, and contours of, Northern objections to slavery.

2. Examine carefully the states' votes on the individual parts of the Williamson motion on July 11. Then look at the Morris/Randolph motion on July 12. How would you expect the various states to vote on the Randolph motion, in light of their votes the previous day? How did they vote? What happened? Keep in mind that the link between taxation and representation had been a fixed principle since before the Revolution, and that neither the Congress nor the Convention itself ever thought the taxable population would be larger than the represented population.

3. What does the discussion of how slaves are to be counted add to earlier materials (in chapters 2 and 5) on the purposes of government? On the nature of the legislature? On the nature of representation? What light does this discussion shed on modern apportionment questions raised by such cases as *Reynolds v. Sims*, 377 U.S. 533, 84 S.Ct. 1362, 12 L.Ed.2d 506 (1964), and *Brown v. Thomson*, 462 U.S. 835, 103 S.Ct. 2690, 77 L.Ed.2d 214 (1983), which established and elaborated the one person, one vote principle?

4. Other than Wilson (in his "cultivation and improvement of the human mind" speech), did any of the delegates deny that protection of property is the primary purpose of government? Why did they decide to allocate representation on the basis of population rather than wealth? Are their assumptions valid today?

5. What was the Convention trying to do in dealing with slavery? Did it work? From the perspective of the modern world, we might condemn their actions as reprehensible. Can you justify what the Convention did from the perspective of 1787? Were there better ways to accomplish their aims?

THE SLAVE TRADE

The Committee on Detail draft (reproduced in the Appendix) also contained other provisions dealing with slavery, and especially with the slave trade. Article VII, sections 4 through 6 provided:

> Sect. 4. No tax or duty shall be laid by the Legislature on articles exported from any State; nor on the migration or importation of such persons as the several States shall think proper to admit; nor shall such migration or importation be prohibited.
> Sect. 5. No capitation tax shall be laid, unless in proportion to the Census herinbefore directed to be taken.
> Sect. 6. No navigation acts shall be passed without the assent of two thirds of the members present in each House.

The prohibition on export taxes was a direct result of Pinckney's earlier threat. The prohibition on capitation taxes was to prevent the Congress from taxing slaves directly. Finally, the supermajority requirement for navigation acts was directed to the Southern fears outlined in the introduction to this chapter.

On August 21, the Convention turned to these provisions.

Tuesday, August 21

Question on Sect: 4. art VII. as far as to "no tax shl. be laid on exports—It passed in the affirmative.

N. H. no. Mas. ay. Ct. ay. N. J. no. Pa. no. Del. no. Md. ay. Va. ay. (Genl. W. & J. M. no) N. C. ay.

S. C. ay. Geo. ay.

Mr. L. Martin, proposed to vary the Sect: 4. art VII. so as to allow a prohibition or tax on the importation of slaves. 1. as five slaves are to be counted as

3 free men in the apportionment of Representatives; such a clause wd. leave an encouragement to this traffic. 2. slaves weakened one part of the Union which the other parts were bound to protect: the privilege of importing them was therefore unreasonable. 3. it was inconsistent with the principles of the revolution and dishonorable to the American character to have such a feature in the Constitution.

Mr. Rutledge did not see how the importation of slaves could be encouraged by this Section. He was not apprehensive of insurrections and would readily exempt the other States from the obligation to protect the Southern against them.—Religion & humanity had nothing to do with this question. Interest alone is the governing principle with nations. The true question at present is whether the Southn. States shall or shall not be parties to the Union. If the Northern States consult their interest, they will not oppose the increase of Slaves which will increase the commodities of which they will become the carriers.

Mr. Elseworth was for leaving the clause as it stands. let every State import what it pleases. The morality or wisdom of slavery are considerations belonging to the States themselves. What enriches a part enriches the whole, and the States are the best judges of their particular interest. The old confederation had not meddled with this point, and he did not see any greater necessity for bringing it within the policy of the new one:

Mr. Pinkney. South Carolina can never receive the plan if it prohibits the slave trade. In every proposed extension of the powers of the Congress, that State has expressly & watchfully excepted that of meddling with the importation of negroes. If the States be all left at liberty on this subject, S. Carolina may perhaps by degrees do of herself what is wished, as Virginia & Maryland have already done.

Wednesday, August 22

Art VII sect 4. resumed. **Mr. Sherman** was for leaving the clause as it stands. He disapproved of the slave trade; yet as the States were now possessed of the right to import slaves, as the public good did not require it to be taken from them, & as it was expedient to have as few objections as possible to the proposed scheme of Government, he thought it best to leave the matter as we find it. He observed that the abolition of Slavery seemed to be going on in the U.S. & that the good sense of the several States would probably by degrees compleat it. He urged on the Convention the necessity of despatching its business.

Col. Mason. This infernal trafic originated in the avarice of British Merchants. The British Govt. constantly checked the attempts of Virginia to put a stop to it. The present question concerns not the importing States alone but the whole Union. The evil of having slaves was experienced during the late war. Had slaves been treated as they might have been by the Enemy, they would have proved dangerous instruments in their hands. But their folly dealt by the slaves, as it did by the Tories. He mentioned the dangerous insurrections of the slaves in Greece and Sicily; and the instructions given by Cromwell to the Commissioners sent to Virginia, to arm the servants & slaves, in case other means of obtaining its submission should fail. Maryland & Virginia he said had already prohibited the importation of slaves expressly. N. Carolina had done the same in substance. All this would be in vain if S. Carolina & Georgia be at liberty to import. The Western people are already calling out for slaves for their new lands, and will fill that Country with slaves if they can be got thro' S. Carolina & Georgia. Slavery discourages arts & manufactures. The poor despise labor when performed by slaves. They prevent the immigration of Whites, who really enrich & strengthen a Country. They produce the most pernicious effect on manners. Every master of slaves is born a petty tyrant. They bring the judgment of heaven on a Country. As nations can not be rewarded or punished in the next world they must be in this. By an inevitable chain of causes & effects providence punishes national sins, by national calamities. He lamented that some of our Eastern brethren had from a lust of gain embarked in this nefarious traffic. As to the States being in possession of the Right to import, this was the case with many other rights, now to be properly given up. He held it essential in every point of view that the Genl. Govt. should have power to prevent the increase of slavery.

Mr. Elsworth. As he had never owned a slave

could not judge of the effects of slavery on character: He said however that if it was to be considered in a moral light we ought to go farther and free those already in the Country.—As slaves also multiply so fast in Virginia & & Maryland that it is cheaper to raise than import them, whilst in the sickly rice swamps foreign supplies are necessary, if we go no farther than is urged, we shall be unjust towards S. Carolina & Georgia. Let us not intermeddle. As population increases poor laborers will be so plenty as to render slaves useless. Slavery in time will not be a speck in our country. Provision is already made in Connecticut for abolishing it. And the abolition has already taken place in Massachusetts. As to the danger of insurrections from foreign influence, that will become a motive to kind treatment of the slaves.

Mr. Pinkney. If slavery be wrong, it is justified by the example of all the world. He cited the case of Greece Rome & other antient States; the sanction given by France England, Holland & other modern States. In all ages one half of mankind have been slaves. If the S. States were let alone they will probably of themselves stop importations. He wd. himself as a Citizen of S. Carolina vote for it. An attempt to take away the right as proposed will produce serious objections to the Constitution which he wished to see adopted.

General Pinkney declared it to be his firm opinion that if himself & all his colleagues were to sign the Constitution & use their personal influence, it would be of no avail towards obtaining the assent of their Constituents. S. Carolina & Georgia cannot do without slaves. As to Virginia she will gain by stopping the importations. Her slaves will rise in value, & she has more than she wants. It would be unequal to require S. C. & Georgia to confederate on such unequal terms. He said the Royal assent before the Revolution had never been refused to S. Carolina as to Virginia. He contended that the importation of slaves would be for the interest of the whole Union. The more slaves, the more produce to employ the carrying trade; The more consumption also, and the more of this, the more of revenue for the common treasury. He admitted it to be reasonable that slaves should be dutied like other imports, but should consider a rejection of the clause as an exclusion of S. Carola. from the Union.

Mr. Baldwin had conceived national objects alone to be before the Convention, not such as like the present were of a local nature. Georgia was decided on this point. That State has always hitherto supposed a Genl. Govermt. to be the pursuit of the central States who wished to have a vortex for every

thing—that her distance would preclude her from equal advantage—& that she could not prudently purchase it by yielding national powers. From this it might be understood in what light she would view an attempt to abridge one of her favorite prerogatives. If left to herself, she may probably put a stop to the evil. As one ground for this conjecture, he took notice of the sect of   which he said was a respectable class of people, who carried their ethics beyond the mere *equality of men*, extending their humanity to the claims of the whole animal creation.

Mr. Wilson observed that if S. C. & Georgia were themselves disposed to get rid of the importation of slaves in a short time as had been suggested, they would never refuse to Unite because the importation might be prohibited. As the Section now stands all articles imported are to be taxed. Slaves alone are exempt. This is in fact a bounty on that article.

Mr. Gerry thought we had nothing to do with the conduct of the States as to Slaves, but ought to be careful not to give any sanction to it.

Mr. Dickenson considered it as inadmissible on every principle of honor & safety that the importation of slaves should be authorised to the States by the Constitution. The true question was whether the national happiness would be promoted or impeded by the importation, and this question ought to be left to the National Govt. not to the States particularly interested. If Engd. & France permit slavery, slaves are at the same time excluded from both those Kingdoms. Greece and Rome were made unhappy by their slaves. He could not believe that the Southn. States would refuse to confederate on the account apprehended; especially as the power was not likely to be immediately exercised by the Genl. Government.

Mr. Williamson stated the law of N. Carolina on the subject, to wit that it did not directly prohibit the importation of slaves. It imposed a duty of £5. on each slave imported from Africa. £10 on each from elsewhere, & £50 on each from a State licensing manumission. He thought the S. States could not be members of the Union if the clause shd. be rejected, and that it was wrong to force any thing down, not absolutely necessary, and which any State must disagree to.

Mr. King thought the subject should be considered in a political light only. If two States will not agree to the Constitution as stated on one side, he could affirm with equal belief on the other, that great & equal opposition would be experienced from the other States. He remarked on the exemption of slaves from duty whilst every other import was subjected to it, as an inequality that could not fail to strike the commercial sagacity of the Northn. & middle States.

Mr. Langdon was strenuous for giving the power to the Genl. Govt. He cd. not with a good conscience leave it with the States who could then go on with the traffic, witout being restrained by the opinions here given that they will themselves cease to import slaves.

Genl. Pinkney thought himself bound to declare candidly that he did not think S. Carolina would stop her importations of slaves in any short time, but only stop them occasionally as she now does. He moved to commit the clause that slaves might be made liable to an equal tax with other imports which he he thought right & wch. wd. remove one difficulty that had been started.

Mr. Rutlidge. If the Convention thinks that N. C. S. C. & Georgia will ever agree to the plan, unless their right to import slaves be untouched, the expectation is vain. The people of those States will never be such fools as to give up so important an interest. He was strenuous agst. striking out the Section, and seconded the motion of Genl. Pinkney for a commitment.

Mr. Govr. Morris wished the whole subject to be committed including the clauses relating to taxes in exports & to a navigation act. These things may form a bargain among the Northern & Southern States.

Mr. Butler declared that he never would agree to the power of taxing exports.

Mr. Sherman said it was better to let the S. States import slaves than to part with them, if they made that a sine qua non. He was opposed to a tax on slaves imported as making the matter worse, because it implied they were *property*. He acknowledged that if the power of prohibiting the importation should be given to the Genl. Government that it would be exercised. He thought it would be its duty to exercise the power.

.   .   .

Mr. Randolph was for committing in order that some middle ground might, if possible, be found. He could never agree to the clause as it stands. He wd. sooner risk the constitution. He dwelt on the dilemma to which the Convention was exposed. By agreeing to the clause, it would revolt the Quakers, the Methodists, and many others in the States having no slaves. On the other hand, two States might be lost to the Union. Let us then, he said, try the chance of a commitment.

The Convention then agreed to send all three clauses to a committee.[12]

That committee reported on August 24, although their report was not taken up until the next day.

Friday, August 24

Governour Livingston, from the Committee of Eleven, to whom were referred the two remaining clauses of the 4th. Sect & the 5 & 6 Sect: of the 7th. art: delivered in the following Report:

"Strike out so much of the 4th Sect: as was referred to the Committee and insert—"The migration or importation of such persons as the several States now existing shall think proper to admit, shall not be prohibited by the Legislature prior to the year 1800, but a tax or duty may be imposed on such migration or importation at a rate not exceeding the average of the duties laid on imports."

"The 5 Sect: to remain as in the Report"

"The 6 Sect to be stricken out"

Saturday, August 25

The Report of the Committee of eleven [see friday the 24th. instant] being taken up.

Genl. Pinkney moved to strike out the words "the year eighteen hundred" as the year limiting the importation of slaves, and to insert the words "the year eighteen hundred and eight"

Mr. Ghorum 2ded. the motion

Mr. Madison. Twenty years will produce all the mischief that can be apprehended from the liberty to import slaves. So long a term will be more dishonorable to the National character than to say nothing about it in the Constitution.

On the motion; which passed in the affirmative.

N. H. ay. Mas. ay. Ct. ay. N. J. no. Pa. no. Del. no. Md. ay. Va. no. N. C. ay. S. C. ay. Geo. ay.

Mr Govr. Morris was for making the clause read at once, " importation of slaves into N. Carolina, S. Carolina & Georgia shall not be prohibited &c." This he said would be most fair and would avoid the ambiguity by which, under the power with regard to naturalization, the liberty reserved to the States might be defeated. He wished it to be known also that this part of the Constitution was a compliance with those States. If the change of language however should be objected to by the members from those States, he should not urge it.

Col: Mason was not against using the term "slaves" but agst. naming N .C. S. C. & Georgia, lest it should give offence to the people of those States.

Mr. Sherman liked a description better than the terms proposed, which had been declined by the old Congs. & were not pleasing to some people. **Mr. Clymer** concurred with Mr. Sherman

Mr. Williamson said that both in opinion & practice he was, against slavery; but thought it more in favor of humanity, from a view of all circumstances, to let in S. C. & Georgia on those terms, than to exclude them from the Union.

Mr. Govr. Morris withdrew his motion.

Mr. Dickenson wished the clause to be confined to the States which had not themselves prohibited the importation of slaves, and for that purpose moved to amend the clause so as to read "The importation of slaves into such of the States as shall permit the same shall not be prohibited by the Leg-islature of the U-S- until the year 1808"—which was disagreed to nem: cont:

The first part of the report was then agreed to, amended as follows.

"The migration or importation of such persons as the several States now existing shall think proper to admit, shall not be prohibited by the Legislature prior to the year 1808."

N. H. Mas. Con. Md. N. C. S. C. Geo: ay

N. J. Pa. Del. Virga..........................no

.   .   .

Mr. Sherman was agst. this 2d. part, as acknowledging men to be property, by taxing them as such under the character of slaves.

Mr. King & **Mr. Langdon** considered this as the price of the 1st. part.

Genl. Pinkney admitted that it was so.

Col: Mason. Not to tax, will be equivalent to a bounty on the importation of slaves.

Mr. Ghorum thought that Mr. Sherman should consider the duty, not as implying that slaves are property, but as a discouragement to the importation of them.

Mr. Govr. Morris remarked that as the clause now stands it implies that the Legislature may tax freemen imported.

Mr. Sherman in answer to Mr. Ghorum observed that the smallness of the duty shewed revenue to be the object, not the discouragement of the importation.

Mr. Madison thought it wrong to admit in the Constitution the idea that there could be property in men. The reason of duties did not hold, as slaves are not like merchandize, consumed, &c

Col. Mason (in answr. to Govr. Morris) the provision as it stands was necessary for the case of Convicts in order to prevent the introduction of them.

It was finally agreed nem: contrad: to make the clause read "but a tax or duty may be imposed on such importation not exceeding ten dollars for each person," and then the 2d. part as amended was agreed to.

Sect 5. art. VII was agreed to nem: con: as reported.

Sect. 6. art. VII. in the Report, was postponed.

Draft notes for a speech John Dickinson had apparently intended to give during an earlier debate explain why he supported the use of the word "slaves": "The omitting the *Word* will be regarded as an Endeavour to conceal a principle of which we are ashamed."[13]

Having reached agreement on at least part of the committee report, the Convention turned to other issues, and did not return to section 6 for several days. One of the intervening debates involved Article XV, which required states to extradite accused criminals to other states. The article itself inspired little debate, but Pierce Butler and Charles Pinckney moved an addition: "to require fugitive slaves and servants to be delivered up like criminals." After Wilson and Sherman both opposed the motion, Butler "withdrew his proposition in order that some particular provision might be made apart from this article." The extradition clause was then approved unanimously and without further debate.

The Convention turned back to the Article VII committee report on August 29. Young Charles Pinckney immediately moved to postpone consideration in order to approve the original supermajority requirement for navigation acts. He was gently reined in by his older cousin:

> General Pinkney said it was the true interest of the S. States to have no regulation of commerce; but considering the loss brought on the commerce of the Eastern States by the revolution, their liberal conduct toward the views of South Carolina, and the interest the weak Southern States had in being united with the strong Eastern States, he thought it proper that no fetters should be imposed on the power of making commercial regulations; and that his constituents though prejudiced against the Eastern States, would be reconciled to this liberality. He had himself, he said, prejudices against the Eastern States before he came here, but would acknowledge that he had found them as liberal and candid as any men whatever.

Lest it be misunderstood why the older Pinckney was willing to concede the point on navigation acts, Madison footnoted Pinckney's reference to the "liberal conduct toward the views of South Carolina." General Pinckney meant, Madison said,

> the permission to import slaves. An understanding on the two subjects of *navigation* and *slavery* had taken place between those parts of the Union, which explains the vote on the motion depending, as well as the language of General Pinkney and others.

Only Martin and Williamson defended the motion to require a supermajority on navigation acts. After eleven other delegates, including Southerners, opposed the motion, it was defeated. The committee's recommendation to strike section 6 was then approved without debate or dissent.

Immediately following the vote on navigation acts—and before the Convention moved on to Article XVII, where they had left off—Butler made another motion:

> Mr. Butler moved to insert after art: XV. "If any person bound to service or labor in any of the U. States shall escape into another State, he or she shall not be discharged from such service or labor, in consequence of any regulations subsisting in the State to which they escape, but shall be delivered up to the person justly claiming their service or labor," which was agreed to nem: con:.

Having adopted the fugitive slave clause without discussion or dissent, the Convention then went back to where they had been before the navigation act interruption: Article XVII, on the admission of new states.

Butler's inelegant language was significantly amended twice. The Committee on Style redrafted the clause to read:

> No person legally held to service or labour in one state, escaping into another, shall in consequence of regulations subsisting therein be discharged from such service or labor, but shall be delivered up on claim of the party to whom such service or labour may be due.

On September 15, the Convention again considered the clause:

> Art. IV. Sect. 2 parag: 3. The term "legally" was struck out, and "under the laws thereof" inserted after the word "State," in compliance with the wish of some who thought the term legal equivocal, and favoring the idea that slavery was legal in a moral view.

Minor changes in wording, unrecorded by Madison, completed the fugitive slave clause.

After satisfactorily resolving—at least temporarily—all the questions regarding slavery, the Convention had only to protect its compromises from future antislavery advocates. On September 15, the delegates approved Article V, which allowed for future amendments. The Committee on Style had already included a proviso prohibiting amendment of the slave trade clause before 1808. Sherman moved to add a further proviso "that no State shall without its consent be affected in its internal police, or deprived of its equal suffrage in the Senate." The motion was rejected eight states to three, and the equal suffrage portion was immediately—and successfully—proposed alone. Mason moved to add "that no law in [the] nature of a navigation act be passed before the year 1808, without the consent of ⅔ of each branch of the Legislature," but it was defeated seven states to three (North Carolina absent from the floor). What William Lloyd Garrison would later call "an agreement with hell" was complete.

Topics for Discussion

1. Are there differences between the delegates' views of slavery and their views of the slave trade? Did their views of the latter influence their views of the former, over time? Return to Morris's "curse of heaven" speech. Was it slavery or the slave trade that was immoral and a "nefarious institution"? Assuming that the Pennsylvania delegation reflected Morris's own views, can you reconcile your answer with Morris's votes?

2. What happened in the Committee of Eleven, which was appointed on August 22 and made its report on August 24? Compare the Committee on Detail draft with the report of the Committee of Eleven. What did the southern states lose? What did they gain? Why would they agree to the Committee of Eleven report? Notice the sequence of events on August 29.

3. Look at the evolution of the language of the fugitive slave clause, and especially at the reason given for the last change (on September 15). Can you explain why there was so little debate on each stage of what we might see as a controversial clause? How might the antislavery delegates have interpreted the changes in the language? How might the proslavery delegates have done so? Note that Butler's version of the clause is the only time a feminine pronoun appears in any draft of the Constitution. What might that suggest about Butler's view of slaves?

4. How far does the slave trade clause extend? Could Congress, prior to 1808, regulate immigration? Could it regulate the interstate transportation and sale of slaves? What about after 1808? What kind of "negative pregnant" can be inferred to give Congress power over slavery or the slave trade? In *Dred Scott v. Sandford*, 60 U.S. (19 How.) 393, 15 L.Ed. 691 (1857), the Supreme Court invalidated Congress' attempt to outlaw slavery in the territories. Do you think the delegates intended to give Congress the power to prohibit slavery in the territories? In the existing states?

5. The debates in the Convention over slavery presaged much of the dispute in Congress prior to the Civil War. Can you see why the Convention's resolution of these questions was inevitably not final? Was the Constitution a "covenant with death and an agreement with hell"? How did it come to be? Review these materials again when you consider the materials on the intellectual origins of Reconstruction (chapter 9) and on the Thirteenth Amendment (chapter 10).

FOOTNOTES

1. James Otis, *The Rights of the British Colonies Asserted and Proved*, in 1 *Pamphlets of the American Revolution, 1750–1776* 439 (Bernard Bailyn ed. 1965).

2. 6 *Journals of the Continental Congress* 1080 (July 30, 1776).

3. 4 Jonathan Elliot, *Debates in the Several State Conventions* 273, 285 (1891).

4. Thomas Jefferson, *Autobiography* (1821), in *The Life and Selected Writings of Thomas Jefferson* 51 (Adrienne Koch & William Peden eds. 1944).

5. Quoted in Duncan J. MacLeod, *Slavery, Race and the American Revolution* 97 (1974).

6. 2 *Journals of the Continental Congress* 221–222 (July 28, 1775).

7. 6 *Journals of the Continental Congress* 1079–1080 (July 30, 1776).

8. *Id.* at 1080.

9. William M. Wiecek, *The Sources of Antislavery Constitutionalism in America, 1760–1848* at 62–63 (1977). The ten clauses are: (1) Article I, section 2, taxation clause; (2) Article I, section 2, three-fifths clause; (3) Article I, section 8, insurrection clause; (4) Article I, section 9, fugitive slave clause; (5) Article I, section 9, direct taxation clause; (6) Article I, section 9, export duty clause; (7) Article I, section 10, export duty clause; (8) Article IV, section 2, fugitive slave clause; (9) Article IV, section 4, republican government clause; (10) Article V, section 9, unamendability clause.

10. *Supplement to Max Farrand's The Records of the Federal Convention of 1787* 44–45 (James H. Hutson ed. 1987) [hereinafter Farrand Supplement].

11. For a discussion of this committee, see chapter 2.

12. The committee, which was "appointed" and consisted of a member from each state, included Langdon, King, Johnson, Livingston, Clymer, Dickinson, Martin, Madison, Williamson, C.C. Pinckney, and Baldwin.

13. *Farrand Supplement* at 158.

CHAPTER SEVEN

The Ratification Process: Federalists and Anti-Federalists

INTRODUCTION

The arduous process of drafting a new Constitution was followed by the even more difficult task of obtaining popular approval. Writing the Constitution took four months; the ratification process took another ten. They were ten months of almost constant public debate, occasionally punctuated by violence. Unlike the Federal Convention itself, the debate over ratification was carried on in the public eye. Newspapers published signed and unsigned tracts by both Federalists (as those advocating ratification called themselves) and Anti-Federalists. The debates in most of the state ratifying conventions were either open to the public, reported in the newspapers, or both. Madison observed in February 1788: "The public here continues to be much agitated by the proposed federal Constitution and to be attentive to little else."[1]

The Federalists began with a minor coup: they successfully appropriated the name "federalist" for themselves. During the Revolution, "federal men" wished to give Congress power to require (rather than merely request) financial contributions from the states. These early "federalists" thus advocated little more than an expansion of congressional authority under the loose union of the Articles of Confederation. The notion of a "federal" government encompassed only limited national powers. By 1787, there was almost universal support for at least some expansion of congressional power, as the very calling of a Federal Convention illustrates. By arrogating the name "federalists," the pro-ratification forces forced on their opponents the unpopular label of "anti-federalists." Anti-Federalists feebly argued that opponents of ratification were the true "federalists": they charged that the new Constitution, which not only granted broad powers to Congress but also established a national executive and judiciary, represented not a federal government but a national or consolidated one. Some early Anti-Federalist writers even called themselves federalists, but the term was soon limited to the advocates of rat-

175

ification. The Anti-Federalist bitterness lingered, however, and Elbridge Gerry (who refused to sign the Constitution and became a prominent Anti-Federalist in Massachusetts) later suggested that a more accurate nomenclature would have been "rats and anti-rats."[2]

Despite this early Federalist success, the battle for ratification was hard fought and the fate of the new Constitution was uncertain throughout much of 1788. Even after New Hampshire in late June became the ninth state —and technically the last required—to ratify, the outcome was still in doubt. New York and Virginia were still debating, and the Federalists knew that the new government would have little prospect of succeeding unless it included both of these large, powerful, and centrally located states.

Throughout the long campaign, both Federalists and Anti-Federalists resorted to questionable tactics. The Anti-Federalists sometimes made scurrilous personal attacks on delegates to the Federal Convention, and occasionally resorted to violence. On July 4, 1788, an Anti-Federalist mob interrupted Independence Day celebrations by burning a Constitution in New York City. The Federalists were not above economic blackmail and political bribery: they cancelled subscriptions to newspapers that supported the Anti-Federalist cause, and they reportedly promised John Hancock, in exchange for his support, the governorship of Massachusetts as well as the presidency if Virginia failed to join the union and thus George Washington became ineligible.

The ratification process officially began on September 28, 1787, when Congress transmitted the proposed Constitution to the states. The conventions in Delaware, New Jersey, and Georgia all ratified, unanimously and with little debate, by early January of 1788. Connecticut soon followed, by an overwhelming majority of one hundred and twenty-eight to forty. Delaware, New Jersey, and Connecticut, small states adjacent to large states, were fearful that if the federal union was unsuccessful, they would be annexed by their larger neighbors. Georgia was in even greater need of federal protection; George Washington said of that state that "if a weak state with the Indians on its back and the Spaniards on its flank does not see the necessity of a general government, there must I think be wickedness or insanity in the way."[3] These early ratifications were thus not surprising.

The first sign of trouble arose in Pennsylvania, which ratified in December 1787. There the Federalists ran a ruthless campaign for ratification, and ultimately won (forty-six to twenty-three) only through coercive tactics. Only hours after the proposed Constitution was received from the Continental Congress, the Federalist majority in the Pennsylvania legislature called for a state ratifying convention. The Anti-Federalists in the legislature tried to prevent passage of the resolution calling for the convention by absenting themselves from the legislature and depriving it of a quorum. Their minority report described how the Federalists ultimately obtained a quorum:

> James M'Calmont, esquire, a member from Franklin, and Jacob Miley, esquire, a member from Dauphin [both Anti-Federalists], were seized by a number of citizens of Philadelphia, who had collected together for that purpose, their lodgings were violently broken open, their cloaths torn, and after much abuse and insult, they were forcibly dragged through the streets of Philadelphia to the State house, and there detained by force, and in the presence of the majority, who had, the day before, voted for the first of the proposed resolutions, treated with the most insulting language; while the house so formed proceeded to finish their resolutions, which

they mean to offer to you as the doings of the legislature of Pennsylvania. On this outrageous proceeding we make no comment.[4]

The Federalist success in Pennsylvania, the first state in which there was a real contest, was thus less encouraging than it might have been had it been achieved by less abusive tactics. It certainly did not bode well for progress in the other large states.

After January 1788 the pace of state ratifications slowed considerably. Although Massachusetts ratified in early February, it did so only by appending "recommendations" for amendments to its ratification. This proved to be a popular device: of the five states that ratified after Massachusetts and before the implementation of the new government in 1789, four made similar recommendations.[5] Moreover, after Massachusetts' action on February 6, there were no further ratifications until Maryland's on April 26. Maryland ratified by a margin of sixty-three to eleven despite Luther Martin's attempts to sabotage ratification of the document he had helped draft but ultimately opposed.

Beginning with Massachusetts, the public debate began to heat up. The three most vital states—Massachusetts, Virginia, and New York—produced some of the liveliest oratory and some of the closest margins. In each state, prominent members of the Federal Convention worked against ratification. In Massachusetts, Elbridge Gerry, who had refused to sign the Constitution in the Convention, publicly opposed ratification. In New York, both Robert Yates and John Lansing attended the state convention and opposed the new Constitution; they had left the Federal Convention in disgust in early July. Of the Virginians present at the Federal Convention, both George Mason and Edmund Randolph had refused to sign. Mason spoke against ratification at the state convention, but Randolph, who had written essays in opposition to ratification, changed his mind and supported the Constitution. He told the state convention that he believed a failure to ratify would result in "the inevitable ruin of the Union." In a nice inversion of Mason's comment during the Federal Convention that he would "sooner chop off his right hand than put it to the Constitution,"[6] Randolph said that he would "assent to the lopping of this limb (meaning his arm)" before he would assent to the dissolution of the union.[7] Mason is reported to have exclaimed "Young Arnold! Young Arnold!" on hearing of Randolph's change of heart. Other popular and eloquent firebrands in these states, including Melancton Smith and Gilbert Livingston in New York, Patrick Henry in Virginia, and James Winthrop in Massachusetts, opposed ratification.

Despite the capabilities and popularity of individual opponents of the Constitution, the Anti-Federalists were a loose and disunified group. They attacked the Constitution from a variety of angles and offered many different solutions, from splitting the union to leaving the Articles of Confederation almost intact. The differences between John Adams, then in London, and Thomas Jefferson, then in Paris, illustrate the variety of views held by critics of the Constitution. Adams wrote to Jefferson:

> The Project of a new Constitution, has Objections against it, to which I find it difficult to reconcile my self, but I am so unfortunate as to differ somewhat from you in the Articles, according to your last kind Letter.

You are afraid of the one—I, of the few. We agree perfectly that the many should have a full fair and perfect Representation.—You are Apprehensive of Monarchy; I, of Aristocracy. I would therefore have given more Power to the President and less to the Senate. . . .

You are apprehensive the President when once chosen, will be chosen again and again as long as he lives. So much the better as it appears to me.—You are apprehensive of foreign Interference, Intrigue, Influence. So am I.—But, as often as Elections happen, the danger of foreign Influence recurs. The less frequently they happen the less danger.—And if the Same Man may be chosen again, it is probable he will be, and the danger of foreign Influence will be less. Foreigners, seeing little Prospect will have less courage for Enterprize.[8]

Despite these differences, there were some common themes. Virtually all the Anti-Federalists argued that the Constitution created a government that was too strong, too national, and too aristocratic. They feared that both the sovereignty of the states and the liberty of the people were in jeopardy. One Anti-Federalist essay, for example, was addressed "To the *real* patriots of America."[9] As the materials below illustrate, the Anti-Federalist concerns took many forms. Many writers criticized the lack of a bill of rights. That criticism will be considered in the next chapter. Others simply attacked the Constitution as a whole, arguing that it created an aristocracy rather than a republic, or that republican principles (such as separation of powers) were insufficiently observed. More analytical essays pointed to defects in specific provisions, concentrating heavily on the small size and broad powers of the federal legislature. Anti-Federalists also revived a dispute that figured heavily in the Federal Convention itself: that the Convention had exceeded its authority.

The Federalists did not remain silent in the face of this Anti-Federalist outpouring. In private, they admitted imperfections. George Washington wrote to his nephew in November 1787:

The warmest friends and the best supporters the Constitution has, do not contend that it is free from imperfections; but they found them unavoidable and are sensible, if evil is likely to arise there from, the remedy must come hereafter; for in the present moment, it is not to be obtained. . . . I do not think we are more inspired, have more wisdom, or possess more virtue, than those who will come after us.[10]

In public, defenders of the Constitution were not so diffident. In general, their writings and speeches sought to answer specific Anti-Federalist objections rather than to defend the entire Constitution.

The Federalist response most familiar to modern scholars is the *Federalist Papers*, written by James Madison, Alexander Hamilton and John Jay under the pseudonym "Publius." Educated eighteenth century readers knew that "Publius" referred to Publius Valerius Publicola, described by Plutarch as a strong leader who supplied the qualities lacking in the populace and thereby saved the republic. The *Federalist Papers*, published between October 1787 and August 1788, were serialized in newspapers in New York, where ratification was thought to be the most seriously in doubt. They were occasionally republished in other states, but their influence elsewhere is uncertain. They are, however, representative of Federalist sentiments in most states. In each state convention, Federalist delegates also gave fiery responses to the Anti-Federalist challenges. Vocal Federalists in the state conventions included

Hamilton in New York, James Wilson in Pennsylvania, and in Virginia, Madison, Edmund Pendleton, and a 32-year-old lawyer named John Marshall.

One factor that played a role in almost every state was the division between urban coastal regions and rural (usually western) regions. The former were heavily Federalist in every state, the latter Anti-Federalist. In Pennsylvania, Philadelphia and the eastern coastal plain were Federalist, and the Appalachian west was Anti-Federalist. In Virginia, the coastal Tidewater region was Federalist, the Piedmont—including the counties that would become Kentucky—heavily Anti-Federalist. New York City was overwhelmingly Federalist, while the rest of the state was peppered with Anti-Federalist strongholds. In Massachusetts, Boston and the surrounding towns were opposed by both the Maine counties and the western counties where Shays' Rebellion had been supported. In New Hampshire the division was between the southern coastal counties and the northern mountainous ones.

Historians have viewed these momentous disputes in different ways, often revealing more about their own biases than about the ratification debates. In the early years of the nineteenth century, when the political emphasis was on pacification and inclusion rather than on domestic infighting, most historians played down the disputes and treated the Anti-Federalists with kind restraint. After the Civil War, by contrast, historians "declared open season on [the Anti-Federalists] and showered them with contempt."[11] In an era when allegiance to state sovereignty was thought to have caused the worst war Americans had ever seen, worship of the Constitution and contempt for the Anti-Federalists was not surprising. By the early years of the twentieth century, the Progressive historians, disgusted with a Constitution that had been interpreted by a conservative Supreme Court to protect the wealthy and to embody laissez-faire economic policies, drew sharp lines between Federalists and Anti-Federalists. Federalists were condemned as conservative aristocrats who created a government tailored to protect their own economic interests; Anti-Federalists were lauded as true democrats fighting a losing battle against a conspiracy of wealth. After World War II, and especially by the middle 1950s, the "consensus historians" began challenging the Progressive interpretation more or less successfully. In an era marked by apparent domestic tranquility and prosperity, these historians looked back at the early turbulent years and maintained that the Federalists and Anti-Federalists were actually more similar than different, both economically and ideologically.

The current historiographical trend, which has gained prominence mostly since the Vietnam War, attempts to draw from both Progressive and consensus historians as well as from British historical scholarship. A number of contemporary historians have suggested an analogy between the Federalist-Anti-Federalist conflict and the seventeenth- and early eighteenth-century dispute between the "Court" and "Country" parties in England, discussed in greater detail in chapter 1. The "Court" party Federalists, according to this view, represented the party in favor of strong government, vigorous commerce, and administrative efficiency. The "Country" party Anti-Federalists were largely agrarian and opposed to the exercise of power by the government. In addition, the "Country" party Anti-Federalists were more distrustful ("jealous" in seventeenth-century language) of power as a corrupting force, although distrust of governments and governors was a common theme among both groups. Neither party, these historians contend, was particularly democratic.

As you read through the materials below, try to identify themes and to evaluate the various historical descriptions of Federalists and Anti-Federalists. To what extent did the Federalists' and Anti-Federalists' views of the purposes of government differ? To what extent were they similar? Where the two parties agreed on the purposes of government, how and why did they disagree over the means to achieve those purposes? How important were different economic views? Different views of human nature? How democratic was each writer or speaker? Were there significant differences within each party? How have modern constitutional interpretations and amendments incorporated the views of Federalists and Anti-Federalists?

GENERAL CRITICISMS

The Amount at Stake

The best overview of the many objections voiced by critics of the Constitution was written by a group of New York Anti-Federalists during the election campaign for delegates to the New York ratifying convention. The *Albany Manifesto* (the Address of the Albany Antifederal Committee) listed virtually all of the Anti-Federalist criticisms of the Constitution.

Address of the Albany Antifederal Committee
April 26, 1788
Storing 6.10.2–18

As we have been informed, that the advocates for the new constitution, have lately travelled through the several districts in the county, and propogated an opinion, that it is a good system of government: we beg leave to state, in as few words as possible, some of the many objections against it. —

The convention, who were appointed for the sole and express purpose of revising and amending the confederation, have taken upon themselves the power of making a new one.

They have not formed a *federal* but a *consolidated* government, repugnant to the principles of a republican government: not founded on the preservation but the destruction of the state governments.

The great and extensive powers granted to the new government over the lives, liberties, and property of every citizen.

These powers in many instances not defined or sufficiently explained, and capable of being interpreted to answer the most ambitious and arbitrary purposes.

The small number of members who are to compose the general legislature, which is to pass laws to govern so large and extensive a continent, inhabited by people of different laws, customs, and opinions, and many of them residing upwards of 400 miles from the seat of government.

The members of the senate are not to be chosen by the people, but appointed by the legislature of each state for the term of six years. This will destroy their reponsibility, and induce them to act like the masters and not the servants of the people.

The power to alter and regulate the time, place, and manner of holding elections, so as to keep them subjected to their influence.

The power to lay poll taxes, duties, imposts, excises, and other taxes.

The power to appoint continental officers to levy and collect those taxes.

Their laws are to be *the supreme law of the land*, and the judges in every state are to be bound thereby, notwithstanding *the constitution or laws* of any state to the contrary.—A sweeping clause, which subjects every thing to the controul of the new government.

Slaves are taken into the computation in apportioning the number of representatives, whereby 50,000 slaves, give an equal representation with 30,000 freemen.

.   .   .

The power to raise, support, and maintain a standing army *in time of peace*. The bane of a republican government; by a standing army most of the once free nations of the globe have been reduced to

bondage; and by this Britain attempted to inforce her arbitrary measures.

.   .   .

Men conscienciously scrupulous of bearing arms, made liable to perform military duty.

.   .   .

The not securing the rights of conscience in matters of religion, of granting the liberty of worshipping God agreeable to the mode thereby dictated; whereas the experience of all ages proves that the benevolence and humility inculcated in the gospel, are no restraint on the love of domination.

The tenor of the *Albany Manifesto* is instructive. The New York Anti-Federalists, like their compatriots in other states, objected both to specific constitutional provisions and to the practical effects of the Constitution as a whole. Their concerns about specific constitutional provisions are addressed in later sections of this chapter. The remaining parts of this section deal with general objections.

As earlier chapters have suggested, the Constitution was a product of the times. It was not, however, based on any particular model or example. As James Wilson noted in the Pennsylvania ratifying convention, the Federal Convention was "almost without precedent or guide, and, consequently, without the benefit of that instruction which, in many cases, may be derived from the constitution, and history, and experience, of other nations."[12] The Constitution was therefore a necessarily imperfect attempt to translate theory into practice, and its critics and defenders often argued over whether the translation was accurate and workable. Many Anti-Federalist critiques of the proposed Constitution attacked it as inadequate to its task: the creation of a federal republic.

Three interwoven concerns dominated the debate over the type of polity the new Constitution would create. Anti-Federalists feared that it would create an *aristocratic, consolidated*, and *energetic* government. Recall the discussion in chapter 1 of the various intellectual influences on the American colonies. Many Americans believed that government by a hereditary aristocracy, or any government that was powerful and active, was likely to lead to corruption and ultimately to decay. In charging that the Constitution would lead to aristocracy, or to energetic government, the loaded language of the Anti-Federalists thus evoked a response far beyond the immediately stated concerns.

Aristocratic Government

The most emotional attack on the Constitution was the charge that it would create an aristocracy. Three factors in particular appeared to Anti-Federalists to create such a danger: the vast size of the new nation, the centralization of power, and the insufficient separation of powers within the national government. Often these criticisms were combined, with little detailed analysis but a solid theoretical foundation and great rhetorical flourish. The essay below by "Montezuma," published in the Philadelphia *Independent Gazeteer* in October 1787, is a good example of the types of arguments made by many Anti-Federalists. "Montezuma" feared that the natural tendency toward corruption, the concentration of power in the central government, and the lack of popular checks on the government would lead to tyranny, not democracy. The essay includes a brief critique of each branch of the federal government. The essay is unusual—and delightful to read—because it is a satire: it purports to be a defense of the Constitution by members of the well-born class, and explains how they have created a government for their own advantage. The identity of "Montezuma" is unknown.

Montezuma
October 17, 1787
Storing 3.4.1–5

We the Aristicratic party of the United States, lamenting the many inconveniencies to which the late confederation subjected the *well-born*, the *better kind* of people bringing them down to the level of the *rabble*, and holding in utter detestation, that frontispiece to every bill of rights—"that all men are born equal," beg leave (for the purpose of drawing a line between such as we think were *ordained* to govern, and such as were *made* to bear the weight of government without having any share in its administration) to submit to *our friends* in the first class for their inspection, the following defence of our *monarchical, aristocratical democracy*.

1st. As a majority of all societies consist of men who (though totally incapable of thinking or acting in governmental matters) are more readily led than driven, we have thought meet to indulge them in something like a democracy in the new constitution, which part we have designated by the popular name of the House of Representatives; but to guard against every possible danger from this *lower house*, we have subjected every bill they bring forward, to the double negative of our *upper house* and president—nor have we allowed the *populace* the right to elect their representatives annually, as usual, lest this body should be too much under the influence and controul of their constituents, and thereby prove the "weatherboard of our grand edefice, to shew the shiftings of every fashionable gale," for we have not yet to learn that little else is wanting, to aristocratize the most democratical representative than to make him somewhat independent of his *political creators*—We have taken away

that rotation of appointment which has so long perplexed us—that *grand engine* of popular influence; every man is eligible into our government, from time to time for life—this will have a two-fold good effect; first it prevents the representatives from mixing with the *lower class*, and imbibing their foolish sentiments, with which they would have come charged on re-election.

2d. They will from the perpetuality of office be under *our* eye, and in a short time will think and act like *us*, independently of popular whims and prejudices; for the assertion "that evil communications corrupt good manners" is not more true than its reverse. We have allowed this house the power to impeach, but we have tenaciously reserved the right to try. We hope gentlemen, you will see the policy of this clause—for what matters it who accuses, if the accused is tried by his friends—In fine, this *plebian house* will have little power, and that little be rightly shaped by our house of *gentlemen*, who will have a very extensive influence, from their being chosen out of the *genteeler class*, and their appointment being almost a life, one as seven years is the calculation on a man's life, and they are chosen for six: It is true, every third senatorial seat is to be vacated duennually, but two-thirds of this influential body will remain in office, and be ready to direct or (if necessary) bring over to the good old way, the young members, if the old ones should not be returned; and whereas many of our brethren, from a laudable desire to support their rank in life above the commonality, have not only deranged their finances, but subjected their persons to indecent treatment (as being arrested for debt, etc.) we have framed a privilege clause, by which they may laugh at the fools who trusted them; but we have given out that this clause was provided, only that the members might be able without interruption, to deliberate on the important business of their country.

We have frequently endeavoured to effect in our respective states, the happy discrimination which pervades this system, but finding we could not bring the states into it individually, we have determined, and in this our general plan we have taken pains to leave the legislature of each *free and independent* state, as they now call themselves, in such a situation that they will eventually be absorbed by our *grand continental vortex*, or dwindle into petty corporations, and have power over little else than *yoaking hogs* or determining the width of *cart wheels*—but (aware that an intention to annihilate state legisla-

tures, would be objected to our favorite scheme) we have made their existence (as a *board of electors*) necessary to ours; this furnishes us and our advocates with a fine answer to any clamours that may be raised on this subject, viz.—We have so interwoven continental and state legislatures that they cannot exist separately; whereas we in truth, only leave them the power of electing us, for what can a provincial legislature do when we possess "the exclusive regulation of external and internal commerce, excise, duties, imposts, post-offices and roads ["]; when we and we alone, have the power to wage war, make peace, coin money (if we can get bullion) if not, borrow money, organize the militia and call them forth to execute our decrees, and crush insurrections assisted by a noble body of veterans subject to our nod, which we have the power of raising and keeping even in the time of peace.

Consolidated Government

The Constitution's concentration of power in the central government also fueled fears of consolidated government. Anti-Federalists pointed to the commerce power and the taxing power to suggest that the federal government would eventually subsume the state governments. They also focused in particular on the necessary and proper clause of Article I, section 8, as evidence that all power would eventually accumulate in the hands of the national government.

Between November 1787 and February 1788, "Agrippa" wrote a series of sixteen essays, which were published in the *Massachusetts Gazette*. Some of the essays were addressed to the people, and some to the Massachusetts ratifying convention, which sat from early January to early February 1788. "Agrippa" was probably James Winthrop, the Harvard librarian and a minor political figure in eastern Massachusetts. In the letter printed below, he argued that the necessary and proper clause confirmed his worst suspicions about the creation of the federal judiciary.

Agrippa, No. 12
January 14, 1788
Storing 4.6.51–52

To the Massachusetts Convention.

Gentlemen:

Let us now consider the probable effects of a consolidation of the separate states into one mass; for the new system extends so far. Many ingenious ex-

planations have been given of it; but there is this defect, that they are drawn from maxims of the common law, while the system itself cannot be bound by any such maxims. A legislative assembly has an inherent right to alter the common law, and to abolish any of its principles, which are not particularly guarded in the constitution. Any system therefore which appoints a legislature without any reservation of the rights of individuals, surrender[s] all power in every branch of legislation to the government. The universal practice of every government proves the justness of this remark; for in every doubtful case it is an established rule to decide in favour of authority. The new system is, therefore, in one respect at least, essentially inferiour to our state constitutions. There is no bill of rights, and consequently a continental law may controul any of those principles, which we consider at present as sacred; while not one of those points, in which it is said that the separate governments misapply their power, is guarded. Tender acts and the coinage of money stand on the same footing of a consolidation of power. It is a mere fallacy, invented by the deceptive powers of Mr. Wilson, that what rights are not given are reserved. The contrary has already been shewn. But to put this matter of legislation out of all doubt, let us compare together some parts of the book; for being an independent system, this is the only way to ascertain its meaning.

In article III, section 2, it is declared, that "the judicial power shall extend to all cases in law and equity arising under this constitution, the laws of the United States, and treaties made or which shall be made under their authority." Among the cases arising under this new constitution are reckoned, "all controversies between citizens of different states," which include all kinds of civil causes between those parties. The giving Congress a power to appoint courts for such a purpose is as much, there being no stipulation to the contrary, giving them power to legislate for such causes, as giving them a right to raise an army, is giving them a right to direct the operations of the army when raised. But it is not left to implication. The last clause of article I, section 8, expressly gives them power "to make all laws which shall be needful and proper for carrying into execution the foregoing powers, and all other powers vested by this constitution in the government of the United States, or in any department or officer thereof." It is, therefore, as plain as words can make it, that they have a right by this proposed form to legislate for all kinds of causes respecting property between citizens of different states.

The Federalist responses to the charge of consolidation differed depending in part on whether the Federalist was speaking in public or private. In private correspondence, Madison and others defended the need for a strong centralized government. In a letter to Jefferson in October of 1787, he observed that the central government was not strong enough, for it lacked a means of controlling state "encroachments":

> If a compleat supremacy somewhere is not necessary in every society, a controuling power at least is so, by which the general authority may be defended against encroachments of the subordinate authorities, and by which the latter may be restrained from encroachments on each other. . . . I mean not by these remarks to insinuate that an esprit de corps will not exist in the National Government, or that opportunities may not occur of extending its jurisdiction in some points. I mean only that the danger of encroachments is much greater from the other side.[13]

In public, however, Federalists denied the charge, and interpreted the necessary and proper clause narrowly. Hamilton took this approach in *Federalist No. 33*, arguing that the clause was tautological:

> What is a power but the ability or faculty of doing a thing? What is the ability to do a thing but the power of employing the means necessary to its execution? What is a *legislative* power, but a power of making *laws*? What are the *means* to execute a *legislative* power but *laws*? What is the power of laying and collecting taxes but a *legislative* power, or a power of *making laws* to lay and collect taxes? What are the proper means of executing such a power but *necessary* and *proper* laws?
>
> This simple train of inquiry furnishes us at once with a test of the true nature of the clause complained of. It conducts us to this palpable truth that a power to lay and collect taxes must be a power to pass all laws *necessary* and *proper* for the exe-

cution of that power; and what does the unfortunate and calumniated provision in question do more than declare the same truth, to wit, that the national legislature to whom the power of laying and collecting taxes had been previously given might, in the execution of that power, pass all laws *necessary* and *proper* to carry it into effect?

Similarly, in a speech to the Pennsylvania ratifying convention, James Wilson said:

> The gentleman in opposition strongly insists that the general clause at the end of the eighth section gives to Congress a power of legislating generally; but I cannot conceive by what means he will render the words susceptible of that expansion. Can the words, "The Congress shall have power to make all laws which shall be necessary and proper to carry into execution the foregoing powers," be capable of giving them general legislative power? I hope that it is not meant to give to Congress merely an illusive show of authority, to deceive themselves or constituents any longer. On the contrary, I trust it is meant that they shall have the power of carrying into effect the laws which they shall make under the powers vested in them by this Constitution.[14]

Despite these assurances, the necessary and proper clause was hotly disputed, and continued to be a source of controversy for many years after ratification. Anti-Federalists who engaged in more detailed critiques of the legislative branch often reserved a special wrath for the necessary and proper clause. History proved that Anti-Federalist predictions about the breadth and elasticity of the clause were justified. In 1819, Chief Justice John Marshall used the clause to uphold the constitutionality of the Second Bank of the United States. His controversial opinion in *McCulloch v. Maryland*, 17 U.S. (4 Wheat.) 316, 4 L.Ed. 579 (1819), strengthened the authority of the national government by interpreting the necessary and proper clause expansively. It drew immediate fire from prominent Anti-Federalists and served to increase the longstanding feud between Marshall and Jefferson.

Marshall read the clause to permit the federal government to use any means "appropriate [and] plainly adapted to [a legitimate] end." His sweeping interpretation of the necessary and proper clause is still the measure of federal power, and has allowed Congress to pass laws that affect virtually every aspect of life. Marshall relied in part on the intent of the framers of the Constitution in reaching his conclusion:

> It must have been the intention of those who gave these powers, to insure, as far as human prudence could insure, their beneficial execution. This could not be done by confining the choice of means to such narrow limits as not to leave it in the power of Congress to adopt any which might be appropriate, and which were conducive to the end.[15]

Is Marshall's construction of the necessary and proper clause consistent with the remarks of Wilson and Hamilton? Was Marshall justified in his expansive interpretation? Why or why not?

Energetic Government

As the preceding excerpts suggest, Anti-Federalist cries of aristocracy and consolidation often hinted at competing theories of government. The most direct glimpses of the contrasting underlying political philosophy of the Federalists and Anti-Federalists, however, came in discussions of the nature of republican government. In particular, the debates focused on two aspects of republican government: how energetic should it be, and how large a territory could it encompass? All but the most superficial discussion of either of these questions led inevitably to debates over what Patrick Henry called the "poor little humble republican maxims," the theories on which republican government ought to be based.[16]

Anti-Federalists saw many violations of their humble republican maxims in the proposed constitution. All were grounded in the failure to provide sufficient checks on the power of the national government. The fear was that without such checks, the government would become too energetic, too powerful.

A common complaint was that the mingling of powers of the different branches was dangerous to liberty:

> It has always been the favorite maxim of princes, to *divide* the people, in order to *govern* them; it is now time that the people should avail themselves of the same maxim, and *divide* power among their rulers, in order to prevent their abusing it[.][17]

More sophisticated Anti-Federalists, however, recognized that strict separation of powers was neither a necessary nor a sufficient condition for preserving liberty. The excerpts below illustrate how two influential Anti-Federalists developed more elaborate theories of republican government.

"Centinel" saw energetic government and aristocratic government as the twin enemies of liberty, but unlike some Anti-Federalists, believed accountability a much more certain principle than separation of powers in combating these evils. Patrick Henry also argued that the Constitution lacked sufficient popular checks on the central government. The essays of "Centinel" originally appeared in Philadelphia newspapers, but enjoyed wide republication. "Centinel" was probably Samuel Bryan, son of one of the leading Pennsylvania Anti-Federalists, George Bryan. Bryan senior was a judge and a legislator, and probably collaborated with his son on the "Centinel" essays.

Centinel, No. 1
October 5, 1787
Storing 2.7.7-10

Mr. Adams's *sine qua non* of a good government is three balancing powers, whose repelling qualities are to produce an equilibrium of interests, and thereby promote the happiness of the whole community. He asserts that the administrators of every government, will ever be actuated by views of private interest and ambition, to the prejudice of the public good; that therefore the only effectual method to secure the rights of the people and promote their welfare, is to create an opposition of interests between the members of two distinct bodies, in the exercise of the powers of government, and balanced by those of a third. This hypothesis supposes human wisdom competent to the task of in-

stituting three co-equal orders in government, and a corresponding weight in the community to enable them respectively to exercise their several parts, and whose views and interests should be so distinct as to prevent a coalition of any two of them for the destruction of the third. Mr. Adams, although he has traced the constitution of every form of government that ever existed, as far as history affords materials, has not been able to adduce a single instance of such a government; he indeed says that the British constitution is such in theory, but this is rather a confirmation that his principles are chimerical and not to be reduced to practice. If such an organization of power were practicable, how long would it continue? not a day—for there is so great a disparity in the talents, wisdom and industry of mankind, that the scale would presently preponderate to one or the other body, and with every accession of power the means of further increase would be greatly extended. The state of society in England is much more favorable to such a scheme of government than that of America. There they have a powerful hereditary nobility, and real distinctions of rank and interests; but even there, for want of that perfect equallity of power and distinction of interests, in the three orders of government, they exist but in name; the only operative and efficient check, upon the conduct of administration, is the sense of the people at large.

Suppose a government could be formed and supported on such principles, would it answer the great purposes of civil society; if the administrators of every government are actuated by views of private interest and ambition, how is the welfare and happiness of the community to be the result of such jarring adverse interests?

Therefore, as different orders in government will not produce the good of the whole, we must recur to other principles. I believe it will be found that the form of government, which holds those entrusted with power, in the greatest responsibility to their constitutents, the best calculated for freeman. A republican, or free government, can only exist where the body of the people are virtuous, and where property is pretty equally divided[;] in such a government the people are the sovereign and their sense or opinion is the criterion of every public measure; for when this ceases to be the case, the nature of the government is changed, and an aristocracy, monarchy or despotism will rise on its ruin. The highest responsibility is to be attained, in a simple structure of government, for the great body of the people never steadily attend to the operations of government, and for want of due information are liable to be imposed on.

Virginia Ratifying Convention
Monday June 9, 1788
Elliot 3:164-169

Mr. Henry: To me it appears that there is no check in that government. The President, senators, and representatives, all, immediately or mediately, are the choice of the people. Tell me not of checks on paper; but tell me of checks founded on self-love. The English government is founded on self-love. This powerful, irresistible stimulus of self-love has saved that government.

It has interposed that hereditary nobility between the king and commons. If the host of lords assist or permit the king to overturn the liberties of the people, the same tyranny will destroy them; they will therefore keep the balance in the democratic branch. Suppose they see the commons encroach upon the king: self-love, that great energetic check, will call upon them to interpose; for, if the king be destroyed, their destruction must speedily follow. Here is a consideration, which prevails, in my mind, to pronounce the British government superior, in this respect, to any government that ever was in any country. Compare this with your congressional checks. I beseech gentlemen to consider whether they can say, when trusting power, that a mere patriotic profession will be equally operative and efficacious as the check of self-love. In consid-

ering the experience of ages, is it not seen that fair, disinterested patriotism, and professions of attachment to rectitude, have never been solely trusted to by an enlightened, free people? If you depend on your President's and senators' patriotism, you are gone. Have you a resting-place like the British government? Where is the rock of your salvation? The real rock of political salvation is self-love, perpetuated from age to age in every human breast, and manifested in every action. If they can stand the temptations of human nature, you are safe. If you have a good President, senators, and representatives, there is no danger. But can this be expected from human nature? Without real checks, it will not suffice that some of them are good. A good President, or senator, or representative, will have a natural weakness. Virtue will slumber.

. . .

Congress, by the power of taxation, by that of raising an army, and by their control over the militia, have the sword in one hand, and the purse in the other. Shall we be safe without either? Congress have an unlimited power over both: they are entirely given up by us. Let him candidly tell me, where and when did freedom exist, when the sword and purse were given up from the people? Unless a miracle in human affairs interposed, no nation ever retained its liberty after the loss of the sword and purse. Can you prove, by any argumentative deduction, that it is possible to be safe without retaining one of these? If you give them up, you are gone.

Federalists replied in many ways. John Marshall at times simply denied the charge: "He says, we wish to have a strong, energetic, powerful government. We contend for a well-regulated democracy."[18] Others argued the necessity of energetic government. They pointed to the role of government in ensuring prosperity, in "form[ing] a national character," and in defending against invasions and insurrections. In the Pennsylvania ratifying convention, James Wilson reminded the delegates of the evils of too little government:

> When we had baffled all the menaces of foreign power, we neglected to establish among ourselves a government that would insure domestic vigor and stability. What was the consequence? The commencement of peace was the commencement of every disgrace and distress that could befall a people in a peaceful state. Devoid of *national power*, we could not prohibit the extravagance of our importations, nor could we derive a revenue from their excess. Devoid of national *importance*, we could not procure, for our exports, a tolerable sale at foreign markets. Devoid of national *credit*, we saw our public securities melt in the hands of the holders, like snow before the sun. Devoid of national *dignity*, we could not, in some instances, perform our treaties, on our part; and, in other instances, we could neither obtain nor compel the performance of them, on the part of others. Devoid of national *energy*, we could not carry into execution our own resolutions, decisions, or laws.
>
> Shall I become more particular still? The tedious detail would disgust me.[19]

Oliver Ellsworth, writing as "The Landholder," added the observation that the potential for abuse is inevitable, and does not always justify withholding power.

> [P]ower when necessary for our good is as much to be desired as the food we eat or the air we breathe. Some men are mightily afraid of giving power lest it should be improved for oppression; this is doubtless possible, but where is the probability. The same objection may be made against the constitution of every state in the union, and against every possible mode of government; because a power of doing good always implies a power to do evil if the person or party be disposed.
>
>   .   .   .
>
> If, my countrymen, you wait for a constitution which absolutely bars a power of doing evil, you must wait long, and when obtained it will have no power of doing good.[20]

The Size of the Republic

One theme running through many Anti-Federalist essays and tying together diverse strands was the theory that only a small territory could function as a republic. This argument was based on Montesquieu's work and on the Anti-Federalist vision of how republican government should function. The Anti-Federalist essay printed below contains an extensive discussion of theories of republican government. It also contains criticisms, derived from the principle of small republics, of various aspects of the proposed Constitution. The Anti-

Federalists' practical distaste for consolidation or nationalization was often supported by a theoretical preference for small republics.

The essays of "Brutus" were among the most influential and important Anti-Federalist writings. Sixteen essays were published in the *New York Journal* between October 1787 and April 1788. They were thus contemporaneous with most of the *Federalist Papers*. The identity of the author is uncertain, but he may have been Robert Yates, one of New York's two Anti-Federalist delegates to the Federal Convention.

Brutus, No. 1
October 18, 1787
Storing 2.9.10-20

To the Citizens of the State of New-York.

If respect is to be paid to the opinion of the greatest and wisest men who have ever thought or wrote on the science of government, we shall be constrained to conclude, that a free republic cannot succeed over a country of such immense extent, containing such a number of inhabitants, and these encreasing in such rapid progression as that of the whole United States.

.   .   .

Not only the opinion of the greatest men, and the experience of mankind, are against the idea of an extensive republic, but a variety of reasons may be drawn from the reason and nature of things, against it. In every government, the will of the sovereign is the law. In despotic governments, the supreme authority being lodged in one, his will is law, and can be as easily expressed to a large extensive territory as to a small one. In a pure democracy the people are the sovereign, and their will is declared by themselves; for this purpose they must all come together to deliberate, and decide. This kind of government cannot be exercised, therefore, over a country of any considerable extent; it must be confined to a single city, or at least limited to such bounds as that the people can conveniently assemble, be able to debate, understand the subject submitted to them, and declare their opinion concerning it.

In a free republic, although all laws are derived from the consent of the people, yet the people do not declare their consent by themselves in person, but by representatives, chosen by them, who are supposed to know the minds of their constituents, and to be possessed of integrity to declare this mind.

In every free government, the people must give their assent to the laws by which they are governed. This is the true criterion between a free government and an arbitrary one. The former are ruled by the will of the whole, expressed in any manner they may agree upon; the latter by the will of one, or a few. If the people are to give their assent to the laws, by persons chosen and appointed by them, the manner of the choice and the number of chosen, must be such, as to possess, be disposed, and consequently qualified to declare the sentiments of the people; for if they do not know, or are not disposed to speak the sentiments of the people, the people do not govern, but the sovereignty is in a few. Now, in a large extended country, it is impossible to have a representation, possessing the sentiments, and of integrity, to declare the minds of the people, without having it so numerous and unwieldly, as to be subject in great measure to the inconveniency of a democratic government.

The territory of the United States is of vast extent; it now contains near three millions of souls, and is capable of containing much more than ten times that number. Is it practicable for a country, so large and so numerous as they will soon become, to elect a representation, that will speak their sentiments, without their becoming so numerous as to be incapable of transacting public business? It certainly is not.

In a republic, the manners, sentiments, and interests of the people should be similar. If this be not the case, there will be a constant clashing of opinions; and the representatives of one part will be continually striving against those of the other. This will retard the operations of government, and prevent such conclusions as will promote the public good. If we apply this remark to the condition of the United States, we shall be convinced that it forbids that we should be one government. The United States includes a variety of climates. The productions of the different parts of the union are very variant, and their interests, of consequence, diverse. Their manners and habits differ as much as their climates and productions; and their sentiments are by no means coincident. The laws and customs of the several states are, in many respects, very diverse, and in some opposite; each would be in favor of its own interests and customs, and, of consequence, a legislature, formed of representatives from the respective parts, would not only be too numerous to act with any care or decision, but would be composed of such heterogenous and discordant principles, as would constantly be contending with each other.

It was in responding to these critiques that the Federalists devised their most elaborate theories of government. The classic response is Madison's *Federalist No. 10*. In it, Madison stole the Anti-Federalists' thunder by turning the size of the republic into an advantage. The real brilliance of *Federalist No. 10*, however, lies in Madison's explication of the theory on which the new governmental structure is based. It is a refutation of virtually every Anti-Federalist argument against the Constitution, because it provides a coherent theory that could be used to elucidate and justify the structure of the whole Constitution as well as its individual parts.

Federalist No. 10
Madison

Among the numerous advantages promised by a well-constructed Union, none deserves to be more accurately developed than its tendency to break and control the violence of faction. The friend of popular governments never finds himself so much alarmed for their character and fare, as when he contemplates their propensity to this dangerous vice.

.   .   .

By a faction, I understand a number of citizens, whether amounting to a majority or minority of the whole, who are united and actuated by some common impulse of passion, or of interest, adverse to the rights of other citizens, or to the permanent and aggregate interests of the community.

There are two methods of curing the mischiefs of faction: the one, by removing its causes; the other, by controlling its effects.

There are again two methods of removing the causes of faction: the one, by destroying the liberty which is essential to its existence; the other, by giving to every citizen the same opinions, the same passions, and the same interests.

It could never be more truly said than of the first remedy, that it was worse than the disease. Liberty is to faction what air is to fire, an aliment without which it instantly expires. But it could not be less folly to abolish liberty, which is essential to political life, because it nourishes faction, than it would be to wish the annihilation of air, which is essential to animal life, because it imparts to fire its destructive agency.

The second expedient is as impracticable as the first would be unwise. As long as the reason of man continues fallible, and he is at liberty to exercise it, different opinions will be formed. As long as the connection subsists between his reason and his self-love, his opinions and his passions will have a reciprocal influence on each other; and the former will be objects to which the latter will attach themselves. The diversity in the faculties of men, from which the rights of property originate, is not less an insuperable obstacle to a uniformity of interests. The protection of these faculties is the first object of government. From the protection of different and unequal faculties of acquiring property, the possession of different degrees and kinds of property immediately results; and from the influence of these on the sentiments and views of the respective proprietors, ensues a division of the society into different interests and parties.

The latent causes of faction are thus sown in the nature of man; and we see them everywhere brought into different degrees of activity, according to the different circumstances of civil society. A zeal for different opinions concerning religion, concerning government, and many other points, as well of speculation as of practice; an attachment to different leaders ambitiously contending for pre-eminence and power; or to persons of other descriptions whose fortunes have been interesting to the human passions, have, in turn, divided mankind into parties, inflamed them with mutual animosity, and rendered them much more disposed to vex and oppress each other than to co-operate for their common good. So strong is this propensity of mankind to fall into mutual animosities, that where no substantial occasion presents itself, the most frivolous and fanciful distinctions have been sufficient to kindle their unfriendly passions and excite their most violent conflicts. But the most common and durable source of factions has been the various and unequal distribution of property. Those who hold and those who are without property have ever formed distinct interests in society. Those who are creditors, and those who are debtors, fall under a like discrimination. A landed interest, a manufacturing interest, a mercantile interest, a moneyed interest, with many lesser interests, grow up of necessity in civilized nations, and divide them into different classes, actuated by different sentiments and views. The regulation of these various and interfering interests forms the principal task of modern legislation, and involves the spirit of party and faction in the necessary and ordinary operations of the government.

No man is allowed to be a judge in his own cause, because his interest would certainly bias his judgment, and, not improbably, corrupt his integrity. With equal, nay with greater reason, a body of men are unfit to be both judges and parties at the same time; yet what are many of the most important acts of legislation, but so many judicial determinations, not indeed concerning the rights of single persons, but concerning the rights of large bodies of citizens? And what are the different classes of legislators but advocates and parties to the causes which they determine? Is a law proposed concerning private debts? It is a question to which the creditors are parties on one side and the debtors on the other. Justice ought to hold the balance between them. Yet the parties are, and must be, themselves the judges;

and the most numerous party, or, in other words, the most powerful faction must be expected to prevail. Shall domestic manufactures be encouraged, and in what degree, by restrictions on foreign manufactures? are questions which would be differently decided by the landed and the manufacturing classes, and probably by neither with a sole regard to justice and the public good. The apportionment of taxes on the various descriptions of property is an act which seems to require the most exact impartiality; yet there is, perhaps, no legislative act in which greater opportunity and temptation are given to a predominant party to trample on the rules of justice. Every shilling with which they overburden the inferior number, is a shilling saved to their own pockets.

It is in vain to say that enlightened statesmen will be able to adjust these clashing interests, and render them all subservient to the public good. Enlightened statesmen will not always be at the helm. Nor, in many cases, can such an adjustment be made at all without taking into view indirect and remote considerations, which will rarely prevail over the immediate interest which one party may find in disregarding the rights of another or the good of the whole.

The inference to which we are brought is, that the *causes* of faction cannot be removed, and that relief is only to be sought in the means of controlling its *effects*.

If a faction consists of less than a majority, relief is supplied by the republican principle, which enables the majority to defeat its sinister views by regular vote. It may clog the administration, it may convulse the society; but it will be unable to execute and mask its violence under the forms of the Constitution. When a majority is included in a faction, the form of popular government, on the other hand, enables it to sacrifice to its ruling passion or interest both the public good and the rights of other citizens. To secure the public good and private rights against the danger of such a faction, and at the same time to preserve the spirit and the form of popular government, is then the great object to which our inquiries are directed. Let me add that it is the great desideratum by which this form of government can be rescued from the opprobrium under which it has so long labored, and be recommended to the esteem and adoption of mankind.

By what means is this object attainable? Evidently by one of two only. Either the existence of the same passion or interest in a majority at the same time must be prevented, or the majority, having such co-existent passion or interest, must be rendered, by their number and local situation, unable to concert and carry into effect schemes of oppression. If the impulse and the opportunity be suffered to coincide, we well know that neither moral nor religious motives can be relied on as an adequate control. They are not found to be such on the injustice and violence of individuals, and lose their efficacy in proportion to the number combined together, that is, in proportion as their efficacy becomes needful.

From this view of the subject it may be concluded that a pure democracy, by which I mean a society consisting of a small number of citizens, who assemble and administer the government in person, can admit of no cure for the mischiefs of faction. A common passion or interest will, in almost every case, be felt by a majority of the whole; a communication and concert result from the form of government itself; and there is nothing to check the inducements to sacrifice the weaker party or an obnoxious individual. Hence it is that such democracies have ever been spectacles of turbulence and contention; have ever been found incompatible with personal security or the rights of property; and have in general been as short in their lives as they have been violent in their deaths. Theoretic politicians, who have patronized this species of government, have erroneously supposed that by reducing mankind to a perfect equality in their political rights, they would, at the same time, be perfectly equalized and assimilated in their possessions, their opinions, and their passions.

A republic, by which I mean a government in which the scheme of representation takes place, opens a different prospect, and promises the cure for which we are seeking. Let us examine the points in which it varies from pure democracy, and we shall comprehend both the nature of the cure and the efficacy which it must derive from the Union.

The two great points of difference between a democracy and a republic are: first, the delegation of the government, in the latter, to a small number of citizens elected by the rest; secondly, the greater number of citizens, and greater sphere of country, over which the latter may be extended.

The effect of the first difference is, on the one hand, to refine and enlarge the public views, by passing them through the medium of a chosen body of citizens, whose wisdom may best discern the true interest of their country, and whose patriotism and love of justice will be least likely to sacrifice it to temporary or partial considerations.

.   .   .

On the other hand, the effect may be inverted. Men of factious tempers, of local prejudices, or of sinister designs, may, by intrigue, by corruption, or by other means, first obtain the suffrages, and then betray the interests, of the people. The question resulting is, whether small or extensive republics are more favorable to the election of proper guardians of the public weal; and it is clearly decided in favor of the latter[.]

.   .   .

[T]he greater number of citizens and extent of territory which may be brought within the compass of republican than of democratic government . . . [is the] circumstance principally which renders factious combinations less to be dreaded in the former than in the latter. The smaller the society the fewer probably will be the distinct parties and interests composing it; the fewer the distinct parties and interests, the more frequently will a majority be found of the same party; and the smaller the number of individuals composing a majority, and the smaller the compass within which they are placed, the more easily will they concert and execute their plans of oppression. Extend the sphere, and you take in a greater variety of parties and interests; you make it less probable that a majority of the whole will have a common motive to invade the rights of other citizens; or if such a common motive exists, it will be more difficult for all who feel it to discover their own strength, and to act in unison with each other. Besides other impediments, it may be remarked that, where there is a consciousness of unjust or dishonorable purposes, communication is always checked by distrust in proportion to the number whose concurrence is necessary.

Hence, it clearly appears, that the same advantage which a republic has over a democracy, in controlling the effects of faction, is enjoyed by a large over a small republic,—is enjoyed by the Union over the States composing it. Does the advantage consist in the substitution of representatives whose enlightened views and virtuous sentiments render them superior to local prejudices and to schemes of injustice? It will not be denied that the representation of the Union will be most likely to possess these requisite endowments. Does it consist in the greater security afforded by a greater variety of parties, against the event of any one party being able to outnumber and oppress the rest? In an equal degree does the increased variety of parties comprised within the Union, increase this security. Does it, in fine, consist in the greater obstacles opposed to the concert and accomplishment of the secret wishes of an unjust and interested majority? Here, again, the extent of the Union gives it the most palpable advantage.

The influence of factious leaders may kindle a

flame within their particular States, but will be unable to spread a general conflagration through the other States. A religious sect may degenerate into a political faction in a part of the Confederacy; but the variety of sects dispersed over the entire face of it must secure the national councils against any danger from that source. A rage for paper money, for an abolition of debts, for an equal division of property, or for any other improper or wicked project, will be less apt to pervade the whole body of the Union than a particular member of it; in the same proportion as such a malady is more likely to taint a particular county or district, than an entire State.

In the extent and proper structure of the Union, therefore, we behold a republican remedy for the diseases most incident to republican government. And according to the degree of pleasure and pride we feel in being republicans, ought to be our zeal in cherishing the spirit and supporting the character of Federalists.

The Lack of Authority

A common Anti-Federalist argument replayed the debates in the Convention itself: that the Convention lacked authority to do more than propose amendments to the Articles of Confederation. Anti-Federalists excoriated the Convention for exceeding its powers:

> The late convention were chosen by the general assembly of each state; they had the sanction of Congress;—for what? To consider what alterations were necessary to be made in the articles of confederation. What have they done? They have made a new constitution for the United States.[21]

Patrick Henry was particularly incensed by the Convention's method of avoiding questions about authority. Like some of the delegates in Philadelphia, he did not agree that authority to frame a new constitution could be given by the people rather than the states.

> And here I would make this inquiry of those worthy characters who composed a part of the late federal Convention. . . . I have the highest veneration for those gentlemen; but, sir, give me leave to demand, What right had they to say, *We the people*? My political curiosity, exclusive of my anxious solicitude for the public welfare, leads me to ask, Who authorized them to speak the language of *We the people*, instead of, *We, the states*? . . . The people gave them no power to use their name. That they exceeded their power is perfectly clear.[22]

Despite Henry's "veneration" of the members of the Convention, other Anti-Federalists virtually accused the delegates of treason. They focused on the secrecy of the Convention to highlight the illegality of the whole proceeding and label it a conspiracy:

> The authors of the new plan, conscious that it would not stand the test of enlightened patriotism, tyrannically endeavoured to preclude all investigation.—If their views were laudable, if they were honest,—the contrary would have been their conduct, they would have invited the freest discussion. . . . Such an attempt does not augur the public good— It carries on the face of it an intention to juggle the people out of their liberties.[23]

The preamble was said to list only the "ostensible" reasons for the new Constitution; the real reason was a longstanding "plan . . . to subvert the confederation."[24]

Federalists tended to ignore the charges of secrecy and to answer personal attacks in kind. Edmund Randolph, attacked in the Virginia convention by Patrick Henry, responded:

> I disdain his aspersions and his insinuations. His asperity is warranted by no principle of parliamentary decency, nor compatible with the least shadow of friendship; and if our friendship must fall, *let it fall, like Lucifer, never to rise again!*[25]

On the more serious issue of the Convention's authority, however, Federalists were forced to defend themselves with more than mere rhetoric. They took two different approaches.

In the Pennsylvania convention, James Wilson argued that the whole question was essentially irrelevant, since popular ratification would legitimate even the greatest usurpation of authority.

> I think the late Convention has done nothing beyond their powers. The fact is, they have exercised no power at all, and, in point of validity, this Constitution, proposed by them for the government of the United States, claims no more than a production of the same nature would claim, flowing from a private pen. It is laid before the citizens of the United States, unfettered by restraint; it is laid before them to be judged by the natural, civil, and political rights of men. By their *fiat*, it will become of value and authority; without it, it will never receive the character of authenticity and power.[26]

Other Federalists, especially the legalistic Madison, argued in addition that the Convention *did* have power to propose a new Constitution. In *Federalist No. 40*, Madison traced the Convention's authority from the recommendations of the Annapolis Convention and the congressional resolution calling for the Philadelphia Convention. He concluded that the latter Convention had the authority "to frame a *national government*, adequate to the *exigencies of government*, and *of the Union*; and to reduce the articles of Confederation into such form as to accomplish these purposes."[27] Using his typical orderly logic, he then argued that the new Constitution was in fact merely an amendment—concededly substantial—of the Articles of Confederation, because there were no changes in principle between the two documents.

Anti-Federalists did see major changes in principle. Their criticism of specific provisions of the new Constitution, the topic of the rest of this chapter, showed just how dissatisfied they were.

DEFECTS OF THE JUDICIAL BRANCH

Anti-Federalists'criticisms of Article III, which established the judicial branch of the federal government, exemplified their criticism of the entire Constitution. In the materials that follow, notice the recurrent objection to centralization of governmental power, which the Anti-Federalists thought detrimental to both individual rights and state sovereignty. The Federalist response is especially interesting, as defenders simultaneously denied that the judiciary had much power and ascribed to it a central and crucial role in the new federal government.

Many of the Anti-Federalist critiques were general objections to federal jurisdiction and to the lack of a jury trial. Unused to a federal judiciary, and frightened by the memory of the Privy Council's appellate power over colonial courts, the Anti-Federalists simply saw no use for a federal judiciary—

especially for lower federal courts. The "Federal Farmer" voiced the sentiments of many Anti-Federalists when he described the ideal court system, which was a far cry from the far-flung, hierarchical system apparently established in Article III:

> I am not for bringing justice so near to individuals as to afford them any temptation to engage in law suits; though I think it one of the greatest benefits in a good government, that each citizen should find a court of justice within a reasonable distance, perhaps, within a day's travel of his home; so that, without great inconveniences and enormous expences, he may have the advantages of his witnesses and jury[.][28]

According to the "Federal Farmer" and other Anti-Federalists, the expense of either original or appellate Supreme Court jurisdiction would be prohibitive, and would deprive citizens of some of their most precious rights as litigants.

Hamilton probably penned *Federalist No. 78* in response to the most general Anti-Federalist complaints, and it therefore contains little detail. It is notable, however, for its defense of judicial review. Compare Hamilton's arguments with those of Chief Justice Marshall in *Marbury v. Madison*, 5 U.S. (1 Cranch) 137, 2 L.Ed. 60 (1803).

Federalist No. 78
Hamilton

Whoever attentively considers the different departments of power must perceive, that, in a government in which they are separated from each other, the judiciary, from the nature of its functions, will always be the least dangerous to the political rights of the Constitution; because it will be least in a capacity to annoy or injure them. The Executive not only dispenses the honors, but holds the sword of the community. The legislature not only commands the purse, but prescribes the rules by which the duties and rights of every citizen are to be regulated. The judiciary, on the contrary, has no influence over either the sword or the purse; no direction either of the strength or of the wealth of the society; and can take no active resolution whatever. It may truly be said to have neither FORCE nor WILL, but merely judgment; and must ultimately depend upon the aid of the executive arm even for the efficacy of its judgments.

This simple view of the matter suggests several important consequences. It proves incontestably, that the judiciary is beyond comparison the weakest of the three departments of power*; that it can never attack with success either of the other two; and that all possible care is requisite to enable it to defend itself against their attacks. It equally proves, that though individual oppression may now and then proceed from the courts of justice, the general liberty of the people can never be endangered from that quarter; I mean so long as the judiciary remains truly distinct from both the legislature and the Executive. For I agree, that "there is no liberty, if the power of judging be not separated from the legislative and executive powers."† And it proves, in the last place, that as liberty can have nothing to fear from the judiciary alone, but would have every thing to fear from its union with either of the other departments; that as all the effects of such a union must ensue from a dependence of the former on the latter, notwithstanding a nominal and apparent separation; that as, from the natural feebleness of the judiciary, it is in continual jeopardy of being overpowered, awed, or influenced by its coordinate branches; and that as nothing can contribute so much to its firmness and independence as permanency in office, this quality may therefore be justly regarded as an indispensable ingredient in its con-

---

*The celebrated Montesquieu, speaking of them, says: "Of the three powers above mentioned, the judiciary is next to nothing."— "Spirit of Laws," vol. i., page 186.—PUBLIUS

†*Idem*, page 181.—PUBLIUS

stitution, and, in a great measure, as the citadel of the public justice and the public security.

The complete independence of the courts of justice is peculiarly essential in a limited Constitution. By a limited Constitution, I understand one which contains certain specified exceptions to the legislative authority; for instance, as that it shall pass no bills of attainder, no *ex-post-facto* laws, and the like. Limitations of this kind can be preserved in practice no other way than through the medium of courts of justice, whose duty it must be to declare all acts contrary to the manifest tenor of the Constitution void. Without this, all the reservations of particular rights or privileges would amount to nothing.

Some perplexity respecting the rights of the courts to pronounce legislative acts void, because contrary to the constitution, has arisen from an imagination that the doctrine would imply a superiority of the judiciary to the legislative power. It is urged that the authority which can declare the acts of another void, must necessarily be superior to the one whose acts may be declared void. As this doctrine is of great importance in all the American constitutions, a brief discussion of the ground on which it rests cannot be unacceptable.

There is no position which depends on clearer principles, than that every act of a delegated authority, contrary to the tenor of the commission under which it is exercised, is void. No legislative act, therefore, contrary to the Constitution, can be valid. To deny this, would be to affirm, that the deputy is greater than his principal; that the servant is above his master; that the representatives of the people are superior to the people themselves; that men acting by virtue of powers, may do not only what their powers do not authorize, but what they forbid.

If it be said that the legislative body are themselves the constitutional judges of their own powers, and that the construction they put upon them is conclusive upon the other departments, it may be answered, that this cannot be the natural presumption, where it is not to be collected from any particular provisions in the Constitution. It is not otherwise to be supposed, that the Constitution could intend to enable the representatives of the people to substitute their *will* to that of their constituents. It is far more rational to suppose, that the courts were designed to be an intermediate body between the people and the legislature, in order, among other things, to keep the latter within the limits assigned to their authority. The interpretation of the laws is the proper and peculiar province of the courts. A constitution is, in fact, and must be regarded by the judges, as a fundamental law. It therefore belongs to them to ascertain its meaning, as well as the meaning of any particular act proceeding from the legislative body. If there should happen to be an irreconcilable variance between the two, that which has the superior obligation and validity ought, of course, to be preferred; or, in other words, the Constitution ought to be preferred to the statute, the intention of the people to the intention of their agents.

Nor does this conclusion by any means suppose a superiority of the judicial to the legislative power. It only supposes that the power of the people is superior to both; and that where the will of the legislature, declared in its statutes, stands in opposition to that of the people, declared in the Constitution, the judges ought to be governed by the latter rather than the former. They ought to regulate their decisions by the fundamental laws, rather than by those which are not fundamental.

More careful critics of Article III focused on the jurisdiction of the federal courts. They were particularly incensed by federal jurisdiction over suits between a state and citizens of a different state, and by the Supreme Court's appellate jurisdiction over law and fact. In addition, both critics and defenders often argued point by point each jurisdictional grant. In the Virginia ratifying convention, George Mason and Patrick Henry used this tactic. As they went through each clause of Article III, they expressed outrage at the havoc that federal jurisdiction would wreak on state governments, state courts, and state citizens. In response, the young John Marshall showed both an affinity for a strong national judiciary and a talent for rhetorical argument; both would later be evident in his opinions as Chief Justice.

Virginia Ratifying Convention
Thursday June 19 and Friday June 20, 1788
Elliot 3:521-29, 539-46, 551-560

Mr. Mason: After having read the first section, Mr. Mason asked, What is there left to the state courts? Will any gentleman be pleased, candidly, fairly, and without sophistry, to show us what remains? There is no limitation. It goes to every thing. The inferior courts are to be as numerous as Congress may think proper. They are to be of whatever nature they please. Read the 2d section, and contemplate attentively the extent of the jurisdiction of these courts, and consider if there be any limits to it.

I am greatly mistaken if there be any limitation whatsoever, with respect to the nature or jurisdiction of these courts. If there be any limits, they must be contained in one of the clauses of this section; and I believe, on a dispassionate discussion, it will be found that there is none of any check. All the laws of the United States are paramount to the laws and constitution of any single state. ''The judicial power shall extend to all cases in law and equity arising under this Constitution.'' What objects will not this expresison extend to? Such laws may be formed as will go to every object of private property.

.   .   .

Their *jurisdiction* further extends to controversies between citizens of different states. Can we not trust our state courts with the decision of these? If I have a controversy with a man in Maryland,—if a man in Maryland has my bond for a hundred pounds.—are not the state courts competent to try it? Is it suspected that they would enforce the payment if unjust, or refuse to enforce it if just? The very idea is ridiculous. What! carry me a thousand miles from home—from my family and business— to where, perhaps, it will be impossible for me to prove that I paid it? Perhaps I have a respectable witness who saw me pay the money; but I must carry him one thousand miles to prove it, or be compelled to pay it again. Is there any necessity for this power? It ought to have no unnecessary or dangerous power. Why should the federal courts have this cognizance? Is it because one lives on one side of the Potomac, and the other on the other? Suppose I have your bond for a thousand pounds: if I have any wish to harass you, or if I be of a litigious disposition, I have only to assign it to a gentleman in

Maryland. This assignment will involve you in trouble and expense.

.   .   .

Mr. Henry: I consider the Virginia judiciary as one of the best barriers against strides of power— against that power which, we are told by the honorable gentleman, has threatened the destruction of liberty. Pardon me for expressing my extreme regret that it is in their power to take away that barrier. Gentlemen will not say that any danger can be expected from the state legislatures. So small are the barriers against the encroachments and usurpations of Congress, that, when I see this last barrier—the independency of the judges—impaired, I am persuaded I see the prostration of all our rights. In what a situation will your judges be, when they are sworn to preserve the Constitution of the state and of the general government! If there be a concurrent dispute between them, which will prevail? They cannot serve two masters struggling for the same object. The laws of Congress being paramount to those of the states, and to their constitutions also, whenever they come in competition, the judges must decide in favor of the former. This, instead of relieving or aiding me, deprives me of my only comfort—the independency of the judges. The judiciary are the sole protection against a tyrannical execution of the laws. But if by this system we lose our judiciary, and they cannot help us, we must sit down quietly, and be oppressed.

.   .   .

As to controversies between a state and the citizens of another state, his [Mr. Madison's] construction of it is to me perfectly incomprehensible. He says it will seldom happen that a state has such demands on individuals. There is nothing to warrant such an assertion. But he says that the state may be plaintiff only. If gentlemen pervert the most clear expressions, and the usual meaning of the language of the people, there is an end of all argument. What says the paper? That it shall have cognizance of controversies between a state and citizens of another state, without discriminating between plaintiff and defendant. What says the honorable gentleman? The contrary—that the state can only be plaintiff. When the state is debtor, there is no reciprocity. It seems to me that gentlemen may put what construction they please on it. What! is justice to be done to one party, and not to the other? If gentlemen take this liberty now, what will they not do when our rights and liberties are in their power? He said it was necessary to provide a tribunal when the case happened, though it would happen but seldom. The power is necessary, because New York could not, before the war, collect money from Connecticut! The state judiciaries are so degraded that they cannot be trusted. This is a dangerous power which is thus instituted. For what? For things which will seldom happen; and yet, because there is a possibility that the strong, energetic government may want it, it shall be produced and thrown in the general scale of power. I confess I think it dangerous.

. . .

Mr. John Marshall. Mr. Chairman, this part of the plan before us is a great improvement on that system from which we are now departing. Here are tribunals appointed for *the decision of controversies* which were before either not at all, or improperly, provided for. That many benefits will result from this to the members of the collective society, every one confesses. Unless its organization be defective, and so constructed as to injure, instead of accommodating, the convenience of the people, it merits our approbation. After such a candid and fair discussion by those gentlemen who support it,—after the very able manner in which they have investigated and examined it,—I conceived it would be no longer considered as so very defective, and that those who opposed it would be convinced of the impropriety of some of their objections. But I perceive they still continue the same opposition. Gentlemen have gone on an idea that the federal courts will not determine the causes which may come before them with the same fairness and impartiality with which other courts decide. What are the reasons of this supposition? Do they draw them from the manner in which the judges are chosen, or the tenure of their office? What is it that makes us trust our judges? Their independence in office, and manner of appointment. Are not the judges of the federal court chosen with as much wisdom as the judges of the state government? Are they not equally, if not more independent? If so, shall we not conclude that they will decide with equal impartiality and candor? If there be as much wisdom and knowledge in the United States as in a particular state, shall

we conclude that the wisdom and knowledge will not be equally exercised in the selection of judges?

. . .

These, sir, are the points of *federal jurisdiction* to which he objects, with a few exception. Let us examine each of them with a supposition that the same impartiality will be observed there as in other courts, and then see if any mischief will result from them. With respect to its cognizance in all cases arising under the Constitution and the laws of the United States, he says that, the laws of the United States being paramount to the laws of the particular states, there is no case but what this will extend to. Has the government of the United States power to make laws on every subject? Does he understand it so? Can they make laws affecting the mode of transferring property, or contracts, or claims, between citizens of the same state? Can they go beyond the delegated powers? If they were to make a law not warranted by any of the powers enumerated, it would be considered by the judges as an infringement of the Constitution which they are to guard. They would not consider such a law as coming under this jurisdiction. They would declare it void. It will annihilate the state courts, says the honorable gentleman. Does not every gentleman here know that the causes in our courts are more numerous than they can decide, according to their present construction? Look at the dockets. You will find them crowded with suits, which the life of man will not see determined. If some of these suits be carried to other courts, will it be wrong? They will still have business enough.

Then there is no danger that particular subjects, small in proportion, being taken out of the jurisdiction of the state judiciaries, will render them useless and of no effect. Does the gentleman think that the state courts will have no cognizance of cases not mentioned here? Are there any words in this Constitution which exclude the courts of the states from those cases which they now possess? Does the gentleman imagine this to be the case? Will any gentleman believe it? Are not controversies respecting lands claimed under the grants of different states the only controversies between citizens of the same state which the federal judiciary can take cognizance of? The case is so clear, that to prove it would be a useless waste of time. The state courts will not lose the jurisdiction of the causes they now decide. They have a concurrence of jurisdiction with the federal courts in those cases in which the latter have cognizance.

. . .

With respect to disputes between a *state and the citizens of another state*, I hope that no gentleman will think that a state will be called at the bar of the federal court. Is there no such case at present? Are there not many cases in which the legislature of Virginia is a party, and yet the state is not sued? It is not rational to suppose that the sovereign power should be dragged before a court. The intent is, to enable states to recover claims of individuals residing in other states. I contend this construction is warranted by the words. But, say they, there will be partiality in it if a state cannot be defendant—if an individual cannot proceed to obtain judgement against a state, though he may be sued by a state. It is necessary to be so, and cannot be avoided. I see a difficulty in making a state defendant, which does not prevent its being plaintiff. If this be only what cannot be avoided, why object to the system of that account? If an individual has a just claim against any particular state, is it to be presumed that, on application to its legislature, he will not obtain satisfaction? But how could a state recover any claim from a citizen of another state, without the establishment of these tribunals?

Although Henry was not at his rhetorical best in these passages, the debates are among the best illustrations of the chasm that divided the Federalists and Anti-Federalists. They are also notable for their presaging of disputes that would soon come before the federal judiciary. For example, Marshall and Henry battled over the construction of a clause that subsequently became very important in constitutional law. Henry contended, and Marshall (and other Federalists) warmly disputed, that the grant of jurisdiction over suits between a state and a citizen of another state would allow individuals to sue states. In 1793, in *Chisholm v. Georgia*, 2 U.S. (2 Dall.) 419, 1 L.Ed. 440 (1793), the Supreme Court adopted Henry's interpretation, only to be reversed two years later by the hastily ratified Eleventh Amendment. The proper construction of that amendment is still in dispute. Compare the majority and dissenting opinions in *Welch v. Texas Department of Highways and Public Transportation*, 483 U.S. 468, 107 S.Ct. 2941, 97 L.Ed.2d 389 (1987).

Marshall was not the only Federalist to defend the various grants of jurisdiction in Article III. Two other lawyers, James Wilson and Alexander Hamilton, also used their considerable legal skills to refute Anti-Federalist criticisms. In one of his many speeches to the Pennsylvania ratifying convention, Wilson appealed to the self-interest of his listeners to defend the much maligned diversity jurisdiction.

But when we consider the matter a little further, is it not necessary, if we mean to restore either public or private credit, that foreigners, as well as ourselves, have a just and impartial tribunal to which they may resort? I would ask how a merchant must feel to have his property lie at the mercy of the laws of Rhode Island. I ask, further, How will a creditor feel who has his debts at the mercy of tender laws in other states?[29]

Hamilton's *Federalist No. 80* is the most extensive and detailed Federalist discussion of the various grants of federal jurisdiction.

Federalist No. 80
Hamilton

It seems scarcely to admit of controversy, that the judiciary authority of the Union ought to extend to these several descriptions of cases: 1st, to all those which arise out of the laws of the United States, passed in pursuance of their just and constitutional powers of legislation; 2d, to all those which concern the execution of the provisions expressly contained in the articles of Union; 3d, to all those in which the United States are a party; 4th, to all those which involve the PEACE of the CONFEDERACY, whether they relate to the intercourse between the United States and foreign nations, or to that between the States themselves; 5th, to all those which originate on the high seas, and are of admiralty or maritime jurisdiction; and lastly, to all those in which the State tribunals cannot be supposed to be impartial and unbiased.

The first point depends upon this obvious consideration, that there ought always to be a constitutional method of giving efficacy to constitutional provisions. What, for instance, would avail restrictions on the authority of the State legislatures, without some constitutional mode of enforcing the observance of them? The States, by the plan of the convention, are prohibited from doing a variety of things, some of which are incompatible with the interests of the Union, and others with the principles of good government. The imposition of duties on imported articles, and the emission of paper money, are specimens of each kind. No man of sense will believe, that such prohibitions would be scrupulously regarded, without some effectual power in the government to restrain or correct the infractions of them. This power must either be a direct negative on the State laws, or an authority in the federal courts to overrule such as might be in manifest contravention of the articles of Union. There is no third course that I can imagine. The latter appears to have been thought by the convention preferable to the former, and, I presume, will be most agreeable to the States.

As to the second point, it is impossible, by any argument or comment, to make it clearer than it is in itself. If there are such things as political axioms, the propriety of the judicial power of a government being coextensive with its legislative, may be ranked among the number. The mere necessity of uniformity in the interpretation of the national laws, decides the question. Thirteeen independent courts of

final jurisdiction over the same causes, arising upon the same laws, is a hydra in government from which nothing but contradiction and confusion can proceed.

Still less need be said in regard to the third point. Controversies between the nation and its members or citizens, can only be properly referred to the national tribunals. Any other plan would be contrary to reason, to precedent, and to decorum.

The fourth point rests on this plain proposition, that the peace of the WHOLE ought not to be left at the disposal of a PART. The Union will undoubtedly be answerable to foreign powers for the conduct of its members. And the responsibility for an injury ought ever to be accompanied with the faculty of preventing it.

. . .

It may be esteemed the basis of the Union, that "the citizens of each State shall be entitled to all the privileges and immunities of citizens of the several States." And if it be a just principle that every government *ought to possess the means of executing its own provisions by its own authority*, it will follow, that in order to the inviolable maintenance of that equality of privileges and immunities to which the citizens of the Union will be entitled, the national judiciary ought to preside in all cases in which one State or its citizens are opposed to another State or its citizens. To secure the full effect of so fundamental a provision against all evasion and subterfuge, it is necessary that its construction should be committed to that tribunal which, having no local attachments, will be likely to be impartial between the different States and their citizens, and which, owing its official existence to the Union, will never be likely to feel any bias inauspicious to the principles on which it is founded.

. . .

The reasonableness of the agency of the national courts in cases in which the State tribunals cannot be supposed to be impartial, speaks for itself. No man ought certainly to be a judge in his own cause, or in any cause in respect to which he has the least interest or bias. This principle has no inconsiderable weight in designating the federal courts as the proper tribunals for the determination of controversies between different States and their citizens. And it ought to have the same operation in regard to some cases between citizens of the same State. Claims to land under grants of different States, founded upon adverse pretensions of boundary, are of this description. The courts of neither of the granting States could be expected to be unbiased. The laws may have even prejudged the question, and tied the courts down to decisions in favor of the grants of the State to which they belonged. And even where this had not been done, it would be natural that the judges, as men, should feel a strong predilection to the claims of their own government.

One theme that runs through the arguments of both Federalists and Anti-Federalists is the trustworthiness of the state courts. Both "Centinel" and Mason protested that Article III cast aspersions on the state courts, implying an "improper distrust." Although both Hamilton and Wilson indirectly denied this charge by giving more neutral justifications for the various grants of jurisdiction, they also implicitly conceded that state courts were unreliable in some areas. Wilson asked whether his listeners would like to "have [their] property lie at the mercy of the laws of Rhode Island." Hamilton, in *Federalist No. 81*, wrote: "State judges, holding their offices during pleasure, or from year to year, will be too little independent to be relied upon for an inflexible execution of the national laws."

The trustworthiness of state courts has remained a controversial issue. As chapters 9 and 10 will show, the failure of state courts to enforce federal rights was one motivating factor in the adoption of the Civil Rights Act of 1866 and the Fourteenth Amendment. The Supreme Court and modern constitutional scholars are no less concerned with the question of whether state courts can be trusted to enforce federal civil rights. In particular, there is a debate over whether litigants seeking to vindicate federal rights should be guaranteed a federal forum. The Supreme Court wavers, declaring in some cases that states courts are fully competent and trustworthy, and implying in others that federal courts are the most appropriate forum for litigating federal rights. Compare *Ex Parte Young*, 209 U.S. 123, 28 S.Ct. 441, 52 L.Ed. 714 (1908), *England v. Louisiana State Board of Medical Examiners*, 375 U.S. 411, 84 S.Ct. 461, 11 L.Ed.2d 440 (1964), and *Mitchum v. Foster*, 407 U.S. 225, 92 S.Ct. 2151, 32 L.Ed.2d 705 (1972), with *Younger v. Harris*, 401 U.S. 37, 91 S.Ct. 746, 27 L.Ed.2d 669 (1971) and its progeny.

Recall the debates over the judiciary in the Federal Convention, discussed in chapter 3. What further light do the disputes between the Federalists and Anti-Federalists shed on this question? Was mistrust of the state courts justified? Is it today? To what extent has the relationship between state and federal courts changed?

DEFECTS OF THE EXECUTIVE BRANCH

The ratification debates over the judiciary, like the debates in the Federal Convention, were sharp and well-defined. Not so the debates over the federal executive. If the delegates to the Federal Convention were uncertain about how best to constitute the executive branch (see chapter 4), the Anti-Federalists were equally confused. Some thought the executive had too much power, some thought it had too little. Some approved of a single magistrate, some preferred a council. One frequently voiced suggestion was periodic ineligibility or rotation in office. The Anti-Federalist writings on the executive branch were perhaps the least focused and most unsophisticated of the Anti-Federalist works. Like the Federal Convention delegates, the Anti-Federalists simply had no clear idea of the nature and function of the executive in a republican government.

The most common Anti-Federalist fears appear to us today as rather quaint. Immersed in the eighteenth-century paradigm of virtue and corruption, the Anti-Federalists viewed a weak president as highly susceptible to the "intrigues" of various corrupting forces: the aristocracy, office-seekers, and foreign powers. A strong president, on the other hand, would become a tyrant. "Philadelphiensis," whose identity is unknown, nicely summarized the dilemma:

> [I]f he be a bold enterprising fellow . . . [t]he two branches of the legislature, will be at his service; no law contrary to his sentiments, however salutary in its operation, dare be mentioned by them. As a body, and as individuals, they will be his sycophants and flatterers. But, if on the contrary he should not be a man of spirit, a thing very improbable, as none but an ambitious man, well versed in the ways of men, could have the address to be raised to that elevated station; if, however, I say, he should not be a man of enterprising spirit, in that case he will be a *minion* of the aristocratics, doing according to their will and pleasure, and confirming every law they may think proper to make, without any regard to their public utility.[30]

Another worry, expressed by the anonymous "Impartial Examiner" in the *Virginia Independent Chronicle*, was that the veto would give the president almost as much control over legislation as Congress, and place him "above all law." The "Federal Farmer" feared that continual eligibility for re-election would lead to corruption. Thomas Jefferson, writing to John Adams (then in London), called the federal executive "a bad edition of a Polish King," because continued eligibility would result in intrigues with foreign powers.[31] The most elaborate responses to these Anti-Federalist criticisms of the executive were Hamilton's primary contributions to the *Federalist Papers*.

Federalist No. 70
Hamilton

There is an idea, which is not without its advocates, that a vigorous Executive is inconsistent with the genius of republican government. The enlightened well-wishers to this species of government must at least hope that the supposition is destitute of foundation; since they can never admit its truth, without at the same time admitting the condemnation of their own principles. Energy in the Executive is a leading character in the definition of good government. It is essential to the protection of the community against foreign attacks; it is not less essential to the steady administration of the laws; to the protection of property against those irregular and high-handed combinations which sometimes interrupt the ordinary course of justice; to the security of liberty against the enterprises and assaults of ambition, of faction, and of anarchy. Every man the least conversant in Roman story, knows how often that republic was obliged to take refuge in the absolute power of a single man, under the formidable title of Dictator, as well against the intrigues of ambitious individuals who aspired to the tyranny, and the seditions of whole classes of the community whose conduct threatened the existence of all government, as against the invasions of external enemies who menaced the conquest and destruction of Rome.

There can be no need, however, to multiply arguments or examples on this head. A feeble Executive implies a feeble execution of the government. A feeble execution is but another phrase for a bad execution; and a government ill executed, whatever it may be in theory, must be, in practice, a bad government.

Those politicians and statesmen who have been the most celebrated for the soundness of their principles and for the justice of their views, have declared in favor of a single Executive and a numerous legislature. They have, with great propriety, considered energy as the most necessary qualification of the former, and have regarded this as most applicable to power in a single hand; while they have, with equal propriety considered the latter, as best adapted to deliberation and wisdom, and best calculated to conciliate the confidence of the people and to secure their privileges and interests.

That unity is conducive to energy will not be disputed. Decision, activity, secrecy, and despatch will generally characterize the proceedings of one man in a much more eminent degree than the proceedings of any greater number; and in proportion as the number is increased, these qualities will be diminished.

Federalist No. 71
Hamilton

The same rule which teaches the propriety of a partition between the various branches of power, teaches us likewise that this partition ought to be so contrived as to render the one independent of the other. To what purpose separate the executive or the judiciary from the legislative, if both the executive and the judiciary are so constituted as to be at the absolute devotion of the legislative? Such a separation must be merely nominal, and incapable of producing the ends for which it was established. It is one thing to be subordinate to the laws, and another to be dependent on the legislative body. The first comports with, the last violates, the fundamental principles of good government; and, whatever may be the forms of the Constitution, unites all power in the same hands. The tendency of the legislative authority to absorb every other, has been fully displayed and illustrated by examples in some preceding numbers. In governments purely republican, this tendency is almost irresistible. The representatives of the people, in a popular assembly, seem sometimes to fancy that they are the people themselves, and betray strong symptoms of impatience and disgust at the least sign of opposition from any other quarter; as if the exercise of its rights, by either the executive or judiciary, were a breach of their privilege and an outrage to their dignity. They often appear disposed to exert an imperious control over the other departments; and as they commonly have the people on their side, they always act with such momentum as to make it very difficult for the other members of the government to maintain the balance of the Constitution.

It may perhaps be asked, how the shortness of the duration in office can affect the independence of the Executive or the legislature, unless the one were possessed of the power of appointing or displacing the other. One answer to this inquiry may be drawn from the principle already remarked—that is, from the slender interest a man is apt to take in a short-lived advantage, and the little inducement it affords him to expose himself, on account of it, to any considerable inconvenience or hazard. Another answer, perhaps more obvious, though not more conclusive, will result from the consideration of the influence of the legislative body over the people; which be employed to prevent the re-election of a man who, by an upright resistance to any sinister project of that body, should have made himself obnoxious to its resentment.

It may be asked also, whether a duration of four years would answer the end proposed; and if it would not, whether a less period, which would at least be recommended by greater security against ambitious designs, would not, for that reason, be preferable to a longer period, which was, at the same time, too short for the purpose of inspiring the desired firmness and independence of the magistrate.

Although the executive branch was not the greatest source of friction, opponents and proponents of the Constitution certainly differed as to its proper character. They did, however, share underlying fears of corruption and faction. What types of "corruption" did these men fear? To what extent would Anti-Federalists and Federalists alike agree with the remark by the Federal Farmer: "It must be admitted, that men, from the monarch down to the porter, are constantly aiming at power and importance"?[32] How accurate have these eighteenth-century fears of power proved? Has the president, over the years, been too weak? Too strong? Corrupt? If their fears were not realized, what prevented the dangers?

Federalist No. 71 is a particularly interesting description of the countermajoritarian purpose of the executive branch. In it Hamilton admonished that the executive must serve as the guardian of long-term values, protecting against the "transient impulses" of the people. Recall debates over the legislature in the Federal Convention: there Madison and others expected that the Senate would serve that function (see also *Federalist No. 62*, reprinted in the next section). Many modern scholars, most notably the late Alexander Bickel, now view the judiciary as the branch best able "to appeal to men's better natures, to call forth their aspirations, which may have been forgotten in the moment's hue and cry."[33] Thus at various times, each of the three branches has been expected to temper principles of popular representation and to protect the people against themselves. Has any branch served this function? How well? Is such a safeguard necessary or desirable? Why or why not? Which branch is best suited to take the long view?

DEFECTS OF THE LEGISLATIVE BRANCH

The most democratic branch of the federal government caused perhaps the greatest controversy in the ratification debates. In addition to criticizing the vast legislative powers granted to the new government, Anti-Federalists attacked the size of the legislature, apportionment of representatives in each house, and the manner of electing those representatives. Detailed Anti-Federalist critiques of all aspects of the federal legislature elaborated and extended many of the arguments presented in earlier sections of this chapter. A common theme of many Anti-Federalist complaints was that the legislature would be insufficiently attentive to interests of the "great body of the people," the "middling classes." This conclusion was based on now-familiar beliefs: the small number of legislators for so large a district would combine with man's natural tendency toward corruption and result in a permanent aristocracy. Anti-Federalists linked these themes together in various ways. "Brutus," for example, found apportionment in the Senate as objectionable as the legislature's small size and overall aristocratic character. Interestingly, "Brutus" eventually came to accept the principle of equal apportionment in the Senate. He wrote on April 10, 1788, in his last essay, that equal apportionment "is proper on the system of confederation—on this principle I approve of it."[34]

Brutus, No. 3
November 15, 1787
Storing 2.9.40-42

There appears at the first view a manifest inconsistency, in the apportionment of representatives in the senate, upon the plan of a consolidated government. On every principle of equity, and propriety, representation in a government should be in exact proportion to the numbers, or the aids afforded by the persons represented. How unreasonable, and unjust then is it, that Delaware should have a representation in the senate, equal to Massachusetts, or Virginia? The latter of which contains ten times her numbers, and is to contribute to the aid of the general government in that proportion? This article of the constitution will appear the more objectionable, if it is considered, that the powers vested in this branch of the legislature are very extensive, and greatly surpass those lodged in the assembly, not only for general purposes, but, in many instances, for the internal police of the states. The other branch of the legislature, in which, if in either, a f[a]int spark of democracy is to be found, should have been properly organized and established—but upon examination you will find, that this branch does not possess the qualities of a just representation, and that there is no kind of security, imperfect as it is, for its remaining in the hands of the people.

It has been observed, that the happiness of society is the end of government—that every free government is founded in compact; and that, because it is impracticable for the whole community to assemble, or when assembled, to deliberate with wisdom, and decide with dispatch, the mode of legislating by representation was devised.

The very term, representative, implies, that the person or body chosen for this purpose, should resemble those who appoint them—a representation of the people of America, if it be a true one, must be like the people. It ought to be so constituted, that a person, who is a stranger to the country, might be able to form a just idea of their character, by knowing that of their representatives. They are the sign—the people are the thing signified. It is absurd to speak of one thing being the representative of another, upon any other principle. The ground and reason of representation, in a free government, implies the same thing. Society instituted government to promote the happiness of the whole, and this is the great end always in view in the delegation of powers. It must then have been intended, that those who are placed instead of the people, should possess their sentiments and feelings, and be governed by their interests, or, in other words, should bear the strongest resemblance of those in whose room they are substituted. It is obvious, that for an assembly to be a true likeness of the people of any country, they must be considerably numerous.— One man, or a few men, cannot possibly represent the feelings, opinions, and characters of a great multitude. In this respect, the new constitution is radically defective.—The house of assembly, which is intended as a representation of the people of America, will not, nor cannot, in the nature of things, be a proper one—sixty-five men cannot be found in the United States, who hold the sentiments, possess the feelings, or are acquainted with the wants and interest of this vast country. This extensive continent is made up of a number of different classes of people; and to have a proper representation of them, each class ought to have an opportunity of choosing their best informed men for the purpose; but this cannot possibly be the case in so small a number.

. . .

The great body of the yeomen of the country cannot expect any of their order in this assembly—the station will be too elevated for them to aspire to—the distance between the people and their representatives, will be so very great, that there is no probability that a farmer, however respectable, will be chosen—the mechanicks of every branch, must expect to be excluded from a seat in this Body—It will and must be esteemed a station too high and exalted to be filled by any but the first men in the state, in point of fortune: so that in reality there will be no part of the people represented, but the rich, even in that branch of the legislature, which is called the democratic.—The well born, and highest orders in life, as they term themselves, will be ignorant of the sentiments of the midling class of citizens, strangers to their ability, wants, and difficulties, and void of sympathy, and fellow feeling.

The method of apportionment, which figured so heavily in the early debates in the Federal Convention, was only one of the common concerns of the Anti-Federalists. Echoing "Brutus" in the essay above, several Anti-Federalists focused also on the effects of the small size of the legislature. Melancton Smith worried that representatives would be of "the natural aristocracy of the country," and not of "the middling class of life." The legislature, moreover, was in his opinion too small to be democratic, and too liable to corruption:

> I confess, to me they hardly wear the complexion of a democratic branch; they appear the mere shadow of representation. The whole number, in both houses, amounts to ninety-one; of these forty-six make a quorum; and twenty-four of those, being secured, may carry any point. Can the liberties of three millions of people be securely trusted in the hands of twenty-four men? Is it prudent to commit to so small a number the decision of the great questions which will come before them? Reason revolts at the idea.[35]

Patrick Henry voiced similar concerns in the Virginia Ratifying Convention.

Virginia Ratifying Convention
Thursday June 12, 1788
Elliot 3:322

Mr. Henry: It has been said, by several gentlemen, that the freeness of elections would be promoted by throwing the country into large districts. I contend, sir, that it will have a contrary effect. It will destroy that connection that ought to subsist between the electors and the elected. If your elections be by districts, instead of counties, the people will not be acquainted with the candidates. They must, therefore, be directed in the elections by those who know them. So that, instead of a confidential connection between the electors and the elected, they will be absolutely unacquainted with each other. A common man must ask a man of influence how he is to proceed, and for whom he must vote. The elected, therefore, will be careless of the interest of the electors. It will be a common job to extort the suffrages of the common people for the most influential characters. The same men may be repeatedly elected by these means. This, sir, instead of promoting the freedom of elections, leads us to an aristocracy. Consider the mode of elections in England. Behold the progress of an election in an English shire. A man of an enormous fortune will spend thirty or forty thousand pounds to get himself elected. This is frequently the case. Will the honorable gentleman say that a poor man, as enlightened as any man in the island, has an equal chance with a rich man, to be elected? He will stand no chance, though he may have the finest understanding of any man in the shire. It will be so here. Where is the chance that a poor man can come forward with the rich? The honorable gentleman will find that, instead of supporting democratical principles, it goes absolutely to destroy them.

The Federal Farmer also predicted the consequences of an aristocratic legislature:

> A virtuous people make just laws, and good laws tend to preserve unchanged a virtuous people. A virtuous and happy people by laws uncongenial to their characters, may easily be gradually changed into servile and depraved creatures. Where the people, or their representatives, make the laws, it is probable they will gener-

ally be fitted to the national character and circumstances, unless the representation be partial, and the imperfect substitute of the people. However, the people may be electors, if the representation be so formed as to give one or more of the natural classes of men in the society an undue ascendency over the others, it is imperfect: the former will gradually become masters, and the latter slaves. It is the first of all among the political balances, to preserve in its proper station each of these classes. We talk of balances in the legislature, and among the departments of government; we ought to carry them to the body of the people.[36]

Several of these authors predicted that the small size of the legislature would ensure that particular classes, especially the wealthy, would be over-represented. Were these predictions accurate? Are federal legislators wealthier, or less representative of the "middling classes," than state legislators? If so, why? Would increasing the size of the legislature change anything? Draft a constitutional amendment to ensure that the federal legislature is representative of a broader segment of the society. Would it work?

Anti-Federalists also complained that the legislature would not be sufficiently accountable to its constituents. The excerpts below from Melancton Smith's remarks in the New York ratifying convention are representative of this common Anti-Federalist sentiment.

New York Ratifying Convention
Wednesday June 5, 1788
Elliot 2:310-313

Mr. Smith: It is a maxim with me that every man employed in a high office by the people, should, from time to time, *return* to them, that he may be in a situation to satisfy them with respect to his conduct and the measures of administration.

I would observe, that, as the senators are the representatives of the *state legislatures*, it is reasonable and proper that they should be under their control. When a state sends an agent commissioned to transact any business, or perform any service, it certainly ought to have a power to recall. These are plain principles, and so far as they apply to the case under examination, they ought to be adopted by us. Form this government as you please, you must, at all events, lodge in it very important powers. These powers must be in the hands of a few men, so situated as to procure a small degree of responsibility. These circumstances ought to put us upon our guard, and the inconvenience of this necessary delegation of power should be corrected, by providing some suitable checks.

Against this part of the amendment a great deal of argument has been used, and with considerable plausibility. It is said, if the amendment takes place,

the senators will hold their office only during the pleasure of the state legislatures, and consequently will not possess the necessary firmness and stability. I conceive, sir, there is a fallacy in this argument, founded upon the suspicion that the legislature of a state will possess the qualities of a mob, and be incapable of any regular conduct. I know that the impulses of the multitude are inconsistent with systematic government. The people are frequently incompetent to deliberate discussion, and subject to errors and imprudences. Is this the complexion of the state legislatures? I presume it is not.

. . .

An honorable gentleman from New York observed yesterday, that the *states* would always maintain their importance and authority, on account of their superior influence over the people. To prove this influence, he mentioned the aggregate number of the state representatives throughout the continent. But I ask him how long the people will retain their confidence for two thousand representatives who shall meet once in a year to make laws for regulating the height of your fences and the repairing of your roads. Will they not, by and by, be saying, Here, we are paying a great number of men for doing nothing; we had better give up all the civil business of our state, with its powers, to Congress, who are sitting all the year round: we had better get rid of the useless burden. That matters will come to this at least, I have no more doubt than I have of my existence. The state governments, without object or authority, will soon dwindle into insignificance, and be despised by the people themselves.

Several of the *Federalist Papers* responded to these objections. Madison, who wrote most of the papers dealing with the legislature, was in a peculiar position. In the Convention, he had argued for proportional representation in the Senate and for a larger legislature. Having lost on both issues, he then, as Publius, had to defend against Anti-Federalist arguments very similar to the ones he himself had made in the Convention. Are his discussions of these two points less analytical, and more rhetorical, than those in which he made arguments congruent with his own beliefs?

Federalist No. 55
Madison

The true question to be decided then is, whether the smallness of the number, as a temporary regulation, be dangerous to the public liberty? Whether sixty-five members for a few years, and a hundred or two hundred for a few more, be a safe depositary for a limited and well-guarded power of legislating for the United States? I must own that I could not give a negative answer to this question, without first obliterating every impression which I have received with regard to the present genius of the people of America, the spirit which actuates the State legislatures, and the principles which are incorporated with the political character of every class of citizens. I am unable to conceive that the people of America, in their present temper, or under any circumstances which can speedily happen, will choose, and every second year repeat the choice of, sixty-five or a hundred men who would be disposed to form and pursue a scheme of tyranny or treachery. I am unable to conceive that the State legislatures, which must feel so many motives to watch, and which possess so many means of counteracting, the federal legislature, would fail either to detect or to defeat a conspiracy of the latter against the liberties of their common constituents. I am equally unable to conceive that there are at this time, or can be in any short time, in the United States, any sixty-five or a hundred men capable of recommending themselves to the choice of the people at large, who would either desire or dare, within the short space of two years, to betray the solemn trust committed to them. What change of circumstances, time, and a fuller population of our country may produce, requires a prophetic spirit to declare, which makes no part of my pretensions. But judging from the circumstances now before us, and from the probable state of them within a moderate period of time, I must pronounce that the liberties of America cannot be unsafe in the number of hands proposed by the federal Constitution.

. . .

As there is a degree of depravity in mankind which requires a certain degree of circumstances and distrust, so there are other qualities in human nature which justify a certain portion of esteem and confidence. Republican government presupposes the existence of these qualities in a higher degree than any other form. Were the pictures which have been drawn by the political jealousy of some among us faithful likenesses of the human character, the inference would be, that there is not sufficient virtue among men for self-government; and that nothing less than the chains of despotism can restrain them from destroying and devouring one another.

Federalist No. 62
Madison

The equality of representation in the Senate is another point, which, being evidently the result of compromise between the opposite pretensions of the large and the small States, does not call for much discussion. If indeed it be right, that among a people thoroughly incorporated into one nation, every district ought to have a *proportional* share in the government, and that among independent and sovereign States, bound together by a simple league, the parties, however unequal in size, ought to have *equal* share in the common councils, it does not appear to be without some reason that in a compound republic, partaking both of the national and federal character, the government ought to be founded on a mixture of the principles of proportional and equal representation. But is is superfluous to try, by the standard of theory, a part of the Constitution which is allowed on all hands to be the result, not of theory, but "of a spirit of amity, and that mutual deference and concession which the peculiarity of our political situation rendered indispensable." A common government, with powers equal to its objects, is called for by the voice, and still more loudly by the political situation, of America. A government founded on principles more consonant to the wishes of the larger States, is not likely to be obtained from the smaller States. The only option, then, for the former, lies between the proposed government and a government still more objectionable. Under this alternative, the advice of prudence must be to embrace the lesser evil; and, instead of indulging a fruitless anticipation of the possible mischiefs which may ensue, to contemplate rather the advantageous consequences which may qualify the sacrifice.

In this spirit it may be remarked, that the equal vote allowed to each State is at once a constitutional recognition of the portion of sovereignty remaining in the individual States, and an instrument for preserving that residuary sovereignty. So far the equality ought to be no less acceptable to the large than to the small States; since they are not less solicitous to guard, by every possible expedient, against an improper consolidation of the States into one simple republic.

Another advantage accruing from this ingredient in the constitution of the Senate is, the additional impediment it must prove against improper acts of legislation. No law or resolution can now be passed without the concurrence, first, of a majority of the people, and then, of a majority of the States. It must be acknowledged that this complicated check on legislation may in some instances be injurious as well as beneficial; and that the peculiar defence which it involves in favor of the smaller States, would be more rational, if any interests common to them, and distinct from those of the other States, would otherwise be exposed to peculiar danger. But as the larger States will always be able, by their power over the supplies, to defeat unreasonable exertions of this prerogative of the lesser State, and as the facility and excess of lawmaking seem to be the diseases to which our governments are most liable, it is not impossible that this party of the Constitution may be more convenient in practice than it appears to many in contemplation.

. . .

The necessity of a senate is not less indicated by the propensity of all single and numerous assemblies to yield to the impulse of sudden and violent passions, and to be seduced by factious leaders into intemperate and pernicious resolutions. Examples on this subject might be cited without number; and from proceedings within the United States, as well as from the history of other nations. But a position that will not be contradicted, need not be proved. All that need be remarked is, that a body which is to correct this infirmity ought itself to be free from it, and consequently ought to be less numerous. It ought, moreover, to possess great firmness, and consequently ought to hold its authority by a tenure of considerable duration.

. . .

The mutability in the public councils arising from a rapid succession of new members, however qualified they may be, points out, in the strongest manner, the necessity of some stable institution in the government. Every new election in the States is found to change one half of the representatives. From this change of men must proceed a change of measures. But a continual change even of good measures is inconsistent with every rule of prudence and every prospect of success. The remark is verified in private life, and becomes more just, as well as more important, in national transactions.

. . .

Another effect of public instability is the unreasonable advantage it gives to the sagacious, the enterprising, and the moneyed few over the industrious and uninformed mass of the people. Every new regulation concerning commerce or revenue, or in any manner affecting the value of the different species of property, presents a new harvest to those who watch the change, and can trace its consequences; a harvest, reared not by themselves, but by the toils and cares of the great body of their fellow-citizens. This is a state of things in which it may be said with some truth that laws are made for the *few*, not for the *many*.

As with general charges that the new constitution failed to establish a true republic, many of the Anti-Federalist writings about the legislature contain well-developed underlying theories of government. Federalists responded not only with specific defenses of the size and composition of the legislature, but with their own theories of government. Notice that virtually all the Anti-Federalists advocated a reflective or mirrorlike legislature, whose members resemble their constituents. Draft several different amendments that might assuage the Anti-Federalist concerns. How did the delegates to the Federal Convention—especially the nationalists—view the purpose and character of a republican legislature? Did they accept the idea of a reflective legislature? What other theories of representation might justify a small, long-tenured Senate? Did Madison accept the Anti-Federalist theory of representation? In framing your answers, reconsider *Federalist No. 10*, reprinted at page 190. Does the theory Madison expounded in *Federalist No. 10* support a small, unreflective legislature?

The following essay should help you understand Madison's cohesive theory. *Federalist No. 51* is Madison's most noteworthy response to Anti-Federalist criticisms of the legislature. In it he expanded and developed the theory of republican government first suggested in *Federalist No. 10*. *Federalist No. 10* offered a new political theory in defense of the Constitution's allocation of power to the national government; in *Federalist No. 51* Madison used a similar theory to justify the Constitutional allocation of power *within* the national government.

Federalist No. 51
Madison

In order to lay a due foundation for that separate and distinct exercise of the different powers of government, which to a certain extent is admitted on all hands to be essential to the preservation of liberty, it is evident that each department should have a will of its own; and consequently should be so constituted that the members of each should have as little agency as possible in the appointment of the members of the others. Were this principle rigorously adhered to, it would require that all the appointments for the supreme executive, legislative, and judiciary magistracies should be drawn from the same fountain of authority, the people, through channels having no communication whatever with one another. Perhaps such a plan of constructing the several departments would be less difficult in practice than it may in contemplation appear. Some difficulties, however, and some additional expense would attend the execution of it. Some deviations, therefore, from the principle must be admitted. In the constitution of the judiciary department in particular, it might be inexpedient to insist rigorously on the principle: first, because peculiar qualifications being essential in the members, the primary consideration ought to be to select that mode of choice which best secures these qualifications; secondly, because the permanent tenure by which the appointments are held in that department, must soon destroy all sense of dependence on the authority conferring them.

It is equally evident, that the members of each department should be as little dependent as possible on those of the others, for the emoluments annexed to their offices. Were the executive magistrate, or the judges, not independent of the legislature in this particular, their independence in every other would be merely nominal.

But the great security against a gradual concentration of the several powers in the same department, consists in giving to those who administer each department the necessary constitutional means and personal motives to resist encroachments of the others. The provision for defence must in this, as in all other cases, be made commensurate to the danger of attack. Ambition must be made to counteract ambition. The interest of the man must be connected with the constitutional rights of the place. It may be a reflection on human nature, that such devices should be necessary to control the abuses of government. But what is government itself, but the greatest of all reflections on human nature? If men were angels, no government would be necessary. If angels were to govern men, neither external nor internal controls on government would be necessary. In framing a government which is to be administered by men over men, the great difficulty lies in this: you must first enable the government to control the governed; and in the next place oblige it to control itself. A dependence on the people is, no doubt, the primary control on the government; but experience has taught mankind the necessity of auxiliary precautions.

This policy of supplying, by opposite and rival interests, the defect of better motives, might be traced through the whole system of human affairs, private as well as public. We see it particularly displayed in all the subordinate distributions of power, where the constant aim is to divide and arrange the several offices in such a manner as that each may be a check on the other—that the private interest of every individual may be a sentinel over the public rights. These inventions of prudence cannot be less requisite in the distribution of the supreme powers of the State.

But it is not possible to give to each department an equal power of self-defence. In republican government, the legislative authority necessarily predominates. The remedy for this inconveniency is to divide the legislature into different branches; and to render them, by different modes of election and different principles of action, as little connected with each other as the nature of their common functions and their common dependence on the society will admit. It may even be necessary to guard against dangerous encroachments by still further precautions. As the weight of the legislative authority requires that it should be thus divided, the weakness of the executive may require, on the other hand, that it should be fortified.

. . .

In a single republic, all the power surrendered by the people is submitted to the administration of a single government; and the usurpations are guarded against by a division of the government into disinct and separate departments. In the compound republic of America, the power surrendered by the people is first divided between two distinct governments, and then the portion allotted to each subdivided among distinct and separate departments. Hence a double security arises to the rights of the people. The different governments will control each other, at the same time that each will be controlled by itself.

In both *No. 51* and *No. 10*, Madison seemed to adopt a pessimistic view of human nature; as he wrote in *No. 51*, "If men were angels, no government would be necessary." His theory of government approached a mechanistic one: if virtue and wisdom are in short supply, construct a government based on vice, and it will run itself. How does this negative outlook compare with the views of Anti-Federalists? With Madison's own views as expressed in the other *Federalist Papers* on the legislative branch? Think about the extent to which the Constitution has or has not functioned as "a machine that would go of itself." Was Madison's pessimism justified? Have his safeguards worked?

SLAVERY

In one context, Madison's pessimism was more than justified. When it came to slavery, he underestimated the depravity and short-sightedness of his fellow citizens. The Constitution's treatment of slavery eventually led abolitionist William Lloyd Garrison to describe the document as "A Covenant with Death and an Agreement with Hell."[37] During the ratification debates, however, the question of slavery was seen more as a political issue than a moral one. The various clauses in the Constitution relating to slavery were not much discussed, and criticism of them served mostly as rhetorical fuel for the Anti-Federalist fire. Other than Quakers and Mennonites in Pennsylvania, most Anti-Federalists were not abolitionists, but used the issue of slavery as a political device. Many Northern Anti-Federalists, including "Brutus," charged that the three-fifths apportionment scheme unfairly increased Southern power in the federal government, and threw in moral arguments almost as an afterthought.

Brutus, No. 3
November 15, 1787
Storing 2.9.38-39

[In the House of Representatives] there is an appearance of justice, in the appointment of its members—but if the clause, which provides for this branch, be stripped of its ambiguity, it will be found that there is really no equality of representation, even in this house.

The words are "representatives and direct taxes, shall be apportioned among the several states, which may be included in this union, according to their respective numbers, which shall be determined by adding to the whole number of free persons, including those bound to service for a term of years, and excluding Indians not taxed, three fifths of all other persons."—What a strange and unnecessary accumulation of words are here used to conceal from the public eye, what might have been expressed in the following concise manner. Representatives are to be proportioned among the states respectively, according to the number of freemen and slaves inhabiting them, counting five slaves for three free men.

"In a free state," says the celebrated Montesquieu, "every man, who is supposed to be a free agent, ought to be concerned in his own government, therefore, the legislature should reside in the whole body of the people, or their representatives." But it has never been alledged that those who are not free agents, can, upon any rational principle, have any thing to do in government, either by themselves or others. If they have no share in government, why is the number of members in the assembly, to be increased on their account? Is it because in some of the states, a considerable part of the property of the inhabitants consists in a number of their fellow men, who are held in bondage, in defiance of every idea of benevolence, justice, and religion, and contrary to all the principles of liberty, which have been publickly avowed in the late glorious revolution? If this be a just ground for representation, the horses in some of the states, and the oxen in others, ought to be represented—for a great share of property in some of them, consists in these animals; and they have as much controul over their own actions, as these poor unhappy creatures, who are intended to be described in the above recited clause, by the words, "all other persons."

Southern Anti-Federalists, particularly Patrick Henry, claimed that the Constitution's grant of broad authority to the federal legislature would allow the federal government to outlaw slavery. Notice how Henry's arguments relate to the doctrine of implied powers, discussed above in connection with the necessary and proper clause.

Virginia Ratifying Convention
Tuesday June 24, 1788
Elliot 3:590-591

Mr. Henry: Slavery is detested. We feel its fatal effects—we deplore it with all the pity of humanity. Let all these considerations, at some future period, press with full force on the minds of Congress. Let that urbanity, which I trust will distinguish America, and the necessity of national defence,—let all these things operate on their minds; they will search that paper, and see if they have power of manumission. And have they not, sir? Have they not power to provide for the general defence and welfare? May they not think that these call for the abolition of slavery? May they not pronounce all slaves free, and will they not be warranted by that power? This is no ambiguous implication or logical deduction. The paper speaks to the point: they have the power in clear, unequivocal terms, and will clearly and certainly exercise it. As much as I deplore slavery, I see that prudence forbids its abolition. I deny that the general government ought to set them free, because a decided majority of the states have not the ties of sympathy and fellow-feeling for those whose interest would be affected by their emancipation. The majority of Congress is to the north, and the slaves are to the south.

In this situation, I see a great deal of the property of the people of Virginia in jeopardy, and their peace and tranquillity gone. I repeat it again, that it would rejoice my very soul that every one of my fellow-beings was emancipated. As we ought with gratitude to admire that decree of Heaven which has numbered us among the free, we ought to lament and deplore the necessity of holding our fellow men in bondage. But is it practicable, by any human means, to liberate them without producing the most dreadful and ruinous consequences? We ought to possess them in the manner we inherited them from our ancestors, as their manumission is incompatible with the felicity of our country. But we ought to soften, as much as possible, the rigor of their unhappy fate. I know that, in a variety of particular instances, the legislature, listening to complaints, have admitted their emancipation. Let me not dwell on this subject. I will only add that this, as well as every other property of the people of Virginia, is in jeopardy, and put in the hands of those who have no similarity of situation with us. This is a local matter, and I can see no propriety in subjecting it to Congress.

Federalist interpretations of the constitutional status of slavery inevitably differed in the North and South. In the Pennsylvania ratifying convention, Wilson defended the Constitution as an antislavery document:

With respect to the clause restricting Congress from prohibiting the *migration or importation of such persons* as any of the states now existing shall think proper to admit, prior to the year 1808, the honorable gentleman says that this clause is not only dark, but intended to grant to Congress, for that time, the power to admit the importation of *slaves*. No such thing was intended. But I will tell you what was done, and it gives me high pleasure that so much was done. Under the present Confederation, the states may admit the importation of slaves as long as they please; but by this article, after the year 1808, the Congress will have power to prohibit such importation notwithstanding the disposition of any state to the contrary. I consider this as laying the foundation for banishing slavery out of this country; and though the period is more distant than I could wish, yet it will produce the same kind, gradual change, which was pursued in Pennsylvania. It is with much satisfaction I view this power in the general government, whereby they may lay an interdiction on this reproachful trade: but an immediate advantage is also obtained; for a tax or duty may be imposed on such importation, not exceeding ten dollars for each person; and this, sir, operates as a partial prohibition; it was all that could be obtained. I am sorry it was no more; but from this I think there is reason to hope, that yet a few years, and it will be prohibited altogether; and in the mean time, the *new* states which are to be formed will be under *the control* of Congress in this particular, and slaves will never be introduced amongst them.[34]

The most detailed refutation of Northern Anti-Federalist charges is contained in Madison's *Federalist No. 54*. In it, he made the standard arguments, rehearsed and perfected in the Federal Convention. Notice, however, that *Federalist No. 54* is unique among the *Federalist Papers* in that Publius purported to be stating not his own views, but those of his "Southern brethren." The entire defense of the three-fifths clause is within quotation marks. No other *Federalist Paper* uses this device. Recall Madison's earlier remarks on slavery. Did he use the quotation marks in *Federalist No. 54* because he found slavery intolerable, or because he thought his readers did? Whatever the cause, Madison's arms-length defense of slavery is an apt illustration of the ambivalence with which the framers, and the nation, viewed the South's peculiar institution.

Federalist No. 54
Madison

Slaves are considered as property, not as persons. They ought therefore to be comprehended in estimates of taxation which are founded on property, and to be excluded from representation which is regulated by a census of persons. This is the objection, as I understand it, stated in its full force. I shall be equally candid in stating the reasoning which may be offered on the opposite side.

"We subscribe to the doctrine," might one of our Southern brethren observe, "that representation relates more immediately to persons, and taxation more immediately to property, and we join in the application of this distinction to the case of our slaves. But we must deny the fact, that slaves are considered merely as property, and in no respect whatever as persons. The true state of the case is, that they partake of both these qualities: being considered by our laws, in some respects, as persons, and in other respects as property. In being compelled to labor, not for himself, but for a master; in being vendible by one master to another master; and in being subject at all times to be restrained in his libery and chastised in his body, by the capricious will of another,—the slave may appear to be degraded from the human rank, and classed with those irrational animals which fall under the legal denomination of property. In being protected, on the other hand, in his life and in his limbs, against the violence of all others, even the master of his labor and his liberty; and in being punishable himself for all violence committed against others,—the slave is no less evidently regarded by the law as a member of the society, not as a part of the irrational creation; as a moral person, not as a mere article of property. The federal Constitution, therefore, decides with great propriety on the case of our slaves, when it views them in the mixed character of persons and of property. This is in fact their true character. It is the character bestowed on them by the laws under which they live; and it will not be denied, that these are the proper criterion; because it is only under the pretext that the laws have transformed the negroes into subjects of property, that a place is disputed them in the computation of numbers; and it is admitted, that if the laws were to restore the rights which have been taken away, the negroes could no longer be refused an equal share of representation with the other inhabitants.

. . .

[T]he votes allowed in the federal legislature to the people of each State, ought to bear some proportion to the comparative wealth of the States. States have not, like individuals, an influence over each other, arising from superior advantages of fortune. If the law allows an opulent citizen but a single vote in the choice of his representative, the respect and consequence which he derives from his fortunate situation very frequently guide the votes of others to the objects of his choice; and through this imperceptible channel the rights of property are conveyed into the public representation. A State possesses no such influence over other States."

Federalist responses to Southern fears of congressional power were minimal and not very coherent. As Henry's remarks indicate, Federalists in the Virginia convention simply denied that the Constitution afforded Congress much power to regulate slavery. To the chagrin of a later generation of nationalists, this disingenuous Federalist position became the law of the land in 1857, when the Supreme Court ruled that Congress had no power to prohibit slavery in the territories.

Chief Justice Taney's infamous opinion in *Dred Scott v. Sandford*, 60 U.S. (19 How.) 393, 15 L.Ed. 691 (1857), despite its copious use of historical references, did not refer to Federalist arguments in determining the scope of federal authority. Would citing Federalist denials of Congressional power have made the *Dred Scott* decision more legitimate? Recall the discussions, earlier in this chapter, on the eventual judicial interpretation of the necessary and proper clause and of the scope of federal jurisdiction. In those cases, as well as in the case of Congressional authority over slavery, Anti-Federalists contended that the Constitution could only be read in a broadly nationalist manner, and thus should be rejected. Federalists responded by offering narrower interpretations of the clauses at issue, to pacify Anti-Federalist fears and ensure ratification. In *Chisholm v. Georgia* and *McCulloch v. Maryland*—both decided before 1820 and discussed earlier in this chapter—the Court ultimately betrayed those Federalist predictions by handing down exactly the rulings feared by the Anti-Federalists. In *Dred Scott*, by contrast, the court kept Federalist promises. Imagine that in each of these decisions, the Court had purported to be guided by the "original intent" of the framers—as evidenced by the statements of proponents—in construing the Constitution. What arguments would you make to criticize or justify each decision, based on the exchanges between Federalists and Anti-Federalists? How persuasive are the arguments? Was each case decided correctly? By what standards?

Dred Scott, or some case like it, was probably inevitable. Federalists like Madison defended the Convention's slavery compromises as necessary to the union, and even some Anti-Federalists agreed. Melancton Smith, in the New York ratifying convention, stated that "accommodation" was necessary if the northern states "meant to be in union with the Southern States," although the compromise was "utterly repugnant to his feelings."[39] But any compromise on such a troubling issue was bound to be short-lived. As we will see, the compromise began disintegrating as early as 1820.

For the short term, however, the various compromises were successful in achieving the Federalists' goal of ratification. In the end, six states ratified unconditionally, and five states ratified with "recommendations" for amendments. Rhode Island refused to call a ratifying convention, and North Carolina's convention voted one hundred and eighty-four to eighty-four against ratification. Both states eventually ratified after the federal government was a fait accompli (See table 7.1).

The superior organization of the Federalists, the largely pro-ratification press, and the promise of subsequent amendments all played a significant role in assuring a Federalist victory. Moreover, in some states many convention delegates were elected not because they were for or against ratification, but rather because they were well-known, respected, and trusted. Such individuals were often war heroes or those involved in national politics, and studies have suggested that such exposure to influences beyond the local sphere promoted Federalist sentiments. Thus in some cases, even where the populace opposed ratification, they elected Federalist delegates to the state convention.

Interestingly, both Gilbert Livingston and Melancton Smith ultimately voted in favor of ratification, despite their anti-ratification diatribes in the

TABLE 7.1   The Ratification Process

State	Date of Action	Decision	Margin
Delaware	December 7, 1787	ratified	30:0
Pennsylvania	December 12, 1787	ratified	46:23
New Jersey	December 18, 1787	ratified	38:0
Georgia	December 31, 1787	ratified	26:0
Connecticut	January 9, 1788	ratified	128:40
Massachusetts	February 6, 1788	ratified with amendments	187:168
Maryland	April 26, 1788	ratified	63:11
South Carolina	May 23, 1788	ratified with amendments	149:73
New Hampshire	June 21, 1788	ratified with amendments	57:47
Virginia	June 25, 1788	ratified with amendments	89:79
New York	July 26, 1788	ratified with amendments	30:27
North Carolina	August 2, 1788 November 21, 1789	rejected ratified with amendments	184:84 194:77
Rhode Island	May 29, 1790	ratified with amendments	34:32

Note: Sources differ on both dates and vote counts. Where there are discrepancies, we have relied on Michael Kammen, *The Origins of the American Constitution: A Documentary History* xxvii-xxix (1986), as the definitive source.

New York convention. Patrick Henry stood his ground and voted against ratification in Virginia. During the last day of debates in the Virginia convention, Henry used a storm outside as a prop. As a bolt of lightning flashed nearby, Henry thundered:

> I see the awful immensity of the dangers with which it is pregnant. I see it. I feel it. I see beings of a higher order anxious concerning our decision. When I see beyond the horizon that bounds human eyes, and look at the final consummation of all human things, and see those intelligent beings which inhabit the ethereal mansions reviewing the political decisions and revolutions which, in the progress of time, will happen in America, and the consequent happiness or misery of mankind, I am led to believe that much of the account, on one side or the other, will depend on what we now decide.[40]

At that point, according to the reporter, "a violent storm arose, which put the house in such disorder, that Mr. Henry was obliged to conclude." The next day, after numerous delegates indicated they would support the Constitution, Henry conceded defeat. His final speech is a model of graciousness and patriotism in defeat:

> If I shall be in the minority, I shall have those painful sensations which arise from a conviction of *being overpowered in a good cause*. Yet I will be a peaceable citizen. My head, my hand, and my heart, shall be at liberty to retrieve the loss of liberty, and remove the defects of that system in a constitutional way. I wish not to go to violence, but will wait with hopes that the spirit which predominated in the revolution is not yet gone, nor the cause of those who are attached to the revolution yet lost. I shall therefore patiently wait in expectation of seeing that government changed, so as to be compatible with the safety, liberty, and happiness, of the people.[41]

It was Anti-Federalist sentiments like these, echoed by the losers in many other states, that helped make the transition from Confederation to Constitution peaceful and successful. And, as the next chapter will show, Henry did not have long to wait.

FOOTNOTES

1. Letter from Madison to Jefferson (February 19, 1788).
2. 1 *Annals of Congress* 731 (August 15, 1789).
3. Quoted in Merrill Jensen, *The Making of the American Constitution* 141-42 (1964).
4. Address of the Minority of the Pennsylvania House of Representatives (October 4, 1787), in 3 *The Complete Anti-Federalist* 11, 13 (H. Storing ed. 1981) [hereinafter Storing].
5. These recommendations are discussed in Chapter 8 on the Bill of Rights.
6. Madison's Notes at 566 (August 31).
7. Virginia Ratifying Convention (June 4, 1788), 3 Jonathan Elliot, *The Debates in the Several State Conventions on the Adoption of the Federal Constitution* 25-26 (1891) [hereinafter Elliot].
8. Letter from Adams to Jefferson (December 6, 1787).
9. Essay by "Alfred" (December 13, 1787), 3 Storing at 141 (emphasis in original).
10. Letter from Washington to Bushrod Washington (November 10, 1787).
11. James J. Hutson, *Country, Court, and Constitution: Antifederalists and the Historians*, 3:38 Wm. & Mary Q. 337, 340 (1981).
12. Pennsylvania Ratifying Convention (November 26, 1787), 2 Elliot at 421-422.
13. Letter from Madison to Jefferson (October 24, 1787).

14. Pennsylvania Ratifying Convention (December 4, 1787), 2 Elliot at 448-49.

15. 17 U.S. (4 Wheat.) at 415.

16. Virginia Ratifying Convention (June 7, 1788), 3 Elliot at 137.

17. "William Penn," No. 2 (January 3, 1788), 3 Storing at 172 (emphasis in original).

18. Virginia Ratifying Convention (June 10, 1788), 3 Elliot at 224.

19. Pennsylvania Ratifying Convention (November 26, 1787), 2 Elliot at 430-31.

20. Oliver Ellsworth, *The Landholder*, No. 3 (November 19, 1787), 1 *The Founders' Constitution* 304 (Philip B. Kurland & Ralph Lerner eds. 1987).

21. An Old Whig, No. 7, 3 Storing at 44 (date uncertain: between October 1787 and February 1788).

22. Virginia Ratifying Convention (June 4, 1788), 3 Elliot at 22-23 (emphasis in original).

23. Centinel, No. 2, 2 Storing at 145 (date uncertain: between October 1787 and April 1788).

24. Address by Sydney (June 13, 1788), 6 Storing at 108.

25. Virginia Ratifying Convention (June 9, 1788), 3 Elliot at 187 (emphasis in original).

26. Pennsylvania Ratifying Convention (December 4, 1787), 2 Elliot at 470 (emphasis in original).

27. Madison, *Federalist No. 40* (emphasis in original).

28. Federal Farmer, No. 2 (October 9, 1787), 2 Storing at 231.

29. Pennsylvania Ratifying Convention (December 7, 1787), 2 Elliot at 491-92.

30. Philadelphiensis, No. 9 (February 7, 1788), 3 Storing at 129.

31. Letter from Jefferson to Adams (November 13, 1787).

32. Federal Farmer, No. 14 (January 17, 1788), 2 Storing at 310-311.

33. Alexander M. Bickel, *The Least Dangerous Branch* 26 (1962).

34. Brutus, No. 16 (April 10, 1788), 2 Storing at 444.

35. New York Ratifying Convention (June 21, 1788), 2 Elliot at 249.

36. Federal Farmer, No. 7 (December 31, 1787), 2 Storing at 266.

37. *Liberator* (September 13, 1844), quoted in Michael Kammen, *A Machine That Would Go of Itself: The Constitution in American Culture* 98 (1986).

38. Pennsylvania Ratifying Convention (December 3, 1787), 2 Elliot at 452.

39. New York Ratifying Convention (June 20, 1788), 2 Elliot at 227.

40. Virginia Ratifying Convention (June 24, 1788), 3 Elliot at 625.

41. Virginia Ratifying Convention (June 25, 1788), 3 Elliot at 652 (emphasis in original).

CHAPTER EIGHT

The Bill of Rights

ANTECEDENTS TO 1789

Historical Origins

By 1787, Americans had long been accustomed to the idea of fundamental and inalienable rights. In theory, if not in practice, British and colonial governments—as well as the infant state governments—lacked power to deprive citizens of certain rights. Such rights belonged inherently to all citizens, even in the absence of written protections. Most written enumerations of rights, in fact, were thought to be *declarations* rather than *enactments* of the listed rights. The language used in these various documents reflected their declaratory character: they "declared" "true, ancient and indubitable rights and liberties" or "self-evident truths," and listed "natural" or "inherent" or "inalienable" rights.

The Magna Carta of 1215 and the Bill of Rights of 1689 declare various rights of Englishmen. Both guarantee trial by a jury of one's peers. The 1689 Bill of Rights also prohibits standing armies in time of peace, and protects the right to petition the king and a limited form of freedom of speech. It also states "[t]hat excessive bail ought not to be required, nor excessive fines imposed; nor cruel and unusual punishments inflicted." These rights—the colonists' most cherished British heritage—formed a core of liberties held dear by Americans.

The English Bill of Rights was not the only written enumeration of fundamental rights by 1787, however. As early as 1774, the newly formed Continental Congress wrote to the inhabitants of Quebec, inviting them to participate in the Congress. The letter, designed to entice the Canadian province away from its already precarious allegiance to England, advised the inhabitants of Quebec to "consult [their] own glory and welfare" in deciding whether to "unite with [the American colonies] in one social compact." Very much an advocate's brief, the congressional letter described the advantages of such a union by listing and explaining the rights enjoyed by the American colonists.

The letter began with a general description of the most fundamental right: the right to a republican form of government.

> In this form, the first grand right, is that of the people having a share in their own government by their representatives chosen by themselves, and, in consequence, of being ruled by *laws*, which they themselves approve, not by *edicts* of *men* over whom they have no controul. This is a bulwark surrounding and defending their property, which by their honest cares and labours they have acquired, so that no portions of it can legally be taken from them, but with their own full and free consent, when they in their judgment deem it just and necessary to give them for public service, and precisely direct the easiest, cheapest, and most equal methods, in which they shall be collected.[1]

The letter then listed and described numerous other rights, including trial by jury, writ of habeas corpus, and freedom of the press. This last was described as important, "besides [in] the advancement of truth, science, morality, and arts in general, in its diffusion of liberal sentiments on the administration of Government, its ready communication of thoughts between subjects, and its consequential promotion of union among them, whereby oppressive officers are shamed or intimidated, into more honourable and just modes of conducting affairs."

After the Revolution, the new American states wrote their own declarations of rights. Most such declarations listed as many as fifteen or twenty "inalienable" and "natural" rights. Many of the them began with some variation on the Declaration of Independence. The 1776 Pennsylvania Declaration of Rights, for example, began:

> That all men are born equally free and independent, and have certain natural, inherent and inalienable rights, amongst which are, the enjoying and defending life and liberty, acquiring, possessing and protecting property, and pursuing and obtaining happiness and safety.

Most state declarations of rights also reflected a commitment to republican government. The Virginia Bill of Rights, for example, after reciting that all men were born free and equal and entitled to certain rights, continued:

> That all power is vested in, and consequently derived from, the People; that magistrates are their trustees and servants, and at all times amenable to them.
>
> That Government is, or ought to be, instituted for the common benefit, protection, and security of the people, nation, or community; of all the various modes and forms of Government that is best which is capable of producing the greatest degree of happiness and safety, and is most effectually secured against the danger of maladministration; and that, whenever any Government shall be found inadequate or contrary to these purposes, a majority of the community hath an indubitable, unalienable, and indefeasible right, to reform, alter, or abolish it, in such manner as shall be judged most conducive to the publick weal.

The state declarations also enumerated specific rights. In addition to the rights already identified in earlier documents, the state declarations of rights included many other rights thought to be fundamental. Among the most common were guarantees of free elections, protections for criminal defendants (including the right to be heard, the right to confront witnesses, and a

privilege against self-incrimination), protections against searches and seizures under general warrants, and broad protection of freedom of speech and
press and rights of assembly. Finally, most state declarations of rights
included the right to worship and protections against compelled worship.
Article II of the Pennsylvania Declaration of Rights is typical:

> That all men have a natural and unalienable right to worship Almighty God accord-
> ing to the dictates of their own consciences and understanding: And that no man
> ought or of right can be compelled to attend any religious worship, or erect or sup-
> port any place of worship, or maintain any ministry, contrary to, or against, his
> own free will and consent: Nor can any man, who acknowledges the being of a
> God, be justly deprived or abridged of any civil right as a citizen, on account of his
> religious sentiments or peculiar mode of religious worship: And that no authority
> can or ought to be vested in, or assumed by any power whatever, that shall in any
> case interfere with, or in any manner controul, the right of conscience in the free
> exercise of religious worship.

Several states also added a proviso protecting those religiously opposed to
bearing arms from having to serve in the militia.

As indicated, a written bill of rights containing many of the rights we still
cherish today was a common feature in Revolutionary-era American constitutions. It is therefore not surprising that the debates over the federal constitution included discussions of the wisdom and necessity of including a bill of
rights.

The Constitutional Convention

The possibility of including a bill of rights in the Constitution was discussed
for the first time late in the Convention. On August 20, Charles Pinckney submitted a plan for consideration by the Committee on Detail. It included the
following provisions:

> The liberty of the Press shall be inviolably preserved.
> No troops shall be kept up in time of peace, but by consent of the Legislature. . . .
> No soldier shall be quartered in any House in time of peace without consent of
> the owner. . . .
> No religious test or qualification shall ever be annexed to any oath of office under
> the authority of the U.S.

The Committee did not include any of Pinckney's suggestions, nor did the
Committee on Style. On September 12, the issue was raised again.

Wednesday, September 12

Mr. **Williamson**, observed to the House that no
provision was yet made for juries in Civil cases and
suggested the necessity of it.

Mr. **Gorham.** It is not possible to discriminate equity cases from those in which juries are proper.
The Representatives of the people may be safely

trusted in this matter.

Mr. **Gerry** urged the necessity of Juries to guard
agst. corrupt Judges. He proposed that the Committee last appointed should be directed to provide a
clause for securing the trial by Juries.

Col: Mason perceived the difficulty mentioned by

Mr. Gorham. The jury cases can not be specified. A general principle laid down on this and some other points would be sufficient. He wished the plan had been prefaced with a Bill of Rights, & would second a Motion if made for the purpose. It would give great quiet to the people; and with the aid of the State declarations, a bill might be prepared in a few hours.

Mr. Gerry concurred in the idea & moved for a Committee to prepare a Bill of Rights. Col: Mason 2ded. the motion.

Mr. Sherman, was for securing the rights of the people where requisite. The State Declarations of Rights are not repealed by this Constitution; and being in force are sufficient. There are many cases where juries are proper which can not be discriminated. The Legislature may be safely trusted.

Col: Mason. The Laws of the U.S. are to be paramount to State Bills of Rights.

On the question for a Come. to prepare a Bill of Rights

N. H. no. Mas. abst. Ct. no. N. J. no. Pa. no. Del. no. Md. no. Va. no. N. C. no. S. C. no. Geo. no.

Undaunted by this unanimous rejection, Gerry tried again two days later. On September 14, he and Pinckney moved "to insert a declaration 'that the liberty of the Press should be inviolably observed.' " Sherman responded that such a provision was "unnecessary" because "the power of Congress does not extend to the Press." The proposal was defeated by a vote of either seven to four or six to five.[2]

Unable to convince their fellow delegates of the need for a bill of rights, the advocates of it tried another tactic. On September 16, Edmund Randolph, objecting generally to "the indefinite and dangerous power given by the Constitution to Congress," proposed to amend the ratification procedure. He moved "that amendments to the plan might be offered by the State Conventions, which should be submitted to and finally decided on by another General Convention." Mason seconded him, without adverting to any specific objections to the present draft. Gerry also supported the Randolph motion. He listed eight miscellaneous objections, and then continued:

> He could however he said get over all these, if the rights of the Citizens were not rendered insecure 1. by the general power of the Legislature to make what laws they may please to call necessary and proper. 2. raise armies and money without limit. 3. to establish a tribunal without juries, which will be a Star-chamber as to civil cases.

Whether or not Charles Pinckney still supported a bill of rights, he could not accept Randolph's proposal. Allowing the states to propose amendments would yield "[n]othing but confusion & contrariety," he argued. As for a second convention, he was adamantly against it: "Conventions are serious things, and ought not to be repeated."

Randolph's motion to permit amendments by the state ratifying conventions was unanimously defeated. Its three supporters then refused to sign the Constitution. The defeat of the Randolph motion in the Convention, however, did not by itself prevent attempts by state ratifying conventions to amend the Convention's work.

Ratification

Opponents of the Constitution sought various changes in the document during the ratification debates. In particular, the absence of a bill of rights troubled many. They feared that without such a limitation, the federal government would infringe the basic rights of the citizenry. In addition to specifying which rights stood in need of protection, many of the Anti-Federalists wrote extended essays on the nature of such rights and their relationship to constitutional government. The essay below, by a New York Anti-Federalist, is a typical example of such arguments.

Brutus, No. 2
November 1, 1787
Storing 2.9.24-32

If we may collect the sentiments of the people of America, from their own most solemn declarations, they hold this truth as self evident, that all men are by nature free. No one man, therefore, or any class of men, have a right, by the law of nature, or of God, to assume or exercise authority over their fellows. The origin of society then is to be sought, not in any natural right which one man has to exercise authority over another, but in the united consent of those who associate. The mutual wants of men, at first dictated the propriety of forming societies; and when they were established, protection and defence pointed out the necessity of instituting government. In a state of nature every individual pursues his own interest; in this pursuit it frequently happened, that the possessions or enjoyments of one were sacrificed to the views and designs of another; thus the weak were a prey to the strong, the simple and unwary were subject to impositions from those who were more crafty and designing. In this state of things, every individual was insecure; common interest therefore directed, that government should be established, in which the force of the whole community should be collected, and under such directions, as to protect and defend every one who composed it. The common good, therefore, is the end of civil government, and common consent, the foundation on which it is established. To effect this end, it was necessary that a certain portion of natural liberty should be surrendered, in order, that what remained should be preserved: how great a proportion of natural freedom is necessary to be yielded by individuals, when they submit to government, I shall now enquire. So much, however, must be given up, as will be sufficient to enable those, to whom the administration of the government is committed, to establish laws for the promoting the happiness of the community, and to carry those laws into effect. But it is not necessary, for this purpose, that individuals should relinquish all their natural rights. Some are of such a nature that they cannot be surrendered. Of this kind are the rights of conscience, the right of enjoying and defending life, etc. Others are not necessary to be resigned, in order to attain the end for which government is instituted, these therefore ought not to be given up. To surrender them, would counteract the very end of government, to wit, the common good. From these observations it appears, that in forming a government on its true principles, the foundation should be laid in the manner I before stated, by expressly reserving to the people such of their essential natural rights, as are not necessary to be parted with. The same reasons which at first induced mankind to associate and institute government, will operate to influence them to observe this precaution. If they had been disposed to conform themselves to the rule of immutable righteousness, government would not have been requisite. It was because one part exercised fraud, oppression, and violence on the other, that men came together, and agreed that certain rules should be formed, to regulate the conduct of all, and the power of the whole community lodged in the hands of rulers to enforce an obedience to them. But rulers have the same propensities as other men; they are as likely to use the power with which they are vested for private purposes, and to the injury and oppression of those over whom they are placed, as individuals in a state of nature are to injure and oppress one another. It is therefore as proper that bounds should be set to their authority, as that government should have at first been instituted to restrain private injuries.

This principle, which seems so evidently founded in the reason and nature of things, is confirmed by universal experience. Those who have governed, have been found in all ages ever active to enlarge their powers and abridge the public liberty. This has induced the people in all countries, where any sense of freedom remained, to fix barriers against the encroachments of their rulers. The country from which we have derived our origin, is an eminent example of this. Their magna charta and bill of rights have long been the boast, as well as the security, of that nation. I need say no more, I presume, to an American, than, that this principle is a fundamental one, in all the constitutions of our own states; there is not one of them but what is either founded on a declaration or bill of rights, or has certain express reservation of rights interwoven in the body of them. From this it appears, that at a time when the pulse of liberty beat high and when an appeal was made to the people to form constitutions for the government of themselves, it was their universal sense, that such declarations should make a part of their frames of government. It is therefore the more astonishing, that this grand security, to the rights of the people, is not to be found in this constitution.

The Federalists responded to these critiques with a number of arguments. They contended that a bill of rights was unnecessary in a government of enumerated powers. They argued, also, that including a bill of rights might be dangerous for two reasons. First, any rights listed might be construed as exceptions to powers not explicitly granted in the Constitution, which would expand federal power. This argument against Anti-Federalist demands for a bill of rights was an implicit renunciation of the doctrine of implied powers, considered more fully in chapter 7. The second perceived threat to liberty posed by a declaration of rights was that an enumeration or listing of rights might be construed as limiting protected rights to those specifically enumerated, thus eliminating other fundamental rights. This argument necessarily presupposes the existence of fundamental rights independent of constitutional affirmation. James Wilson argued to the Pennsylvania ratifying convention, for example:

> In all societies, there are many powers and rights which cannot be particularly enumerated. A bill of rights annexed to a constitution is *an enumeration of the powers* reserved. If we attempt an enumeration, every thing that is not enumerated is presumed to be given. The consequence is, that an imperfect enumeration would throw all implied power into the scale of the government, and the rights of the people would be rendered incomplete.[3]

James Iredell told the North Carolina ratifying convention:

> [I]t would be not only useless, but dangerous, to enumerate a number of rights which are not intended to be given up; because it would be implying, in the strongest manner, that every right not included in the exception might be impaired by the government without usurpation; and it would be impossible to enumerate every one. Let any one make what collection or enumeration of rights he pleases, I will immediately mention twenty or thirty more rights not contained in it.[4]

Some Anti-Federalists engaged in careful constitutional construction to expose the fallacy of the Federalist arguments. The "Federal Farmer" (probably Richard Henry Lee of Virginia) pointed to such clauses as the prohibition on titles of nobility, the protection of the writ of habeas corpus, and the prohibition of ex post facto laws. He asked why *these* protections were thought necessary, since the Constitution nowhere granted Congress the power to confer titles of nobility, to suspend habeas corpus, or to enact ex post facto laws.

Edmund Randolph responded to this argument in the Virginia ratifying convention. He argued that "every exception here mentioned is an exception, not from general powers, but from particular powers therein vested." He suggested, for example, that the restriction on suspension of habeas corpus was an exception to the congressional power of regulating federal courts. The prohibitions against ex post facto laws and bills of attainder were exceptions to Congress' power to pass criminal laws, as "attainders and *ex post facto* laws have always been the engines of criminal jurisprudence."[5]

The battle over theory ultimately persuaded no one, and the Constitution was ratified—without a bill of rights—on the basis of a series of very practical compromises. To the Federalists' fallback position that the Constitution could always be amended after ratification, Anti-Federalists responded that it would be safer to make ratification conditional on the acceptance of various amendments. Anti-Federalists adopting this argument, however, were faced with the problem of different states submitting different "conditional" amendments. When various prominent Federalists (including James Madison in Virginia) promised to seek amendments immediately after ratification, the Anti-Federalists compromised: five states submitted proposed amendments along with their unconditional ratifications. These state wish lists were long and diverse, and included provisions not only guaranteeing individual rights but also rectifying many other problems Anti-Federalists had identified during the debates. Proposed amendments reducing the power of the federal judiciary, guaranteeing separation of powers, and otherwise attempting to disable the new federal government were not uncommon. Again, one of the most common features of the state wish lists was a declaration of natural rights. The Virginia wish list began with the following:

> First, That there are certain natural rights of which men, when they form a social compact cannot deprive or divest their posterity, among which are the enjoyment of life and liberty, with the means of acquiring, possessing and protecting property, and pursuing and obtaining happiness and safety.
>
> Second. That all power is naturally vested in and consequently derived from the people; that Magistrates, therefore, are their trustees and agents and at all times amenable to them.
>
> Third, That Government ought to be instituted for the common benefit, protection and security of the People; and that the doctrine of non-resistance against arbitrary power and oppression is absurd slavish, and destructive of the good and happiness of mankind.

Other proposed amendments mirrored the rights enumerated in the earlier state declarations of rights.

Topics for Discussion

1. How would you describe the theory of rights propounded in such documents as the Virginia wish list and the Pennsylvania Declaration of Rights? Was this theory shared by Anti-Federalists such as "Brutus"? By Federalist opponents of a bill of rights? Compare these views with views expressed in the early cases of judicial review (discussed in chapter 3) and with the sentiments of delegates to the Federal Convention (in various chapters). Can you suggest reasons for such broad underlying agreement?

2. The notion that inherent fundamental rights exist independent of the written constitution, though common to Federalists and Anti-Federalists alike, is unfamiliar in modern constitutional law. Instead, the modern Supreme Court has hesitated to protect rights not listed in the Constitution, and has been roundly criticized when it does so. What light might the eighteenth-century view of fundamental rights shed on modern disputes over such controversial cases as *Lochner v. New York*, 198 U.S. 45, 25 S.Ct. 539, 49 L.Ed. 937 (1905), which established a right to enter into contracts free of state regulation (such as minimum wage and maximum hours legislation), and *Roe v. Wade*, 410 U.S. 113, 93 S.Ct. 705, 35 L.Ed.2d 147 (1973), which established a right to abortion? How might a court identify fundamental or inalienable rights?

3. Consider the argument between the "Federal Farmer" and Edmund Randolph regarding the rights listed in the body of the 1787 Constitution. Who has the better argument?

THE CONGRESSIONAL DEBATES

The House of Representatives

In 1788, five states submitted demands for amendments to the new Constitution along with their ratifications. These clamorous demands might not have succeeded, however, had the states not had a powerful weapon at their disposal. On May 5, 1789, Virginia submitted to Congress an application for the calling of a second constitutional convention. New York followed suit the next day. North Carolina and Rhode Island still refused to ratify the Constitution, partly on the ground that it did not contain a bill of rights.

The Federalists were determined both to bring the stray states into the union and to prevent a second constitutional convention, which they were certain would result in disaster. Realizing that adoption of a bill of rights might be the only way to achieve either object, James Madison took steps to fulfill his ratification-era promise to shepherd a bill of rights through the new Congress.

Madison—elected to the House of Representatives from Virginia—took his task seriously. On May 4, 1789, just over a month after the first Congress began its work, he gave notice that he intended to bring amendments to the Constitution before the House in late May. The House became embroiled in discussion of a revenue bill and other pressing matters, however, and Madison did not have an opportunity to present his proposed amendments until June 8.

Madison had great difficulty in persuading his fellow Congressmen even to address the issue of amendments; compared to the business of establishing a judiciary and creating sources of revenue for the new government, the bill of rights was a minor matter. Half a dozen representatives wasted the better part of the day arguing that the House had no time to consider Madison's proposals. One of his supporters noted that "[i]f no objection had been made to [Madison's] motion, the whole business might have been finished before this." Madison and his supporters urged the House to make an initial good faith effort to consider the amendments pressed by the states, as such consideration "would tend to tranquilize the public mind." He suggested that the people would subsequently "wait with patience" until the House was "at leisure to resume" consideration. A refusal to consider the amendments at all might instead "irritate many . . . constituents."

Surprisingly, some prominent Anti-Federalists in Congress opposed the bill of rights they had so vigorously championed only a year before. With Madison urging adoption and Anti-Federalists opposing it, the positions of 1787 were now reversed. This peculiar configuration was largely the result of the Federalist fear, and the Anti-Federalist hope, that a failure to adopt a bill of rights would lead to a second constitutional convention.

Late on June 8, 1789, Madison ignored the opposition and presented his amendments to the assembled House.

Monday, June 8

Mr. Madison.—I am sorry to be accessary to the loss of a single moment of time by the House. If I had been indulged in my motion, and we had gone into a Committee of the Whole, I think we might have rose and resumed the consideration of other business before this time; that is, so far as it depended upon what I proposed to bring forward. As that mode seems not to give satisfaction, I will withdraw the motion, and move you, sir, that a select committee be appointed to consider and report such amendments as are proper for Congress to propose to the Legislatures of the several States, conformably to the fifth article of the Constitution.

It will be a desirable thing to extinguish from the bosom of every member of the community, any apprehensions that there are those among his countrymen who wish to deprive them of the liberty for which they valiantly fought and honorably bled. And if there are amendments desired of such a nature as will not injure the Constitution, and they can be ingrafted so as to give satisfaction to the doubting part of our fellow-citizens, the friends of the Federal Government will evince that spirit of deference and concession for which they have hitherto been distinguished.

It cannot be a secret to the gentlemen in this House, that, notwithstanding the ratification of this system of Government by eleven of the thirteen United State, in some cases unanimously, in others by large majorities; yet still there is a great number of our constituents who are dissatisfied with it; among whom are many respectable for their talents and patriotism, and respectable for the jealousy they have for their liberty, which, though mistaken in its object, is laudable in its motive. There is a great body of the people falling under this description, who at present feel much inclined to join their support to the cause of Federalism, if they were

satisfied on this one point. We ought not to disregard their inclination, but, on principles of amity and moderation, conform to their wishes, and expressly declare the great rights of mankind secured under this Constitution.

.   .   .

But I will candidly acknowledge, that, over and above all these considerations, I do conceive that the Constitution may be amended; that is to say, if all power is subject to abuse, that then it is possible the abuse of the powers of the General Government may be guarded against in a more secure manner than is now done, while no one advantage arising from the exercise of that power shall be damaged or endangered by it. We have in this way something to gain, and, if we proceed with caution, nothing to lose.

.   .   .

I believe that the great mass of the people who opposed it, disliked it because it did not contain effectual provisions against the encroachments on particular rights, and those safeguards which they have been long accustomed to have interposed between them and the magistrate who exercises the sovereign power; nor ought we to consider them safe, while a great number of our fellow-citizens think these securities necessary.

It is a fortunate thing that the objection to the Government has been made on the ground I stated; because it will be practicable, on that ground, to obviate the objection, so far as to satisfy the public mind that their liberties will be perpetual, and this without endangering any part of the Constitution, which is considered as essential to the existence of the Government by those who promoted its adoption.

The amendments which have occurred to me, proper to be recommended by Congress to the State Legislatures, are these:

First. That there be prefixed to the Constitution a declaration, that all power is orginally vested in, and consequently derived from, the people.

That Government is instituted and ought to be exercised for the benefit of the people; which consists in the enjoyment of life and liberty, with the right of acquiring and using property, and generally of pursuing and obtaining happiness and safety.

That the people have an indubitable, unalienable, and indefeasible right to reform or change their Government, whenever it be found adverse or inadequate to the purposes of its institution.

Secondly. That in article 1st, section 2, clause 3, these words be struck out, to wit: "The number of Representatives shall not exceed one for every thirty thousand, but each State shall have at least one Representative, and until such enumeration shall be made," and that in place thereof be inserted these words, to wit: "After the first actual enumeration, there shall be one Representative for every thirty thousand, until the number amounts to ____, after which the proportion shall be so regulated by Congress, that the number shall never be less than , nor more than ____, but each State shall, after the first enumeration, have at least two Representatives; and prior thereto."

Thirdly. That in article 1st, section 6, clause 1, there be added to the end of the first sentence, these words, to wit: "But no law varying the compensation last ascertained shall operate before the next ensuing election of Representatives."

Fourthly. That in article 1st, section 9, between clauses 3 and 4, be inserted these clauses, to wit: The civil rights of none shall be abridged on account of religious belief or worship, nor shall any national religion be established, nor shall the full and equal rights of conscience be in any manner, or on any pretext, infringed.

The people shall not be deprived or abridged of their right to speak, to write, or to publish their sentiments; and the freedom of the press, as one of the great bulwarks of liberty, shall be inviolable.

The people shall not be restrained from peaceably assembling and consulting for their common good; nor from applying to the Legislature by petitions, or remonstrances, for redress of their grievances.

The right of the people to keep and bear arms shall not be infringed; a well armed and well regulated militia being the best security of a free country: but no person religiously scrupulous of bearing arms shall be compelled to render military service in person.

No soldier shall in time of peace be quartered in any house without the consent of the owner; nor at any time, but in a manner warranted by law.

No person shall be subject, except in cases of impeachment, to more than one punishment or one trial for the same offence; nor shall be compelled to be a witness against himself; nor be deprived of life, liberty, or property without due process of law; nor be obliged to relinquish his property, where it may be necessary for public use, without a just compensation.

Excessive bail shall not be required, nor excessive fines imposed, nor cruel and unusual punishments inflicted.

The rights of the people to be secured in their persons, their houses, their papers, and their other property, from all unreasonable searches and seizures, shall not be violated by warrants issued, without probable cause, supported by oath or affirmation, or not particularly describing the places to be searched, or the persons or things to be seized.

In all criminal prosecutions, the accused shall enjoy the right to a speedy and public trial, to be informed of the cause and nature of the accusation, to be confronted with his accusers, and the witnesses against him; to have a compulsory process for obtaining witnesses in his favor; and to have the assistance of counsel for his defence.

The exceptions here or elsewhere in the Constitution, made in favor of particular rights, shall not be so construed as to diminish the just importance of other rights retained by the people, or as to enlarge the powers delegated by the Constitution; but either as actual limitations of such powers, or as inserted merely for greater caution.

Fifthly. That in article 1st, section 10, between clauses 1 and 2, be inserted this clause, to wit:

No State shall violate the equal rights of conscience, or the freedom of the press, or the trial by jury in criminal cases.

Sixthly. That, in article 3d, section 2, be annexed to the end of clause 2d, these words, to wit:

But no appeal to such court shall be allowed where the value in controversy shall not amount to ____ dollars: nor shall any fact triable by jury, according to the course of common law, be otherwise re-examinable than may consist with the principles of common law.

Seventhly. That in article 3d, section 2, the third clause be struck out, and in its place be inserted the clauses following, to wit:

The trial of all crimes (except in cases of impeachments, and cases arising in the land or naval forces, or the militia when on actual service, in time of war or public danger) shall be by an impartial jury of freeholders of the vicinage, with the requisite of unanimity for conviction, of the right of challenge, and other accustomed requisites; and in all crimes punishable with loss of life or member, presentment or indictment by a grand jury shall be an essential preliminary, provided that in cases of crimes committed within any county which may be in possession of an enemy, or in which a general insurrection may prevail, the trial may by law be authorized in some other county of the same State, as near as may be to the seat of the offence.

In cases of crimes committed not within any county, the trial may by law be in such county as the laws shall have prescribed. In suits at common law, between man and man, the trial by jury, as one of the best securities to the rights of the people, ought to remain inviolate.

Eighthly. That immediately after article 6th, be inserted, as article 7th, the clauses following, to wit:

The powers delegated by this Constitution are appropriated to the departments to which they are respectively distributed: so that the Legislative Department shall never exercise powers vested in the Executive or Judicial, nor the Executive exercise the powers vested in the Legislative or Judicial, nor the Judicial exercise the powers vested in the Legislative or Executive Departments.

The powers not delegated by this Constitution, nor prohibited by it to the States, are reserved to the States respectively.

Ninthly. That article 7th be numbered as article 8th.

.   .   .

The people of many States have thought it necessary to raise barriers against power in all forms and departments of Government, and I am inclined to believe, if once bills of rights are established in all the States as well as the Federal Constitution, we shall find, that, although some of them are rather unimportant, yet, upon the whole, they will have a salutary tendency. It may be said, in some instances, they do no more than state the perfect equality of mankind. This, to be sure, is an absolute truth, yet it is not absolutely necessary to be inserted at the head of a Constitution.

In some instances they assert those rights which are exercised by the people in forming and establishing a plan of Government. In other instances, they specify those rights which are retained when particular powers are given up to be exercised by the Legislature. In other instances, they specify positive rights, which may seem to result from the nature of the compact. Trial by jury cannot be considered as a natural right, but a right resulting from a social compact, which regulates the action of the community, but is as essential to secure the liberty of the people as any one of the pre-existent right of

nature. In other instances, they lay down dogmatic maxims with respect to the construction of the Government; declaring that the Legislative, Executive, and Judicial branches, shall be kept separate and distinct. Perhaps the best way of securing this in practice is, to provide such checks as will prevent the encroachment of the one upon the other.

.   .   .

But I confess that I do conceive, that in a Government modified like this of the United States, the great danger lies rather in the abuse of the community than in the Legislative body. The prescriptions in favor of liberty ought to be levelled against that quarter where the greatest danger lies, namely, that which possesses the highest prerogative of power. But this is not found in either the Executive or Legislative departments of Government, but in the body of the people, operating by the majority against the minority.

.   .   .

It is true, the powers of the General Government are circumscribed, they are directed to particular objects; but even if Government keeps within those limits, it has certain discretionary powers with respect to the means, which may admit of abuse to a certain extent, in the same manner as the powers of the State Governments under their constitutions may to an indefinite extent; because in the Constitution of the United States, there is a clause granting to Congress the power to make all laws which shall be necessary and proper for carrying into execution all the powers vested in the Government of the United States, or in any department or officer thereof; this enables them to fulfil every purpose for which the Government was established. Now, may not laws be considered necessary and proper by Congress, (for it is for them to judge of the necessity and propriety to accomplish those special purposes which they may have in contemplation,) which laws in themselves are neither necessary nor proper; as well as improper laws could be enacted by the State Legislatures, for fulfilling the more extended objects of those Governments? I will state an instance, which I think in point, and proves that this might be the case. The General Government has a right to pass all laws which shall be necessary to collect its revenue; the means for enforcing the collection are within the direction of the Legislature: may not general warrants be considered necessary for this purpose, as well as for some purposes which it was supposed at the framing of their constitutions the State Governments had in view? If there was reason for restraining the State Governments from exercising this power, there is like reason for restraining the Federal Government.

It may be said, indeed it has been said, that a bill of rights is not necessary, because the establishment of this Government has not repealed those declarations of rights which are added to the several State constitutions; that those rights of the people which had been established by the most solemn act, could not be annihilated by a subsequent act of that people, who meant and declared at the head of the instrument, that they ordained and established a new system, for the express purpose of securing to themselves and posterity the liberties they had gained by an arduous conflict.

I admit the force of this observation, but I do not look upon it to be conclusive. In the first place, it is too uncertain ground to leave this provision upon, if a provision is at all necessary to secure rights so important as many of those I have mentioned are conceived to be, by the public in general, as well as those in particular who opposed the adoption of this Constitution. Besides, some States have no bills of rights, there are others provided with very defective ones, and there are others whose bills of rights are not only defective, but absolutely improper; instead of securing some in the full extent which republican principles would require, they limit them too much to agree with the common ideas of liberty.

It has been objected also against a bill of rights, that, by enumerating particular exceptions to the grant of power, it would disparage those rights which were not placed in that enumeration; and it might follow by implication, that those rights which were not singled out, were intended to be assigned into the hands of the General Government, and were consequently insecure. This is one of the most plausible arguments I have ever heard urged against the admission of a bill of rights into this system; but, I conceive, that it may be guarded against. I have attempted it, as gentlemen may see by turning to the last clause of the fourth resolution.

It has been said that it is unnecessary to load the Constitution with this provision, because it was not found effectual in the constitution of the particular States. It is true, there are a few particular States in which some of the most valuable articles have not, at one time or other, been violated; but it does not follow but they may have to a certain degree, a salutary effect against the abuse of power. If they are incorporated into the Constitution, independent tribunals of justice will consider themselves in a peculiar manner the guardians of those rights; they will be an impenetrable bulwark against every assumption of power in the Legislative or Executive; they will be naturally led to resist every encroachment

upon rights expressly stipulated for in the Constitution by the declaration of rights. Besides this security, there is a great probability that such a declaration in the federal system would be enforced; because the State Legislatures will jealously and closely watch the operations of this Government, and be able to resist with more effect every assumption of power, than any other power on earth can do; and the greatest opponents to a Federal Government admit the State Legislatures to be sure guardians of the people's liberty. I conclude, from this view of the subject, that it will be proper in itself, and highly politic, for the tranquillity of the public mind, and the stability of the Government, that we should offer something, in the form I have proposed, to be incorporated in the system of Government, as a declaration of the rights of the people.

. . .

I wish, also, in revising the Constitution, we may throw into that section, which interdicts the abuse of certain powers in the State Legislatures, some other provisions of equal, if not greater importance than those already made. The words, "No State shall pass any bill of attainder, *ex post facto* law," &c., were wise and proper restrictions in the Constitution. I think there is more danger of those powers being abused by the State Governments than by the Government of the United States. The same may be said of other powers which they possess, if not controlled by the general principle, that laws are unconstitutional which infringe the rights of the community. I should, therefore, wish to extend this interdiction, and add, as I have stated in the 5th resolution, that no State shall violate the equal right of conscience, freedom of the press, or trial by jury in criminal cases; because it is proper that every Government should be disarmed of powers which trench upon those particular rights.

. . .

[T]he State Governments are as liable to attack these invaluable privileges as the General Government is, and therefore ought to be as cautiously guarded against.

I think it will be proper, with respect to the judiciary powers, to satisfy the public mind on those points which I have mentioned. Great inconvenience has been apprehended to suitors from the distance they would be dragged to obtain justice in the Supreme Court of the United States, upon an appeal on an action for a small debt. To remedy this, declare that no appeal shall be made unless the matter in controversy amounts to a particular sum; this, with the regulations respecting jury trials in criminal cases, and suits at common law, it is to be hoped, will quiet and reconcile the minds of the people to that part of the Constitution.

I find, from looking into the amendements proposed by the State conventions, that several are particularly anxious that it should be declared in the Constitution, that the powers not therein delegated should be reserved to the several States. Perhaps other words may define this more precisely than the whole of the instrument now does. I admit they may be deemed unnecessary; but there can be no harm in making such a declaration, if gentlemen will allow that the fact is as stated. I am sure I understand it so, and do therefore propose it.

At this point, the House again engaged in a lengthy debate over the wisdom and propriety of considering Madison's proposals, and the best method of doing so. Opponents worried that foreign powers would not regard the United States as a serious trading partner as long as it was still tinkering with its Constitution instead of organizing its government. Elbridge Gerry objected to the notion that the amendments were necessary to maintain the trust of the people:

> Some gentlemen consider it necessary to do this to satisfy our constituents. I think referring the business to a special committee will be attempting to amuse them with trifles. Our fellow-citizens are possessed of too much discernment not to be able to discover the intention of Congress by such procedures.

Various suggestions were made, including referring the matter to a select committee and simply tabling the proposals. The House eventually agreed to consider Madison's proposals as a Committee of the Whole.

More than a month elapsed before the House turned again to the proposals. On July 21, Madison "begged the House to indulge him in the further consideration of Amendments to the Constitution." Several members opposed consideration by a Committee of the Whole, on the ground that "the members from the several States proposing amendments would, no doubt, drag the House through the consideration of every one." After further argument in this vein, the House voted to send the matter to a select committee of a member from each state.[6] The committee reported on July 28.

The committee report (reprinted in the Appendix) was similar to Madison's original proposal. Some of the language was changed, though it is not clear in every case whether the committee intended to alter the meaning of Madison's suggestions. For example, the committee draft condensed Madison's more extensive protection of religious worship to "No religion shall be established by law, nor shall the equal rights of conscience be infringed." Also, the clauses of what eventually became the Second Amendment were reversed; the committee placed first the words stressing the importance of a militia to the security of a free state, followed by the clause protecting the right to bear arms. Other provisions, such as the retention of unenumerated rights, were shortened but not altered in meaning. Some rights were eliminated, including Madison's "indefeasible right to reform [the] Government."

Little is known about the workings of the committee that produced this draft. It may be assumed that Madison played a major role in the drafting process, as the report differed little from his original proposals. One intermediate draft, in Roger Sherman's handwriting, is extant. It is substantively similar to the committee's version. A few differences are noteworthy: Sherman's draft prohibits Congress from granting monopolies, and also contains the boilerplate natural rights language of the earlier state declarations. There is a striking difference in form, however. Sherman's draft is meant to be appended to the end of the Constitution, rather than inserted in it. Each of his amendments stands alone as an independent provision.

The committee's report was tabled until August 3, when Madison successfully moved that the report be "made the order of the day" for August 12. In fact, the House did not take up the report until August 13.

Again Madison had difficulty convincing many of his colleagues of the importance of the matter. Theodore Sedgwick of Massachusetts reminded the House that they had "much other and more important business requiring attention," and William Smith of Maryland suggested that "the Judicial bill . . . deserved the first attention of the House." Elbridge Gerry, reversing the position he had taken in the Convention, speculated that the proposed amendments would "inevitably produce a more copious debate than the gentleman [Madison] contemplates," and indicated his hope "that the honorable gentlemen would no longer press the motion." John Vining of Delaware, who had presented the committee's report, supported its immediate consideration, but his remarks suggest the minimal importance with which the amendments were viewed even by proponents:

> Mr. Vining, impressed by the anxiety which the honorable gentleman from Virginia had discovered for having the subject of amendments considered, had agreed, in his own mind, to waive, for the present, the call he was well authorized to make, for the House to take into consideration the bill for establishing a Land Office for the disposal of the vacant lands in the Western Territory. In point of time, his motion had the priority; in point of importance, every candid mind would acknowledge its preference[.]

Despite attempts at delay or abandonment, however, the House voted to consider the amendments and resolved itself into a Committee of the Whole. The members immediately began squabbling over the form the amendments should take.

Sherman, in keeping with the draft he had favored in committee, objected to inserting the amendments in the existing Constitution, and proposed an alternative procedure. He argued that:

> [I]t is questionable whether we have the right to propose amendments in this way. The Constitution is the act of the people, and ought to remain entire. But the amendments will be the act of the State Governments. Again, all the authority we possess is derived from that instrument; if we mean to destroy the whole, and establish a new Constitution, we remove the basis on which we mean to build.

Madison opposed Sherman's motion, arguing that the Constitution should "remain uniform and entire." He suggested that placing the amendments at the end would make interpretation of the document difficult and would invite "unfavorable comparisons" between the 1787 document and subsequent amendments. Others echoed his sentiments, stressing the need for simplicity. Gerry argued, for example:

> If we proceed in the way proposed by [Sherman], I presume the title of our first amendment will be, a supplement to the Constitution of the United States; the next a supplement to the supplement, and so on, until we have supplements annexed five times in five years, wrapping up the Constitution in a maze of perplexity; and as great an adept as that honorable gentleman is at finding out the truth, it will take

him, I apprehend, a week or a fortnight's study to ascertain the true meaning of the Constitution.

John Vining of Delaware ridiculed Sherman's motion by referring to an act he had seen entitled "an act to amend a supplement to an act entitled an act for altering part of an act entitled an act for certain purposes therein mentioned."

Sherman's supporters argued that the interlineation method required Congress to repeal or suspend the first Constitution pending ratification of the new, cleanly amended Constitution; this, they said, Congress lacked the power to do. Moreover, any laws enacted by Congress during the pendency of the ratification process might be without constitutional foundation. They also argued that interlineating amendments would suggest "that George Washington, and the other worthy characters who composed the convention, signed an instrument which they never had in contemplation." Sherman himself spoke on the necessity of his motion, forcefully stating the objections to interlineation:

> If I had looked upon this question as a mere matter of form, I should not have brought it forward, or troubled the committee with such a lengthy discussion. But, sir, I contend that amendments made in the way proposed by the committee are void. No gentleman ever knew an addition and alteration introduced into an existing law, and that any part of such law was left in force; but if it was improved or altered by a supplemental act, the original retained all its validity and importance, in every case where the two were not incompatible. But if these observations alone should be thought insufficient to support my motion, I would desire gentlemen to consider the authorities upon which the two Constitutions are to stand. The original was established by the people at large, by conventions chosen by them for the express purpose. The preamble to the Constitution declares the act; but will it be a truth in ratifying the next Constitution, which is to be done perhaps by the State Legislatures, and not conventions chosen for the purpose? Will gentlemen say it is "We the people["] in this case? Certainly they cannot; for, by the present Constitution, we, nor all the Legislatures in the Union together, do not possess the power of repealing it. All that is granted us by the 5th article is, that whenever we shall think it necessary, we may propose amendments to the Constitution; not that we may propose to repeal the old, and substitute a new one.

Sherman's motion was defeated and the House finally turned, on August 14 (three months after Madison's original proposal), to the substance of the proposed amendments. It once again resolved itself into a Committee of the Whole, and considered the select committee report one item at a time.

After a brief debate on whether the preamble was a part of the Constitution—and thus subject to amendment—and whether its "neatness and simplicity" was in need of amendment, the House voted twenty-seven to twenty-three to adopt the first proposal.

The members then turned to the second proposal, to increase the size of the House of Representatives. Fisher Ames of Massachusetts immediately moved to amend the measure by requiring one representative for every forty thousand, rather than the committee's proposal of one for every thirty thousand. He made a long speech essentially opposing the increase in size, using many of the arguments the Convention delegates had made in support of a small House in the first place. He suggested that increasing the size of the House would "diminish the individual usefulness" of representatives, that it would "lessen the chance of selecting men of the greatest wisdom and abilities," and would cause the members to "fall the prey of party spirit [and] cabal to carry measures which they would be unable to get through by fair and open argument." Larger legislative bodies, he argued, were "less under the guidance of reason than smaller ones," and more "confused" in their deliberations. Madison countered that larger legislatures also had advantages: "if they are more exposed to passion and fermentation, they are less subject to venality and corruption."

James Jackson of Georgia also opposed Ames's motion, on the ground that reducing the number of representatives, whether to one hundred or to one, was inconsistent with democratic principles:

> Can one man, however consummate his abilities, however unimpeachable his integrity, and however superior his wisdom, be supposed capable of understanding, combining, and managing interests so diversified as those of the people of America? It has been complained of, that the representation is too small at one for thirty thousand; we ought not therefore attempt to reduce it.
>
> In a Republic, the laws should be founded upon the sense of the community; if every man's opinion could be obtained it would be the better.

Other members made similar arguments, and Ames's motion was defeated "by a large majority." Sedgwick's motion to increase the minimum number of representatives from one hundred to two hundred (and presumably the maximum from 175 to 275) was then carried. The whole proposal passed by a vote of twenty-seven to twenty-two. The next proposal, to require an intervening election before any legislative salary increase became effective, was also approved after a brief debate.

On August 15, the House continued its consideration of the committee report.

Saturday, August 15

The fourth proposition being under consideration, as follows:

Article 1. Section 9. Between paragraphs two and three insert "no religion shall be established by law, nor shall the equal rights of conscience be infringed."

Mr. Sylvester had some doubts of the propriety of the mode of expression used in this paragraph. He apprehended that it was liable to a construction different from what had been made by the committee. He feared it might be thought to have a tendency to abolish religion altogether.

Mr. Vining suggested the propriety of transposing the two members of the sentence.

Mr. Gerry said it would read better if it was, that no religious doctrine shall be established by law.

Mr. Sherman thought the amendment altogether unnecessary, inasmuch as Congress had no authority whatever delegated to them by the Constitution to make religious establishments; he would, therefore, move to have it struck out.

Mr. Carroll.—As the rights of conscience are, in their nature, of peculiar delicacy, and will little bear the gentlest touch of governmental hand; and as many sects have concurred in opinion that they are not well secured under the present Constitution, he said he was much in favor of adopting the words. He thought it would tend more towards conciliating the minds of the people to the Government than almost any other amendment he had heard proposed. He would not contend with gentlemen about the phraseology, his object was to secure the substance in such a manner as to satisfy the wishes of the honest part of the community.

Mr. Madison said, he apprehended the meaning of the words to be, that Congress should not establish a religion, and enforce the legal observation of it by law, nor compel men to worship God in any manner contrary to their conscience. Whether the words are necessary or not, he did not mean to say, but they had been required by some of the State Conventions, who seemed to entertain an opinion that under the clause of the Constitution, which gave power to Congress to make all laws necessary and proper to carry into execution the Constitution, and the laws made under it, enabled them to make laws of such a nature as might infringe the rights of conscience, and establish a national religion; to prevent these effects he presumed the amendment was intended, and he thought it as well expressed as the nature of the language would admit.

Mr. Huntington said that he feared, with the gentleman first up on this subject, that the words might be taken in such latitude as to be extremely hurtful to the cause of religion. He understood the amendment to mean what had been expressed by the gentleman from Virginia; but others might find it convenient to put another construction upon it. The ministers of their congregations to the Eastward were maintained by the contributions of those who belonged to their society; the expense of building meeting-houses was contributed in the same manner. These things were regulated by by-laws. If an action was brought before a Federal Court on any of these cases, the person who had neglected to perform his engagements could not be compelled to do it; for a support of ministers or building of places of worship might be construed into a religious establishment.

By the charter of Rhode Island, no religion could be established by law; he could give a history of the effects of such a regulation; indeed the people were now enjoying the blessed fruits of it. He hoped, therefore, the amendment would be made in such a way as to secure the rights of conscience, and a free exercise of the rights of religion, but not to patronise those who professed no religion at all.

Mr. Madison thought, if the word "national" was inserted before religion, it would satisfy the minds of honorable gentlemen. He believed that the people feared one sect might obtain a pre-eminence, or two combine together, and establish a religion to which they would compel others to conform. He thought if the word "national" was introduced, it would point the amendment directly to the object it was intended to prevent.

Mr. Livermore was not satisfied with that amendment; but he did not wish them to dwell long on the subject. He thought it would be better if it were altered, and made to read in this manner, that Congress shall make no laws touching religion, or infringing the rights of conscience.

Mr. Gerry did not like the term national, pro-

posed by the gentleman from Virginia, and he hoped it would not be adopted by the House. It brought to his mind some observations that had taken place in the conventions at the time they were considering the present Constitution. It had been insisted upon by those who were called anti-federalists, that this form of Government consolidated the Union; the honorable gentleman's motion shows that he considers it in the same light. Those who were called anti-federalists at that time, complained that they had injustice done them by the title, because they were in favor of a Federal Government, and the others were in favor af a national one; the federalists were for ratifying the Constitution as it stood, and the others not until amendments were made. Their names then ought not to have been distinguished by federalists and anti-federalists, but rats and anti-rats.

Mr. Madison withdrew his motion, but observed that the words "no national religion shall be established by law," did not imply that the Government was a national one; the question was then taken on Mr. Livermore's motion, and passed in the affirmative, thirty-one for, and twenty against it.

The next clause of the fourth proposition was taken into consideration, and was as follows: "The freedom of speech and of the press, and the right of the people peaceably to assemble and consult for their common good, and to apply to the Government for redress of grievances, shall not be infringed."

Mr. Sedgwick submitted to those gentlemen who had contemplated the subject, what effect such an amendment as this would have; he feared it would tend to make them appear trifling in the eyes of their constituents; what, said he, shall we secure the freedom of speech, and think it necessary, at the same time, to allow the right of assembling? If people freely converse together, they must assemble for that purpose; it is a self-evident, unalienable right which the people possess; it is certainly a thing that never would be called in question; it is derogatory to the dignity of the House to descend to such minutiæ; he therefore moved to strike out "assemble and."

Mr. Benson.—The committee who framed this report proceeded on the principle that these rights belonged to the people; they conceived them to be inherent; and all that they meant to provide against was their being infringed by the Government.

Mr. Sedgwick replied, that if the committee were governed by that general principle, they might have gone into a very lengthy enumeration of rights; they might have declared that a man should have a right to wear his hat if he pleased; that he might get up when he pleased, and go to bed when he thought proper; but he would ask the gentleman whether he thought it necessary to enter these trifles in a declaration of rights, in a Government where none of them were intended to be infringed.

. . .

Mr. Page.—The gentleman from Massachusetts, (Mr. Sedgwick,) who made this motion, objects to the clause, because the right is of so trivial a nature. He supposes it no more essential than whether a man has a right to wear his hat or not; but let me observe to him that such rights have been opposed, and a man has been obliged to pull off his hat when he appeared before the face of authority; people have also been prevented from assembling together on their lawful occasions, therefore it is well to guard against such stretches of authority, by inserting the privilege in the declaration of rights. If the people could be deprived of the power of assembling under any pretext whatsoever, they might be deprived of every other privilege contained in the clause.

Mr. Vining said, if the thing were harmless, and it would tend to gratify the States that had proposed amendments, he should agree to it.

. . .

The question was now put upon Mr. Sedgwick's motion, and lost by a considerable majority.

At this point in the debates, Thomas Tudor Tucker of South Carolina moved to insert the right of the people "to instruct their representatives." An extensive debate ensued. Opponents of Tucker's motion argued that federal legislators should be presumed to know and respect the wishes of constituents, and that if they did not, a divided legislature and short terms of office would keep them in check. Opponents also suggested that adoption of Tucker's motion would allow the "passions of the people" too much influence. Tucker's supporters countered with arguments about the popular nature of democratic government. The division was sharp between those who viewed the legislature as Burkean and deliberative, and those who viewed it as a mirrorlike reflection of the people's desires. Roger Sherman adhered to the former view:

> It appears to me, that the words are calculated to mislead the people, by conveying an idea that they have a right to control the debates of the Legislature. This cannot be admitted to be just, because it would destroy the object of their meeting. I think, when the people have chosen a representative, it is his duty to meet others from the different parts of the Union, and consult, and agree with them to such acts as are for the general benefit of the whole community. If they were to be guided by instructions, there would be no use in deliberation; all that a man would have to do, would be to produce his instructions, and lay them on the table, and let them speak for him.

John Page of Virginia took the opposite approach:

> [Tucker's motion is] strictly compatible with the spirit and the nature of the Government; all power vests in the people of the United States; it is therefore, a Government of the people, a democracy. If it were consistent with the peace and tranquility of the inhabitants, every freeman would have a right to come and give his vote upon the law; but, inasmuch as this cannot be done by reason of the extent of territory, and some other causes, the people have agreed that their representatives shall exercise a part of their authority. To pretend to refuse them the power of instructing their agents, appears to me to deny them a right.

In response to an argument by Michael Jenifer Stone of Maryland that Tucker's motion would change the government "from a representative one to a democracy," Elbridge Gerry countered that "he had always heard that it was a democracy; but perhaps he was misled, and the honorable gentleman was right in distinguishing it by some other appellation; perhaps an aristocracy was a term better adapted to it."

Some of the legislators made less theoretical arguments. Madison cautioned against approving amendments "of a doubtful nature," lest such amendments cause the whole list to fail. Several members raised practical problems about how constituents would decide what instructions to give. Proponents pointed to the fact that many state constitutions provided for a right of instruction, as did several of the state wish lists.

Tucker's motion was ultimately defeated by a vote of forty-one to ten, and the rest of the proposition was agreed to. Fisher Ames of Massachusetts immediately moved "to discharge the committee from any further proceeding," and the debate over the wisdom of considering amendments at all resumed. Ames eventually withdrew his motion, and the House adjourned for the day. They returned to the committee's proposals the following day.

Monday, August 17

The House again resolved itself into a committee, Mr. Boudinot in the Chair, on the proposed amendments to the Constitution. The third clause of the fourth proposition in the report was taken into consideration, being as follows: "A well regulated militia, composed of the body of the people, being the best security of a free state, the right of the people to keep and bear arms shall not be infringed; but no person religiously scrupulous shall be compelled to bear arms."

. . .

Mr. Jackson did not expect that all the people of the United States would turn Quakers or Moravians; consequently one part would have to defend the other in case of invasion. Now, this in his opinion, was unjust, unless the Constitution secured an equivalent: for this reason, he moved to amend the clause, by inserting at the end of it, "upon paying an equivalent, to be established by law."

. . .

Mr. Sherman conceived it difficult to modify the clause and make it better. It is well known that those who are religiously scrupulous of bearing arms, are equally scrupulous of getting substitutes or paying an equivalent. Many of them would rather die than do either one or the other; but he did not see an absolute necessity for a clause of this kind. We do not live under an arbitrary Government, said he, and the States, respectively, will

have the government of the militia, unless when called into actual service; besides, it would not do to alter it so as to exclude the whole of any sect, because there are men amongst the Quakers who will turn out, notwithstanding the religious principles of the society, and defend the cause of their country. Certainly it will be improper to prevent the exercise of such favorable dispositions, at least whilst it is the practice of nations to determine their contests by the slaughter of their citizens and subjects.

Mr. Vining hoped the clause would be suffered to remain as it stood, because he saw no use in it if it was amended so as to compel a man to find a substitute, which, with respect to the Government, was the same as if the person himself turned out to fight.

Mr. Stone inquired what the words "religiously scrupulous" had reference to: was it of bearing arms? If it was, it ought so to be expressed.

Mr. Benson moved to have the words "but no person religiously scrupulous shall be compelled to bear arms" struck out. He would always leave it to the benevolence of the Legislature, for, modify it as you please, it will be impossible to express it in such a manner as to clear it from ambiguity. No man can claim this indulgence of right. It may be a religious persuasion, but it is no natural right, and therefore ought to be left to the discretion of the Government. If this stands part of the Constitution, it will be a question before the Judiciary on every regulation you make with respect to the organization of the militia, whether it comports with this declaration or not. It is extremely injudicious to intermix matters of doubt with fundamentals.

I have no reason to believe but the Legislature will always possess humanity enough to indulge this class of citizens in a matter they are so desirous of; but they ought to be left to their discretion.

The motion to strike the clause failed twenty-four to twenty-two, and the House continued to discuss both the militia clause and the prohibition against quartering soldiers. A motion to add a clause prohibiting a standing army was rejected. The House then proceeded to consider the clause on punishments: "Excessive bail shall not be required, nor excessive fines imposed, nor cruel and unusual punishments inflicted."

Monday, August 17

Mr. Smith, of South Carolina, objected to the words "nor cruel and unusual punishments;" the import of them being too indefinite.

Mr. Livermore.—The clause seems to express a great deal of humanity, on which account I have no objection to it; but as it seems to have no meaning in it, I do not think it necessary. What is meant by the terms excessive bail? Who are to be the judges? What is understood by excessive fines? It lies with the court to determine. No cruel and unusual punishment is to be inflicted; it is sometimes necessary to hang a man, villains often deserve whipping, and perhaps having their ears cut off; but are we in future to be prevented from inflicting these punishments because they are cruel? If a more lenient mode of correcting vice and deterring others from the commission of it could be invented, it would be very prudent in the Legislature to adopt it; but until we have some security that this will be done, we ought not to be restrained from making necessary laws by any declaration of this kind.

The question was put on the clause, and it was agreed to by a considerable majority.

.   .   .

The committee went on to the consideration of the seventh clause of the fourth proposition, being as follows: "The right of the people to be secured in their persons, houses, papers, and effects, shall not be violated by warrants issuing without probable cause, supported by oath or affirmation, and not particularly describing the place to be searched and the persons or things to be seized."

Mr. Gerry said he presumed there was a mistake in the wording of this clause; it ought to be "the right of the people to be secure in their persons, houses, papers, and effects, against unreasonable seizures and searches," and therefore moved that amendment.

This was adopted by the committee.

Mr. Benson objected to the words "by warrants issuing." This declaratory provision was good as far as it went, but he thought it was not sufficient; he therefore proposed to alter it so as to read "and no warrant shall issue."

The question was put on this motion, and lost by a considerable majority.

The clause as amended being now agreed to,

The eighth clause of the fourth proposition was taken up, which was "The enumeration in this Constitution of certain rights, shall not be construed to deny or disparage others retained by the people."

Mr. Gerry said, it ought to be "deny or impair," for the word "disparage" was not of plain import; he therefore moved to make that alteration, but not being seconded, the question was taken on the clause, and it passed in the affirmative.

The committee then proceeded to the fifth proposition:

Article 1, section 10, between the first and second paragraph, insert "no State shall infringe the equal rights of conscience, nor the freedom of speech, or of the press, nor of the right of trial by jury in criminal cases."

Mr. Tucker.—This is offered, I presume, as an amendment to the Constitution of the United States, but it goes only to the alteration of the constitutions of particular States. It will be much better, I apprehend, to leave the State Governments to themselves, and not to interfere with them more than we already do; and that is thought by many to be rather too much. I therefore move, sir, to strike out these words.

Mr. Madison conceived this to be the most valuable amendment in the whole list. If there were any reason to restrain the Government of the United States from infringing upon these essential rights, it was equally necessary that they should be secured against the State Governments. He thought that if they provided against the one, it was as necessary to provide against the other, and was satisifed that it would be equally grateful to the people.

Mr. Livermore had no great objection to the sentiment, but he thought it not well expressed. He wished to make it an affirmative proposition; "the equal rights of conscience, the freedom of speech or of the press, and the right of trial by jury in criminal cases, shall not be infringed by any State."

This transposition being agreed to, and Mr. Tucker's motion being rejected, the clause was adopted.

The next day, Gerry moved to consider *all* the amendments proposed by the states, even those which had not been adopted by the select committee. His motion was defeated by a vote of thirty-four to sixteen, and the House returned to the substance of the select committee's report.

Tuesday, August 18

The 8th proposition in the words following was considered, "Immediately after article 6, the following to be inserted as article 7:"

"The powers delegated by this Constitution to the Government of the United States, shall be exercised as therein appropriated, so that the Legislative shall not exercise the powers vested in the Executive or Judicial; nor the Executive the power vested in the Legislative or Judicial; nor the Judicial the powers vested in the Legislative or Executive."

Mr. Sherman conceived this amendment to be altogether unnecessary, inasmuch as the Constitution assigned the business of each branch of the Government to a separate department.

Mr. Madison supposed the people would be gratified with the amendment, as it was admitted that the powers ought to be separate and distinct; it might also tend to an explanation of some doubts that might arise respecting the construction of the Constitution.

Mr. Livermore, thinking the clause subversive of the Constitution, was opposed to it, and hoped it might be disagreed to.

On the motion being put, the proposition was carried.

The 9th proposition, in the words following, was considered, "The powers not delegated by the Constitution, nor prohibited by it to the States, are reserved to the States respectively."

Mr. Tucker proposed to amend the proposition, by prefixing to it "all powers being derived from the people." He thought this a better place to make this assertion than the introductory clause of the Constitution, where a similar sentiment was proposed by the committee. He extended his motion also, to add the word "expressly," so as to read "the powers not expressly delegated by this Constitution."

Mr. Madison objected to this amendment, because it was impossible to confine a Government to the exercise of express powers; there must necessarily be admitted powers by implication, unless the Constitution descended to recount every minutiæ. He remembered the word "expressly," had been moved in the convention of Virginia, by the opponents to the ratification, and, after full and fair discussion, was given up by them, and the system allowed to retain its present form.

Mr. Sherman coincided with Mr. Madison in opinion, observing that corporate bodies are supposed to possess all powers incident to a corporate capacity, without being absolutely expressed.

Mr. Tucker did not view the word "expressly" in the same light with the gentleman who opposed him; he thought every power to be expressly given that could be clearly comprehended within any accurate definition of the general power.

Mr. Tucker's motion being negatived,

Mr. Carroll proposed to add to the end of the proposition, "or to the people;" this was agreed to.

The 10th proposition, "Article 7 to be made Article 8," agreed to.

The committee then rose, and reported the amendments as amended by the committee.

Tucker then moved a long list of miscellaneous amendments, which the House declined to consider.

Having completed consideration of the amendments as a Committee of the Whole, the House began formal consideration of the Committee of the Whole's report at the end of the day on August 19. It quickly rejected the first proposition—amending the preamble—with little debate. Roger Sherman renewed his motion to append the amendments to the end of the Constitution rather than integrating them into the body of the document; this time his motion succeeded. Unfortunately, the Annals of Congress contain no record of the debates over Sherman's motion, but report only that "a debate similar to what took place in the Committee of the Whole" ensued. Fisher Ames also renewed his motion to limit the increase in the size of the House, but the House adjourned without coming to any decision. The next day they took up Ames's proposal as well as the rest of the report.

Thursday, August 20

The House resumed the consideration of the report of the Committee of the Whole on the subject of amendment to the Constitution.

Mr. Ames's proposition was taken up. Five or six other members introduced propositions on the same point, and the whole were, by mutual consent, laid on the table. After which, the House proceeded to the third amendment, and agreed to the same.

On motion of Mr. Ames, the fourth amendment was altered so as to read "The Congress shall make no law establishing religion, or to prevent the free exercise thereof, or to infringe the rights of conscience." This being adopted,

The first proposition was agreed to.

Mr. Scott objected to the clause in the sixth amendment, "No person religiously scrupulous shall be compelled to bear arms." He observed that if this becomes part of the Constitution, such persons can neither be called upon for their service, nor can an equivalent be demanded; it is also attended with still further difficulties, for a militia can never be depended upon. This would lead to the violation of another article in the Constitution, which secures to the people the right of keeping arms, and in this case recourse must be had to a standing army. I conceive it, said he, to be a Legislative right altogether. There are many sects I know, who are religiously scrupulous in this respect; I do not mean to deprive them of any indulgence the law affords; my design is to guard against those who are of no religion.

It has been urged that religion is on the decline; if so, the argument is more strong in my favor, for when the time comes that religion shall be discarded, the generality of persons will have recourse to these pretexts to get excused from bearing arms.

Mr. Boudinot thought the provision in the clause, or something similar to it, was necesssary. Can any dependence, said he, be placed in men who are conscientious in this respect? or what justice can there be in compelling them to bear arms, when, according to their religious principles, they would rather die than use them? He adverted to several instances of oppression on this point, that occurred during the war. In forming a militia, an effectual defence ought to be calculated, and no characters of this religious description ought to be compelled to take up arms. I hope that in establishing this Government, we may show the world that proper care is taken that the Government may not interfere with the religious sentiments of any person. Now, by striking out the clause, people may be led to believe that there is an intention in the General Government to compel all its citizens to bear arms.

Some further desultory conversation arose, and it was agreed to insert the words "in person," to the end of the clause; after which, it was adopted, as was the fourth, fifth, sixth, seventh, and eighth clauses of the fourth proposition; then the fifth, sixth, and seventh propositions were agreed to, and the House adjourned.

Friday, August 21

The ninth proposition **Mr. Gerry** proposed to amend by inserting the word "expressly," so as to read "the powers not expressly delegated by the Constitution, nor prohibited to the States, are reserved to the States respectively, or to the people." As he thought this an amendment of great importance, he requested the yeas and nays might be taken. He was supported in this by one-fifth of the members present; whereupon they were taken, and were as follows:

Yeas—Messrs. Burke, Coles, Floyd, Gerry, Grout, Hathorn, Jackson, Livermore, Page, Parker, Partridge, Van Rensselaer, Smith, (of South Carolina,) Stone, Sumter, Thatcher, and Tucket—17.

Nays—Messrs. Ames, Benson, Boudinot, Brown, Cadwalader, Carroll, Clymer, Fitzsimons, Foster, Gale, Gilman, Goodhue, Hartley, Heister, Lawrence, Lee, Madison, Moore, Muhlenburg, Schureman, Scott, Sedgwick, Seney, Sherman, Sylvester, Sinnickson, Smith, (of Maryland,) Sturges, Trumbull, Vining, Wadsworth, and Wynkoop—32.

Mr. Sherman moved to alter the last clause, so as to make it read, "the powers not delegated to the United States by the Constitution nor prohibited by it to the States, are reserved to the States respectively, or to the people."

This motion was adopted without debate.

Aedanus Burke of South Carolina moved to add a provision prohibiting Congress from modifying the time, place, or manner of elections. His motion was defeated twenty-eight to twenty-three. The House resumed discussion of Ames's proposal on the ratio of representation, but the Annals record only that "after some desultory conversation," the following language was agreed to:

> After the first enumeration, required by the first article of the Constitution, there shall be one representative for every thirty thousand, until the number shall amount to one hundred. After which, the proportion shall be not less than one hundred representatives, nor less than one representative for every forty thousand persons, until the number of representatives shall amount to two hundred, after which, the proportion shall be so regulated by Congress, that there shall not be less than two hundred representatives, nor less than one representative for fifty thousand persons.

The House then adjourned for the day.

The next day, August 22, Tucker moved an amendment prohibiting Congress from imposing direct taxes until other revenues—including revenues from requisitions to states—should prove insufficient. After a long and uninteresting debate, the motion was defeated. A few members unsuccessfully moved other miscellaneous provisions. The House then referred their work to a committee consisting of Benson, Sherman, and Sedgwick to arrange the resolutions and put them in proper form to send to the Senate. On August 24, that committee's report (reprinted in the Appendix) was approved without debate.

The Senate

On August 25, the House resolution was transmitted to the Senate, which took up consideration of the matter on September 2. Unfortunately, the Senate sat in closed session until 1794, so no record of its debates exists. The *Sen-*

ate Journal, which contains a record of motions and votes, is the best record of Senate consideration of the bill of rights.

The Senate made few substantive changes. It altered the apportionment article, again changing the number of persons per representative. It rejected the language protecting conscientious objectors from having to serve in the military, the article prohibiting states from violating the most important rights, and the article requiring strict separation of powers in the national government.

Several unsuccessful motions in the Senate duplicated some of those proposed in the House: a motion to include a right to "instruct representatives" failed by a vote of fourteen to two, a motion to limit standing armies failed nine to six, and a motion to insert "expressly" into what became the Tenth Amendment failed by an unknown margin. The Senate also considered and rejected a miscellany of other amendments, including, among other things, general provisions that all power is derived from the people and should be exercised for their benefit, an oblique reference to the right to revolt against unjust governments, a two-thirds requirement for commercial treaties and navigation acts, limitations on the military, elimination of the power to establish inferior courts, limitations on the Supreme Court's jurisdiction, and a prohibition against congressional modification of election practices.

Not content to rely on the House's wording, the Senate altered the style of almost every article and combined various articles. This tinkering produced essentially the amendments that were ultimately contained in the Bill of Rights.

The most interesting aspect of the Senate's consideration of the proposed amendments was an attempt to alter what eventually became the establishment clause of the First Amendment. Several amendments were proposed and rejected when the Senate first considered the clause:

> The third article, as it passed the house, stands thus: "Congress shall make no law establishing religion, or prohibiting the free exercise thereof; *nor shall the rights of conscience be infringed.*" The first motion to amend this article was by striking out these words: "Religion, or prohibiting the free exercise thereof," and inserting these words: "One religious sect or society in preference to others." This motion was negatived. A motion for reconsideration then prevailed, and it was moved to strike out the third article altogether; but this motion was decided in the negative. An unsuccessful attempt was then made to adopt, as a substitute for the third article, the following: "Congress shall not make any law infringing the rights of conscience, or establishing any religious sect or society." The question was then taken on the adoption of the third article, as it came from the House of Representatives, when it was decided in the negative. Finally, the words, "Nor shall the rights of conscience be infringed," were stricken out; and, in this form, the article was agreed to.

When the Senate returned to the clause the next day, it amended the House's language to read: "Congress shall make no law establishing articles of faith, or a mode of worship, or prohibiting the free exercise of religion."

Conference Committee

A conference committee was immediately appointed to work out the differences between the House and Senate versions of the amendments. Madison,

Sherman, and Vining represented the House, and Ellsworth, Carroll and Paterson represented the Senate.

There is virtually no record of the proceedings of that committee. It arranged the amendments in the order they were eventually transmitted to the states: first the reapportionment amendment, then the legislative salaries amendment, then the ten amendments (in order) that became the Bill of Rights. The committee apparently resolved the differences between the House and Senate through various compromises reflected in the September 24 House debates and the *Senate Journal*. Those debates show that three changes were made. The reapportionment article was changed to limit the ultimate number of representatives to not more than one for every fifty thousand people. Criminal defendants were entitled to not only a speedy and public trial, but also one "by an impartial jury" in the district where the crime was committed.

Finally, the conference committee reached an agreement on what eventually became the First Amendment:

> Art. 3. Congress shall make no law respecting an establishment of religion, or prohibiting the free exercise thereof, or abridging the freedom of speech, or of the press, or the right of the people peaceably to assemble, and to petition the Government for a redress of grievances.

On October 2, 1789, the amendments were transmitted to the several states for ratification, pursuant to Article V. The first two articles, ultimately rejected, read as follows:

> ARTICLE I. After the first enumeration required by the first article of the Constitution, there shall be one Representative for every thirty thousand, until the number shall amount to one hundred, after which the proportion shall be so regulated by Congress, that there shall be not less than one hundred Representatives, nor less than one Representative for every forty thousand persons, until the number of Representatives shall amount to two hundred; after which the proportion shall be so regulated by Congress, that there shall not be less than two hundred Representatives, nor more than one Representative for every fifty thousand persons.
>
> ARTICLE II. No law varying the compensation for the services of the Senators and Representatives shall take effect, until an election of Representatives shall have intervened.

The remaining articles consisted of the text of the first ten amendments to the Constitution, and are reprinted in the Appendix.

STATE RATIFICATION

President Washington officially transmitted the twelve proposed amendments to the states on October 2, 1789. The state legislative history on ratification of the Bill of Rights is virtually nonexistent. Only a few states even have records of their final vote. Maryland apparently ratified the amendments unanimously, the New York lower house by a vote of fifty-two to five. None of the state legislatures kept any records of debates.

New Jersey, on November 20, 1789, was the first state to ratify the amendments. When Virginia, on December 15, 1791, became the eleventh state to ratify, the ratification of Articles III through XII was complete. The timing and results of the state ratifications are presented in Table 8.1.

TABLE 8.1   **State Ratification of the Bill of Rights**

State	Date of Action	Ratified	Rejected
New Jersey	November 20, 1789	I, III-XII	II
Maryland	December 19, 1789	I-XII	
North Carolina	December 22, 1789	I-XII	
South Carolina	January 19, 1790	I-XII	
New Hampshire	January 25, 1790	I, III-XII	II
Delaware	January 28, 1790	II-XII	I
New York	February 24, 1790*	I, III-XII	II
Pennsylvania	March 10, 1790	III-XII	I, II
Rhode Island	June 7, 1790	I, III-XII	II
Vermont	November 3, 1791	I-XII	
Virginia	November 3, 1791 December 15, 1791	I II-XII	
Massachusetts	March 2, 1939**	III-XII	I, II
Georgia	March 18, 1939	III-XII	I, II
Connecticut	April 19, 1939	III-XII	I, II

*The New York Assembly voted its approval on February 22, and the New York Senate on February 24. On February 27, the New York Council of Revision, headed by Governor Clinton, signified its assent to the actions of the legislature. It is a nice constitutional question whether New York's ratification was completed on February 24 or 27, since Article V of the United States Constitution provides that amendments become part of the Constitution when ratified by *"the Legislatures* of three fourths of the several States." Different sources list different dates for New York's ratification.

**The Massachusetts senate voted in favor of Articles III–XII on January 29, 1790, and the house in favor of Articles III–XI on February 2, 1790. However, according to a letter from Christopher Gore of Boston to Secretary of State Jefferson (August 18, 1791), the Massachusetts legislature never formally enacted a bill signifying assent. As with the case of New York, this raises the question whether Massachusetts' ratification should have been considered completed on February 2, 1790.

Topics for Discussion

1. What evidence can you find in the debates that members of Congress shared the view of natural rights described in the first section of this chapter? That they disagreed with it?

2. Notice that the House spent more time debating whether to consider a bill of rights and how to do it than they spent on the proposed amendments themselves. In enacting a proposed bill of rights, what did most members of Congress think they were doing? Was it an important task? If not, why did they engage in it? How could members of Congress believe that protecting individual rights was unimportant? Does their view of the nature of rights help explain their lackadaisical attitude?

3. The Ninth Amendment, which says that rights not enumerated are not "disparaged or denied," is so rarely used that it has been labeled "The Forgotten Amendment." No modern Supreme Court case has relied on it to support any holding, although Justice Goldberg did rely on it in his concurring opinion in *Griswold v. Connecticut*, 381 U.S. 479, 85 S.Ct. 1678, 14 L.Ed.2d 510 (1965), invalidating restrictions on the use of contraceptives. What do you think the Ninth Amendment means? Look at Madison's original explanation of it. Consider the eighteenth-century view of natural rights. Does this help explain its meaning, and why it hasn't been used more often? In what circumstances might the Court find the Ninth Amendment useful?

4. There is great dispute about the meaning of the Establishment Clause of the First Amendment, which prohibits Congress from enacting any law "respecting an establishment of religion." Some interpreters argue that the clause prohibits any government support of religion, even where that support is even-handed among many religions. Others suggest that the clause prohibits only discrimination among religions, but that it permits the government to offer financial and other support to all religions equally. Which interpretation is supported by the debates in the House? In the Senate? The Conference Committee reports?

5. Choose one amendment and follow it through all its permutations. How did it change? What reasons, if any, were given for the changes? What significance do you attribute to the specific language of the amendment as ultimately adopted? How helpful are the debates to your interpretation of the amendment?

6. What role did the members of Congress (especially Madison) seem to envision for the judiciary? Is this role consistent with Madison's earlier expressed views?

7. If amendments had in fact been interlineated in the Constitution, rather than appended to the end of it, what difference might that have made? Is it a purely technical dispute? Did the Congress think so?

FOOTNOTES

1. 1 *Journals of the Continental Congress* 107 (October 1774).

2. Madison's notes report that New Hampshire voted against, but the Convention Journal recorded an affirmative vote by New Hampshire.

3. Pennsylvania Ratifying Convention (October 28, 1787), in 2 *The Debates in the Several State Conventions on the Adoption of the Federal Constitution* 436 (Jonathan Elliot ed. 1891) [hereinafter Elliot].

4. North Carolina Ratifying Convention (July 29, 1788), 4 Elliot at 167.

5. Virginia Ratifying Convention (June 17, 1788), 3 Elliot at 464-65.

6. The members of the committee were Nicholas Gilman of New Hampshire, Benjamin Goodhue of Massachusetts, Roger Sherman of Connecticut, Egbert Benson of New York, Elias Boudinot of New Jersey, George Clymer of Pennsylvania, John Vining of Delaware, George Gale of Maryland, James Madison of Virginia, Aedanus Burke of South Carolina, and Abraham Baldwin of Georgia.

PART TWO

The Reconstruction Amendments: 1865-1873

INTRODUCTION TO PART TWO

With the ratification of the first ten amendments, the immediate problems of the new Constitution were remedied, and the federal government returned to ordinary politics. Inferior federal tribunals were established, commercial regulations enacted, cabinet officers selected, money minted, taxes imposed, and the new nation began increasing in size and prestige. This untroubled state of affairs did not last long, however.

In 1793, the Supreme Court decided a case that sent the nation into an uproar. Recall the debates during ratification over whether the Article III grant of federal jurisdiction in cases ''between a state and citizens of another state'' would allow an individual to sue a state in federal court. In 1792, a South Carolina citizen brought a federal suit against the state of Georgia, demanding payment for war supplies he had sold the state during the Revolution. In February 1793, in *Chisholm v. Georgia*, 2 U.S. (2 Dall.) 419, 1 L.Ed. 440 (1793), the Supreme Court held that the suit was permissible. Many of those who had been prominent delegates to the federal and state conventions participated in the decision. Edmund Randolph, the United States attorney general, served as counsel for the South Carolina plaintiff. James Wilson, James Iredell, and John Blair were all Supreme Court justices. Wilson and Blair each wrote an opinion upholding the right to sue; Iredell dissented, although the grounds for his dissent are somewhat ambiguous.

The negative public reaction was immediate and almost universal. The day after the Court's decision, a constitutional amendment to overturn *Chisholm* was introduced in the House. A similar amendment was introduced in the Senate the next day. As eventually ratified by the states, the amendment read: ''The Judicial power of the United States shall not be construed to extend to any suit in law or equity, commenced or prosecuted against one of the United States by citizens of another State, or by citizens or subjects of any foreign State.''[1]

The Senate approved the amendment within a year, and the House soon followed. By February of 1795 (two years after *Chisholm*), the necessary twelve states had ratified the Eleventh Amendment. Because some states delayed notifying the federal government of ratification, however, the amendment did not officially become part of the Constitution until 1798. A significant body of law has since developed interpreting the Eleventh Amendment, but most suits against states and their agents are still barred.

Chisholm himself never benefited from his suit. Although the Court entered a judgment in his favor, he never tried to collect. One reason might have been a bill passed by the Georgia House of Representatives in November 1793. It provided that any person attempting to execute the judgment in *Chisholm v. Georgia* would be declared "guilty of felony and shall suffer death, without benefit of clergy, by being hanged."

Only a few years passed before another crisis necessitated amending the Constitution again. Unforeseen events of the presidential election of 1800 led to the Twelfth Amendment, which changed slightly the electoral college system. In that election, Thomas Jefferson and Aaron Burr ran on the Republican ticket, handily defeating Federalist incumbent John Adams. It is probable (though Burr denied it the rest of his life) that the Republican party intended Jefferson—who was the incumbent vice president—to be president, and Burr to be vice president.

When it came time for the electors to cast their two ballots, as specified in Article II, section 1, the system did not work as expected. Unable to foresee the development of political parties, and thus of party tickets, the authors of the Constitution had inadvertently created a system in which party-affiliated electors would all vote for the same two candidates. Each Republican elector in 1800 thus cast one vote for Jefferson and one for Burr, resulting in a tie vote. The election went to the House of Representatives, where 36 ballots were taken to resolve the deadlock.

Congress immediately began considering ways to avoid the problem before the next presidential election. In December 1803, it proposed what became the Twelfth Amendment, which provided that the electors "shall name in their ballots the person voted for as President, and in distinct ballots the person voted for as Vice-President." Within three weeks, the first state (North Carolina) had ratified the amendment; ratification was completed by June 1804.

After these two amendments, the Constitution remained unchanged for almost half a century. No further amendments were made until after the Civil War. During the Constitution's first half-century, however, three major Supreme Court cases significantly influenced its actual operation.

The election of 1800, in which Republicans swept Federalists out of the Congress and the presidency, created more than the electoral problem noted above. In March 1801, just days before the newly elected Republicans were to take office, the outgoing Federalist Congress and President Adams tried to extend Federalist influence by creating new judicial positions and appointing Federalists to those positions. Some judges were in fact appointed just before midnight on March 3, the last day of the Adams administration. The lame duck judicial commissions were hurriedly signed, sealed, and delivered, but in the last-minute rush, a few commissions remained undelivered when Jefferson took office on March 4.

President Jefferson and his new secretary of state, James Madison, refused to deliver the remaining commissions. Some of the disappointed appointees, including one William Marbury (who had been named as a justice of the peace for the District of Columbia), sued Madison in the Supreme Court for delivery of their commissions. Madison refused to respond, and there was speculation that if the Supreme Court ordered delivery of the commissions, Jefferson and Madison would ignore the order. A constitutional crisis seemed imminent.

In the 1803 decision of *Marbury v. Madison*, 5 U.S. (1 Cranch) 137, 2 L.Ed. 60 (1803), the Supreme Court simultaneously averted a constitutional crisis and inserted a permanent fixture in our constitutional system. The chief justice, John Marshall, was a Virginia Federalist who had been appointed by Adams. Marshall was a distant cousin and a political and personal enemy of President Jefferson. During the last days of the Adams administration, Marshall had also been Adams's acting secretary of state (while simultaneously serving as chief justice). He had been responsible for failing to deliver the last-minute commissions.

Despite his personal involvement in the case, Marshall wrote the opinion for a unanimous court. In it, he declared that Marbury was entitled to his commission, but that bringing suit in the Supreme Court was not a constitutionally authorized way of obtaining it. His opinion thus chastised Jefferson and Madison while still avoiding issuance of an order that might be ignored. In addition, *Marbury* is the first Supreme Court opinion explicitly asserting the power of judicial review: the power to strike down federal statutes that violate the Constitution. A federal statute had authorized suits like Marbury's to be brought in the Supreme Court, but Marshall interpreted Article III as allowing only a few specified types of suits to begin in the Supreme Court. Marshall thus held the statute unconstitutional. As you will recall, state courts had exercised judicial review over state statutes prior to 1787, and the delegates to the federal convention had assumed that federal courts would have the same power. It was not until *Marbury*, however, that the Supreme Court explicitly endorsed this assumption.[2] Since that time, federal courts have routinely examined the constitutionality of federal statutes, and have invalidated many.

The next development was the assertion of federal power to review the constitutionality of *state* statutes. Again, a complicated procedural tangle led to a significant Supreme Court case. This time, the dispute was over land. Lord Fairfax, a British subject who died in 1781, willed some of his vast northern Virginia land holdings to another British citizen, Denny Martin, who in turn left the property to his American brother, Thomas Martin. The elder Martin's year of death was not recorded (which caused some of the dispute). The state of Virginia claimed that it owned the land, having confiscated it from Fairfax during the Revolution because he was a British loyalist. Virginia then granted the land to David Hunter, a Virginian. Two treaties between the United States and Great Britain also influenced the question; the Peace Treaty of 1783 and the Jay Treaty of 1794 both provided that land owned by British citizens would no longer be confiscated.

The lawsuit between Hunter and Martin to determine who owned the land began in the Virginia state courts and first reached the United States Supreme Court in 1813. The Supreme Court, reversing the Virginia court, held that the land had not been properly confiscated prior to the 1783 treaty. It thus ruled that Virginia's attempted confiscation was in violation of the treaty. Under the Supremacy Clause of the Constitution, the treaty was paramount to the Virginia confiscation statute, so Martin owned the land.

Virginians were outraged by the ruling, and Virginia's highest court refused to obey the mandate of the United States Supreme Court. It reaffirmed its prior ruling that Hunter owned the land and held that the Supreme Court had no authority to rule on the actions of states or to review the decisions of state courts.

Martin took his case back to the Supreme Court, and in 1816 that Court decided *Martin v. Hunter's Lessee*, 14 U.S. (1 Wheat.) 304, 4 L.Ed. 97 (1816). Justice Story, writing for the Court, held that the Supreme Court *did* have the authority to review state court decisions, and to determine whether state statutes violated federal law (including the federal Constitution as well as federal statutes and treaties). That ruling has remained undisturbed, and federal courts in fact invalidate many more state statutes than federal statutes.

The final major Supreme Court case of that era involved the power of Congress, rather than the power of the Supreme Court. In 1816, Congress chartered the Second Bank of the United States. Congress' power to establish a national bank had been hotly debated since 1791. Parties to the controversy included many notable politicians: Jefferson was opposed, Hamilton was in favor, and Washington and Madison both wavered. The significant opposition to the First Bank led to a hiatus between its expiration in 1811 and establishment of the Second Bank in 1816. After the Second Bank was chartered, the opposition grew more fierce, in part because of the bank's mismanagement and fiscal irresponsibility.

One of the most active and controversial branches of the bank was in Baltimore. In April 1818, the Maryland legislature adopted an annual fifteen thousand dollar minimum tax on all banks not chartered by the state legislature itself. Penalties were to be assessed personally against bank officers, and ranged up to five hundred dollars for each bank note issued. Payment of either the tax or the penalties would have bankrupted the Baltimore branch, and might have brought down the whole bank.

When the Baltimore branch refused to pay the tax, Maryland sued the cashier of the Baltimore branch, James McCulloch, for the statutory penalties. McCulloch was not only the chief Baltimore bank officer, he was also the bank's main legislative lobbyist in Washington. He was also, as it later turned out, embezzling from it on a massive scale. Rumors of his misconduct were circulating as early as 1818, although he was not removed from office until after the Supreme Court decided the case.

After the Maryland trial and appellate courts decided against McCulloch, he took the case to the United States Supreme Court. The oral arguments took nine days. Daniel Webster was one of the lawyers for the bank, and Maryland's attorney general, Luther Martin, was lead counsel for Maryland. It has been rumored that Martin was drunk when he made his two-day-long argument. If he was, it apparently did not affect his acuity: he closed his argument by reading from John Marshall's own speeches in the Virginia ratifying convention (which are reprinted in chapter 7).

Three days after the oral arguments, Chief Justice Marshall delivered the unanimous decision of the Supreme Court in *McCulloch v. Maryland*, 17 U.S. (4 Wheat.) 316, 4 L.Ed. 579 (1819), upholding the validity of the second Bank and invalidating the tax. In an eloquent opinion, Marshall relied on principles of general reasoning, as well as on the necessary and proper clause of Article I, section 8, to find that the Constitution permitted Congress to exercise broad implied powers. In a phrase still repeated and applied in cases today, he found few limits on Congressional power:

> Let the end be legitimate, let it be within the scope of the constitution, and all means which are appropriate, which are plainly adapted to that end, which are not prohibited, but consist with the letter and spirit of the constitution, are constitutional.

Interpreting the Constitution any less expansively, he said, would turn the document into "a splendid bauble."

There was an immediate harsh reaction of Anti-Federalists (and others), based more on the sweeping breadth of Marshall's language than on opposition to the holding on the bank. Virginia Judge Spencer Roane, who had been one of the defiant judges involved in the controversy over *Hunter's Lessee*, wrote a series of pseudonymous essays in the Richmond *Enquirer*, attacking Marshall and the *McCulloch* decision. Marshall responded in the Alexandria Gazette, writing under the pseudonym "A Friend of the Constitution."[3] Marshall's broad reading of congressional powers eventually won. With the exception of a brief period from 1887 to 1937, there have been few objects beyond the reach of congressional regulation.

With the basic framework of the Constitution now in place and operating smoothly, the nation began focusing attention on the one significant issue the framers had so carefully avoided. The slavery question was repeatedly brought back on the national agenda by events relating to the country's western expansion. In 1819, controversy erupted over the admission of Missouri to the union. The result was a compromise: slavery would be allowed only south of the line forming Missouri's southern border. The annexation of Texas, and the Mexican war, brought the slavery issue back to the political forefront. In the course of the war, a congressional debate on slavery had erupted over the Wilmot Proviso. This amendment to an appropriations bill by Representative David Wilmot would have banned slavery in any territory that might be acquired from Mexico. Although it never passed, the Wilmot Proviso reopened the slavery issue in national politics.

For the next ten years, the nation was plagued by disputes over the status of slavery in the territories. The 1850 Compromise engineered by Henry Clay and Daniel Webster seemed for a time to quiet the dispute by admitting California as a free state, establishing territorial governments in the rest of the territory acquired from Mexico, taking over the public debt of Texas, and enacting the Fugitive Slave Law. But, as a by-product of the plans to build a transcontinental railroad, Stephen Douglas proposed the Kansas-Nebraska Act, which allowed slavery in an area in which it had been prohibited under the earlier Missouri Compromise of 1820. This statute exploded the relative calm that had prevailed after the 1850 Compromise. The resulting turmoil earned the territory the nickname "Bleeding Kansas" and also polarized Congress.

Enforcement of the fugitive slave laws encountered increasingly violent Northern resistance. As antislavery forces became more powerful in the North, pro-slavery forces in the South became more extreme, advocating slavery in the territories, annexation of new territory in Latin America, and reopening the slave trade. By the end of the 1850s, the slavery issue had seemingly passed any hope of compromise, and talk of secession was rampant. The Supreme Court had not helped the situation with its 1857 *Dred Scott* decision, which held that blacks could never become citizens and that Congress lacked any power to ban slavery in the territories.[4]

The same period was also marked by party realignment. The Whigs collapsed as a viable political party; the Democrats suffered schisms, such as the Barnburner faction; and the Know-Nothing Party emerged temporarily as a powerful political force. In 1848, a coalition of antislavery groups formed the Free Soil Party, in some respects a precursor of the Republican Party. In 1856, after much shifting of coalitions and political infighting, the Republican Party held its first national convention. In 1860, following a four-way contest between the Republicans, the Northern Democrats, the Southern Democrats, and the short-lived Constitutional Union Party, Abraham Lincoln was elected president with only a plurality of the national popular vote but a majority in the electoral college. Except for Virginia, he did not receive a single popular vote in any of the states that ultimately joined the Confederacy. By the end of the following month, a South Carolina state convention had voted to secede, and the stage was set for civil war.[5]

FOOTNOTES

1. The original proposal omitted the words "be construed," which were added in the course of congressional debate.

2. In an earlier case, the Supreme Court had reviewed a federal statute and found it constitutional; there was no discussion of the power itself. *Hylton v. U.S.*, 3 U.S. (3 Dall.) 171, 1 L.Ed. 556 (1796). In another early case, the Supreme Court issued a judgment that might have rested on a finding that a federal statute was unconstitutional, but the case was unreported and no reason for the judgment was given. *U.S. v. Yale Todd* (1794), unreported but described in *U.S. v. Ferreira*, 54 U.S. 40, 52, 14 L.Ed. 40 (1851).

3. Marshall's essays are reprinted in *John Marshall's Defense of McCulloch v. Maryland* (Gerald Gunther ed. 1969).

4. For a good introduction to the history of this period, see Donald Potter, *Impending Crisis* (1976).

5. On the origins and rise of the Republican Party, see William Gienapp, *The Origins of the Republican Party, 1852-1856* (1987); Eric Foner, *Free Soil, Free Labor, Free Men: The Ideology of the Republican Party* (1970).

CHAPTER NINE

The Ideological Origins of the Reconstruction Amendments

This part of the book focuses on the three amendments adopted during the Reconstruction period after the Civil War: the Thirteenth Amendment, abolishing slavery; the Fourteenth Amendment, guaranteeing due process and equal protection; and the Fifteenth Amendment, giving blacks the right to vote. Together, these amendments transformed the constitutional structure. As a famous editorial in the *Nation* argued at the centennial of the Constitution, the constitutional system took its final form only after the Civil War.[1] In seeking to understand these key amendments, a natural starting point is to examine the ideas the Republicans brought with them to power in 1861. This chapter, by synthesizing the work of recent historians, places the amendments in their intellectual context.

THE ANTISLAVERY REPUBLICANS AND THEIR PLATFORM

When it assumed power, the Republican party's platform included provisions on the federal budget, naturalization, a Pacific railroad, and other matters having little relation to constitutional issues. These provisions were undoubtedly more important than the slavery problem to many supporters. On the slavery issue itself, there was some divergence of opinion within the party. As we shall see in later chapters, the Reconstruction amendments were largely the product of moderate and radical Republicans, many of whom had taken an active role in the antislavery movement of the 1850s. Consequently, our focus will be on this antislavery wing of the pre-War Republican party.

The most important members of this group were probably Charles Sumner, William Seward (who as secretary of state later acquired Alaska from Russia), and Salmon Chase (later chief justice). Other important figures included Henry Wilson, Ben Wade, Charles Adams, Joshua Giddings, and John Hale. Toward the end of the decade, new leaders such as Lincoln began to emerge.

253

By and large, unlike the major figures in the American Revolution and Constitutional Convention, these have not become household names. However, like the Revolutionary patriots and the Convention delegates, these men transformed American society. To help you keep track of the major figures in the pre-War and Reconstruction periods, we have included a biographical dictionary in the Appendix.

Despite their shared antislavery sentiments, members of this group had divergent views. Some began their careers as Democrats; others were former Whigs. They engaged in prolonged feuds and political battles among themselves. Giddings and Chase, for instance, conducted a lengthy duel for control of the Ohio antislavery movement; Wilson, Sumner, and Adams in Massachusetts shifted coalitions with bewildering frequency.

Nevertheless, the antislavery leadership was connected by background as well as by ideological ties. Many had worked together in the Free Soil party before becoming Republicans. Lincoln, when he was in Congress, lived at the same rooming house as Giddings; Lincoln's law partner corresponded with Sumner and others. Giddings was also a close friend of Sumner, who in turn looked to John Quincy Adams as a father figure. Sumner's law office was a meeting place for Charles Francis Adams and Henry Wilson; Sumner also carried on a "confidential correspondence" with Chase and Hale. Seward and Adams were close personal friends. Because antislavery leaders were ostracized by Southern-dominated Washington society, they were driven together socially, thus strengthening their ties.

A graphic example of Southern hostility toward the antislavery leaders is provided by a brutal assault on Senator Charles Sumner on the Senate floor. In retaliation for some offensive remarks about a Southern Senator, his nephew, Representative Preston Brooks, beat Sumner with a cane while Sumner struggled to get up from the desk where he had been sitting. Eventually Sumner wrenched loose the desk, which had been screwed to the floor. Southerners generally approved of this attack, while Northerners were shocked. After the beating, Cameron, Wade, and Chandler agreed to use deadly force if necessary to repel attacks. They are said to have stalked the halls of Congress with handguns bulging under their coats (an ominous harbinger of the Civil War).

The Republican antislavery leaders shared a basic attitude toward slavery and belonged to a fairly well-defined social group. They were, moreover, seen by others as a cohesive group, even a conspiracy. Hence, in enumerating the views of this group, we are doing more than collating statements by unconnected individuals.

Before considering their views in detail, two additional points must be made. First, despite what sometimes sounds to modern ears as naive language, these men were far from unsophisticated idealists. Lincoln, it is often forgotten, was a shrewd and highly successful railroad lawyer. Seward has been called the ablest constitutional law scholar of the period. Wilson was a self-educated cobbler who became a successful manufacturer, senator, and later a historian. Charles Adams, the son of one president and grandson of another, was intimately familiar with American history and politics. Chase was a leading lawyer before becoming governor of Ohio. Sumner was a close friend of Justice Story, wrote a number of law review articles, and was a lecturer at Harvard Law School. Wade, at one time a law partner of Giddings, was a leading Ohio judge. These were not simply starry-eyed dreamers.

A second point to keep in mind is that their statements were widely distributed among the public. Interest in politics was high, with voter turnouts as high as eighty-four percent of qualified voters. The public followed Senate debates closely. In 1857 to 1858 alone, free state senators distributed 680,000 copies of their speeches. Seward's famous "Higher Law" speech was distributed to 100,000 people. In the 1860 campaign, the Republican party issued large editions of the Lincoln-Douglas debates in order to publicize Lincoln's views. These speeches would not have been circulated so heavily unless politicians were convinced that they would appeal to large segments of the public. Antislavery views were also popularized at public rallies. For instance, Charles Francis Adams addressed a Philadelphia rally that comprised nearly a majority of the city's voters. The antislavery leaders were also highly successful in getting their views incorporated into early Republican state platforms. Much of their ideology was represented in the 1856 and 1860 national platforms. When the North elected Lincoln in 1860, it could hardly have been ignorant of his views and those of many of his party's leaders on the crucial issue of slavery.

The political program that unified this group can be simply stated. They favored a prohibition on the extension of slavery into new territories, but opposed direct attempts at abolition in the South. Both parts of this program were important. Lincoln considered the nonextension principle so important that he rejected all compromises on this issue proposed to avoid civil war. On the other hand, many antislavery Republicans like Adams were willing to support the proposed thirteenth amendment, which would have permanently protected existing slave states from federal interference. That amendment would have banned any federal interference with slavery in the states, and would itself have been unamendable. This position can be best labeled "anti-extensionism."

Ironically, the anti-extensionists favored prohibiting slavery in the territories, where there were few slaves, but opposed intervention in the South, where there were millions. To understand this peculiar position, we must consider in some detail the reasons for their opposition to extension, their stress on the extension issue, and their opposition to intervention in the South.

We may begin by considering the reasons for Northern opposition to the expansion of slavery. Although the reasons were varied, four were of particular significance: racism, economics, the slave-power theory, and moral objections to slavery.

There is no doubt that racism was widespread in the North. For many, the issue was not so much an objection to slavery as a desire to keep all blacks out of the territories. Moreover, many Republicans repeatedly found it necessary to reaffirm publicly their disinclination toward miscegenation and their belief in white supremacy. Savvy politicians like Lincoln were careful not to offend racist audiences. This was a constant theme in the Lincoln-Douglas debates, most notably in the Charleston, Illinois, debate, where Lincoln denied being "in favor of bringing about in any way the social and political equality of the white and black races."[2] He also stressed that simply because he wanted to free black women from slavery didn't mean he wanted to marry one.

Nevertheless, it is important not to overstate the influence of racism on the Republican leadership. Lincoln himself stressed his view that blacks were equally entitled to fundamental economic and legal rights, if not equal social status. Men such as Adams, Hale, Wilson, Seward, and Chase vigorously supported black rights in the North. The antislavery faction used its political leverage in Ohio to repeal the harsher provisions of the state's black code, and strong Republican support existed for suffrage. In Massachusetts, a ban on racial intermarriage was repealed. Stevens went so far as to direct that he be buried in a black cemetery. Prominent antislavery Republicans, including John Bingham, objected strongly to the exclusion of free blacks from homestead rights in Oregon. While a racist desire to reserve the territories for whites may have played a primary role with the rank-and-file, it was seemingly a secondary influence on the Republican antislavery leadership.

Apart from racism, there was great concern about the economic and political effects of slavery on whites. Northern antislavery writers portrayed the South as an economically backward area. Echoing Gouverneur Morris's stirring "curse of Heaven" speech, in which he described the "desert increasing" as one traveled southward, the antislavery writers compared run-down conditions in Kentucky with the prosperous New England economy and blamed the difference on slavery. They also compared ambitious white workers of the North with their less educated and allegedly less motivated counterparts in the South, and concluded that slavery caused stagnation in working class whites. They were anxious to shield the promising new territories of the West from this economic blight. In short, Republicans accused slavery of perhaps the greatest of all nineteenth-century sins: opposition to progress. Antislavery beliefs were reinforced by visions of manifest destiny and of America's role as a world leader.

Besides its adverse economic effects on whites, slavery was also thought to pose a political threat to the freedom of whites. As Thaddeus Stevens put it, "laws which oppress the black man, and deprive him of all safeguards of liberty, will eventually enslave the white man."[3] Republicans commonly believed that the South was controlled by a slave-owning oligarchy known as the slavocracy or the slave power, whose members were morally corrupted by their absolute power over their slaves. Through its control of the Democratic Party, its representation in the Senate, and its over-representation in the House under the three-fifths rule, the slave power had supposedly seized control of the country. In the Lincoln-Douglas debates, for example, Lincoln portrayed Douglas as a member of a conspiratorial Southern plot to extend slavery nationwide.

Like conspiracy theories in other periods of the nation's history, the slave power theory held that the hour was late and that only immediate action could halt the extinction of the nation's freedom. This view of the aggressive nature of slavery was reinforced by a number of Southern actions: assaults on free speech rights (discussed later in this chapter), demands for affirmative protection of slavery in the territories, attempts to annex Cuba or other parts of Latin America as new slave states, the *Dred Scott* decision, and the Kansas-Nebraska bill. Lincoln predicted a "second Dred Scott" decision that would extend slavery nationwide.

This concern about the corrupting effect of slavery on the nation's economic and political life is reminiscent of eighteenth-century "republicanism." It also resembles the republican stress on economic independence and self-discipline as the foundation of a republican society, though the pre-Civil War Republicans tended to stress the self-reliant working man at least as much as the yeoman farmer.[4] But antislavery supporters may have been somewhat more oriented toward individualism than the earlier republicans; the abolitionists have often been viewed as successors of the Federalist Party.[5] As you read the debates in the next three chapters, look for Lockean and republican elements, as well as more modern strains of thought such as utilitarianism.

A final reason for opposing the expansion of slavery was simply moral opposition to slavery. For many Republicans, this opposition was religiously based. Hale viewed slavery as a sin, forbidden by the word of God. On the other hand, he was sure that aiding escaped slaves, despite its unlawfulness, could not be seen as a sin by God. Giddings referred to opponents of the Republicans as "infidels." He had turned to antislavery after a quasi-religious personal crisis. Chase joined him in proclaiming that the "cause of human freedom was the cause of God." Others believed that slavery was prohibited by the Bible because God gave Adam dominion over the beasts, but not over his fellow men. These religious views on slavery were shared by many Northern clergy. As we will see later, many of the antislavery leaders also based their views on the Declaration of Independence, with its stress on inalienable rights and inherent equality. This moral opposition to slavery was clearly an important factor in motivating antislavery Republicans. Lincoln, for example, proclaimed this moral stance to be the primary difference between himself and Douglas.

Given this moral position, why did the antislavery Republicans focus their energy on the seemingly unimportant question of slavery in the territories? There are two parts to the answer: they thought the territorial issue was important, and they thought slavery in the states was beyond their reach.

They believed the territorial issue was important partly for symbolic reasons, but they were also seriously concerned that slavery might expand westward. It had taken hold in Missouri and might do so elsewhere in the Great Plains. If so, the result might be the ultimate economic ruin of this vital area. Moreover, the South had shown interest in expanding into Latin America and the Caribbean, where the plantation system was well-suited to slavery. Historians today disagree about how seriously these threats should have been taken, but they may well have seemed real at the time.

The Republicans also believed that if slavery was confined, it would die. After all, slave-owners were only a small portion of the Southern population. Poor Southerners, Republicans believed, had to be deceived into accepting a system that was in many ways against their interests, since it required them to compete against unpaid labor. If diminishing political power in the national arena weakened the slavocracy's power in the South, the mail would be opened to antislavery literature that would soon enlighten poor whites. Federal patronage might help develop an opposition party in the South. Equally important, without room to expand the South would lack an outlet for its excess population of slaves. The growing population would make slavery increasingly unprofitable. Meanwhile, national recognition of the immorality of slavery would undermine the ideology essential to the maintenance of slavery. Thus, as Lincoln said, confining slavery would cause its eventual extinction. Sumner put it somewhat more graphically: slavery would die "as a poisoned rat dies of rage in its hole."[6] Though many were more discreet, Seward spoke for others when he proclaimed that slavery "can and must be abolished, and you and I can and must do it."[7]

The antislavery Republicans agreed with the abolitionists' ultimate goal, the elimination of slavery. Some historians, however, such as tenBroek, have tended to confuse the antislavery and abolitionist factions. It is true that contacts existed between the two groups, but most Republicans were strongly opposed to the abolitionists and went to great lengths to disassociate themselves from that position. Unlike radical abolitionists such as Garrison, the Republicans were unwilling to condemn the Constitution as an "agreement with hell," a pro-slavery document. They rejected abolitionist proposals such as secession by the North and personal withdrawal from involvement with existing government. Indeed, practical politicians could find little to commend in a man like Garrison, who refused to hold any governmental office because the presence of the war power in the Constitution violated his pacifist beliefs.

Antislavery Republicans also rejected the view of some abolitionists that the Constitution prohibited slavery in the states. This view was repudiated as simple crankism by men like Hale. Instead, most antislavery Republicans took the entirely realistic view that the Constitution left decisions about slavery to the states. Men like Lincoln believed they were giving away nothing by pledging not to use federal power to abolish slavery in the South, for they believed the federal government lacked this power anyway. They were willing neither to abandon the Constitution nor to distort its meaning. Their stress on states' rights cut them off from their abolitionist friends. In short, they were against slavery, but would consider only means to abolish it consistent with their perception of the existing constitutional scheme. As Owen Lovejoy said, being against monarchy didn't mean he favored "a naval armament to dethrone Queen Victoria."[8] Ultimately, of course, events were to force their hands.

THE INTELLECTUAL FRAMEWORK: NATURAL LAW
AND THE LAW OF NATIONS

The antislavery Republicans needed a framework to support their view that slavery was an immoral aberration from the normal legal order, yet one that would leave untouched the legality of slavery where established by state law. Such an intellectual framework had to satisfy several requirements. It had to provide a point of moral reference outside the status quo from which they could assess the morality of slavery, yet leave unchallenged the right of the South to remain free of Northern interference within the federalist system. The antislavery Republicans were professional politicians rather than original thinkers and would not have been capable of inventing this framework. None of them had the intellectual powers of a Jefferson or Madison. Furthermore, like other reformers in our history, they were anxious to portray themselves as guardians of the original American tradition, not as inventors of a novel ideology.

Fortunately, a system of thought was at hand that satisfied all these requirements. The antislavery Republicans found what they needed in the natural law theories that had formed part of the ideological basis for the American Revolution.

Of the natural law writers of the Enlightenment, Locke is the best remembered today. Since we have already discussed his views in chapter 1, we will just briefly summarize them here. His *Second Treatise* opens with a discussion of the state of nature, in which men are free from all government. In this state of nature, men are subject to certain natural duties and possess certain natural rights. Among these natural rights are the right to continued life and the right to whatever property is created by one's own labor. All men are equal in the sense of having an equal right to this natural freedom. In the state of nature, each man has the power to punish transgressions of natural law by others. Unfortunately, this power cannot be effectively exercised by unorganized individuals. So, political society is formed when men delegate their enforcement powers to a central authority by means of a social compact. This authority has only the power it is granted through this delegation or compact, that is, the power to protect men in their natural rights. "[T]he law of nature stands as an eternal rule to all men, legislators as well as others."[9] If the government should exceed these powers and turn against the people, nothing remains but an "appeal to Heaven," i.e., revolution. The people must be the ultimate judges of whether the compact is violated.

Just as it provided an almost perfect justification for the Revolution, Lockean theory was remarkably congruent with Republican ideology. Locke's labor theory of property accorded well with the Republican stress on free labor in the territories and their generally conservative views on the right to property. Except for free trade, Republican views on many economic matters have shown remarkable continuity from Abraham Lincoln to Ronald Reagan. More importantly, although Locke tolerated slavery under very limited circumstances, his theories provided powerful arguments against it. First, and perhaps most fundamentally, ownership of one person by another is inconsistent with their basic human equality. Second, the slave's natural right to life was allegedly not protected under slavery. Many Republicans believed that slaves were at the mercy of their owners. Third, slaves were denied their natural right to property in the fruit of their own labor. Fourth, slaves were excluded from the social compact.

Although they have been largely forgotten today, three other writers of the natural law school were highly influential in eighteenth- and early nineteenth-century America. These were Pufendorf, Vattel, and Burlamaqui. As his major modern commentator says, "Samuel Pufendorf is known to American students—when he is known at all—as an obscure German with a funny name who followed Grotius in the early development of international law."[10] Nevertheless, despite having an admittedly funny name, he was a highly influential figure. His natural law system stressed the social nature of human beings and their duty to protect each other's welfare. Like Locke, he also stressed human equality and the compact theory of government.

Burlamaqui's theory shared the same theological foundation underlying Locke's work. In his view, since God gave men life and the desire for happiness, he must have willed these as their goals, thereby imposing on others the duty not to deprive them of these rights. Like Pufendorf and Locke, Burlamaqui adopted a compact theory of government under which government acts in excess of the granted power were invalid.

Vattel's work mainly involved international law but contained some important observations on natural law. He postulated that the object of civil society

is to procure the happiness of its citizens by assuring them peaceful possession of their property, justice, and mutual defense. Hence, a nation is obliged
to preserve its members and cannot override their natural right to self-
defense. If the sovereign violates fundamental rights, the nation as a whole
can withdraw its obedience. Even individuals have a right to resist in cases of
extreme injustice, for self-preservation is not only a right, but an obligation
imposed by nature.

These early continental natural law theorists created two distinct but linked
lines of "higher law" thought. One was the American adoption of natural law
and social compact theories of government discussed in chapter 1. The other
was the "law of nations," a set of legal norms governing the rights and duties
of nations. Both lines of thought persisted into the nineteenth century and
became part of antislavery Republican ideology.

The law of nations has no exact counterpart today. It was a blend of what
we would now call public international law, political theory, conflicts of law,
and commercial law. The law of nations was linked with natural law primarily
by the idea that nations have no common sovereign and therefore are in a
state of nature with respect to one another. According to Kent, the law of nations derived from "principles of right reason, the same views of the nature
and constitution of man, and the same sanction of Divine revelation, as those
from which the science of morality is deduced."[11] He added that one element
of the law of nations was the "general principles of right and justice, equally
suitable to the government of individuals in a state of natural equality, and to
the relations and conduct of nations[.]"[12]

The idea of an unwritten international law was very much in tune with the
thinking of the legal community in the nineteenth century. This was the age
of *Swift v. Tyson*, 41 U.S. (16 Pet.) 1, 19, 10 L.Ed. 865 (1842), in which the Supreme Court held that federal courts would apply the "general common law"
rather than the rulings of any particular state court on matters of contract and
tort law, even when the case involved matters of state rather than federal concern. (Today, the Court has repudiated that view; contract and tort cases are
governed by state law rather than any federal common law.) Justice Story declared in Swift:

> The law respecting negotiable instruments may be truly declared in the language of
> Cicero . . . to be in a great measure, not the law of a single country only, but of the
> commercial world. Non erit alia lex Romae, alia Athenis, alia nunc, alia posthac sed
> et apud omnes gentes, et omni tempore, una eademque lex obtenebit.

Few judges today would invest the law of negotiable instruments with such
universalistic grandeur!

The extraordinary influence of these ideas can best be seen in *Watson v. Tar-
pley*, 59 U.S. (18 How.) 517, 521, 15 L.Ed. 509 (1855). *Watson* was a case
brought on a negotiable instrument by a Mississippi citizen in the federal circuit court for Mississippi. It was a routine commercial matter that would be
covered by state law today. The Supreme Court refused to follow a Mississippi statute governing suits to collect on these negotiable instruments because:

> The general commercial law being circumscribed within no local limits, . . . it
> must follow by regular consequence, that any state law or regulation, the effect of
> which would be to impair the rights thus secured, or to divest the federal courts of

cognizance thereof, in their fullest acceptation under the commercial law, must be nugatory and unavailing.

A requisition like this would be a violation of the general commercial law, which a State would have no power to impose, and which the courts of the United States would be bound to disregard.

Other Supreme Court decisions applied a similar theory to state insolvency laws, holding them valid in the courts of the legislating state but not in the courts of any other state or of the United States. The idea of an unwritten law, controlling except when a court was directed otherwise by its own legislature, was deeply embedded in the legal thinking of the time.

For our purposes, the most important aspect of the law of nations was its relevance to the slavery debate. Justice Story condemned slavery as immoral and argued that "every doctrine, that may be fairly deduced [from] the nature of moral obligation, may theoretically be said to exist in the law of nations; and unless it be relaxed or waived by the consent of nations, . . . it may be enforced by a court of justice[.]"[13] He concluded that a slave ship is considered guilty of piracy under international law, except when the flag state permits the slave trade. Similarly, in *The Antelope*, 23 U.S. (10 Wheat.) 66, 6 L.Ed. 268 (1825), Chief Justice Marshall began with this premise concerning the slave trade:

> That it is contrary to the law of nature will scarcely be denied. That every man has a natural right to the fruits of his own labour, is generally admitted; and that no other person can rightfully deprive him of those fruits, and appropriate them against his will, seems to be the necessary result of this admission.

He found, however, that the practice of nations fell lamentably short of this standard and hence that the slave trade did not violate international law. The same ambivalence was reflected by Kent, who declared the slave trade to be immoral and unjust, but not piracy unless so declared by treaty or municipal law. These American writers were probably influenced by a desire not to support British claims of a right to board American ships on the high seas.

Unhampered by this consideration, Story was able to state a clearer view with respect to the extraterritorial effect of slavery:

> Suppose a person to be a slave in his own country, having no personal capacity to contract there, is he, upon his removal to a foreign country, where slavery is not tolerated, to be still deemed a slave? If so, then a Greek or Asiatic, held in slavery in Turkey, would, upon his arrival in England, or in Massachusetts, be deemed a slave, and be there subject to be treated as mere property, and be under the uncontrollable despotic power of his master. The same rule would exist as to Africans and others, held in slavery in foreign countries. But we know, that no such general effect has in practice ever been attributed to the state of slavery. There is a uniformity of opinion among foreign jurists, and foreign tribunals, in giving no effect to the state of slavery of a party, whatever it might have been in the country of his birth or of that, in which he had been previously domiciled, unless it is also recognized by the laws of the country of his actual domicile, and where he is found, and it is sought to be enforced. . . . This is also the undisputed law of England. It has been solemnly decided, that the law of England abhors, and will not endure the existence of slavery within the nation: and consequently, as soon as a slave lands, in England, he becomes *ipso facto* a freeman; and discharged from the state of servitude. Independent of the provisions of the Constitution of the United States, for the protection of the rights of masters in regard to domestic fugitive slaves, there is no

doubt, that the same principle pervades the common law of the non-slave-holding States in America; that is to say, foreign slaves would no longer be deemed such after their removal thither.[14]

This position ultimately derived from Lord Mansfield's famous statement that:

> The state of slavery is of such a nature, that it is incapable of being introduced on any reasons . . . but only [by] positive law. . . . It's so odious, that nothing can be suffered to support it, but positive law.[15]

A wealth of American cases supported the view that slavery could exist only when supported by local, positive law.

Until just before the Civil War, this position was held even by Southern courts. In cases where slaves had been brought to free states for more than a brief sojourn, Southern courts generally ruled that they remained free even on their return to slave states.

The Republicans made strong use of this "slavery local, freedom national" view. Indeed, without it, anti-extensionism would have been an untenable position, for the slave relationship would have been automatically transported from Southern states into the territories whenever slaves were brought there. Under the law of nations, however, slavery was not a status that traveled with the slave's person. Instead, it had to be continuously imposed by positive legislation.

The natural law tradition became part of antislavery thought by an additional route. The natural law writers discussed earlier, along with various English legal and political writers discussed in chapters 1 and 3, played a critical role in creating the ideology underlying the American Revolution. Thus it was unnecessary for antislavery thinkers to research these ideas for themselves; much of the research and synthesis had already been done by the founding fathers. As understood by the pre-Civil War Republicans, the Declaration of Independence stood as the capstone of the pre-Revolutionary natural law ideology. As we shall see, the Declaration played a crucial role in the Republican antislavery ideology. When they adopted the Declaration of Independence as the basis of their platform, the antislavery Republicans were incorporating a synthesis of eighteenth-century natural law.

As we saw in chapter 3, natural law continued to play an important role in American law well into the nineteenth century. One of the best-known early instances was Justice Chase's opinion in *Calder v. Bull*, 3 U.S. (3 Dall.) 386, 388, 1 L.Ed. 648 (1798), in which he declared that even without express constitutional limitations, state governments were limited by "certain vital principles in our free Republican governments, which will determine and overrule an apparent and flagrant abuse of legislative power." Less well-known are opinions by Chief Justice Marshall asserting the same position. In *Fletcher v. Peck*, 10 U.S. (6 Cranch) 87, 139, 3 L.Ed. 162 (1810), for instance, not content to rest on the contract clause, he also relied on "general principles which are common to our free institutions."[16] A number of state court decisions asserted a similar view in the earlier part of the nineteenth century.

Natural law theories were also adopted by commentators during this period. For example, Kent took the position that the rights of personal security, liberty, and property were "natural, inherent, and unalienable." Based on natural law writers like Pufendorf, Kent held that the power of the legislature to take private property was limited by principles of natural equity. Natural law concepts also found expression by notable lawyers in their briefs and arguments before judges.

Nevertheless, by the 1850s, a somewhat diminished degree of belief in natural law became apparent. Skepticism grew about the reality of the social compact. The compact was more and more referred to as a convenient fiction. State courts ruled in this period that they had no inherent power to declare laws void because of conflict with natural law. Intellectually, the tide was turning against natural law and in favor of utilitarianism.

There seem to have been several reasons for this shift. First, growing reliance on express constitutional provisions like the due process clause made reliance on natural law superfluous. Second, the ideas of Jacksonian democracy were hostile to such assertions of power by judges. Third, conservatives (especially Southerners) were increasingly troubled by the potential of natural law theories to spark secession, rebellion, or civil disobedience. Finally, newer ideas like utilitarianism were beginning to influence American scholars. Natural law ideas were not dead in legal circles. They were still argued by lawyers and still used in strongly worded dissents by judges. But the legal trend seems to have been in the other direction.

Many of the antislavery Republicans, however, remained faithful to the older, natural law tradition. Like many other reformers from Luther onward, they rejected modern innovations and sought to return to what they saw as a more exalted tradition.

NATURAL LAW AND REPUBLICAN THOUGHT

In a famous speech, Seward said:

> We [Congress] hold no arbitrary authority over anything, whether acquired lawfully, or seized by usurpation. The Constitution regulates our stewardship; the Constitution devotes the domain to union, to justice, to defence, to welfare, and to liberty.
>
> But there is a higher law than the Constitution, which regulates our authority over the domain, and devotes it to the same noble purposes.[17]

Later in the same speech, he spoke of slavery as incompatible with natural rights. Elsewhere, he spoke of "the law of God, the only law which is paramount to [the] Constitution,"[18] and on yet another occasion, he proclaimed that "[t]he Constitution of the United States confers no power upon Congress to deprive men of their natural rights and inalienable liberty."[19] Speaking of the Wilmot Proviso, he said: "If it ever was right at any time, in any place, under any circumstances, it is right always, in all places, and under all circumstances."[20]

He was not alone in believing that governments are limited by a higher law. Wade said he would never recognize the right of one man to own another "[u]ntil the laws of nature and of nature's God are changed."[21] The Mexican War, Sumner said, was "wrong by the law of nations, and by the higher law of God."[22] Giddings proclaimed that a "law of right . . . implanted in the breast of every intelligent human being" called upon him to scorn the 1850 Compromise.[23] John Bingham, who later played a crucial role in drafting the

Fourteenth Amendment, replied to criticisms of the "higher law" theory as follows:

> I know this remark may be met with the sneer that this is the "higher law." Pray, did not Madison recognize a higher law when, in the convention of 1787, he declared that it was *WRONG* to admit in the Constitution that there can be property in man? . . . No, sir; the fathers of the Republic never would have . . . borne the sacred ark of liberty through a seven years' war, if they had not believed in a higher law—in the eternal verities of truth and justice. That law is of perpetual and of universal obligation. It is obligatory alike upon individual and collective man; upon the citizen and upon the State.[24]

In a similar vein, Charles Francis Adams said that the "cardinal principle" of the Revolution was that "the individual man, whether in or out of the social organization, . . . has certain rights which his fellow-man all over the globe is bound to respect."[25] Chase gave perhaps the clearest exposition of these principles. In a lengthy court argument, he said:

> The provisions of the constitution, contained in the amendments, like the provisions of the ordinance, contained in the articles of the compact, were mainly designed to establish as written law, certain great principles of natural right and justice, which exist independently of all such sanction. They rather announce restrictions upon legislative power, imposed by the very nature of society and of government, than create restrictions, which, were they erased from the constitution, the Legislature would be at liberty to disregard. No Legislature is omnipotent. No Legislature can make right wrong; or wrong, right. No Legislature can make light, darkness; or darkness, light. No Legislature can make men, things; or things, men. Nor is any Legislature at liberty to disregard the fundamental principles of rectitude and justice. Whether restrained or not by constitutional provisions, there are acts beyond any legitimate or binding legislative authority. There are certain vital principles, in our national government, which will ascertain and overrule an apparent and flagrant abuse of legislative power. The Legislature cannot authorize injustice by law; cannot nullify private contracts; cannot abrogate the securities of life, liberty and property, which, it is the very object of society, as well as of our constitution of government, to provide; cannot make a man judge in his own case; cannot repeal the laws of nature; cannot create any obligation to do wrong, or neglect duty. No court is bound to enforce unjust law; but, on the contrary, every court is bound, by prior and superior obligations, to abstain from enforcing such law. It must be a clear case, doubtless, which will warrant a court in pronouncing a law so unjust that it ought not to be enforced; but, in a clear case, the path of duty is plain.[26]

For moderates like Abraham Lincoln, belief in natural law did not imply immunity from the duties imposed by positive law. For example, Lincoln maintained that if elected to Congress, it would be his duty to pass legislation enforcing the fugitive slave clause. For him, natural law was like the law of nations, interstitial and capable of being displaced by positive law.

Others took a sterner view of the commands of natural law. John Hale argued that a New Hampshire jury was no more obliged to give effect to a law recognizing slavery than it would to a law recognizing ownership of moonbeams. Of the fugitive slave law, Giddings said, "[l]et no man tell you that there is no higher law than this . . . bill," and he vowed to resist its enforcement.[27] He also thought slaves had the legal and moral right to use force to escape. He defended an uprising and murder by slaves aboard the slave ship *Creole*:

> The slaves on board the Creole were conscious of this, from intuitive conviction. Their own immortal natures spurned the doctrine asserted in the Senate, and, under the guidance and promptings of that innate love of liberty which throbs in every human heart, they asserted the rights bestowed upon them by the Creator. One of the slave-dealers attempted forcibly to maintain the doctrine avowed in the Senate. Here, again, that God-given reason, which every man possesses, taught these people, reared in ignorance, in slave-holding stupidity, that the slave-dealer was a *pirate*, had incurred the just penalty attached to that crime, and they at once inflicted upon the miscreant the punishment due to his iniquity. I leave it for casuists to determine whether he was more guilty than those that encouraged him in his accursed vocation. These quondam slaves, now freemen, taking possession of the ship, extended mercy to the other slave-dealers on board, and directed their course to Nassau, in the island of New Providence, and went on shore, seeking their own happiness.[28]

Ben Wade, later a leading Radical Republican, was elected to the Senate on a platform of disobedience of the fugitive slave law. These sentiments were not confined to a few senators. In Massachusetts, Ohio, and Wisconsin, there were notable instances of forcible resistance to the fugitive slave laws, sometimes with the support of the state courts. As Governor of New York, Seward refused to extradite individuals accused of helping slaves to escape, reasoning that stealing slaves cannot be theft because no law can convert men into property.

For many Republicans the "higher law" had a religious basis. The Republicans' intellectual roots seemed rooted more in the religious revival of the early nineteenth century than in the Enlightenment. The *Rockford Register* said, for example, that the equality of man was a "truth not obvious to the senses, but one that is hidden in God, and revealed to those only who in all sincerity approach Him."[29] It went on to say that the basis of human equality is that "when life in all is derived from God, no one can have a claim to superiority over another." Combining religious ideas with principles drawn from the law of nations, Representative Walton said:

> God gave to man "dominion over the fish of the sea, and over the fowls of the air, and over every living thing that *creepeth* upon the earth"—not over man. (Genesis i, 28). There may be, and there is, *legal* dominion; but only by force of arbitrary power, expressed in governmental law, having no sort of force beyond the governmental line.[30]

Seeking support elsewhere in the Bible, Lovejoy (brother of the famous abolitionist editor), expounded upon the passage, "He that stealeth a man and selleth him . . . he shall surely be put to death."[31] Later in the same speech, Lovejoy admonished Southerners, "Instead of chattering your gibberish in my ear about negro equality, go look the Son of God in the face and reproach him with favoring negro equality because he poured out his blood for the most abject and despised of the human family." Giddings accused Southerners of authorizing the sale of "the Savior of mankind in the person of his followers."[32] He held to the view that "all human governments, are subjected to the 'higher law' of the Creator, and authorized to legislate only for the protection of the rights which God has conferred on mankind."[33] In keeping with these views, the Free Soil party's platform proclaimed slavery a sin. For any Southerners who missed the message, Hamlin warned that "nations, like individuals, must answer to a higher power for the wrongs they perpetrate,"[34] a warning echoed by Senator Clark, who said that when a government forsakes the higher law, it is on the road to ruin. The religious beliefs of these men not only provided a foundation for their antislavery views, but also added an emotional resonance that could hardly have been obtained by quoting Pufendorf or Vattel.

For many Republicans, however, the wellsprings of natural law were to be found with the founding fathers rather than the biblical patriarchs. As Wade once said:

> I do not understand that . . . I claim anything more than was claimed by the founders of this Republic. I am not the advocate of any new doctrine. I stand upon the principles of the fathers of our Constitution.[35]

The Republicans went to great lengths to demonstrate the antislavery sentiments of the founding fathers. Much reliance was placed on Madison's opposition to the use of the word "slavery" in the Constitution, as showing that the Constitution gave no sanction to slavery. Based on the statements of the framers, the constitutional debates, and the *Federalist Papers*, Seward stated the basic Republican position:

> I deem it established . . . that the Constitution does not recognize property in man, but leaves that question, as between the States, to the law of nature and of nations. That law, as expounded by Vattel, is founded in the reason of things.[36]

In one 1858 speech, Howard collected antislavery statements from Jefferson, Patrick Henry, James Monroe, John Randolph, and others. In another 1858 speech, Hale cited opinions by Jefferson, Patrick Henry, William Pinckney, and John Jay. A Connecticut newspaper stressed Jefferson's statement (now chiseled into the Jefferson Memorial) that he trembled for his country when he remembered that God is just. Jefferson's role in excluding slavery from the Northwestern territory also was cited, as well as a 1787 declaration that America stood for "the cause of human nature."

Perhaps the most important source of antislavery Republicanism was the Declaration of Independence. Giddings and Adams both thought it part of the law of nations or American public law. Other Republicans drew lengthy parallels between the actions of the slavocracy and the list of grievances in the Declaration. Adherence to the Declaration became a kind of touchstone for Republicans. In the 1860 platform, the party officially affirmed its belief: -

> That the maintenance of the principles promulgated in the Declaration of Independence and embodied in the Federal Constitution, "That all men are created equal; that they are endowed by their Creator with certain inalienable rights; that among these are life, liberty and the pursuit of happiness; that to secure these rights, governments are instituted among men, deriving their just powers from the consent of the governed," is essential to the preservation of our Republican institutions; and that the Federal Constitution, the Rights of the States, and the Union of the States must and shall be preserved.

This provision was not boilerplate, but instead was adopted out of parliamentary order when Giddings threatened a walk-out.

This platform comported well with the candidate's views. Lincoln repeatedly stressed the Declaration in his debates with Douglas. In one speech, for example, he said:

> I adhere to the Declaration of Independence. If Judge Douglas and his friends are not willing to stand by it, let them come up and amend it. Let them make it read that all men are created equal except negroes. Let us have it decided whether the Declaration of Independence, in this blessed year of 1858, shall be thus amended.[37]

In another debate he argued that "[i]f [the] Declaration is not the truth, let us get the statute book, in which we find it, and tear it out!"[38] Lincoln used this attack on Douglas again and again in the debates, perhaps most powerfully in the following passage:

> The Judge has alluded to the Declaration of Independence, and insisted that negroes are not included in that Declaration; and that it is a slander upon the framers of that instrument to suppose that negroes were meant therein; and he asks you: Is it possible to believe that Mr. Jefferson, who penned the immortal paper, could have supposed himself applying the language of that instrument to the negro race, and yet hold a portion of that race in slavery? Would he not at once have freed them? I only have to remark upon this part of the Judge's speech (and that, too, very briefly, for I shall not detain myself, or you upon that point for any great length of time), that I believe the entire records of the world, from the date of the Declaration of Independence up to within three years ago, may be searched in vain for one single affirmation, from one single man, that the negro was not included in the Declaration of Independence; I think I may defy Judge Douglas to show that he ever said so, that Washington ever said so, that any President ever said so, that any member of Congress ever said so, or that any living man upon the whole earth ever said so, until the necessities of the present policy of the Democratic party, in regard to slavery, had to invent that affirmation. And I will remind Judge Douglas and this audience that while Mr. Jefferson was the owner of slaves, as undoubtedly he was, in speaking upon this very subject he used the strong language that "he trembled for his country when he remembered that God was just;" and I will offer the highest premium in my power to Judge Douglas if he will show that he, in all his life, ever uttered a sentiment at all akin to that of Jefferson.[39]

As we now know, Lincoln's view of Jefferson is supported by Jefferson's attempt to include an antislavery clause in the Declaration.

Lincoln's views are particularly significant. His fight for the Republican nomination was successful because of his acceptability to all factions of the party. Because he was at the center of the party, historians view him as an example of the thinking of average Republicans.

For Lincoln, as for many others, the most important aspect of the Declaration was its affirmation that "all men are created equal." This stress on equality is found repeatedly in Republican speeches, not just those by well-known speakers, such as Chase, Wade, and Adams, but also those by lesser-known men. Seward said that the United States was "founded in the natural equality of *all* men . . . not made equal by human laws, but born equal."[40] He said elsewhere (idealistically, if not in complete accord with the framers' record on slavery) that the Constitution was based on the "absolute and inherent equality of all men."[41] In his view, the central idea of the Republican Party was the equality of all men before the law, an idea he also thought as native to the Constitution as "the blood is . . . native to the heart."[42] Sumner's belief in legal equality was strong enough to lead him to argue, over a century before the Supreme court finally adopted this view in *Brown v. Board of Education*, 347 U.S. 483, 74 S.Ct. 686, 98 L.Ed. 873 (1954), that school segregation violated "that fundamental right of all citizens, Equality before the Law," because it branded "a whole race with the stigma of inferiority."[43]

What the Republicans meant by equality was legal equality. Wilson praised his home state of Massachusetts as "a commonwealth that throws over the poor, the weak, the lowly, upon whom misfortune has laid its iron hand, the protection of just and equal laws."[44] Wade declared that he stood "upon the Declaration of Independence" in support of the idea that before the law all men are equal.[45] In a similar vein, Bingham said that the "Constitution is based upon the EQUALITY of the human race."[46] Bingham saw in the Constitution several affirmations of equality:

> It must be apparent that the absolute equality of all, and the equal protection of each, are principles of our Constitution, which ought to be observed and enforced in the organization and admission of new States. The Constitution provides, as we have seen, that *no person* shall be deprived of life, liberty, or property, without due process of law. It makes no distinction either on account of complexion or birth—it secures these rights to all persons within its exclusive jurisdiction. This is equality. It protects not only life and liberty, but also property, the product of labor. It contemplates that no man shall be wrongfully deprived of the fruit of his toil any more than of his life. The Constitution also provides that no title of nobility shall be granted by the United States, nor by any State of the Union. Why this restriction? Was it not because all are equal under the Constitution; and that no distinctions should be tolerated, except those which merit originates, and no nobility except that which springs from the practice of virtue, or the honest, well-directed effort of brain, or heart, or hand? There is a profound significance in this restriction of the Constitution. It is an announcement of the equality and brotherhood of the human race.

Keep this statement in mind in chapter 11 when we consider Bingham's role in drafting the Fourteenth Amendment.

It was Lincoln, however, who spoke most fully on the subject of equality. His position was as follows:

> My declarations upon this subject of negro slavery may be misrepresented, but cannot be misunderstood. I have said that I do not understand the Declaration to mean that all men were created equal in all respects. They are not our equal in color; but I suppose that it does mean to declare that all men are equal in some respects; they are equal in their right to "life, liberty, and the pursuit of happiness." Certainly the negro is not our equal in color,—perhaps not in many other respects; still, in the right to put into his mouth the bread that his own hands have earned, he is the equal of every other man, white or black.[47]

The Declaration of Independence rested on a view about the relationship of government and the people that many Republicans were willing to adopt. There was wide agreement among Republicans that governments derived their powers from the consent of the governed. They viewed the federal constitution as a compact by the people (rather than the states). Even on the eve of secession, Bingham conceded that the right of revolution was a "sacred and indefeasible" right, though he argued that the South had no just grounds for rebellion. He also opposed the proposed thirteenth amendment, a last-ditch effort to avoid civil war which would have precluded future antislavery amendments. The proposed amendment, he said, struck at the "inherent right of the people to alter or amend [the Constitution] at their pleasure."[48] Hale's belief in revolution found expression in praise for Cromwell and the regicides. Belief in popular self-rule did not, however, lead to a belief in unqualified majoritarian supremacy. Giddings believed that governments are "authorized to legislate only for the protection of the rights which God has conferred on mankind."[49] Bingham agreed that government's "object must be to protect each human being within its jurisdiction in the free and full enjoyment of his natural rights."[50]

THE CONTENT OF NATURAL LAW

What were these natural rights? The Republicans found it less necessary to define them than to affirm their existence. Nevertheless, a few clues exist as to their thinking on particular rights. In attempting to determine what rights they considered fundamental, we may look to a long period of Republican attacks on the South for denying a variety of human rights. It is also useful to examine the legal literature and case law of the period, which were generally consistent with what we can determine about Republican thinking.

There is fairly strong evidence for listing freedom of speech and religion among the fundamental rights recognized by the Republicans in the 1850s. The legal literature of the nineteenth century contains strong support for these First Amendment rights. Kent stressed that free speech concerning governmental officials is essential to the "control over their rulers, which resides in the free people of the United States."[51] He also believed that "[c]ivil and religious liberty generally go hand in hand."[52] Rawle agreed that "[t]he foundation of a free government begins to be undermined when freedom of speech on political subjects is restrained," and that when such rights are denied, "life is indeed of little value."[53] As to religious freedom, he felt that the First Amendment merely restated Congress' lack of power in the area, since no one could reasonably believe that *the general welfare of a nation* could be promoted by religious intolerance."[54] Similar views were expressed by Francis Lieber, who also supported the right to petition and freedom of association.

The Republicans stressed their agreement with these principles and attacked the South as an enemy of free speech. Giddings attacked it for keeping slaves ignorant and restricting freedom of speech in order to enslave the public mind. Lovejoy accused the South of a despotism like Napoleon's in crushing freedom of speech and the press. These assertions, which were echoed by other Republican leaders and by the press, had deep historical roots. The antislavery movement gained much of its strength from Northern reaction to Southern attempts to limit freedom of speech. Note that the slogan of the Free Soil party was "Free Soil, Free Labor, Free Speech, Free Men."

The Kansas controversy in the late 1850s provided an important opportunity to express civil liberties views. The pro-slavery LeCompton government attempted to suppress antislavery speech. Its attempts to do so were bitterly attacked by the Republicans. Wilson accused the LeCompton government of striking down free speech, imposing "[t]est oaths, against which reason and humanity revolt," and reducing the people of Kansas "to the pitiable condition of conquered menials of the slave power."[55] Seward accused the Kansas legislature of making it "a crime to think what one pleased, and to write and print what one thought," thereby borrowing "all the enginery of tyranny, but the torture, from the practice of the Stuarts."[56] "Before you hold this enactment to be law," Bingham proclaimed, "burn our immortal Declaration and our free-written Constitution, fetter our free press, and finally penetrate the human soul and put out the light of that understanding which the breath of the Almighty hath kindled."[57]

In addition to First Amendment rights, some property rights may also have been considered fundamental. Protection of property rights was an important part of early nineteenth-century legal thought. Kent viewed property as one of the "natural, inherent, and unalienable" rights, while Lieber viewed the unrestricted right to acquire and produce property as an important fundamental right. Similarly, Sedgwick argued that legislation destroying vested rights in land would violate the takings clause, the due process clause, and inherent limits on the legislative power.

This view of the sanctity of property was shared by many Republicans. Fessenden and Hale argued that the true "foundation of the law of property" was divine, a view embraced by Bliss (who also embraced Locke's labor theory of property). According to Tappan, slaves were not held on "the same ground of natural right" as that by which other property was held, and a similar distinction was made by Brenton. As we have already seen, one of the objections to slavery stressed by Lincoln and others was that it deprived slaves of the right to the fruits of their labor.

It is unclear whether the due process clause was viewed as a source of substantive protection of property. The due process clauses in state constitutions were given varying interpretations by state courts. With the notable exception of New York's highest court,[58] many state courts rejected substantive due process, the theory that the due process clause not only requires fair judicial or administrative procedures, but also allows courts to review the substance of legislative policy decisions. On the other hand, the 1860 Republican platform adopted the view that the due process clause prohibited Congress from imposing slavery in the territories. This view of due process, which obviously went beyond the merely procedural, was strongly endorsed by Bingham. Having imported at least some substantive content into the clause, the Republicans might have been willing to find protection for other fundamental rights in the same place. The evidence on this score seems too weak to be conclusive.

The evidence is not as clear as one might like as to just what rights were considered fundamental or the degree to which those rights could be regulated. Because so much attention was focused on slavery, and because slaves had essentially no legal rights at all, the pre-war Republicans had little reason to specify the precise contour of natural rights.

As we have seen, a powerful wing of the Republican party had a strong belief in the concept of natural law. The point should not, however, be overstated. It should not be forgotten that other strands of thought were present at the same time; that many Republicans were swayed by racism, by attachment to federalism, and by political expediency; and that for at least some, natural law must have been as much a source for slogans as a basis for serious belief. Despite these qualifications, however, natural law remained part of the party's ideological baggage when it assumed power. The social compact, natural equality, and the law of nations were part of the intellectual toolbox to which Republicans could turn when faced with new problems. In reading the next three chapters you will find many of these ideas expressed, but you will also find them being modified to fit the needs of Reconstruction.

Topics for Discussion

1. How did the law of nations theories of the nineteenth century differ from the natural law theories of the previous century?
2. Why did the slavery compromise in the original Constitution break down?
3. What assumptions about federalism underlie pre-War Republican thought?
4. How were Republican views on property rights related to those of the eighteenth century?

FOOTNOTES

1. *See* Michael Kammen, *A Machine That Would Go of Itself* 141 (1986).

2. *See* Don M. Fehrenbacher, *Lincoln in Text and Context: Collected Essays* 101 (1987) (discussing Lincoln's racial attitudes).

3. Hans L. Trefousse, *The Radical Republicans: Lincoln's Vanguard for Racial Justice* 56 (1969) [hereinafter *Radical Republicans*].

4. Eric Foner, *Politics and Ideology in the Age of the Civil War* 24-25, 58-59, 101, 135 (1980).

5. *Id.* at 22-23, 40, 64-65. For a discussion of how Lincoln's views differed from classical republican thought, *see* John P. Diggins, *The Lost Soul of American Politics: Virtue, Self-Interest, and the Foundations of Liberalism* 296-333 (1984).

6. David H. Donald, *Charles Sumner and the Coming of the Civil War* 361 (1960) [hereinafter *Sumner*].

7. Frederick J. Blue, *The Free Soilers: Third Party Politics 1848-54*, 112 (1973) [hereinafter *Free Soilers*]. Seward, oddly enough, made this statement in a speech urging adherence to the Whig Party and opposition to the Free Soil Party.

8. Trefousse, *Radical Republicans*, at 16-17.

9. John Locke, *Two Treatises of Government*, 2d Treatise § 135 (1690).

10. Leonard Kreiger, *The Politics of Discretion: Pufendorf and the Acceptance of Natural Law* 1 (1965).

11. 1 James Kent, *Commentaries on American Law* *2 (1896) [hereinafter *Commentaries*].

12. *Id.* at *3.

13. *United States v. La Jeune Eugenia*, 26 Fed. Cas. 832, 846 (C.C.D. Mass. 1822) (No. 15,551). For background on this case, see Robert M. Cover, *Justice Accused: Antislavery and the Judicial Process* 100-16 (1975).

14. Joseph Story, *Commentaries on the Conflict of Laws, Foreign and Domestic* § 96 (5th ed. Boston 1857) (citing numerous cases) (footnotes omitted).

15. *Somerset v. Stewart*, 98 Eng. Rep. 499, 510 (K.B. 1772). Lord Mansfield today is considered one of the great creators of modern commercial law.

16. For further discussion, see G. Edward White, *The American Judicial Tradition* 14-17 (1976); William E. Nelson, *The Eighteenth-Century Background of John Marshall's Constitutional Jurisprudence*, 76 Mich. L. Rev. 893, 932, 936 (1978).

17. *Cong. Globe*, 31st Cong., 1st Sess., App. 265 (1850).

18. *Cong. Globe*, 34th Cong., 1st Sess. 1417 (1856).

19. *Cong. Globe*, 31st Cong., 1st Sess., App. 1023 (1850). *See generally* Glyndon G. Van Deusen, *William Henry Seward* 584 n.14 (1967) [hereinafter *Seward*].

20. *Cong. Globe*, 31st Cong., 1st Sess., App. 1023 (1850).

21. Hans L. Trefousse, *Benjamin Franklin Wade* 36 (1963) [hereinafter Wade].

22. Donald, *Sumner*, at 146.

23. Russell B. Nye, *William Lloyd Garrison and the Humanitarian Reformers* 157 (1955). Giddings also called on "good Christians" to violate the fugitive slave law. *See* James B. Stewart, *Joshua R. Giddings and the Tactics of Radical Politics* 196 (1970) [hereinafter *Radical Politics*]. *See also Cong. Globe*, 33d Cong., 2d Sess., App. 35 (1854).

24. *Cong. Globe*, 36th Cong., 2d Sess., App. 83 (1861) (emphasis in original).

25. *Id.* at 36th Cong., 1st Sess. 2514 (1860).

26. William H. Pease & Jane H. Pease, *The Antislavery Argument* 391-92 (1965) [hereinafter *Argument*]. Chase was "astonished" at the view that a majority could rightfully enslave a minority. *See* Eric Foner, *Free Soil, Free Labor, Free Men: The Ideology of the Republican Party Before the Civil War* 132 (1970). For more on Chase's views, see Albert B. Hart, *Salmon Portland Chase* 67-81, 127-28 (1899).

27. Russell B. Nye, *Fettered Freedom: Civil Liberties and the Slavery Controversy*, 1830-1860, at 269 (1963) [hereinafter *Fettered Freedom*]. *See also* Blue, *Free Soilers*, at 204.

28. *Cong. Globe*, 35th Cong., 1st Sess., App. 543 (1858) (emphasis in original).

29. 1 Howard C. Perkins, *Northern Editorials on Secession* 505 (April 13, 1861) (1942).

30. *Cong. Globe*, 35th Cong., 1st Sess., App. 334 (1858) (emphasis in original); *see also id.* at 34th Cong., 1st Sess., App. 971 (1856) (Rep. Kelsey).

31. *Id.* at 35th Cong., 2d Sess., App. 197 (1859). Despite his strongly antislavery stance, Lovejoy enjoyed a high degree of popularity in his district. *See* Willard L. King, *Lincoln's Manager David Davis* 113-14, 117-19 (1960).

32. *Cong. Globe*, 33rd Cong., 2d Sess., App. 3 (1854).

33. *Cong. Globe*, 35th Cong., 1st Sess., App. 65 (1858). Later in the same passage, he said that certain rights are "an element of the human soul; they cannot be alienated by the individual; nor can any association of men, or any earthly power, separate the humblest of the human race from them."

34. *Cong. Globe*, 35th Cong., 1st Sess. 1003 (1858).

35. *Cong. Globe*, 34th Cong., 1st Sess., App. 749 (1856). Wade particularly relied on Thomas Jefferson for support. *See* Trefousse, *Wade*, at 88. *See also*, 2 Allan Nevins, *Ordeal of the Union* 489 (1947) (Republican stress on framers' views); Kenneth Stampp, *The Imperiled Union: Essays on the Background of the Civil War* 151-52 (1980). Even early in his career, Wade believed that slavery violated the principles of the Declaration. *See* Trefousse, Wade, at 31.

36. *Cong. Globe*, 31st Cong., 1st Sess., App. 264 (1850).

37. *The Political Debates Between Abraham Lincoln and Stephen A. Douglas* (Part I) 175 (G. Putnam ed. 1913) [hereinafter Lincoln-Douglas Debates].

38. *Id.* at 64.

39. *Id.* (Part II) at 113-14.

40. Nye, *Fettered Freedom*, at 229 (emphasis in original).

41. *See* Van Deusen, Seward, at 135. *See also Cong. Globe*, 35th Cong., 1st Sess. 944 (remarks of Sen. Seward) (1858). Legal equality has been called Seward's dominant idea. *See* 1 Allan Nevins, *The Emergence of Lincoln* 410-11 (1950).

42. *Cong. Globe*, 31st Cong., 1st Sess., App. 1023 (1850). In a somewhat similar vein, Rep. Leiter suggested that the drafters of the Declaration "submitted their principles to Almighty God, and received His righteous approval." *Id.* at 34th Cong., 1st Sess., App. 1171 (1856).

43. Oral argument of Charles Sumner in *Roberts v. Boston* (1849), quoted in Pease & Pease, *Argument*, at 288.

44. *Cong. Globe*, 34th Cong., 1st Sess., App. 393 (1856).

45. *Id.* at 751.

46. *Cong. Globe*, 34th Cong., 3d Sess., App. 139, 140 (1857) (emphasis in original).

47. *Lincoln-Douglas Debates*, (Part I) at 176. *See also id.* (Part II) at 115-16. Lovejoy expressed a similar view. *See Cong. Globe*, 35th Cong., 2d Sess., App. 199 (1859). According to Richard Sewell, *Ballots for Freedom: Antislavery Politics in the United States*,

1837-1860 327-29 (1976), Lincoln's statement would have been endorsed by most Republicans.

48. *Cong. Globe*, 36th Cong., 2d Sess., App. 82 (1861).

49. *Cong. Globe*, 35th Cong., 1st Sess., App. 65 (1858). *See also* Stewart, *Radical Politics*, at 171-72.

50. *Cong. Globe*, 34th Cong., 3d Sess., App. 139 (1857).

51. 2 Kent, *Commentaries*, at *17.

52. *Id*. at *34-35.

53. W. Rawle, *A View of the Constitution of the United States* 123 (2d ed. 1829).

54. *Id*. at 121 (emphasis in original).

55. *Cong. Globe*, 34th Cong., 1st Sess., App. 854 (1856).

56. *Id*. at 35th Cong., 1st Sess. 941 (1858). Similar statements were made by Hale, *id*. at 317.

57. *Id*. at 34th Cong., 1st Sess., App. 124 (1856).

58. The cases were reviewed at length in Edward S. Corwin, *The Doctrine of Due Process of Law Before the Civil War*, 24 Harv. L. Rev. 366 (1911). (It should be noted that some of the cases Corwin discusses are from states such as Rhode Island in which the language of the state due process clause limited the clause to criminal cases.) It seems clear that "procedural" due process had at least been expanded to require the legislature to act through general rules of prospective application. *See* Theodore Sedgwick, *A Treatise on the Rules Which Govern the Interpretation and Application of Statutory and Constitutional Law* 537 (1857).

The Thirteenth Amendment

INTRODUCTION

Perhaps nothing separates us so much from the constitutional world of the original framers as the passage of the Thirteenth Amendment, which put an end to slavery. Slavery was not only a major issue in the framing of the Constitution (see especially chapter 6), but it also subtly influenced debate on many other issues relating to national power and states' rights. Once the slavery issue was resolved, the framework of constitutional debate shifted irrevocably.

Today, the Thirteenth Amendment is only rarely invoked to resolve constitutional disputes, but the Fourteenth Amendment, with which it was closely bound historically, forms the foundation of most modern constitutional decisions. Yet the Fourteenth Amendment is difficult to understand without understanding the Thirteenth, for the later amendment perfected the freedom mandated by its predecessor.

This chapter focuses on the views of the framers of the Thirteenth Amendment on issues such as federalism and individual rights, for these views (as opposed to the specific historical decision to abolish slavery) can shed light on continuing constitutional debates.

The debates on the Thirteenth Amendment are lengthy, and we unfortunately do not have the benefit of a Madison to boil them down to pithy notes. Reprinting them would occupy hundreds of pages of this book; even with heavy editing, the material would take far too much space. Instead, we will present extensive excerpts from the final House debates on the amendment. Because these debates took place just before passage, the speakers could summarize and respond to much of what had preceded. Thus these final arguments tended to be somewhat shorter and less bombastic than the earlier ones. We will also attempt to summarize some of the other significant aspects of the debates.

Before turning to the amendment itself, however, we will begin in the next section by sketching its historical background. The events of the Civil War forced a rethinking of the roles of the state and federal governments, which influenced the framers of the Reconstruction amendments.

THE HISTORICAL CONTEXT

Lincoln was inaugurated on March 4, 1861. His inaugural address was conciliatory and contained an endorsement of a proposed constitutional amendment that was intended to halt secession. Ironically, this proposed thirteenth amendment would have forever guaranteed the *legality* of slavery in the states, putting it beyond the reach of later constitutional amendments. Lincoln took the position that the Union was perpetual and that secession was unconstitutional. Consequently, he pledged to hold those Southern forts still in Union possession, the most important of which were Fort Pickens in Florida and Fort Sumter in Charleston. On April 12, the Confederates opened fire on Sumter, beginning the Civil War.

The North could hardly have been less prepared for war. It had virtually no army; it lacked a modern fiscal system with which to finance the war; and it had no bureaucracy with which to organize the war effort. Worse, the president had no clear legal authority to stop secession, let alone take drastic measures to improve the situation. Nevertheless, Lincoln did take decisive action. He proclaimed a blockade of Southern ports, disbursed funds to antisecessionists without legal authorization, suspended the writ of habeas corpus, and hastily mustered an army consisting of volunteers and state militias. Slowly and clumsily, the North mobilized for war.

Lincoln also faced monumental political problems. Northern Democrats were at best unenthusiastic about the war. The border states, which had to be held if the Union was to survive, had strong leanings toward the South and slavery. While attempting to pacify them, Lincoln also had to maintain the support of his own party, which contained strong antislavery forces. The party itself was less than a decade old and had never before held a national position. So Lincoln had to fight a war, mold a political party, and create the machinery of wartime government, all at the same time. Even more difficult was the constant fear that England might recognize the Confederacy, putting the world's greatest naval power on the side of the South.

As we saw in chapter 9, the Republicans came to power with a strong ideological opposition to slavery. The relatively even strength of the two parties, combined with the need for maintaining the loyalty of the border states, required Lincoln to take a cautious position on slavery. His position was supported by political realists and by those politicians who were tied to his administration by patronage. From the point of view of the antislavery wing of the party, the pro-administration wing seemed conservative. Nevertheless, most recent historians believe that the divisions among Republicans concerned tactics rather than ideology. Though some were more cautious than others and wanted to move more slowly, they were united in opposing slavery. In any event, conservative and moderate Republicans joined the Democrats during the early stages of the conflict in disavowing abolition as a Northern war aim.

Inevitably, however, Republicans came to believe that emancipation was necessary to achieve the avowed goal of preserving the Union. In 1862, Congress took a timid step toward emancipation with the Confiscation Act, which provided for the seizure of rebel property, including slaves. That same year it prohibited slavery in the Territories (apparently undeterred by the *Dred Scott* decision holding such prohibitions unconstitutional). Slavery was also abolished in the District of Columbia. On September 22, 1862, Lincoln issued a preliminary proclamation, which he made final in the Emancipation Proclamation on January 1, 1863. Historians are not entirely in agreement on Lincoln's motives. He was apparently influenced by a combination of military necessity (the public explanation), a desire to influence foreign public opinion and prevent English recognition of the Confederacy, and his longstanding antislavery beliefs. The Emancipation Proclamation applied only to the Confederacy, not the border states.

By mid-1863, Republicans were ready for a permanent solution to the slavery problem. No longer did they disavow abolition as an independent objective of the war. Indeed, most Republicans had become convinced that abolition was necessary to ensure the Union's future security. In their minds, slavery and rebellion had become one. And the only way to abolish the institution itself was through a change in the fundamental law.

The Thirteenth Amendment provides that "[n]either slavery nor involuntary servitude, except as a punishment for crime whereof the party shall have been duly convicted, shall exist within the United States, or any place subject to their jurisdiction." Section 2 gives Congress the power to enforce the Amendment "by appropriate legislation." The language of the amendment was drawn from the Northwest Ordinance of 1787. The sponsors vigorously resisted attempts to modify this familiar, time-worn language, including Senator Sumner's effort to add a declaration that "all persons are equal before the law."

The amendment was debated in both Houses of Congress in the spring of 1864. It passed the Senate easily but failed to obtain the necessary two-thirds majority in the House. It then became an issue in the presidential campaign of 1864, with Lincoln vigorously backing it. After his victory, the amendment passed in the next session of the House.

THE FINAL HOUSE DEBATES

As we noted at the beginning of this chapter, the debates on the Thirteenth Amendment are lengthy. A summary cannot adequately convey the tenor of the arguments. In this section, we will present excerpts from the final debates in the House in January of 1865, in which the House reconsidered its previous rejection of the amendment.

The proceedings on the amendment reopened on January 6, 1865, with some minor parliamentary maneuvering. Representative Ashley announced his desire to call up for debate a motion for reconsideration of the vote rejecting the amendment. The day had been scheduled for the presentation of private bills (laws for the benefit of particular individuals, such as laws providing for compensation of injuries caused by the government). Hence, the first order of business was whether to set aside the consideration of private bills; a majority voted to do so. Ashley then opened the debate with a long speech, of which about fifteen percent is included here, followed by excerpts from another long speech by another proponent.

January 6, 1865

Mr. Ashley. Mr. Speaker, *"If slavery is not wrong, nothing is wrong."* Thus simply and truthfully has spoken our worthy Chief Magistrate.

The proposition before us is, whether this universally acknowledged wrong shall be continued or abolished. Shall it receive the sanction of the American Congress by the rejection of this proposition, or shall it be condemned as an intolerable wrong by its adoption?

. . .

As for myself, I do not believe any constitution can legalize the enslavement of men. I do not believe any Government, democratic or despotic, can rightfully make a single slave, and that which a Government cannot rightfully do it cannot rightfully or legally authorize or even permit its subject to do. I do not believe that there can be legally such a thing as property in man. A majority in a republic cannot rightfully ensale the minority, nor can the accumulated decrees of courts or the musty precedents of Governments make oppression just. I do not, however, wish to go into a discussion of the question of slavery as an abstract question. It is a system so at war with human nature, so revolting and brutal, and is withal so at variance with the precepts of Christianity and every idea of justice, so absolutely indefensible in itself, that I will not uncover its hideous blackness and thus harrow up my own and the feelings of others by a description of its disgusting horrors, or an attempted recital of its terrible barbarism and indescribable villainy.

It is enough for me to know that slavery has forced this terrible civil war upon us; a war which we could not have avoided, if we would, without an unconditional surrender to its degrading demands. It has thus attempted to strike a deathblow at the national life. It has shrouded the land in mourning and filled it with widows and orphans. It has publicly proclaimed itself the enemy of the Union and our unity as a free people. Its barbarities have no parallel in the world's history. The enormities committed by it upon our Union prisoners of war were never equaled in atrocity since the creation of man.

For more than thirty years past there is no crime known among men which it has not committed under the sanction of law. It has bound men and women in chains, and even the children of the slave-master, and sold them in the public shambles like beasts. Under the plea of Christianizing them it has enslaved, beaten, maimed, and robbed millions of men for whose salvation the Man of sorrows died. It so constituted its courts that the complaints and appeals of these people could not be heard by reason of the decision "that black men had no rights which white men were bound to respect." It has for many years defied the Government and trampled upon the national Constitution, by kidnapping, imprisoning, mobbing, and murdering white citizens of the United States guilty of no offense except protesting against its terrible crimes. It has silenced every free pulpit within its control, and debauched thousands which ought to have been independent. It has denied the masses of poor white children within its power the privilege of free schools, and made free speech and a free press impossible within its domain; while ignorance, poverty, and vice are almost universal wherever it dominates. Such is slavery, our mortal enemy, and these are but a tithe of its crimes. No nation could adopt a code of laws which would sanction such enormities, and live. No man deserves the name of statesman who would consent that such a monster should live in the Republic for a single hour.

My colleague from the first district, [Mr. Pendleton,] in a speech which he made at the last session against the passage of this amendment, raised the question as to the constitutional power of Congress to propose, and three fourths of the Legislatures of the States to adopt, an amendment of the character of the one now under consideration. He claimed that, though Congress passed the proposed amendment by the requisite two thirds, and three fourths of the Legislatures of the several States adopted it, or, indeed, all the States save one, it would not legally become a part of the national Constitution. These are his words:

"But neither three fourths of the States, nor all the States save one, can abolish slavery in that dissenting State, because it lies within the domain reserved entirely to each State for itself, and upon it the other states cannot enter."

Is this position defensible? If I read the Constitution aright and understand the force of language, the section which I have just quoted is today free from all limitations and conditions save two, one of which provides that the suffrage of the several States in the Senate shall be equal, and that no State shall lose this equality by any amendment of the Constitution without its consent; the other relates to taxation. These are the only conditions and limitations.

In my judgment, Congress may propose, and three fourths of the States may adopt, any amendment, republican in its character and consistent with the continued existence of the nation, save in the two particulars just named.

If they cannot, then is the clause of the Constitution just quoted a dead letter; the States sovereign, the Government a confederation, and the United States not a nation.

The extent to which this question of State rights and State sovereignty has aided this terrible rebellion and manacled and weakened the arm of the national Government can hardly be estimated. Certainly doctrines so at war with the fundamental principles of the Constitution could not be accepted and acted upon by any considerable number of our citizens without eventually culminating in rebellion and civil war.

. . .

It is past comprehension how any man with the Constitution before him, and the history of the convention which formed that Constitution within his reach, together with the repeated decisions of the Supreme Court against the assumption of the State rights pretensions, can be found at this late day defending the State sovereignty dogmas, and claiming that the national constitution cannot be amended as to prohibit slavery, even though all the States of the Union save one give it their approval.

That provision of the national Constitution which imposes upon Congress the duty of guarantying to the several States of the Union a republican form of government is one which impresses me as forcibly as any other with the idea of the utter indefensibility of the State sovereignty dogmas, and of the supreme power intended by the framers of the Constitution to be lodged in the national Government.

In this connection we ought not to overlook that provision of the Constitution which secures nationality of citizenship. The Constitution guaranties that the citizens of each State shall enjoy all the rights and privileges of citizens of the several States. It is a universal franchise which cannot be confined to States, but belongs to the citizens of the Republic. We are fighting to maintain this national franchise and prevent its passing under the control of a foreign Power, where this great privilege would be denied us or so changed as to destroy its value. The nationality of our citizenship makes our Army a unit, although from distant States, and makes them also invincible.

. . .

Mr. Orth. Congress cannot amend the Constitution, and hence, if this bill should pass, the question will then simply be referred to the people of the several States for their action. In other words, we, by our action here, simply authorize the people to determine for themselves whether they will ratify or reject the proposed amendment. To me it seems that on such a proposition there should not be a dissenting voice. Whatever questions may otherwise divide us, we all assent to the proposition that our people are capable of self-government, and have the right to alter their laws, fundamental as well as statutory.

Is slavery, then, too sacred to be submitted to the ordeal and judgment of our people? What is this institution of American slavery? A system of fraud, of injustice, of crime, and of tyranny. In the comprehensive language of an eminent divine, it is the "sum of all villainies." It tramples upon every moral precept, sets at defiance every divine law, and destroys every natural right of man. Like the poisonous upas, it diffuses its deadly malaria, and slave and master alike become its victims. It has debased the social circle, polluted the sanctuary, defiled the judicial ermine, and corrupted every department of the Government. It was the evil genius which troubled the fathers in their labors of patriotism, and produced dissension where concord alone should have reigned. Like the old serpent, it entered our Garden of Eden and seduced from their loyalty many of the sons and daughters of the Republic. Winding its deadly folds around the goddess of Liberty, it claimed and exercised despotic power in the very *sanctum sanctorum* of her temples. It laid its hand upon our nervous system and the nation became palsied. For eighty years it has been the deadly enemy of republican institutions; for eighty years it has molded the legislation of the country; for eighty years it has controlled the foreign policy of the Government; for eighty years it has crippled the power and energies of an otherwise free people; for eighty years it has ruled the executive and influenced the judicial departments; for eighty years it has commanded the Army and the Navy; for eighty years it has muzzled free speech and free press; for eighty years it has poisoned public opinion and repressed every aspiration of freedom; for eighty years it has made the American name a hissing and a by-word among the nations of the earth; for eighty years it robbed the American people of their rights under the Constitution; for eighty years it has ruthlessly trampled upon every principle of the Declaration of Independence; for the last four years it has waged a fiendish, malignant, remorseless war against us, striking with death the first-born in almost every loyal household, bringing untold misery upon the nation, demanding from our people sacrifices of blood and treasure to an extent that might well appall and crush the spirit of any other people on earth; and yet with this glaring and damnable record against this institution, we have gentlemen within the hall of freedom, sitting beneath the folds of that thrice glorious flag of liberty, Representatives of a free people, who hesitate to strike this last blow which shall exterminate the monster forever and ever.

This Congress may not heed the public voices; it may refuse to respond to the known sentiment of our constituents; but before the close of this year, so recently ushered into existence, another Congress, fresh from the people, will obey their voice, and secure to themselves, by such act, an honorable fame, and be remembered with gratitude by untold millions who are hereafter to enjoy its blessings.

January 7, 1865

Mr. Bliss. The pretense of a humanitarian motive toward the negroes amounts to nothing but a display of systematic and intense hypocricy. All sensible men perceive that the negro slaves, whether held under the new bondage of the so-called freedmen, on confiscated plantations, or scattered in want and undeserved suffering over the North, are the much-abused and unfortunate victims of an unlawful interference with the protection and support to the benefits of which they were born; and that the best possible disposition of them is to restore them to their primal condition. They have been used as a party political instrumentality to their bitter cost, and they have sense enough to know that politicians cannot reverse the decree of Almighty God and make their race equal, socially or politically, with white men. Such may be the opinion of the fanatical politician; but the more sane mind of the negro, weak as it may be, has too much perspicacity not to perceive the deceptive bait which is thrown him. Many of them are now sighing for the happy homes from which they have been seduced.

Let us take honest counsel together and agree to let the Constitution alone, with the hope of restoring the happy old constitutional regime. . . .

.   .   .

Mr. Rogers. If the position in reference to the amendments of the Constitution taken by gentlemen on the other side of the House be true, then the other relations of the States, the marital rights, the rights of husband and wife, of parents and child, of master and servants; the right of licensing hotels, the right of making private contracts, the rights of courts, the manner in which they shall obtain evidence, the allowance of parties to be witnesses, the jurisdiction and powers of State courts, the rights of suffrage for State officers, constitutions of States and all the rights which now belong to the States, upon the same principle may be interfered with, abolished, and annulled. Those rights, like those connected with the institution of slavery, belong solely and exclusively to the jurisdiction of the States, and were never delegated to the General Government. Does any man here believe that Congress, by a constitutional amendment, can so far alter the organic law of the land as to interfere with marital relations in the States; interfere with the manner in which evidence shall be given; take away the constitutional provision that a man shall enjoy property by descent in certain ways defined by the organic law of a State and blot all States laws out of existence? I ask, do gentlemen here believe that by constitutional amendment the General Government would have a right to do away with all those express and reserved rights of the States, and which were never delegated to that General Government, and never constituted a part of the jurisdiction of the Congress of the United States or of the people, except that the people of each State could act and legislate upon those individual concerns according to their own judgment exclusively, and the dictates of their own consciences?

. . .

Now, it does seem to me that the decision of the Supreme Court of the United States in the celebrated Dred Scott case, although not upon this particular point, yet goes clearly to show that there is no authority by amending the Constitution of the country, to interfere with rights of the States which never were delegated to the General Government. I will read a part of the judgment of the court in the case, as well to show that slavery cannot be abolished in this way, as for the purpose of showing that it is a well-settled principle of law, which can hardly be denied by any living man, that slaves are held as goods and chattels, and can be bought and sold like any other property.

But it is proclaimed that because the Declaration of Independence declares that all men are born equal, having certain inalienable rights, among which are life, liberty, and the pursuit of happiness, it never was intended that slavery should exist lawfully. I presume that no right-minded man will pretend that the framers of the Declaration of Independence, when they said that all men were born equal and had certain inalienable rights, intended to include slaves, because slaves at that time never had held any political rights. Slaves had been held long before the formation of the Constitution; the institution had been transmitted by England and other European nations to the colonies here; slaves were treated here as property liable to be bought and sold, and not as citizens within the meaning of the Declaration of Independence or of the original laws of the country. [He then read from the *Dred Scott* opinion.]

. . .

No man, though he search till the end of time, can show me an instance in which an amendment has been allowed which did not come within the plain letter or the spirit of the Consitution. Examine, if you choose, the amendments which were adopted after the Constitution had been ratified, and the Government established. Those amendments, which were adopted by the people because they apprehended that their personal rights, their life, liberty, or property which they had fought to maintain during the mighty strife of the Revolution might be invaded, were germane to the Constitution itself.

You will find none but such as came within the powers delegated to the General Government, either by the spirit or the letter of the Constitution. For, sir, the Constitution is to be interpreted, not only by its letter, but, like all other laws, by its spirit, and the object had in view by its framers when they made it, which object was to preserve the rights of themselves and their posterity for all time to come.

. . .

Mr. Davis, of New York. Mr. Speaker, I did not intend to trespass upon the time of this House during the discussion of this bill, but I have heard from the lips of two or three gentlemen whose views have been expressed here sentiments which are not in accordance with my own, and I think it due to myself and to my constituents that I should place upon record the sentiments which will control my action and determine my vote. Having lived more than half a century, I have never, until this morning understood to its full and perfect extent the definition of *civil liberty*. I find, by the commentary of the gentleman from New Jersey, [Mr. Rogers,] that civil liberty consists in the right of one people to enslave another people to whom nature has given equal rights of freedom. Sir, civil liberty, in my judgment, has no such interpretation, no such meaning; and no man who regards himself as made in the image of his Maker, solely responsible to his Maker for his thoughts and actions, can recognize a sentiment which lowers him in his own estimation, in the estimation of Heaven, and before the face of the whole world. Nature made all men free, and entitled them to equal rights before the law; and this Government of ours must stand upon this principle, which, sooner or later, will be recognized throughout the civilized world.

. . .

I am not, sir, one of those who believe that the emancipation of the black race is of itself to elevate them to an equality with the white race. I believe in the distinction of races as existing in the providence of God for his wise and beneficent designs to man; but I would make every race free and equal before the law, permitting to each the elevation to which its own capacity and culture should entitle it, and securing to each the fruits of its own progression.

This we can do only by removing every vestige of African slavery from the American Republic.

The focus remained on congressional power for several days. Opponents contended that Congress lacked the power to tamper with property law, while proponents argued that slavery was not a legitimate form of property and that in any event the amendment power was subject to no such limitation.

Janauary 11, 1865

Mr. C. A. White. The very term "amendment" is itself a word of limitation. This is not a change, an alteration, a modification, an enlargement, or a diminution of any provision already existing in the Constitution, but it is a supplement added to the. Constitution—a separate, independent, distinct, substantive clause, disconnected with any grant or delegation of power written down in the Constitution.

Did the States, when they ratified the Constitution of the United States, intend by the fifth article of that Constitution to confer upon two thirds of Congress and three fourths of the States unlimited power? If the construction claimed by gentlemen upon the other side be true, it is so. All then that you would have to do in order to make the Congress of the United States as omnipotent as the Parliament of Great Britain would be to change the fifth article of the Constitution, and provide that a majority of a quorum in Congress might amend the Constitution, and that would confer upon the Congress of the United States as plenary, omnipotent, unlimited power over every subject of legislation, ay, sir, it would make the Congress of the United States as omnipotent as the English Parliament. Does any man believe that the people of the States who adopted this Constitution, jealous as they were of the encroachments of centralized power, would have incorporated any such provision as that in the Constitution if they had so understood it?

I maintain, therefore, that the proposed amendment of the Constitution cannot be made of binding force and effect upon the States except by the ratification and consent of the States given in the exercise of the sovereign power of the States; that even the Legislatures of the States have not the power to give the consent. Sir, it is written down in the Constitution, tenth amendment, that "no person shall be deprived of life, liberty, or property except by due process of law."

What is "process of law?" It imports day in court and trial by jury. Is not the right of the master to the service of the slave property? Those who made our Constitution for us and the States that ratified it so understood. I will not allude to the express provisions of the Constitution in which we have a direct recognition of the right to service in slaves as property in fixing the basis of taxation and representation, and in other respects. Every one of the original thirteen States while the constitutional Convention was laboring to effect the completion of that instrument was a slave State; and at the time of its adoption each State except one was a slave State.

That is property which the local municipal law recognizes as property. I cannot accept the doctrine of the gentleman from Illinois, [Mr. Farnsworth,] that that is property which God makes property. Why, sir, I think that he would have great difficulty in tracing the title of his land if he would attempt to trace it to that omnipotent source. Adopting that doctrine, he would find a link missing in the chain of almost every title in the land.

Mr. Farnsworth. I wish to inquire of the gentleman whether if the municipal law should declare him property that would make him property?

Mr. C.A. White. My answer is, that if the local, municipal law provided that another man should have property in my service, my service would be his property. The guarantee of the Constitution is for the enforcement of the local municipal laws by the concentration of the power of the whole people. The parent has the right to the service of his child; he has a property in the service of that child. A husband has a right of property in the service of his wife; he has the right to the management of his household affairs. The master has a right of property in the service of his apprentice. All these rights rest upon the same basis as a man's right of property in the service of slaves. The relation is clearly and distinctly defined by the law, and as clearly and distinctly recognized by the Consitution of the United States.

Mr. Farnsworth. I would like to put another inquiry to the gentleman. I understand him to announce the doctrine that any man is property who is made so by municipal law.

Mr. C. A. White. That, sir, is not the question.

Mr. Farnsworth. I wish now to ask the gentleman what he understands by the phrase in the Declaration of Independence in regard to man's "inalienable right to liberty." In the opinion of the gentleman, has any man an "inalienable right to liberty?"

Mr. C. A. White. I will come directly to that question—the doctrine of inalienability of rights.

As I was proceeding to argue, that is property which the local municipal law makes property. Everything that we have in this material universe is the gift of God to man for his sustenance, for his support, and for his comfort. This beautiful world and all its treasures were given to mankind in general. They were originally no more the property of one man than another. They were given for the common use of all. But the necessities of society required that there should be separate and distinct rights of individuals with reference to this world and its products; and the appropriation of them by individuals is recognized by the municipal customary law and by the fundamental law of the land. Gentlemen who claim that it is a violation of "the inalienable rights of man" for one man to hold property in the labor of another, might as well claim that it was a violation of "inalienable rights" for one man to appropriate to himself to the exclusion of others any part of this common gift of God to man, bestowed as a common heritage. This is the result of the doctrine. It is a leveling principle; it is agrarian in its character, and once entered upon there is no telling when to stop.

. . .

Mr. Smithers. The immediate practical effect of this measure is to abrogate the possibility of slavery in Kentucky and Delaware, and it is in view of the fact that I have the honor to represent the people of the latter State, that I feel it incumbent on me to offer any suggestion in relation to it. Satisfied that the measure is constitutional and beneficial, not only to the Republic, but eminently to my immediate constituency, I cheerfully accord my vote to the passage of the bill.

Mr. Speaker, I am no apologist for slavery, but I cannot be false to truth by willfully perverting history. The necessary characteristics of slavery are bad enough; it is of itself and in itself wrong enough; its concomitants and consequences are injurious enough to deserve universal condemnation without attributing to the master qualities which sink him below the level of mankind.

It is not true that wanton cruelty and unmitigated oppression were universally or even ordinarily exercised toward the slave. The fact that from four hundred thousand, at the adoption of the Constitution, the race has increased to four million in the space of less than eighty years, is a sufficient evidence that their treatment has been generally humane.

In this respect the slave-owners of the South present a marked and laudable contrast to those of the West Indies, where a different policy prevailed. In the latter it was the accepted maxim that it was cheaper to import than to raise; more profitable to kill than to maintain. The result was visible in the effect. While in those islands at the time of the emancipation there were fewer slaves than had been imported, in the States they have increased to tenfold their original number.

The title by which they are held, and the nature of the property recognized and protected, form the material subjects for our consideration in answering or avoiding the objections proposed to the pending measure. Whatever this right is, it exists only by the laws of the States in which the institution obtains. It has no warrant in nature; it finds no sanction in the enumeration of the subjects of property over which dominion was given to man by the Creator. Whether existing by force of custom, or by immemorial usage, or by positive enactment, its origin is human and not divine. So existing it was confined to the locality in which the custom obtained, or over which the law recognizing it was capable of enforcement. If the slave escaped beyond this jurisdiction, if the master carried him beyond its confines, the bond which obliged him was loosed, the tenure by which he was held was dissolved. The owner could neither retake or detain. That such was the light in which it was regarded by the framers of the Constitution is manifest from the necessity of the clause authorizing the recapture and requiring the surrender. The language in which it is couched is guardedly framed. In this provision it is expressly and intentionally declared that—

"No person held to service or labor in any State under the laws thereof shall, by escaping into another, be deemed to be discharged."

The tenure by which such person was held was declared to be the municipal law of the State—that and that only was recognized as the foundation of the claim. When such law ceased to exist, either by the act of the constituted authorities of the State or by the intervention of a superior power rendering it null, the right was at an end by the abrogation of the authority by which alone it had existence. The property or thing is not taken, but the law is repealed under and by virtue of which we could set up any claim to a slave.

. . .

Mr. Holman. [U]nder the present policy of the Government, if the armed rebellion is overthrown African slavery is dead. I do not discuss the subject, but assert what must be apparent to all. If the South arms her slaves in the cause of the rebellion African slavery is dead, no matter what are the fortunes of the war. In my judgment the fate of slavery is sealed. It dies by the rebellious hand of its votaries, untouched by the law. Its fate is determined by the war, by the measures of the war, by the results of the war; these, sir, must determine it, even if the Constitution were amended. Therefore I oppose the amendment, because, admitting the full force of your arguments, it is unnecessary, a dangerous precedent without a benefit.

. . .

The men who commenced and have continued the agitation of slavery up to the time of its culmination in the present civil war will not be content to let the subject rest with the mere abolishment of slavery by constitutional amendment; it will still be the apple of discord while there is any considerable number of that poor and unfortunate African race on our soil. I have nothing to satisfy my mind that it is any part of the policy of the abolitionist to deport these people when they are liberated; they must therefore be diffused through the free States or allowed to remain where they are. I believe, as a general proposition, that the people of the free States are opposed to the diffusion of emancipated negroes among them. They must then remain where they are; and that being the case, who does not at once see the many perplexing and dangerous questions which are to grow out of the adoption of the amendment at this time?

If we assume the responsibility of liberating three or four million slaves by the operation of this amendment, will we not impose upon ourselves the moral obligation to provide for and support all that large number of helpless women and children, decrepit and old, who would become mendicants or wandering outcasts without such protection from us? To my mind this duty is plain; and I do not desire to incur such fearful responsibilities in the face of the obligations resting on us to provide for and look after the comfort and welfare of those of our own race who, in large numbers, have been rendered helpless by the operations of this terrible war.

. . .

Mr. Broomall. I remember that, at the last session

of Congress, a question was propounded to one of my colleagues [Mr. Thayer] something like this: whether he maintained that there existed power in the people of the United States, under the provision of the Constitution allowing them to alter their organic law, to so alter it as to establish slavery in any State where it does not now exist. The answer to that question is easy. Power can do anything that is possible to it, and when the people of the United States resolve by the physical force to enslave any portion of a free people, I know of no means but resistance with the sword to prevent it. But I do say that there are some things that are not within the limits of human legislation. It is not within the limits of human laws to legislate away the soul of man; we cannot deprive him, by any process of legislation, constitutional or otherwise, of his free agency; we cannot legislate away his liberty. No man can sell himself. Hence no man can empower his Government to sell him.

. . .

But it is said, again, that we ought not so to alter the Constitution and to abolish slavery in the absence of the seceded States. It seems to me that that argument comes with a very bad grace from those who are even the apologists of the doctrine of secession. It is not our fault that those States are not represented here. We did not drive them away. But for their own mad act their own Representatives might be here engaging in this discussion and aiding the gentleman from Kentucky in preserving his darling institution and keeping his specimens of humanity.

. . .

But the gentleman from Kentucky [Mr. Mallory] takes high ground upon this question. He opposes the resolution upon the ground of humanity? He says that it would be a cruel act to turn upon the world all of these negroes. It is strange that an appeal should be made to humanity in favor of an institution which allows the husband to be separated from the wife, that allows the children to be taken from the mother; ah! that allows the very children of the deceased slaveholder himself to be sold to satisfy his merciless creditors.

We are told that cruelties do not often occur under the institution of slavery. I grant that. I believe that as a body the slaveholders are a humane class of men. When I know the regard I have for my horse I can entirely assent to the proposition that the slaveholder shall be kind to his own negro, shall feed him well, clothe him and be proud of him. But that does not take away my dislike of the whole institution. The very danger of the evils which I have described, arising from the institution, is enough to cause me to do away with it. I would not rest in my bed if I believed the next morning, in the event of my death, my children might be sold to pay some creditor, though they might be darker than I and offspring of my crime.

Events like this gentlemen on the other side will not deny have occurred, are occurring, and will constantly occur so long as the institution of slavery exists in the land.

. . .

Mr. Pendleton. I have endeavored to maintain that the right of amendment granted by this Constitution is limited in two ways. First by the letter of the Constitution itself, and next by the spirit and intent and scope of that instrument, and by the idea which underlies it all as a foundation.

. . .

Can three fourths of the States so amend the Constitution of the States to make the northern States of this Union slaveholding States? The gentleman from Pennsylvania [Mr. Thayer] at the last session said that in his judgment it might be done. I know that the majority of this House would repudiate that doctrine. I would repudiate it myself. Believing, as I do, that the Federal Government can no more make a slave than it can make a king, I, for one, would be ready to resist it to the last extremity.

Mr. Thayer. I think the gentleman from Ohio does not precisely quote the answer that I gave to the question that he has just referred to. If I recollect rightly the answer which I gave to the question upon the occasion referred to, it was that so far as slavery could be rendered lawful, a constitutional provision making it lawful in all parts of the United States would have a binding and legal effect upon the people of the Unites States.

Mr. Pendleton. I understood that to be the position of the gentleman from Pennsylvania, and if I expressed myself clearly I meant so to represent him, and I meant in behalf of myself to repudiate that proposition, for I do not believe that it lies within the power of three fourths of the States to give to the Federal Government the power to make the citizens of a State slaves within its jurisdiction.

Mr. Thayer. The gentleman still, I think, fails to apprehend the character of the answer which I gave to his question. I have never conceded that an amendment or a law of the barbarous character suggested by the question would have a moral force or a moral obligation upon the people of the United States. But what I said, in answer to the question of the gentleman from Ohio was, that it would have

the force of law, the force of an amendment of the Constitution; that the law, if it was opposed to the inalienable rights of the people of the United States, would be, if I may use a contradictory expression, an unlawful law, a law which you could not enforce, a law contravening the inalienable rights of the citizens of this country.

I hope, sir, that I have made myself understood. I do not wish to be placed in the position which the last remark of the gentleman from Ohio assigned to me, of saying that either a law of Congress or any amendment of the Constitution which could be adopted by the people of the United States could introduce slavery into a State, but I say that so far as it would have the effect of law it would legalize it.

Mr. Pendleton. Mr. Speaker, I would not do injustice to the gentleman from Pennsylvania, as I believe he well knows. I go a step further than he does. I say that it would not be binding in morals; I say that it would not be binding in law. It would be illegal. It would be void. It would have no more sanction than that which the power of those who choose to impose it would be able to give to it. It would be binding on those who would come within the power of the sword of those who made it, and on no other.

. . .

Mr. Kasson. Mr. Speaker, I rose a moment ago, as the gentleman knows the esteem in which I hold his ability on these questions, to state this to him, and to make an inquiry. It seems to me that he has taken the extreme ground of the extremest abolitionists, so frequently denounced by his political associates on this floor and at the other end of the Capitol, of a higher law than the Constitution itself.

. . .

Mr. Boutwell. I understand the gentleman from Ohio [Mr. Pendleton] to say that he dissented from the doctrine that the power to amend the Constitution was an unlimited power. I wish to say that I also dissent from that doctrine. I do not agree that under the article of the Constitution authorizing amendments we have the right to amend the Constitution so as to establish slavery, or to invite the King of Dahomey to rule over this country. I think the limitation, if the gentleman from Ohio [Mr. Pendleton] will bear with me a moment longer, is found in the preamble, as follows:

"We, the people of the United States, in order to form a more perfect union, establish justice, insure domestic tranquility, provide for the common defense, promote the general welfare, and secure the blessings of liberty to ourselves and our posterity, do ordain and establish this Constitution."

One provision of the Constitution is that in a certain way it may be amended. Whenever it is amended it must be amended, in order that it may have both moral and legal force, in conformity with the objects for which the Constitution was framed, as set forth in the preamble. And an amendment which tends to "a more perfect union, to establish justice, to insure domestic tranquillity, to provide for the common defense, to promote the general welfare, and to secure the blessings of liberty to ourselves and our posterity," is an amendment which, when made according to the form prescribed in the Constitution, is both morally and legally binding upon the people of the country. But if it be made in violation of those great objects, although it may be legally operative, it has no moral force. The argument would be, in my mind, that the amendment we now advocate is in conformity with those objects, while an amendment to establish slavery would be contrary to them.

Surprisingly little was said in the debates about the future status of the newly freed slaves. One of the more interesting discussions of this issue was that of Representative Patterson in the course of the following lengthy speech about the validity and wisdom of the proposed amendment.

January 28, 1865

Mr. Patterson. [S]ir, are there any limitations except those specified in the Constitution to the right of amendment? One gentleman asserts that limitations are "to be found in its intent, and its spirit, and its foundation idea." Another tells us we are to look for limitations in the preamble to the Constitution. But as the preamble is only a general expression of the intent, and spirit, and underlying idea of the instrument itself, the difference between the honorable gentlemen is one of definitions, and not of ideas. Justice, tranquillity, defense, the general welfare, and liberty are the ends of government; but the English definition of justice and liberty in the twelfth century is not the definition of the nineteenth. Our interpretation of these terms in the future of our history will vary with education and local prejudices. The means which we should feel authorized to employ for the public defense and general welfare might have been deemed extravagant, and possibly revolutionary in the piping days of peace.

To say that this power is limited by the idea of the Constitution, however or wherever expressed or implied, is as indefinite as to say that extension is limited by space. Who, sir, is to determine the intent of the organic law, and the proper means by which its objects are to be secured, but the people themselves? And will not their ideas advance and change with the progress of civilization? That there are moral limitations to legislation and to popular sovereignty, I should be the last to deny. This constitutes the higher law, which when violated either by legislative assemblies or by popular majorities, justifies, nay sanctifies the exercise of the right of revolution. But our fathers were not guilty of the extreme folly of attempting the impossible task of enumerating all possible applications of the divine law of limitations.

.   .   .

The right of amendment and the system of representation, by which men familiar with public opinion and the wants and prejudices of the masses are brought to the work of legislation, enables us to mold and adapt our Government and laws by peaceful methods to the progressive changes of society. This was not accident, but a wise provision of political sagacity. Again it is claimed that the passage of this resolution would interfere with the rights of property, and is therefore unconstitutional. I might reply that the municipal act upon which the right to property in man is predicated is in contravention to the law of natural justice, and cannot establish a claim which "white men are bound to respect." Theft and robbery, though sanctioned by legislative authority, cannot absolve man from his allegiance to that law which is supreme and infallible. The enactment which reduces an accountable being, however humble and degraded, to the condition of a chattel, that subjects him to unrequited toil and hopeless ignorance, that multiplies men for the market, oblivious of domestic ties, and presses the cup of mixed and measureless woe to the lips of helpless women and innocent children without pity and without remorse, has no force as law. I diffidently, but fearlessly, deny, upon this door, that any assembly of human law-makers ever possessed the power to create a right of property in man which we, as men, or citizens of the Republic, are bound to respect.

. . .

In seeking to purge our institutions of the mortal taint of slavery, in seeking to rescue our liberties by an organic change from the fatal *imperium in imperio*, it is not necessary to fix the ethnological position of the African or to prove his equality with the white races. Remembering that the descendants of the sons of Israel are now a by-word and a hissing among the Gentiles; that the barbarian whom the proud old Greek despised has become his master in all the arts and virtues of a Christian civilization; that the offspring of the half-civilized and bloody men whom the Roman historian located in the forests of Germany and Britain are now giving literature and science, liberty and law, to the nations, let us deferentially leave to the African, who since the building of the monuments of Egypt has borne the burdens of the world, to solve the vexed problem, and, under Providence, to determine for himself his appointed place in the social scale. If the poets and orators of the sable race, whose light has fallen upon our horizon, are the morning stars of a brighter day that is to dawn upon that benighted family of men, let not us who have grown rich upon their docile labor and long-suffering, be found fighting against the counsels of Him who should "work within us both to will and to do of His own good pleasure."

. . .

Some gentlemen, too, seem to fear a fair competition between free white and black labor. Now, if the black man belongs to a more intellectual and vigorous race than we, then he ought to triumph in the conflict, and will. But if the white man has a larger brain, stronger and more enduring muscles, and a more active temperament than the black, then he will conquer in this legitimate conflict, and will gradually push the weaker race from the continent, leaving this heritage of liberties to our children after us to the latest generation. Can any man doubt the result? Why, sir, the present servile condition of four millions of this people is a prophecy of the future. Let the negro be free, and if he had no Africa to flee to as a refuge from the restless and insatiable Saxon, he would repeat the sad history of the proud but fading people that once played upon these waters and ruled with a native majesty of power where we now sit in council and sway the destinies of a great empire.

The final day of debates gave the Democrats one last chance to go on record with their position on the issue. As we shall see, some of them recognized that their party needed to rethink its views.

January 31, 1865

Mr. Herrick. Mr. Speaker, at the last session of Congress I voted against this resolution from a solemn conviction of duty. And as I shall now vote for it from a similar conviction, it becomes me to explain to the House and the country what considerations prompt me to assume a new attitude upon the question before us. Events which will now govern my action have superseded the arguments which influenced the vote I recorded last year. The considerations which then rendered the amendment proposed impolitic, in my view, have ceased to operate, and reasons of great force, which were not then in existence, have arisen to make it now expedient, and to warrant me in reversing my former action.

In my humble judgment the rejection of this measure at that time was demanded by the best interests of the country, which now, on the contrary, seems to call for its adoption. Mr. Speaker, circumstances have changed, and I shall now vote for the resolution, as I formerly voted against it, because I think such action on my part is best calculated to assist in the maintenance of the Government, the preservation of the Union, and the perpetuation of the free institutions which we inherited from our fathers. These are the great objects for which the loyal people of this country have struggled during the last four years with a courage and self-devotion to which history affords no parallel, and poured forth their blood and treasure with an unhesitating patriotism that has astonished the world. So long as a Representative seeks these objects, regardless of partisan or political prejudices, he cannot be rightfully charged with inconsistency, no matter how widely the means he may find it necessary to employ at one time or another, to adapt himself in ever-varying circumstances, may differ. I believe this is the only consistency that is truly desirable. It is certainly the only one to which I make any pretensions.

I have no doubt of the power to make this amendment to the Constitution in the manner proposed. It is altogether immaterial, for the purposes of this discussion, whether the power of three fourths of the States to alter the organic law is altogether unlimited, except by the reservation in the amending clause of the Constitution. It may well be doubted whether the people do not possess certain inalienable rights, of which a minority, however small, cannot be divested by a majority, however large. But the States formed the Federal Government by a grant to it of their sovereignty over certain specified subjects, and it must seem to follow that they can also confer upon it any other rights or powers which they themselves possess, in the manner prescribed by the Constitution itself. By the adoption of that Constitution the States transferred to three fourths of their number their entire sovereignty, which can be at any time exerted to augment or diminish the functions of the General Government, save in the two particulars excepted by special limitation. Three fourths of the States can, by an amendment of the Constitution, exercise throughout the United States any power that a State individually can exercise within its own limits.

The institution of slavery is purely a creation of law, and completely under the control of the State in which it may exist, at whose pleasure it may be modified or abolished. What the State may do, the higher power to which by the adoption of the Constitution the State voluntarily ceded its whole sovereignty, except in two particulars, is certainly competent to do, whenever it chooses to assert its authority. In amending the Constitution, three fourths of the States actually represent the whole; and the agent is invested with all the powers that belong to his principal.

That this was the view entertained by the founders of our Government is conclusively established by the fact that a proviso, declaring that "no State shall, without its consent, be affected in its internal police," was defeated in the Convention which framed the Constitution by a decisive majority. The power thus acknowledged was never disputed from that day until the abolition of slavery by a constitutional amendment became a practical question in the politics of the country. I have never entertained a doubt of the existence of this power, and I am now convinced that the time has arrived when it is expedient to exercise it in consummating the amendment proposed in the resolution now under consideration.

.   .   .

Looking at the subject as a party man, from a party point of view, as one who hopes soon to see the Democratic party again in power, this proposition seems to present a desirable opportunity for the Democracy to rid itself at once and forever of the incubus of slavery, and to banish its preplexing issues beyond the pale of party politics, no longer to distract our counsels and disturb the harmony of our movements. It has been our seeming adherence to slavery, in maintaining the principle of State rights, that has, year by year, depleted our party ranks until our once powerful organization has trailed its standard in the dust and sunk into a hopeless minority in nearly every State of the Union; and every year and every day we are growing weaker and weaker in popular favor, while our opponents are strengthening, because we will not venture to cut loose from the dead carcass of negro slavery. The institution of slavery was cruelly murdered in the house of its friends when they raised the standard of rebellion against the constitutional Government which had ever protected it from the popular disfavor that always attached to it in the North. When the Representatives of the slaveholding States, with base ingratitude, deserted the Democracy, which has always sustained their rights, and left their seats in Congress, while, with our cooperation, they had ample power to protect slavery even from such a measure as that now before the House, they not only gave a death-stab to the institution, but forever absolved the Democratic party, which had always protected it, from any further obligations to break the storm of popular sentiment which will continue to rage against it in all the northern States until its prohibition, as contemplated in the resolution now before the House, shall have been incorporated into the Constitution. It is plain enough to my mind that if the Democratic party would regain its supremacy in the Government of the nation it must now let slavery "slide."

. . .

Mr. Brown. [W]hile for the reasons stated I cannot vote for the amendment, I have been extremely doubtful whether I ought to vote against it. I recognize the absolute fealty due from a member of Congress to the interests of his country and his constituents. Not only is it his duty, as a matter of conscience, not to vote for a bad measure, but he is bound, when he cannot defeat bad legislation, not to increase the evil by useless opposition. We all know that in the next Congress there is a majority of extreme men. They will, without regard to the effect of this measure upon the country, pass it. And whatever may be the personal wishes of the President, he is so committed to the radicals on this question that he must call a special session of Congress. A session of Congress unsettles all the business interests of the country. No man seeking legitimate profits can know what course to pursue. Some new freak of legislation may tax him into bankruptcy, or so depreciate the currency as to effect the same result. Better a pestilence than a session of Congress, so far as business is concerned. If a session is pernicious to the business interests, it is ten times more so to our armies. Each day politicians throw stumbling-blocks in their path. It was only yesterday that this House passed a resolution impliedly censuring the most successful general of the war—a complete soldier in his plans, a hero in the field, a statesman in council. I mean General Sherman.

If, then, there is no hope of great advantage by the mere delay of this measure, it is the duty of those opposed to it not to vote.

. . .

Mr. Ashley. I cannot yield any further. I desire this morning to be heard on this question, and came into the House intending to close the debate, as under the rules I had a right to do. The time, the subject, and the occasion, all united to make it desirable; but I yielded the time to gentlemen on the other side, until it is now nearly four o'clock, and members on all sides of the House demand a vote. I therefore decline to take up the time of the House, and demand that the main question shall now be put.

. . .

The Speaker. The constitutional majority of two thirds voted in the affirmative, the joint resolution is passed.

[The announcement was received by the House and by the spectators with an outburst of enthusiasm. The members on the Republican side of the House instantly sprung to their feet, and, regardless of parliamentary rules, applauded with cheers and clapping of hands. The example was followed by the male spectators in the galleries, which were crowded to excess, who waved their hats and cheered loud and long, while the ladies, hundreds of whom were present, rose in their seats and waved their handkerchiefs, participating in and adding to the general excitement and intense interest of the scene. This lasted for several minutes.]

Mr. Ingersoll. Mr. Speaker, In honor of this immortal and sublime event I move that the House do now adjourn.

The Speaker declared the motion carried, and again the cheering and demonstrations of applause were renewed.

The jubilation over the passage of the amendment reflected the relief of having finally settled an issue that had vexed the nation since its birth. But as some of the speakers realized, a whole new set of problems was created, for, having freed the slaves, the government would soon be faced with the problem of what to do with them.

AN OVERVIEW OF THE DEBATES

The themes expressed in the final House debates figured heavily in the more extensive earlier debates in both chambers. In this section we will highlight some of the key statements from those debates.

The Evils of Slavery

The debates on the amendment show a clear continuity with pre-war anti-slavery thought. As before the war, slavery opponents used the slavocracy theory as a major part of their arguments. In initiating the Senate debates, Trumbull attributed all the Union's problems to the failure of slavery to disappear as the framers had expected and to the slavocracy's demand for control of the nation:

> Without stopping to inquire into all the causes of our troubles, and of the distress, desolation and death which have grown out of this atrocious rebellion, I suppose it will be generally admitted that they sprung from slavery. If a large political party in the North attribute these troubles to the impertinent interference of northern philanthropists and fanatics with an institution in the southern States with which they had no right to interfere, I reply, if there had been no such institution there could have been no such alleged impertinent interference; if there had been no slavery in the South, there could have been no abolitionists in the North to interfere with it. If, upon the other hand, it be said that this rebellion grows out of the attempt on the part of those in the interest of slavery to govern this country so as to perpetuate and increase the slaveholding power, and failing in this that they have endeavored to overthrow the Government and set up an empire of their own, founded upon slavery as its chief corner-stone, I reply, if there had been no slavery there could have been no such foundation on which to build. If the freedom of speech and of the press, so dear to freemen everywhere, and especially cherished in this time of war by a large part in the North who are now opposed to interfering with slavery, has been denied us all our lives in one half the States of the Union, it was by reason of slavery.
>
> If these Halls have resounded from our earliest recollections with the strifes and contests of sections, ending sometimes in blood, it was slavery which almost always occasioned them. No superficial observer, even, of our history North or South, or of any party, can doubt that slavery lies at the bottom of our present troubles. Our fathers who made the Constitution regarded it as an evil, and looked forward to its early extinction. They felt the inconsistency of their position, while proclaiming the equal rights of all to life, liberty, and happiness, they denied liberty, happiness, and life itself to a whole race, except in subordination to them. . . . The history of the last seventy years has proved that the founders of the Republic were mistaken in their expectations; and slavery, so far from gradually disappearing as they had anticipated, had so strengthened itself that in 1860 its advocates demanded the control of the nation in its interests, failing in which they attempted its overthrow. This attempt brought into hostile collision the slaveholding aristocracy, who made the right to live by the toil of others the chief article of their faith, and the free laboring masses of the North, who believed in the right of every man to eat the bread his own hands had earned.[1]

Senator Wilson, too, stressed the expansionism of the slave power, which had aggressively sought to extend slavery into the territories. "So long as slavery shall live," he said, "it will infuse its deadly and fatal poison into the southern brain, heart, and soul."[2] In the House, Representative Farnsworth reiterated the view that the framers had hoped for an end to slavery but that instead it grew until "the slave power got the control of the Government."[3] Similar views were stated by Representative Ashley and Senator Clark.

Like the pre-war antislavery Republicans, the members of the Thirty-eighth Congress also stressed the burden slavery placed on the rights of non-slaves. As Trumbull noted in his introductory remarks, slavery had brought about a denial of freedom of speech and the press in half the Union.[4] In a speech titled "The Death of Slavery Is the Life of the Nation," Senator Wilson catalogued the evils that slavery had led to:

Slaves were held in the District of Columbia, and slave pens and the slave trade polluted and dishonored the national capital under the color of laws for which the people of America were responsible in the forum of nations and before the throne of Almighty God. Christian men and women, oppressed with the sin and shame, humbly petitioned Congress to relieve them from that sin and shame by making the national capital free. Slavery bade its tools—its Pattons, its Pinckneys, and its Athertons—violate the constitutional right of petition, and willing majorities hastened to register its decree. Slavery arraigned before the bar of the House of Representatives John Quincy Adams, the illustrious champion of the right of petition and the freedom of speech, and it expelled the fearless and faithful Giddings for the offense of daring to construe the Constitution of his country and interpret the law of nations. Slavery stepped upon the decks of Massachusetts ships in the harbor of Charleston, seized colored seamen, citizens of the Commonwealth, and consigned them to prisons, to be fined, to be lashed, and to be sold into perpetual bondage. Massachusetts, mindful of the rights of all her citizens, sent Samuel Hoar, one of her most honored sons, to test the constitutional rights of her imprisoned citizens in the judicial tribunals. Slavery cast him violently from South Carolina, and enacted that whoever should attempt to defend the rights of colored seamen in the courts of that Commonwealth should suffer the ignominy of imprisonment. . . .

Slavery instinctively feels that the achieved institutions of twenty million free people, their free speech, free presses, their political, moral, and religious convictions, their permanent interests, all forbid that its policy should continue to control the national Government. Slavery realizes, too, that every enduring element of the Constitution, every permanent principle of national policy and interest, is and must continue to be hostile to the ascendancy of its principles and its policy.[5]

To the list of the harms created by slavery, Representative Wilson added infractions of freedom of religion and the right of assembly.[6] In the House, Representatives Kelley, Farnsworth, Ingersol, and Orth all stressed the ill effects that slavery had had upon freedom of speech.[7]

Federalism

As we saw in the final House debates, one of the major arguments of the opponents to the Thirteenth Amendment was that the amending power was subject to inherent limits. Some of these arguments were based on concepts of federalism. Senator Saulsbury argued, for example, that the amendment process should not be construed to give unlimited power to three-fourths of the states to override the laws of a minority:

Mr. President, if the ratification of your proposed amendment by three fourths of the States can give it the validity of a constitutional provision, obligatory upon a protesting State, then would a ratification by three fourths of the people in reference to any other matter, except that simple one that each State shall have two Senators, be obligatory. . . . If that be so, then I ask you, could three fourths of the States say that you should have no manufactories, that you should plant no corn, that you should not have property in anything else which is the subject of property?

I go further. If it would be competent for them to make such a provision as this the paramount law of the land, as the constitution of that land, and if this theory be true, that omnipotent power, so far as the purposes of government are concerned, resides with three fourths of the States, then they could blot out of existence any State in this Union. Does any gentleman suppose that it would be competent for a convention to so frame the Constitution, and for three fourths of the States to ratify it, that property should not be held in any State of this Union, or that all existing property should be swept away? . . .

   Sir, property is not regulated and was not intended to be regulated by the Constitution of the United States. Property is the creature of the law of the State, and whenever this Government undertakes, either by legislative enactment or operating through and by three fourths of the States, to say to the people of any State, "We will say what shall be property and what shall not be property within your midst; that subject shall be regulated by a Federal Constitution or by a Federal law," they violate the purposes and objects for which the Constitution was framed, and do that which, if they had proclaimed had been their object in the beginning, would have prevented the formation of that Constitution and of the Union.[8]

Opponents like Saulsbury viewed federalism as an implicit limitation on the amendment process.

   In response, Senator Clark pointed out that the reference to the slave trade in Article V of the constitution

   shows conclusively that the framers of the Constitution had the subject of slavery directly under their thought and control when they said, you shall not amend it in regard to the slave trade for twenty years, but was silent as to everything else in regard to it. . . . There is no provision here that you shall not abolish domestic servitude. . . . The implication is clear and forcible that you may do it whenever two thirds of both Houses of Congress see fit to propose the amendment and three fourths of the States to accept it.[9]

He went on to add that tolerance of slavery was a fatal flaw in the original Constitution; "[t]o restore this Union with slavery in it when we have subdued the rebel armies, would be again to build your house on its smoking ruins when you had not put out the fire which burned it down."[10]

Natural Law

As they had before the war, opponents of slavery looked to the Declaration of Independence for support. Reverdy Johnson, a clear-headed constitutional lawyer not normally given to flights of rhetoric said:

   We mean that the Government in future shall be as it has been in the past, . . . an example of human freedom for the light and example of the world, and illustrating in the blessings and the happiness it confers the truth of the principles incorporated into the Declaration of Independence, that life and liberty are man's inalienable right.[11]

As seen earlier, Trumbull also noted the inconsistency between the Declaration, which proclaimed "the equal rights of all to life, liberty, and happiness," and the denial of "liberty, happiness, and life itself to a whole race."[12]

   There were also more direct appeals to higher law. Representative Ingersoll, for example, favored the amendment

   because it will secure to the oppressed slave his natural and God-given rights. I believe that the black man has certain inalienable rights. . . . I believe he has a right to live, and live in a state of freedom. . . . He has a right to till the soil, to earn his bread by the sweat of his brow, and enjoy the rewards of his own labor. He has a right to the endearments and enjoyment of family ties. . . .[13]

Representative Ashley, too, maintained that no "constitution can legalize the enslavement of men."[14] Representative Patterson argued that

the municipal act upon which the right to property in man is predicated is in contravention to the law of natural justice, and cannot establish a claim which "white men are bound to respect." Theft and robbery, though sanctioned by legislative authority, cannot absolve man from his allegiance to that law which is supreme and infallible.[15]

He denied "that any assembly of human law-makers ever possessed the power to create a right of property in man which we as men, or citizens of the Republic, are bound to respect."[16]

Ironically, opponents of the amendment also relied on natural law. They used it to argue that the amendment clause of the Constitution did not extend to matters such as slavery. For example, Representative Fernando Wood argued that governments are under a duty to protect property, that the proposed amendment struck at property, and that the states could not have delegated what they did not possess—the power to destroy individual rights without compensation. He concluded that the Thirteenth Amendment was beyond the power of the government.[17] In other words, Wood claimed that abolition of slavery would violate the natural law of property.

Supporters of the amendment gave two responses to this argument. Some answered that the amendment power was simply not limited by ideas such as natural law.[18] Others responded that the amendment did not impermissibly affect a vested property right because slavery itself violated natural law. Representative Farnsworth, for example, argued that God gave man no right to property in man.[19] In the same vein, Representative Smithers contended that property in slaves "exists only by the laws of the States" in which it is found, but "has no warrant in nature; it finds no sanction in the enumeration of the subjects of property over which dominion was given to man by the Creator. . . . [I]ts origin is human and not divine."[20] As we saw in chapter 9, this view was supported by judicial rulings predating the Civil War. Senator Harlan argued that slavery violated other natural rights, because it did not allow slaves to be legally married and did not protect the integrity of their families:

The existence of this institution therefore requires the existence of a law that annuls the law of God establishing the relation of man and wife, which is taught by the churches to be a sacrament as holy in its nature and its designs as the eucharist itself. If informed that in these Christian States of the Union men were prohibited by positive statute law from partaking of the emblems of the broken body and shed blood of the Saviour, what Senator could hesitate to vote for their repeal and future inhibition? And yet here one of these holy sacraments that we are taught to regard with the most sacred feelings, equally holy, instituted by the Author of our being, deemed to be necessary for the preservation of virtue in civil society, is absolutely inhibited by the statute laws of the States where slavery exists. . . .

Another incident [of slavery] is the abolition practically of the parental relation, robbing the offspring of the care and attention of his parents, severing a relation which is universally cited as the emblem of the relation sustained by the Creator to the human family.[21]

Opponents of the amendment taunted Republicans with the question whether the Constitution could be amended to establish slavery in free states.[22] This drew heated responses from several members of the House. Some seemed to concede that such an amendment would be legally effective though immoral. Others agreed with Representative Morris that such an amendment would violate the higher law and that "any human law that conflicts with the laws of God should be pronounced of no binding force by our courts."[23]

The debates on the Thirteenth Amendment make clear the continued adherence of large segments of the Republican Party to higher law doctrines. The same themes which we found in our study of pre-war antislavery Republicans reappear in these debates. Like their predecessors, many of the Republicans in the Thirty-eighth Congress believed that slavery violated fundamental rights. They hoped that with slavery ended, these fundamental rights would no longer be suppressed.[24] Events were to show, however, that ending the formal relationship of slavery was not enough to bring about freedom for blacks. After emancipation, Congress was faced with the problem of providing protection for blacks' fundamental rights. The next chapter examines the efforts of Congress to solve this problem.

Topics for Discussion

1. While reading the Reconstruction period debates, you should consider not only the views of the framers about the meaning of the specific measures before them, but also their views of the proper methods of constitutional interpretation. For example, in discussing the amendment power, Ashley referred both to the text of the Constitution and to the "history of the convention which formed that Constitution . . . together with the repeated decisions of the Supreme Court" as support for his interpretation. He also seemed to view the Constitution as subject to some implicit limitations. (For instance, he said that only amendments "republican in character" are valid under Article V). To what extent should our choice of a method of interpretation be influenced by these views about interpretive methods? For instance, does Patterson's speech about evolving views of "justice and liberty" argue against an "original intent" approach to the Reconstruction Amendments?

2. One of the major themes of the Thirteenth Amendment debates involved nationalism versus states' rights. Both sides appealed to the "founding fathers" for support. Based on your own reading of the historical record, which side was right?

3. Another topic raised in the debates was the status of the seceding states. Opponents of the amendment argued that Congress could not validly amend the Constitution with so many states unrepresented in Congress, since the requisite two-thirds of all members could not be mustered; those states would at least have to be counted in determining the number needed for ratification. The question of how to conceptualize secession caused great puzzlement on all sides. Had the Southern states reverted to the status of territories, were they without lawful governments, or were the state governments themselves still in existence (although temporarily in the hands of criminals)? Varying views on these issues were related to the broader issues of nationalism and states' rights.

4. The debates on January 7 and 11 reflect a variety of views about the "higher law," its existence, status, and content. Should these views be taken seriously, or should they be dismissed as rhetorical flourishes? If remarks about the higher law are taken seriously, what significance might they have for understanding the Thirteenth and Fourteenth amendments? Should the views of the framers about the nature of property, in particular, be given any weight today in determining the degree of constitutional protection to be accorded property rights?

5. Ironically, as the war came to a close, the Confederacy was being forced toward abolition, not by the North, but to increase the pool of military manpower by including blacks and to gain greater European support. Was there any practical necessity for the Thirteenth Amendment if the only purpose was to eliminate slavery? If not, should it be viewed as purely symbolic? Or should we assume (as some historians have argued) that the purpose was not just to end slavery but to bestow freedom by protecting the fundamental rights of the newly freed slaves? To what extent does the addition of section 2, granting Congress legislative power to enforce the amendment, support the argument that the amendment was intended to do more than invalidate state slave laws?

FOOTNOTES

1. *Cong. Globe*, 38th Cong., 1st Sess. 1313 (1864).

2. *Id.* at 1322.

3. *Id.* at 2979.

4. *See id.* at 1313.

5. *Id.* at 1320-21.

6. *See id.* at 1202.

7. *See id.* at 2978-79 (remarks of Rep. Farnsworth); *id.* at 2984 (remarks of Rep. Kelley); *id.* at 2990 (remarks of Rep. Ingersoll); *id.*, 38th Cong., 2d Sess. 142 (1865) remarks of Rep. Orth). To the same effect, *see id.* 38th Cong., 1st Sess. 1439 (1864) (remarks of Sen. Harlan).

8. *Id.*, 38th Cong., 1st Sess. 1366 (1864).

9. *Id.* at 1368.

10. *Id.* at 1370.

11. *Id.* at 1424. Other references to the Declaration can be found in Sen. Henderson's remarks, *id.* at 1461; in Sen. Sumner's remarks, *id.* at 1482-83; and in Rep. Orth's remarks, *id.*, 38th Cong., 2d Sess. 142 (1865). In the 1864 enabling acts for Colorado, Nevada, and Nebraska, Congress required them to follow the Declaration of Independence.

12. *Cong. Globe*, 38th Cong., 1st Sess. 1313 (1864).

13. *Id.* at 2990.

14. *Id.*, 38th Cong., 2d Sess. 138 (1865). For other general references to natural law, see *id.* at 142-43 (remarks of Rep. Orth), *id.* at 154-55 (remarks of Rep. Davis).

15. *Id.* at 484.

16. *Id.*

17. *See id.*, 38th Cong., 1st Sess. 2940-41 (1864). *See also id.* at 2952 (remarks of Rep. Coffroth); *id.*, 38th Cong., 2d Sess. 151 (remarks by Rep. Rogers).

18. *See id.*, 38th Cong., 1st Sess. 2943 (1864) (remarks of Rep. Higby); *id.* at 2980 (remarks of Rep. Thayer).

19. *See id.* at 2978.

20. *Id.*, 38th Cong., 2d Sess. 217 (1865). A similar natural law view of property was expressed by Sen. Harlan. *See id.*, 38th Cong., 1st Sess. 1437 (1864).

21. *Cong. Globe,* 38th Cong., 1st Sess. 1439 (1864).

22. *See, e.g., Cong. Globe,* 38th Cong., 2d Sess. 222 (1865) (remarks of Rep. Pendelton).

23. *Id.* at 486.

24. *See, e.g., id.*, 38th Cong., 1st Sess. 2989 (1864) (remarks of Rep. Ingersoll); *id.*, 38th Cong., 2d Sess. 142-43 (1865) (remarks of Rep. Orth); *id.* at 155 (remarks of Rep. Davis).

The Fourteenth Amendment

INTRODUCTION

The Fourteenth Amendment consists of five sections. Section 1 overturns the *Dred Scott* decision by making all persons born in the United States States citizens. It then goes on to forbid states from depriving individuals of their rights to the privileges and immunities of citizens of the United States, to due process of law, and to the equal protection of the laws. This section gives rise to virtually all of the Supreme Court's constitutional docket. Sections 2, 3, and 4, as we shall see, were Reconstruction-era measures of no lasting significance. They were, however, more extensively debated than section 1. Section 5 gives Congress power to enforce the amendment through appropriate legislation.

Perhaps few provisions of the Constitution have given rise to as much debate about original intent as section 1 of the Fourteenth Amendment. The historical record has been scrutinized for indications of whether the framers meant to prohibit school segregation, to incorporate the provisions of the Bill of Rights within section 1, to limit regulation of business through the due process clause, to allow affirmative action, or to allow Congress to define new rights or prohibit discrimination by private individuals. As you can see, these issues are central to important developments in twentieth-century constitutional law. Not surprisingly, most of these historical issues are still hotly disputed today.

We will begin our examination of the Fourteenth Amendment's passage with a description of the historical context. To do justice to the complexities of Reconstruction would take us far beyond the scope of this book. We will content ourselves with a sketch of developments through 1866, with particular attention to the Civil Rights Act, which was closely linked with the amendment. We will then consider the debates about the amendment itself.

HISTORICAL CONTEXT:
RECONSTRUCTION AND THE CIVIL RIGHTS ACT

The process of Reconstruction started well before the defeat of the South when the Union military began governing conquered areas. In December 1863, Lincoln established a procedure for Southern states to reenter the Union. New state governments would be organized when ten percent of the voters had taken a loyalty oath and adopted a state constitution renouncing secession and accepting emancipation. Congress would retain only the power to decide when to seat Southern representatives.

Congress responded to Lincoln's lenient proposal with the Wade-Davis bill, in which it attempted to gain greater control of Reconstruction. The bill required a majority of the state's white male citizens to take a loyalty oath as the first step in forming a reconstructed state government. They would then elect delegates to a constitutional convention, who were required to take a more stringent oath. The new state constitution would forbid participation in state government by certain classes of rebels deemed most disloyal. If a majority of the voters ratified the constitution, then the state would be entitled to representation in Congress. Lincoln pocket-vetoed the bill, apparently in order to retain more flexibility during Reconstruction. Congress, however, continued to assert its authority in Reconstruction matters. It created the Freedmen's Bureau to provide protection for blacks and other refugees in the South, and declined to seat representatives of the Banks government in Louisiana.

When the war ended in April of 1865, Republicans were confident that restoration of the Southern states could be achieved without any national guarantees other than ratification of the Thirteenth Amendment. Even the assassination of Lincoln did not immediately dim their optimism. When Andrew Johnson assumed office, he was not viewed as an implacable foe of the congressional Republicans. When he announced his Reconstruction plan at the end of May, however, it became clear that he would take an extremely conservative position on Reconstruction, requiring little from the South beyond ratification of the Thirteenth Amendment. The Republican euphoria of the immediate post-war period began to wane with the implementation of Johnson's program over the summer. The state governments created under the plan were dominated by leading rebels.

Even more disturbing were the reports, widely publicized in the North, of black codes in the Southern states. These codes included provisions prohibiting blacks from renting land, providing for the arrest and return to their employers of blacks who breached labor contracts, prohibiting servants from leaving their masters' premises, and authorizing the hiring out of black children and of blacks unable to pay vagrancy fines. The codes also made certain conduct criminal only when done by blacks. Predictably, Republicans considered the codes attempts by the Southern states to deprive the North of the fruits of victory by reimposing slavery in a more subtle form. Republicans were now convinced that additional guarantees were needed to secure the future of the Union. A consensus existed that these should include adequate protection of freedom in the South.

When the Thirty-ninth Congress convened on December 2, 1865, the moderate Republicans immediately went about formulating a Reconstruction plan they thought would be acceptable to Johnson and the American people. Congress established a Joint Committee on Reconstruction to coordinate consideration of the issue. The most immediate results of the Republican consensus regarding the need for federal protection of blacks and loyal whites in the South were the second Freedmen's Bureau bill and the Civil Rights bill. The Freedmen's Bureau, which was part of the War Department, was charged with providing welfare relief to blacks and protecting their legal rights by use of special military courts. The primary purpose of the Freedmen's Bureau bill was to extend the Bureau's life. The bill also made an attempt to provide land for the freedmen, as well as additional protection of their civil rights. The second measure, the Civil Rights bill, was a peacetime measure, unlike the Freedmen's bill which was based on the war power. Both measures sailed through Congress easily.

In mid-February, Johnson shocked moderate Republicans with his veto of the Freedmen's Bureau bill. Although his opposition to the bill had been clear for some time, the breadth of his objections came as a surprise. His veto message denied Congress power to pass any such bill in peacetime and seemed to indicate that peace had arrived. The next evening, he made an impromptu speech vituperatively attacking not only radicals but also a number of moderates who had supported him. Conservative and moderate Republicans felt betrayed.

Following the veto of the Freedmen's Bureau bill, moderates were under intense pressure to get Reconstruction moving again. Their response was to push through the Civil Rights bill.

Senator Trumbull, who chaired the Senate Judiciary Committee, introduced the Civil Rights bill in the Senate on January 5, 1866. As amended by Trumbull when the bill first came up for debate, section 1 contained four provisions. First, blacks were declared to be citizens of the United States. Second, the bill prohibited "discrimination in civil rights or immunities among the inhabitants of any State or Territory" on account of race. Third, all inhabitants were to have the same rights as whites to contract, to sue, and to engage in various real estate and personal property transactions. Fourth, all inhabitants were to have "full and equal benefit of all laws and proceedings for the security of person and property" and were to be subject to the same punishments. As amended, the bill passed the Senate on February 2, 1866.

In the House, Representative Wilson, on behalf of the Judiciary Committee, reported certain additional amendments to the bill, beyond those already made in the Senate. The most important change was to replace the word "inhabitants" with "citizens," so that the protection of the bill extended only to citizens.

The most important subsequent change took place at the initiative of Representative Bingham. On March 8, he moved to have the general prohibition on "discrimination in civil rights or immunities" struck from the bill because he believed that Congress lacked power to pass it. On March 13, when the House resumed consideration of the bill, Representative Wilson agreed on behalf of the committee to strike the general anti-discrimination clause from the section. He explained that in his view the change did not materially affect the bill, but "some gentlemen were apprehensive that the words we propose to strike out might give warrant for a latitudinarian construction not intended."[1] On March 15, on the recommendation of the Senate Judiciary Committee, the Senate concurred in the House changes.

On March 27, President Johnson vetoed the Civil Rights bill. He contended that the matters covered by the bill were within the exclusive jurisdiction of the states, and that the bill was thus unconstitutional. Johnson had retained some party support after vetoing the Freedmen's Bureau bill, but the reaction was far more severe when he vetoed the Civil Rights bill. The Senate overrode the presidential veto on April 6, and the House did the same on April 9.

There is an unmistakable shift in the rhetoric of the debates over the Civil Rights bill and the Freedmen's Bureau bill compared to the debates over the Thirteenth Amendment. While many Republicans observed that the bills were designed to protect natural rights belonging to all human beings, they more often referred to these rights as belonging to United States citizens. The reason for the change in rhetoric was not a sudden disbelief in natural rights. Republicans continued to believe that all people were entitled to these rights. But they had always distinguished between the existence of natural rights and the question of federal power. Prior to the Civil War, their position had been that the government had power to deal with slavery only in the territories, but not in the South.

Similarly, in adopting the Civil Rights bill, what Republicans needed was not a defense of human rights, but a justification for federal intervention to protect those rights against state abridgement. Many Republicans relied on the Thirteenth Amendment as a source of power, on the theory that deprivation of the rights set forth in the bill was a denial of the freedom guaranteed by the amendment. Opponents replied that the Thirteenth Amendment only authorized Congress to abolish the formal slave relationship. The Republicans responded by arguing that *all* governments have a duty, and therefore the inherent power, to protect the fundamental rights of their citizens. (Based on your reading of chapter 10, which interpretation do you agree with?)

While considering these arguments about the scope of federal power, it is important to keep in mind the changes the Civil War had caused in constitutional thinking. The Constitution, after all, said nothing about secession. It also said nothing about waging civil war, nor did it speak to the question of reconstructing a defeated South. Strict constructionists like President Buchanan believed that the North was powerless to oppose secession, to wage civil war, or to conclude it by Reconstruction. Fortunately, the Republicans were not such strict constructionists. During the war people came to believe that the national government's powers were adequate to resolve problems facing the nation. The Civil War had called for unprecedented actions by the president and Congress. By the end of the war, Republicans were accustomed to finding some source of constitutional authority for whatever actions they thought necessary. This is not to say, however, that they had completely abandoned older ways of thinking about national power and states' rights.

Nevertheless, the Civil War also caused undeniable changes in prevailing views about the relationship between the individual citizen and the national government. Prior to the war, the state governments were primarily responsible for meeting the basic needs of American citizens. The national government had little impact on the daily lives of most Americans. Consequently, before the war, state citizenship was paramount. From this premise, it was a small step to the conclusion that allegiance to the state came before allegiance to the federal government. But such concepts obviously could not survive the Civil War, a war for the primary allegiance of the citizen. The decision to defeat secession by force necessarily implied that the citizen's relationship to the national government took precedence over his or her relationship to the state.

The significance attached to national citizenship and allegiance became evident early in the war. In the *Prize Cases*,[2] for example, the Supreme Court was required to determine not only the president's power to impose a blockade, but also the relationship of Southerners to the federal government after the outbreak of war.[3] In deciding the case, the Court strongly affirmed presidential power to react to the emergency without waiting for congressional approval or a declaration of war. When war broke out, "[t]he President was bound to meet it in the shape it presented itself, without waiting for Congress to baptize it with a name; and no name given to it by him or them could change the fact." As to the question of the status of the citizens in the South, the Court said, "[t]hey have cast off their allegiance and made war on their Government, and are none the less enemies because they are traitors." In an affirmation of nationalism, the Court also said that citizens owe "supreme allegiance" to the federal government and only "qualified allegiance" to their states.

In the Confiscation Act of 1862, Congress provided a new punishment for treason and created the lesser crime of giving aid to the rebellion. Throughout the debates Republicans characterized the rebels as traitors who could be punished for their "broken allegiance." The importance attached to citizenship and allegiance is also evidenced by the frequent resort to loyalty oaths. Under the Confiscation Act and other legislation, rights under the fugitive slave clause depended on the claimant's taking an "iron-clad" loyalty oath, requiring not just a pledge of future loyalty but also a statement of complete past loyalty. And in the Wade-Davis Reconstruction bill, Congress made participation in the process of formulating new state governments dependent on loyalty oaths. In addition, the Wade-Davis bill stripped certain classes of Confederate officeholders of their United States citizenship. Finally, Congress provided that congressmen-elect from the Southern states would have to take an iron-clad oath of past loyalty to the Union.

Given the emotional significance of allegiance during the sectional conflict and the expansion of national power under the stress of war, it is not remarkable that Republicans used the concept of national citizenship to justify their support of the Civil Rights bill.

Republicans had little difficulty connecting the natural rights they sought to protect with the status of national citizenship. They asserted that the "comity clause" in Article IV, section 2, of the original Constitution had already established the connection between United States citizenship and fundamental rights. Article IV, section 2, provides that "the citizens of each State shall be entitled to all Privileges and Immunities of Citizens in the several States." Republicans interpreted the clause to mean that "the citizens of each state shall be entitled to all the privileges and immunities of citizens [of the United States] in the several states." They found support for this reading in some pre-Civil War cases, the most noteworthy of which was *Corfield v. Coryell*.[4] In *Corfield*, Justice Washington said that the comity clause was confined to "those privileges and immunities which are, in their nature, fundamental; which belong, of right, to the citizens of all free governments; and which have, at all times, been enjoyed by the citizens of the several states." Among these rights were "[p]rotection by the government; the enjoyment of life and liberty, with the right to acquire and possess property of every kind, and to pursue and obtain happiness and safety; subject nevertheless to such restraints as the government may justly prescribe for the general good of the whole."[5]

There are several examples of this interpretation of the comity clause in the debates on the Thirteenth Amendment. This interpretation also figured prominently in the debates on the Civil Rights bill. One purpose of the Fourteenth Amendment was to "constitutionalize" the Civil Rights Act, so the debates on that statute are particularly relevant to understanding the amendment.

In the Senate debate, Senator Trumbull referred to the comity clause in order to demonstrate that

> the rights of a citizen of the United States were certain great fundamental rights, such as the right to life, to liberty, and to avail one's self of all the laws passed for the benefit of the citizen to enable him to enforce his rights; inasmuch as this was the definition given to the term as applied in that part of the Constitution, I reasoned from that, that when the Constitution had been amended and slavery abolished, and we were about to pass a law declaring every person, no matter of what color, born in the United States a citizen of the United States, the same rights would then appertain to all persons who were clothed with American citizenship.[6]

In the House, Representative Wilson argued that the rights protected in the bill were not new because they were already contained in the comity clause as construed in *Corfield*. In his opinion, that clause represented a "general citizenship" which "entitles every citizen to security and protection of personal rights."[7] He argued that the bill protected rights belonging to "citizens of the United States, as such."[8] Speaking at great length, Representative Lawrence responded to the president's veto with a defense of the bill, discussing in detail the role of the comity clause. He maintained that Congress had the power to secure citizens "in the enjoyment of their inherent right of life, liberty, and property, and the means essential to that end, . . . to enforce the observance of the provisions of [the comity clause], and the equal civil rights which it recognizes or by implication affirms to exist among citizens of the same state."[9] He concluded, after a discussion of some of the cases and writers dealing with the comity clause, that it embodies "equal fundamental civil rights for all citizens."[10] Some congressmen also referred to the Fifth Amendment's due process clause as a source of the rights that Congress could protect.

Another concept played an important role in the debates. Natural law and law-of-nations thinkers had stressed the idea that citizens owe allegiance to their government in exchange for the government's grant of protection to them. Thus, one of the most important rights of citizenship is the right to receive such protection. This concept served not only as a possible source of rights, but also as a source of power to protect the rights of citizens, whether those rights derived from the law of nations or from constitutional provisions such as the comity clause.

Early in the debates on the Civil Rights Act, Senator Johnson raised the law-of-nations argument that the government had a duty to protect its citizens:

> If I am right . . . that we can authorize them [blacks] to sue, authorize them to contract, authorize them to do everything short of voting, it is not because there is anything in the Constitution of the United States that confers the authority to give to a

negro the right to contract, but it is because it is a necessary, incidental function of a Government that it should have authority to provide that the rights of everybody within its limits shall be protected, and protected alike.[11]

Johnson concluded that it "would have been a disgrace to the members of the [Constitutional] Convention" if they had foreseen the abolition of slavery and "had denied to the Congress of the United States the authority to pass laws for the protection of all the rights incident to the condition of a free man."[12] His argument was echoed by Senator Morrill.

A similar argument was made in the House by Representative Broomall. He first noted that it was a "strange" view that the government could protect its citizens abroad but not at home. He found such a power in the Article I, section 8, grant of power to Congress to provide for the general welfare, and in the necessary and proper clause. Then he made a more sweeping, non-textual argument:

> But throwing aside the letter of the Constitution, there are characteristics of Governments that belong to them as such, without which they would cease to be Governments. The rights and duties of allegiance and protection are corresponding rights and duties. . . . [Wherever] I owe allegiance to my country, there it owes me protection, and wherever my Government owes me no protection I owe it no allegiance and can commit no treason.[13]

Broomall attacked the idea that such protection could be left to the states, inasmuch as "everybody knows that the rights and immunities of citizens were habitually and systematically denied in certain States to the citizens of other States: the right of speech, the right of transit, the right of domicil, the right to sue, the writ of *habeas corpus*, and the right of petition." Broomall also argued that the necessity for the bill was not limited to blacks, since loyal whites were being denied their basic rights in the South.

Representative Wilson made one of the most forceful arguments based on the duty to protect. In his view, the rights protected by the Civil Rights Act were "simply the absolute rights of individuals" or "the natural rights of man." He argued that the bill did not establish new rights, but instead protected and enforced those which already belonged to every citizen. In his opinion, the comity clause entitled every citizen to protection of personal rights. He summarized his defense of congressional power as follows:

> I reassert that the possession of these rights by the citizen raises by necessary implication the power in Congress to protect them. If a citizen of the United States should go abroad, and while within the jurisdiction of a foreign Power be despoiled of his rights of personal security, personal liberty, or personal property contrary to the due course of law of the nation inflicting the wrong, this Government would espouse his cause and enforce redress even to the extremity of war. . . .
>
> Well, if all the terrible powers of war may be resorted to for the protection of the rights of our citizens when those rights are disregarded and trampled on beyond our jurisdiction, is it possible that our Constitution is so defective that we have no power under it to protect our citizens within our own jurisdiction through the peaceful means of statutes and courts? . . .
>
> Under this broad principle I rest my justification of this bill. I assert that we possess the power to do those things which Governments are organized to do; that we may protect a citizen of the United States against a violation of his rights by the law of a single State; . . . that this power permeates our whole system, is a part of it, without which the States can run riot over every fundamental right belonging to

citizens of the United States; that the right to exercise this power depends upon no express delegation, but runs with the rights it is designed to protect. . . . [14]

Representative Thayer made a similar argument, as did Representative Shellabarger, who stressed that since citizens owe their primary allegiance to the federal government, the government's primary duty correspondingly was to protect them. Like Wilson, Shellabarger argued that if the states could abridge those rights which the United States is bound to protect, even by a declaration of war in the case of violations by foreign governments, then "the United States is no nation."[15]

After President Johnson's veto, Trumbull made an important speech in the Senate defending the bill against Johnson's charges. He asserted that

> [t]o be a citizen of the United States carries with it some rights; . . . They are those inherent, fundamental rights which belong to free citizens or free men in all countries, such as the rights enumerated in this bill, and they belong to them in all the States of the Union. The right of American citizenship means something.[16]

Trumbull stated that citizens are entitled to protection within the states as well as abroad. He contended that the rights of life, liberty, and property are "inalienable rights, belonging to every citizen of the United States, as such, no matter where he may be." He asserted that "American citizenship would be little worth" if it did not carry protection with it. He stated:

> How is it that every person born in these United States owes allegiance to the Government? Everything that he is or has, his property and his life, may be taken by the Government of the United States in its defense . . . and can it be that . . . we have got a Government which is all-powerful to command the obedience of the citizen, but has no power to afford him protection? Is that all that this boasted American citizenship amounts to? . . . Sir, it cannot be. Such is not the meaning of our Constitution. Such is not the meaning of American citizenship. This Government, which would go to war to protect its meanest—I will not say citizen—inhabitant . . . in any foreign land whose rights were unjustly encroached upon, has certainly some power to protect its own citizens in their own country. Allegiance and protection are reciprocal rights.

Senator Johnson responded to Trumbull's arguments with a line of reasoning that probably would have been convincing prior to the Civil War. He conceded that citizenship carried with it certain rights and that a nation is bound to protect its own citizens. But he added that this was true only when the nation has such power under its form of government, such as when another nation has invaded a citizen's rights. But under the American Constitution, Johnson said, the states have exclusive jurisdiction over matters covered by section 1 of the bill. Trumbull's theory that it was the business of every government to protect its own citizens begged the question, Johnson argued; it was the business of the federal government to protect its citizens, but only with respect to matters within federal jurisdiction. Trumbull responded by repeating his original argument, and the Senate voted to override the president's veto.

In the House, Representative Lawrence responded to the president's veto with a lengthy defense of the bill. Lawrence defended congressional power to pass the bill by asserting that it protected rights "recognized by the Constitution as existing anterior to and independently of all laws and all constitutions."[17] It was, he maintained, "idle to say that a citizen shall have the right to life, yet to deny him the right to labor, whereby alone he can live." More, "[i]t is worse than mockery to say that men may be clothed by the national authority with the character of citizens, yet may be stripped by State authority of the means by which citizens may exist." In his view, "Congress has the incidental power to enforce and protect the equal enjoyment in the States of civil rights which are inherent in national citizenship."[18]

The arguments on behalf of the Civil Rights Act were irresistible. The nation had fought a civil war to establish that citizens owe their primary allegiance to the federal government rather than to the states. In this war, the government had sent thousands of men, many of them draftees, to their deaths. The South was still in essence a militarily occupied territory. Under these circumstances, it seemed simply unacceptable to say that a government that had demanded such sacrifices from its citizens was powerless to give them in return the slightest protection of their most fundamental rights. The Civil Rights Act was the product of this new shift in constitutional understanding. Its provisions still operate today as a basis for federal court lawsuits attacking racial discrimination.

BINGHAM'S PROPOSED AMENDMENT

Before the Civil Rights bill was taken up in the House, that body considered a constitutional amendment proposed by Representative Bingham from the Joint Committee on Reconstruction on February 26, 1866. It provided:

> The Congress shall have power to make all laws which shall be necessary and proper to secure to the citizens of each State all privileges and immunities of citizens in the several States, and to all persons in the several States equal protection in the rights of life, liberty, and property.[19]

Bingham called "the attention of the House to the fact that the amendment proposed stands in the very words of the Constitution," except the portion conferring power on Congress. The remainder, he argued, was in the comity clause and the due process clause of the Fifth Amendment. As we have seen, the majority view among Republicans was that Congress already had the power to protect these rights. Bingham, however, disagreed. He believed that under the original Constitution state officers were obligated by oath to comply with the Fifth Amendment and the privileges and immunities clause, but that enforcement of these rights rested solely with the states.[20]

Debate on the proposed amendment was not extensive, but it was spirited, filled with "points of order" and heated personal interchanges, as well as spots of humor (such as one representative's admission that apparently he was one of the only members of the House who *wasn't* an expert on constitutional law).

The amendment's supporters argued variously that the national government already had the power to defend the rights of citizens but that the amendment would remove any doubts;[21] that the amendment would give Congress the power to enforce only the original comity clause;[22] and that the amendment merely gave Congress power to protect "the natural rights which necessarily pertain to citizenship."[23]

Bingham denied that the provision would take away from any state any right belonging to it. Rather, it simply would arm Congress with the power to enforce "the bill of rights as it stands in the Constitution to-day." He then quoted the comity clause and the Fifth Amendment. He derided the notion that any state could reserve the right to deny these rights. He contended that the rights of liberty and life "are universal and independent of all local State legislation" and "belong, by the gift of God," to all.[24] He found it anomalous that the federal government had power to vindicate the rights of citizens abroad, but not power in peacetime to enforce those rights within the limits of the states.

In the course of the discussion, some members of Congress began to grapple with the problem of defining equality. The most interesting discussions involved laws which reduced or eliminated the ability of married women to own or control property.[25]

February 27, 1866

Mr. Hale: What is the effect of the amendment which the committee on reconstruction propose for the sanction of this House and the States of the Union? I submit that it is in effect a provision under which all State legislation, in its codes of civil and criminal jurisprudence and procedure, affecting the individual citizen, may be overridden, may be repealed or abolished, and the law of Congress established instead. I maintain that in this respect it is an utter departure from every principle ever dreamed of by the men who framed our Constitution.

Mr. Stevens. Does the gentleman mean to say that, under this provision, Congress could interfere in any case where the legislation of a State was equal, impartial to all? Or is it not simply to provide that, where any State makes a distinction in the same law between different classes of individuals, Congress shall have power to correct such discrimination and inequality? Does this proposition mean anything more than that?

Mr. Hale. I will answer the gentleman. In my judgment it does go much further than the remarks of the gentleman would imply: but even if it goes no further than that—and I will discuss this point more fully before I conclude—it is still open to the same objection, that it proposes an entire departure from the theory of the Federal Government in meddling with these matters of State jurisdiction at all.

.   .   .

Now, I say to the gentleman from Pennsylvania [Mr. Stevens] that reading the language in its grammatical and legal construction it is a grant of the fullest and most ample power to Congress to make all laws "necessary and proper to secure to all persons in the several States protection in the rights of life, liberty, and property," with the simple proviso that such protection shall be equal. It is not a mere provision that when the States undertake to give protection which is unequal Congress may equalize it: it is a grant of power in general terms—a grant of the right to legislate for the protection of life, liberty and property, simply qualified with the condition that it shall be equal legislation. That is my construction of the proposition as it stands here. It may differ from that of other gentlemen.

Mr. Eldridge. Mr. Speaker, let me go a little further here. If it be true that the construction of this amendment, which I understand to be claimed by the gentlemen from Ohio. [Mr. Bingham.] who introduced it, and which I infer from his question is claimed by the gentleman from Pennsylvania. [Mr. Stevens:] if it be true that that is the true construction of this article, is it not even then introducing a power never before intended to be conferred upon Congress. For we all know it is true that probably every State in this Union fails to give equal protection to all persons within its borders in the rights of life, liberty, and property. It may be a fault in the States that they do not do it. A reformation may be desirable, but by the doctrines of the school of politics in which I have been brought up, and which I have been taught to regard was the best school of political rights and duties in this Union, reforms of this character should come from the States, and not be forced upon them by the centralized power of the Federal Government.

Take a single case by way of illustration, and I

take it simply to illustrate the point, without expressing any opinion whatever on the desirability or undesirability of a change in regard to it. Take the case of the rights of married women: did any one ever assume that Congress was to be invested with the power to legislate on that subject, and to say that married women, in regard to their rights of property, should stand on the same footing with men and unmarried women? There is not a State in the Union where disability of married women in relation to the rights of property does not to a greater or less extent still exist. Many of the States have taken steps for the partial abolition of that distinction in years past, some to a greater extent and others to a less. But I apprehend there is not to-day a State in the Union where there is not a distinction between the rights of married women, as to property, and the rights of *femmes sole* and men.

Mr. Stevens. If I do not interrupt the gentleman I will say a word. When a distinction is made between two married people or two *femmes sole*, then it is unequal legislation: but where all of the same class are dealt with in the same way then there is no pretense of inequality.

Mr. Hale. The gentleman will pardon me: his argument seems to me to be more specious than sound. The language of the section under consideration gives to *all persons* equal protection. Now, if that means you shall extend to one married woman the same protection you extend to another, and not the same you extend to unmarried women or men, then by parity of reasoning it will be sufficient if you extend to one negro the same rights you do to another, but not those you extend to a white man. I think, if the gentleman from Pennsylvania claims that the resolution only intends that all of a certain class shall have equal protection, such class legislation may certainly as easily satisfy the requirements of this resolution in the case of the negro as in the case of the married woman. The line of distinction is, I take it, quite as broadly marked between ne-

groes and white men as between married and unmarried women.

.   .   .

Mr. Hale. It is claimed that this constutitional amendment is aimed simply and purely toward the protection of "American citizens of African descent" in the States lately in rebellion. I understand that to be the whole intended practical effect of the amendment.

Mr. Bingham. It is due to the committee that I should say that it is proposed as well to protect the thousands and tens of thousands and hundreds of thousands of loyal white citizens of the United States whose property, by State legislation, has been wrested from them under confiscation, and protect them also against banishment.

Mr. Hale. I trust that when the gentlemen comes to reply, he will give me as much of his time as he takes of mine. As he has the reply, I do not think he ought to interject his remarks into my speech. I will modify my statement and say that this amendment is intended to apply solely to the eleven States lately in rebellion, so far as any practical benefit to be derived from it is concerned. The gentleman from Ohio can correct me if I am again in error.

Mr. Bingham. It is to apply to other States also that have in their constitutions and laws to-day provisions in direct violation of every principle of our Constitution.

Mr. Rogers. I suppose the gentleman refers to the State of Indiana!

Mr. Bingham. I do not know: it may be so. It applies unquestionably to the State of Oregon.

Mr. Hale. Then I will again modify my correction and say that it is intended to apply to every State which, in the judgment of the honorable member who introduced this measure, has failed to provide equal protection to life, liberty, and property. And here we come to the very thing for which I denounce this proposition, that it takes away from these States the right to determine for themselves what their institutions shall be.

Apparently dissatisfied with the discussion the preceding day, Bingham returned to the subject of the Married Women's Acts at the end of the debate on his proposal. He was then questioned about his views by Representative Hale.

February 28, 1866

Mr. Bingham. Excuse me. Mr. Speaker, we have had some most extraordinary arguments against the adoption of the proposed amendment.

.   .   .

But, say the gentleman, if you adopt this amendment you give to Congress the power to enforce all the rights of married women in the several States. I beg the gentleman's pardon. He need not be alarmed at the condition of married women. Those rights which are universal and independent of all local State legislation belong, by the gift of God, to every woman, whether married or single. The rights of life and liberty are theirs whatever States may enact. But the gentleman's concern is as to the right of property in married women.

Although this word property has been in your bill of rights from the year 1789 until this hour, who ever heard it intimated that anybody could have property protected in any State until he owned or acquired property there according to its local law or according to the law of some other State which he may have carried thither? I undertake to say no one.

As to real estate, every one knows that its acquisition and transmission under every interpretation ever given to the word property, as used in the Constitution of the country, are dependent exclusively upon the local law of the States, save under a direct grant of the United States. But suppose any person has acquired property not contrary to the laws of the State, but in accordance with its law, are they not to be equally protected in the enjoyment of it, or are they to be denied all protection? That is the question, and the whole question, so far as that part of the case is concerned.

.   .   .

Mr. Speaker. I speak in behalf of this amendment in no party spirit, in no spirit of resentment toward any State or the people of any State, in no spirit of innovation, but for the sake of a violated Constitution and a wronged and wounded country whose heart is now smitten with a strange, great sorrow. I urge the amendment for the enforcement of these essential provisions of your Constitution, divine in their justice, sublime in their humanity, which declare that all men are equal in the rights of life and liberty before the majesty of American law.

Representatives, to you I appeal, that hereafter, by your act and the approval of the loyal people of this country, every man in every State of the Union, in accordance with the written words of your Constitution, may, by the national law, be secured in the equal protection of his personal rights. Your Constitution provides that no man, no matter what his color, no matter beneath what sky he may have been born, no matter in what disastrous conflict or by what tyrannical hand his liberty may have been cloven down, no matter how poor, no matter how friendless, no matter how ignorant, shall be deprived of life or liberty or property without due process of law—law in its highest sense, that law which is the perfection of human reason, and which is impartial, equal, exact justice; that justice which requires that every man shall have his right: that justice which is the highest duty of nations as it is the imperishable attribute of the God of nations.

Mr. Hale. Before the gentleman takes his seat will he allow me to ask a single question pertinent to this subject?

Mr. Bingham. Yes sir.

Mr. Hale. I desire after hearing the gentleman's argument, in which I have been much interested as a very calm, lucid, and logical vindication of the amendment, to ask him, as an able constitutional lawyer, which he has proved himself to be, whether in his opinion this proposed amendment to the Constitution does not confer upon Congress a general power of legislation for the purpose of securing to all persons in the several States protection of life, liberty, and property, subject only to the qualification that that protection shall be equal.

Mr. Bingham. I believe it does in regard to life and liberty and property as I have heretofore stated it: the right to real estate being dependent on the State law except when granted by the United States.

Mr. Hale. Excuse me. If I understand the gentleman, he now answers that it does confer a general power to legislate on the subject in regard to life and libery, but not in regard to real estate. I desir_ to know if he means to imply that it extends to personal estate.

Mr. Bingham. Undoubtedly it is true. Let the gentleman look to the great Mississippi case. Slaughter and another, which is familiar doubtless, to all the members of the House, and he will find that under the Constitution the personal property of a citzen follows its owner, and is entitled to be protected in the State into which he goes.

Mr. Hale. The gentleman misapprehends my

point, or else I misapprehend his answer. My question was whether this provision, if adopted, confers upon Congress general powers of legislation in regard to the protection of life, liberty, and personal property.

Mr. Bingham. It certainly does this: it confers upon Congress power to see to it that the protection given by the laws of the United States shall be equal in respect to life and liberty and property to all persons.

Mr. Hale. Then will the gentleman point me to that clause or part of this resolution which contains the doctrine he here announces?

Mr. Bingham. The words "equal protection" contain it, and nothing else.

After this exchange, debate rapidly drew to a close. At the end of the debate, Representative Hotchkiss took the floor to state his position on the proposed amendment. He explained that he would vote to postpone consideration of the amendment until it could be modified. In his view, it was possible that Congress might fall into the control of the former rebels. To secure the rights described in the amendment, they should be directly protected by the Constitution:

> I have no doubt that I desire to secure every privilege and every right to every citizen in the United States that the gentleman who reports this resolution desires to secure. As I understand it, his object in offering this resolution and proposing this amendment is to provide that no State shall discriminate between its citizens and give one class of citizens greater right than it confers upon another. If this amendment secured that, I should vote very cheerfully for it to-day; but as I do not regard it as permanently securing those rights, I shall vote to postpone its consideration until there can be a further conference between the friends of the measure, and we can devise some means whereby we shall secure those rights beyond a question. . . .
>
> Now, I desire that the very privileges for which the gentleman [Bingham] is contending shall be secured to the citizens; but I want them secured by a constitutional amendment that legislation cannot override. Then if the gentleman wishes to go further, and provide by laws of Congress for the enforcement of these rights, I will go with him. . . .
>
> This amendment provides that Congress may pass laws to enforce these rights. Why not provide by an amendment to the Constitution that no State shall discriminate against any class of its citizens; and let that amendment stand as part of the organic law of the land, subject only to be defeated by another constitutional amendment. We may pass laws here to-day, and the next Congress may wipe them out.[26]

Representative Conkling then moved to postpone consideration of the measure. The motion passed with almost all Republicans, including Bingham, voting in favor.[27]

THE HOUSE DEBATES ON THE FOURTEENTH AMENDMENT

On April 9, 1866, the House overrode the President's veto and the Civil Rights bill became law. On April 21, Representative Stevens placed before the joint committee a Reconstruction plan proposed by Robert Owen. One aspect of the plan was a proposed constitutional amendment.[28] After some maneuvering in committee,[29] Bingham successfully had the original language of the proposal replaced by his own formulation:

> No state shall make or enforce any law which shall abridge the privileges or immunities of citizens of the United States; nor shall any state deprive any person of life, liberty or property without due process of law, nor deny to any person within its jurisdiction the equal protection of the laws.[30]

This language was similar to that contained in Bingham's earlier proposal. The significant difference was that the earlier proposal was phrased as a grant of congressional power whereas the new proposal was phrased as a limitation on state power. Years later, Bingham explained that, after the debates on his original proposal, he had read Chief Justice Marshall's opinion in *Barron v. Baltimore*,[31] which had convinced him that the existing Constitution did not protect fundamental rights against the action of the states. He explained that the privileges and immunities he had had in mind in 1866 were largely defined in the first eight amendments to the Constitution.[32]

Most of the debate on the Fourteenth Amendment concerned the now-forgotten provisions of sections 2 and 3. Moderate Republicans were apparently not yet prepared to mandate black suffrage immediately. As a substitute, they proposed a three-part solution to the problem of protecting blacks. Section 1 would ensure protection for fundamental civil rights, presumably excluding suffrage. Section 2 would reduce Southern representation in the House if and to the extent that Southern states denied blacks the right to vote. Section 3 would compensate for a possible lack of black suffrage by removing the right of certain Confederate supporters to vote. In the course of the debates, this last provision was watered down to prohibiting these individuals from holding federal office.[33]

Despite the focus on other sections, some significant statements were made about section 1 in the House, particularly on the opening day of the debate.

May 8, 1866

Mr. Stevens: Let us now refer to the provisions of the proposed amendment.

The first section prohibits the States from abridging the privileges and immunities of citizens of the United States, or unlawfully depriving them of life, liberty, or property, or of denying to any person within their jurisdiction the "equal" protection of the laws.

I can hardly believe that any person can be found who will not admit that every one of these provisions is just. They are all asserted, in some form or other, in our DECLARATION or organic law. But the Constitution limits only the action of Congress, and is not a limitation on the States. This amendment supplies that defect, and allows Congress to correct the unjust legislation of the States, so far that

the law which operates upon one man shall operate *equally* upon all. Whatever law punishes a white man for a crime shall punish the black man precisely in the same way and to the same degree. Whatever law protects the white man shall afford "equal" protection to the black man. Whatever means of redress is afforded to one shall be afforded to all. Whatever law allows the white man to testify in court shall allow the man of color to do the same. These are great advantages over their present codes. Now different degrees of punishment are inflicted, not on account of the magnitude of the crime, but according to the color of the skin. Now color disqualifies a man from testifying in courts, or being tried in the same way as white men. I need not enumerate these partial and oppressive laws. Unless the Constitution should restrain them those States will all, I fear, keep up this discrimination, and crush to death the hated freedmen. Some answer. "Your civil rights bill secures the same things." That is partly true, but a law is repealable by a majority. And I need hardly say that the first time that the South with their copperhead allies obtain the command of Congress it will be repealed. The veto of the President and their votes on the bill are conclusive evidence of that.

.   .   .

Mr. Garfield: Sir. I believe that the right to vote, if it be not indeed one of the natural rights of all men, is so necessary to the protection of their natural rights as to be indispensable, and therefore equal to natural rights. I believe that the golden sentence of John Stuart Mill, in one of his greatest works, ought to be written on the constitution of every State, and on the Constitution of the United States as the greatest and most precious of truths. "That the ballot is put into the hands of men, no so much to enable them to govern others as that he may not be misgoverned by others." I believe that suffrage is the shield, the sword, the spear, and all the panoply that best befits a man for this own defense in the great social organism to which he belongs. And I profoundly regret that we have not been enabled to write it and engrave it upon our institutions, and imbed it in the imperishable bulwarks of the Constitution as a part of the fundamental law of the land.

But I am willing, as I said once before in this presence, when I cannot get all I wish to take what I can get. And therefore I am willing to accept the propositions that the committee have laid before us, though I desire one amendment which I will mention presently.

I am glad to see this first section here which proposes to hold over every American citizen, without regard to color, the protecting shield of law. The gentleman who as just taken his seat [Mr. Finck] un-dertakes to show that because we propose to vote for this section we therefore acknowledge that the civil rights bill was unconstitutional. He was anticipated in that objection by the gentleman from Pennsylvania [Mr. Stevens.] The civil rights bill is now a part of the law of the land. But every gentleman knows it will cease to be a part of the law whenever the sad moment arrives when that gentleman's party comes into power. It is precisely for that reason that we propose to lift that great and good law above the reach of political strife, beyond the reach of the plots and machinations of any party, and fix it in the serene sky, in the eternal firmament of the Constitution, where no storm of passion can shake it and no cloud can obscure it. For this reason, and not because I believe the civil rights bill unconstituional, I am glad to see that first section here.

.   .   .

Mr. Thayer: With regard to the second section of the proposed amendment to the Constitution, it simply brings into the Constitution what is found in the bill of rights of every State of the Union. As I understand it, it is but incorporating in the Constitution of the United States the principle of the civil rights bill which has lately become a law, and that, not as the gentleman from Ohio [Mr. Finck] suggested, because in the estimation of this House that law cannot be sustained as constitutional, but in order, as was justly said by the gentleman from Ohio who last addressed the House [Mr. Garfield.] that that provision so necessary for the equal administration of the law, so just in its operation, so necessary for the protection of the fundamental rights of citizenship, shall be forever incorporated in the Constitution of the United States. But, sir, that subject has already been fully discussed. I have upon another occasion expressed my views upon it, and I do not propose to detain the House with any further remarks of my own upon it.

Several other speakers noted that they had supported the Civil Rights Acts and believed it to be constitutional, but were supporting the amendment to remove any possible doubts.[34] Some speakers referred to the Declaration of Independence as the source of the rights protected by the amendment.[35]

Near the close of the debates on section 1, Representative Bingham took the floor in a final attempt to explain the meaning of the amendment.

May 10, 1866

Mr. Bingham: The necessity for the first section of this amendment to the Constitution, Mr. Speaker, is one of the lessons that have been taught to your committee and taught to all the people of this country by the history of the past four years of terrific conflict—that history in which God is, and in which He teaches the profoundest lessons to men and nations. There was a want hitherto, and there remains a want now, in the Constitution of our country, which the proposed amendment will supply. What is that? It is the power in the people, the whole people of the United States, by express authority of the Constitution to do that by congressional enactment which hitherto they have not had the power to do, and have never even attempted to do; that is, to protect by national law the privileges and immunities of all the citizens of the Republic and the inborn rights of every person within its jurisdiction whenever the same shall be abridged or denied by the unconstitutional acts of any State.

Allow me, Mr. Speaker, in passing, to say that this amendment takes from no State any right that ever pertained to it. No State ever had the right, under the forms of law or otherwise, to deny to any freeman the equal protection of the laws or to abridge the privileges or immunities of any citizen of the Republic, although many of them have assumed and exercised the power, and that without remedy. The amendment does not give, as the second section shows, the power to Congress of regulating suffrage in the several States.

The second section excludes the conclusion that by the first section suffrage is subjected to congressional law: save, indeed, with this exception, that as the right in the people of each State to a republican government and to choose their Representatives in Congress is of the guarantees of the Constitution, by this amendment a remedy might be given directly for a case supposed by Madison, where treason might change a State government from a republican to a despotic government, and thereby deny suffrage to the people. Why should any American citizen object to that? But, sir, it has been suggested, not here, but elsewhere, if this section does not confer suffrage the need of it is not perceived. To all such I beg leave again to say, that many instances of State injustice and oppression have already occurred in the State legislation of this Union, of flagrant violations of the guarantied privileges of citizens of the United States, for which the national

Government furnished and could furnish by law no remedy whatever. Contrary to the express letter of your Constitution, "cruel and unusual punishments" have been inflicted under State laws within this Union upon citizens, not only for crimes committed, but for sacred duty done, for which and against which the Government of the United States had provided no remedy and could provide none.

Sir, the words of the Constitution that "the citizens of each State shall be entitled to all privileges and immunities of citizens in the several States" include, among other privileges, the right to bear true allegiance to the Constitution and laws of the United States, and to be protected in life, liberty, and property. Next, sir, to the allegiance which we all owe to God our Creator, is the allegiance which we owe to our common country.

The time was in our history, thirty-three years ago, when, in the State of South Carolina, by solemn ordinance adopted in a convention held under the authority of State law, it was ordained, as a part of the fundamental law of that State, that the citizens of South Carolina, being citizens of the United States as well, should abjure their allegiance to every other government or authority than that of the State of South Carolina.

That ordinance contained these words:

"The allegiance of the citizens of this State is due to the State: and no allegiance is due from them to any other Power or authority: and the General Assembly of said State is hereby empowered from time to time, when they may deem it proper, to provide for the administration to the citizens and officers of the State, or such of the said officers, as they may think fit, of suitable oaths or affirmations, binding them to the observance of such allegiance, and abjuring all other allegiance; and also to define what shall amount to a violation of their allegiance, and to provide the proper punishment for such violation."

There was also, as gentlemen know, an attempt made at the same time by that State to nullify the revenue laws of the United States. What was the legislation of Congress in that day to meet this usurpation of authority by that State, violative alike of the rights of the national Government and of the rights of the citizen?

In that hour of danger and trial to the country there was as able a body of men in this Capitol as was ever convened in Washington, and of these were Webster, Clay, Benton, Silas Wright, John

Quincy Adams, and Edward Livingston. They provided a remedy by law for the invasion of the rights of the Federal Government and for the protection of its officials and those assisting them in executing the revenue laws. (See 4 Statutes-at-Large, 632-33.) No remedy was provided to protect the citizen. Why was the act to provide for the collection of the revenue passed, and to protect all acting under it, and no protection given to secure the citizen against punishment for fidelity to his country? But one answer can be given. There was in the Constitution of the United States an express grant of power to the Federal Congress to lay and collect duties and imposts and to pass all laws necessary to carry that grant of power into execution. But, sir, that body of great and patriotic men looked in vain for any grant of power in the Constitution by which to give protection to the citizens of the United States resident in South Carolina against the infamous provision of the ordinance which required them to abjure the allegiance which they owed their country. It was an opprobrium to the Republic that for fidelity to the United States they could not by national law be protected against the degrading punishment inflicted on slaves and felons by State law. That great want of the citizen and stranger, protection by national law from unconstitutional State enactments, is supplied by the first section of this amendment. That is the extent that it hath, no more; and let gentlemen answer to God and their country who oppose its incorporation into the organic law of the land.

Do you find Bingham's speech illuminating? Just what rights did he think were protected by the proposed amendment? Or is his vagueness an indication of the potential flexibility of the amendment?

Shortly after Bingham's speech, the House passed the joint resolution proposing the constitutional amendment.[36]

THE SENATE DEBATES

On May 23, the Senate began consideration of the proposed amendment. Since the Senate chairman of the joint committee, Senator Fessenden, was ill, the joint resolution was presented by Senator Howard.

May 23, 1866

Mr. Howard: The first clause of this section relates to the privileges and immunities of citizens of the United States as such, and as distinguished from all other persons not citizens of the United States.

.   .   .

It would be a curious question to solve what are the privileges and immunities of citizens of each of the States in the several States. I do not propose to go at any length into that question at this time. It would be a somewhat barren discussion. But it is certain the clause was inserted in the Constitution for some good purpose. It has in view some results beneficial to the citizens of the several States, or it would not be found there; yet I am not aware that the Supreme Court have ever undertaken to define either the nature or extent of the privileges and immunities thus guarantied. Indeed, if my recollection serves me, that court, on a certain occasion not many years since, when this question seemed to present itself to them, very modestly declined to go into a definition of them, leaving questions arising under the clause to be discussed and adjudicated when they should happen practically to arise. But we may gather some intimation of what probably will be the opinion of the judiciary by referring to a case adjudged many years ago in one of the circuit courts of the United States by Judge Washington: and I will trouble the Senate but for a moment by reading what that very learned and excellent judge says about these privileges and immunities of the citizens of each State in the several States. It is the case of Corfield vs. Coryell.

.   .   .

Such is the character of the privileges and immunities spoken of in the second section of the fourth article of the Constitution. To these privileges and immunities, whatever they may be—for they are not and cannot be fully defined in their entire extent and precise nature—to these should be added the personal rights guarantied and secured by the first eight amendments of the Constitution; such as the freedom of speech and of the press; the right of the people peaceably to assemble and petition the Government for a redress of grievances, a right appertaining to each and all the people; the right to keep and to bear arms; the right to be exempted from the quartering of soldiers in a house without the consent of the owner; the right to be exempt from unreasonable searches and seizures, and from any search or seizure except by virtue of a warrant issued upon a formal oath or affidavit: the right of an accused person to be informed of the nature of the accusation against him, and his right to be tried by an impartial jury of the vicinage; and also the right to be secure against excessive bail and against cruel and unusual punishments.

Now, sir, here is a mass of privileges, immunities, and rights, some of them secured by the second section of the fourth article of the Constitution, which I have recited, some by the first eight amendments of the Constitution; and it is a fact well worthy of attention that the course of decision of our courts and the present settled doctrine is, that all these immunities, privileges, rights, thus guarantied by the Constitution or recognized by it, are secured to the citizen solely as a citizen of the United States and as a party in their courts. They do not operate in the slightest degree as a restraint or prohibition upon State legislation. States are not affected by them, and it has been repeatedly held that the restriction contained in the Constitution against the taking of private property for public use without just compensation is not a restriction upon State legislation, but applies only to the legislation of Congress.

Now, sir, there is no power given in the Constitution to enforce and to carry out any of these guarantees. They are not powers granted by the Constitution to Congress, and of course do not come within the sweeping clause of the Constitution authorizing Congress to pass all laws necessary and proper for carrying out the foregoing or granted powers, but they stand simply as a bill of rights in the Constitution, without power on the part of Congress to give them full effect; while at the same time

the States are not restrained from violating the principles embraced in them except by their own local constitutions, which may be altered from year to year. The great object of the first section of this amendment is, therefore, to restrain the power of the States and compel them at all times to respect these great fundamental guarantees. How will it be done under the present amendment? As I have remarked, they are not powers granted to Congress, and therefore it is necessary, if they are to be effectuated and enforced, as they assuredly ought to be, that additional power should be given to Congress to that end. This is done by the fifth section of this amendment, which declares that "the Congress shall have power to enforce by appropriate legislation the provisions of this article." Here is a direct affirmative delegation of power to Congress to carry out all the principles of all these guarantees, a power not found in the Constitution.

The last two clauses of the first section of the amendment disable a State from depriving not merely a citizen of the United States, but any person, whoever he may be, of life, liberty, or property without due process of law, or from denying to him the equal protection of the laws of the State. This abolishes all class legislation in the States and does away with the injustice of subjecting one caste of persons to a code not applicable to another. It prohibits the hanging of a black man for a crime for which the white man is not be be hanged. It protects the black man in his fundamental rights as a citizen with the same shield which it throws over the white man. Is it not time, Mr. President, that we extend to the black man, I had almost called it the poor privilege of the equal protection of the law? Ought not the time to be now passed when one measure of justice is to be meted out to a member of one caste while another and a different measure is meted out to the member of another caste, both castes being alike citizens of the United States, both bound to obey the same laws, to sustain the burdens of the same Government, and both equally responsible to justice and to God for the deeds done in the body?

But, sir, the first section of the proposed amendment does not give to either of these classes the right of voting. The right of suffrage is not, in law, one of the privileges or immunities thus secured by the Constitution. It is merely the creature of law. It has always been regarded in this country as the result of positive local law, not regarded as one of those fundamental rights lying at the basis of all society and without which a people cannot exist except as slaves, subject to a depotism.

As I have already remarked, section one is a restriction upon the States, and does not, of itself, confer any power upon Congress. The power which Congress has, under this amendment, is derived, not from that section, but from the fifth section, which gives it authority to pass laws which are appropriate to the attainment of the great object of the amendment. I look upon the first section, taken in connection with the fifth, as very important. It will, if adopted by the States, forever disable every one of them from passing laws trenching upon those fundamental rights and privileges which pertain to citizens of the United States, and to all persons who may happen to be within their jurisdiction. It establishes equality before the law, and it gives to the humblest, the poorest, the most despised of the race the same rights and the same protection before the law as it gives to the most powerful, the most wealthy, or the most haughty. That, sir, is republican government, as I understand it, and the only one which can claim the praise of a just Government. Without this principle of equal justice to all men and equal protection under the shield of the law, there is no republican government and none that is really worth maintaining.

Another clue about Howard's views is contained in an exchange relating to voting rights, which were indirectly protected by the proposed rules reducing House representation for states that disenfranchised their citizens. In defending this provision, he read a passage by Madison about the right of all persons to vote. Asked whether this included women, he replied:

> I believe Mr. Madison was old enough and wise enough to take it for granted there was such a thing as the law of nature which has a certain influence even in political affairs, and that by that law women and children were not regarded as the equals of men. Mr. Madison would not have quibbled about the question of women's voting or of an infant's voting. He lays down a broad democratic principle, that those who are to be bound by the laws ought to have a voice in making them; and everywhere mature manhood is the representative type of the human race.[37]

After the Senate debate on May 23, Republican senators met in caucus to agree on a course of action regarding the proposed constitutional amendment. The joint resolution came before the Senate again on May 29. As a result of the caucus, amendments were made to sections 2 and 3, and the citizenship clause was added to section 1. Opponents complained bitterly that the key decisions had been made secretly.

After the caucus amendments to the joint resolution were passed by party vote, significant Senate debate on the Fourteenth Amendment was brief. This seems largely due to the fact that Senate Republicans had resolved their differences in secret party caucus, about which we know very little.

At various points in the debate, references were made to the reciprocal nature of allegiance and protection, as well as to the fundamental rights protected by the comity clause.[38] Again, reference was made to the need for an assured constitutional basis for the Civil Rights Act.

In the course of the debates, Senator Howard explained that in his view the amendment was "simply declaratory of what I regard as the law of the land already, that every person born within the limits of the United States, and subject to their jurisdiction, is by virtue of natural law and national law a citizen of the United States."[39] He also engaged in the following exchange about the reasons for section 1.

May 30, 1866

Mr. Doolittle. As I understand, a member from Ohio, Mr. Bingham, who in a very able speech in the House maintained that the civil rights bill was without any authority in the Constitution, brought forward a proposition in the House of Representatives to amend the Constitution so as to enable Congress to declare the civil rights of all persons, and that the constitutional amendment, Mr. Bingham being himself one of the committee of fifteen, was referred by the House to that committee, and from the committee it has been reported. I say I have a right to infer that it was because Mr. Bingham and others of the House of Representatives and other persons upon the committee had doubts, at least, as to the constitutionality of the civil rights bill that this proposition to amend the Constitution now appears to give it validity and force. It is not an imputation upon any one.

Mr. Grimes. It is an imputation upon every member who voted for the bill, the inference being legitimate and logical that they violated their oaths and knew they did so when they voted for the civil rights bill.

Mr. Doolittle. The Senator goes too far. What I say is that they had doubts.

Mr. Fessenden. I will say to the Senator one thing: whatever may have been Mr. Bingham's motives in bringing it forward, he brought it forward some time before the civil rights bill was considered at all and had it referred to the committee, and it was discussed in the committee long before the civil rights bill was passed. Then I will say to him further, that during all the discussion in the committee that I heard nothing was ever said about the civil rights bill in connection with that. It was placed on entirely different grounds.

Mr. Doolittle. I will ask the Senator from Maine this question: if Congress, under the Constitution now has the power to declare that "all persons born in the United States, and not subject to any foreign Power, excluding Indians not taxed, are hereby declared to be citizens of the United States," what is the necessity of amending the Constitution at all on this subject?

Mr. Fessenden. I do not choose that the Senator shall get off from the issue he presented. I meet him right there on the first issue. If he wants my opinion upon other questions, he can ask it afterward. He was saying that the committee of fifteen brought this proposition forward for a specific object.

Mr. Doolittle. I said the committee of fifteen brought it forward because they had doubts as to the consitutional power of Congress to pass the civil rights bill.

Mr. Fessenden. Exactly: and I say, in reply, that if they had doubts, no such doubts were stated in the committee of fifteen, and the matter was not put on that ground at all. There was no question raised about the civil rights bill.

Mr. Dootlittle. Then I put the question to the Senator: if there are no doubts, why amend the Constitution on that subject?

Mr. Fessenden. That question the Senator may answer to suit himself. It has no reference to the civil rights bill.

Mr. Doolittle. That does not meet the case at all. If my friend maintains that at this moment the Constitution of the United States, without amendment, gives all the power you ask, why do you put this new amendment into it on that subject?

Mr. Howard. If the Senator from Wisconsin wishes an answer, I will give him one such as I am able to give.

Mr. Doolittle. I was asking the Senator from Maine.

Mr. Howard. I was a member of the same committee, and the Senator's observations apply to me equally with the Senator from Maine. We desired to put this question of citizenship and the right of citizens and freedmen under the civil rights bill beyond the legislative power of such gentlemen as the Senator from Wisconsin, who would pull the whole system up by the roots and destroy it, and expose the freedmen again to the oppressions of their old masters.

On June 13, the joint resolution as amended in the Senate was taken up again in the House, the question being whether the House would approve the Senate amendments. There was little discussion of section 1. Then began a long and tortuous struggle for ratification. Because that struggle reveals more about changing political forces after 1866 than about the intended scope of the amendment, we will consider the ratification process in the next chapter.

Topics for Discussion

1. How much weight should be given to Howard's views? Some writers have argued that they should be discounted because he only presented the amendment in Fessenden's absence. Do his remarks seem hasty or ill-considered? Is it significant that no one thought to correct his views about section 1 (for example, with respect to incorporation of the Bill of Rights)?

2. What was Bingham's position? Should his views be given decisive weight because of his role in drafting section 1? Or should they be discounted because his speeches sometimes seemed muddled or vague?

3. The discussion of the scope of section 1 took up very little time, and much that did take place related to the drafting of the citizenship clause, particularly regarding its application to Indian tribes. What can we infer from this? That the equal protection clause, privileges and immunities clause, and due process clause were considered insignificant? That everyone assumed their content had been fixed by the list of rights in the Civil Rights Act? That the rights were thought to exist independently of the amendment, so that only a new enforcement mechanism was involved? Or simply that other matters seemed more pressing in the context of Reconstruction?

4. What guidance do you find in the debates regarding present-day constitutional issues like affirmative action, or earlier controversies about school segregation and incorporation of the Bill of Rights? How much weight should "original intent" be given in these matters? Should any weight be given to the widespread racism and sexism of the 1860s in determining how to apply the amendment today?

5. The Supreme Court's first opportunity to interpret the Fourteenth Amendment came in the *Slaughter-House Cases*, 83 U.S. (16 Wall.) 36, 21 L.Ed. 394 (1873), which involved the validity of a Louisiana statute creating a monopoly over slaughtering in the New Orleans area. A five-justice majority upheld the Louisiana law. The "privileges and immunities" clause was narrowly construed to include only a few rights involving the individual's relationship with the federal government, such as the right to communicate with federal authorities. In contrast, those rights described in *Corfield* remained exclusively subject to state control. A contrary ruling, the majority said, would destroy the entire basis of federalism. The dissent insisted that the *Corfield* rights were now protected by the Fourteenth Amendment. Which view comes closest to the original understanding of the framers? Do you agree with historian William Nelson that the majority's approach was "flatly inconsistent"[40] with the amendment's history?

FOOTNOTES

1. *Cong. Globe*, 39th Cong., 1st Sess. 1366 (1866).

2. 67 U.S. (2 Black) 635, 17 L.Ed. 459 (1862).

3. In attempting to uphold the blockade, the federal government was put in a difficult position. On the one hand, it was committed to the position that secession was legally void and that Southerners remained citizens of the United States subject to American municipal law. The implication of this view was that the Civil War was in effect a police action against a band of criminals. But such a police action would not give the United States the right under the law of nations to impose a blockade on neutrals on the high seas, nor would it give the Government the right under the Constitution to seize the property of citizens who were not proved to be members of the criminal group.

4. 6 Fed. Cas. 546 (C.C.E.D. Pa. 1823) No. 3,230. *See also Douglas v. Stephens*, 1 Del. Ch. 465, 469-74, 477-78 (1821). *Corfield* is close to the Supreme Court's current view of the comity clause, which also uses a fundamental rights analysis. For a recent discussion of the relationship between the Fourteenth Amendment and evolving concepts of national citizenship, see Robert J. Kaczorowski, *Revolutionary Constitutionalism in the Era of the Civil War and Reconstruction*, 61 N. Y. U. L. Rev. 863 (1986).

5. 6 Fed. Cas. at 551-52.

6. *Cong. Globe*, 39th Cong., 1st Sess. 600 (1866). *See also id*. at 476 (bill protects "fundamental rights belonging to every man as a free man"). Trumbull used somewhat similar language in connection with the Freedmen's Bureau bill. See *id*. 319, 322.

7. *Id*. at 1118.

8. *Id*. at 1294.

9. *Id*. at 1835.

10. *Id*. at 1836. See also *id*. at 1263 (remarks by Rep. Broomall listing free speech as one of the "rights and immunities of citizens"); *id*. at 1266 (remarks of Rep. Raymond listing "right to bear arms" as a right of citizens); *id*. at 1293-94 (remarks of Rep. Shellabarger, right of petition is an "indipensable" right of citizenship).

11. *Id*. at 530. See also Johnson's expostulation in response to a contrary argument by Sen. Henderson, *id*. at 572.

12. *Id*. at 530.

13. *Id*. at 1263.

14. *Id*. at 1119. Wilson reiterated essentially the same argument, *id*. at App. 157 and *id*. at 1294.

15. *Id*. at 1293.

16. *Id*. at 1757.

17. *Id*. at 1833.

18. *Id*. at 1835.

19. *Id*. at 1033-34.

20. *Id*. at 1034. *See also id*. at 1292.

21. *Id*. at 1062-63 (remarks of Rep. Kelley).

22. *Id*. at 1066 (remarks of Rep. Price).

23. *Id*. at 1088 (remarks of Rep. Woodbridge).

24. *Id*. at 1088-89.

25. Such laws would unquestionably be struck down by the Supreme Court today as violations of the equal protection clause.

26. *Cong. Globe*, 39th Cong., 1st Sess. 1095 (1866).

27. *Id*.

28. *See* Benjamin B. Kendrick, *The Journal of the Joint Committee of Fifteen on Reconstruction*, 83-84 (1914) [hereinafter Committee Journal]; Charles Fairman, *Reconstruction and Reunion 1864-88* 1282 (1971) [hereinafter Reconstruction].

29. *See* Kendrick, *Committee Journal*, at 85-88.

30. *Id*. at 87.

31. 32 U.S. (7 Pet.) 243, 8 L.Ed. 672 (1833).

32. *See* Joseph B. James, *The Framing of the Fourteenth Amendment* 104-06 (1956).

33. *See* Fairman, *Reconstruction*, at 1296.

34. See *Cong. Globe*, 39th Cong., 1st Sess. 2498 (1866) (remarks of Rep. Broomall); *id*. at 2468 (remarks of Rep. Kelley); *id*. at 2502 (remarks of Rep. Raymond); *id*. at 2511 (remarks of Rep. Eliot).

35. See *id.* at 2510 (remarks of Rep. Miller); *id.* at 2539 (remarks of Rep. Farnsworth).

36. *Id.* at 2545.

37. *Id.* at 2767.

38. *Id.* 2918 (remarks of Sen. Willey); *id.* at 2919 (remarks of Sen. Davis); *id.* at 2892 (remarks of Sen. Conness); *id.* at 2896 (remarks of Sen. Howard); *id.* at 2961 (remarks of Sen. Poland); *id.* at App. 219 (remarks of Sen. Howe); *id.* at 3031-35 (remarks of Sen. Henderson). *See also id.* at App. 256 (remarks of Rep. Baker); *id.* at App. 293 (remarks of Rep. Shellabarger).

39. *Id.* at 2890.

40. William Nelson, *The Fourteenth Amendment* 163 (1988).

CHAPTER TWELVE

The Fifteenth Amendment

INTRODUCTION

As we saw in the previous chapter, black suffrage was on the minds of the Congressmen who enacted the Fourteenth Amendment. They apparently did not feel, however, that a direct attack on the problem was politically feasible. Instead, they provided in section 1 of the amendment protection of the fundamental rights of southern blacks, while in section 2 they encouraged suffrage by reducing congressional representation for states that denied blacks the vote. Four years later, however, a changing political landscape made a constitutional amendment on suffrage not only feasible but imperative.[1]

This chapter will explore the complex events leading up to the passage of the Fifteenth Amendment. We will begin by discussing the historical background, including the process of ratifying the Fourteenth Amendment. Next, we will turn to the enactment itself, considering first the amendment's tangled procedural history in Congress and then the debates. The debates are of interest partly for the light they shed on the amendment, and partly for what they tell us about changing concepts of political representation and federalism. After describing the debates, we will consider the ratification and then round off the story of the Reconstruction amendments by briefly describing the end of Reconstruction.

The Fifteenth Amendment can be seen in either of two lights. First, it can be seen as a crucial step in Reconstruction and in the larger history of American race relations. But it was also an important step in another story, that of the gradual expansion of popular suffrage and majority rule. That story continued with several later constitutional amendments, which we consider briefly in the final section of this chapter. We bring the two aspects of the story together with a brief discussion of the 1965 Voting Rights Act, which finally made real the amendment's promise that political participation would encompass all segments of American society.

HISTORICAL BACKGROUND

Ratification of the Fourteenth Amendment

The story of the Fifteenth Amendment really begins with the ratification of the Fourteenth Amendment, which itself is a fascinating chapter in American history. Ratification turned on issues of raw political power rather than on intellectual disputes about the amendment. As a result, the ratification debates shed little light on the amendment's meaning. They are crucial, however, to understanding the political forces behind the amendment's successor.

Tennessee's early ratification was important and accomplished through extraordinary means. Tennessee was the only former member of the Confederacy to ratify quickly. The governor told a special session of the legislature that ratification was the price of readmission to the Union. Congress had never explicitly promised readmission on these terms, and some radicals were opposed to making ratification the sole condition for readmission. Nevertheless, the governor's statement reflected the common understanding.

The Tennessee Senate moved with dispatch and little debate. But the House could not assemble a quorum to consider the amendment. As the number present decreased rather than increased, the House issued a summons to its absent members. One was arrested after a "wild night-chase by mule and on foot through the hills. . . ."[2] Others were said to have eluded detectives. A writ of habeas corpus was issued to obtain the release of two members, but the legislature refused to comply. When the two refused to take their seats, they were kept in custody in a nearby room, being marked "present" for the vote, thereby securing the existence of a quorum.

The governor sent a telegram to Bingham announcing, "Battle fought and won. . . . Two of Johnson's tools refused to vote. Give my compliments to the dead dog in the White House."[3] Congress promptly agreed to seat the Tennessee delegation.

The other former members of the Confederacy were more obdurate. In Texas, for example, the amendment was rejected on a variety of grounds, including its inconsistency with the Tenth Amendment and the "loss of honor as a people" that would have been entailed by ratification.[4] In general, as the leading historian of ratification puts it, "Southerners felt that they could not voluntarily bring humiliation and dishonor upon themselves by approving the proposal."[5] Mississippi not only refused to ratify the Fourteenth Amendment, it had never even agreed to ratify the Thirteenth. Several border states joined the South in rejecting the amendment, but a wave of Northern states voted to ratify.

After the South rejected the amendment, there was a period of negotiation in which (with the support of President Johnson and others) various compromise amendments were suggested, softening the impact of sections 2 and 3 on the South. These compromise measures went nowhere.

Southern ratification of the amendment was secured only through congressional reconstruction of the governments of the Southern states. The Arkansas case is illustrative. During military Reconstruction, the state was under the jurisdiction of General Ord, who supervised a state election calling for a state constitutional convention. Republicans elected most of the delegates, including three blacks. The election for adoption of the new state constitution was held under military supervision. After the new state constitution was adopted, ratification of the Fourteenth Amendment quickly followed, but the amendment was ratified before the new legislature had been approved by the federal government. Accepting the ratification, Congress overlooked numerous election irregularities, as well as the presence for some days of duplicate state governments. Elsewhere in the South, the ratification process was also messy, chaotic, and accomplished only as part of the larger process of forcibly revamping Southern society.

The ratification process raised many legal concerns at the time. Ohio and New Jersey passed resolutions rescinding their ratification, but these resolutions were ignored. Southern ratification can be called voluntary only in the broadest sense, given the fact that it was the price of readmission. Some members of Congress believed that the Southern states did not count as part of the total number of states needed, but others believed that three-fourths of all the states (including the former Confederacy) was needed. The secretary of state issued several announcements demonstrating that he was puzzled about whether the amendment had or had not been ratified. Congress then passed a concurrent resolution to the effect that it had been ratified. The secretary of state then issued a very peculiar announcement that the amendment was in force, but based this announcement on the congressional resolution rather than on his own judgment that ratification had been achieved.

This highly irregular ratification process is somewhat reminiscent of the ratification of the original Constitution. Recall that the legality of the Constitution was subject to much dispute. As with the original Constitution, the adoption of the Fourteenth Amendment strained the norms of legalism. In the end, however, the political will of the nation proved more significant than legalities.

Congressional Reconstruction

For Bingham and other moderates, the ratification of the Fourteenth Amendment was the key to Reconstruction. The initial rejection of the amendment in the South made it clear that more vigorous action by Congress was necessary. It was only this more radical Reconstruction program that ultimately, as we have just seen, led to the ratification of the amendment by the Southern states.

The question of black suffrage, temporarily put aside in the drafting of the Fourteenth Amendment, again returned to the forefront. By the time the Fourteenth Amendment was finally ratified, black suffrage in the South had already been instituted through congressional action.

By January of 1867, ten Southern states had rejected the Fourteenth Amendment, and there were disturbing reports of violence against freedmen. Clearly, further action was necessary. A variety of Reconstruction proposals were made by Republicans of varying degrees of radicalism.

The first Military Reconstruction Act was passed in 1867. It divided the South into five military districts. National protection for the rights of citizens, later to be secured judicially through the Fourteenth Amendment, was to be enforced by the cruder but perhaps more powerful mechanism of the military. The commanding general for each district was in charge not only of maintaining order but also of supervising the creation of new state governments. As in the Arkansas episode discussed above, a new state constitution was to be drafted and then ratified by the voters, after which new state officers would be elected. Also, the state would have to ratify the Fourteenth Amendment. Once these steps were completed, the state's congressional delegation would be readmitted.

The most dramatic innovation of the act was its requirement of black suffrage. Blacks were entitled to vote in the elections for delegates to the state constitutional conventions and in the elections to adopt the constitutions. Moreover, the new state constitutions themselves were required to provide for black suffrage. Thus, well before the passage of the Fifteenth Amendment, Southern blacks had received the right to vote from Congress.

President Johnson vetoed the first Military Reconstruction Act. He attacked it as beyond congressional power, a violation of the rights of Southerners, and a dangerous step toward giving blacks undue status in society. His veto was overridden. Supplementary legislation soon followed, filling in the details of congressional Reconstruction.

Because the new constitutions adopted under the Reconstruction statutes gave blacks equal status, they were vigorously resisted by whites, who also had other objections to the new state governments. The new governments had a checkered record. Corruption was widespread, as it was in Northern cities. Whites who participated in the governments were scorned as "scala-wags" and "carpetbaggers," epithets that survive in our language. The recon-structed governments did have genuine achievements, though, such as intro-ducing public education in the South.

The subject of southern Reconstruction remains controversial today. While there may never be a complete consensus on it, the following comments by a noted historian are a fairly balanced appraisal:

> The post-war period was one of low political morality, and there was no reason to expect that newly enfranchised blacks would prove any less attracted by the profits of politics than anybody else. Petty corruption prevailed in all the Southern state governments. Louisiana legislators voted themselves an allowance for stationery— which covered purchases of hams and bottles of champagne. The South Carolina legislature ran up a bill of more than $50,000 in refurbishing the state house with such costly items as a $750 mirror, $480 clocks, and 200 porcelain spittoons at $8 apiece. The same legislature voted $1,000 to the speaker of the house of represen-tatives to repay his losses on a horse race.
>
> Bad as these excesses were, Southern Democrats were angered less by them than by the legitimate work performed by the new state governments. Unwilling to rec-ognize that Negroes were now equal members of the body politic, they objected to expenditures for hospitals, jails, orphanages, and asylums to care for blacks. Most of all they objected to the creation of a public school system. Throughout the South, there was considerable hostility to the idea of educating any children at the cost of the taxpayer, and the thought of paying taxes in order to teach black children seemed wild and foolish extravagance. "It is worse than throwing money away to give it to the education of niggers," announced the Livingston (Louisiana) *Herald* in 1870.[6]

The Johnson Impeachment

The impeachment of Andrew Johnson was a unique event in American his-tory. The only other president ever to be seriously threatened with impeach-ment, Richard Nixon, resigned rather than face trial in the Senate. Johnson was actually tried on articles of impeachment, and he was very nearly convicted. This episode is not only an important part of the political developments leading up to the Fifteenth Amendment, it is in its own right an event of constitutional import.

As we saw in the previous chapter, congressional Republicans had some hopes for President Johnson when he took office. His veto of the 1866 Civil Rights Act marked the beginning of a rift, which was broadened by his opposition to the Fourteenth Amendment. This rift was exacerbated by the fact that, because the South was under military occupation, control of Reconstruction required control of military officials. The president, as commander-in-chief of armed forces under Article II of the Constitution, naturally claimed exclusive power over these officers. From the congressional point of view, however, his actions obstructed genuine reconstruction. The Military Reconstruction Act of 1867 made matters worse by reinforcing the responsibility of the military commanders.

Congress in 1867 took steps to restrict presidential authority over military Reconstruction. Two 1867 statutes concentrated military authority in the general of the army. The president could not issue orders directly to subordinate officers, appoint those officers, or remove the commanding general without the Senate's consent.

The Tenure of Office Act prohibited the president from removing any official who had been appointed with the Senate's advice and consent unless he obtained senatorial consent for the removal. A provision that would later prove important gave the president authority to remove officials when the Senate was not in session, but those officials would resume office if the Senate declined to consent to the removal after it was in session again. Presidents had always claimed the power to remove their subordinates, and the First Congress had given some support to that view. Relying on that history, Johnson vetoed the act, but his veto was quickly overridden.

By this time, radical Republicans were already interested in the possibility of removing Johnson from office. They were unable to find a basis for impeachment that would command sufficiently broad support, and the House actually voted down one impeachment effort. But in February 1868 Johnson gave the radicals the ammunition they needed. He had previously removed Secretary of War Stanton from office while the Senate was not in session. When the Senate returned and refused to consent to the removal, Stanton resumed office. Johnson again removed Stanton while the Senate was still in session.

Within two weeks, the House had settled on articles of impeachment. Several of the articles charged Johnson with criminally conspiring with the new appointee to violate the Tenure Act. The act made it a crime for the new appointee to hold office, but did not provide a criminal penalty for the president; the conspiracy charge was a way of criminalizing the president's conduct as well. Other articles charged Johnson with subverting Reconstruction and bringing Congress into public contempt.

The trial began at the end of March. Johnson had several defenses to the charge of violating the Tenure of Office Act. One was technical, the fact that Stanton was originally appointed by Lincoln and therefore arguably subject to a special statutory exception. More importantly, Johnson argued, the statute itself was an unconstitutional intrusion on presidential prerogatives. Finally, he contended, his action was only intended as a test case to determine the constitutionality of the statute.

The impeachment effort failed by a single vote. The decisive votes were cast by seven Republican senators, several of whom (Fessenden and Trumbull, in particular) are familiar names from previous chapters. By the time of the vote, Johnson had already begun to cooperate more fully on Reconstruction. Also, conservative Republicans were not pleased at the prospect that Ben Wade, then president pro tem of the Senate, would succeed to the presidency. And some may well have agreed with Johnson's legal arguments.

It is hard to guess what the long-term effects of a successful impeachment would have been. Perhaps it would have been viewed as a unique event, or perhaps it would have established the right of Congress to remove any president it viewed as hostile to its policies. That would have been an important step toward a parliamentary regime. Another result might have been to establish the right of Congress to control presidential removals of subordinates, which might well have weakened the executive branch. Less speculatively, a successful impeachment would surely have changed the further path of Reconstruction.

Political Forces and the Suffrage Issue

The suffrage issue did not disappear while these events were occurring. Rather, beginning even before 1866, it posed substantial political problems for the Republicans. Northern voters rejected black suffrage in a number of critical races in 1865. In 1866, Nebraska voters rejected it, and so did Kansas and Minnesota voters. Ohio was another major defeat for supporters of suffrage for blacks. There were, however, some victories in the North. Iowa and Minnesota adopted black suffrage in 1868, and Wisconsin adopted it by judicial decree. These states did not, however, have significant black populations.

Congress also took some cautious steps toward black suffrage. In 1866, after Johnson's supporters suffered major electoral defeats, Congress provided for black suffrage in the District of Columbia, overruling another unsuccessful veto by Johnson. Following this defeat, Johnson acquiesced in a bill granting black suffrage in the territories. And in 1867, as we have seen, the Military Reconstruction Act granted blacks the right to vote in the South.

The 1867 "off-year" elections were a serious setback to the Northern Republicans and caused them to rethink their position. They decided to hold the issue of black suffrage in abeyance until after the next presidential election. The 1868 Republican convention witnessed a platform fight over it, but the moderates succeeded in adopting a plank that left Northern suffrage to the states while guaranteeing suffrage in the South. Grant won the election by a margin of only 300,000 votes, less than the number of Southern blacks voting.

At this point, Republicans had several reasons to take immediate steps toward black suffrage. First, a federal guarantee of black suffrage would help hold the Southern black vote. Otherwise, blacks might defect to the Democrats if the Republicans failed to maintain their loyalty, or the South might succeed in disenfranchising them. Disturbing accounts of white terrorism and electoral intimidation were reaching Washington. Second, black voters in the border and middle states might well provide a key Republican margin in the Northern states. Third, prompt action was necessary. The Democrats had made substantial gains in the new House. If the Republicans were going to pass a constitutional amendment, they had to do so in the "lame duck" session of Congress before the newly elected members of Congress took office.

Topics for Discussion

1. To what extent was the Republican Reconstruction effort consistent with the constitutional scheme as envisioned by the original framers? If the ratification of the Fourteenth Amendment was accomplished only by a disruption of the original scheme of federalism, does this have any implications for the interpretation of the amendment?

2. Was the Tenure of Office Act consonant with the framers' views on the role of the executive branch?

3. The Fourteenth Amendment has long been construed by the courts to give some protection of the right to vote. (For example, the equal protection clause is the basis for the "one-person, one-vote" rule in modern reapportionment cases.) Does history suggest anything about whether its framers shared this understanding?

PASSAGE OF THE FIFTEENTH AMENDMENT

The Complex Path Through Congress

The procedural history of the Fifteenth Amendment is complicated. Most of the infighting involved divisions among the Republicans, since there were only a dozen Democrats in the Senate. As finally proposed, the amendment was a victory for moderates in the Republican party.

On January 15, 1869, Senator Stewart reported Senate Joint Resolution 8, which provided that "the right to vote and hold office" could not be denied on the basis of race. While debate was held on that resolution, another version was under consideration in the House. House Joint Resolution 402 provided that the "right to vote shall not be denied by reasons of race." Unsuccessful amendments by Shellabarger and Bingham attempted to change the resolution into a guarantee of universal male suffrage. On January 30, H. J. Res. 402 passed the House.

The House resolution was then amended in the Senate to prohibit discrimination "in suffrage or holding office on account of race, nativity, property, education, or creed." The House refused to accept the amendments and sought a conference committee. The Senate majority then voted to replace the amended version of the House resolution with the original version, but the original version failed to obtain the necessary two-thirds majority.

At this point, the Senate dropped the House resolution, took up S. J. Res. 8 again, and adopted it. The Senate resolution went back to the House, where it was again amended, first by adding the right to hold office, and second by including "nativity, property, creed, or previous condition of servitude" as well as race. The Senate refused to accept these amendments and sought a conference committee; the House agreed. The conference committee's proposal excluded the right to hold office and covered only racial discrimination; thus, both chambers had at some point endorsed stronger versions of the amendment. Nevertheless, on February 25 and 26, the House and Senate both voted to adopt the conference committee report.

Rather than attempt to follow the debates through this complicated procedural tangle, we will focus on the main issues raised in them: reasons for giving blacks the vote, views on control of suffrage as a component of federalism, and arguments over whether to strengthen the amendment by including office-holding and various voter qualifications. Finally, we will include some brief discussions of an issue that was to remain unresolved for fifty years: whether women should have a constitutional right to vote.

Reasons for Black Suffrage

The rationale for the amendment was explained by Senator Boutwell when he introduced the proposal:

January 23, 1869

Mr. Boutwell. If we rely exclusively upon a bill which when enacted is merely a law, and subject to congressional control and to all the vicissitudes of politics and changes of opinion, we cannot be assured of its fate in some future Congress. Therefore, if we have power to do what is contemplated in this bill, let us act. Having given to the colored people in several of the States the power to vote we have put into the politics of the country an element by which the amendment itself can be carried. I speak very plainly, because I have no processes in my own mind in reference to this or any other public measure which I am not at all times willing to disclose. There are one hundred and fifty thousand citizens of the United States who by this bill will be entitled to the elective franchise but who are now disfranchised—seventeen hundred in Connecticut, ten thousand in New York, five thousand in New Jersey, fourteen thousand in Pennsylvania, seven thousand in Ohio, twenty-four thousand in Missouri, forty-five thousand in Kentucky, four thousand in Delaware, thirty-five thousand in Maryland—who will rally to the support of this constitutional amendment if by the law they are enfranchised. These men have by the Constitution and by the judgment of the people of this country been declared citizens and entitled to all the rights of citizens. Now, in this struggle for the establishment of manhood suffrage in the country are we to decline the services of one hundred and fifty thousand men who are ready to do battle for us at the ballot-box in favor of human rights: not of their own rights

merely, but of the rights of all men on this continent?

Sir, there can be no safety while we continue the wrong. If one hundred and fifty thousand black men may be disfranchised in ten States of this Union, if hundreds or thousands of naturalized citizens may be disfranchised in Rhode Island, where is the security? The foreigners naturalized in this country have acted under an opinion or impulse or prejudice against enfranchising the negroes; but when they see that their own class may be disfranchised, what security have they better than the negro who in Maryland is disfranchised? Some day or another the foreigners may desire to settle in South Carolina. South Carolina has a majority of black people. Suppose they disfranchise the natives of Ireland, or Germany, or the Scandinavian States. In view of such a contingency will the foreign citizens hesitate in this crisis when they have the power to settle this great question of human rights, not for negroes merely, but for white men? To white men born in this country, to white men born in other countries and coming here, as well as to negroes, there is no security while this great wrong continues. If we fail to act, and if, sir, there be a day of retribution for our omission to do our duty, as there has been a day of retribution for those men who omitted to do their duty upon another great question involving public crime, there can be no defense for us.

Mr. Welker. I desire to inquire whether there is anything in this bill that will prevent any of the

States from requiring of voters a property or an educational qualification?

Mr. Boutwell. I do not suppose there is.

Mr. Welker. Then the States may, under this bill, require such a qualification?

Mr. Boutwell. I suppose they may. Mr. Speaker, there is a special duty which we owe to these black people. There is a special duty which we owe to the white people of the South. To-day the blacks in the South are laboring under special disadvantages due to the circumstance that in Ohio and in other States of the North their kindred are not allowed to vote. When we shall have established universal manhood suffrage for the whole country we shall have given the black people in the South a position in the affairs of their respective States which they cannot command while their race is the subject of an unjust discrimination in other States of the Union. This question goes home as well to the white people of the South. Many of this class have been before a committee of this House asking for the removal of their political disabilities. I, for one, am not influenced by any resentment, by any malice, by any desire conceivable to myself, to delay for one moment their restoration to all the rights they formerly enjoyed. But, sir, I do not see how this House or this country can consent to relieve these men from their disabilities while those with whom they associate, and for whose conduct they are in some degree responsible, are oppressing our friends, the loyal men of the South.

Whenever we do justice to the black man in the North we improve his position, his capacity to take care of himself in the South. I know very well, from personal interviews with conservative men of the South, that to-day they are influenced in their opposition to negro suffrage by the fact that negro suffrage is not established in the old free States of the Union. The measures before us are a part of the great work of harmonizing the country, of pacifying all classes, of reconciling all interests.

Two weeks later, Senator Willey offered a particularly succinct summary of the arguments for the amendment:

February 5, 1869

Mr. Willey. My reasons, then, for supporting this bill, are—

1. Because I accept as true the maxim of the fathers of the Republic, that all just government must rest on the consent of the governed. If, therefore, the colored people of this country are to be recognized as citizens and held subject to our laws, then they ought to have a right to a voice in the enactment of those laws and to a participation in the administration of the Government. To deprive them of this would be an infraction of one of the well settled fundamental principles of our political institutions.

2. Taxation without representation is tyranny. If the negro race are to be taxed to support the Government they ought to be allowed an equal voice in the selection of their rulers, who impose and disburse the taxes. If they are to be compelled to bear arms in defense of the Government at the peril of their lives they ought not only to be regarded worthy of political power, but they should be allowed to exercise it.

3. The welfare of the white race no less than of the black race requires the speediest moral, intellectual, and physical improvement and development of the negro which are practicable. While he remains unenfranchised it were idle to hope for much advancement in these respects. He will be a freeman only in name. The incubus of slavery will still cling to him, repressing all the nobler aspirations and energies of his nature, and suppressing, more or less, all effort to rise to respectability, usefulness, or honorable distinction.

4. This amendment, when adopted, will settle the question for all time of negro suffrage in the insurgent States, where it has lately been extended under the pressure of congressional legislation, and will preclude the possibility of any future denial of this privilege by any change of the constitutions of those States.

5. In those States where the colored race are numerous and remain unenfranchised, the adoption of this amendment will remove a source of disquiet and danger. An emancipated race, subject to our laws, with no voice in ordaining them—subject to

taxation, and yet without representation—required to bear all the burdens of civil society without any authority to impose or regulate those burdens, must, in the course of time, if they ever rise to any considerable degree of intelligence, become dissatisfied and restive under a sense of their degradation, and thus be disposed to revolt against the injustice and tyranny which oppress them; or, sinking under this injustice and tyranny into a state of hopeless despondency, they will degenerate into a class of mere lazzaroni, and become pests to society and a burden to the State.

6. The enfranchisement of the negro will remove him from the arena of national politics, and finally relieve the country from those conflicts of opinion and passion which have been disturbing the public tranquillity and retarding the progress and prosperity of the nation ever since the Revolution. He will then not only be made equal before the law, but equally entitled, with all others, to make and administer the law. "Let us have peace."

7. Suffrage is the only sure guarantee which the negro can have, in many sections of the country, in the enjoyment of his civil rights. Without it his free-dom will be imperfect, if not in peril of total over-thow. The ballot will be a safer shield than the laws.

8. The adoption of this amendment will place all the States on an equality in respect of negro suffrage. The exigencies growing out of the late rebellion made it necessary to impose this suffrage on ten of the insurgent States, where a large majority of the colored race dwell. Several of the other States have voluntarily enfranchised the negro. He is now entitled to vote in eighteen or twenty States. If he is entitled to vote in these States, why not in all? The adoption of this amendment will remove all complaint of unjust discrimination, and the remonstrance of the southern States that the other States have imposed on them burdens and evils which the latter were unwilling to share, will be met and answered.

9. Summing up the whole, I believe the political enfranchisement of the colored race in this country is required not only by considerations of policy and expediency, but also by the demands of justice to the negro, by the principles of human liberty, and by the spirit of Christian civilization.

Apart from issues of federalism, which we will come to shortly, the primary argument of the opponents was simple racism: blacks lacked the intellectual ability and moral character needed to be voters. Perhaps the most notable statement of this position is that of Senator Vickers, given immediately before Willey's speech. What makes Vickers's statement so interesting is his resurrection of the language of eighteenth-century republicanism:

February 5, 1869

Mr. Vickers. Public virtue and intelligence are the foundations of a republic; it can rest on no others; can exist and be perpetuated by no other means. It is a government of opinion, of principle; its officers and agents must be wise, capable, and patriotic. The people who select them must, to a great extent, possess the same elements; they are to exercise sagacity, discrimination, knowledge of men, of motives, and of character; their judgment and ability are to be judiciously exercised in the election of officers to conduct and manage the affairs of a nation; they must have some knowledge of statesmanship, of political economy, of trade, commerce, manufactures, agriculture, and mechanic arts, and of the re-sources and wealth of the country, and withal a fund of experience and common sense. Will the introduction of the negro into our political affairs add to the intelligence, statesmanship, wisdom, and judgment of the country? Will it not weaken our institutions and the confidence we have had in their stability and lay another and different foundation than that which was laid by our fathers? The negro as a class, as a race, is unfortunately ignorant and superstitious; with some exceptions, he cannot read nor understand your Constitution, is unacquainted with your laws, institutions, history, and policy; he at present lacks independence and that high sense of honor and integrity which every voter should possess to shield him from sinister or unworthy influences. He needs the very qualities and qualifications essential to a free, fair, and sensible exercise of the elective franchise. If you had a house to build would you procure ignorant and unskillful hands to erect it? If you desired to have transacted business which required experience, judgment, and prudence, would you employ the illiterate, the inexperienced, and the unskillful? And yet, in so grave a matter as legislation, statesmanship, and the affairs, internal and external, of a great country, and in choosing Representatives and officers to discharge the most difficult and momentous duties, we are to call to our aid the power of numbers only, which possess not the moral or intellectual strength to render the slightest assistance. They may be made the dupes and instruments of interested persons, but it should be recollected that, like the elephants in battle, they will be as likely to trample upon friends as upon foes. No one political organization can long hold them, and they will become a *tertium quid* which will enervate rather than strengthen the body politic.

Sumner later answered the "public virtue" argument by conceding that "public intelligence and public virtue are essential to a Republic" but arguing that external features such as skin color are no guide to the possession of virtue.[7]

The Federalism Issue

Besides their argument about racial inferiority, the opponents of the amendment made the most of the federalism issue. Control of the suffrage, they argued, was crucial to the existence of the states as independent entities within the federalist system. Supporters of the amendment argued that this was simply a remnant of discredited notions of state sovereignty. The following two speeches exemplify the opposing positions.

January 29, 1869

Mr. Dixon. What is the question? It is not merely a question of suffrage. That of itself is a subject of vast importance, and is now agitating the public mind of this country to a very great extent. The question whether the female sex should be permitted to participate in the privilege of suffrage, whether other restrictions should be removed, the question of age, the question of property, a multitude of questions are or may be raised which are vastly important and interesting in connection with the right of suffrage. But, sir, we are not now dealing merely with the qualification of voters. The question is not what shall be the qualifications of the voter, but who shall create, establish, and prescribe those qualifications; not who shall be the voter, but who shall make the voter.

In considering that question we ought to remember that it is utterly impossible that any State should be an independent republic which does not entirely control its own laws with regard to the right of suffrage. Nor does it make the slightest difference with regard to this that any abdication or abnegation of its power is voluntary. It may be said that it is proposed that the States shall voluntarily relinquish their power to control the subject of suffrage within their respective limits. Sir, suppose a State should voluntarily assume upon itself a foreign yoke, or declare by a majority of its own people, or even by a unanimous vote, that it would prefer a monarchy, would the fact of its being voluntary at all affect the question whether it was still an independent republic?

Now, sir, it may be that the people of this country in their present condition of mind are ready to relinquish the power in the States of regulating their own laws with regard to suffrage: and if it should so prove, and the result should show that your own State (Ohio) and my State, (Connecticut.) having once or twice voted against extending the right to suffrage to the negro race, should now consent that a central power should regulate that question, and should do this voluntarily and freely, nevertheless they would by that action lose their character as republican governments. And, sir, that is the reason why it was that in the formation of the Constitution of the United States there was an entire neglect to interfere in the slightest degree with the question of suffrage in the several states.

.   .   .

Sir, when we view the question in this light it must be acknowledged that it rises far above the question of any mere detail as to suffrage; far higher in importance than the question even of abolishing slavery in the States; far higher than any proposition which has ever been made with regard to the amendment of the Constitution, because it is in its truest sense radical and revolutionary. It strikes at the very root and foundation of the Government; it removes its corner stone, and changes the entire character of the State governments.

February 8, 1869

Mr. Morton. Now, sir, I wish to call the attention of the Senate for one moment to the character of the whole train of argument that has been offered against this amendment. Take that of the Senator from Kentucky, the Senator from Delaware, and other Senators that I might refer to. I say that the whole train of argument is based upon those broad doctrines and those old theories upon which the right of secession rested. We were not told by the Senator from Kentucky and the Senator from Delaware that they believed in the right of secession, but they advocated the same theories, urged the same arguments, and cited the same history upon which the right of secession has been based for the last twenty years.

Mr. Saulsbury. Will the honorable Senator allow me to ask him a question?

Mr. Morton. Yes, sir.

Mr. Saulsbury. I ask whether the historical references that I made were not true references; and whether the facts in relation to the formation of the Federal Constitution are not evidenced by the records of the Convention which framed it?

Mr. Morton. Mr. President, I might admit the Senator's references, but I should deny his deductions. The Senator told us today frankly that we were not one people. He said in the Senate of the United States, after the culmination of a war that cost this nation six hundred thousand lives, that we were not a nation. He gave us to understand that we were as many separate nationalities as we have States; that one State is different from another as one nation in Europe is different from another. He denied expressly that we were a nation. He gave us to understand that he belonged to the tribe of the Delawares, an independent and sovereign tribe living on a reservation up here near the city of Philadelphia, [laughter] but he denied his American nationality. The whole argument from first to last has proceeded upon that idea, that this is a mere confederacy of States; to use the language of the Senator to-day, a partnership of States. What is the deduction? If that is true there was the right of secession; the South was right and we were wrong. He did not draw that deduction, but it is one that springs inevitably from his premises.

Sir, the heresy of secession is not dead; it lives. It lives after this war, although it ought to have been settled by the war. It exists even as snow sometimes exists in the lap of summer when it is concealed behind the cliffs and the hedges and in the clefts of the rocks. It has come forth during this debate. We have heard the very premises, the very arguments, the very historical references upon which the right of secession was argued for thirty years. The whole fallacy lies in denying our nationality. I assert that we are one people and not thirty-seven different peoples; that we are one nation, and as such we have provided for ourselves a national Constitution, and that Constitution has provided the way by which it may be amended.

The Right to Hold Office

Some of the early versions of the Fifteenth Amendment protected not only the right to vote but also the right to hold office. There was spirited discussion in the Senate on whether to agree to the House version, which did not offer such protection.

February 17, 1869

Mr. Frelinghuysen. It seems to me that this whole difficulty can be settled very easily and very quickly. The question is now whether we shall adopt the proposition that comes to us from the House of Representatives. If we adopt that, we have a constitutional amendment. As to the objection that it does not provide eligibility to office for the colored people I will only say that if you give seven hundred and fifty thousand men the right to the ballot they will look out for their own rights as to office. Therefore, I shall vote for that proposition: but I confess that I prefer the proposition that originally came from the Senate committee. If the proposition now pending fails all that we have to do is to take up that which came from the Judiciary Committee of the Senate and pass it within an hour.

Mr. Edmunds. The trouble about the argument of my friend on this pending question is that the seven hundred and fifty thousand colored voters are not altogether in the southern States; they are divided up among all the States; and if you do not give them the right to hold office as well as to vote you immediately create a white aristocracy in every one of those States with the negroes divided among them, which will work as bad a resolution as my friend from Pennsylvania [Mr. Buckalew] referred to in South America, totally destructive of the liberties of that people. Now, as my friend from New Jersey says, all we have to do to do right in this matter is to reject this proposition of the House or lay it on the table, and then take up and pass the Senate resolution which the Judiciary Committee have perfected and reported.

.   .   .

Mr. Welch. I most distinctly hope that this proposition will pass, and what is further, I hope that adequate time will be taken for its discussion. It has been charged here by the honorable Senator from Nevada [Mr. Nye] that the gentlemen recently from the southern states have voted with their political enemies against the proposition of the House of Representatives. We are ready to give a reason for the faith that is in us. We did not cast that vote from mere caprice. We so voted because we believe that the negro should have full and impartial justice, and because the proposed amendment that was voted down when the Senate refused to concur does not give complete and impartial justice. By implication it deprives him of the right to hold office, and puts the Senate in the absurd position, contrary to all true philosophy, that a man cannot hold office in this Republic, not because of what is in him, but because he belongs to a certain race, because he has a skin not colored like our own. I believe that men should vote and hold office because they have the capacity to vote and to hold office, and that every such question should be decided upon some general principles that will be justified by their general intelligence or general virtue, not because of their forefathers, and not because their forefathers have or have not made inventions. The negroes have the right to vote by the State constitutions in the reconstructed States; but in all those States they have not the right to hold office.

Voting Qualifications

Another hotly disputed issue was whether to impose some version of universal male suffrage by banning voting qualifications, or merely to prohibit discrimination on the basis of race. The various viewpoints are well represented in this series of remarks.

February 8, 1869

Mr. Edmunds. Therefore, we say that negroes shall have the same rights and privileges as the white electors there. Very well. Now, you go to another State, for instance New Hampshire, and you find a different rule prevailing. Then you go to Rhode Island. There the question of the Celt or any other alien comes in, and if the negro possesses certain qualification of property he may vote, if he is to be put upon the grade of the naturalized citizen. If he does not possess a certain qualification of property, if you make the natural born citizen the standard, then he may vote. Now, "Under which king, Bezonian?" as the proverb is. Why, sir, it leads you to infinite confusions and difficulty. But what is worse, it undertakes to leave with the States, after all, the regulation of suffrage, the conferring or withholding it entirely, and therefore you merely turn the African alone, to speak of nobody else, over to every State of which he is an inhabitant or a citizen to fix qualification of property, of intelligence, of religion, of landholding, of anything that may reduce a State government to an aristocracy, as it has been in South Carolina and many of the other States under old influences; and where is the benefit to the African, then?

.   .   .

Mr. Warner. I hope this amendment will not be adopted. I hope the Congress of this country will not single out one race for protection; but that we shall go at once to the broad, grand, affirmative proposition which shall secure the object the Senator from Vermont so well states—that of securing to all the citizens of this country their rights. I think this proposition to single out one race is the weakest one that can be put before the country. If we want to strengthen it and give it a chance of adoption, we ought to amend it and insert the Irish and Germans. I think to single out one race is unworthy of the country and unworthy of the great opportunity now presented to us. We ought to go to the root of the matter by putting in the fundamental law a provision which will make the Constitution beyond doubt mean what the Senators from Vermont and Massachusetts now understand it to mean.

Mr. Patterson, of New Hampshire. I hope that this proposition will be adopted; for of all the amendments which have been offered I think it is the best. Our object is to meet a wrong done to a class of black native citizens; to give them the same privileges that other citizens of the United States possess. The Constitution gives to the United States the right to establish a uniform system of naturalization; so that Europeans and Asiatics coming to our coast may be naturalized upon the same conditions in California and in New York. So by the passage of this proposition we shall relieve these black citizens, native to the soil, from the wrong which is done them, without doing any wrong to the Asiatics who may flow in upon our western shores. I prefer, for one, to leave that question open, so that if a war springs up in Asia and these increasing tides of immigration from Asia pour upon our Pacific coast in such numbers as to endanger the welfare of those States, they may have it in their power to guard themselves against the threatened evils, and then, if any evil should result, it will be in our power to remedy it. "Sufficient unto the day is the evil thereof." Let us meet this evil, and not in attempting to meet it provide others that we know not of.

Women's Suffrage

The developing concepts of democracy and equality underlying the Fifteenth Amendment led a few speakers to argue for women's suffrage.

January 28, 1869

Mr. Fowler. Besides that, there is another objection in my mind to this provision going into the Constitution, and that is this: if it is intended to be an expression of the fact that the American people have risen to the point of acknowledging the freedom of the individual—if this is to be an expression of individual freedom, it does not go far enough. While I am in favor of all citizens of the United States having the right to vote and hold office, without respect to race or color, I would rather go a little further than that. I would not by any means be willing to debar the women of the country from giving their suffrage or their expression in regard to the authority of laws to control or govern them, as I do not believe that any responsible person can be controlled by the authority of any other one. There is no reason why you, sir, should be governed by any other person; and if there is any argument why you should vote, that argument will apply equally well to any intelligent woman in the country. I cannot see the force of the argument which would give to natives of China, of Africa, and of India a right to control the destinies of the women of this country—and recollect I am an advocate of that right—and exclude from a voice my mother or my sister or my wife, an American woman, from the exercise of this inestimable privilege. I intend, when the proper stage is reached, to move an amendment to this proposition for the benefit of the women of this country.

January 29, 1869

Mr. Pomeroy. I ask the ballot for woman, not on account of her weakness or on account of her strength; not because she may be above or below a man; that has nothing to do with the question. I ask it because she is a citizen of the Republic, amenable to its laws, taxed for its support, and a sharer in its destiny. There are no reasons for giving the ballot to a man that do not apply to a woman with equal force. She may use it or neglect it, as many men do; still it should be hers whenever she chooses to exercise the right. This would tend to its elevation and purification; for when the sacredness of the ballot is preserved it would not soil a woman's heart, hand, or dress, or the place of voting any more than when she uses the Bible and the prayer-book in the congregation of honorable worshipers. In all the walks of life, retired or public, she adds grace, elegance, and purity to every step of her pathway, to every work of her hand, and to every love of her heart. I am for the enfranchisement fully and without restrictions of every man in the land who has the rights and discharges faithfully the duties of a citizen of the Republic, no matter how depressed or oppressed he may have been. The way of his elevation is by the way of the ballot, and that should be as fixed and as settled as the fundamental law itself. But I would put in the form of law precisely the same provision for every woman in the land; for it is as safe in her hands as in his; it will be used with as much intelligence and with as good results. And besides all that, the distinctive character of our republican Government on the basis of the original design can be perpetuated in no other way. The highest justice is the only safety. Let it come, then, by one comprehensive amendment striking out all inequalities among citizens, and the dream of the fathers of a free and pure Republic shall be realized, and there shall be peace throughout the land and good will among men.

Later in the debates, the question of female suffrage was briefly discussed again.

February 8, 1869

Mr. Sawyer. Now, Mr. President, the war has made all the slaves citizens. When the war opened the great majority of the black men in the country were slaves. The rebellion came on, and in the process of the rebellion, as a consequence of the rebellion, under the Providence of God they became freemen. By the sense of justice of the American people they were made citizens of the United States. They are citizens of the United States wherever they are found to-day. Now, whatever class of men we make citizens of the United States, it is, in my opinion, a public danger to keep from participation in the active powers of government.

Mr. Davis. Are not women citizens?

Mr. Sawyer. Woman are represented through their husbands or brothers.

Mr. Davis. Are not our negroes represented?

Mr. Sawyer. Through their masters. I know that the theory is that the negroes should be represented by those who have so long represented them in pro-viding for their animal wants and taking the proceeds of the labor of their muscle. I know that it is a favorite theory of the Senator that the negro should be represented in that way; but I claim that we have a right to exact from the male negro citizen his duties toward his country, that we have a right to call upon him to perform his part of the labors and burdens of the citizen. We tax him; the clothes that he wears pay a revenue to the Government; the food that he eats is in many cases taxed for the aid of the Government; almost everything that he consumes is taxed. He pays a tax to the Government; he is liable to be called into the service of the Government. They have, in immense numbers, volunteered to aid the Government in its time of trial. Demanding of the negro citizen the performances of these duties, claiming from him these taxes, I assume that it is our duty to see that he has the same rights that any other man who pays the same taxes enjoys.

Later that day, Senator Edmunds attempted to explain why language enfranchising "citizens" would not extend the franchise to women. He first cited a Kentucky decision holding that while women were in some sense citizens, they were not citizens in the sense of being entitled to participate in the political community. He was then questioned about the distinction.

February 8, 1869

Mr. Howe. But I wish, if my friend will allow me, to ask him if the decision of the supreme court of Kentucky, to which he refers, pronounced twenty-five years ago, is not reversed by this very clause of the Constitution, which says that all persons born or naturalized in the United States and subject to the jurisdiction thereof are citizens of the United States and of the States in which they reside.

Mr. Edmunds. Not reversed at all; for that is exactly what the decision holds. It holds that everybody, subject to the qualification I have named, is a citizen of the country for that purpose: that there belongs to everybody who, as a part of the highest class in community, may exercise political privileges, equal political rights; and therefore, as the case was in Kentucky, a male person cannot be a citizen unless, being a citizen, he has breathed into him at the same moment with the fact that he is a citizen the right to vote. That is perhaps a sufficient definition of citizenship in the narrow sense we are now speaking of, as distinguishing between the rights of citizens, rather than defining what they are. A citizen is a person in community who, other things being equal, is invested with all the privileges that belong to the highest class in community, by whatever name you may call them.

I admit that this method of argument to show that a citizen must necessarily possess the privileges that belong to the highest class, and that that is the true definition of the term, and at the same time to hold that that does not comprehend an adult female, is a somewhat artificial and, philosophically speaking, a somewhat unsound argument; but I say that judicial decisions have determined that these are the qualities that inhere in the very nature and definition of citizenship as applied to the political subjects which relate to any citizenship at all, and that this qualification, as I call it, is equally well settled.

We may, therefore, set aside, for the purpose of considering what I am speaking of, the question whether by a true and philosophical construction of the definition of the term "citizen," a female would be entitled to vote or not. That is not the question now before us. I should not cry very much if we could extend the true and philosophic idea of citizenship to giving females the right to vote. I think they would vote quite as well as we do if they would only go and do it. The great difficulty that I have on

that question—but I am not going into a dissertation on it—is that I am very much afraid when it is extended to them all the bad women will vote and the good women will stay at home. It is somewhat so with men. The non-voting class in a community, as you and I well know, sir, who are entitled to vote, as a rule are those who, when they would go and vote, would exercise the most salutary and beneficial influence upon society; and they commit crime, in a certain sense, against society if they do not do it. You never see a bad man or a wicked man or a man who is a tool in the hands of somebody else absent from the polls on election day. He is there and counts to the last vote. It is not so with the other class of the community. That is a defect in the men who compose and should rule and control our institutions. But that is apart from my present purpose.

The language of the amendment was ultimately limited to race, and the question of women's suffrage would wait another half century.

Topics for Discussion

1. Why were the provisions on office-holding and voting qualifications eliminated? The Southern abuse of voting qualifications was to prove especially troublesome in practice. Was a stronger amendment politically feasible? Would it be proper for a twentieth-century court to declare poll taxes or literacy requirements unconstitutional?

2. Was the Fifteenth Amendment purely an act of political expediency, or did it reflect a theory of democratic representation? If the supporters of the amendment did have a consistent view of the nature of representation, how did it compare with the views of the framers of the original Constitution?

3. Some members of Congress believed that voting was one of the "privileges and immunities" of American citizenship, and that the Fourteenth Amendment gave Congress the power to legislate on the subject. Do the materials in chapter 11 support this view?

4. Was the Fifteenth Amendment, as its opponents charged, an abandonment of the core concepts of federalism? Or, as some historians have argued, was it an attempt to restore the autonomy of the states by terminating the need for ongoing congressional intervention in the Southern states?

5. Why was women's suffrage rejected? If the supporters of the amendment had been logically consistent, should they have agreed to extend the franchise to women? What do you suppose would have happened to the amendment had they done so? Might it have affected interpretation of the *Fourteenth* Amendment in cases involving women's rights?

RATIFICATION AND BEYOND

Ratification and Enforcement of the Fifteenth Amendment

When the Fifteenth Amendment was proposed, only twenty states allowed blacks to vote, not enough states to ratify the amendment. Moreover, of these twenty states, eleven had adopted black suffrage only under duress as part of Reconstruction. Democrats, who stood to lose politically from the amendment, needed only ten states to block ratification, and they controlled five state legislatures. According to the amendment's leading historian,

> In late March it seemed likely that the Amendment would be ratified. But ratification bogged down during the summer and fall, and by the winter of 1869-70 the situation became very critical for those favoring it. Trouble brewed among Republicans, while Democrats tried every device to defeat ratification. However, the formidable Republican advantages overcame fierce opposition, and by the beginning of February the fight was over.[8]

Among the Republican advantages was the belief that Southern states would not be readmitted unless they ratified, an understanding that Congress made explicit a few months after the amendment was sent to the states. In fact, the amendment was easily ratified in the South, with higher percentages of affirmative votes than it received elsewhere in the country. Republicans dominated many of the Southern legislatures, but even where they did not, Southerners had little reason to oppose ratification. Southern blacks had already received the ballot under the Military Reconstruction Act, so the immediate effect of the Fifteenth Amendment would be felt most in other parts of the country.

The other stronghold of the amendment was New England, where the Republican party was most influential. But the amendment met heavy resistance in the border states, parts of the Midwest, and the West (where anti-Chinese prejudice played a role). One particularly bitter fight took place in Indiana, where the Democrats tried to prevent a quorum by resigning en masse. Some of them made the mistake of remaining in the Senate chamber after their resignations, whereupon the Republicans locked the doors. The Republicans then counted them toward a quorum on the ground that they had failed to submit written resignations to the presiding officer. (The Democrats had sent their written resignations to the governor instead.) In the House, the Republicans were unable to muster a quorum but simply proceeded anyway.[9] In Ohio, Republicans had to overcome a filibuster and a flood to obtain a vote; several Republicans commandeered a freight train to get to Columbus for the vote, while another was tricked into returning to Cincinnati but discovered his mistake in time to return for the vote.[10]

The success of the ratification movement was due to several factors. First, Republican legislators were well-organized and under firm national control. Second, Reconstruction assured ratification in the South. Third, Democrats were hindered by their fear that if the amendment was ratified, they might need the black vote to get re-elected.

The End of Reconstruction

Several important Reconstruction statutes were enacted after 1870. In the Enforcement Acts, Congress provided penalties for racial discrimination by state election officials and intimidation of voters, as well as federal supervision of congressional elections in Southern cities. The Ku Klux Klan Act of 1871 outlawed conspiracies to deprive citizens of their rights under the Fourteenth Amendment. Finally, the 1875 Civil Rights Act, passed in a lame duck session after the Republicans lost control of the House, prohibited discrimination in public accommodations such as inns and railroads. It was later held unconstitutional by the Supreme Court.

Reconstruction ended with the 1876 election. Although Samuel Tilden, the Democratic candidate, won a popular majority and had a larger number of clear electoral votes, there were disputed results in enough states to leave the electoral contest in doubt. A commission of five representatives, five senators, and five justices was appointed to decide the results in the disputed states. The commission decided all of the disputed states in favor of Rutherford B. Hayes, the Republican, by a straight party vote of eight to seven. Democrats accepted this outcome as a result of hard bargaining at behind-the-scenes negotiations with the Republicans at the Wormley Hotel in Washington. Ironically, the hotel was owned by a black—ironic because the crux of the bargain was the Republican agreement that if elected, Hayes would deal "justly and generously" with the South. In other words, he would stop enforcing Reconstruction. This bargain gave the election to Hayes, who promptly removed the remaining federal troops from the South as soon as he took office. In a series of cases shortly afterward, the Supreme Court reinforced the return to pre-Reconstruction "business as usual" by striking down several Reconstruction statutes because the statutes either failed to limit themselves to racially motivated conduct or attempted to prohibit discriminatory conduct by private individuals.

With federal enforcement of Reconstruction virtually abandoned, the South adopted measures to disenfranchise blacks. A one or two dollar poll tax might seem reasonable enough on its face, but since the median Southern income was well under sixty dollars per year in 1880, it was a substantial barrier to voting, particularly for blacks. The Twenty-Fourth Amendment would ultimately ban poll taxes in federal elections, and a 1966 Supreme Court decision held them unconstitutional in state elections as well.[11] Other devices adopted to complicate balloting took advantage of the high rate of illiteracy among blacks. Even after 1870, however, most eligible blacks continued to vote. For example, over seventy percent of eligible blacks voted in the 1880 presidential election in Virginia and four other Southern states. In the 1890s, however, Southern legislatures moved decisively to end black voting by adopting literacy tests and reinforcing existing barriers to black suffrage. For the next fifty years, white political supremacy in the South was virtually uncontested.

Further Steps Toward Extending Majority Rule

The Fifteenth Amendment was one of a series of measures extending the franchise and reinforcing the concept of majority rule. As John Hart Ely has pointed out, there has been a long-term trend toward increased constitutional emphasis on majoritarianism:

> Populist critics like to stress the Constitution's provisions for the election of Senators by the state legislatures and the election of the President by an Electoral Col-

lege. . . . There have also existed throughout our history limits on the extent of the franchise and thus on government by majority. But the development again, and again it has been a *constitutional* development, has been continuously, even relentlessly, away from that state of affairs: as Tocqueville observed in 1848, "[o]nce a people begins to interfere with the voting qualification, one can be sure that sooner or later it will abolish it altogether."[12]

The Fifteenth Amendment was a major part of this expansion, but other developments also reflected the growing irresistibility of majoritarianism. Ironically, although the Fifteenth Amendment was formally ratified early in this process, it was one of the last expansions of the franchise to take practical effect, because of the strength of white resistance to black suffrage. After a look at other developments on the road to universal suffrage, we will close this chapter with a brief discussion of the legislation that in some sense truly "ratified" the Fifteenth Amendment by making its promise a reality.

The Seventeenth Amendment. An important part of the original conception of the Senate was the selection of Senators by state legislatures rather than popular election. This method of selection, it was thought, both provided an additional "filter" to assure merit and ensured that the interests of the states would be represented in Congress. By the end of the nineteenth century, however, this selection process was attacked as antidemocratic. First the Populists and then the Progressives agitated for direct election of senators.

From 1893 to 1902, the House repeatedly passed constitutional amendments calling for direct election of senators. Each time, the amendments were defeated in the Senate. The states themselves, however, began to adopt direct election by holding senatorial primaries binding on the legislature from each district, or statewide elections, the results of which were "rubber stamped" by the state legislatures. By 1912, twenty-nine of the forty-eight states had adopted one of these techniques. Finally, in 1911, after a scandal involving the fraudulent election of an Illinois senator, the Senate agreed to direct election. The amendment was ratified in 1913.

Although it was intended to make the Senate more democratic and limit the control of political parties over the selection of senators, the switch to popular selection does not seem to have had any great practical effect. By reducing the link between state governments and Congress, however, the amendment may represent an important shift in conceptions of federalism.

The Nineteenth Amendment. We have already seen that the question of women's suffrage did not attract widespread support in the Reconstruction-era Congress. Indeed, the Fourteenth Amendment explicitly sanctioned male suffrage, and for that reason was opposed by some feminists of the era. But the struggle for women's suffrage was already under way.

Actually, women's suffrage was not unheard of in the early years of the Republic. The New Jersey constitution granted the right to vote to "inhabitants" who met certain property requirements. Women took advantage of this provision to vote. In the early nineteenth century, however, the New Jersey legislature brought the state back into line with the rest of the states by outlawing women's suffrage.

In 1848, three hundred people gathered in Seneca Falls, New York, at the invitation of Elizabeth Cady Stanton and Lucretia Mott. Stanton drafted several resolutions, which received unanimous support with one exception: that calling for women's suffrage. Mott asked her not to submit this resolution to the convention, for fear of making the group look ridiculous, but black leader Frederick Douglass encouraged her to proceed. This alliance between the causes of black rights and women's suffrage was to prove an uneasy one, however. Later, Stanton and Susan B. Anthony would refuse to support black voting rights; as Anthony put it, "I will cut off this right arm before I will ever work for or demand the ballot for the Negro and not the woman."[13]

In 1872, Anthony succeeded in voting despite a provision of the New York constitution limiting the franchise to men. She was then charged with the crime of election fraud for casting a ballot in a federal election in which she was not an eligible voter. Two years later, the Supreme Court ruled in *Minor v. Happersett*, 88 U.S. (21 Wall) 162, 22 L.Ed. 627 (1874), that the right to vote was not protected by the Constitution except when it was denied on the basis of race.

Nevertheless, women's suffrage began to make headway, especially in the West. In 1870, Wyoming's territorial legislature adopted women's suffrage. Utah adopted it but was overridden by federal statute (as part of the same statute outlawing polygamy). Wyoming's state constitution then called for women's suffrage. In 1897, Colorado gave women the vote. The Progressive Party endorsed women's suffrage in 1912. By 1914, twelve Western states had given women the vote, and Illinois allowed women to vote in presidential elections.

Several groups opposed women's suffrage. The liquor industry believed that women would favor prohibition. Southerners feared that any expansion in federal power over voting would encourage new efforts on behalf of black voters. Traditionalists associated women's suffrage with other feminist issues such as birth control, "free love," and other challenges to Victorianism. As a result, suffragettes narrowed their program by abandoning many earlier feminists' concerns.

When women entered the work force in record numbers during World War I, pressure to give them the vote increased. In 1918, despite strong opposition from Southern Democrats, Wilson announced his support for women's suffrage. In 1919, with strong Republican support, Congress proposed the Nineteenth Amendment, and it was ratified the following year. One of the voters in the 1920 election was a woman who had attended the 1848 meeting in Seneca Falls as a nineteen-year-old.[14]

The Twenty-Sixth Amendment. Three other amendments extended the suffrage by allowing residents of the District of Columbia to vote for president (the Twenty-Third Amendment), abolishing poll taxes (the Twenty-Fourth Amendment), and giving eighteen-year-olds the vote (the Twenty-Sixth Amendment). Of these, the Twenty-Sixth Amendment is particularly interesting.

In addition to its place in the development of universal suffrage, the Twenty-Sixth Amendment's background raises interesting questions about federalism and Congressional power in suffrage decisions.

In 1970, Congress amended the Voting Rights Act to prohibit states from denying any citizen the right to vote in any election "on account of age if such citizen is eighteen years of age or older." The Supreme Court upheld this provision by a five to four vote for federal elections, but another coalition of five justices held it unconstitutional for state elections.[15]

Justice Black, the swing voter, concluded that Congress had the power under Article I, section 4, to alter state rules governing voting in federal elections. On the other hand, he believed that the power to control their own elections was crucial to the separate existence of the states, and held that Congress had no power to invade this area except in cases of racial discrimination. Another group of three justices, led by Justice Brennan, argued that Congress had the power under the Fourteenth Amendment to determine that discrimination against eighteen-year-old voters violated the equal protection clause. In a separate opinion, Justice Douglas reached much the same conclusion as Brennan. The remaining justices believed that Congress lacked the power to determine voting qualifications in either federal or state elections. Justice Harlan argued at some length, as we will see in a later chapter, that the historical record precluded any application of the Fourteenth Amendment to voting, as well as any congressional power under Article I to control suffrage in federal elections.

Congress responded to the Court's decision by proposing the Twenty-Sixth Amendment, which was submitted to the states three months after the Court's decision. In another three months, the amendment had been ratified.

Voting Rights and the "Second Reconstruction"

Despite the Fifteenth Amendment, Southern states adopted a variety of devices to prevent blacks from voting. Gerrymandering, delegation of political authority to "private," all-white associations, poll taxes, and literacy tests were among the methods used by the South to defeat the Fifteenth Amendment's guarantee of black suffrage. Literacy tests were often coupled with special exemptions (such as "grandfather clauses") to ensure that white illiterates would still be entitled to vote. After years of litigation, many of these devices were struck down by the Supreme Court,[16] but these victories only seemed to spur the South to greater ingenuity. Literacy tests were upheld by the Court as a legitimate means of ensuring intelligent voting.[17]

In the early 1960s, the federal government made a serious attempt to use the courts to enfranchise blacks. These cases proved difficult and expensive, because in most localities the explicit voting requirements were perfectly constitutional but were administered in a highly discriminatory fashion. The results were disappointing. For example, in Selma, Alabama, despite major efforts by civil rights groups and four years of litigation by the Justice Department, which succeeded in obtaining two judicial rulings in its favor, black voting registration inched up from one to two percent. The Fifteenth Amendment seemed as far from realization as it had at the turn of the century.

Congress responded with new legislation reminiscent of the Reconstruction Era. The Voting Rights Act of 1965 represented one of the most drastic intrusions of the federal government into state operations since the Hayes election of 1876 marked the end of Reconstruction. Under section 5 of the Act, "covered jurisdictions" could not implement any change in voting requirements without the approval of the United States attorney general. To escape from this "preclearance" requirement, the state was required to obtain a federal court judgment that the voting change lacked any discriminatory purpose or effect. Other provisions of the statute authorized the appointment of federal voting examiners and prohibited the use of literacy tests in covered jurisdictions.

Covered jurisdictions were defined by a two-part test. First, the attorney general had to determine that a jurisdiction used a "test or device" to limit voting rights, a term which was defined to include any literacy or character test. Second, he had to determine that less than half of the jurisdiction's voting age residents were registered in 1964 or had voted in the 1964 presidential election. These findings were not judicially reviewable. The covered jurisdiction could escape this status only by persuading a federal court in Washington, D.C., that it had not used tests or devices to abridge the right to vote for five years. At the time the Supreme Court considered the constitutionality of the act, the covered jurisdictions were South Carolina, Alabama, Alaska, Georgia, Louisiana, Mississippi, Virginia, and some counties in North Carolina, Arizona, Hawaii, and Idaho.[18]

Despite the innovative and intrusive nature of the act, the Supreme Court upheld its constitutionality in no uncertain terms. Quoting language used by Chief Justice Marshall in a different context, the Court observed that the congressional enforcement power under section 2 of the Fifteenth Amendment "is complete in itself, may be exercised to its utmost extent, and acknowledges no limitations, other than are prescribed in the constitution." The aggressive nature of the remedy was justified because "[a]fter enduring nearly a century of systematic resistance to the Fifteenth Amendment, Congress might well decide to shift the advantage of time and inertia from the perpetrators of the evil to its victims." And the statute's geographical focus (largely on the old states of the Confederacy) was also justified, for Congress was entitled to "limit its attention to the geographic areas where immediate action seemed necessary." Now, the Court concluded, the promise of the Fifteenth Amendment might finally become a reality:

> After enduring nearly a century of widespread resistance to the Fifteenth Amendment, Congress has marshalled an array of potent weapons against the evil, with authority in the Attorney General to employ them effectively. . . . Hopefully, millions of non-white Americans will now be able to participate for the first time on an equal basis in the government under which they live. We may finally look forward to the day when truly "[t]he right of citizens of the United States to vote shall not be denied or abridged by the United States or by any State on account of race, color or previous condition of servitude."[19]

Topics for Discussion

1. Is the 1965 Voting Rights Act consistent with the intent of the framers of the Fifteenth Amendment? To what extent was the later legislation necessitated by the compromises made in drafting the amendment? By the 1876 Compromise?

2. The Nineteenth Amendment presents an interesting contrast with the Fifteenth. Women obtained a constitutional guarantee of suffrage later than blacks, but afterward, women had little difficulty exercising their rights. How do you explain the differences?

3. The division of responsibility for enforcing constitutional rights between Congress and the federal courts was one of the key issues in *South Carolina v. Katzenbach*, 383 U.S. 301, 86 S.Ct. 803, 15 L.Ed.2d 769 (1966) (in which the

Court upheld the Voting Rights Act), and in *Oregon v. Mitchell*, 400 U.S. 112, 91 S.Ct. 260, 27 L.Ed.2d 272 (1970) (in which the Court held that Congress lacked the power to give eighteen-year-olds the right to vote in state elections). Does the history we have reviewed in part 2 of this book shed any light on this problem?

4. Some historians have suggested that the Reconstruction effort was handicapped by the desire to intrude on state prerogatives no more than absolutely necessary. Do you agree with this characterization of the framers' motives or this appraisal of the results?

FOOTNOTES

1. For overviews of this period of Reconstruction history, see Eric Foner, *Reconstruction: America's Unfinished Revolution 1863-1877* (1988); Michael Les Benedict, *A Compromise of Principle: Congressional Republicans and Reconstruction 1863-1869* (1974). For a good review of Reconstruction historiography, see Randall Kennedy, *Reconstruction and the Politics of Scholarship*, 98 Yale L.J. 521 (1989).

2. Joseph J. James, *The Ratification of the Fourteenth Amendment* 21 (1984).

3. *Id.* at 23.

4. *Id.* at 60-61.

5. *Id.* at 113.

6. David H. Donald, *Liberty and Union: The Crisis of Popular Government, 1830-1890* 209-210 (1978). The concluding portion of this paragraph is also of some interest:

> Adding to all these hostilities was a fear that a system of public education might some day lead to a racially integrated system of education. These apprehensions had little basis in fact, for during the entire period of Reconstruction in the whole South there were significant numbers of children in racially mixed schools only in New Orleans between 1870 and 1874.

Id. at 210. For a more recent appraisal of the Reconstruction governments, *see* Richard Current, *Those Terrible Carpetbaggers* (1988).

7. *Cong. Globe*, 40th Cong., 3d Sess. 909 (1869).

8. William Gillette, *The Right to Vote: Politics and the Passage of the Fifteenth Amendment* 81 (1965).

9. *Id.* at 136-38.

10. *Id.* at 143.

11. *Harper v. Virginia Bd. of Elections*, 383 U.S. 663, 86 S.Ct. 1079, 16 L.Ed.2d 169 (1966).

12. John Hart Ely, *Democracy and Distrust: A Theory of Judicial Review* 6-7 (1980) (emphasis in original).

13. Louis H. Pollack, *Voting Rights*, in 4 *Encyclopedia of the American Constitution* 1982 (Leonard W. Levy, Kenneth L. Karst & Dennis J. Mahoney, eds. 1986).

14. *Id.* at 1983.

15. *Oregon v. Mitchell*, 400 U.S. 112, 91 S.Ct. 260, 27 L.Ed.2d 272 (1970).

16. Some of the leading cases are *Gomillion v. Lightfoot*, 364 U.S. 339, 81 S.Ct. 125, 5 L.Ed.2d 110 (1960); *Terry v. Adams*, 345 U.S. 461, 73 S.Ct. 809, 97 L.Ed.2d 1152 (1953); *Nixon v. Herndon*, 273 U.S. 536, 47 S.Ct. 446, 71 L.Ed. 759 (1927).

17. *Lassiter v. Northampton County Board of Elections*, 360 U.S. 45, 79 S.Ct. 985, 3 L.Ed.2d 1072 (1959); *Guinn v. United States* 238 U.S. 347, 35 S.Ct. 926, 59 L.Ed. 1340 (1915).

18. Later amendments to the statute extended its life and expanded its coverage. The most important change was in section 2 of the act, which covers preexisting voting rules (as opposed to the new rules subject to preclearance under section 5). Under the 1982 amendments, the statute prohibits voting rules that "result in a denial or abridgement of the right to vote on account of race or color'' even if no racially discriminatory purpose is present. The statute is intended to ensure that minority groups have an equal opportunity to participate in the political process and elect representatives of their choice, but Congress disclaimed any intention of requiring proportionate representation.

19. *South Carolina v. Katzenbach*, 383 U.S. 301, 337 (1966).

PART THREE

The Uses of History

INTRODUCTION TO PART THREE

At the end of Reconstruction, the Constitution as we know it today was virtually complete. Some further amendments were made, expanding the franchise and modifying structural matters such as presidential succession. But the basic allocation of power between the states and the federal government, the division of authority within the branches of the federal government, and basic individual rights were left untouched by these later amendments. Considered as a text, the Constitution reached maturity over a century ago.

And yet, constitutional law has changed enormously in the century since Reconstruction. The written text is nearly what it was, but much else has been transformed. A brief summary cannot do justice to the complexities of evolving judicial doctrines, but can at least provide some perspective on the extent of the changes.[1]

As we have seen, in the period following Reconstruction, the Supreme Court interpreted the Reconstruction amendments narrowly, leaving blacks with relatively little constitutional protection against racial discrimination. In the *Slaughter House Cases*, 83 U.S. (16 Wall.) 36, 21 L.Ed. 394 (1873), the Court also refused to use the Fourteenth Amendment to protect the economic freedom of all citizens, black or white. By the end of the nineteenth century, however, the Court assumed a more activist role, aggressively protecting "freedom of contract" as a constitutional right. In several cases in the 1890s, the Court invalidated some state limits on railroad rates as deprivations of private property without due process of law.[2]

During the era of economic libertarianism at the beginning of the twentieth century, the Supreme Court vigilantly guarded against what it considered excessive government regulation, such as state laws governing minimum wages or maximum hours for workers. Federalism decisions also sharply limited the ability of the federal government to engage in economic regulation.[3] Although economic libertarianism held sway until 1937, the most notorious example dates from 1905. In *Lochner v. New York*, 198 U.S. 45, 25 S.Ct. 539, 49

L.Ed. 937 (1905), the Court struck down a statute limiting bakers to a sixty-hour workweek. The Court found no reason to think that longer hours were harmful to bakers, and rejected the statute as an intolerable intrusion on the bakers' freedom of contract. In a famous dissent, Justice Holmes protested that the Court had read its own preferred economic theories into the Constitution.

The climax of economic libertarianism occurred in the early 1930s, when the Court struck down important New Deal legislation. President Roosevelt then proposed to "pack" the Court with additional appointees. Although his proposal was rejected by Congress, his view of the Constitution triumphed, first because of a switch in the views of a key justice and then because of new appointments. As a result, for many years the Court almost entirely withdrew from judicial review of economic regulations. It also left Congress free to regulate areas previously left to the states.

Gradually, the Court began to assume a new role as the guardian of other individual rights. The process began during the 1940s and flowered during the Warren Court. Perhaps the most notable Warren Court decision was *Brown v. Board of Education*, 347 U.S. 483, 74 S.Ct. 686, 98 L.Ed. 873 (1954), overturning the "separate but equal" doctrine and ending Jim Crow laws in the South. Other important decisions greatly increased the procedural rights of criminal defendants and aggressively expanded First Amendment freedoms. The Warren Court ended in 1968 amid expectations of a "constitutional counterrevolution." The Burger Court that followed was cautious about expanding individual rights and often read Warren Court precedents narrowly, but it rarely overruled important Warren Court decisions. Indeed, it sometimes went well beyond the Warren Court, particularly regarding issues relating to women. The most controversial decision of the Burger Court was *Roe v. Wade*, 410 U.S. 113, 93 S.Ct. 705, 35 L.Ed.2d 147 (1973), which gave constitutional protection to women seeking abortions. The direction of the Rehnquist Court is as yet unclear, but the one thing we can be sure of is that judicial doctrines will continue to evolve.

Plainly, the judicial interpretation of the Constitution has evolved in ways that the framers and ratifiers could not have predicted. One question raised by this history of dramatic judicial transformation is whether the original understanding of the Constitution has any continuing legal relevance today. Of course, even someone who believes the "original intent" irrelevant to contemporary constitutional issues might well consider the historical record interesting in its own right. Many, however, believe that the original intent has more than merely historical interest.

In chapter 13, we will examine how the Supreme Court has used—or misused—historical evidence of intent. We will then discuss in chapter 14 the spirited debate among scholars about the relevance of original intent.

FOOTNOTES

1. Readers seeking further detail about changing judicial doctrines should consult one of the excellent texts on constitutional law, such as Alfred H. Kelley, Winfred A. Harbison & Herman Belz, *The American Constitution: Its Origins and Development* (6th ed. 1983); John E. Nowak, Ronald D. Rotunda & J. Nelson Young, *Constitutional Law* (3d ed. 1986); and Laurence H. Tribe, *American Constitutional Law* (2d ed. 1988).

2. In a similar effort to protect private property, the Supreme Court held the federal income tax unconstitutional, on the theory that a tax on the income from property was a "direct tax" and therefore had to be apportioned among the states on the basis of population. This decision ultimately led to the passage of the Sixteenth Amendment authorizing Congress to tax income from all sources. As a matter of legal theory, the amendment was only a minor modification of Article I, but its practical ramifications were far-reaching indeed.

3. These federalism decisions, and the Court's later reversal of its views on congressional power, are discussed in detail in the first section of chapter 13.

CHAPTER THIRTEEN

The Supreme Court's Use of History

INTRODUCTION

In the final chapter of this book, we will examine the views of scholars about the extent to which the "original intent" should control constitutional interpretation. In this chapter, we will see how views about original intent have already affected the Supreme Court's interpretation of the Constitution.

In reading the cases in this chapter, you should consider several points. The first, of course, is whether the Justices are indeed placing any reliance on original intent. Because some of the historical materials relevant to these cases were studied in earlier chapters, you should also consider the plausibility of the historical arguments made by various justices. If you conclude that the justices do a poor job of historical analysis, for example, that conclusion may suggest something about how much weight they should give to original intent.

The cases also raise some subtler questions about the use of history. Sometimes the question of intent has to do with the level of generality. For example, one might inquire whether the framers approved or disapproved of a particular practice, or one might inquire about the general principles held by the framers. You should keep this distinction in mind when reading the cases and should give particular attention to any statements by the justices about the appropriate level of abstraction.

Another issue about the use of history is what kinds of history to consider. By now, the Court is rarely writing on a clean slate. Besides whatever information it may have about the original intent, it may also wish to consider the history of later judicial decisions and perhaps also later practices by the other branches of government. The opinions contain some interesting discussions about the weight to be given to this post-ratification history.

Finally, many writers have suggested that an important part of the Supreme Court's role is to keep the Constitution "up to date" with changing times. After all, the United States today bears little resemblance to the thirteen states of 1787; even the century since Reconstruction has dramatically changed American society. If documents written so long ago are to continue to provide a viable foundation for our scheme of government, these writers argue, the Supreme Court must creatively remold the document to fit contemporary needs. In reading the cases, you should consider whether the Court's decisions can be justified on this basis.

GOVERNMENTAL STRUCTURE

Federalism

Today, the most important source of legislative power for Congress is the commerce clause. Until around 1890, however, that clause functioned mostly as a restriction on the authority of the states. The Court's theory, roughly speaking, was that if interstate commerce was under federal jurisdiction then it could not be within state jurisdiction. Under this so-called "dormant commerce clause" doctrine, even if Congress has not exercised its regulatory power, the states are forbidden to regulate interstate commerce. Drawing a rigid line between state and federal jurisdiction proved unworkable in practice. Today, although courts still view the commerce clause as a limit on state authority, application of this doctrine is much more pragmatic.[1]

The reason that most of the early judicial decisions involved the "dormant commerce clause" is that Congress was not very aggressive about exercising its authority over commerce, so most of the controversies involved cases in which Congress had been silent and states had stepped in to regulate. Beginning with the Civil War era a trend began toward greater congressional activity. This trend has continued to the present.

The initial judicial reception to this new legislation was hostile. From 1890 until 1937, the Supreme Court adopted a restrictive view of congressional power under the commerce clause. For example, in *United States v. E.C. Knight Co.*, 156 U.S. 1, 15 S.Ct. 249, 39 L.Ed. 325 (1895), the Court held that Congress could not prevent a nationwide monopoly in sugar manufacturing. The rationale was that manufacturing (unlike interstate shipment) was an inherently local concern, reserved to the states under the Tenth Amendment. Any effect on later interstate sales was only "indirect" and therefore insufficient to give Congress jurisdiction. In an important later case, the Court ruled that Congress lacked the power to prohibit child labor in factories that sold goods in interstate commerce.[2] During this period, however, the Court was not consistent in ruling against Congress, leading some commentators to criticize its decisions as unprincipled.

In the first half of the 1930s, the Court applied its expansive view of states' rights to strike down important portions of the New Deal, including labor legislation and agricultural price supports. These decisions led to a constitutional crisis in 1937. After President Roosevelt threatened to "pack" the Court with new appointments, Justice Owen Roberts changed his views and voted to uphold New Deal legislation. In key decisions in 1937, the Supreme Court upheld the National Labor Relations Act and the Social Security Act.

Even today, historians debate whether the Court changed course because of political pressure or because the justices came to realize that national economic problems required national solutions. In the end, both explanations may be valid, for the enormous political pressure on the Court was caused by a widespread belief in the need for national measures to counter the Great Depression.

Since 1937, the scope of congressional power under the commerce clause has steadily expanded. In *Wickard v. Filburn*, 317 U.S. 111, 63 S.Ct. 82, 87 L.Ed. 122 (1942), the Court held that Congress could restrict the amount of wheat a farmer grew for his own use. The rationale was that when many farmers divert grain from market for their own use, there is a cumulative effect on interstate commerce. In an even more striking application of the commerce clause, the Court held in *Heart of Atlanta Motel v. United States*, 379 U.S. 241, 85 S.Ct. 348, 13 L.Ed.2d 258 (1964), that Congress could use the commerce clause as the basis for civil rights legislation prohibiting racial discrimination by private businesses. The rationale was that racial discrimination has a significant cumulative effect on the national economy.

Since 1937, the Supreme Court has never struck down any federal regulation of private conduct as a violation of the Tenth Amendment or as exceeding congressional power under the commerce clause. But in one important case, *National League of Cities v. Usery*, 426 U.S. 833, 96 S.Ct. 2465, 49 L.Ed.2d 245 (1976), the Court did hold that Congress lacked the power to impose minimum wage requirements on state and local governments. This federal legislation was held to be an undue intrusion on state sovereignty. In a series of later cases, the Court struggled to define the limits of this doctrine.

The following case, *EEOC v. Wyoming*, was one of the Court's efforts to define the *League of Cities* doctrine. The issue before the Court was whether Congress could prohibit certain forms of age discrimination by state governments, such as mandatory retirement of state employees. The state of Wyoming claimed that it had a Tenth Amendment right to discharge state park rangers at age fifty-five. The majority opinion by Justice Brennan found the case distinguishable from *League of Cities* on the ground that the age discrimination statute was not as inflexible as the minimum wage law. This argument was sufficient to persuade Justice Blackmun, who had cast the decisive fifth vote for the majority in *League of Cities*, thereby giving Brennan a five-justice majority. For our purposes, however, the most interesting aspect of the case is not the doctrinal dispute about *League of Cities* and its proper application, but rather a debate between Justices Stevens (concurring) and Powell (in dissent) about the original understanding of federalism.

EQUAL EMPLOYMENT OPPORTUNITY COMMISSION v. WYOMING
Supreme Court of the United States, 1983
460 U.S. 226, 103 S.Ct. 1054, 75 L.Ed.2d 18

Justice Stevens, concurring.

In final analysis, we are construing the scope of the power granted to Congress by the Commerce Clause of the Constitution. It is important to remember that this Clause was the Framers' response to the central problem that gave rise to the Constitution itself. As I have previously noted, Justice Rutledge described the origins and purpose of the Commerce Clause in these words:

"If any liberties may be held more basic than others, they are the great and indispensable democratic freedoms secured by the First Amendment. But it was not to assure them that the Constitution was framed and adopted. Only later were they added, by popular demand. It was rather to secure freedom of trade, to break down the barriers to its free flow, that the Annapolis Convention was called, only to adjourn with a view to Philadelphia. Thus the generating source of the Constitution lay in the rising volume of restraints upon commerce which the Confederation could not check. These were the proximate cause of our national existence down to today."

.   .   .

There have been occasions when the Court has given a miserly construction to the Commerce Clause. But as the needs of a dynamic and constantly expanding national economy have changed, this Court has construed the Commerce Clause to reflect the intent of the Framers of the Constitution—to confer a power on the National Government adequate to discharge its central mission. In this process the Court has repeatedly repudiated cases that had narrowly construed the Clause. The development of judicial doctrine has accommodated the transition from a purely local, to a regional, and ultimately to a national economy. Today, of course, our economy is merely a part of an international mechanism no single nation could possibly regulate.

In the statutes challenged in this case and in *National League of Cities v. Usery*, 426 U.S. 833 (1976), Congress exercised its power to regulate the American labor market. There was a time when this Court would have denied that Congress had any such power, but that chapter in our judicial history has long been closed. Today, there should be universal agreement on the proposition that Congress has ample power to regulate the terms and conditions of employment throughout the economy. Because of the interdependence of the segments of the economy and the importance and magnitude of government employment, a comprehensive congressional policy to regulate the labor market may require coverage of both public and private sectors to be effective.

Powell, J., dissenting.

.   .   .

Justice Stevens begins his concurring opinion with the startling observation that the Commerce Clause "was the Framers' response to the *central*

problem that gave rise to the Constitution itself." At a subsequent point in his opinion, he observes that "this Court has construed the Commerce Clause to reflect the *intent of the Framers* . . . to confer a power on the national Government adequate to discharge its *central mission*." Justice Stevens further states that "*National League of Cities* not only was incorrectly decided, but also is inconsistent with the *central purpose* of the Constitution itself . . . ."

No one would deny that removing trade barriers between the States was *one* of the Constitution's purposes. I suggest, however, that there were other purposes of equal or greater importance motivating the statesmen who assembled in Philadelphia and the delegates who debated the ratification issue in the state conventions. No doubt there were differences of opinion as to the principal shortcomings of the Articles of Confederation. But one can be reasonably sure that few of the Founding Fathers thought that trade barriers among the States were "the central problem," or that their elimination was the "central mission" of the Constitutional Convention. Creating a National Government within a federal system was far more central than any 18th-century concern for interstate commerce.

It is true, of course, that this Court properly has construed the Commerce Clause, and extended its reach, to accommodate the unanticipated and unimaginable changes, particularly in transportation and communication, that have occurred in our country since the Constitution was ratified. If Justice Stevens had written that the Founders' intent in adopting the Commerce Clause nearly two centuries ago is of little relevance to the world in which we live today, I would not have disagreed. But his concurring opinion purports to rely on their intent. I therefore write—briefly, in view of the scope of the subject—to place the Commerce Clause in proper historical perspective, and further to suggest that even today federalism is not, as Justice Stevens appears to believe, utterly subservient to that Clause.

The Constitution's central purpose was, as the name implies, to constitute a government. The most important provisions, therefore, are those in the first three Articles relating to the establishment of that government. The system of checks and balances, for example, is far more central to the larger perspective than any single power conferred on any branch. Indeed, the Virginia Plan, the initial proposal from which the entire Convention began its work, focuses on the framework of the National Government without even mentioning the power to regulate commerce.

Although *EEOC v. Wyoming* was not the last of the Court's efforts to apply *League of Cities*, it became increasingly obvious that the outcome in Tenth Amendment cases turned largely on the views of Justice Blackmun, who was often the decisive swing voter. By 1985, he was apparently convinced that no principled way to apply *League of Cities* could be found.

In another case involving the federal minimum wage, this time in the context of local transit workers, Justice Blackmun wrote the opinion overruling *League of Cities*. He relied heavily on the difficulty of drawing principled lines between permissible federal regulation and impermissible intrusions on state sovereignty. His opinion (and those of the dissenters) also devoted considerable attention to the original understanding of federalism, as the following excerpts show.

GARCIA v. SAN ANTONIO METROPOLITAN TRANSIT AUTHORITY
Supreme Court of the United States, 1985
469 U.S. 528, 105 S.Ct. 1005, 83 L.Ed.2d 1016

Justice Blackmun delivered the opinion of the Court.

. . .

The States unquestionably do "retai[n] a significant measure of sovereign authority." *EEOC v. Wyoming*, 460 U.S., at 269 (Powell, J., dissenting). They do so, however, only to the extent that the Constitution has not divested them of their original powers and transferred those powers to the Federal Government. In the words of James Madison to the Members of the First Congress: "Interference with the power of the States was no constitutional criterion of the power of Congress. If the power was not given, Congress could not exercise it; if given, they might exercise it, although it should interfere with the laws, or even the Constitution of the States." 2 Annals of Cong. 1897 (1791). . . .

As a result, to say that the Constitution assumes the continued role of the States is to say little about the nature of that role. Only recently, this Court recognized that the purpose of the constitutional immunity recognized in *National League of Cities* is not to preserve "a sacred province of state autonomy." *EEOC v. Wyoming*, 460 U.S., at 236. With rare exceptions, like the guarantee, in Article IV, § 3, of state territorial integrity, the Constitution does not carve out express elements of state sovereignty that Congress may not employ its delegated powers to displace. James Wilson reminded the Pennsylvania ratifying convention in 1787: "It is true, indeed, sir, although it presupposes the existence of state gov-

ernments, yet this Constitution does not suppose them to be the sole power to be respected."

. . .

When we look for the States' "residuary and inviolable sovereignty," The Federalist No. 39, p. 285 (B. Wright ed. 1961) (J. Madison), in the shape of the constitutional scheme rather than in predetermined notions of sovereign power, a different measure of state sovereignty emerges. Apart from the limitation on federal authority inherent in the delegated nature of Congress' Article I powers, the principal means chosen by the Framers to ensure the role of the States in the federal system lies in the structure of the Federal Government itself. It is no novelty to observe that the composition of the Federal Government was designed in large part to protect the States from overreaching by Congress.

. . .

The extent to which the structure of the Federal Government itself was relied on to insulate the interests of the States is evident in the views of the Framers. James Madison explained that the Federal Government "will partake sufficiently of the spirit [of the States], to be disinclined to invade the rights of the individual States, or the prerogatives of their governments." The Federalist No. 46, p. 332 (B. Wright ed. 1961). Similarly, James Wilson observed that "it was a favorite object in the Convention" to provide for the security of the States against federal encroachment and that the structure of the Federal

Government itself served that end. 2 Elliot, at 438-439. Madison placed particular reliance on the equal representation of the States in the Senate, which he saw as "at once a constitutional recognition of the portion of sovereignty remaining in the individual States, and an instrument for preserving that residuary sovereignty." The Federalist No. 62, p. 408 (B. Wright ed. 1961). He further noted that "the residuary sovereignty of the States [is] implied *and secured* by that principle of representation in one branch of the [federal] legislature" (emphasis added). The Federalist No. 43, p. 315 (B. Wright ed. 1961). See also *McCulloch v. Maryland*, 4 Wheat. 316, 435 (1819). In short, the Framers chose to rely on a federal system in which special restraints on federal power over the States inhered principally in the workings of the National Government itself, rather than in discrete limitations on the objects of federal authority. State sovereign interests, then, are more properly protected by procedural safeguards inherent in the structure of the federal system than by judicially created limitations on federal power.

. . .

Powell, J., dissenting.

. . .

In our federal system, the States have a major role that cannot be pre-empted by the National Government. As contemporaneous writings and the debates at the ratifying conventions make clear, the States' ratification of the Constitution was predicated on this understanding of federalism. Indeed, the Tenth Amendment was adopted specifically to ensure that the important role promised the States by the proponents of the Constitution was realized.

Much of the initial opposition to the Constitution was rooted in the fear that the National Government would be too powerful and eventually would eliminate the States as viable political entities. This concern was voiced repeatedly until proponents of the Constitution made assurances that a Bill of Rights, including a provision explicitly reserving powers in the States, would be among the first business of the new Congress. Samuel Adams argued, for example, that if the several States were to be joined in "one entire Nation, under one Legislature, the Powers of which shall extend to every Subject of Legislation, and its Laws be supreme & controul the whole, the Idea of Sovereignty in these States must be lost." Letter from Samuel Adams to Richard Henry Lee (Dec. 3, 1787), reprinted in Anti-Federalists versus Federalists 159 (J. Lewis ed.

1967). Likewise George Mason feared that "the general government being paramount to, and in every respect more powerful than the state governments, the latter must give way to the former." Address in the Ratifying Convention of Virginia (June 4-12, 1788), reprinted in Anti-Federalists versus Federalists, *supra*, at 208-209.

Antifederalists raised these concerns in almost every state ratifying convention. See generally 1-4 Debates in the Several State Conventions on the Adoption of the Federal Constitution (J. Elliot 2d. ed. 1876). As a result, eight States voted for the Constitution only after proposing amendments to be adopted after ratification. All eight of these included among their recommendations some version of what later became the Tenth Amendment.

. . .

The Framers had definite ideas about the nature of the Constitution's division of authority between the Federal and State Governments. In The Federalist No. 39, for example, Madison explained this division by drawing a series of contrasts between the attributes of a "national" government and those of the government to be established by the Constitution. While a national form of government would possess an "indefinite supremacy over all persons and things," the form of government contemplated by the Constitution instead consisted of "local or municipal authorities [which] form distinct and independent portions of the supremacy, no more subject within their respective spheres to the general authority, than the general authority is subject to them, within its own sphere." *Id.*, at 256 (J. Cooke ed. 1961). Under the Constitution, the sphere of the proposed government extended to jurisdiction of "certain enumerated objects only, . . . leav[ing] to the several States a residuary and inviolable sovereignty over all other objects."

. . .

Thus, the harm to the States that results from federal overreaching under the Commerce Clause is not simply a matter of dollars and cents. *National League of Cities*, 426 U.S. at 846-851. Nor is it a matter of the wisdom or folly of certain policy choices. Rather, by usurping functions traditionally performed by the States, federal overreaching under the Commerce Clause undermines the constitutionally mandated balance of power between the States and the Federal Government, a balance designed to protect our fundamental liberties.

Garcia was decided by a five to four margin, with the dissenters vowing that the majority opinion would in its turn be overruled someday. While it would be a mistake to view the question as settled, at present there are no significant, judicially enforceable federalism restrictions on congressional power.[3]

Separation of Powers

Although the Supreme Court currently gives Congress almost complete leeway when the issue is federalism, it is more aggressive about enforcing the separation of powers doctrine.

The following case, *United States v. Curtiss-Wright Corp.*, is frequently cited by presidents as the basis for claiming inherent authority over foreign affairs matters. The specific issue before the Court, however, was rather different: whether Congress could delegate to the president the authority to declare an arms embargo over sales to a foreign country. In a case involving purely *domestic* legislation, at least at that time, the Court might have been less willing to allow Congress to delegate its authority to the executive branch. In explaining the difference, the Court discussed constitutional history in some detail, partly in order to establish the special nature of federal authority over international affairs. Thus, the opinion approaches a separation-of-powers issue on the basis of history that seems to bear more directly on federalism concerns.

UNITED STATES v. CURTISS-WRIGHT CORP.
Supreme Court of the United States, 1936
299 U.S. 304, 57 S.Ct. 216, 81 L.Ed.2d 255

Justice Sutherland delivered the opinion of the Court.

. . .

As a result of the separation from Great Britain by the colonies acting as a unit, the powers of external sovereignty passed from the Crown not to the colonies severally, but to the colonies in their collective and corporate capacity as the United States of America. Even before the Declaration, the colonies were a unit in foreign affairs, acting through a common agency—namely the Continental Congress, composed of delegates from the thirteen colonies. That agency exercised the powers of war and peace, raised an army, created a navy, and finally adopted the Declaration of Independence. Rulers come and go; governments end and forms of government change; but sovereignty survives. A political society cannot endure without a supreme will somewhere. Sovereignty is never held in suspense. When, therefore, the external sovereignty of Great Britain in re-

spect to the colonies ceased, it immediately passed to the Union. *See Penhallow v. Doane*, 3 Dall. 54, 80-81. That fact was given practical application almost at once. The treaty of peace, made on September 23, 1783, was concluded between his Britanic Majesty and the "United States of America."

The Union existed before the Constitution, which was ordained and established among other things to form "a more perfect Union." Prior to that event, it is clear that the Union, declared by the Articles of Confederation to be "perpetual," was the sole possessor of external sovereignty and in the Union it remained without change save in so far as the Constitution in express terms qualified its exercise. The Framers' Convention was called and exerted its powers upon the irrefutable postulate that though the states were several their people in respect of foreign affairs were one. In that convention, the entire absence of state power to deal with those affairs was thus forcefully stated by Rufus King:

"The states were not 'sovereigns' in the sense

contended for by some. They did not possess the peculiar features of sovereignty,—they could not make war, nor peace, nor alliances, nor treaties. Considering them as political beings, they were dumb, for they could not speak to any foreign sovereign whatever. They were deaf, for they could not hear any propositions from such sovereign. They had not even the organs or faculties of defence or offence, for they could not of themselves raise troops, or equip vessels for war." 5 Elliott's Debates 212.

It results that the investment of the federal government with the powers of external sovereignty did not depend upon the affirmative grants of the Constitution. The powers to declare and wage war, to conclude peace, to make treaties, to maintain diplomatic relations with other sovereignties, if they had never been mentioned in the Constitution, would have vested in the federal government as necessary concomitants of nationality.

.   .   .

Not only, as we have shown, is the federal power over external affairs in origin and essential character different from that over internal affairs, but participation in the exercise of the power is significantly limited. In this vast external realm, with its important, complicated, delicate and manifold problems, the President alone has the power to speak or listen as a representative of the nation. He *makes* treaties with the advice and consent of the Senate; but he alone negotiates. Into the field of negotiation the Senate cannot intrude; and Congress itself is pow-

erless to invade it. As Marshall said in his great argument of March 7, 1800, in the House of Representatives, "The President is the sole organ of the nation in its external relations, and its sole representative with foreign nations." Annals, 6th Cong., col. 613.

.   .   .

The result of holding that the joint resolution here under attack is void and unenforceable as constituting an unlawful delegation of legislative power would be to stamp [a] multitude of comparable acts and resolutions as likewise invalid. [These statutes are discussed in detail in a deleted portion of the opinion.] And while this court may not, and should not, hesitate to declare acts of Congress, however many times repeated, to be unconstitutional if beyond all rational doubt it finds them to be so, an impressive array of legislation such as we have just set forth, enacted by nearly every Congress from the beginning of our national existence to the present day, must be given unusual weight in the process of reaching a correct determination of the problem. A legislative practice such as we have here, evidenced not by only occasional instances, but marked by the movement of a steady stream for a century and a half of time, goes a long way in the direction of proving the presence of unassailable ground for the constitutionality of the practice, to be found in the origin and history of the power involved, or in its nature, or in both combined.

Curtiss-Wright is one of only a handful of important separation-of-powers decisions prior to 1970. In the last twenty years, however, the Court has become more actively involved in resolving disputes over the separation of powers. Perhaps because there is less of a developed body of precedent to guide the Court here than in the area of federalism, the Court seems more often to refer to the original understanding of the Constitution as a basis for decision.

In the following case, the Court struck down the "legislative veto" provisions in numerous federal statutes. These provisions had allowed Congress (or sometimes one branch of Congress or a committee) to override action taken by administrators in implementing congressional statutes. Under federal immigration law, an administrative law judge (technically an executive official rather than a member of the judicial branch) could suspend an alien's deportation if certain conditions were met, but either house of Congress could pass a resolution overruling the suspension. This resolution did not require approval by the other branch and was not submitted to the president for possible veto. The dissent listed over two hundred other federal statutes with similar legislative vetoes, all of them now presumably unconstitutional. The majority relied heavily on history in reaching the conclusion that the legislative veto was unconstitutional.

IMMIGRATION AND NATURALIZATION SERVICE v. CHADHA
Supreme Court of the United States, 1983
462 U.S. 919, 103 S.Ct. 2764, 77 L.Ed.2d 317

Chief Justice Burger delivered the opinion of the Court.

. . .

The Presentment Clauses

The records of the Constitutional Convention reveal that the requirement that all legislation be presented to the President before becoming law was uniformly accepted by the Framers. Presentment to the President and the Presidential veto were considered so imperative that the draftsmen took special pains to assure that these requirements could not be circumvented. During the final debate on Art. I, § 7, cl. 2, James Madison expressed concern that it might easily be evaded by the simple expedient of calling a proposed law a "resolution" or "vote" rather than a "bill." 2 Farrand 301-302. As a consequence, Art. I, § 7, cl. 3, was added. 2 Farrand 304-305.

The decision to provide the President with a limited and qualified power to nullify proposed legislation by veto was based on the profound conviction of the Framers that the powers conferred on Congress were the powers to be most carefully circumscribed. It is beyond doubt that lawmaking was a power to be shared by both Houses and the President. In The Federalist No. 73 (H. Lodge ed. 1888), Hamilton focused on the President's role in making laws:

"If even no propensity had ever discovered itself in the legislative body to invade the rights of the Executive, the rules of just reasoning and theoretic propriety would of themselves teach us that the one ought not to be left to the mercy of the other, but ought to possess a constitutional and effectual power of self-defense." *Id.*, at 458.

. . .

Bicameralism

The bicameral requirement of Art. I, §§ 1, 7, was of scarcely less concern to the Framers than was the Presidential veto and indeed the two concepts are interdependent. By providing that no law could take effect without the concurrence of the prescribed majority of the Members of both Houses, the Framers reemphasized their belief, already remarked upon in connection with the Presentment Clauses, that legislation should not be enacted unless it has been carefully and fully considered by the Nation's elected officials. In the Constitutional Convention debates on the need for a bicameral legislature, James Wilson, later to become a Justice of this Court, commented:

"Despotism comes on mankind in different shapes, sometimes in an Executive, sometimes in a military, one. Is there danger of a Legislative despotism? Theory & practice both proclaim it. If the Legislative authority be not restrained, there can be neither liberty nor stability; and it can only be restrained by dividing it within itself, into distinct and independent branches. In a single house there is no check, but the inadequate one, of the virtue & good sense of those who compose it." 1 Farrand 254.

Hamilton argued that a Congress comprised of a single House was antithetical to the very purposes of the Constitution. Were the Nation to adopt a Constitution providing for only one legislative organ, he warned:

"[We] shall finally accumulate, in a single body, all the most important prerogatives of sovereignty, and thus entail upon our posterity one of the most execrable forms of government that human infatuation ever contrived. Thus we should create in reality that very tyranny which the adversaries of the new Constitution either are, or affect to be, solicitous to avert." The Federalist No. 22, p. 135 (H. Lodge ed. 1888).

. . .

We see therefore that the Framers were acutely conscious that the bicameral requirement and the Presentment Clauses would serve essential constitutional functions. The President's participation in the legislative process was to protect the Executive Branch from Congress and to protect the whole people from improvident laws. The division of the Congress into two distinctive bodies assures that the legislative power would be exercised only after opportunity for full study and debate in separate settings. The President's unilateral veto power, in turn, was limited by the power of two-thirds of both Houses of Congress to overrule a veto thereby precluding final arbitrary action of one person. *See id.*, at 99-104. It emerges clearly that the prescription for legislative action in Art. I, §§ 1, 7, represents the

Framers' decision that the legislative power of the Federal Government be exercised in accord with a single, finely wrought and exhaustively considered, procedure.

. . .

Justice White, dissenting.

The reality of the situation is that the constitutional question posed today is one of immense difficulty over which the Executive and Legislative Branches—as well as scholars and judges—have understandably disagreed. That disagreement stems from the silence of the Constitution on the precise question: The Constitution does not directly authorize or prohibit the legislative veto. Thus, our task should be to determine whether the legislative veto is consistent with the purposes of Art. I and the principles of separation of powers which are reflected in that Article and throughout the Constitution. We should not find the lack of a specific constitutional authorization for the legislative veto surprising, and I would not infer disapproval of the mechanism from its absence. From the summer of 1787 to the present the Government of the United States has become an endeavor far beyond the contemplation of the Framers. Only within the last half century has the complexity and size of the Federal Government's responsibilities grown so greatly that the Congress must rely on the legislative veto as the most effective if not the only means to insure its role as the Nation's lawmaker. But the wisdom of the Framers was to anticipate that the Nation would grow and new problems of governance would require different solutions. Accordingly, our Federal Government was intentionally chartered with the flexibility to respond to contemporary needs without losing sight of fundamental democratic principles.

Topics for Discussion

1. It seems clear that the framers would have been shocked if the First Congress had used the commerce clause to pass national civil rights laws or minimum wage laws. Does this mean that such laws violate the "original understanding"? Or should we interpret the framers' understanding at a higher level of generality, as encompassing the power to pass whatever laws are appropriate to meet national economic needs?

2. If in fact the modern expansion of federal power does violate the original understanding of the Constitution, what should the Court do about it? Would it be feasible today for the Court to return to its pre-1937 view of federal power?

3. The relationship between the president and Congress has been a small but now rapidly growing part of the Supreme Court's docket. For instance, in *Bowsher v. Synar*, 478 U.S. 714, 106 S.Ct. 3181, 92 L.Ed.2d 583 (1986), the Court struck down a key provision of the Gramm-Rudman-Hollings Act, which was intended to balance the federal budget by delegating certain budget-cutting authority to the comptroller general. The Court held this delegation invalid because of an unconstitutional provision making the comptroller general removable by Congress. In another important recent case, the Supreme Court upheld the "independent counsel" act, even though the act restricted the attorney general's power to remove independent counsels. *Morrison v. Olson*, 483 U.S. ___ ,108 S.Ct. 2597, 101 L.Ed.2d 569 (1988). Based on your readings, what, if anything, was the original intent about who could remove executive officials? Also, is there any evidence that the framers intended the courts to police relationships between the other two branches? Or is judicial enforcement of the separation of powers provisions simply inherent in the framers' general acceptance of judicial review?

4. In deciding separation of powers issues such as those presented by *Morrison*, *Bowsher*, *Chadha*, and *Curtiss-Wright*, how useful is a consideration of the "original intent"? Had the framers' understanding of the office of the presidency crystallized sufficiently to provide a useful basis for judicial decisions today?

5. If the framers, in solving early separation of powers puzzles, engaged in a freewheeling, flexible analysis of the relevant Constitutional provisions, what guidance might that offer modern interpreters of other separation of powers provisions? In other words, does recourse to the "framers' intent" mean looking at the *answers* the framers reached to particular questions, or at the *methods* they used to answer questions? *See* Gerhard Casper, *An Essay in Separation of Powers: Some Early Versions and Practices*, 30 Wm. & M. L. Rev. 211 (1989); Suzanna Sherry, *Separation of Powers: Asking a Different Question*, 30 Wm. & M. L. Rev. 287 (1989).

6. Should the Court's methods of constitutional interpretation be the same in every case? In a famous opinion, Justice Frankfurter suggested that different clauses of the Constitution might require different methods of interpretation:

> Broadly speaking, two types of constitutional claims come before this Court. Most constitutional issues derive from the broad standards of fairness written into the Constitution (*e.g.* "due process," "equal protection of the laws," "just compensation"), and the division of power as between States and Nation. Such questions, by their very nature, allow a relatively wide play for individual legal judgment. The other class gives no such scope. For this second class of constitutional issues derives from very specific provisions of the Constitution. These had their source in definite grievances and led the Fathers to proscribe against recurrence of their experience. These specific grievances and the safeguards against their recurrence were not defined by the Constitution. They were defined by history. Their meaning was so settled by history that definition was superfluous. Judicial enforcement of the Constitution must respect these historic limits.[4]

If this distinction is valid, would it suggest that the Court should use different techniques in construing the presentment clause in *Chadha* than it uses in cases involving individual rights such as free speech?

INDIVIDUAL RIGHTS

Most of the Supreme Court's constitutional docket involves litigation challenging state laws and policies. Most claims that a state has violated an individual's constitutional rights must be based on the Reconstruction amendments, for the body of the Constitution has little to say about individual rights, and the Bill of Rights was enacted as a limitation on only the federal government. Thus, many of the Court's most celebrated decisions have involved the Reconstruction amendments, particularly the Fourteenth Amendment. As we will see in this section, the justices have on occasion engaged in heated debates about the relationship between their decisions and the intentions of the framers.

The Thirteenth Amendment

The immediate purpose of the Thirteenth Amendment was, of course, to abolish involuntary servitude. This purpose still occasionally gives rise to litigation today, when employers are found to be forcibly keeping workers in conditions resembling those of slave days.[5] But the amendment has also been invoked as a basis for dealing with racial discrimination.

The Fourteenth Amendment's equal protection clause is another, more commonly used basis for attacks on racial discrimination. The language of the Fourteenth Amendment, however, suggests one significant restriction on the application of the equal protection clause. The amendment provides that "no state shall . . . deprive any person within its jurisdiction of the equal protection of the laws." Thus, the Fourteenth Amendment seems to require some sort of state involvement in discrimination. This "state action" requirement has given rise to a large body of case law. One particularly unclear area is the extent to which Congress can use its power under section 5 of the Fourteenth Amendment to prohibit racial discrimination by private parties.

Because the language of the Thirteenth Amendment contains no similar reference to state action, attempts have sometimes been made to invoke it as a basis for restrictions on private discrimination. The following case is the basis for modern applications of the amendment; it has been adhered to and extended in a series of later cases. The issues before the Court were whether the Civil Rights Act of 1866 prohibited racial discrimination by private parties in the sale of real estate, and whether Congress had the power to prohibit such private discrimination. The defendant was a real estate developer who refused to sell to blacks. The case is particularly interesting because, as we saw in chapter 11, the Civil Rights Act was a crucial part of the background of the Fourteenth Amendment as well.

JONES v. MAYER CO.

Supreme Court of the United States, 1968

392 U.S. 409, 88 S.Ct. 2186, 20 L.Ed.2d 1189

Justice Stewart delivered the opinion of the Court.

. . .

In its original form, 42 U. S. C. § 1982 was part of § 1 of the Civil Rights Act of 1866. That section was cast in sweeping terms. . . .

The crucial language for our purposes was that which guaranteed all citizens "the same right, in every State and Territory in the United States, . . . to inherit, purchase, lease, sell, hold, and convey real and personal property . . . as is enjoyed by white citizens. . . ." To the Congress that passed the Civil Rights Act of 1866, it was clear that the right to do these things might be infringed not only by "State or local law" but also by "custom, or prejudice." Thus, when Congress provided in § 1 of the Civil Rights Act that the right to purchase and lease property was to be enjoyed equally throughout the United States by Negro and white citizens alike, it plainly meant to secure that right against interfer-

ence from any source whatever, whether governmental or private.

That broad language, we are asked to believe, was a mere slip of the legislative pen. We disagree. For the same Congress that wanted to do away with the Black Codes *also* had before it an imposing body of evidence pointing to the mistreatment of Negroes by private individuals and unofficial groups, mistreatment unrelated to any hostile state legislation.

. . .

As its text reveals, the Thirteenth Amendment "is not a mere prohibition of State laws establishing or upholding slavery, but an absolute declaration that slavery or involuntary servitude shall not exist in any part of the United States." *Civil Rights Cases*, 109 U.S. 3, 20. It has never been doubted, therefore, "that the power vested in Congress to enforce the article by appropriate legislation," *ibid.*, includes the power to enact laws "direct and primary, operating upon the acts of individuals, whether sanctioned by State legislation or not." *Id.*, at 23.

Thus, the fact that § 1982 operates upon the unofficial acts of private individuals, whether or not sanctioned by state law, presents no constitutional problem. If Congress has power under the Thirteenth Amendment to eradicate conditions that prevent Negroes from buying and renting property because of their race or color, then no federal statute calculated to achieve that objective can be thought to exceed the constitutional power of Congress simply because it reaches beyond state action to regulate the conduct of private individuals. The constitutional question in this case, therefore, comes to this: Does the authority of Congress to enforce the Thirteenth Amendment "by appropriate legislation" include the power to eliminate all racial barriers to the acquisition of real and personal property? We think the answer to that question is plainly yes.

. . .

Those who opposed the passage of the Civil Rights Act of 1866 argued in effect that the Thirteenth Amendment merely authorized Congress to dissolve the legal bond by which the Negro slave was held to his master. Yet many had earlier opposed the Thirteenth Amendment on the very ground that it would give Congress virtually unlimited power to enact laws for the protection of Negroes in every State. And the majority leaders in Congress—who were, after all, the authors of the Thirteenth Amendment—had no doubt that its Enabling Clause contemplated the sort of positive legislation that was embodied in the 1866 Civil Rights Act.

Justice Harlan, dissenting:

The Court rests its opinion chiefly upon the legislative history of the Civil Rights Act of 1866. I shall endeavor to show that those debates do not, as the Court would have it, overwhelmingly support the result reached by the Court, and in fact that a contrary conclusion may equally well be drawn.

. . .

On January 29, Senator Trumbull uttered the first of several remarkably similar and wholly unambiguous statements which indicated that the bill was aimed only at "state action." He said:

"[This bill] may be assailed as drawing to the Federal Government powers that properly belong to 'States'; but I apprehend, rightly considered, it is not obnoxious to that objection. *It will have no operation in any State where the laws are equal, where all persons have the same civil rights without regard to color or race. It will have no operation in the State of Kentucky when her slave code and all her laws discriminating between persons on account of race or color shall be abolished.*"

. . .

The House debates are even fuller of statements indicating that the civil rights bill was intended to reach only state-endorsed discrimination. Representative Wilson was the bill's sponsor in the House. On the very first day of House debate, March 1, Representative Wilson said in explaining the bill:

"[I]f the States, seeing that we have citizens of different races and colors, would but shut their eyes to these differences and legislate, so far at least as regards civil rights and immunities, as though all citizens were of one race or color, our troubles as a nation would be well-nigh over. . . . It will be observed that *the entire structure of this bill rests on the discrimination relative to civil rights and immunities made by the States* on 'account of race, color, or previous condition of slavery.' "

. . .

Residential segregation was the prevailing pattern almost everywhere in the North. There were no state "fair housing" laws in 1866, and it appears that none had ever been proposed. In this historical context, I cannot conceive that a bill thought to prohibit purely private discrimination not only in the sale or rental of housing but in *all* property transactions would not have received a great deal of criticism explicitly directed to this feature. The fact that the 1866 Act received *no* criticism of this kind is for me strong additional evidence that it was not regarded as extending so far.

Jones has since been extended to another provision of the 1866 Civil Rights Act prohibiting racial discrimination in the making of contracts. In *Runyon v. McCrary*, 427 U.S. 160, 96 S.Ct. 2586, L.Ed.2d 415 (1976), the Court held that the 1866 Act prohibits discriminatory admission policies by private schools. Interestingly enough, two justices who joined the majority said specifically that they considered *Jones* to have been wrongly decided. Justice Stevens's position is particularly interesting:

> *Jones v. Alfred H. Mayer Co.*, 392 U.S. 409, and its progeny have unequivocally held that § 1 of the Civil Rights Act of 1866 prohibits private racial discrimination. There is no doubt in my mind that that construction of the statute would have amazed the legislators who voted for it. Both its language and the historical setting in which it was enacted convince me that Congress intended only to guarantee all citizens the same legal capacity to make and enforce contracts, to obtain, own, and convey property, and to litigate and give evidence. Moreover, since the legislative history discloses an intent not to outlaw segregated public schools at that time, it is quite unrealistic to assume that Congress intended the broader result of prohibiting segregated private schools. Were we writing on a clean slate, I would therefore vote to reverse [the lower court decision against the private school.]

> .   .   .

> The policy of the Nation as formulated by Congress in recent years has moved constantly in the direction of eliminating racial segregation in all sectors of society. This Court has given a sympathetic and liberal construction to such legislation. For the Court now to overrule *Jones* would be a significant step backwards, with effects that would not have arisen from a correct decision in the first instance. Such a step would be so clearly contrary to my understanding of the mores of today that I think the Court is entirely correct in adhering to *Jones*.

Ironically, twelve years later, the Court announced its willingness to reconsider *Runyon*. Over the bitter dissent of four justices, the Court ordered that the issue be argued by the parties in a pending case, even though none of the parties had raised the issue. *Patterson v. McLean Credit Commission*, 485 U.S. 617, 108 S.Ct. 1419, 99 L.Ed.2d 879 (1988).[6] After reargument, however, the Court unanimously reaffirmed *Runyon*. __ U.S. __, 109 S.Ct. 2363, __ L.Ed.2d __ (1989).

The Fourteenth Amendment: Equal Protection

Perhaps one of the most significant examples of the Supreme Court's attitude toward the use of history is a case in which the Court decided *not* to rely on historical evidence. After hearing oral arguments in *Brown v. Board of Education*, 347 U.S. 483, 74 S.Ct. 686, 98 L.Ed. 873 (1954), the famous school desegregation case, the Court asked for an additional round of briefs on the original intent of the framers regarding segregated schools. The parties responded with detailed historical arguments on the subject. Chief Justice Warren's opinion, however, brushed aside the question of original intent with the explanation that the historical arguments were at best inconclusive.

Another major innovation by the Warren Court involved voting rights. In a series of cases, the Court created and rigorously applied the principle of "one person, one vote." The result was nationwide reapportionment, often shifting political power away from rural areas toward cities and suburbs. The Court's decisions were based on the equal protection clause. As in *Brown*, it paid little heed to questions of original intent.

Justice Harlan protested that applying the equal protection clause to voting violated the original understanding of the Fourteenth Amendment. For years, his detailed historical arguments were simply ignored by the majority.

In the following case, however, Justice Harlan's arguments finally got a response. The case was not about apportionment but instead involved an effort by Congress to give eighteen-year-olds the right to vote in state and national elections. Because the justices were sharply divided on the issue, there was no majority opinion.[7]

OREGON v. MITCHELL
Supreme Court of the United States, 1970
400 U.S. 112, 91 S.Ct. 260, 27 L.Ed.2d 272

. . .

Opinion of **Justice Harlan**:

. . .

Debate in the House [on the Fourteenth Amendment] was substantially concluded by Bingham, the man primarily responsible for the language of § 1. Without equivocation, he stated:

"The amendment does not give, as the second section shows, the power to Congress of regulating suffrage in the several States.

"The second section excludes the conclusion that by the first section suffrage is subjected to congressional law; save, indeed, with this exception, that as the right in the people of each State to a republican government and to choose their Representatives in Congress is of the guarantees of the Constitution, by this amendment a remedy might be given directly for a case supposed by Madison, where treason might change a State government from a republican to a despotic government, and thereby deny suffrage to the people." Globe 2542.

. . .

[In introducing the Amendment in the Senate,] Howard minced no words. He stated that

"the first section of the proposed amendment does not give to either of these classes the right of voting. The right of suffrage is not, in law, one of the privileges or immunities thus secured by the Constitution. It is merely the creature of law. It has always been regarded in this country as the result of positive local law, not regarded as one of those fundamental rights lying at the basis of all society and without which a people cannot exist except as slaves, subject to a depotism [sic]. Globe 2766.

. . .

The history of the Fourteenth Amendment with respect to suffrage qualifications is remarkably free of the problems which bedevil most attempts to find a reliable guide to present decision in the pages of the past. Instead, there is virtually unanimous agreement, clearly and repeatedly expressed, that § 1 of the Amendment did not reach discriminatory voter qualifications.

Opinion of **Justices Brennan**, **White**, and **Marshall**:

. . .

Meeting in the winter and spring of 1866 and facing elections in the fall of the same year, the Republicans in Congress thus faced a difficult dilemma: they desperately needed Negro suffrage in order to prevent total Democratic resurgence in the South, yet they feared that by pressing for suffrage they might create a reaction among northern white voters that would lead to massive Democratic electoral gains in the North. Their task was thus to frame a policy that would prevent total southern Democratic resurgence and that simultaneously would serve as a platform upon which Republicans could go before their northern constituents in the fall. What ultimately emerged as the policy and political platform of the Republican Party was the Fourteenth Amendment.

. . .

The purpose of § 1 in relation to the suffrage emerges out of the debates on the floor of Congress with an equal obscurity.

. . .

Howard, with that "lack of legal precision" typical of the period, stated that the right of suffrage was not one of the privileges and immunities protected by the Constitution, Globe 2766, immediately after he had read into the record an excerpt from the case of *Corfield v. Coryell*, 6 F. Cas. 546 (No. 3230)

(CCED Pa. 1825), an excerpt which listed the elective franchise as among the privileges and immunities. Globe 2765. Bingham was equally ambiguous, for he too thought that the elective franchise was a constitutionally protected privilege and immunity. Globe 2542[.]

. . .

The historical record left by the framers of the Fourteenth Amendment, because it is a product of differing and conflicting political pressures and conceptions of federalism, is thus too vague and imprecise to provide us with sure guidance in deciding the pending cases. We must therefore conclude that its framers understood their Amendment to be a broadly worded injunction capable of being interpreted by future generations in accordance with the vision and needs of those generations.

For a variety of reasons, a majority of the justices agreed with Harlan that Congress lacked the power to give eighteen-year-olds the vote in state elections. As we saw in chapter 12, the Court's decision in this case led to a constitutional amendment, one of a series of amendments broadening the franchise.

The Fourteenth Amendment: Individual Liberty

Although the Warren Court de-emphasized original intent in the segregation and reapportionment cases, considerations of original intent played a major role in its adoption of the view that the Bill of Rights can be applied to the states through the Fourteenth Amendment. It comes as a surprise to many people that the Bill of Rights does not directly apply to the states. Indeed, as we saw in chapter 11, it seems to have been something of a surprise to John Bingham, the drafter of section 1 of the Fourteenth Amendment.

Today, there is even greater ground for confusion on this point, because newspapers are full of accounts about application to the states of the First Amendment, the Fourth Amendment, and the Fifth Amendment. Technically, however, these amendments apply to the states only to the extent that the Fourteenth Amendment "incorporates" the Bill of Rights.

Before the Warren Court, the accepted rule was that the due process clause of the Fourteenth Amendment did impose substantive restrictions on state legislation, but not necessarily the same restrictions that the Bill of Rights imposes on the federal government. The usual formula was that states could not violate fundamental rights "inherent in ordered liberty." Some of those fundamental rights, such as free speech, coincided with provisions of the Bill of Rights, but other provisions of the Bill of Rights were held not to be inherent in ordered liberty. For example, in *Adamson v. California*, 332 U.S. 46, 67 S.Ct. 1672, 91 L.Ed. 1903 (1947), the Fifth Amendment privilege against self-incrimination was held by the majority of the Court not to apply to the states. The holding was later overruled, and today the Fifth Amendment privilege *is* applicable to the states.

Adamson is still important today, however, primarily because of Justice Black's dissent, in which he began a successful campaign for incorporation of the Bill of Rights. His dissent argued forcefully for a return to what he considered the original intent. A lengthy appendix to Black's dissent marshalled the historical evidence in favor of incorporation. Much of that evidence is reprinted in chapter 11 of this book. An important opinion by Justice Frankfurter took issue with Justice Black. Frankfurter argued that the "plain language" of the amendment could not have been understood at the time to mean that every detail of the Bill of Rights would apply to the states.

The Supreme Court has never explicitly adopted Justice Black's historical analysis, but his campaign for incorporation of the Bill of Rights did achieve its goal. Today, with only minor exceptions—such as the rights to jury trials in civil cases, to indictment by a grand jury, and perhaps the right to bear arms—all of the provisions of the Bill of Rights apply to the states by way of the Fourteenth Amendment. Since many of the Bill of Rights' provisions relate to criminal trials, this has meant a revolution in the law of criminal procedure, which in important respects has become a matter more of federal constitutional law than of state law.

One effect of the incorporation doctrine has been to increase significantly the number of occasions on which the Court must interpret the provisions of the Bill of Rights. The major provisions—the First, Fourth, Fifth, and Sixth Amendments—have all given rise to large bodies of case law, substantial historical investigation, and considerable public controversy. Here, we will focus on only one provision, the establishment clause of the First Amendment. As some recent commentators have observed, "[t]here is a seemingly irresistible impulse to appeal to history when analyzing issues under the religion clauses."[8]

The following case is the foundation of modern establishment clause doctrines. The Court relied heavily on the historical record as the basis for its broad view of the scope of the clause. Ironically, the particular establishment clause claim made by the plaintiffs was rejected by the Court. The state was providing school buses to students attending parochial school. The majority viewed this as a matter of public safety rather than a form of affirmative support for religion. But the case is remembered today less for its specific holding than for its enthusiastic reading of the original intent regarding religious freedom.

EVERSON v. BOARD OF EDUCATION
Supreme Court of the United States, 1947
330 U.S. 1, 67 S.Ct. 504, 91 L.Ed. 711

Justice Black delivered the opinion of the Court.

. . .

A large proportion of the early settlers of this country came here from Europe to escape the bondage of laws which compelled them to support and attend government-favored churches. The centuries immediately before and contemporaneous with the colonization of America had been filled with turmoil, civil strife, and persecutions, generated in large part by established sects determined to maintain their absolute political and religious suprem-

acy. With the power of government supporting them at various times and places, Catholics had persecuted Protestants, Protestants had persecuted Catholics, Protestant sects had persecuted other Protestant sects, Catholics of one shade of belief had persecuted Catholics of another shade of belief, and all of these had from time to time persecuted Jews. In efforts to force loyalty to whatever religious group happened to be on top and in league with the government of a particular time and place, men and women had been fined, cast in jail, cruelly tortured, and killed. Among the offenses for which these punishments had been inflicted were such things as speaking disrespectfully of views of ministers of government-established churches, non-attendance at those churches, expressions of non-belief in their doctrines, and failure to pay taxes and tithes to support them.

These practices of the old world were transplanted to and began to thrive in the soil of the new America. The very charters granted by the English Crown to the individuals and companies designated to make the laws which would control the destinies of the colonials authorized these individuals and companies to erect religious establishments which all, whether believers or non-believers, would be required to support and attend. An exercise of this authority was accompanied by a repetition of many of the old-world practices and persecutions.

. . .

These practices became so commonplace as to shock the freedom-loving colonials into a feeling of abhorrence. The imposition of taxes to pay ministers' salaries and to build and maintain churches and church property aroused their indignation. It was these feelings which found expression in the First Amendment. No one locality and no one group throughout the Colonies can rightly be given entire credit for having aroused the sentiment that culminated in adoption of the Bill of Rights' provisions embracing religious liberty. But Virginia, where the established church had achieved a dominant influence in political affairs and where many excesses attracted wide public attention, provided a great stimulus and able leadership for the movement. The people there, as elsewhere, reached the conviction that individual religious liberty could be achieved best under a government which was stripped of all power to tax, to support, or otherwise to assist any or all religions, or to interfere with the beliefs of any religious individual or group.

The movement toward this end reached its dramatic climax in Virginia in 1785-86 when the Virginia legislative body was about to renew Virginia's tax levy for the support of the established church. Thomas Jefferson and James Madison led the fight against this tax. Madison wrote his great Memorial and Remonstrance against the law. In it, he eloquently argued that a true religion did not need the support of law; that no person, either believer or non-believer, should be taxed to support a religious institution of any kind; that the best interest of a so-

ciety required that the minds of men always be wholly free; and that cruel persecutions were the inevitable result of government-established religions. Madison's Remonstrance received strong support throughout Virginia, and the Assembly postponed consideration of the proposed tax measure until its next session. When the proposal came up for consideration at that session, it not only died in committee, but the Assembly enacted the famous "Virginia Bill for Religious Liberty" originally written by Thomas Jefferson. The preamble to that Bill stated among other things that

"Almighty God hath created the mind free; that all attempts to influence it by temporal punishments or burthens, or by civil incapacitations, tend only to beget habits of hypocrisy and meanness, and are a departure from the plan of the Holy author of our religion, who being Lord both of body and mind, yet chose not to propagate it by coercions on either . . .; that to compel a man to furnish contributions of money for the propagation of opinions which he disbelieves, is sinful and tyrannical; that even the forcing him to support this or that teacher of his own religious persuasion, is depriving him of the comfortable liberty of giving his contributions to the particular pastor, whose morals he would make his pattern. . . ."

And the statute itself enacted

"That no man shall be compelled to frequent or support any religious worship, place, or ministry whatsoever, nor shall be enforced, restrained, molested, or burthened in his body or goods, nor shall otherwise suffer on account of his religious opinions or belief. . . ."

This Court has previously recognized that the provisions of the First Amendment, in the drafting and adoption of which Madison and Jefferson played such leading roles, had the same objective and were intended to provide the same protection against governmental intrusion on religious liberty as the Virginia statute.

. . .

The "establishment of religion" clause of the First Amendment means at least this: Neither a state nor the Federal Government can set up a church. Neither can pass laws which aid one religion, aid all religions, or prefer one religion over another. Neither can force nor influence a person to go to or to remain away from church against his will or force him to profess a belief or disbelief in any religion.

Justice Black's "wall of separation" reading of both the clause and its framers' intent gave rise to spirited controversy. Debating this issue became something of a "cottage industry" among constitutional historians. The following case gave rise to perhaps the only serious critique of Justice Black's history by a member of the Supreme Court itself. The issue before the Court was the constitutionality of a state law that mandated a moment of silence "for meditation or voluntary prayer" in public classrooms. The majority held the statute unconstitutional. In dissent, Justice Rehnquist, now chief justice, argued that the establishment clause prohibits only discrimination among religions, not laws aiding all religions equally. Note that he relies heavily on evidence of original intent, while the majority relegates historical evidence to a footnote.

WALLACE v. JAFFREE
Supreme Court of the United States, 1985
472 U.S. 38, 105 S.Ct. 2479, 86 L. Ed.2d 29

Justice Stevens delivered the opinion of the Court:

. . .

As is plain from its text, the First Amendment was adopted to curtail the power of Congress to interfere with the individual's freedom to believe, to worship, and to express himself in accordance with the dictates of his own conscience. Until the Fourteenth Amendment was added to the Constitution, the First Amendment's restraints on the exercise of federal power simply did not apply to the States. But when the Constitution was amended to prohibit any State from depriving any person of liberty without due process of law, that Amendment imposed the same substantive limitations on the States' power to legislate that the First Amendment had always imposed on the Congress' power. This Court has confirmed and endorsed this elementary proposition of law time and time again.

Just as the right to speak and the right to refrain from speaking are complementary components of a broader concept of individual freedom of mind, so also the individual's freedom to choose his own creed is the counterpart of his right to refrain from accepting the creed established by the majority. At one time it was thought that this right merely proscribed the preference of one Christian sect over another, but would not require equal respect for the conscience of the infidel, the atheist, or the adherent of a non-Christian faith such as Islam or Judaism. But when the underlying principle has been examined in the crucible of litigation, the Court has unambiguously concluded that the individual free-

dom of conscience protected by the First Amendment embraces the right to select any religious faith or none at all. This conclusion derives support not only from the interest in respecting the individual's freedom of conscience, but also from the conviction that religious beliefs worthy of respect are the product of free and voluntary choice by the faithful,* and from recognition of the fact that the political interest in forestalling intolerance extends beyond intolerance among Christian sects—or even intolerance among "religions"—to encompass intolerance of the disbeliever and the uncertain.

. . .

Justice Rehnquist, dissenting.

It is impossible to build sound constitutional doctrine upon a mistaken understanding of constitu-

---

*In his "Memorial and Remonstrance Against Religious Assessments, 1785." James Madison wrote in part:

"1. Because we hold it for a fundamental and undeniable truth, that Religion or the duty which we owe to our Creator and the [Manner of discharging it, can be directed only by reason and] conviction, not by force or violence. The Religion then of every man must be left to the conviction and conscience of every man; and it is the right of every man to exercise it as these may dictate. This right is in its nature an unalienable right. It is unalienable: because the opinions of men, depending only on the evidence contemplated by their own minds, cannot follow the dictates of other men: It is unalienable also: because what is here a right towards men, is a duty towards the Creator. It is the duty of every man to render to the Creator such homage, and such only as he believes to be acceptable to him. . . . We maintain therefore that in matters of Religion, no man's right is abridged by the institution of Civil Society, and that Religion is wholly exempt from its cognizance." [Footnote by the Court]

tional history, but unfortunately the Establishment Clause has been expressly freighted with Jefferson's misleading metaphor for nearly 40 years. Thomas Jefferson was of course in France at the time the constitutional Amendments known as the Bill of Rights were passed by Congress and ratified by the States. His letter to the Danbury Baptist Association was a short note of courtesy, written 14 years after the Amendments were passed by Congress. He would seem to any detached observer as a less than ideal source of contemporary history as to the meaning of the Religion Clauses of the First Amendment.

Jefferson's fellow Virginian, James Madison, with whom he was joined in the battle for the enactment of the Virginia Statute of Religious Liberty of 1786, did play as large a part as anyone in the drafting of the Bill of Rights. He had two advantages over Jefferson in this regard: he was present in the United States, and he was a leading Member of the First Congress. But when we turn to the record of the proceedings in the First Congress leading up to the adoption of the Establishment Clause in the Constitution, including Madison's significant contributions thereto, we see a far different picture of its purpose than the highly simplified "wall of separation between church and State."

. . .

On the basis of the record of these proceedings in the House of Representatives, James Madison was undoubtedly the most important architect among the Members of the House of the Amendments which became the Bill of Rights, but it was James Madison speaking as an advocate of sensible legislative compromise, not as an advocate of incorporating the Virginia Statute of Religious Liberty into the United States Constitution. During the ratification debate in the Virginia Convention, Madison had actually opposed the idea of any Bill of Rights. His sponsorship of the Amendments in the House was obviously not that of a zealous believer in the necessity of the Religion Clauses, but of one who felt it might do some good, could do no harm, and would satisfy those who had ratified the Constitution on the condition that Congress propose a Bill of Rights. His original language "nor shall any national religion be established" obviously does not conform to the "wall of separation" between church and State idea which latter-day commentators have ascribed to him. His explanation on the floor of the meaning of his language—"that Congress should not establish a religion, and enforce the legal observation of it by law" is of the same ilk. When he replied to Huntington in the debate over the proposal which came from the Select Committee of the House, he urged that the language "no religion shall be established by law" should be amended by inserting the word "national" in front of the word "religion."

It seems indisputable from these glimpses of Madison's thinking, as reflected by actions on the floor of the House in 1789, that he saw the Amendment as designed to prohibit the establishment of a national religion, and perhaps to prevent discrimination among sects. He did not see it as requiring neutrality on the part of government between religion and irreligion. Thus the Court's opinion in *Everson*—while correct in bracketing Madison and Jefferson together in their exertions in their home State leading to the enactment of the Virginia Statute of Religious Liberty—is totally incorrect in suggesting that Madison carried these views onto the floor of the United States House of Representatives when he proposed the language which would ultimately become the Bill of Rights.

The materials presented in this chapter are only a sample of the numerous discussions of original intent by Supreme Court justices. It is, of course, far from true that the Court's views of constitutional law have been solely based on considerations of original intent. Many landmark cases, like *Brown v. Board of Education*, have simply bypassed consideration of original intent. On the other hand, it also seems clear that discussions of original intent have figured in some leading constitutional decisions. In the following chapter, we will consider scholarly arguments about whether the Court should be more faithful to original intent.

Topics for Discussion

1. Chapter 11 contains much of the historical evidence relevant to Justice

Black's incorporation theory and Justice Harlan's theory regarding voting rights. What is your own evaluation of the historical record on these points?

2. In interpreting the Fourteenth Amendment, to what extent should the Court be concerned with its broader intellectual context (such as that discussed in chapter 9)? Do evolving concepts of federalism during the Civil War and Reconstruction shed any light on the original understanding with respect to the issues involved in the cases in this section?

3. The main disagreement in *Jones* involves the interpretation of a statute. Should original intent play the same role in interpreting statutes as in interpreting the Constitution? Or should it be given more (or less) of a role in statutory construction?

4. Which reading of the establishment clause do you find most plausible, Black's or Rehnquists's? Do the materials in chapter 8 shed light on this problem?

5. Do the justices' discussions of the historical record give their decisions greater legitimacy in the eyes of the public? How likely is it that even lawyers or lower court judges will read lengthy historical narratives with any care?

6. If the courts are going to rely on original intent, would it be useful to obtain expert testimony by historians while the case is still in the trial court? Would this improve the quality of decision making by the Supreme Court?

7. Based on the materials in this chapter, what is your impression of the Court's actual reliance on history? Are historical discussions merely window-dressing, or do the justices pay serious attention to them? If original intent does play a role, how much weight does it carry as compared to a judge's own sense of justice or commitment to judicial precedent?

FOOTNOTES

1. For a brief survey and critique of current doctrine, see Daniel A. Farber, *State Regulation and the Dormant Commerce Clause*, 3 Constitutional Commentary 395 (1986).

2. *Hammer v. Dagenhart*, 247 U.S. 251, 38 S.Ct. 529, 62 L.Ed. 1101 (1918).

3. For insightful recent discussions of the original understanding of federalism, see Michael McConnell, *Book Review*, 54 U. Chi. L. Rev. 484 (1987); H. Jefferson Powell, *Book Review*, 54 U. Chi. L. Rev. 1513 (1987). Both essays discuss Raoul Berger's book, *Federalism: The Founders' Design* (1987). Another reviewer of that book commented that "[f]or those of us who continue to attach some importance to the views of the Framers, . . . this book is a considerable embarrassment." Daniel A. Farber, *Book Review*, The Washington Monthly, September 1987 at 59.

4. *United States v. Lovett*, 328 U.S. 303, 321 (1946) (Frankfurter, J., concurring).

5. For a recent decision giving a restrictive interpretation of the anti-peonage statute, see *United States v. Kozminski*, ___ U.S. ___, 108 S.Ct. 2751, 101 L.Ed.2d 788 (1988).

6. For commentary on the reargument order, see Daniel A. Farber, *Statutory Interpretation, Legislative Inaction, and Civil Rights*, 87 Mich. L. Rev. 2 (1988). A historical argument in favor of *Runyon* and *Jones* can be found in Barry Sullivan, *Historical Reconstruction, Reconstruction History, and the Proper Scope of Section 1981*, 98 Yale L.J. 541 (1989).

7. Four justices voted to uphold the entire statute, while four voted to strike it down. Justice Black, the swing voter, believed that regulation of age requirements in state elections exceeded congressional power under section 5 of the Fourteenth Amendment, but that Congress did have the power under Article I, section 4, to set voting qualifications in federal elections.

8. John E. Nowak & Ronald D. Rotunda, *Constitutional Law* 1031 (3d ed. 1986).

CHAPTER FOURTEEN

The Relevance of Original Intent

INTRODUCTION

The role of historical evidence in constitutional law has always been of interest to scholars. Recently, however, it has become a matter of more pressing concern, as Professor Murray Dry explains:

> How can a Constitution that was written two hundred years ago properly be said to govern us today, in light of the massive changes in our territory as well as our population's size and heterogeneity? This question has given rise to what is commonly known as the battle between interpretivism and noninterpretivism. The scholars who introduced these terms a decade ago meant by "interpretivism" that constitutional adjudication must be limited to norms inferable from the text, those demonstrably expressed or implied by the framers. Finding this inadequate to justify decisions they thought were correctly decided, notably the abortion case but also the apportionment and school desegregation decisions, they advocated "noninterpretivism," which licenses courts to apply contemporary norms not demonstrably expressed or implied in the text.[1]

This debate, as Professor Dry goes on to explain, soon extended beyond academics to include judges and other government officials:

> This important debate came out of the academic closet in 1985, when Attorney General Edwin Meese gave public addresses on constitutional jurisprudence. In one, after noting that the new terms replaced the older ones of strict versus loose construction, he quipped, "Under the old system the question was *how* to read the Constitution; under the new approach, the question is *whether* to read the Constitution." He called for a return to a "jurisprudence of original intention," (a clearer term for interpretivism). Acting on that principle, he said the Justice Department stood prepared to challenge the incorporation doctrine, according to which nearly all of the provisions of the original Bill of Rights have been applied against the states under the fourteenth amendment. This drew from Justice Brennan a defense of an activist approach to individual rights and a twentieth-century reading of the

Constitution. For Justice Brennan and his supporters, the choice is between being ruled by the dead hand of the past or the living present; for Attorney General Meese and his supporters, the choice is between courts that say what the law is, which is their job, and courts that make law and policy, which is the job of legislatures.[2]

This debate about constitutional interpretation is the subject of this chapter.

It is useful to begin by defining some terms. Instead of the term "interpretivism," we will call supporters of Meese's position "originalists." The latter term is found more frequently in current writings on the subject because it emphasizes that the issue is the role of *original* intent in constitutional interpretation. Most opponents of originalism also claim to be "interpreting" the Constitution; they simply have a different view of the appropriate methods of doing so. We will call them non-originalists because they do not find original intent dispositive of contemporary constitutional questions.

A great deal of ink has been spilled over the question of originalism. It is important to realize, however, that the area of dispute is narrow. Almost no one believes that original understanding is wholly irrelevant to modern-day constitutional interpretation. For example, here are the views of Professor Michael Perry, a leading non-originalist:

> Given the nonauthoritative status of the original (the ratifiers') understanding of particular textual provisions, is the Court's frequent reference to the original understanding merely a self-protective formality?
>
> Of course not. The ratifiers and their polity were participants in the tradition too. In their day, they were the stewards of the tradition. The ways in which they shaped and responded to the aspiration of the tradition may well shed light on how we should shape and respond to those aspirations. Why assume we have nothing to learn from our past? The Court is right to consult the ratifiers' normative judgments.
>
> To consult their judgments is one thing, however; to accord them authoritative status is something else. As Alexander Bickel observed, "as time passes, fewer and fewer relevantly decisive choices are to be divined out of the tradition of our founding. Our problems have grown radically different from those known to the Framers, and we have had to make value choices that are effectively new, while maintaining continuity with tradition."[3]

It is the final paragraph of this passage that distinguishes originalists from non-originalists. Originalists are committed to the view that original intent is not only relevant but authoritative, that we are in some sense obligated to follow the intent of the framers.

Among originalists, we can distinguish shades of belief about the binding effect of original intent and about how to define "intent." One extreme view would be that the *only* relevant factor is original intent; whichever side has the best historical evidence should always win. A moderate originalist might well view other factors as potentially important, particularly in cases where the evidence of intent is unclear. The minimum originalist view would be that *clear* evidence of original intent is controlling on any "open" question of constitutional law; that is, any question that has not already been decisively resolved by entrenched Supreme Court doctrine.[4] Originalists also differ about the level of generality at which they define original intent. Those who focus on the framers' general principles are quite different from those who emphasize the framers' views of particular governmental practices. Moderate originalists may be difficult to distinguish from non-originalists, as Dean Paul Brest explains:

> The only difference between moderate originalism and nonoriginalist adjudication is one of attitude toward the text and original understanding. For the moderate originalist, these sources are conclusive when they speak clearly. For the nonoriginalist, they are important but not determinative. Like an established line of precedent at common law, they create a strong presumption, but one which is defeasible in the light of changing public values.[5]

Similar divisions can be drawn among non-originalists based on the degree of deference they are inclined to give historical intent. Non-originalists have in common a rejection of the binding authority of original intent, but this leaves room for considerable disagreement about how much weight to give intent in comparison with other factors. Another important ground of distinction among non-originalists is how they supplement consideration of original intent. Some non-originalists trace their intellectual lineage to Enlightenment rationalists. They seek general theories that will provide logical answers in particular cases. Others trace their lineage to Burke, placing their faith in evolving traditions and time-tested institutions rather than abstract theories. And some, of course, combine both approaches.

In considering the debate on originalism discussed in the remainder of this chapter, it is important to keep these distinctions in mind. When reading a particular argument against originalism, you should always ask: Which form of originalism is most vulnerable to this criticism? If this criticism is valid, what form of non-originalism does it support?

We will begin in the next section by asking whether originalism is workable. Then we will consider its normative basis. Finally, we will offer a tentative resolution of the originalism debate.

Topics for Discussion

1. Currently, the debate about originalism has a strong ideological component: conservatives tend to be originalist, while liberals tend to be non-originalist. Is the question of originalism inherently ideological, or under other circumstances might the roles of the debaters be reversed? Is it, as Judge Ruth Bader Ginsburg has suggested, simply a matter of "whose ox is being gored"?[6]

2. Based on your readings in the previous chapter, which of the positions discussed in this section comes closest to the Supreme Court's approach to history?

3. Questions of interpretation arise in other contexts, for example, in discussing literature. Is originalism the proper approach to literary interpretation? Is literary interpretation at all analogous to the problem of constitutional interpretation? Does the fact that the Supreme Court, unlike the Yale English Department, gives a *binding* interpretation of a text, influence your decision?

4. Most of the originalism debate has involved the individual rights provisions of the Constitution. To what extent do the same arguments apply when the issue is federalism or separation of powers?

5. In choosing nominees for the Supreme Court, should the president consider an individual's views on topics like originalism? Is it proper for the Sen-

ate to consider these views? To what extent does the choice between originalism and non-originalism carry implications about what kinds of qualifications
a nominee should have?

6. Is originalism consistent with the way most people think of the Supreme
Court's functions? Or do people expect the Court to exercise a greater degree
of moral leadership? Do popular expectations matter in determining the appropriate role for the Court?

7. If Madison knew about the Court's current methods of interpretation and
the results the Court had reached, would he feel vindicated or betrayed? How
would John Bingham have felt about what the Court has created out of his
language in section 1 of the Fourteenth Amendment? Or is there simply no
way of guessing the answers to these questions?

IS ORIGINALISM WORKABLE?

Methodological Problems

One initial problem is whether we can determine the original intent of the
framers with any confidence. Various methodological problems may make it
difficult to do so, and of course, if we cannot determine original intent, we
cannot make it the basis for interpretation.

The framers of various provisions often failed to discuss the issues in which
we are interested today. Recall the discussions of the executive branch in
chapter 4. Much time was spent discussing how the executive would be appointed, what the term of office would be, and so forth. Little thought was
given to questions that today hold greater interest, such as the president's
power to send troops into combat without congressional approval or power to
remove subordinate officers. Similarly, as we observed in chapter 11, the debates about the Fourteenth Amendment focused on the now forgotten sections 2 and 3, which were of immediate concern in the context of Reconstruction but had no lasting importance. Section 1 of the amendment, which today
looms larger in judicial application than any other provision of the Constitution, received only cursory attention. This is not to say that the record is
wholly silent on these issues. Indeed, even the conspicuous lack of attention
given to these questions may itself carry a message about the original understanding, although it may also indicate a failure to consider or contemplate
particular issues. But the originalist task would certainly be easier if the framers had addressed these issues in detail.

Another question is whether the documentary evidence we do have is reliable. There have been recurring charges that Madison significantly altered
his notes at a later date, perhaps to reflect his own changing views of the
meaning of the Constitution. After a careful recent investigation, based on
matters such as the watermarks on Madison's paper, historian James Hutson
concluded that any alterations were not significant. But Hutson points out
that Madison gave only a highly abbreviated account of the proceedings:

> Madison's notes then, stand alone as the key to the Framers' intentions. If his
> notes on any given day are compared to the fragmentary records of debates left by
> other delegates that Farrand printed or that have been discovered more recently, a
> rough approximation between the different accounts is evident—demonstrating

that Madison was not inventing dialogue, but was trying to capture what was said. Still, there is an enigma about Madison's note-taking methods. . . .

If read aloud, Madison's notes for any particular day consume only a few minutes, suggesting that he may have recorded only a small part of each day's proceedings. . . . Madison averaged 2,740 words per session in June. Because sessions lasted five hours . . . he averaged 548 words per hour, a figure which can be rounded up to 600 words per hour to simplify calculations. At this rate Madison recorded only 600 of a possible 8,400 words per hour, or seven percent of each hour's proceedings. Even if the possible words per hour are reduced to 6,000, Madison recorded only ten percent of each hour's proceedings.[7]

There is also some reason to suspect Madison's accounts of his own speeches; he may have improved them somewhat in writing after he had already delivered them orally.

Hutson points out even more severe problems with other parts of the documentary record. He concludes that the records of the ratification debates are too "corrupt . . . [to] be relied upon to reveal the intentions of the Framers." For example, the Pennsylvania and Maryland debates were recorded by ardent Federalist Thomas Lloyd, who was paid by the Federalists to delete all the Anti-Federalist speeches. He reported only selective Federalist speeches and even those seem to have been significantly revised.[8]

The same Thomas Lloyd was responsible for the *Annals of Congress* volume covering the Bill of Rights. "Far from improving by 1789, Lloyd's technical skills had become dulled by excessive drinking."[9] And the *Annals* cover only the House debates, because the Senate did not permit its proceedings to be reported.

The potential unreliability of parts of the historical record does not mean that historical investigation is hopeless. If historians were reduced to studying impeccably documented events, they would have little to do with their time. But a significant part of a professional historian's training is learning how to assess the validity of various documents. Historians learn to make sophisticated credibility judgments based not only on the documents themselves and their drafting, but also on a knowledge of the culture and politics of the period. Credibility judgments must also be made to determine which of various possible interpretations of the historical record is the most plausible. But judges may be ill-prepared to make such judgments:

> [J]udicial judgments about the credibility of various accounts of the constitutional past may be idiosyncratic and otherwise unsound. While judges have fulsome experience in regard to the behavioral patterns of the sorts of people who typically appear before them, they know little about how people behaved in the distant past. Thus they may reason anachronistically when they use their present-day behavioral assumptions to assess the accuracy of a particular interpretation of the past.
>
> After all, judges are not selected for office because they have special skill in reconstructing the intentions of individuals in the past. . . . [A] judge who decides constitutional cases on the basis of credibility is likely to mislead both himself and his audience as to the ultimate basis of his decisions.[10]

The difficulty of determining the plausibility of a historical interpretation is increased by the need to interpret the views of a diverse group of individuals. These individuals may not have agreed with each other on the interpretation of a provision. Some may have voted for a package such as the Constitution or Bill of Rights having approved of some portions but having no particular view about the meaning or desirability of other parts. How can we aggregate the views of a diverse group in order to determine a collective intent? Of course, the framers were not randomly drawn from different societies or even different segments of the same society. Their shared common culture should be reflected in some degree of consensus about the meaning of texts. Even where this is true, however, discerning that consensus may require extensive knowledge of a historical period, which may be beyond the reach of anyone but historians specializing in the period.

The problems of reconstructing original intent do not prove that the task is impossible or unimportant. They do suggest, however, that determining the original understanding may be a much more difficult task than many originalists assume.

Was Originalism the Original Understanding?

The question of originalism can itself be approached from an originalist perspective, by asking whether the framers expected their intentions to control subsequent interpretation of the Constitution. Although earlier scholars had mentioned this problem, it was investigated in the greatest detail in an influential 1985 article by Professor H. Jefferson Powell.[11]

Powell began by exploring the common law's methods of interpreting various documents such as statutes, wills, and contracts. He argued that "intent" generally referred to the objective meaning of the language used in the document, not the subjective intentions of the authors:

> At common law, then, the "intent" of the maker of a legal document and the "intent" of the document itself were one and the same; "intent" did not depend upon the subjective purposes of the author. The late eighteenth century common lawyer conceived an instrument's "intent"—and therefore its meaning—not as what the drafters meant by their words but rather as what judges, employing the "artificial reason and judgment of law," understood "the reasonable and legal meaning" of those words to be. . . .
>
> The courts likewise looked to "rules of law" and to "common understanding" when interpreting statutes. The modern practice of interpreting a law by reference to its legislative history was almost wholly nonexistent, and English judges professed themselves bound to honor the true import of the "express words" of Parliament. The "intent of the act" and the "intent of the legislature" were interchangeable terms; neither term implied that the interpreter looked at any evidence concerning that "intent" other than the words of the text and the common law background of the statute. . . .
>
> The common law tradition did admit the propriety of looking beyond the statute's wording where the text was defective on its face. In such situations judges were free to substitute coherence for gibberish. A more serious interpretive problem occurred when the statute's wording was ambiguous, rather than clear but in conflict with its apparent intent. It was generally agreed that such *ambiguitas patens* could not be resolved by extrinsic evidence as to Parliament's purpose. . . .[12]

Because the common law adopted different methods of interpretation for different kinds of documents, however, interpretation of the new Constitution posed something of a problem. To interpret it, the eighteenth-century lawyer first had to determine what kind of document it was. In the debates over ratification, according to Powell, the Federalists took the position that the text would be interpreted like a statute, on the basis of the meaning of its words to a reasonable reader. Even after the Constitution was in effect, according to Powell, references to history were viewed with some suspicion as an innovation in methods of interpretation. A newer approach to interpretation, based on the understandings of the ratifiers, was crystallized by Madison:

> The text itself, of course, was the primary source from which that intention was to be gathered, but Madison's awareness of the imperfect nature of human communication led him to concede that the text's import would frequently be unclear. Madison thought it proper to engage in structural inference in the classic contractual mode of the Virginia and Kentucky Resolutions, and to consult the direct expressions of state intention available in the resolutions of the ratifying conventions. He regarded the debates in those conventions to be of real yet limited value for the interpreter: evidentiary problems with the surviving records and Madison's insistence on distinguishing the binding public intention of the state from the private opinions of any individual or group of individuals, including those gathered at a state convention, led him to conclude that the state debates could bear no more than indirect and corroborative witness to the meaning of the Constitution. . . . Last and least in value were the records of the Philadelphia convention.[13]

Madison's objection to reliance on the Convention debates was based on two factors: the possible defects in the historical record and the status of the ratifiers as the true sources of the Constitution's authority.

Powell's historical evidence has been carefully examined by Professor Charles Lofgren. Lofgren agrees with him about the nature of common law interpretative methods and about Madison's position.[14] The crux of the disagreement between these two scholars relates to timing. Powell believes that the view of interpretation adopted by Madison did not become prevalent until well after ratification. Lofgren argues, however, that this theory of interpretation based on the ratifiers' intent was adopted earlier, by the time the Constitution was ratified or soon thereafter. Both scholars agree that the Convention debates themselves were not considered to have any authority as a source of meaning.

The Convention debates have at best a dubious claim as an authoritative source of constitutional interpretation. As we saw earlier in this book, one important concern of the framers was that they had exceeded their authority in proposing such radical constitutional change. Partly in response, they developed the theory that the Constitution took its authority from its adoption by the sovereign People: "We, the People" referred to the ratifiers, not the members of the Convention. Given this understanding, the framers themselves were merely scriveners, drafting a document for possible use by others—little different in principle from staff members in Congress who help draft legislation for Congress to consider. It seems somewhat unlikely that the intent of the scriveners was thought to be binding on the ratifiers, especially when the framers were so careful to keep the proceedings of the Convention secret from the ratifiers themselves.

Of course, even if it is correct, this conclusion would not mean that the Convention debates should be disregarded. Besides their intrinsic interest, they are also strong evidence of the understanding of reasonable readers of the period. But even in the framers' own views, the Convention debates were probably not considered authoritative

Even assuming, however, that only the intent of the ratifiers counts, and taking into account the defective historical record concerning that intent, some areas remain in which original intent might be decisive. For example, it might well be possible to establish that no intelligent eighteenth-century reader would have thought that the phrase "cruel and unusual punishment" included execution by hanging, or that no mid-nineteenth century reader would have thought that "equal protection of the laws" had anything to do with the right to vote. Thus, the problems with originalism considered above do not undermine the originalist thesis that original intent controls where it can be determined.

Anti-Originalist Clauses

Another argument against originalism, related to that considered in the previous section, is that the framers anticipated that the courts would defend human rights beyond those expressly listed in the Bill of Rights. The basis for this enforcement of unwritten rights might either be natural law or certain "open-ended" clauses of the Constitution.

As one writer has recently explained, natural law was considered a legitimate basis for judicial decision in the period leading up to the framing of the Constitution:

> [F]or American judges in the late eighteenth century, the sources of fundamental law were as open-ended as they were in English opposition theory. The colonists inherited a tradition that provided not only a justification for judicial review but also guidelines for its exercise. As Bolingbroke proposed in theory and the new American states translated into action, judges were to look to natural law and the inherent rights of man, as well as to the written constitution, in determining the validity of a statute. Where the written constitution affirmatively addressed a problem—most often in governmental structure cases . . . but even in cases where the constitution provided clear protection of individual rights—it was dispositive, but in other cases, judges looked outside the written constitution.[15]

Chapters 1 and 3 indicate that natural rights theories persisted into the 1780s. Indeed, as we saw in chapter 9, belief in the existence of an unwritten "higher law" continued well into the nineteenth century. Some writers argue that the framers accepted natural law as a judicially enforceable restriction on governmental power.[16]

Recall that the Federalists argued during the ratification debates that a Bill of Rights was unnecessary. This may imply that the powers granted in Article I carry implicit limitations. If read at face value, for example, the grant of general legislative authority over the seat of government would presumably include the right to establish an official religion there or allow the use of coerced confessions or Star Chamber proceedings. Similar abuses of other powers, such as the power to control interstate commerce, can also be imagined. It would not be an unreasonable interpretation, however, to suggest that some framers expected these grants of power to be read against the background of accepted assumptions about natural rights. Thus, the grant of power to Congress to govern the District of Columbia or to regulate interstate commerce might have been understood to be subject to inherent limitations. Such an interpretation may underlie the Federalist argument against the need for a Bill of Rights. Indeed, some of the Federalist arguments rested explicitly on natural rights as inherent limitations.

Chapter 8 shows that the Federalist argument was not considered wholly convincing. One response was the move to add a Bill of Rights immediately after ratification. As chapter 8 also shows, many legislators seemed to view the Bill of Rights as unnecessary. Moreover, one of its provisions lends itself naturally to non-originalist judicial review: the Ninth Amendment. On one interpretation, the Ninth Amendment is a response to widespread concerns that an enumeration of rights might be taken as exclusive. The Federalists had made this argument in opposing inclusion of a list of the rights. It also figured in the debates in Congress on the Bill of Rights. To be sure, other readings of the Ninth Amendment are possible. It can be read as a clone of the Tenth Amendment, protecting against the existence of implied federal powers, or as a means of rebutting any argument that the federal constitution somehow undermined other nonconstitutional rights. But these other interpretations strain the language of the amendment.

The privileges and immunities clause of the Fourteenth Amendment is another possible source of unenumerated rights. Perhaps the leading spokesman for this argument is Dean John Ely.[17] If Ely's historical interpretation is correct—a question you should consider in connection with the readings in chapter 11—then at least some clauses of the Constitution seem to require judges to protect rights that are not themselves listed in the Constitution. Even if correct, however, that conclusion does not necessarily invalidate originalism. For it may still be possible to give an originalist reading to these clauses themselves. For example, we might look to the understandings of the times to find out precisely what rights were then considered fundamental (and therefore presumably protected by the Ninth Amendment or the privileges and immunities clause).

Neither those who discussed the need for a Bill of Rights in the late eighteenth century, nor those who framed the Fourteenth Amendment seventy years later, seem to have spent much time worrying about whether the unwritten fundamental rights were static or subject to change.[18] Thus, an originalist interpretation of these provisions might be limited to the specific fundamental rights of the time, or it might require an evolving list of rights. The original understanding of the "higher law" may be even more elusive than that of more specific constitutional language. Nevertheless, it might be possible to establish with some degree of confidence, for instance, that abortion was not considered a fundamental right in 1866 and that the list of fundamental rights was considered static. The question would then remain whether that historical understanding is binding today.

The Ambiguity of Intent

One difficulty of implementing originalism is deciding exactly what level of intent we are interested in. At its simplest level, we might consider the "original intent" to be a kind of examination administered to the framers, in which all the questions look like this: "Constitutional provision X covers fact-pattern Y. True or false?"

One problem with this approach is that it may be very difficult to find out the answers, for the reasons discussed in the preceding sections. Moreover, some fact-patterns will involve situations that the framers could not have considered. For example, the framers had no occasion to consider whether the Fourth Amendment applied to electronic eavesdropping, whether electrocution was cruel and unusual punishment, or whether the manufacture of computer chips is part of interstate commerce. If we seek to address these issues in terms of original intent, we will have to define our inquiry at a higher level of generality.

The view of original intent as a sort of checklist of specific prohibitions is vulnerable to another attack. Presumably, the checklist is not entirely arbitrary; it reflects some underlying beliefs or values of the framers. But this underlying belief system may be more complex than the checklist indicates, and in particular may contain some inner tensions or inconsistencies. Ignoring these complexities may fail to do justice to the original understanding. Yet, the more we understand the intellectual and cultural matrix in which a provision arose, the more difficult we may find the task of projecting its meaning into the contemporary world.[19]

The question of whether the death penalty is a form of cruel and unusual punishment exemplifies some of the problems. As Professor David Richards explains in criticizing the work of Raoul Berger, a leading originalist:

> The nature of the historiographical distortion in Berger's approach is brought out by comparing . . . Berger's *Death Penalties* [and] John McManners' *Death and the Enlightenment*, a study of changing attitudes toward death (including natural deaths, executions, and suicides) in eighteenth century France. . . . For McManners, the historiography of death in eighteenth-century France requires the broadest integration of diverse sources and perspectives bearing on deep shifts in the moral and human sensibilities surrounding death in its various forms. The consequence is remarkable: McManners, writing of France with no particular focus on legal issues, enables us to understand the moral norms implicit in the eighth amendment in exhaustive depth, in a way that Berger does not remotely approximate.[20]

As Richards explains, these different approaches to history have potential significance when applying the Eighth Amendment today:

> If the Enlightenment thought the death penalty acceptable in certain cases, the period was more historically remarkable in its skepticism about the extent and forms of the penalty's use and in its special concern with abuse of the death penalty for terroristic degradation. Berger's "meaning" of the eighth amendment therefore is not the eighteenth century's meaning. . . . Why, then, should it be our meaning on the issue of the death penalty when many of the eighteenth century's grounds for skepticism, implicit in the principles of the eighth amendment, may, given the contemporary context with shifts in many relevant features (alternative ways of securing deterrence, the greater value of life, etc.), dictate a complete repudiation of the death penalty?[21]

Thus, examined at a higher level of generality, the framers' views about what is cruel and unusual punishment might lead to a rejection of the death penalty today, while their more specific views are to the contrary. As Dean Robert Bennett suggests, it may not be true "that knowing specific intentions allows one to project the intenders' values or process of decision over time, even as applied to phenomena very similar to the subjects of the specific intentions."[22]

A crucial question for originalists, then, is to determine the proper level of generality. Does the Eighth Amendment require judges to apply some general concept of "cruel and unusual"? Or does it address only what specific punishments the framers meant to forbid? One answer is to determine the framers' views about the appropriate level of generality. For example, we might investigate whether the framers expected judges to rely on the general concepts or the specific examples discussed in the debates. As Dean Paul Brest explains, the reality is that the framers probably intended that both their general principles and their specific examples be given some weight:

> A principle does not exist wholly independently of its author's subjective, or his society's conventional exemplary applications, and is always limited to some extent by the applications they found conceivable. Within these fairly broad limits, however, the adopters may have intended their examples to constrain more or less. To the intentionalist interpreter falls the unenviable task of ascertaining, for each provision, how much more or less.[23]

The difficulties of this historical inquiry are obvious, since the framers are unlikely to have discussed the precise balance between general principles and specific examples.

Another originalist solution is to specify a nonhistorical rule for determining the proper level of abstraction. For example, Judge Robert Bork suggests that "the problem of levels of generality may be solved by choosing no level of generality higher than that which interpretation of the words, structure, and history of the Constitution fairly support.[24] His argument for adopting this rule is that higher levels of generality would give judges increasing amounts of leeway in deciding cases, so the presumption should be in favor of specificity rather than generality. Unlike the approach discussed by Brest, this one does not look to the framers to establish *their* views about the proper level of generality. Rather than look to history, Bork looks to his own political theory to answer this question.

Judge Bork's test for the proper level of generality is, apart from the presumption, vague and may prove very difficult to apply. Moreover, since the ultimate question before a court is the extent to which a constitutional provision limits majority rule, Bork's test amounts to a presumption that all limits on governmental power should be read narrowly. But this is a rather far-reaching principle of interpretation that Bork provides no support for, historical or otherwise, so his analysis at least must be considered incomplete.

The Problem of Change

Probably the most prevalent argument against originalism is that it is too static, and thereby disregards the need to keep the Constitution up to date. Originalism is unworkable, then, even if the original intent can be reliably determined, because it would make the Constitution itself unworkable. According to Justice Brennan, the judicial approach to interpretation must be nonoriginalist:

> Current Justices read the Constitution in the only way we can: as twentieth-century Americans. We look to the history of the time of framing and to the intervening history of interpretation. But the ultimate question must be: What do the words of the text mean in our time? For the genius of the Constitution rests not in

any static meaning it might have had in a world that is dead and gone, but in the adaptability of its great principles to cope with current problems and current needs. What the constitutional fundamentals meant to the wisdom of other times cannot be the measure of the vision of our time.[25]

Non-originalists argue that the Supreme Court has always functioned this way, and that it is now too late to change the "rules of the game." For example, Professor Thomas Grey argues that there is only a shaky originalist basis for doctrines such as the application of the Bill of Rights to the states and the prohibition on racial discrimination by the federal government.[26] Indeed, Grey suggests, the potential implications are even broader:

> [T]here is serious question how much of the law prohibiting state racial discrimination can survive honest application of the interpretive model. It is clear that the equal protection clause was meant to prohibit *some* forms of state racial discrimination, most obviously those enacted in the Black Codes. It is equally clear from the legislative history that the clause was *not* intended to guarantee equal political rights, such as the right to vote or to run for office, and perhaps including the right to serve on juries.
>
> It is at least doubtful whether the clause can fairly be read as intending to bar any form of state-imposed racial segregation, so long as equal facilities are made available. . . .
>
> While one might disagree with this rough catalogue on points of detail, it should be clear that an extraordinarily radical purge of established constitutional doctrine would be required if we candidly and consistently applied the pure interpretive model. Surely that makes out at least a prima facie practical case against the model.[27]

Some originalists may be undismayed or even pleased by the thought of such a radical uprooting of current doctrine. Originalism need not, however, require such radical doctrinal change. First, for all the reasons we have explored in this chapter, history is rarely clear, and many of Grey's specific conclusions are subject to dispute. So the originalist may be able in good conscience to uphold the correctness of many current constitutional doctrines.

Second, originalism may be tempered by an appreciation of the importance of stability in the law, so that an originalist who agrees with Grey's list of mistaken doctrines might nonetheless oppose overruling them. Professor Henry Monaghan says,

> I accept as a premise that the illustrations cited are not consistent with original intent. . . . The expectations so long generated by this body of constitutional law render unacceptable a full return to original intent theory in any pure, unalloyed form. While original intent may constitute the starting point for constitutional interpretation, it cannot now be recognized as the only legitimate mode of constitutional reasoning. To my mind, some theory of stare decisis is necessary to confine its reach. Of course, this is to accord an authoritative status to tradition in "supplementing or derogating from" the constitutional text, at least if that "tradition" has worked its way into judicial opinions. But a stare decisis theory has its limits, at least for those who take original intent seriously. . . . [T]his concession to reality would not be taken to entail, also in the name of reality, the further concession that our constitutional law now sanctions the general, nontextual mode of constitutional analysis. . . .[28]

Third, an originalist might take into account not only judicial precedents, but also the changing views of those adopting later constitutional provisions.

For example, the people who ratified the Fourteenth Amendment's due process clause may well have had a broader concept of the meaning of due process than their predecessors who adopted the Fifth Amendment's due process clause. Yet it would be incongruous to give the two due process clauses different interpretations today.

Even defeated constitutional amendments may count for something. For example, an amendment to allow Congress to regulate child labor failed to obtain ratification because it became clear that the Supreme Court had changed its mind on this issue. Or, to take another example, one argument against the proposed equal rights amendment was that it was unnecessary because the Supreme Court was already attacking sex discrimination by using the equal protection clause. After these amendments failed to obtain ratification, it seems dubious that the Court would feel free to abandon the positions on which the public relied.[29] As with Monaghan's treatment of precedent, however, these points could be conceded without abandoning originalism as a general principle.

Topics for Discussion

1. Which of the difficulties of implementing originalism is the most serious? What is the best originalist response to that objection?
2. If the Constitution should be kept up to date, why shouldn't this be done through the amendment process rather than by judicial interpretation? Is the Supreme Court now an ongoing constitutional convention, as some critics have charged? Or is the Court's role in "updating" the Constitution more constrained than these critics suggest? What constrains originalist judges? Non-originalist judges?
3. One key issue relating to originalism is the level of abstraction at which the original intent is to be viewed. Viewed at an extremely abstract level, a constitutional provision does little more than identify a general goal the courts should pursue. Viewed at an extremely particular level, the provision may have a few specific examples on which the framers agreed, examples that will often fail to fit the case before the court. Is there a middle ground?
4. As we saw in the last chapter, some have argued that the Constitution contains some originalist clauses and other clauses that require an evolving interpretation. Is this view intellectually tenable? Is it an attractive solution to the originalism problem?

THE NORMATIVE ARGUMENTS FOR ORIGINALISM

There are three basic normative arguments in favor of originalism. The first is that legitimate authority in a democracy must be based on majority rule. Hence, a court is justified in overruling one majority decision only on the basis of another, even more authoritative, majority decision. In exercising judicial review, a judge is merely doing the will of the majority as contained in the Constitution, and the judge's job is simply to understand that majority will. The second argument is more general: that the job of the judge is to interpret legal documents like the Constitution, and that interpreting any document is simply a matter of determining the author's intentions. The third argument is that there is no principled alternative to originalism. We will consider these arguments in turn.

Majoritarianism

As former Attorney General Edwin Meese explains, majoritarianism is one of the fundamental underpinnings of originalism:

> The Constitution represents the consent of the governed to the structures and powers of the government. The Constitution is the fundamental will of the people; that is the reason the Constitution is the fundamental law. To allow the courts to govern simply by what it views at the time as fair and decent, is a scheme of government no longer popular; the idea of democracy has suffered.[30]

Reduced to its essence, the argument is this: If judges derive authority from the Constitution, and the Constitution derives authority from the majority vote of the ratifiers, then the role of the judge is to carry out the will of the ratifiers.

Dean John Ely is not an originalist, but he has given one of the best explanations of the majoritarian basis of originalism:

> We have as a society from the beginning, and now almost instinctively, accepted the notion that a representative democracy must be our form of government. The very process of adopting the Constitution was designed to be, and in some respects it was, more democratic than any that had preceded it. . . .
>
> All this belabors the obvious part: whatever the explanation, and granting the qualifications, rule in accord with the consent of a majority of those governed is the core of the American governmental system. Just as obviously, however, that cannot be the whole story, since a majority with untrammeled power to set governmental policy is in a position to deal itself benefits at the expense of the remaining minority. . . .
>
> Of course, [the originalists] would answer, the majority can tyrannize the minority, and that is precisely the reason that in the Bill of Rights and elsewhere the Constitution designates certain rights for protection. . . . Thus the judges do not check the people, the Constitution does, which means the people are ultimately checking themselves.[31]

The majoritarian argument for originalism has three premises: that our society's "master norm" is democracy; that the Constitution gets its legitimacy solely from the majority will as expressed at the time of enactment; and that judicial decisions are less "democratic" than those of the elected branches of government. We will consider these in turn.

Democracy as a "Master Norm."   A non-originalist might question the status of democracy as the unique fundamental norm of our society. Since this response leads to far-reaching inquiries into political theory, we will not pursue it in detail here, but the general concept can be easily sketched. Why, one might ask, do we believe in democracy? Isn't it because of underlying beliefs in human dignity and equality, beliefs that are also the bases for judicial protection of individual rights? In this view, individual rights should not be viewed as conflicting with democracy. Rather, majority rule and individual rights are both part of a harmonious vision of democratic government.

Perhaps identifying democracy with unlimited majority rule is too simplistic. Instead, as one political theorist has put it, democracy may mean creating and maintaining "a society whose adult members are, and continue to be, equipped by their education and authorized by political structures to share in ruling."[32] Thus, majority-approved policies that deprive some citizens of their right or ability to participate in governance are contrary to the ideal of democracy.

This structure of constrained majoritarianism is reflected in the Constitution itself (mostly in the Bill of Rights and other amendments). As Justice Jackson recognized:

> The very purpose of a Bill of Rights was to withdraw certain subjects from the vicissitudes of political controversy, to place them beyond the reach of majorities and officials and to establish them as legal principles to be applied by the courts.[33]

Those who recognize that the Constitution does not establish unmodified majoritarianism often talk about the "counter-majoritarian premise" of the Constitution.

Of course, the mere existence of a counter-majoritarian premise does not specify how it is to be applied, and originalists argue that it should be limited to the specific rights protected by the amendments. However, the existence of a counter-majoritarian premise, coupled with the political theory of democracy, suggests that the originalist reliance on "pure" majoritarianism may not work.

The Basis of Constitutional Legitimacy.   Non-originalists can also question the claim that majority ratification in the past is a valid source of majoritarian legitimacy in the present. After all, the adoption process had defects that today would be considered fatal to legitimacy:

> The drafting, adopting, or amending of the Constitution may itself have suffered from defects of democratic process which detract from its moral claims. To take an obvious example, the interests of black Americans were not adequately represented in the adoption of the Constitution of 1787 or the fourteenth amendment. Whatever moral consensus the Civil War Amendments embodied was among white male property-holders and not the population as a whole.[34]

In addition, the ratifiers had no claim at all to represent those of us alive today, so it is unclear how their majority vote can override the will of current majorities: "We did not adopt the Constitution, and those who did are dead and gone."[35]

Thus, in seeking a majoritarian source of legitimacy, we perhaps should look not to the vote of the drafters but rather to the popular support of the Constitution today. Since most people aren't historians, that popular support may be based on the current legal understanding of the Constitution rather than that on its original understanding. This assumes, of course, that the populace knows something about current constitutional judicial doctrines.

Even if part of the Constitution's legitimacy does rest on the fact that it was adopted by past majorities, this may not be the only source of its current authority. Individuals today may accept the Constitution partly because of its pedigree but also because they think it is a *good* Constitution and therefore one worthy of continuing support. This additional source of legitimacy may not mandate abandonment of original intent, but it does support some degree of supplementation: we would want to give the Constitution a reading tied to its origins but that also makes it worthy of continuing allegiance.

Majority Rule and the Judicial Branch.   The crux of the majoritarian argu-

ment is the incongruity in a democratic society of having major societal decisions made by nonelected federal judges. In response, some non-originalists
downplay the undemocratic nature of the judiciary. Federal judges, as a practical matter, are not removable from office, but they are subject to subtler influence by public opinion. Also, over time, new appointments tend to bring
the court in line with public opinion. As a last resort, there is the possibility of
constitutional amendment. While these factors do tend to limit the divergence
between public opinion and the courts, it is still clear that courts are less dem-
ocratically responsive than other branches of government.

Non-originalists also point out special attributes of the judicial role that may
give judges a comparative advantage in dealing with questions of principle.
Among these traits are relative isolation from immediate public pressure, the
requirement that all decisions be explained with reasoned opinions, and the
utility of the adversary process in giving both sides a fair hearing. Other aspects of the judicial system may also be conducive to principled decision making. Examples include the use of multimember appellate courts, trial records
compiled with elaborate evidentiary rules, and the limitation of judicial power
to concrete disputes. It is hard to assess the cumulative significance of these
points, especially given the possibility that our elected officials would give
more thought to matters of constitutional principle if they did not rely on
judges to do so for them. Recall from part 1 of the book that various framers
expected other branches of government, the Senate and the executive, to take
the long view.

Although a great deal has been written about these issues, the conclusions
seem fairly simple: federal courts are not as unresponsive to the public as they
first appear, but they are still less democratic than the other branches; and
federal courts have some advantage as forums in which to decide matters of
principle relating to individual rights, but perhaps not so much as many people believe. Whether the gain in principled decision making is worth the cost
in democratic responsiveness is a question not susceptible to proof one way or
the other.

The majoritarianism issue, then, proves to be much more subtle than it initially appears. Fully resolving it, if such a resolution is possible, would require
a fairly complete theory of democratic legitimacy. Perhaps the best we can say
without such a theory is that majoritarianism provides originalists with a
powerful argument, but the non-originalists' replies are not insubstantial.

Intentionalism

Originalism can also be based on a broader theory of interpretation, one that
has strong roots in our legal culture:

> [Originalism] fits our usual conceptions of what law is and the way it works. In
> interpreting a statute, in order to decide whether certain private behavior is autho-
> rized or whether (and this is closer to the constitutional review situation) it conflicts
> with another statute, a court obviously will limit itself to a determination of the pur-
> poses and prohibitions expressed by or implicit in its language. Were a judge to
> announce in such a situation that he was not content with those references and in-
> tended additionally to enforce, in the name of the statute in question, those funda-
> mental values he believed America had always stood for, we would conclude that

he was not doing his job, and might even consider a call to the lunacy commission.[36]

Originalism is closely linked to the Constitution's status as a legal text, and that status itself has been an important part of the argument for judicial review:

> The Constitution is, among other things, a legal document, and it is on the Constitution's status as written law that justification of the practice of judicial review has largely rested. As Edwin Corwin once wrote, "The first and most obvious fact about the Constitution of the United States is that it is a document." Justice Black began his lectures on constitutional interpretation by saying "It is of paramount importance to me that our country has a written constitution." With words like these, contemporary constitutional interpreters hark back to John Marshall's original argument for judicial review in *Marbury v. Madison*, an argument permeated with reliance on the *"writtenness"* of the Constitution.[37]

Since people often think of a document's meaning as consisting of the author's intentions in writing it, this stress on the Constitution's status as a written text provides strong support for originalism.

Still, while the Constitution is a text, it is a very special kind of text.[38] Unlike most texts, it was written by one group of people for adoption by another, then amended over two centuries by yet other groups. Furthermore, as we have seen, its various authors and adopters may perhaps have intended that the text refer to norms outside itself. All of this makes it more difficult to identify a specific set of authors whose intent controls. More fundamentally, the Constitution plays a unique role in our culture, not only giving a set of instructions but literally constituting our national identity. Given that unique role, a special approach to interpretation could well be appropriate.

Moreover, it is not clear that the meaning even of ordinary texts is derived from the author's intent rather than the reader's understanding. Theories of interpretation are presently the subject of hot dispute among philosophers and literary theorists, and to enter into this debate would be far beyond our present purpose. Indeed, the complexity and subtlety of the debate caution against any expectation that general theories of interpretation will provide simple means of resolving the dispute about originalism.

As in many debates, one of the most difficult problems of assessing originalism is deciding just what is in dispute. Some advocates of originalism make it clear that the original intent they have in mind is not a psychological state of the framers:

> Dworkin is scornful, and I think properly so, of the notion that in interpreting poetry or the Constitution we should seek to discern authorial intent as a mental fact of some sort. As to poetry, his argument rightly holds that we would not consider an account of Shakespeare's mental state at the time he wrote a sonnet to be a more complete or better account of the sonnet than the sonnet itself. Dworkin would certainly disagree, as would I, with the notion that when we consider the Constitution we are really interested in the mental state of each of the persons who drew it up and ratified it. In this view, which we both reject, the texts of a sonnet or of the Constitution would be a kind of second-best; we would prefer to take the top off the heads of authors and framers—like soft-boiled eggs—to look inside for the truest account of their brain states at the moment that the texts were created.[39]

Yet, the author of this passage champions the "attempt to understand the Constitution according to the intention of those who conceived it. . . ."[40] But at this point, the precise meaning of originalism becomes a bit murky.

On the whole, the earlier, majoritarian argument for originalism seems stronger than the argument based on the primacy of authorial intent. The problem is not just that the primacy of intent is disputable, but that attempting to define precisely what we mean by authorial intent is difficult, even apart from the special problems of attributing a unified authorial intention to a document like the Constitution.

Moreover, even a successful theory of authorial intent might not be enough to justify originalism. A general theory of interpretation should work equally well for interpreting a sonnet, the Constitution, the Bible, and a laundry list. It seems unlikely that such a theory would have decisive implications regarding the differences that separate originalism and non-originalism. After all, the dispute between originalists and non-originalists is not over the relevance of intent, on which both agree, but on specific rules for considering intent in deciding constitutional cases. There is no reason to think that the same specific rules about intent should apply to all written documents.

Are There Principled Alternatives?

One important normative argument in favor of originalism is the difficulty of specifying another principled basis for deciding cases. The literature on the alternatives to originalism is as large as that on originalism itself—indeed, the two overlap substantially—and we can only touch on them here.

One suggested alternative looks to natural law or moral philosophy as a basis for judicial enforcement of individual rights. The difficulty is that our culture has no consensus on these matters:

> "[A]ll theories of natural law have a singular vagueness which is both an advantage and disadvantage in the application of the theories." The advantage, one gathers, is that you can invoke natural law to support anything you want. The disadvantage is that everybody understands that. . . .
>
> The constitutional literature that has dominated the past thirty years has often insisted that judges, in seeking constitutional value judgments, should employ, in Alexander Bickel's words, "the method of reason familiar to the discourse of moral philosophy.". . .
>
> The error here is one of assuming that something exists called "the method of moral philosophy" whose contours sensitive experts will agree on. . . . That is not the way things are. Some moral philosophers think utilitarianism is the answer; others feel just as strongly it is not. Some regard enforced economic redistribution as a moral imperative; others find it morally censurable. . . . There simply does not exist *a* method of moral philosophy.[41]

Similar attacks can be made on attempts to use tradition or consensus as the basis of decisionmaking. The American tradition is diverse, and contemporary American society contains an enormous variety of groups with strikingly different views of the world. Even the argument that the Constitution should promote the democratic process falters in the light of the lack of agreement on any precise understanding of democracy.

As Dean Brest points out, these criticisms of non-originalist approaches are all rather similar, and all reminiscent of the attacks on originalism:

My point so far is not that any of these theories are untenable, but that all are vulnerable to similar criticisms based on their indeterminacy, manipulability, and, ultimately, their reliance on judicial value choices that cannot be "objectively" derived from text, history, consensus, natural rights, or any other source. No theory of constitutional adjudication can defend itself against self-scrutiny. Each critic's assessment of the alternative theories seems rather like an aesthetic judgment issued from the Warsaw Palace of Culture.[42]

A footnote then recounts a joke from Poland: "Why is the best view of Warsaw from the Palace of Culture?" "Because that's the only place in Warsaw where you can't *see* the Palace of Culture."

Both originalists and non-originalists seem to be highly effective in critiquing each others' theories. Perhaps the lesson is that the standards they set are inherently unattainable. The real problem may be that both sides have demanded too much. We may have to be content with an approach to constitutional law that leaves some room for judicial discretion while attempting to channel that discretion. In other words, the real problem may not be that originalism is less desirable than some other global theory of constitutional law, but that no global theory can work. If so, we might do better to abandon the attempt to create a theory of constitutional interpretation, and get on with the business of actually interpreting the Constitution. Perhaps, in other words, constitutional interpretation is best thought of as an activity that one can do well or poorly, rather than as an application of some explicit general theory.

Topics for Discussion

1. When judges apply to a case the terms of a legal document like a contract or will, to what extent should they search for the intent of the drafters? Why might intent be relevant in this situation? Do the same reasons apply to the Constitution?

2 Suppose, as Justice Harlan argued in his *Oregon v. Mitchell* opinion (see chapter 13), that the framers of the Fourteenth Amendment did not intend the equal protection clause to cover voting. Does this make the Supreme Court's decisions on voting (such as the "one person, one vote" rule) anti-majoritarian? Or is the relationship between majoritarianism and original intent more complex? How well do the circumstances under which the Fourteenth Amendment was adopted and ratified fit the standard concept of representative democracy?

3. Germany's and Japan's current written constitutions were imposed as part of the Allied occupation. Would you expect originalism to be an appealing theory of interpretation to the courts of those nations? Should it be? Does the role of military force in securing the ratification of the Reconstruction Amendments make them analogous to the constitutions of those countries?

4. How persuasive are the arguments against non-originalist interpretation? Assuming that cases like *Brown v. Board of Education* are not justified on the basis of original intent, do the arguments against non-originalism give you serious doubts about the correctness of *Brown*? Or is non-originalism less troubling in practice than in theory?

5. How important is the originalism debate? If moderates on one side, like Monaghan, concede the relevance of other factors such as respect for precedent, and moderates on the other side concede that original intent is relevant (but not authoritative), then how much difference does it make which side is right? Is the dispute really just over a matter of degree? Then why is the debate so heated?

6. How much of the dispute about constitutional interpretation turns on the fact that nonelected judges are doing the interpreting? Should different methods of interpretation be used in the state courts, where judges are often elected and normally serve for limited terms? What about situations in which the president or Congress confronts a constitutional question (such as, for example, whether impeachable offenses are limited to crimes)? Should those officials adopt originalism?

7. What view of constitutional interpretation fits best with the framers' own conception of what they were doing in 1787 or 1866? Were they laying down a code of specifics or establishing a framework for future development?

8. Some scholars associated with the Critical Legal Studies movement have argued that neither originalist nor non-originalist methods of interpretation place any meaningful constraints on judicial decisions. Does this argument imply that judicial review is illegitimate, or instead that judicial activism is proper? Is this view of the judicial process too jaundiced?

CONCLUSION

It is not our purpose, either in this chapter or elsewhere in this book, to convert readers to our our views. For that reason, we have largely avoided any attempt to propound our positions. But it seems only fair to give the reader some idea of where we stand on an issue as fundamental as the proper relationship between original intent and modern constitutional law.

The strongest form of originalism—that all constitutional issues should be decided on the basis of original intent—seems particularly untenable. As we have seen, the original intent is often hard to ascertain because of blanks in the historical record (particularly concerning the views of the ratifiers of constitutional provisions), the divergent views of those involved in making crucial decisions, and the usual difficulties of interpreting any text (particularly texts of ancient vintage). Beyond these practical problems is the question of just what kind of intent to look for. For example, do we look for the framers' philosophical theory of equality, their general views of racial discrimination, their (possibly nonexistent) specific views about affirmative action, or the views they would have had about affirmative action if they had thought about it then or if they were alive today? And more fundamentally, why is the intent of the long-dead authors of the Constitution binding on present-day Americans, many of whom would have been disenfranchised in 1789 or 1866 anyway? None of these arguments is individually devastating, nor do they demonstrate that original intent is irrelevant. Cumulatively, however, they make it highly unlikely that original intent can provide an adequate basis for *all* constitutional decisions.

Inevitably, we think, other considerations will have to enter into many constitutional decisions. To resolve issues in constitutional law, judges will have to obtain guidance from other sources such as judicial precedents, American traditions, and contemporary social values. Purists may be dismayed that this process is so unstructured, but that may simply be the nature of the beast. This pragmatic approach is typical not just of constitutional law but also of judicial decision making in general, as Justice Holmes explained in a famous passage:

> It is something to show that the consistency of a system requires a particular result, but it is not all. The life of the law has not been logic: it has been experience. The felt necessities of the time, the prevalent moral and political theories, intuitions of public policy, avowed or unconscious, even the prejudices which judges share with their fellow-men, have had a good deal more to do than the syllogism in determining the rules by which men should be governed. The law embodies the story of a nation's development through many centuries, and it cannot be dealt with as if it contained only the axioms and corollaries of a book of mathematics. In order to know what it is, we must know what it has been, and what it tends to become. We must alternately consult history and existing theories of legislation. But the most difficult labor will be to understand the combination of the two into new products at every stage.[43]

This blend of principle and policy, of tradition and innovation, is the essence of pragmatic constitutionalism.[44]

This process may seem disturbingly open-ended. Yet, it is not clear that originalism could provide more coherent or predictable results. Originalist judges would be as likely to differ in their interpretations of the historical record as professional historians themselves. Rather than debating the virtues and vices of affirmative action, they would debate the proper interpretation of the debates on the Freedmen's Bureau.[45] Not only would the results be likely to reflect political predispositions, but the real values at stake would be concealed beneath historiographic debates.

The distinctions between pragmatic constitutionalism and originalism are real, but should not be exaggerated. Thoughtful originalists like Monaghan concede that factors other than original intent must be given some weight in decisions. In turn, pragmatic constitutionalism leaves open the possibility that clear evidence of intent will sometimes prove decisive.

In this respect, pragmatic constitutionalism differs only in degree from the minimal version of originalism, under which clear original intent is binding in open cases. Although this would not be the invariable result under pragmatic constitutionalism, it might well happen, for any of three reasons. First, in dealing with an old constitutional provision, an "open" case may be open precisely because no relevant developments (such as judicial precedents or entrenched governmental practices) have arisen in the meantime. Thus, original intent may recommend itself as a basis for decision simply because there is little other basis for deciding the case.

Second, intent may be clear in some cases that are otherwise difficult to decide because the other factors are evenly balanced. Even judges who do not accept evidence of intent as totally binding on them may often be inclined to give it heavy weight, and nothing in pragmatic constitutionalism precludes this result.

Third, the question may be open because the provision in question is relatively new, and few questions about it have had time to be settled. Most of the arguments against originalism, however, assume that some substantial amount of time has passed since an enactment. When dealing with a relatively new enactment, original intent should weigh much more heavily. For non-originalists, the "text and original understanding exert the strongest claims when they are contemporary and thus likely to reflect current values and beliefs, or simply the expressed will of a current majority. . . ."[46] Otherwise, new amendments might be discouraged because of fears that their judicial interpretations will be unpredictable.[47] Indeed, this was one of the arguments made against the unsuccessful equal rights amendment. Thus, originalism may under some circumstances make good pragmatic sense.

Pragmatic constitutionalism will only sometimes give history decisive weight, but that does not mean that history will be ignored in the remaining cases. While pragmatic constitutionalism does not, unlike originalism, make modern constitutional interpretation subservient to original intent, neither is it blind to the views of those who adopted constitutional provisions. We can learn much from history. The framers' views define much of the tradition in which modern judges place themselves. By rediscovering old ideas (such as republicanism), we can find new directions for future development. By identifying flaws in the framers' views (such as the influence of the institution of slavery on various parts of the Constitution), we understand better where our tradition has been led astray.

It is a truism—but true nonetheless—that to decide where we should be going, we must first know where we have been.

FOOTNOTES

1. Murray Dry, *Federalism and the Constitution: The Founders' Design and Contemporary Constitutional Law*, 4 Constitutional Commentary 233, 233–34 (1987).

2. *Id.* at 234 (emphasis in original). For a recent summary of the arguments for originalism, see Earl M. Maltz, *The Failure of Attacks on Constitutional Originalism*, 4 Constitutional Commentary 43 (1987).

3. Michael J. Perry, *The Authority of Text, Tradition, and Reason: A Theory of Constitutional 'Interpretation'*, 58 S. Cal. L. Rev. 551, 569–70 (1985).

4. An even looser use of the term "originalist" might include anyone who believes that the starting point of analysis should be original intent but that original intent is not necessarily controlling even when it is clear. At this point, however, it becomes difficult to tell the difference between an originalist of this school and a non-originalist like Michael Perry.

5. Paul Brest, *The Misconceived Quest for the Original Understanding*, 60 B. U. L. Rev. 204, 229 (1980) [hereinafter *Misconceived Quest*].

6. Ruth Bader Ginsburg, *Limiting Judicial Activism*, 15 Ga. L. Rev. 539, 546 (1981).

7. James H. Hutson, *The Creation of the Constitution: The Integrity of the Documentary Record*, 65 Tex. L. Rev. 1, 33–34 (1986).

8. *Id.* at 22—24.

9. *Id.* at 36.

10. William E. Nelson, *History and Neutrality in Constitutional Adjudication*, 72 Va. L. Rev. 1237, 1250—51 (1986).

11. H. Jefferson Powell, *The Original Understanding of Original Intent*, 98 Harv. L. Rev. 885 (1985).

12. *Id.* at 895—98.

13. *Id.* at 937–38.

14. Charles A. Lofgren, *The Original Understanding of Original Intent?*, 5 Constitutional Commentary 77 (1988).

15. Suzanna Sherry, *The Founders' Unwritten Constitution*, 54 U. Chi. L. Rev. 1127, 1145–46 (1987).

16. *See id.;* Thomas C. Grey, The Original Understanding and the Unwritten Con-

stitution, in Neil L. York, ed., *Toward A More Perfect Union: Six Essays on the Constitution* 145 (1988).

17. Dean Ely argues that:

[T]he legislative history argument is one neither side can win. It really shouldn't be critical, however. What is most important here, as it has to be everywhere, is the actual language of the provision that was proposed and ratified. On that score Justice Black argued that: "No State shall make or enforce any law which shall abridge the privileges or immunities of citizens of the United States" was an "eminently reasonable way of expressing the idea that henceforth the Bill of Rights shall apply to the States.". . . . There is another edge to this, and that is that nothing in the material that has been discussed supports Justice Black's *limitation* of the Fourteenth Amendment's Privileges or Immunities Clause to the function of incorporating the Bill of Rights. There is some legislative history suggesting an intention to incorporate the Bill of Rights: there is none at all suggesting that was *all* the Privileges or Immunities Clause was designed to do, and indeed Howard's speech, which is Black's strongest proof of incorporation, is quite explicitly against him on the limitation point. The words of the clause *are* an "eminently reasonable" way of applying the Bill of Rights to the States, but apter language could have been found had that been the *only* content intended.

John Hart Ely, *Democracy and Distrust: A Theory of Judicial Review* 27–28 (1980) (emphasis in original) [hereinafter *Democracy and Distrust*].

18. See Henry P. Monaghan, *Our Perfect Constitution*, 56 N. Y. U. L. Rev. 353, 367 (1981) [hereinafter *Perfect Constitution*].

19. In this hermeneutic approach to history, "[t]he historian must enter the minds of his or her subjects, see the world as they saw it, and understand it in their own terms." Mark Tushnet, *Following the Rules Laid Down: A Critique of Interpretation and Neutral Principles*, 96 Harv. L. Rev. 781, 798 (1983). As Professor Tushnet explains, hermeneutics has potentially important implications for constitutional interpretation:

The intellectual world of the framers is one that bears some resemblance, which is more than merely genetic, to ours. A hermeneutic interpretivism would force us to think about the social contexts of the resemblances and dissimilarities. It would lead us not to despair over the gulf that separates the framers' world from ours, but rather to the crafting of creative links between their ideals and our own. But in recognizing the magnitude of the creative component, we inevitably lose faith in the ability of interpretivism to provide the constraints on judges that liberal constitutional theory demands. . . .

We can gain an interpretive understanding of the past by working from commonalities in the use of large abstractions to reach the unfamiliar particulars of what those abstractions really meant in the past. The commonalities are what make the past *our* past; they are the links between two segments of a single community that extends over time. . . . Interpretivism goes wrong in thinking that the commonalities are greater than they really are, but we would go equally wrong if we denied that they exist.

Id. at 803–04 (emphasis in original).

20. David A. J. Richards, *Interpretation and Historiography*, 58 S. Cal. L. Rev. 489, 513–14 (1985).

21. *Id.* at 514–15.

22. Robert W. Bennett, *Objectivity in Constitutional Law*, 132 U. Pa. L. Rev. 445, 463 (1984).

23. Brest, *Misconceived Quest*, at 217.

24. Robert Bork, *The Constitution, Original Intent, and Economic Rights*, 23 San Diego L. Rev. 823, 828 (1986).

25. William Brennan, *The Constitution of the United States: Contemporary Ratification*, 27 S. Tex. L. Rev. 433, 438 (1986). For the contrasting view of another justice, see William H. Rehnquist, *The Idea of a Living Constitution*, 54 Tex. L. Rev. 693 (1976). The primary line of response available to originalists is to agree that changing times must be accommodated somewhere in the system of government, but to ask why the courts' performance of constitutional review is the appropriate place. If people today have broader views of individual rights than those who drafted the Fourteenth Amendment, they can prevail upon their legislators to recognize those rights. The Supreme Court's function, the originalist can maintain, is limited to enforcing the original understanding; social change simply must find its expression elsewhere.

26. Thomas C. Grey, *Do We Have an Unwritten Constitution?*, 27 Stan. L. Rev. 703, 711–14 (1975).

27. *Id.* (emphasis in original).

28. Monaghan, *Perfect Constitution*, at 382.

29. For some other illustrations, *see* Akhil R. Amar, *Our Forgotten Constitution: A Bicentennial Comment*, 97 Yale L. J. 281, 291–92 (1987).

30. Edwin Meese, *The Supreme Court of the United States: Bulwark of a Limited Constitution*, 27 S. Tex. L. Rev. 455, 464 (1986).

31. Ely, *Democracy and Distrust*, at 5–8.

32. Amy Gutmann, *Democratic Education*, at xi (1987).

33. *West Virginia Board of Educ. v. Barnette*, 319 U.S. 624, 638 (1943).

34. Brest, *Misconceived Quest*, at 230.

35. *Id.* at 225.

36. Ely, *Democracy and Distrust*, at 3.

37. Thomas C. Grey, *The Constitution as Scripture*, 37 Stan. L. Rev. 1, 14 (1984). Grey continues with a description of *Marbury*:

> Marshall began by noting that the people had not only created institutions of government, but had also placed limits on their power. He continued: "and that those limits may not be mistaken or forgotten, the constitution is *written*. To what purpose are powers limited, and to what purpose is that limitation *committed to writing*, if these limits may, at any time, be passed by those intended to be restrained?" He added that those who frame "*written* constitutions" act on the theory that legislation repugnant to the constitution is void; indeed "[t]his theory is essentially attached to a *written* constitution." . . . This point alone would suffice to establish judicial review "in America, where *written* constitutions have been viewed with so much reverence."

38. *See* Stephen R. Munzer & James W. Nickel, *Does the Constitution Mean What It Always Meant?*, 77 Colum. L. Rev. 1029, 1044 (1977).

39. Charles Fried, *Sonnett LXV and the "Black Ink" of the Framers' Intention*, 100 Harv. L. Rev. 751, 758–59 (1987).

40. *Id.* at 756.

41. Ely, *Democracy and Distrust*, at 50–58 (emphasis in original).

42. Paul Brest, *The Fundamental Rights Controversy: The Essential Contradictions of Normative Constitutional Scholarship*, 90 Yale L. J. 1063, 1096 (1981).

43. Oliver Wendell Homes, *The Common Law* 1–2 (1881).

44. For further discussion of the role of pragmatism in constitutional law, see Daniel A. Farber, *Legal Pragmatism and the Constitution*, 72 Minn. L. Rev. 1331 (1988).

45. *See* Herman Belz, *The Civil War Amendments to the Constitution: The Relevance of Original Intent*, 5 Constitutional Commentary 115, 133–141 (1988).

46. Brest, *Misconceived Quest*, at 229. *See also* Larry G. Simon, *The Authority of the Framers of the Constitution: Can Originalist Interpretation Be Justified?*, 73 Cal. L. Rev. 1482, 1537 (1985).

47. It seems much less likely, however, that anyone would vote against an amendment because of fears that, over the course of a century or two, it would become subject to novel interpretations.

Constitution of the United States

We the People of the United States, in Order to form a more perfect Union, establish Justice, insure domestic Tranquility, provide for the common defence, promote the general Welfare, and secure the Blessings of Liberty to ourselves and our Posterity, do ordain and establish this Constitution for the United States of America.

ARTICLE I

Section 1. All legislative Powers herein granted shall be vested in a Congress of the United States, which shall consist of a Senate and House of Representatives.

Section 2. [1] The House of Representatives shall be composed of Members chosen every second Year by the People of the several States, and the Electors in each State shall have the Qualifications requisite for Electors of the most numerous Branch of the State Legislature.

[2] No Person shall be a Representative who shall not have attained to the Age of twenty five Years, and been seven Years a Citizen of the United States, and who shall not, when elected, be an Inhabitant of that State in which he shall be chosen.

[3] Representatives and direct Taxes shall be apportioned among the several States which may be included within this Union, according to their respective Numbers, which shall be determined by adding to the whole Number of free Persons, including those bound to Service for a Term of Years, and excluding Indians not taxed, three fifths of all other Persons. The actual Enumeration shall be made within three Years after the first Meeting of the Congress of the United States, and within every subsequent Term of ten Years, in such Manner as they shall by Law direct. The Number of Representatives shall not exceed one for every thirty Thousand, but each State shall have at Least one

Representative; and until such enumeration shall be made, the State of New Hampshire shall be entitled to chuse three, Massachusetts eight, Rhode Island and Providence Plantations one, Connecticut five, New York six, New Jersey four, Pennsylvania eight, Delaware one, Maryland six, Virginia ten, North Carolina five, South Carolina five, and Georgia three.

[4] When vacancies happen in the Representation from any State, the Executive Authority thereof shall issue Writs of Election to fill such Vacancies.

[5] The House of Representatives shall chuse their Speaker and other Officers; and shall have the sole Power of Impeachment.

Section 3. [1] The Senate of the United States shall be composed of two Senators from each State, chosen by the Legislature thereof, for six Years; and each Senator shall have one Vote.

[2] Immediately after they shall be assembled in Consequence of the first Election, they shall be divided as equally as may be into three Classes. The Seats of the Senators of the first Class shall be vacated at the Expiration of the second Year, of the second Class at the Expiration of the fourth Year, and of the third Class at the Expiration of the sixth Year, so that one third may be chosen every second Year; and if Vacancies happen by Resignation, or otherwise, during the Recess of the Legislature of any State, the Executive thereof may make temporary Appointments until the next Meeting of the Legislature, which shall then fill such Vacancies.

[3] No Person shall be a Senator who shall not have attained to the Age of Thirty Years, and been nine Years a Citizen of the United States, and who shall not, when elected, be an Inhabitant of that State for which he shall be chosen.

[4] The Vice President of the United States shall be President of the Senate, but shall have no Vote, unless they be equally divided.

[5] The Senate shall chuse their other Officers, and also a President pro tempore, in the absence of the Vice President, or when he shall exercise the Office of President of the United States.

[6] The Senate shall have the sole Power to try all Impeachments. When sitting for that purpose, they shall be on Oath or Affirmation. When the President of the United States is tried, the Chief Justice shall preside: And no Person shall be convicted without the Concurrence of two thirds of the Members present.

[7] Judgment in Cases of Impeachment shall not extend further than to removal from Office, and disqualification to hold and enjoy any Office of honor, Trust or Profit under the United States: but the Party convicted shall nevertheless be liable and subject to Indictment, Trial, Judgment and Punishment, according to Law.

Section 4. [1] The Times, Places and Manner of holding Elections for Senators and Representatives, shall be prescribed in each State by the Legislature thereof; but the Congress may at any time by Law make or alter such Regulations, except as to the Places of chusing Senators.

[2] The Congress shall assemble at least once in every Year, and such Meeting shall be on the first Monday in December, unless they shall by Law appoint a different Day.

Section 5. [1] Each House shall be the Judge of the Elections, Returns and Qualifications of its own Members, and a Majority of each shall constitute a Quorum to do Business; but a smaller Number may adjourn from day to day, and may be authorized to compel the Attendance of absent Members, in such Manner, and under such Penalties as each House may provide.

[2] Each House may determine the Rules of its Proceedings, punish its Members for disorderly Behavior, and, with the Concurrence of two thirds, expel a Member.

[3] Each House shall keep a Journal of its Proceedings, and from time to time publish the same, excepting such Parts as may in their Judgment require Secrecy; and the Yeas and Nays of the Members of either House on any question shall, at the Desire of one fifth of those Present, be entered on the Journal.

[4] Neither House, during the Session of Congress, shall, without the Consent of the other, adjourn for more than three days, nor to any other Place than that in which the two Houses shall be sitting.

Section 6. [1] The Senators and Representatives shall receive a Compensation for their Services, to be ascertained by Law, and paid out of the Treasury of the United States. They shall in all Cases, except Treason, Felony and Breach of the Peace, be privileged from Arrest during their Attendance at the Session of their respective Houses, and in going to and returning from the same; and for any Speech or Debate in either House, they shall not be questioned in any other Place.

[2] No Senator or Representative shall, during the Time for which he was elected, be appointed to any civil Office under the Authority of the United States, which shall have been created, or the Emoluments whereof shall have been encreased during such time; and no Person holding any Office under the United States, shall be a Member of either House during his Continuance in Office.

Section 7. [1] All Bills for raising Revenue shall originate in the House of Representatives; but the Senate may propose or concur with Amendments as on other Bills.

[2] Every Bill which shall have passed the House of Representatives and the Senate, shall, before it become a Law, be presented to the President of the United States; If he approve he shall sign it, but if not he shall return it, with his Objections to the House in which it shall have originated, who shall enter the Objections at large on their Journal, and proceed to reconsider it. If after such Reconsideration two thirds of that House shall agree to pass the Bill, it shall be sent, together with the Objections, to the other House, by which it shall likewise be reconsidered, and if approved by two thirds of that House, it shall become a Law. But in all such Cases the Votes of both Houses shall be determined by yeas and Nays, and the Names of the Persons voting for and against the Bill shall be entered on the Journal of each House respectively. If any Bill shall not be returned by the President within ten Days (Sundays excepted) after it shall have been presented to him, the Same shall be a Law, in like Manner as if he had signed it, unless the Congress by their Adjournment prevents its Return, in which Case it shall not be a Law.

[3] Every Order, Resolution, or Vote to Which the Concurrence of the Senate and House of Representatives may be necessary (except on a question of Adjournment) shall be presented to the President of the United States; and before the Same shall take Effect, shall be approved by him, or being disapproved by him, shall be repassed by two thirds of the Senate and House of

Representatives, according to the Rules and Limitations prescribed in the Case of a Bill.

Section 8. [1] The Congress shall have Power To lay and collect Taxes, Duties, Imposts and Excises, to pay the Debts and provide for the common Defence and general Welfare of the United States; but all Duties, Imposts and Excises shall be uniform throughout the United States;

[2] To borrow money on the credit of the United States;

[3] To regulate Commerce with foreign Nations, and among the several States, and with the Indian Tribes;

[4] To establish an uniform Rule of Naturalization, and uniform Laws on the subject of bankruptcies throughout the United States;

[5] To coin Money, regulate the Value thereof, and of foreign Coin, and fix the Standard of Weights and Measures;

[6] To provide the Punishment of counterfeiting the Securities and current Coin of the United States;

[7] To establish Post Offices and post Roads;

[8] To promote the Progress of Science and useful Arts, by securing for limited Times to Authors and inventors the exclusive Right to their respective Writings and Discoveries;

[9] To constitute Tribunals inferior to the supreme Court;

[10] To define and punish Piracies and Felonies committed on the high Seas, and Offenses against the Law of Nations:

[11] To declare War, grant Letters of Marque and Reprisal, and make Rules concerning Captures on Land and Water;

[12] To raise and support Armies, but no Appropriation of Money to that Use shall be for a longer Term than two Years;

[13] To provide and maintain a Navy;

[14] To make Rules for the Government and Regulation of the land and naval Forces;

[15] To provide for calling forth the Militia to execute the Laws of the Union, suppress Insurrections and repel Invasions;

[16] To provide for organizing, arming, and disciplining, the Militia, and for governing such Part of them as may be employed in the Service of the United States, reserving to the States respectively, the Appointment of the Officers, and the Authority of training the Militia according to the discipline prescribed by Congress;

[17] To exercise exclusive Legislation in all Cases whatsoever, over such District (not exceeding ten Miles square) as may, by Cession of particular States, and the Acceptance of Congress, become the Seat of the Government of the United States, and to exercise like Authority over all Places purchased by the Consent of the Legislature of the State in which the Same shall be, for the Erection of Forts, Magazines, Arsenals, dock-Yards, and other needful Buildings;—And

[18] To make all Laws which shall be necessary and proper for carrying into Execution the foregoing Powers, and all other Powers vested by this Constitution in the Government of the United States, or in any Department or Officer thereof.

Section 9. [1] The Migration or Importation of such Persons as any of the States now existing shall think proper to admit, shall not be prohibited by the Congress prior to the Year one thousand eight hundred and eight, but a Tax or duty may be imposed on such Importation, not exceeding ten dollars for each Person.

[2] The privilege of the Writ of Habeas Corpus shall not be suspended, unless when in Cases of Rebellion or Invasion the public Safety may require it.

[3] No Bill of Attainder or ex post facto Law shall be passed.

[4] No Capitation, or other direct, Tax shall be laid, unless in Proportion to the Census or Enumeration herein before directed to be taken.

[5] No Tax or Duty shall be laid on Articles exported from any State.

[6] No Preference shall be given by any Regulation of Commerce or Revenue to the Ports of one State over those of another: nor shall Vessels bound to, or from, one State, be obliged to enter, clear, or pay Duties in another.

[7] No Money shall be drawn from the Treasury, but in Consequence of Appropriations made by Law; and a regular Statement and Account of the Receipts and Expenditures of all public Money shall be published from time to time.

[8] No Title of Nobility shall be granted by the United States: And no Person holding any Office of Profit or Trust under them, shall, without the Consent of the Congress, accept of any present, Emolument, Office, or Title, of any kind whatever, from any King, Prince, or foreign State.

Section 10. [1] No State shall enter into any Treaty, Alliance, or Confederation; grant Letters of Marque and Reprisal; coin Money; emit Bills of Credit; make any Thing but gold and silver Coin a Tender in Payment of Debts; pass any Bill of Attainder, ex post facto Law, or Law impairing the obligation of Contracts, or grant any Title of Nobility.

[2] No State shall, without the Consent of the Congress, lay any Imposts or Duties on Imports or Exports, except what may be absolutely necessary for executing its inspection Laws: and the net Produce of all Duties and Imposts, laid by any State on Imports or Exports, shall be for the Use of the Treasury of the United States; and all such Laws shall be subject to the Revision and Controul of the Congress.

[3] No State shall, without the Consent of Congress, lay any Duty of Tonnage, keep Troops, or Ships of War in time of Peace, enter into any Agreement or Compact with another State, or with a foreign Power, or engage in War, unless actually invaded, or in such imminent Danger as will not admit of delay.

ARTICLE II

Section 1. [1] The executive Power shall be vested in a President of the United States of America. He shall hold his Office during the Term of four Years, and, together with the Vice President, chosen for the same Term, be elected, as follows:

[2] Each State shall appoint, in such Manner as the Legislature thereof may direct, a Number of Electors, equal to the whole Number of Senators and Representatives to which the State may be entitled in the Congress: but no Senator or Representative, or Person holding an Office of Trust or Profit under the United States, shall be appointed an Elector.

[3] The Electors shall meet in their respective States, and vote by Ballot for two Persons, of whom one at least shall not be an Inhabitant of the same State with themselves. And they shall make a List of all the Persons voted for, and

of the Number of Votes for each; which List they shall sign and certify, and transmit sealed to the Seat of the Government of the United States, directed to the President of the Senate. The President of the Senate shall, in the Presence of the Senate and House of Representatives, open all the Certificates, and the Votes shall then be counted. The Person having the greatest Number of Votes shall be the President, if such Number be a Majority of the whole Number of Electors appointed; and if there be more than one who have such Majority, and have an equal Number of Votes, then the House of Representatives shall immediately chuse by Ballot one of them for President; and if no Person have a Majority, then from the five highest on the List the said House shall in like Manner chuse the President. But in chusing the President, the Votes shall be taken by States, the Representation from each State having one Vote; a quorum for this Purpose shall consist of a Member or Members from two thirds of the States, and a Majority of all the States shall be necessary to a Choice. In every Case, after the choice of the President, the Person having the greatest Number of Votes of the electors shall be the Vice President. But if there should remain two or more who have equal Votes, the Senate shall chuse from them by Ballot the Vice President.

[4] The Congress may determine the Time of chusing the Electors, and the Day on which they shall give their Votes; which Day shall be the same throughout the United States.

[5] No person except a natural born Citizen, or a Citizen of the United States, at the time of the Adoption of this Constitution, shall be eligible to the Office of President; neither shall any Person be eligible to that Office who shall not have attained to the Age of thirty five Years, and been fourteen Years a Resident within the United States.

[6] In case of the removal of the President from Office, or of his Death, Resignation or Inability to discharge the Powers and Duties of the said Office, the Same shall devolve on the Vice President, and the Congress may by Law provide for the case of Removal, Death, Resignation or Inability, both of the President and Vice President, declaring what Officer shall then act as President, and such Officer shall act accordingly, until the disability be removed, or a President shall be elected.

[7] The President shall, at stated Times, receive for his Services, a Compensation, which shall neither be increased nor diminished during the Period for which he shall have been elected, and he shall not receive within that Period any other Emolument from the United States, or any of them.

[8] Before he enter on the execution of his Office, he shall take the following Oath or Affirmation: "I do solemnly swear (or affirm) that I will faithfully execute the Office of President of the United States, and will to the best of my Ability, preserve, protect and defend the constitution of the United States."

Section 2. [1] The President shall be Commander in Chief of the Army and Navy of the United States, and of the Militia of the several States, when called into the actual Service of the United States; he may require the Opinion, in writing, of the principal Officer in each of the executive Departments, upon any subject relating to the Duties of their respective Offices, and he shall have Power to grant Reprieves and Pardons for Offenses against the United States, except in Cases of Impeachment.

[2] He shall have Power, by and with the Advice and Consent of the Senate, to make Treaties, provided two thirds of the Senators present concur; and he

shall nominate, and by and with the Advice and Consent of the Senate, shall appoint Ambassadors, other public Ministers and Consuls, Judges of the supreme Court, and all other Officers of the United States, whose Appointments are not herein otherwise provided for, and which shall be established by Law: but the Congress may by Law vest the Appointment of such inferior Officers, as they think proper, in the President alone, in the Courts of Law, or in the Heads of Departments.

[3] The President shall have Power to fill up all Vacancies that may happen during the Recess of the Senate, by granting Commissions which shall expire at the End of their next Session.

Section 3. He shall from time to time give to the Congress Information of the State of the Union, and recommend to their Consideration such Measures as he shall judge necessary and expedient; he may, on extraordinary Occasions, convene both Houses, or either of them, and in Case of Disagreement between them, with Respect to the Time of Adjournment, he may adjourn them to such Time as he shall think proper; he shall receive Ambassadors and other public Ministers; he shall take Care that the Laws be faithfully executed, and shall Commission all the Officers of the United States.

Section 4. The President and all civil Officers of the United States, shall be removed from Office on Impeachment for, and Conviction of, Treason, Bribery, or other high Crimes and Misdemeanors.

ARTICLE III

Section 1. The judicial Power of the United States, shall be vested in one supreme Court, and in such inferior Courts as the Congress may from time to time ordain and establish. The Judges, both of the supreme and inferior Courts, shall hold their Offices during good Behaviour, and shall, at stated Times, receive for their Services, a Compensation, which shall not be diminished during their Continuance in Office.

Section 2. [1] The Judicial Power shall extend to all Cases, in Law and Equity, arising under this Constitution, the Laws of the United States, and Treaties made, or which shall be made, under their Authority;—to all Cases affecting Ambassadors, other public Ministers and Consuls;—to all Cases of admiralty and maritime Jurisdiction;—to Controversies to which the United States shall be a Party;—to Controversies between two or more States;—between a State and Citizens of another State;—between Citizens of different States;— between Citizens of the same State claiming Lands under Grants of different States, and between a State, or the Citizens thereof, and foreign States, Citizens or Subjects.

[2] In all Cases affecting Ambassadors, other public Ministers and Consuls, and those in which a State shall be a Party, the supreme Court shall have original Jurisdiction. In all the other Cases before mentioned, the supreme Court shall have appellate Jurisdiction, both as to Law and Fact, with such Exceptions, and under such Regulations as the Congress shall make.

[3] The trial of all Crimes, except in Cases of Impeachment, shall be by Jury, and such Trial shall be held in the State where the said Crimes shall have been committed; but when not committed within any State, the Trial shall be at such Place or Places as the Congress may by Law have directed.

Section 3. [1] Treason against the United States, shall consist only in levying War against them, or in adhering to their Enemies, giving them Aid and Comfort. No person shall be convicted of Treason unless on the Testimony of two Witnesses to the same overt Act, or on Confession in open Court.

[2] The Congress shall have Power to declare the Punishment of Treason, but no Attainder of Treason shall work Corruption of Blood, or Forfeiture except during the life of the Person attainted.

ARTICLE IV

Section 1. Full Faith and Credit shall be given in each State to the public Acts, Records, and judicial Proceedings of every other State. And the Congress may by general Laws prescribe the Manner in which such Acts, Records and Proceedings shall be proved, and the Effect thereof.

Section 2. [1] The Citizens of each State shall be entitled to all Privileges and Immunities of Citizens in the several States.

[2] A Person charged in any State with Treason, Felony, or other Crime, who shall flee from Justice, and be found in another State, shall on demand of the executive Authority of the State from which he fled, be delivered up, to be removed to the State having Jurisdiction of the Crime.

[3] No Person held to Service or Labour in one State, under the Laws thereof, escaping into another, shall, in Consequence of any Law or Regulation therein, be discharged from such Service or Labour, but shall be delivered up on Claim of the Party to whom such Service or Labour may be due.

Section 3. [1] New States may be admitted by the Congress into this Union; but no new State shall be formed or erected within the Jurisdiction of any other State; nor any State be formed by the Junction of two or more States, or Parts of States, without the Consent of the Legislatures of the States concerned as well as of the Congress.

[2] The Congress shall have Power to dispose of and make all needful Rules and Regulations respecting the Territory or other Property belonging to the United States; and nothing in this Constitution shall be so construed as to Prejudice any Claims of the United States, or of any particular State.

Section 4. The United States shall guarantee to every State in this Union a Republican Form of Government, and shall protect each of them against Invasion; and on Application of the Legislature, or of the Executive (when the Legislature cannot be convened) against domestic Violence.

ARTICLE V

The Congress, whenever two thirds of both Houses shall deem it necessary, shall propose Amendments to this Constitution, or, on the Application of the Legislatures of two thirds of the several States, shall call a Convention for proposing Amendments, which, in either Case, shall be valid to all Intents and Purposes, as part of this Constitution, when ratified by the Legislatures of three fourths of the several States, or by Conventions in three fourths thereof, as the one or the other Mode of Ratification may be proposed by the Congress; Provided that no Amendment which may be made prior to the Year One thousand eight hundred and eight shall in any Manner affect the first and fourth Clauses in the Ninth Section of the first Article; and that no State, without its Consent, shall be deprived of its equal Suffrage in the Senate.

ARTICLE VI

[1] All Debts contracted and Engagements entered into, before the Adoption of this Constitution, shall be as valid against the United States under this Constitution, as under the Confederation.

[2] This Constitution, and the Laws of the United States which shall be made in Pursuance thereof; and all Treaties made, or which shall be made, under the Authority of the United States, shall be the supreme Law of the Land; and the Judges in every State shall be bound thereby, any Thing in the Constitution or Laws of any State to the Contrary notwithstanding.

[3] The Senators and Representatives before mentioned, and the Members of the several State Legislatures, and all executive and judicial Officers, both of the United States and of the several States, shall be bound by Oath or Affirmation, to support this Constitution; but no religious test shall ever be required as a Qualification to any Office or public Trust under the United States.

ARTICLE VII

The Ratification of the Conventions of nine States shall be sufficient for the Establishment of this Constitution between the States so ratifying the Same.

Done in Convention by the Unanimous Consent of the States present the Seventeenth Day of September in the Year of our Lord one thousand seven hundred and Eighty seven and of the Independence of the United States of America the Twelfth.

ARTICLES IN ADDITION TO, AND AMENDMENT OF, THE CONSTITUTION OF THE UNITED STATES OF AMERICA, PROPOSED BY CONGRESS, AND RATIFIED BY THE LEGISLATURES OF THE SEVERAL STATES, PURSUANT TO THE FIFTH ARTICLE OF THE ORIGINAL CONSTITUTION

AMENDMENT I [1791]

Congress shall make no law respecting an establishment of religion, or prohibiting the free exercise thereof; or abridging the freedom of speech, or of the press; or the right of the people peaceably to assemble, and to petition the Government for a redress of grievances.

AMENDMENT II [1791]

A well regulated Militia, being necessary to the security of a free State, the right of the people to keep and bear Arms, shall not be infringed.

AMENDMENT III [1791]

No Soldier shall, in time of peace be quartered in any house, without the consent of the Owner, nor in time of war, but in a manner to be prescribed by law.

AMENDMENT IV [1791]

The right of the people to be secure in their persons, houses, papers, and effects, against unreasonable searches and seizures, shall not be violated, and no Warrants shall issue, but upon probable cause, supported by Oath or affirmation, and particularly describing the place to be searched, and the persons or things to be seized.

AMENDMENT V [1791]

No person shall be held to answer for a capital, or otherwise infamous crime, unless on a presentment of indictment of a Grand Jury, except in cases arising in the land or naval forces, or in the Militia, when in actual service in time of War or public danger; nor shall any person be subject for the same offence to be twice put in jeopardy of life or limb; nor shall be compelled in any criminal case to be a witness against himself, nor be deprived of life, liberty, or property, without due process of law; nor shall private property be taken for public use, without just compensation.

AMENDMENT VI [1791]

In all criminal prosecutions, the accused shall enjoy the right to a speedy and public trial, by an impartial jury of the State and district wherein the crime shall have been committed, which district shall have been previously ascertained by law, and to be informed of the nature and cause of the accusation; to be confronted with the witnesses against him; to have compulsory process for obtaining witnesses in his favor, and to have the Assistance of Counsel for his defence.

AMENDMENT VII [1791]

In Suits at common law, where the value in controversy shall exceed twenty dollars, the right of trial by jury shall be preserved, and no fact tried by a jury, shall be otherwise re-examined in any Court of the United States, than according to the rules of the common law.

AMENDMENT VIII [1791]

Excessive bail shall not be required, nor excessive fines imposed, nor cruel and unusual punishments inflicted.

AMENDMENT IX [1791]

The enumeration in the Constitution, of certain rights, shall not be construed to deny or disparage others retained by the people.

AMENDMENT X [1791]

The powers not delegated to the United States by the Constitution, nor prohibited by it to the States, are reserved to the States respectively, or to the people.

AMENDMENT XI [1798]

The Judicial power of the United States shall not be construed to extend to any suit in law or equity, commenced or prosecuted against one of the United States by Citizens of another State, or by Citizens or Subjects of any Foreign State.

AMENDMENT XII [1804]

The Electors shall meet in their respective states and vote by ballot for President and Vice-President, one of whom, at least, shall not be an inhabitant of the same state with themselves; they shall name in their ballots the person voted for as President, and in distinct ballots the person voted for as Vice-President, and they shall make distinct lists of all persons voted for as President, and of all persons voted for as Vice-President, and of the number of votes for each, which lists they shall sign and certify, and transmit sealed to the seat of the government of the United States, directed to the President of the Senate;—The President of the Senate shall, in the presence of the Senate and House of Representatives, open all the certificates and the votes shall then be counted;—The person having the greatest number of votes for President, shall be the President, if such number be a majority of the whole number of Electors appointed; and if no person have such majority, then from the persons having the highest numbers not exceeding three on the list of those voted for as President, the House of Representatives shall choose immediately, by ballot, the President. But in choosing the President, the votes shall be taken by states, the representation from each state having one vote; a quorum for this purpose shall consist of a member or members from two-thirds of the states, and a majority of all the states shall be necessary to a choice. And if the House of Representatives shall not choose a President whenever the right of choice shall devolve upon them, before the fourth day of March next following, then the Vice-President shall act as President, as in the case of the death or other constitutional disability of the President.—The person having the greatest number of votes as Vice-President, shall be the Vice-President, if such number be a majority of the whole number of Electors appointed, and if no person have a majority, then from the two highest numbers on the list, the Senate shall choose the Vice-President; a quorum for the purpose shall consist of two-thirds of the whole number of Senators, and a majority of the whole number shall be necessary to a choice. But no person constitutionally ineligible to the office of President shall be eligible to that of Vice-President of the United States.

AMENDMENT XIII [1865]

Section 1. Neither slavery nor involuntary servitude, except as a punishment for crime whereof the party shall have been duly convicted, shall exist within the United States, or any place subject to their jurisdiction.

Section 2. Congress shall have power to enforce this article by appropriate legislation.

AMENDMENT XIV [1868]

Section 1. All persons born or naturalized in the United States, and subject to the jurisdiction thereof, are citizens of the United States and of the State wherein they reside. No State shall make or enforce any law which shall abridge the privileges or immunities of citizens of the United States; nor shall any State deprive any person of life, liberty, or property, without due process of law; nor deny to any person within its jurisdiction the equal protection of the laws.

Section 2. Representatives shall be apportioned among the several States according to their respective numbers, counting the whole number of persons in each State, excluding Indians not taxed. But when the right to vote at any election for the choice of electors for President and Vice President of the United States, Representatives in Congress, the Executive and Judicial officers of a state, or the members of the Legislature thereof, is denied to any of the male inhabitants of such State, being twenty-one years of age, and citizens of the United States, or in any way abridged, except for participation in rebellion, or other crime, the basis of representation therein shall be reduced in the proportion which the number of such male citizens shall bear to the whole number of male citizens twenty-one years of age in such State.

Section 3. No person shall be a Senator or Representative in Congress, or elector of President and Vice President, or hold any office, civil or military, under the United States, or under any State, who, having previously taken an oath, as a member of Congress, or as an officer of the United States, or as a member of any State legislature, or as an executive or judicial officer of any State, to support the Constitution of the United States, shall have engaged in insurrection or rebellion against the same, or given aid or comfort to the enemies thereof. But Congress may by a vote of two-thirds of each House, remove such disability.

Section 4. The validity of the public debt of the United States, authorized by law, including debts incurred for payment of pensions and bounties for services in suppressing insurrection or rebellion, shall not be questioned. But neither the United States nor any State shall assume or pay any debt or obligation incurred in aid of insurrection or rebellion against the United States, or any claim for the loss of emancipation of any slave, but all such debts, obligation and claims shall be held illegal and void.

Section 5. The Congress shall have power to enforce, by appropriate legislation, the provisions of this article.

AMENDMENT XV [1870]

Section 1. The right of citizens of the United States to vote shall not be denied or abridged by the United States or by any State on account of race, color, or previous condition of servitude.

Section 2. The Congress shall have power to enforce this article by appropriate legislation.

AMENDMENT XVI [1913]

The Congress shall have power to lay and collect taxes on incomes, from whatever source derived, without apportionment among the several States, and without regard to any census or enumeration.

AMENDMENT XVII [1913]

[1] The Senate of the United States shall be composed of two Senators from each State, elected by the people thereof, for six years; and each Senator shall have one vote. The electors in each State shall have the qualifications requisite for electors of the most numerous branch of the State legislatures.

[2] When vacancies happen in the representation of any State in the Senate, the executive authority of such State shall issue writs of election to fill such vacancies: Provided, That the legislature of any State may empower the executive thereof to make temporary appointments until the people fill the vacancies by election as the legislature may direct.

[3] This amendment shall not be so construed as to affect the election or term of any Senator chosen before it becomes valid as part of the Constitution.

AMENDMENT XVIII [1919]

Section 1. After one year from the ratification of this article the manufacture, sale, or transportation of intoxicating liquors within, the importation thereof into, or the exportation thereof from the United States and all territory subject to the jurisdiction thereof for beverage purposes is hereby prohibited.

Section 2. The Congress and the several States shall have concurrent power to enforce this article by appropriate legislation.

Section 3. This article shall be inoperative unless it shall have been ratified as an amendment to the Constitution by the legislatures of the several States, as provided in the Constitution, within seven years from the date of submission hereof to the States by the Congress.

AMENDMENT XIX [1920]

[1] The right of citizens of the United States to vote shall not be denied or abridged by the United States or by any State on account of sex.

[2] Congress shall have power to enforce this article by appropriate legislation.

AMENDMENT XX [1933]

Section 1. The terms of the President and Vice President shall end at noon on the 20th day of January, and the terms of Senators and Representatives at noon on the 3d day of January, of the years in which such terms would have ended if this article had not been ratified; and the terms of their successors shall then begin.

Section 2. The Congress shall assemble at least once in every year, and such meeting shall begin at noon on the 3d day of January, unless they shall by law appoint a different day.

Section 3. If, at the time fixed for the beginning of the term of the President, the President elect shall have died, the Vice President elect shall become President. If a President shall not have been chosen before the time fixed for the beginning of his term, or if the President elect shall have failed to qualify, then the Vice President elect shall act as President until a President shall have qualified; and the Congress may by law provide for the case wherein neither a President elect nor a Vice President elect shall have qualified, declaring who shall then act as President, or the manner in which one who is to act shall be selected, and such person shall act accordingly until a President or Vice President shall have qualified.

Section 4. The Congress may by law provide for the case of the death of any of the persons from whom the House of Representatives may choose a President whenever the right of choice shall have devolved upon them and for the case of the death of any of the persons from whom the Senate may choose a Vice President whenever the right of choice shall have devolved upon them.

Section 5. Sections 1 and 2 shall take effect on the 15th day of October following the ratification of this article.

Section 6. This article shall be inoperative unless it shall have been ratified as an amendment to the Constitution by the legislatures of three-fourths of the several States within seven years from the date of its submission.

AMENDMENT XXI [1933]

Section 1. The eighteenth article of amendment to the Constitution of the United States is hereby repealed.

Section 2. The transportation or importation into any State, Territory, or possession of the United States for delivery or use therein of intoxicating liquors, in violation of the laws thereof, is hereby prohibited.

Section 3. This article shall be inoperative unless it shall have been ratified as an amendment to the Constitution by conventions in the several States, as provided in the Constitution, within seven years from the date of the submission hereof to the States by the Congress.

AMENDMENT XXII [1951]

Section 1. No person shall be elected to the office of the President more than twice, and no person who has held the office of President, or acted as President, for more than two years of a term to which some other person was elected President shall be elected to the office of the President more than once. But this Article shall not apply to any person holding the office of President when this Article was proposed by the Congress, and shall not prevent any person who may be holding the office of President, or acting as President, during the term within which the Article becomes operative from holding the office of president or acting as President during the remainder of such term.

Section 2. This article shall be inoperative unless it shall have been ratified as an amendment to the Constitution by the legislatures of three-fourths of the several States within seven years from the date of its submission to the States by the Congress.

AMENDMENT XXIII [1961]

Section 1. The District constituting the seat of Government of the United States shall appoint in such manner as the Congress may direct: A number of electors of President and Vice President equal to the whole number of Senators and Representatives in Congress to which the District would be entitled if it were a State, but in no event more than the least populous State; they shall be in addition to those appointed by the States, but they shall be considered, for the purposes of the election of President and Vice President, to be electors appointed by a State; and they shall meet in the District and perform such duties as provided by the twelfth article of amendment.

Section 2. The Congress shall have power to enforce this article by appropriate legislation.

AMENDMENT XXIV [1964]

Section 1. The right of citizens of the United States to vote in any primary or other election for President or Vice President, for electors for President or Vice President, or for Senator or Representative in Congress, shall not be denied or abridged by the United States or any State by reason of failure to pay any poll tax or other tax.

Section 2. The Congress shall have power to enforce this article by appropriate legislation.

AMENDMENT XXV [1967]

Section 1. In case of the removal of the President from office or of his death or resignation, the Vice President shall become President.

Section 2. Whenever there is a vacancy in the office of the Vice President, the President shall nominate a Vice President who shall take office upon confirmation by a majority vote of both Houses of Congress.

Section 3. Whenever the President transmits to the President pro tempore of the Senate and the Speaker of the House of Representatives his written declaration that he is unable to discharge the powers and duties of his office, and until he transmits to them a written declaration to the contrary, such powers and duties shall be discharged by the Vice President as Acting President.

Section 4. Whenever the Vice President and a majority of either the principal officers of the executive departments or of such other body as Congress may by law provide, transmit to the President pro tempore of the Senate and the

Speaker of the House of Representatives their written declaration that the President is unable to discharge the powers and duties of his office, the Vice President shall immediately assume the powers and duties of the office as Acting President. Thereafter, when the President transmits to the President pro tempore of the Senate and the Speaker of the House of Representatives his written declaration that no inability exists, he shall resume the powers and duties of his office unless the Vice President and a majority of either the principal officers of the executive department or of such other body as Congress may by law provide, transmit within four days to the President pro tempore of the Senate and the Speaker of the House of Representatives their written declaration that the President is unable to discharge the powers and duties of his office. Thereupon Congress shall decide the issue, assembling within forty-eight hours for that purpose if not in session. If the Congress, within twenty-one days after receipt of the latter written declaration, or, if Congress is not in session, within twenty-one days after Congress is required to assemble, determines by two-thirds vote of both Houses that the President is unable to discharge the powers and duties of his office, the Vice President shall continue to discharge the same as Acting President; otherwise, the President shall resume the powers and duties of his office.

AMENDMENT XXVI [1971]

Section 1. The right of citizens of the United States, who are eighteen years of age or older, to vote shall not be denied or abridged by the United States or by any State on account of age.

Section 2. The Congress shall have power to enforce this article by appropriate legislation.

Drafts of the 1787 Constitution

1. Randolph Resolutions
(presented May 29)

1. Resolved that the Articles of Confederation ought to be so corrected & enlarged as to accomplish the objects proposed by their institution; namely, "common defence, security of liberty and general welfare."

2. Resd. therefore that the rights of suffrage in the National Legislature ought to be proportioned to the Quotas of contribution, or to the number of free inhabitants, as the one or the other rule may seem best in different cases.

3. Resd. that the National Legislature ought to consist of two branches.

4. Resd. that the members of the first branch of the National Legislature ought to be elected by the people of the several States every   for the term of   ; to be of the age of   years at least, to receive liberal stipends by which they may be compensated for the devotion of their time to public service; to be ineligible to any office established by a particular State, or under the authority of the United States, except those peculiarly belonging to the functions of the first branch, during the term of service, and for the space of   after its expiration; to be incapable of reelection for the space of   after the expiration of their term of service, and to be subject to recall.

5. Resold. that the members of the second branch of the National Legislature ought to be elected by those of the first, out of a proper number of persons nominated by the individual Legislatures, to be of the age of   years at least; to hold their offices for a term sufficient to ensure their independency; to receive liberal stipends, by which they may be compensated for the devotion of their time to public service; and to be ineligible to any office established by a particular State, or under the authority of the United States, except those peculiarly belonging to the functions of the second branch, during the term of service, and for the space of   after the expiration thereof.

6. Resolved that each branch ought to possess the right of originating Acts; that the National Legislature ought to be impowered to enjoy the Legislative Rights vested in Congress by the Confederation & moreover to legislate in all cases to which the separate States are incompetent, or in which the harmony of the United States may be interrupted by the exercise of individual Legislation; to negative all laws passed by the several States, contravening in the opinion of the National Legislature the articles of Union; and to call forth theforce of the Union agst. any member of the

Union failing to fulfill its duty under the articles thereof.

7. Resd. that a National Executive be instituted; to be chosen by the National Legislature for the term of   years, to receive punctually at stated times, a fixed compensation for the services rendered, in which no increase or diminution shall be made so as to affect the Magistracy, existing at the time of increase or diminution, and to be ineligible a second time; and that besides a general authority to execute the National laws, it ought to enjoy the Executive rights vested in Congress by the Confederation.

8. Resd. that the Executive and a convenient number of the National Judiciary, ought to compose a Council of revision with authority to examine every act of the National Legislature before it shall operate, & every act of a particular Legislature before a Negative thereon shall be final; and that the dissent of the said Council shall amount to a rejection, unless the Act of the National Legislature be again passed, or that of a particular Legislature be again negatived by   of the members of each branch.

9. Resd. that a National Judiciary be established to consist of one or more supreme tribunals, and of inferior tribunals to be chosen by the National Legislature, to hold their offices during good behaviour; and to receive punctually at stated times fixed compensation for their services, in which no increase or diminution shall be made so as to affect the persons actually in office at the time of such increase or diminution. that the jurisdiction of the inferior tribunals shall be to hear & determine in the first instance, and of the supreme tribunal to hear and determine in the dernier resort, all piracies & felonies on the high seas, captures from an enemy; cases in which foreigners or citizens of other States applying to such jurisdictions may be interested, or which respect the collection of the National revenue; impeachments of any National officers, and questions which may involve the national peace and harmony.

10. Resolvd. that provision ought to be made for the admission of States lawfully arising within the limits of the United States, whether from a voluntary junction of Government & Territory or otherwise, with the consent of a number of voices in the National legislature less than the whole.

11. Resd. that a Republican Government & the territory of each State except in the instance of a voluntary junction of Government & territory ought to be guarantied by the United States to each State

12. Resd. that provision ought to be made for the continuance of Congress and their authorities and privileges, until a given day after the reform of the articles of Union shall be adopted, and for the completion of all their engagements.

13. Resd. that provision ought to be made for the amendment of the Articles of Union whensoever it shall seem necessary, and that the assent of the National Legislature ought not to be required thereto.

14. Resd. that the Legislative Executive & Judiciary powers within the several States ought to be bound by oath to support the articles of Union

15. Resd. that the amendments which shall be offered to the Confederation, by the Convention ought at a proper time, or times, after the approbation of Congress to be submitted to an assembly or assemblies of Representatives, recommended by the several Legislatures to be expressly chosen by the people, to consider & decide thereon.

2. Randolph Plan
(adopted by Committee of the Whole June 13 and June 19)

1. RESOLVED that it is the opinion of this Committee that a national government ought to be established consisting of a Supreme Legislative, Judiciary, and Executive.

2. RESOLVED. that the national Legislature ought to consist of Two Branches.

3. RESOLVED that the members of the first branch of the national Legislature ought to be elected by the People of the several States for the term of Three years. to receive fixed stipends, by which they may be compensated for the devotion of their time to public service to be paid out of the National-Treasury. to be ineligible to any Office established by a particular State or under the authority of the United-States (except those peculiarly belonging to the functions of the first branch) during the term of service, and under the national government for the space of one year after it's expiration.

4. RESOLVED. that the members of the second Branch of the national Legislature ought to be chosen by the individual Legislatures. to be of the age of thirty years at least. to hold their offices for a term sufficient to ensure their independency, namely seven years. to receive fixed stipends, by which they may be compensated for the devotion of their time to public service—to be paid out of the National Treasury to be ineligible to any office established by a particular State, or under the authority of the United States (except those peculiarly belonging to the functions of the second branch) during the term of service, and under the national government, for the space of one year after it's expiration.

5. RESOLVED that each branch ought to possess the right of originating acts.

6. RESOLVED. that the national Legislature ought to be empowered to enjoy the legislative rights vested in Congress by the confederation—and moreover to legislate in all cases to which the separate States are incompetent: or in which the harmony of the United States may be interrupted by the exercise of individual legislation. to negative all laws passed by the several States contravening, in the opinion of the national Legislature, the articles of union, or any treaties subsisting under the authority of the union.

7. RESOLVED. that the right of suffrage in the first branch of the national Legislature ought not to be according to the rule established in the articles of confederation: but according to some equitable ratio of representation—namely, in proportion to the whole number of white and other free citizens and inhabitants of every age, sex, and condition including those bound to servitude for a term of years, and three fifths of all other persons not comprehended in the foregoing description, except Indians, not paying taxes in each State.

8 RESOLVED. that the right of suffrage in the second branch of the national Legislature ought to be according to the rule established for the first.

9 RESOLVED. that a national Executive be instituted to consist of a single person. to be chosen by the National Legislature. for the term of seven years. with power to carry into execution the national Laws, to appoint to Offices in cases not otherwise provided for to be ineligible a second time, and to be removable on impeachment and conviction of mal practice or neglect of duty. to receive a fixed stipend, by which he may be compensated for the devotion of his time to public service to be paid out of the national Treasury.

10 RESOLVED. that the national executive shall have a right to negative any legislative act: which shall not be afterwards passed unless by two third parts of each branch of the national Legislature.

11 RESOLVED. that a national Judiciary be established to consist of One Supreme Tribunal. The Judges of which to be appointed by the second Branch of the National Legislature. to hold their offices during good behaviour to receive, punctually, at stated times, a fixed compensation for their services: in which no encrease or diminution shall be made so as to affect the persons actually in office at the time of such encrease or diminution

12 RESOLVED. That the national Legislature be empowered to appoint inferior Tribunals.

13 RESOLVED. that the jurisdiction of the national Judiciary shall extend to cases which respect the collection of the national revenue: impeachments of any national officers: and questions which involve the national peace and harmony.

14. RESOLVED. that provision ought to be made for the admission of States, lawfully arising within the limits of the United States, whether from a voluntary junction of government and territory, or otherwise, with the consent of a number of voices in the national Legislature less than the whole.

15. RESOLVED that provision ought to be made for the continuance of Congress and their authori-

ties until a given day after the reform of the articles of Union shall be adopted; and for the completion of all their engagements.

16. RESOLVED. that a republican constitution, and its existing laws, ought to be guaranteed to each State by the United States.

17. RESOLVED that provision ought to be made for the amendment of the articles of Union, whensoever it shall seem necessary.

18. RESOLVED. that the Legislative, Executive, and Judiciary powers within the several States ought to be bound by oath to support the articles of Union.

19 RESOLVED. that the amendments which shall be offered to the confederation by the Convention, ought at a proper time or times, after the approbation of Congress to be submitted to an assembly or assemblies of representatives, recommended by the several Legislatures, to be expressly chosen by the People to consider and decide thereon.

3. New Jersey Plan
(presented June 14)

1. Resd. that the articles of Confederation ought to be so revised, corrected & enlarged, as to render the federal Constitution adequate to the exigencies of Government & the preservation of the Union.

2. Resd. that in addition to the powers vested in the U. States in Congress, by the present existing articles of Confederation, they be authorized to pass acts for raising a revenue, by levying a duty or duties on all goods or merchandizes of foreign growth or manufacture, imported into any part of the U. States, by Stamps on paper, vellum or parchment, and by a postage on all letters or packages passing through the general post-office, to be applied to such federal purposes as they shall deem proper & expedient; to make rules & regulations for the collection thereof; and the same from time to time, to alter & amend in such manner as they shall think proper: to pass Acts for the regulation of trade & commerce as well with foreign nations as with each other: provided that all punishments, fines, forfeitures & penalties to be incurred for contravening such acts rules and regulations shall be adjudged by the Common law Judiciaries of the State in which any offence contrary to the true intent & meaning of such Acts rules & regulations shall have been committed or perpetrated, with liberty of commencing in the first instance all suits & prosecutions for that purpose in the superior common law Judiciary in such State, subject nevertheless, for the correction of all errors, both in law & fact in rendering Judgment, to an appeal to the Judiciary of the U. States.

3. Resd. that whenever requisitions shall be necessary, instead of the rule for making requisitions mentioned in the articles of Confederation, the United States in Congs. be authorized to make such requisitions in proportion to the whole number of white & other free citizens & inhabitants of every age sex and condition including those bound to servitude for a term of years & three fifths of all other persons not comprehended in the foregoing description, except Indians not paying taxes; that if such requisitions be not complied with, in the time specified therein, to direct the collection thereof in the non complying States & for that purpose to devise and pass acts directing & authorizing the same; provided that none of the powers hereby vested in the U. States in Congs. shall be exercised without the consent of at least   States, and in that pro-

portion if the number of Confederated States should hereafter be increased or diminished.

4. Resd. that the U. States in Congs. be authorized to elect a federal Executive to consist of persons, to continue in office for the term of years, to receive punctually at stated times a fixed compensation for their services, in which no increase or diminution shall be made so as to affect the persons composing the Executive at the time of such increase of diminution, to be paid out of the federal treasury; to be incapable of holding any other office or appointment during their time of service and for   years thereafter; to be ineligible a second time, & removable by Congs. on application by a majority of the Executives of the several States; that the Executives besides their general authority to execute the federal acts ought to appoint all federal officers not otherwise provided for, & to direct all military operations; provided that none of the persons composing the federal Executive shall on any occasion take command of any troops, so as personally to conduct any enterprise as General or in other capacity.

5. Resd. that a federal Judiciary be established to consist of a supreme Tribunal the Judges of which to be appointed by the Executive, & to hold their offices during good behaviour, to receive punctually at stated times a fixed compensation for their services in which no increase or diminution shall be made, so as to affect the persons actually in office at the time of such increase or diminution; that the Judiciary so established shall have authority to hear & determine in the first instance on all impeachments of federal officers, & by way of appeal in the dernier resort in all cases touching the rights of Ambassadors, in all cases of captures from an enemy, in all cases of piracies & felonies on the high Seas, in all cases in which foreigners may be interested, in the construction of any treaty or treaties, or which may arise on any of the Acts for regulation of trade, or the collection of the federal Revenue: that none of the Judiciary shall during the time they remain in office be capable of receiving or holding any other office or appointment during their time of service, or for   thereafter.

6. Resd. that all Acts of the U. States in Congs. made by virtue & in pursuance of the powers hereby & by the articles of Confederation vested in them, and all Treaties made & ratified under the au-

thority of the U. States shall be the supreme law of the respective States so far forth as those Acts or Treaties shall relate to the said States or their Citizens, and that the Judiciary of the several States shall be bound thereby in their decisions, any thing in the respective laws of the Individual States to the contrary notwithstanding; and that if any State, or any body of men in any State shall oppose or prevent ye. carrying into execution such acts or treaties, the federal Executive shall be authorized to call forth ye. power of the Confederated States, or so much thereof as may be necessary to enforce and compel an obedience to such Acts, or an observance of such Treaties.

7. Resd. that provision be made for the admission of new States into the Union.

8. Resd. the rule for naturalization ought to be the same in every State.

9. Resd. that a Citizen of one State committing an offense in another State of the Union, shall be deemed guilty of the same offense as if it had been committed by a Citizen of the State in which the offense was committed.

Adjourned.

4. Amended Randolph Plan
(adopted by Convention July 29)

I. RESOLVED, That the Government of the United States ought to consist of a supreme legislative, judiciary, and executive.

II. RESOLVED, That the legislature consist of two branches.

III. RESOLVED, That the members of the first branch of the legislature ought to be elected by the people of the several states for the term of two years; to be paid out of the publick treasury; to receive an adequate compensation for their services; to be of the age of twenty-five years at least; to be ineligible and incapable of holding any office under the authority of the United States (except those peculiarly belonging to the functions of the first branch) during the term of service of the first branch.

IV. RESOLVED, That the members of the second branch of the legislature of the United States ought to be chosen by the individual legislatures; to be of the age of thirty years at least; to hold their offices for six years, one third to go out biennally; to receive a compensation for the devotion of their time to the publick service; to be ineligible to and incapable of holding any office, under the authority of the United States (except those peculiarly belonging to the functions of the second branch) during the term for which they are elected, and for one year thereafter.

V. RESOLVED, That each branch ought to possess the right of originating acts.

VI. RESOLVED, That the national legislature ought to possess the legislative rights vested in Congress by the confederation; and moreover, to legislate in all cases for the general interests of the union, and also in those to which the states are separately incompetent, or in which the harmony of the United States may be interrupted by the exercise of individual legislation.

VII. RESOLVED, That the legislative acts of the United States, made by virtue and in pursuance of the articles of union, and all treaties made and ratified under the authority of the United States, shall be the supreme law of the respective states, as far as those acts or treaties shall relate to the said states, or their citizens and inhabitants; and that the judiciaries of the several states shall be bound thereby in their decisions, any thing in the respective laws of the individual states to the contrary, notwithstanding.

VIII. RESOLVED, That in the original formation of the legislature of the United States, the first branch thereof shall consist of sixty-five members; of which number

New Hampshire shall send three,
Massachusetts ....eight,
Rhode Island ....one,
Connecticut ....five,
New York ....six,
New Jersey ....four,
Pennsylvania................................eight,
Delaware.....................................one,
Maryland.....................................six,
Virginia......................................ten,
North Carolina ....five,
South Carolina ....five,
Georgia ....three.

But as the present situation of the states may probably alter in the number of their inhabitants, the legislature of the United States shall be authorized, from time to time, to apportion the number of representatives; and in case any of the states shall hereafter be divided, or enlarged by addition of territory, or any two or more states united, or any new states created within the limits of the United States, the legislature of the United States shall possess authority to regulate the number of representatives, in any of the foregoing cases, upon the principle of their number of inhabitants according to the provisions hereafter mentioned, namely—Provided always, that representation ought to be proportioned according to direct taxation. And in order to ascertain the alteration in the direct taxation, which may be required from time to time by the changes in the relative circumstances of the states—

IX. RESOLVED, That a census be taken within six years from the first meeting of the legislature of the United States, and once within the term of every ten years afterwards, of all the inhabitants of the United States, in the manner and according to the ratio recommended by Congress in their resolution of April 18, 1783; and that the legislature of the United States shall proportion the direct taxation accordingly.

X. RESOLVED, That all bills for raising or appropriating money, and for fixing the salaries of the officers of the government of the United States, shall originate in the first branch of the legislature of the United States, and shall not be altered or amended by the second branch; and that no money shall be drawn from the publick treasury, but in pursuance of appropriations to be originated by the first branch.

XI. RESOLVED, That in the second branch of the legislature of the United States, each state shall have an equal vote.

XII. RESOLVED, That a national executive be instituted, to consist of a single person; to be chosen by the national legislature, for the term of seven years; to be ineligible a second time; with power to carry into execution the national laws; to appoint to offices in cases not otherwise provided for; to be removable on impeachment, and conviction of malpractice or neglect of duty; to receive a fixed compensation for the devotion of his time to publick service; to be paid out of the publick treasury.

XIII. RESOLVED, That the national executive shall have a right to negative any legislative act, which shall not be be afterwards passed, unless by two third parts of each branch of the national legislature.

XIV. RESOLVED, That a national judiciary be established, to consist of one supreme tribunal, the judges of which shall be appointed by the second branch of the national legislature; to hold their offices during good behaviour; to receive punctually, at stated times, a fixed compensation for their services, in which no diminution shall be made, so as to affect the persons actually in office at the time of such diminution.

XV. RESOLVED, That the national legislature be empowered to appoint inferior tribunals.

XVI. RESOLVED, That the jurisdiction of the national judiciary shall extend to cases arising under laws passed by the general legislature; and to such other questions as involve the national peace and harmony.

XVII. RESOLVED, That provision ought to be made for the admission of states lawfully arising within the limits of the United States, whether from a voluntary junction of government and territory, or otherwise, with the consent of a number of voices in the national legislature less than the whole.

XVIII. RESOLVED, That a republican form of government shall be guarantied to each state; and that each state shall be protected against foreign and domestick violence.

XIX. RESOLVED, That provision ought to be made for the amendment of the articles of union, whensoever it shall seem necessary.

XX. RESOLVED, That the legislative, executive, and judiciary powers, within the several states, and of the national government, ought to be bound, by oath, to support the articles of union.

XXI. RESOLVED, That the amendments which shall be offered to the confederation by the convention ought, at a proper time or times after the approbation of Congress, to be submitted to an assembly or assemblies of representatives, recommended by the several legislatures, to be expressly chosen by the people to consider and decide thereon.

XXII. RESOLVED, That the representation in the second branch of the legislature of the United States consist of two members from each state, who shall vote per capita.

XXIII. RESOLVED, That it be an instruction to the committee, to whom were referred the proceedings of the convention for the establishment of a national government, to receive a clause or clauses, requiring certain qualifications of property and citizenship, in the United States, for the executive, the judiciary, and the members of both branches of the legislature of the United States.

5. Committee on Detail Draft (presented August 6)

ARTICLE I

The stile of the Government shall be, "The United States of America."

II

The Government shall consist of supreme legislative, executive; and judicial powers.

III

The legislative power shall be vested in a Congress, to consist of two separate and distinct bodies of men, a House of Representatives and a Senate; each of which shall in all cases have a negative on the other. The Legislature shall meet on the first Monday in December every year.

IV

Sect. 1. The members of the House of Representatives shall be chosen every second year, by the people of the several States comprehended within this Union. The qualifications of the electors shall be the same, from time to time, as those of the electors in the several States, of the most numerous branch of their own legislatures.

Sect. 2. Every member of the House of Representatives shall be of the age of twenty five years at least; shall have been a citizen in the United States for at least three years before his election; and shall be, at the time of his election, a resident of the State in which he shall be chosen.

Sect. 3. The House of Representatives shall, at its first formation, and until the number of citizens and inhabitants shall be taken in the manner herein after described, consist of sixty five Members, of whom three shall be chosen in New-Hampshire, eight in Massachusetts, one in Rhode-Island and Providence Plantations, five in Connecticut, six in New-York, four in New-Jersey, eight in Pennsylvania, one in Delaware, six in Maryland, ten in Virginia, five in North-Carolina, five in South-Carolina, and three in Georgia.

Sect. 4. As the proportions of numbers in different States will alter from time to time; as some of the States may hereafter be divided; as others may be enlarged by addition of territory; as two or more States may be united; as new States will be erected within the limits of the United States, the Legislature shall, in each of these cases, regulate the number of representatives by the number of inhabitants, according to the provisions herein after made, at the rate of one for every forty thousand.

Sect. 5. All bills for raising or appropriating money, and for fixing the salaries of the officers of Government, shall originate in the House of Representatives, and shall not be altered or amended by the Senate. No money shall be drawn from the Public Treasury, but in pursuance of appropriations that shall originate in the House of Representatives.

Sect. 6. The House of Representatives shall have the sole power of impeachment. It shall choose its Speaker and other officers.

Sect. 7. Vacancies in the House of Representatives shall be supplied by writs of election from the executive authority of the State, in the representation from which it shall happen.

V

Sect. 1. The Senate of the United States shall be chosen by the Legislatures of the several States. Each Legislature shall chuse two members. Vacancies may be supplied by the Executive until the next meeting of the Legislature. Each member shall have one vote.

Sect. 2. The Senators shall be chosen for six years; but immediately after the first election they shall be divided, by lot, into three classes, as nearly as may be, numbered one, two and three. The seats of the members of the first class shall be vacated at the expiration of the second year, of the second class at the expiration of the fourth year, of the third class at the expiration of the sixth year, so that a third part of the members may be chosen every second year.

Sect. 3. Every member of the Senate shall be of the age of thirty years at least; shall have been a citizen in the United States for at least four years before his election; and shall be, at the time of his election, a resident of the State for which he shall be chosen.

Sect. 4. The Senate shall chuse its own President and other officers.

VI

Sect. 1. The times and places and manner of holding

the elections of the members of each House shall be prescribed by the Legislature of each State; but their provisions concerning them may, at any time be altered by the Legislature of the United States.

Sect. 2. The Legislature of the United States shall have authority to establish such uniform qualifications of the members of each House, with regard to property, as to the said Legislature shall seem expedient.

Sect. 3. In each House a majority of the members shall constitute a quorum to do business; but a smaller number may adjourn from day to day.

Sect. 4. Each House shall be the judge of the elections, returns and qualifications of its own members.

Sect. 5. Freedom of speech and debate in the Legislature shall not be impeached or questioned in any Court or place out of the Legislature; and the members of each House shall, in all cases, except treason felony and breach of the peace, be privileged from arrest during their attendance at Congress, and in going to and returning from it.

Sect. 6. Each House may determine the rules of its proceedings; may punish its members for disorderly behaviour; and may expel a member.

Sect. 7. The House of Representatives, and the Senate, when it shall be acting in a legislative capacity, shall keep a journal of their proceedings, and shall, from time to time, publish them: and the yeas and nays of the members of each House, on any question, shall at the desire of one-fifth part of the members present, be entered on the journal.

Sect. 8. Neither House, without the consent of the other, shall adjourn for more than three days, nor to any other place than that at which the two Houses are sitting. But this regulation shall not extend to the Senate, when it shall exercise the powers mentioned in the   article.

Sect. 9. The members of each House shall be ineligible to, and incapable of holding any office under the authority of the United States, during the time for which they shall respectively be elected: and the members of the Senate shall be ineligible to, and incapable of holding any such office for one year afterwards.

Sect. 10. The members of each House shall receive a compensation for their services, to be ascertained and paid by the State, in which they shall be chosen.

Sect. 11. The enacting stile of the laws of the United States shall be. "Be it enacted by the Senate and Representatives in Congress assembled."

Sect. 12. Each House shall possess the right of originating bills, except in the cases beforementioned.

Sect. 13. Every bill, which shall have passed the House of Representatives and the Senate, shall, before it become a law, be presented to the President of the United States for his revision: if, upon such revision, he approve of it, he shall signify his approbation by signing it: But if, upon such revision, it shall appear to him improper for being passed into a law, he shall return it, together with his objections against it, to that House in which it shall have originated, who shall enter the objections at large on their journal and proceed to reconsider the bill. But if after such reconsideration, two thirds of that House shall, notwithstanding the objections of the President, agree to pass it, it shall together with his objections, be sent to the other House, by which it shall likewise be reconsidered, and if approved by two thirds of the other House also, it shall become a law. But in all such cases, the votes of both Houses shall be determined by yeas and nays; and the names of the persons voting for or against the bill shall be entered on the journal of each House respectively. If any bill shall not be returned by the President within seven days after it shall have been presented to him, it shall be a law, unless the legislature, by their adjournment, prevent its return; in which case it shall not be a law.

VII

Sect. 1. The Legislature of the United States shall have the power to lay and collect taxes, duties, imposts and excises;

To regulate commerce with foreign nations, and among the several States;

To establish an uniform rule of naturalization throughout the United States;

To coin money;

To regulate the value of foreign coin;

To fix the standard of weights and measures;

To establish Post-offices;

To borrow money, and emit bills on the credit of the United States;

To appoint a Treasurer by ballot;

To constitute tribunals inferior to the Supreme Court;

To make rules concerning captures on land and water;

To declare the law and punishment of piracies and felonies committed on the high seas, and the punishment of counterfeiting the coin of the United States, and of offenses against the law of nations;

To subdue a rebellion in any State, on the application of its legislature;

To make war;

To raise armies;

To build and equip fleets;

To call forth the aid of the militia, in order to execute the laws of the Union, enforce treaties, suppress insurrections, and repel invasions;

And to make all laws that shall be necessary and proper for carrying into execution the foregoing powers, and all other powers vested, by this Constitution, in the government of the United States, or in any department or officer thereof;

Sect. 2. Treason against the United States shall consist only in levying war against the United States, or any of them; and in adhering to the enemies of the United States, or any of them. The Legislature of the United States shall have power to declare the punishment of treason. No person shall be convicted of treason, unless on the testimony of two witnesses. No attainder of treason shall work corruption of blood, nor forfeiture, except during the life of the person attainted.

Sect. 3. The proportions of direct taxation shall be regulated by the whole number of white and other free citizens and inhabitants of every age, sex and condition, including those bound to servitude for a term of years, and three fifths of all other persons not comprehended in the foregoing description, (except Indians not paying taxes) which number shall, within six years after the first meeting of the Legislature, and within the term of every ten years afterwards, be taken in such manner as the said Legislature shall direct.

Sect. 4. No tax or duty shall be laid by the Legislature on articles exported from any State; nor on the migration or importation of such persons as the several States shall think proper to admit; nor shall such migration or importation be prohibited.

Sect. 5. No capitation tax shall be laid, unless in proportion to the Census hereinbefore directed to be taken.

Sect. 6. No navigation act shall be passed without the assent of two thirds of the members present in the each House.

Sect. 7. The United States shall not grant any title of Nobility.

VIII

The Acts of the Legislature of the United States made in pursuance of this Constitution, and all treaties made under the authority of the United States shall be the supreme law of the several States, and of their citizens and inhabitants; and the judges in the several States shall be bound thereby in their decisions; any thing in the Constitutions or laws of the several States to the contrary notwithstanding.

IX

Sect. 1. The Senate of the United States shall have power to make treaties, and to appoint Ambassadors, and Judges of the Supreme Court.

Sect. 2. In all disputes and controversies now subsisting, or that may hereafter subsist between two or more States, respecting jurisdiction or territory, the Senate shall possess the following powers. Whenever the Legislature, or the Executive authority, or lawful agent of any State, in controversy with another, shall by memorial to the Senate, state the matter in question, and apply for a hearing; notice of such memorial and application shall be given by order of the Senate, to the Legislature or the Executive authority of the other State in Controversy. The Senate shall also assign a day for the appearance of the parties, by their agents, before the House. The Agents shall be directed to appoint, by joint consent, commissioners or judges to constitute a Court for hearing and determining the matter in question. But if the Agents cannot agree, the Senate shall name three persons out of each of the several States; and from the list of such persons each party shall alternately strike out one, until the number shall be reduced to thirteen; and from that number not less than seven nor more than nine names, as the Senate shall direct, shall in their presence, be drawn out by lot; and the persons whose names shall be so drawn, or any five of them shall be commissioners or Judges to hear and finally determine the controversy; provided a majority of the Judges, who shall hear the cause, agree in the determination. If either party shall neglect to attend at the day assigned, without shewing sufficient reasons for not attending, or being present shall refuse to strike, the Senate shall proceed to nominate three persons out of each State, and the Clerk of the Senate shall strike in behalf of the party absent or refusing. If any of the parties shall refuse to submit to the authority of such Court; or shall not appear to prosecute or defend their claim or cause, the Court shall nevertheless proceed to pronounce judgment. The judgment shall be final and conclusive. The proceedings shall be transmitted to the President of the Senate, and shall be lodged among the public records, for the security of the parties concerned. Every Commissioner shall, before he sit in judgment, take an oath, to be administred by one of the Judges of the Supreme or Superior Court of the State where the cause shall be tried, "well and truly to hear and determine the matter in question according to the best of his judgment, without favor, affection, or hope of reward."

Sect. 3. All controversies concerning lands claimed under different grants of two or more States, whose jurisdictions, as they respect such lands shall have been decided or adjusted subsequent to such grants, or any of them, shall, on application to the Senate, be finally determined, as near as may be, in the same manner as is before prescribed for deciding controversies between different States.

X

Sect. 1. The Executive Power of the United States shall be vested in a single person. His stile shall be, "The President of the United States of America," and his title shall be, "His Excellency." He shall be elected by ballot by the Legislature. He shall hold his office during the term of seven years; but shall not be elected a second time.

Sect. 2. He shall, from time to time, give information to the Legislature, of the state of the Union: he may recommend to their consideration such measures as he shall judge necessary, and expedient: he may convene them on extraordinary occasions. In case of disagreement between the two Houses, with regard to the time of adjournment, he may adjourn them to such time as he thinks proper: he shall take care that the laws of the United States be duly and faithfully executed: he shall commission all the officers of the United States; and shall appoint officers in all cases not otherwise provided for by this Constitution. He shall receive Ambassadors, and may correspond with the supreme Executives of the several States. He shall have power to grant reprieves and pardons; but his pardon shall not be pleadable in bar of an impeachment. He shall be commander in chief of the Army and Navy of the United States, and of the Militia of the several States. He shall, at stated times, receive for his services, a compensation, which shall neither be increased nor diminished during his continuance in office. Before he shall enter on the duties of his department, he shall take the following oath or affirmation, "I _____ solemnly swear, (or affirm) that that I will faithfully execute the office of President of the United States of America." He shall be removed from his office on impeachment by the House of Representatives, and conviction in the supreme Court, of treason, bribery, or corruption. In case of his removal as aforesaid, death, resignation, or disability to discharge the powers and duties of his office, the President of the Senate shall exercise those powers and duties, until another President of the United States be chosen, or until the disability of the President be removed.

XI

Sect. 1. The Judicial Power of the United States shall be vested in one Supreme Court, and in such inferior Courts as shall, when necessary, from time to time, be constituted by the Legislature of the United States.

Sect. 2. The Judges of the Supreme Court, and of the Inferior Courts, shall hold their offices during good behaviour. They shall, at stated times, receive for their services, a compensation, which shall not be diminished during their continuance in office.

Sect. 3. The Jurisdiction of the Supreme Court shall extend to all cases arising under laws passed by the Legislature of the United States; to all cases affecting Ambassadors, other Public Ministers and Consuls; to the trial of impeachments of officers of the United States; to all cases of Admiralty and maritime jurisdiction; to controversies between two or more States, (except such as shall regard Territory or Jurisdiction) between a State and Citizens of another State, between Citizens of different States, and between a State or the Citizens thereof and foreign States, citizens or subjects. In cases of impeachment, cases affecting Ambassadors, other Public Ministers and Consuls, and those in which a State shall be party, this jurisdiction shall be original. In all the other cases beforementioned, it shall be appellate, with such exceptions and under such regulations as the Legislature shall make. The Legislature may assign any part of the jurisdiction abovementioned (except the trial of the President of the United States) in the manner, and under the limitations which it shall think proper, to such Inferior Courts, as it shall constitute from time to time.

Sect. 4. The trial of all criminal offences (except in cases of impeachments) shall be in the State where they shall be committed; and shall be by Jury.

Sect. 5. Judgment, in cases of Impeachment, shall not extend further than to removal from office, and disqualification to hold and enjoy any office of honour, trust or profit, under the United States. But the party convicted shall, nevertheless be liable and subject to indictment, trial, judgment and punishment according to law.

XII

No State shall coin money; nor grant letters of marque and reprisal; nor enter into any Treaty, alliance, or confederation; nor grant any title of Nobility.

XIII

No State, without the consent of the Legislature of the United States, shall emit bills of credit, or make any thing but specie a tender in payment of debts; nor lay imposts or duties on imports; nor keep troops or ships of war in time of peace; nor enter into any agreement or compact with another State, or with any foreign power; nor engage in any war, unless it shall be actually invaded by enemies, or the danger of invasion be so imminent, as not to admit of delay, until the Legislature of the United States can be consulted.

XIV

The Citizens of each State shall be entitled to all privileges and immunities of citizens in the several States.

XV

Any person charged with treason, felony or high misdemeanor in any State, who shall flee from justice, and shall be found in any other State, shall, on demand of the Executive power of the State from which he fled, be delivered up and removed to the State having jurisdiction of the offence.

XVI

Full faith shall be given in each State to the acts of the Legislatures, and to the records and judicial proceedings of the Courts and magistrates of every other State.

XVII

New States lawfully constituted or established within the limits of the United States may be admitted, by the Legislature, into this Government; but to such admission the consent of two thirds of the members present in each House shall be necessary. If a new State shall arise within limits of any of the present States, the consent of the Legislatures of such States shall be also necessary to its admission. If the admission be consented to, the new States shall be admitted on the same terms with the original States. But the Legislature may make conditions with the new States, concerning the public debt which shall be then subsisting.

XVIII

The United States shall guaranty to each State a Republican form of Government; and shall protect each State against foreign invasions, and, on the application of its Legislature, against domestic violence.

XIX

On the application of the Legislatures of two thirds of the States in the Union, for an amendment of this Constitution, the Legislature of the United States shall call a Convention for that purpose.

XX

The members of the Legislatures, and the Executive and Judicial officers of the United States, and of the several States, shall be bound by oath to support this Constitution.

XXI

The ratifications of the Conventions of   States shall be sufficient for organizing this Constitution.

XXII

This Constitution shall be laid before the United States in Congress assembled, for their approbation; and it is the opinion of this Convention, that it should be afterwards submitted to a Convention chosen, under the recommendation of its legislature, in order to receive the ratification of such Convention.

XXIII

To introduce this government, it is the opinion of this Convention, that each assenting Convention should notify its assent and ratification to the United States in Congress assembled; that Congress, after receiving the assent and ratification of the Conventions of   States, should appoint and publish a day, as early as may be, and appoint a place for commencing proceedings under this Constitution; that after such publication, the Legislatures of the several States should elect members of the Senate, and direct the election of members of the House of Representatives; and that the members of the Legislature should meet at the time and place assigned by Congress, and should, as soon as may be, after their meeting, choose the President of the United States, and proceed to execute this Constitution.

6. Committee on Style Draft
(presented September 12)

WE, THE PEOPLE OF THE UNITED STATES, IN ORDER TO FORM a more perfect union, to establish justice, insure domestic tranquility, provide for the common defence, promote the general welfare, and secure the blessings of liberty to ourselves and our posterity, do ordain and establish this Constitution for the United States of America.

ARTICLE I

Sect. 1. ALL legislative powers herein granted shall be vested in a Congress of the United States, which shall consist of a Senate and House of Representatives.

Sect. 2. The House of Representatives shall be composed of members chosen every second year by the people of the several states, and the electors in each state shall have the qualifications requisite for electors of the most numerous branch of the state legislature.

No person shall be a representative who shall not have attained to the age of twenty-five years, and been seven years a citizen of the United States, and who shall not, when elected, be an inhabitant of that state in which he shall be chosen.

Representatives and direct taxes shall be apportioned among the several states which may be included within this Union, according to their respective numbers, which shall be determined by adding to the whole number of free persons, including those bound to servitude for a term of years, and excluding Indians not taxed, three-fifths of all other persons. The actual enumeration shall be made within three years after the first meeting of the Congress of the United States, and within every subsequent term of ten years, in such manner as they shall by law direct. The number of representatives shall not exceed one for every forty thousand, but each state shall have at least one representative: and until such enumeration shall be made, the state of New-Hampshire shall be entitled to chuse three, Masschusetts eight, Rhode-Island and Providence Plantations one, Connecticut five, New-York six, New-Jersey four, Pennsylvania eight, Deleware one, Maryland six, Virginia ten, North-Carolina five, South-Carolina five, and Georgia three.

When vacancies happen in the representation from any state, the Executive authority thereof shall issue writs of election to fill such vacancies.

The House of Representatives shall choose their Speaker and other officers; and they shall have the sole power of impeachment.

Sect. 3. The Senate of the United States shall be composed of two senators from each state, chosen by the legislature thereof, for six years: and each senator shall have one vote. Immediately after they shall be assembled in consequence of the first election, they shall be divided [by lot] as equally as may be into three classes. The seats of the senators of the first class shall be vacated at the expiration of the second year, of the second class at the expiration of the fourth year, and of the third class at the expiration of the sixth year, so that one-third may be chosen every second year: and if vacancies happen by resignation, or otherwise, during the recess of the Legislature of any state, the Executive thereof may make temporary appointments until the next meeting of the Legislature.

No person shall be a senator who shall not have attained to the age of thirty years, and been nine years a citizen of the United States, and who shall not, when elected, be an inhabitant of that state for which he shall be chosen.

The Vice-President of the United States shall be, ex officio President of the senate, but shall have no vote, unless they be equally divided.

The Senate shall choose their other officers, and also a President pro tempore, in the absence of the Vice-President, or when he shall exercise the office of President of the United States.

The Senate shall have the sole power to try all impeachments. When sitting for that purpose, they shall be on oath. When the President of the United States is tried, the Chief Justice shall preside: And no person shall be convicted without the concurrence of two-thirds of the members present.

Judgment in cases of impeachment shall not extend further than to removal from office, and disqualification to hold and enjoy any office of honor, trust or profit under the United States: but the party convicted shall nevertheless be liable and subject to indictment, trial, judgment and punishment, according to law.

Sect. 4. The times, places and manner of holding elections for senators and representatives, shall be prescribed in each state by the legislature thereof: but the Congress may at any time by law make or alter such regulations.

The Congress shall assemble at least once in every year, and such meeting shall be on the first Monday in December, unless they shall by law appoint a different day.

Sect. 5. Each house shall be the judge of the elections, returns and qualifications of its own members, and a majority of each shall constitute a quorum to do business: but a smaller number may adjourn from day to day, and may be authorized to compel the attendance of absent members, in such manner, and under such penalties as each house may provide.

Each house may determine the rules of its proceedings; punish its members for disorderly behaviour, and, with the concurrence of two-thirds, expel a member.

Each house shall keep a journal of its proceedings, and from time to time publish the same, excepting such parts as may in their judgment require secrecy; and the yeas and nays of the members of either house on any question shall, at the desire of one-fifth of those present, be entered on the journal.

Neither house, during the session of Congress shall, without the consent of the other, adjourn for more than three days, nor to any other place than that in which the two houses shall be sitting.

Sect. 6. The senators and representatives shall receive a compensation for their services, to be ascertained by law, and paid out of the treasury of the United States. They shall in all cases, except treason, felony and breach of the peace, be privileged from arrest during their attendance at the session of their respective houses, and in going to and returning from the same; and for any speech or debate in either house, they shall not be questioned in any other place.

No senator or representative shall, during the time for which he was elected, be appointed to any civil office under the authority of the United States, which shall have been created, or the emoluments whereof shall have been encreased during such time; and no person holding any office under the United States, shall be a member of either house during his continuance in office.

Sect. 7. The enacting stile of the laws shall be, "Be it enacted by the senators and representatives in Congress assembled."

All bills for raising revenue shall originate in the house of representatives: but the senate may propose or concur with amendments as on other bills.

Every bill which shall have passed the house of representatives and the senate, shall, before it become a law, be presented to the president of the United States. If he approve he shall sign it, but if not he shall return it, with his objections to that house in which it shall have originated, who shall enter the objections at large on their journal, and proceed to reconsider it. If after such reconsideration two-thirds of that house shall agree to pass the bill, it shall be sent, together with the objections, to the other house, by which it shall likewise be reconsidered, and if approved by two-thirds of that house, it shall become a law. But in all such cases the votes of both houses shall be determined by yeas and nays, and the names of the persons voting for and against the bill shall be entered on the journal of each house respectively. If any bill shall not be returned by the President within ten days (Sundays excepted) after it shall have been presented to him, the same shall be a law, in like manner as if he had signed it, unless the Congress by their adjournment prevent its return, in which case it shall not be a law.

Every order, resolution, or vote to which the concurrence of the Senate and House of Representatives may be necessary (except on a question of adjournment) shall be presented to the President of the United States; and before the same shall take effect, shall be approved by him, or, being disapproved by him, shall be repassed by three-fourths of the Senate and House of Representatives, according to the rules and limitations prescribed in the case of a bill.

Sect. 8. The Congress may by joint ballot appoint a treasurer. They shall have power

To lay and collect taxes, duties, imposts and excises; to pay the debts and provide for the common defence and general welfare of the United States.

To borrow money on the credit of the United States.

To regulate commerce with foreign nations, among the several states, and with the Indian tribes.

To establish an uniform rule of naturalization, and uniform laws on the subject of bankruptcies throughout the United States.

To coin money, regulate the value thereof, and of foreign coin, and fix the standard of weights and measures.

To provide for the punishment of counterfeiting the securities and current coin of the United States.

To establish post offices and post roads.

To promote the progress of science and useful arts, by securing for limited times to authors and inventors the exclusive right to their respective writings and discoveries.

To constitute tribunals inferior to the supreme court.

To define and punish piracies and felonies committed on the high seas, and [punish] offences against the law of nations.

To declare war, grant letters of marque and reprisal, and make rules concerning captures on land and water.

To raise and support armies: but no appropriation of money to that use shall be for a longer term than two years.

To provide and maintain a navy.

To make rules for the government and regulation of the land and naval forces.

To provide for calling forth the militia to execute the laws of the union, suppress insurrections and repel invasions.

To provide for organizing, arming and disciplining the militia, and for governing such part of them as may be employed in the service of the United States, reserving to the States respectively, the appointment of the officers, and the authority of training the militia according to the discipline prescribed by Congress.

To exercise exclusive legislation in all cases whatsoever, over such district (not exceeding ten miles square) as may, by cession of particular States, and the acceptance of Congress, become the seat of the government of the United States, and to exercise like authority over all places purchased by the consent of the legislature of the state in which the same shall be, for the erection of forts, magazines, arsenals, dock-yards, and other needful buildings— And

To make all laws which shall be necessary and proper for carrying into execution the foregoing powers, and all other powers vested by this constitution in the government of the United States, or in any department or officer thereof.

Sect. 9. The migration or importation of such persons as the several states now existing shall think proper to admit, shall not be prohibited by the Congress prior to the year one thousand eight hundred and eight, but a tax or duty may be imposed on such importation, not exceeding ten dollars for each person.

The privilege of the writ of habeas corpus shall not be suspended, unless when in cases of rebellion or invasion the public safety may require it.

No bill of attainder shall be passed, nor any ex post facto law.

No capitation tax shall be laid, unless in proportion to the census herein before directed to be taken.

No tax or duty shall be laid on articles exported from any state.

No money shall be drawn from the treasury, but in consequence of appropriations made by law.

No title of nobility shall be granted by the United States. And no person holding any office of profit or trust under them, shall, without the consent of the Congress, accept of any present, emolument, office, or title, of any kind whatever, from any king, prince, or foreign state.

Sect. 10. No state shall coin money, nor emit bills of credit, nor make any thing but gold or silver coin a tender in payment of debts, nor pass any bill of attainder, nor ex post facto laws, nor laws altering or impairing the obligation of contracts; nor grant letters of marque and reprisal, nor enter into any treaty, alliance, or confederation, nor grant any title of nobility.

No state shall, without the consent of Congress, lay imposts or duties on imports or exports, nor with such consent, but to the use of the treasury of the United States. Nor keep troops nor ships of war in time of peace, nor enter into any agreement or compact with another state, nor with any foreign power. Nor engage in any war, unless it shall be actually invaded by enemies, or the danger of invasion be so imminent, as not to admit of delay until the Congress can be consulted.

II

Sect. 1. The executive power shall be vested in a president of the United States of America. He shall hold his office during the term of four years, and, together with the vice-president, chosen for the same term, be elected in the following manner:

Each state shall appoint, in such manner as the legislature thereof may direct, a number of electors, equal to the whole number of senators and representatives to which the state may be entitled in Congress: but no senator or representative shall be appointed an elector, nor any person holding an office of trust or profit under the United States.

The electors shall meet in their respective states, and vote by ballot for two persons, of whom one at least shall not be an inhabitant of the same state with themselves. And they shall make a list of all the persons voted for, and of the number of votes for each; which list they shall sign and certify, and transmit sealed to the seat of the general government, directed to the president of the senate. The president of the senate shall in the presence of the senate and house of representatives open all the certificates, and the votes shall then be counted. The person having the greatest number of votes shall be the president, if such number be a majority of the whole number of electors appointed; and if there be more than one who have such majority, and have an equal number of votes, then the house of representatives shall immediately chuse by ballot one of them for president; and if no person have a majority, then from the five highest on the list the said house shall in like manner choose the president. But in choosing the president, the votes shall be taken by states and not per capita, the representation from each state having one vote. A quorum for this purpose shall consist of a member or members from two-thirds of the states, and a majority of all the states shall be necessary to a choice. In every case, after the choice of the president by the representatives, the person having the greatest number of votes of the electors shall be the vice-president. But if there should remain two or more who have equal votes, the senate shall choose from them by ballot the vice-president.

The Congress may determine the time of chusing the electors, and the time in which they shall give their votes; but the election shall be on the same day throughout the United States.

No person except a natural born citizen, or a citizen of the United States, at the time of the adoption of this constitution, shall be eligible to the office of president; neither shall any person be eligible to that office who shall not have attained to the age of thirty-five years, and been fourteen years a resident within the United States.

In case of the removal of the president from office, or of his death, resignation, or inability to discharge the powers and duties of the said office, the same shall devolve on the vice-president, and the Congress may by law provide for the case of removal, death, resignation or inability, both of the president and vice-president, declaring what officer shall then act as president, and such officer shall act accordingly, until the disability be removed, or the period for chusing another president arrive.

The president shall, at stated times, receive a fixed compensation for his services, which shall neither be encreased nor diminished during the period for which he shall have been elected.

Before he enter on the execution of his office, he shall take the following oath or affirmation: "I _____, do solemnly swear (or affirm) that I will faithfully execute the office of president of the United States, and will to the best of my judgment and power, preserve, protect and defend the constitution of the United States."

Sect. 2. The president shall be commander in chief of the army and navy of the United States, and of the militia of the several States when called into the actual service of the United States, he may require the opinion, in writing, of the principal officer in each of the executive departments, upon any subject relating to the duties of their respective offices, and he shall have power to grant reprieves and par-

dons for offences against the United States, except in cases of impeachment.

He shall have power, by and with the advice and consent of the senate, to make treaties, provided two-thirds of the senators present concur; and he shall nominate, and by and with the advice and consent of the senate, shall appoint ambassadors, other public ministers and consuls, judges of the supreme court, and all other officers of the United States, whose appointments are not herein otherwise provided for.

The president shall have power to fill up all vacancies that may happen during the recess of the senate, by granting commissions which shall expire at the end of their next session.

Sect. 3. He shall from time to time give to the Congress information of the state of the union, and recommend to their consideration such measures as he shall judge necessary and expedient: he may, on extraordinary occasions, convene both houses, or either of them, and in case of disagreement between them, with respect to the time of adjournment, he may adjourn them to such time as he shall think proper: he shall receive ambassadors and other public ministers: he shall take care that the laws be faithfully executed, and shall commission all the officers of the United States.

Sect. 4. The president, vice-president and all civil officers of the United States, shall be removed from office on impeachment for, and conviction of treason, bribery, or other high crimes and misdemeanors.

III

Sect. 1. The judicial power of the United States, both in law and equity, shall be vested in one supreme court, and in such inferior courts as the Congress may from time to time ordain and establish. The judges, both of the supreme and inferior courts, shall hold their offices during good behaviour, and shall, at stated times, receive for their services, a compensation, which shall not be diminished during their continuance in office.

Sect. 2. The judicial power shall extend to all cases, both in law and equity, arising under this constitution, the laws of the United States, and treaties made, or which shall be made, under their authority. To all cases affecting ambassadors, other public ministers and consuls. To all cases of admiralty and maritime jurisdiction. To controversies to which the United States shall be a party. To controversies between two or more States; between a state and citizens of another state; between citizens of different States; between citizens of the same state claiming lands under grants of different States, and between a state, or the citizens thereof, and foreign States, citizens or subjects.

In cases affecting ambassadors, other public ministers and consuls, and those in which a state shall be party, the supreme court shall have original jurisdiction. In all the other cases before mentioned, the supreme court shall have appellate jurisdiction, both as to law and fact, with such exceptions, and under such regulations as the Congress shall make.

The trial of all crimes, except in cases of impeachment, shall be by jury; and such trial shall be held in the state where the said crimes shall have been committed; but when not committed within any state, the trial shall be at such place or places as the Congress may by law have directed.

Sect. 3. Treason against the United States, shall consist only in levying war against them, or in adhering to their enemies, giving them aid and comfort. No person shall be convicted of treason unless on the testimony of two witnesses to the same overt act, or on confession in open court.

The Congress shall have power to declare the punishment of treason, but no attainder of treason shall work corruption of blood nor forfeiture, except during the life of the person attainted.

IV

Sect. 1. Full faith and credit shall be given in each state to the public acts, records, and judicial proceedings of every other state. And the Congress may by general laws prescribe the manner in which such acts, records and proceedings shall be proved, and the effect thereof.

Sect. 2. The citizens of each state shall be entitled to all privileges and immunities of citizens of the several states.

A person charged in any state with treason, felony, or other crime, who shall flee from justice, and be found in another state, shall on demand of the executive authority of the state from which he fled be delivered up, and removed to the state having jurisdiction of the crime.

No person legally held to service or labour in one state, escaping into another, shall in consequence of regulations subsisting therein be discharged from such service or labor, but shall be delivered up on claim of the party to whom such service or labour may be due.

Sect. 3. New states may be admitted by the Congress into this union; but no new state shall be formed or erected within the jurisdiction of any other state; nor any state be formed by the junction of two or more states, or parts of states, without the consent of the legislatures of the states concerned as well as of the Congress.

The Congress shall have power to dispose of and make all needful rules and regulations respecting the territory or other property belonging to the United States: and nothing in this Constitution shall be so construed as to prejudice any claims of the United States, or of any particular state.

Sect. 4. The United States shall guarantee to every state in this union a Republican form of government, and shall protect each of them against invasion; and on application of the legislature or executive, against domestic violence.

V

The Congress, whenever two-thirds of both houses shall deem necessary, or on the application of two-thirds of the legislatures of the several states, shall propose amendments to this constitution, which shall be valid to all intents and purposes, as part thereof, when the same shall have been ratified by three-fourths at least of the legislatures of the several states, or by conventions in three-fourths thereof, as the one or the other mode of ratification may be proposed by the Congress: Provided, that no amendment which may be made prior to the year 1808 shall in any manner affect the   and   section of   article

VI

All debts contracted and engagements entered into before the adoption of this Constitution shall be as valid against the United States under this Constitution as under the confederation.

This constitution, and the laws of the United States which shall be made in pursuance thereof; and all treaties made, or which shall be made, under the authority of the United States, shall be the supreme law of the land; and the judges in every state shall be bound thereby, any thing in the constitution or laws of any state to the contrary notwithstanding.

The senators and representatives beforementioned, and the members of the several state legislatures, and all executive and judicial officers, both of the United States and of the several States, shall be bound by oath or affirmation, to support this constitution; but no religious test shall ever be required as a qualification to any office or public trust under the United States.

VII

The ratification of the conventions of nine States, shall be sufficient for the establishment of this constitution between the States so ratifying the same.

Drafts of the Bill of Rights

1. House Select Committee Draft
(presented July 28, 1789)

Mr. VINING, *from the Committee of eleven, to whom it was referred to take the subject of* AMENDMENTS *to the* CONSTITUTION *of the* UNITED STATES, *generally into their consideration, and to report thereupon, made a report, which was read, and is as followeth:*

In the introductory paragraph before the words, "*We the people*," add, "Government being intended for the benefit of the people, and the rightful establishment thereof being derived from their authority alone."

ART. 1, SEC. 2, PAR. 3—Strike out all between the words, "direct" and "and until such," and instead thereof insert, "After the first enumeration there shall be one representative for every thirty thousand until the number shall amount to one hundred; after which the proportion shall be so regulated by Congress that the number of Representatives shall never be less than one hundred, nor more than one hundred and seventy-five, but each State shall always have at least one Representative."

ART. I, SEC. 6—Between the words "United States," and "shall in all cases," strike out "they," and insert, "But no law varying the compensation shall take effect until an election of Representatives shall have intervened. The "members.""

ART. I, SEC. 9—Between PAR. 2 and 3 insert, "No religion shall be established by law, nor shall the equal rights of conscience be infringed."

"The freedom of speech, and of the press, and the right of the people peaceably to assemble and consult for their common good, and to apply to the government for redress of grievances, shall not be infringed."

"A well regulated militia, composed of the body of the people, being the best security of a free State, the right of the people to keep and bear arms shall not be infringed, but no person religiously scrupulous shall be compelled to bear arms."

"No soldier shall in time of peace be quartered in any house without the consent of the owner, nor in time of war but in a manner to be prescribed by law."

"No person shall be subject, except in case of impeachment, to more than one trial or one punishment for the same offence, nor shall be compelled to be a witness against himself, nor be deprived of life, liberty, or property without due process of law; nor shall private property be taken for public use without just compensation."

"Excessive bail shall not be required, nor excessive fines imposed, nor cruel and unusual punishments inflicted."

"The right of the people to be secure in their person, houses, papers and effects, shall not be violated by warrants issuing, without probable cause supported by oath or affirmation, and not particularly describing the places to be searched, and the persons or things to be seized."

"The enumeration in this Constitution of certain rights shall not be construed to deny or disparage others retained by the people."

ART. I, SEC. 10, between the 1st and 2d PAR. insert, "No State shall infringe the equal rights of conscience, nor the freedom of speech, or of the press, nor of the right of trial by jury in criminal cases."

ART. 3, SEC. 2, add to the 2d PAR. "But no appeal to such court shall be allowed, where the value in controversy shall not amount to one thousand dollars; nor shall any fact, triable by a Jury according to the course of the common law, be otherwise reexaminable than according to the rules of common law."

ART. 3, SEC. 2—Strike out the whole of the 3d paragraph, and insert—"In all criminal prosecutions the accused shall enjoy the right to a speedy and public trial, to be informed of the nature and cause of the accusation, to be confronted with the witnesses against him, to have compulsory process for obtaining witnesses in his favor, and to have the assistance of counsel for his defence."

"The trial of all crimes (except in cases of impeachment, and in cases arising in the land or naval forces, or in the militia, when in actual service in time of war or public danger) shall be by an impartial jury of freeholders of the vicinage, with the requisite of unanimity for conviction, the right of challenge and other accustomed requisites; and no person shall be held to answer for a capital, or otherwise infamous crime, unless on a presentment or indictment by a Grand Jury; but if a crime be committed in a place in the possession of an enemy, or in which an insurrection may prevail, the indictment and trial may by law be authorized in some other place within the same State; and if it be committed in a place not within a State, the indictment and trial may be at such place or places as the law may have directed."

"In suits at common law the right of trial by jury shall be preserved."

"Immediately after ART. 6, the following to be inserted as ART. 7."

"The powers delegated by this Constitution to the government of the United States, shall be exercised as therein appropriated, so that the Legislative shall never exercise the powers vested in the Executive or the Judicial; nor the Executive the powers vested in the Legislative or Judicial; nor the Judicial the powers vested in the Legislative or Executive."

"The powers not delegated by this Constitution, nor prohibited by it to the States, are reserved to the States respectively."

ART. 7 to be made ART. 8.

2. House Resolution
(adopted August 24, 1789)

ARTICLES in addition to, and amendment of, the Constitution of the United States of America, proposed by Congress, and ratified by the Legislatures of the several States, pursuant to the fifth Article of the original Constitution.

ARTICLE THE FIRST.

After the first enumeration, required by the first Article of the Constitution, there shall be one Representative for every thirty thousand, until the number shall amount to one hundred, after which the proportion shall be so regulated by Congress, that there shall be not less than one hundred Representatives, nor less than one Representative for every forty thousand persons, until the number of Representatives shall amount to two hundred, after which the proportion shall be so regulated by Congress, that there shall not be less than two hundred Representatives, nor less than one Representative for every fifty thousand persons.

ARTICLE THE SECOND.

No law varying the compensation to the members of Congress, shall take effect, until an election of Representatives shall have intervened.

ARTICLE THE THIRD.

Congress shall make no law establishing religion or prohibiting the free exercise thereof, nor shall the rights of Conscience be infringed.

ARTICLE THE FOURTH.

The Freedom of Speech, and of the Press, and the right of the People peaceably to assemble, and consult for their common good, and to apply to the Government for a redress of grievances, shall not be infringed.

ARTICLE THE FIFTH.

A well regulated militia, composed of the body of the People, being the best security of a free State, the right of the People to keep and bear arms, shall not be infringed, but no one religiously scrupulous of bearing arms, shall be compelled to render military service in person.

ARTICLE THE SIXTH

No soldier shall, in time of peace, be quartered in any house without the consent of the owner, nor in time of war, but in a manner to be prescribed by law.

ARTICLE THE SEVENTH

The right of the People to be secure in their persons, houses, papers and effects, against unreasonable searches and seizures, shall not be violated, and no warrants shall issue, but upon probable cause supported by oath or affirmation, and particularly describing the place to be searched, and the persons or things to be seized.

ARTICLE THE EIGHTH.

No person shall be subject, except in case of impeachment, to more than one trial, or one punishment for the same offence, nor shall be compelled in any criminal case, to be a witness against himself, nor be deprived of life, liberty or property, without due process of law; nor shall private property be taken for public use without just compensation.

ARTICLE THE NINTH.

In all criminal prosecutions, the accused shall enjoy the right to a speedy and public trial, to be informed of the nature and cause of the accusation, to be confronted with the witnesses against him, to have compulsory process for obtaining witnesses in his favor, and to have the assistance of counsel for his defence.

ARTICLE THE TENTH

The trial of all crimes (except in cases of impeachment, and in cases arising in the land or naval forces, or in the militia when in actual service in time of War or public danger) shall be by an Impartial Jury of the Vicinage, with the requisite of unanimity for conviction, the right of challenge, and other accustomed requisites; and no person shall be held to answer for a capital, or otherways infamous crime, unless on a presentment or indictment by a Grand Jury; but if a crime be committed in a place in the possession of an enemy, or in which an insurrection may prevail, the indictment and trial may by law be authorised in some other place within the same State.

ARTICLE THE ELEVENTH.

No appeal to the Supreme Court of the United States, shall be allowed, where the value in controversy shall not amount to one thousand dollars, nor shall any fact, triable by a Jury according to the course of the common law, be otherwise re-examinable, than according to the rules of common law.

ARTICLE THE TWELFTH.

In suits at common law, the right of trial by Jury shall be preserved.

ARTICLE THE THIRTEENTH

Excessive bail shall not be required, nor excessive fines imposed, nor cruel and unusual punishments inflicted.

ARTICLE THE FOURTEENTH

No State shall infringe the right of trial by Jury in criminal cases, nor the rights of conscience, nor the freedom of speech, or of the press.

ARTICLE THE FIFTEENTH

The enumeration in the Constitution of certain rights, shall not be construed to deny or disparage others retained by the people.

ARTICLE THE SIXTEENTH

The powers delegated by the Constitution to the government of the United States, shall be exercised as therein appropriated, so that the Legislative shall never exercise the powers vested in the Executive or Judicial; nor the Executive the powers vested in the Legislative or Judicial; nor the Judicial the powers vested in the Legislative or Executive.

ARTICLE THE SEVENTEENTH

The powers not delegated by the Constitution, nor prohibited by it, to the States, are reserved to the States respectively.

Biographical Dictionary

1. Delegates to the Constitutional Convention

Baldwin, Abraham (1754–1807) (Georgia).

Yale graduate. Chaplin in Revolutionary Army. Declined professorship of divinity at Yale to study and practice law. United States House of Representatives, 1789–99. United States Senator, 1799–1807. Called Father of the University of Georgia for arranging endowment from the Georgia Assembly.

Bassett, Richard (1745–1815) (Delaware).

Captain in Revolutionary War. Delegate to Annapolis Convention. Leading member of Delaware ratifying convention, the first state to accept the new Constitution. United States Senator, 1789–93. Governor of Delaware, 1799–1801. One of president Adams' "midnight appointees" to the bench, 1801.

Bedford, Gunning (1747–1812) (Delaware).

Princeton graduate, classmate of James Madison. Practiced law. Continental Congress, 1783–85. Delegate to Annapolis Convention. Member of Delaware ratifying convention. Attorney general of Delaware, 1784–89.

Blair, John (1732–1800) (Virginia).

Judge of Virginia Court of Appeals, which decided *Commonwealth v. Caton* (1782), first reported case of judical review. Appointed by Washington to the U.S. Supreme Court, 1789–96.

Blount, William (1749–1800) (North Carolina).

North Carolina House of Commons 1780–89. Continental Congress, 1782, 1786. Appointed territorial governor of Tennessee, 1790. First senator from state of Tennessee, 1796. Expelled from Senate in 1797 for allegedly planning to help Great Britain gain control of Spanish Florida and Louisiana. State senator until death.

Brearly, David (1745–1790) (New Jersey).

Arrested for outspoken Whig sentiments at beginning of Revolutionary War. Chief Justice of Supreme Court of New Jersey, 1779. Decided *Holmes v. Walton*, 1780, which overturned a legislative act as unconstitutional. Presided over New Jersey state ratifying convention. United States district court judge, 1789 until death.

Broom, Jacob (1752–1810) (Delaware).

Delegate to Annapolis Convention.

Butler, Pierce (1744–1822) (South Carolina).

Born in Ireland. Major in British army until he married a South Carolinian, 1771. Representative in state legislature, 1778–82, 1784–89. United States Senator, 1789–96, when he resigned. Reelected in 1802, denounced the Twelfth Amendment. Resigned again in 1806.

Carroll, Daniel (1730–1796) (Maryland).

Continental Congress, 1781. Aligned with large property holders, heir to father's large estate. United States Senator, 1789–91. Named by Washington as one of three commissioners to survey and locate the District of Columbia.

Clymer, George (1739–1813) (Pennsylvania).

Orphaned at age one, succeeded guardian uncle in business and became prosperous Philadelphia merchant. Early and ardent patriot. Signed the Declaration of Independence. Continental Congress, 1775–77, 1780–82. United States House of Representatives, 1789–91.

Davie, William R. (1756–1820) (North Carolina).

Born in England, adopted by South Carolina uncle in 1763. Princeton graduate. Colonel in Revolutionary War. Circuit lawyer for fifteen years. North Carolina legislature, 1786–98. Appointed by President Adams as peace commissioner to France, 1799. Lost United States congressional election in 1803, retired from politics to plantation in South Carolina.

Dayton, Jonathan (1760–1824) (New Jersey).

Captain at battle of Yorktown. New Jersey Assembly, 1786–87. Father declined appointment in his favor to Constitutional Convention. United States House of Representatives, 1791–99. United States Senator, 1799–1805. Opposed Twelfth Amendment. Owned quarter-million acre tract in Ohio subsequently named Dayton, Ohio. Indicted for high treason with Aaron Burr but not prosecuted, 1807. Political career ended with stigma.

Dickinson, John (1732–1808) (Delaware).

One of the leaders of the opposition to the Stamp Act. Published patriot pamphlets. Continental Congress, 1774–79. Helped draft address to the people of Canada and Declaration of the Causes of Taking up Arms, but voted against Declaration of Independence, hoping for reconciliation with Great Britain. President of Supreme Executive Council of Delaware, 1781.

Ellsworth, Oliver (1745–1807) (Connecticut).

Dismissed from Yale. Graduated from Princeton. Leader of the Connecticut bar, although he supported himself during the first three years of his practice by chopping wood. Governor's Council, 1780–84. Judge of the Supreme Court of Errors, 1784. Continental Congress, 1777–83. United States Senator, 1789–96; chaired committee that drafted Judiciary Act. Chief justice of the United States Supreme Court, 1796–1800. Commissioner to France, 1799–1800.

Few, William (1748–1828) (Georgia).

Continental Congress, 1780–82, 1785–88. General Assembly of Georgia, three terms. United States Senator, 1788–93. Federal judge in Georgia, 1796–99. Moved to New York and held public positions until death: General Assembly, prison inspector, city alderman.

Fitzsimons, Thomas (1741–1811) (Pennsylvania).

Born in Ireland. Mercantile career in Philadelphia. Continental Congress, 1782–83. United States House of Representatives, 1789–95. Influential in establishing first Bank of North America.

Franklin, Benjamin (1706–1790) (Pennsylvania).

Expert printer at 17. Owner of *Pennsylvania Gazette* at 24. Wrote *Poor Richard's Almanac*, 1732, establishing fame in America and Europe. Community leader; established libraries, hospitals, educat'onal institutions. Inventor, scientist. Spent 25 years as colonial agent, peace commissioner in France, Great Britain. First postmaster general. Continental Congress, 1775–76; helped draft Declaration of Independence.

Gerry, Elbridge (1744–1814) (Massachusetts).

Harvard graduate. Merchant and supplier during Revolutionary War. Continental Congress, 1776–80,

1783–85; signed the Declaration of Independence. Refused to attend Annapolis Convention because thought its scope was too restricted. Although not elected to Massachusetts ratifying convention, invited to answer questions. Declared out of order for speaking out of turn, refused to return. United States House of Representatives, 1789–93. Governor of Massachusetts, 1810. Administration led to term "gerrymander" because of redistricting scheme to keep Republican state senators in office. Defeated in 1812 election. Served as Madison's vice president, 1813–14, and died in office.

Gilman, Nicholas (1755–1814) (New Hampshire).

Captain in Revolutionary War. Continental Congress, 1786–88. United States House of Representatives, 1789–97. United States Senator, 1804–14.

Gorham, Nathaniel (1738–1796) (Massachusetts).

Leading businessman in Massachusetts. Colonial legislature, 1771–75. State senate and house, 1779–85. Continental Congress, 1782–83, 1785–87. Member of state ratifying convention. Died insolvent when partnership holding 6 million acres of land collapsed.

Hamilton, Alexander (1757–1804) (New York).

Born into financially troubled family, sent to college by aunts. Early patriot, pamphleteer. Secretary and aide to General Washington. Delegate to Annapolis Convention. Wrote influential *Federalist Papers* advocating ratification. Appointed secretary of treasury, 1789. Lifelong feud with Thomas Jefferson. Returned to law practice in New York, 1795. Challenged to duel by Aaron Burr in 1804, shot and killed.

Houston, William C. (1740–1788) (New Jersey).

Graduate of College of New Jersey (now Princeton) and later professor of math and natural philosophy there. Captain of New Jersey militia. Continental Congress, 1779–82, 1784–86. Resigned professorship to practice law, 1783. Clerk of New Jersey Supreme Court, 1781–88.

Houstoun, William (1748–1833) (Georgia).

Member of loyalist family. Decided to join the pa-

triot cause while studying law in London. Continental Congress, 1784, 1787. One of only ten framers who refused to serve in the new United States government. Lived the rest of his life in relative obscurity, leading Madison to declare himself the last living framer in 1831, two years before Houstoun died.

Ingersoll, Jared (1749–1822) (Pennsylvania).

Yale graduate. Studied law in England, 1773. Returned to Philadelphia, 1781. Attorney opposing Alexander Hamilton in one of the first cases involving the constitutionality of a congressional act before the Supreme Court, *Hylton v. United States* (1796). Attorney general of Pennsylvania, 1790–99, 1811–17.

Jenifer, Daniel of St. Thomas (1723–1790) (Maryland).

Governor's Council of Maryland, 1773–75. President of state senate, 1777. Continental Congress, 1778–82. Close personal friend of George Washington.

Johnson, William Samuel (1727–1819) (Connecticut).

Yale graduate. Practiced law. Connecticut delegate to Stamp Act Congress. Colonial agent in London, 1767–71. Judge of Connecticut Superior Court. Continental Congress, 1785–87. United States Senator, 1789–91. First president of Columbia College, 1787–1800.

King, Rufus (1755–1827) (Massachusetts).

Harvard graduate. Practiced law. Continental congress, 1784–86. United States Senator, 1789–91, 1795–96, 1813–20. Director of first Bank of North America, 1791. Appointed by Washington to be minister to Great Britain, 1796–1803. Unsuccessful vice presidential candidate with Pinckney, 1804 and 1808. Presidential candidate, 1816, defeated by Monroe.

Langdon, John (1741–1819) (New Hampshire).

Grammar school education. After apprenticeship as clerk, became sucessful businessman. Continental Congress, 1775, 1783. State legislature, 1777–81, 1786–87. State senator, 1784. President of New Hampshire, 1785, 1788. United States Senator, 1789–1801. State legislature, 1801–05. Ran for governor annually starting in 1802 until he finally won in 1805. Served as governor until 1812. Declined Republican nomination for vice presidency, 1812.

Lansing, John (1754–1814) (New York).

Albany lawyer. New York Assembly, 1780–88. Continental Congress, 1784–85. New York Supreme Court justice, 1790–1801. Chancellor of New York, 1801–14. Disappeared mysteriously in 1814; went to New York City on business and never returned.

Livingston, William (1723–1790) (New Jersey).

Yale graduate. Practiced law. Active liberal politician in New York, 1772. Moved to New Jersey estate, 1772. Continental Congress, 1774–76. Assumed command of New Jersey militia, 1776. First governor of New Jersey, 1776–90.

Madison, James (1750–1836) (Virginia).

Princeton graduate. Member of committee that drafted Virginia constitution, 1776. Continental Congress, 1780–83. Delegate to Annapolis Convention. Author of many of the *Federalist Papers*. United States House of Representatives, 1789–97. Leader in framing and passing Bill of Rights. Fourth president of United States, 1809–17.

Martin, Alexander (1740–1807) (North Carolina).

Colonel in Revolutionary War, but was arrested for cowardice in the battle of Germantown. Court-martialed and acquitted, but resigned command, 1777. State senator, 1778–82, 1785, 1787–88. Governor of North Carolina, 1782–85, 1789–92. Continental Congress, 1786.

Martin, Luther (1748–1826) (Maryland).

Trained as teacher, became lawyer in Virginia. Delegate to Annapolis Convention. Pamphleteer during Revolutionary War. Attorney general of Maryland, 1778–1805, 1818–22. Continental Congress, 1785. As Maryland attorney general, opposed Daniel Webster and William Pinckney in *McCulloch v. Maryland*.

Mason, George (1725–1792) (Virginia).

Plantation owner, fourth generation of original Virginia family of settlers. Influential writer: Fairfax Resolves of 1774, helped frame Declaration of Rights in Virginia. Appointed to but did not attend Annapolis Convention.

McClurg, James (1746–1823) (Virginia).

Physician. Studied medicine at University of Edinburgh, 1770. Chief surgeon with Virginia's patriot militia. Professor of anatomy and medicine at William and Mary, 1779–83. Rumored to have been selected for Convention because advanced age of many of the delegates made presence of physician useful.

McHenry, James (1753–1816) (Maryland).

Born in Ireland. Emigrated to Philadelphia, 1771. Inherited father's import business,1790. Studied medicine. Medical Staff of military hospital during Revolutionary War. Secretary to General Washington, 1778, Lafayette, 1780. State senate in Maryland, 1781–86. Member of Maryland ratifying convention. Secretary of war under President Washington, 1796. Continued under President Adams who subsequently demanded his resignation, 1800.

Mercer, John Francis (1759–1821) (Maryland).

William and Mary graduate. Captain in Revolutionary War. Continental Congress, 1782–88. Opposed ratification in Maryland convention. United States House of Representatives, 1791–94. Governor of Maryland, 1801–03.

Mifflin, Thomas (1744–1800) (Pennsylvania).

Member of Quaker merchant family. One of the youngest members of the First Continental Congress. Brigadier general in Revolutionary War. Read out of Quaker meeting for serving in military. Quartermaster general of army; negligence led to calls for court-martial, but General Washington never proceeded against him. Continental Congress, 1782–84. Chairman of state constitutional convention. Pennsylvania governor, 1790–99. Died penniless.

Morris, Gouverneur (1752–1816) (Pennsylvania).

Member of landed aristocracy. Admitted to bar at age 19. Helped draft New York constitution. Continental Congress 1778–79. Moved to Pennsylvania, resumed law practice. Lived in Europe, 1789–98, negotiating trade relations and land purchases. United States Senator, 1800–02.

Morris, Robert (1734–1806) (Pennsylvania).

Born in England. Emigrated to Maryland at age 13. Worked for shipping merchant in Philadelphia, eventually becoming partner. Financier/supplier to Revolutionary Army. Superintendent of finance, 1781, during Confederation's financial crisis. Delegate to Annapolis Convention. Offered secretary of treasury under President Washington, but declined. United States Senator, 1789–95. Became deeply involved in land speculation, which eventually drained his fortune. Spent three years in a debtors' prison.

Paterson, William (1745–1806) (New Jersey).

Born in Ireland. Emigrated as a child. Practiced law. Attorney general of New Jersey, 1776–83. Elected to Continental Congress, 1780, but declined to serve. United States Senator, 1789–90. Helped draft Judiciary Act of 1789 with Oliver Ellsworth. Governor of New Jersey, 1790–93. Justice of United States Supreme Court, 1793–1806.

Pierce, William (1740–1789) (Georgia).

Revolutionary soldier. Continental Congress, 1787.

Pinckney, Charles (1757–1824) (South Carolina).

Second counsin to Charles Cotesworth Pinckney. Practiced law. Soldier and prisoner of war in Revolutionary War. Continental Congress, 1784–87. Lied about his age so he could claim to be youngest member of Convention. Governor of South Carolina, 1789–92. United States Senator, 1798–1801. Minister to Spain, 1801–05.

Pinckney, Charles Cotesworth (1746–1825) (South Carolina).

Educated in England where father was colonial agent for South Carolina. Admitted to English bar. Returned to South Carolina to practice law, 1769. Commanded Revolutionary regiment. Offered cabinet positions by President Washington, declined. Accepted mission to France, 1796. Unsuccessful candidate for vice president, 1800. Unsuccessful candidate for president, 1804, 1808.

Randolph, Edmund (1753–1813) (Virginia).

Father and grandfather were king's attorneys in Virginia. Continental Congress, 1779. Governor of Virginia, 1786. Delegate to Annapolis Convention. Appointed United States attorney general by President Washington, 1789. Resigned in 1795 under accusations that he had improperly provided information to the French government. Practiced law in Richmond. Senior counsel for Aaron Burr in his trial for treason.

Read, George (1733–1798) (Delaware).

Admitted to Philadelphia bar at 20. Moved his practice to Delaware, 1754. Continental Congress, 1774–76. Presided over Delaware constitutional convention, 1776. Called to serve as president of Delaware when previous president was captured by the British, 1777. Delegate to Annapolis Convention. United States Senator, 1788–93. Resigned to become chief justice of Delaware Supreme Court, 1793–98.

Rutledge, John (1739–1800) (South Carolina).

Continental Congress, 1774–76. Helped write South Carolina constitution. Elected president of South Carolina's first general assembly. Appointed justice of United States Supreme Court by President Washington. Resigned to sit on South Carolina court, 1791, without having heard any Supreme Court cases. Recess appointment as chief justice of United States Supreme Court, 1795, but subsequently rejected by Senate.

Sherman, Roger (1721–1793) (Connecticut).

No formal education, self-educated. Published almanacs with astronomy, philosophy, and poetry, 1750–61. Studied law. State legislature, 1755–61. Judge of Superior Court of Connecticut, 1766–89. Continental Congress, 1774–81. Member of committee that drafted Declaration of Independence and Articles of Confederation. United States House of Representatives, 1789–91. United States Senator, 1791–93.

Spaight, Richard Dobbs (1758–1802) (North Carolina).

Orphaned at eight. Sent to Ireland for education; advanced studies at University of Glasgow. Returned to North Carolina, 1778. Soldier in Revolutionary War. Continental Congress, 1783–85. Governor of North Carolina, 1792–95. United States House of Representatives, 1798–1801. State senator, 1801–02. Died in duel with political opponent.

Strong, Caleb (1745–1819) (Massachusetts).

Harvard graduate. Smallpox as a young adult permanently impaired his sight. Admitted to the Massachusetts bar, 1772. Delegate to Massachusetts state constitutional convention, 1779. State senator, 1780–89. United States Senator, 1789–96. Governor of Massachusetts, 1800–07, 1812–16.

Washington, George (1732–1799) (Virginia).

Commander in chief of all Virginia forces at age 23. Developed estate of Mount Vernon, 1759–74. Continental Congress, 1774–76. Selected to command Revolutionary Army, 1775–83. Returned to Mount Vernon to renew estate, establish Potomac Company, 1784. First president of United States, 1789–97.

Williamson, Hugh (1735–1819) (North Carolina).

Graduated in the first class of the College of Philadelphia (now the University of Pennsylvania), 1757. Studied theology, mathematics, medicine. Professor of mathematics, College of Philadelphia. Continental Congress, 1782–85, 1787. United States House of Representatives, 1789–93. Moved to New York in 1793, devoted rest of life to literary, scientific pursuits earning greatest reputation for research on climate. Close friend of Benjamin Franklin.

Wilson, James (1742–1798) (Pennsylvania).

Born in Scotland. Studied at University of Edinburgh. Emigrated to New York, 1765. Admitted to New York bar, 1767. Continental Congress, 1774–76. Pamphleteer during Revolutionary War. Helped draft Pennsylvania state constitution, 1790. Appointed to United States Supreme Court by President Washington, 1789–98. Speculated in land. Moved to New Jersey in 1797 to avoid arrest for debt.

Wythe, George (1726–1806) (Virginia).

Practiced law. Chancellor of Virginia, 1778–1801. Judge of Virginia Court of Appeals, which decided *Commonwealth v. Caton* (1782), first reported case of judicial review. Held first chair of law in an American college, the College of William and Mary, 1779. Poisoned with arsenic-laced coffee by grandnephew, principal beneficiary of his will.

Yates, Robert (1738–1801) (New York).

Admitted to bar in Albany, 1760. Lifetime resident of Albany. Justice of New York Supreme Court, 1777–98. Wrote a number of Anti-Federalist papers and worked against ratification in New York convention. Unsuccessfully ran for governor, 1789, 1795.

2. Members of the First Congress

Delegates to the 1787 Federal Constitutional Convention are marked with an asterisk.

House of Representatives:

Ames, Fisher (Massachusetts)
Ashe, John Baptista (North Carolina)
Baldwin, Abraham (Georgia)*
Benson, Egbert (New York)
Bland, Theodorick (Virginia)[1]
Bloodworth, Timothy (North Carolina)
Boudinot, Elias (New Jersey)
Bourn, Benjamin (Rhode Island)
Brown, John (Virginia)
Burke, Aedenus (South Carolina)
Cadwalader, Lambert (New Jersey)
Carroll, Daniel (Maryland)*
Clymer, George (Pennsylvania)*
Coles, Isaac (Virginia)
Contee, Benjamin (Maryland)
Fitzsimons, Thomas (Pennsylvania)*
Floyd, William (New York)
Foster, Abiel (New Hampshire)
Gale, George (Maryland)
Gerry, Elbridge (Massachusetts)*
Giles, William B. (Virginia)[2]
Gilman, Nicholas (New Hampshire)*
Goodhue, Benjamin (Massachusetts)
Griffin, Samuel (Virginia)
Grout, Jonathan (Massachusetts)
Hartley, Thomas (Pennsylvania)
Hathorn, John (New York)
Hiester, Daniel (Pennsylvania)
Huger, Daniel (South Carolina)
Huntington, Benjamin (Connecticut)
Jackson, James (Georgia)
Laurance, John (New York)

Lee, Richard Bland (Virginia)
Leonard, George (Massachusetts)
Livermore, Samuel (New Hampshire)
Madison, James (Virginia)*
Mathews, George (Georgia)
Moore, Andrew (Virginia)
Muhlenberg, Frederick A. (Pennsylvania)
Muhlenberg, Peter (Pennsylvania)
Page, John (Virginia)
Parker, Josiah (Virginia)
Partridge, George (Massachusetts)
Schureman, James (New Jersey)
Scott, Thomas (Pennsylvania)
Sedgwick, Theodore (Massachusetts)
Seney, Joshua (Maryland)
Sevier, John (North Carolina)
Sherman, Roger (Connecticut)*
Silvester, Peter (New York)
Sinnickson, Thomas (New Jersey)
Smith, William (Maryland)
Smith, William (South Carolina)
Steele, John (North Carolina)
Stone, Michael Jenifer (Maryland)
Sturges, Jonathan (Connecticut)
Sumter, Thomas (South Carolina)
Thatcher, George (Massachusetts)
Trumbull, Jonathan (Connecticut)
Tucker, Thomas Tudor (South Carolina)
Van Rensselaer, Jeremiah (New York)
Vining, John (Delaware)
Wadsworth, Jeremiah (Connecticut)
White, Alexander (Virginia)
Williamson, Hugh (North Carolina)*
Wynkoop, Henry (Pennsylvania)

---

1. Died June 1, 1790.
2. Seated December 7, 1790, replacing Theodorick Bland.

Senate

Bassett, Richard (Delaware)*
Butler, Pierce (South Carolina)*
Carroll, Charles (Maryland)
Dalton, Tristam (Massachusetts)
Dickinson, Philemon (New Jersey)[3]
Ellsworth, Oliver (Connecticut)*
Elmer, Jonathan (New Jersey)
Few, William (Georgia)*
Foster, Theodore (Rhode Island)
Grayson, William (Virginia)[4]
Gunn, James (Georgia)
Hawkins, Benjamin (North Carolina)
Henry, John (Maryland)
Izard, Ralph (South Carolina)
Johnson, William Samuel (Connecticut)*

Johnston, Samuel (North Carolina)
King, Rufus (New York)*
Langdon, John (New Hampshire)*
Lee, Richard Henry (Virginia)
Maclay, William (Pennsylvania)
Monroe, James (Virginia)[5]
Morris, Robert (Pennsylvania)*
Paterson, William (New Jersey)*[6]
Read, George (Delaware)*
Schuyler, Philip (New York)
Stanton, Joseph (Rhode Island)
Strong, Caleb (Massachusetts)*
Walker, John (Virginia)[7]
Wingate, Paine (New Hampshire)

---

3. Seated December 6, 1790, replacing William Paterson.
4. Died March 12, 1790.

5. Seated December 6, 1790, replacing William Grayson.
6. Resigned November 13, 1790.
7. Interim appointment to replace William Grayson. Served from March 31 to November 9, 1790.

3. Major Political Figures in the Civil War and Reconstruction Periods

Adams, Charles (1807–1886) (Massachusetts).

Served in House of Representatives, 1858–61. Ambassador to Great Britain, 1861–68. Son of John Quincy Adams. Active member of the antislavery movement.

Ashley, John (1824–1896) (Ohio)

Served in House of Representatives, 1859–69. Former Democrat whose antislavery beliefs compelled him to become a Republican. Initiated Johnson's impeachment.

Bingham, John (1815–1900) (Ohio).

Served in House of Representatives, 1854–63, 1865–73. Drafted Section 1 of Fourteenth Amendment.

Boutwell, George (1818–1905) (Massachusetts).

Served in House of Representatives, 1863–69. Served in the Senate, 1873–77. Secretary of the treasury, 1869–73. Free Soil party member who became a radical Republican. A central figure in the Johnson impeachment.

Chase, Salmon (1808–1873) (Ohio).

Served in the Senate, 1849–55. Secretary of the treasury, 1861–64. Chief justice, United States Supreme Court, 1864–73. Before entering the Senate, Chase frequently served as counsel for fugitive slaves.

Clay, Henry (1777–1852) (Kentucky).

Served in House of Representatives, 1811–21, 1823–25. Served in the Senate, 1831–42, 1849–52. A leading political figure in the first half of the nineteenth century. Sponsored the Missouri Compromise (1820), the Compromise of 1833, and the Compromise of 1850.

Douglas, Stephen (1813–1861) (Illinois).

Served in the Senate, 1847–61. Ran as Democratic candidate against Lincoln in 1860. Remembered now largely for a series of debates with Lincoln in 1858. Became a strong Lincoln supporter.

Farnsworth, John (1820–1897) (Illinois).

Served in House of Representatives, 1857–61, 1863–73. Radical Republican activist. During the years between his House membership, he served as a high-ranking Union Army officer.

Fessenden, William (1806–1869) (Maine).

Served in House of Representatives, 1841–43. Served in the Senate, 1854–64, 1865–69. Secretary of the treasury, 1864–65. A Lincoln supporter.

Giddings, Joshua (1795–1864) (Ohio).

Served in House of Representatives, 1838–42, 1842–59. Dedicated antislavery activist. Resigned from House in 1842 after being censured for his actions against slavery, but returned to Congress later that year.

Hale, John (1806–1873) (New Hampshire).

Served in House of Representatives, 1843–45. Served in the Senate, 1847–53, 1855–65. First avowed antislavery candidate elected to the Senate.

Howard, Jacob (1805–1871) (Michigan).

Served in House of Representatives, 1841–43. Served in the Senate, 1862–71. Helped establish the Republican party in the 1850s. A strong supporter of congressional Reconstruction policy.

Johnson, Reverdy (1796–1876) (Maryland).

Served in the Senate, 1845–49, 1863–68. Attorney general, 1849–50. Represented slave-owner Sanford in the famous slave case, *Dred Scott v. Sanford* (1857).

Lovejoy, Owen (1811–1864) (Illinois).

Served in House of Representatives, 1856–64. A Congregational minister and enthusiastic Lincoln supporter. His brother, Elijah, was a radical abolitionist murdered by a mob in 1861.

Patterson, James (1823–1893) (New Hampshire).

Served in House of Representatives, 1864–67. Served in the Senate, 1867–73. Republican. Sponsored a bill to establish schools for black children in the District of Columbia. Almost expelled from the Senate for his involvement in the Credit Mobilier scandal.

Seward, William (1801–1872) (New York).

Served in the Senate, 1849–61. Secretary of state, 1861–69. A leading antislavery activist. Played a central role in keeping foreign powers out of involvement in the Civil War.

Story, Joseph (1779–1845) (Massachusetts).

Served in House of Representatives, 1808–09. Associate justice, United States Supreme Court, 1811–45. An influential jurist and legal educator. Known for a conservative Yankee temperament.

Sumner, Charles (1811–74) (Massachusetts).

Served in the Senate, 1851–74. Powerful antislavery activist. Played a large role in President Johnson's impeachment proceedings.

Trumbull, Lyman (1813–1896) (Illinois).

Served in the Senate, 1855–73. Drafted Civil Rights Act of 1866. Introduced the resolution that became the Thirteenth Amendment.

Wade, Benjamin (1800–1878) (Ohio).

Served in the Senate, 1851–69. Important antislavery advocate. Co–author, with Henry Davis, a House member, of the Wade-Davis bill. Severe critic of President Johnson.

Webster, Daniel (1782–1852) (Massachusetts).

Served in House of Representatives, 1813–17, 1823–27. Served in the Senate, 1827–41, 1845–50. Secretary of state, 1841–43, 1850–52. A leading figure in nineteenth-century law and letters. Supported Clay's Compromise of 1850.

Wilmot, David (1814–1868) (Pennsylvania).

Served in House of Representatives, 1845–61. Served in the Senate, 1861–63. Author of the Wilmot Proviso. Republican party founder and Lincoln supporter.

Wilson, Henry (1812–1875) (Massachusetts).

Served in the Senate, 1855–73. Major antislavery activist. Helped found the Free Soil and Republican parties. Strong opponent of President Johnson.

Wood, Fernando (1812–1881) (New York).

Served in House of Representatives, 1841–43, 1863–65, 1867–81. A Tammany Hall member with ties to the Democratic party. Opposed the war effort and advocated coexistence with the slave-holding South.

Recommended Further Reading

Note: This is not an exhaustive list of the voluminous literature on the periods and events discussed in this book. We have tried to include a balanced collection of materials. Students are urged to consult larger bibliographies and to use the sources listed below as a method of gaining entry into the literature.

PART ONE:

Willi P. Adams, *The First American Constitutions: Republican Ideology and the Making of the State Constitutions in the Revolutionary Era* (Univ. of North Carolina 1973)

Bernard Bailyn, *The Ideological Origins of the American Revolution* (Belknap 1967)

Lance Banning, *The Jeffersonian Persuasion: Evolution of a Party Ideology* (Cornell 1978)

John Diggins, *The Lost Soul of American Politics: Virtue, Self-Interest and the Foundations of Liberalism* (Basic Books 1984)

Edward Dumbauld, *The Bill of Rights and What it Means Today* (Univ. of Oklahoma 1957)

Lawrence M. Friedman, *A History of American Law* (Simon & Schuster 1973)

Julius Goebel, Jr., *History of the Supreme Court of the United States: Antecedents and Beginnings to 1801* (Macmillan 1971)

Jack P. Greene, *Peripheries and Center* (Univ. of Georgia 1986)

Jack P. Greene (ed.), *The Reinterpretation of the American Revolution 1763–1789* (Greenwood 1968)

Morton J. Horwitz, *The Transformation of American Law, 1780–1860* (Harvard 1977)

James H. Hutson, *Country, Court and Constitution: Antifederalism and the Historians*, 3:38 Wm. & M.Q. 337 (1981)

Jackson Turner Main, *The Anti-Federalists: Critics of the Constitution 1781–1788* (Univ. of North Carolina 1961)

Richard Morris, *The Forging of the Union, 1781–89* (Harper & Row 1987)

Forrest McDonald, *Novus Ordo Seclorum: The Intellectual Orgins of the Constitution* (Kansas 1986)

Jack N. Rakove, *The Beginnings of National Politics: An Interpretive History of the Continental Congress* (Johns Hopkins 1983)

Clinton Rossiter, *1787: The Grand Convention* (Macmillan 1966)

Robert A. Rutland, *The Birth of the Bill of Rights, 1776–1791* (New England Univ. Press 1983)

Robert A. Rutland, *The Ordeal of the Constitution: The Antifederalists and the Ratification Struggle of 1787–1788* (Univ. of Oklahoma 1966)

Bernard Schwartz (ed.), *The Roots of the Bill of Rights*, Volume I (Scribner 1980)

Herbert Storing (ed.), *The Complete Anti-Federalist* (vol. 1) (Univ. of Chicago 1981)

William M. Wiecek, *The Sources of Antislavery Constitutionalism in America, 1760–1848* (Cornell 1977)

Garry Wills, *Inventing America: Jefferson's Declaration of Independence* (Doubleday 1978)

Gordon S. Wood (ed.), *The Confederation and the Constitution: The Critical Issues* (Little, Brown 1973)

Gordon S. Wood, *The Creation of the American Republic, 1776–1787* (Univ. of North Carolina 1969)

PART TWO:

Herman Belz, *Emancipation and Equal Rights: Politics and Constitutionalism in the Civil War Era* (Norton 1978)

Herman Belz, *A New Birth of Freedom: The Republican Party and Freedmen's Rights, 1861–1866* (Greenwood 1976)

Michael Benedict, *A Compromise of Principle: Congressional Republicans and Reconstruction, 1863–1869* (Norton 1974)

Robert Cover, *Justice Accused* (Yale 1978)

David H. Donald, *Charles Sumner and the Coming of the Civil War* (Knopf 1960)

David H. Donald, *Liberty and Union: The Crisis of Popular Government, 1830–1890* (Little, Brown 1978)

Don E. Fehrenbacher, *Lincoln in Text and Context: Collected Essays* (Stanford 1987)

Eric Foner, *Free Soil, Free Labor, Free Men: The Ideology of the Republican Party* (Oxford 1970)

William Gienapp, *The Origins of the Republican Party, 1852–1856* (Oxford 1987)

William Gillette, *The Right to Vote: Politics and the Passage of the Fifteenth Amendment* (Johns Hopkins 1965)

Charles Haines, *The Revival of Natural Law Concepts* (Harvard 1930)

Harold Hyman & William Wiecek, *Equal Justice Under Law: Constitutional Development, 1835–1875* (Harper & Row 1982)

Joseph James, *The Ratification of the Fourteenth Amendment* (Mercer 1984)

David Potter, *Impending Crisis 1848–1861* (Harper & Row 1976)

William Nelson, *The Fourteenth Amendment* (Harvard 1988)

Allan Nevins, *Ordeal of the Union* (Scribner 1947)

Aviam Soifer, *Protecting Civil Rights: A Critique of Raoul Berger's History*, 54 N. Y. U. L. Rev. 651 (1979)

Kenneth Stampp, *Imperiled Union: Essays on the Background of the Civil War* (Oxford 1980)

Benjamin Wright, *American Interpretations of Natural Law: A Study in the History of Political Thought* (Harvard 1931)

Charles Fairman, *History of the Supreme Court of the United States: Reconstruction and Reunion, 1861–88, Part One* (Macmillan 1971)

PART THREE:

Herman Belz, *The Civil War Amendments to the Constitution: the Relevance of Original Intent*, 5 Constitutional Comm. 115 (1988)

Raoul Berger, *Government by Judiciary: The Transformation of the Fourteenth Amendment* (Harvard 1977)

Paul Brest, *The Misconceived Quest for the Original Understanding*, 60 B. U. L. Rev. 204 (1980)

John Hart Ely, *Democracy and Distrust: A Theory of Judicial Review* (Harvard 1980)

Charles Fairman, *Does the Fourteenth Amendment Incorporate the Bill of Rights? The Original Understanding*, 2 Stan. L. Rev. 5 (1949)

Alfred Kelly, *Clio and the Court: An Illicit Love Affair*, 1965 Supreme Court Review 119 (1965)

Earl Maltz, *The Failure of Attacks on Constitutional Originalism*, 4 Constitutional Comm. 43 (1987)

H. Jefferson Powell, *The Original Understanding of Original Intent*, 98 Harv. L. Rev. 885 (1985)

William Rehnquist, *The Idea of a Living Constitution*, 54 Tex. L. Rev. 693 (1976)

Suzanna Sherry, *The Founders' Unwritten Constitution*, 54 U. Chi. L. Rev. 1127 (1987)

Mark Tushnet, *Red, White, and Blue: A Critical Analysis of Constitutional Law* (Harvard 1988)

Index